Lecture Notes in Computer Science

T0238816

Commenced Publication in 1973
Founding and Former Series Editors:
Gerhard Goos, Juris Hartmanis, and Jan van Leeuwen

Vikram Adve
María Jesús Garzarán
Paul Petersen (Eds.)

Languages and Compilers for Parallel Computing

20th International Workshop, LCPC 2007
Urbana, IL, USA, October 11-13, 2007
Revised Selected Papers

 Springer

Volume Editors

Vikram Adve
María Jesús Garzarán
University of Illinois at Urbana-Champaign
Department of Computer Science
Thomas M. Siebel Center for Computer Science
201 N. Goodwin Ave, Urbana, IL, 61801, USA
E-mail: {vadve,garzaran}@cs.uiuc.edu

Paul Petersen
Intel Corporation
1906 Fox Drive, Champaign, IL, 61820, USA
E-mail: paul.petersen@intel.com

Library of Congress Control Number: 2008932585

CR Subject Classification (1998): D.1.3, C.2.4, D.4.2, H.3.4, D.2

LNCS Sublibrary: SL 1 – Theoretical Computer Science and General Issues

ISSN   0302-9743
ISBN-10   3-540-85260-3 Springer Berlin Heidelberg New York
ISBN-13   978-3-540-85260-5 Springer Berlin Heidelberg New York

Springer is a part of Springer Science+Business Media

springer.com

© Springer-Verlag Berlin Heidelberg 2008
Printed in Germany

Typesetting: Camera-ready by author, data conversion by Scientific Publishing Services, Chennai, India
Printed on acid-free paper   SPIN: 12455096   06/3180   5 4 3 2 1 0

Preface

It is our pleasure to present the papers from the 20th International Workshop on Languages and Compilers for Parallel Computing! For the past 19 years, this workshop has been one of the primary venues for presenting and learning about a wide range of current research in parallel computing. We believe that tradition has continued in this, the 20th year of the workshop.

This year, we received 49 paper submissions from 10 countries. About a quarter of the papers (12 out of 49) included authors from industry. We selected 23 papers to be presented at the workshop, for an acceptance rate of 47%, which was similar to that of the last two years. Each paper received at least three reviews, with about two-thirds of the papers getting four or more reviews each. Most papers also received at least one review from an external reviewer. The committee held a full-day teleconference to discuss the reviews and select papers. Program Committee members who had a conflict with a paper left the call when that paper was being discussed. There were seven submissions that included Program Committee members as co-authors. These papers were evaluated more stringently and four of seven were accepted.

The workshop this year also included two exciting special events. First, David Kirk, Chief Scientist of nVidia and a member of the National Academy of Engineering, gave a keynote talk on using highly multithreaded graphics processors for accelerating general-purpose parallel computing applications. Kirk and nVidia have led the drive to make the high parallelism in graphics processors more easily accessible for a wide range of applications beyond traditional graphics processing, and this talk gave LCPC attendees a valuable perspective on the potential of this work.

Second, a special panel was held on Friday morning to commemorate the 20th year of LCPC. This panel, organized and moderated by Steering Committee Chair David Padua, was scheduled for an entire session to allow seven leaders in parallel computing to give their perspective on how the field has evolved over the past 20 years, and what the major challenges are for the future. The panel included a number of luminaries in parallel computing – Arvind (MIT), David Kuck (Intel), Monica Lam (Stanford University), Alexandru Nicolau (University of California Irvine), Keshav Pingali (University of Texas, Austin), Burton Smith (Microsoft Research), and Michael Wolfe (The Portland Group). Our thanks to David Padua for organizing this panel.

We would like to thank the many people who contributed valuable time and effort to making LCPC 2007 a success. Most importantly, we want to thank all the members of the community who submitted papers to the workshop. This workshop is, in the end, an (incomplete) representation of the results of their hard work. Second, the Program Committee worked hard to review 12–13 papers each and to participate in the all-day Program Committee teleconference. The quality of the technical program owes much to their effort. In his role as Steering Committee Chair, David Padua provided valuable guidance and support. He also lent his stack of 19 previous LCPC proceedings to mark the occasion!

Finally, Sheila Clark put in tremendous effort behind the scenes to manage many organizational details for the workshop and we would not have been able to pull it off without all her help.

October 2007   Vikram Adve
                                                      María Jesús Garzarán
                                                            Paul Petersen

Organization

LCPC 2007 was organized by the Steering and Program Committees.

General/Program Co-chairs

Vikram Adve   University of Illinois at Urbana-Champaign
María Jesús Garzarán   University of Illinois at Urbana-Champaign
Paul Petersen   Intel Corporation

Program Committee

Vikram Adve   University of Illinois at Urbana-Champaign
Gheorghe Almási   IBM Research
José Nelson Amaral   University of Alberta, Canada
Eduard Ayguadé   Universitat Politécnica de Catalunya, Spain
Gerald Baumgartner   Louisiana State University
Călin Caşcaval   IBM Research
María Jesús Garzarán   University of Illinois at Urbana-Champaign
Sam Midkiff   Purdue University
Paul Petersen   Intel Corporation
J. Ramanujam   Louisiana State University
P. Sadayappan   Ohio State University
Peng Wu   IBM Research

Steering Committee

Rudolf Eigenmann   Purdue University
Alex Nicolau   UC Irvine
David Padua   University of Illinois at Urbana-Champaign
Lawrence Rauchwerger   Texas A&M University

Sponsoring Institution

University of Illinois at Urbana-Champaign
Siebel Center for Computer Science
Urbana, Illinois, October 11–13, 2007

Referees

V. Adve
G. Agrawal
G. Almasi
J.N. Amaral
E. Ayguadé
M. Baskaran
G. Baumgartner
P. Berube
R. Bocchino
U. Bondhugula
J. Brodman
C. Caşcaval
L. Ceze
A. Chakravarti
A. Cohen
G. Dozsa
A. Eichenberger
R. Eigenmann
B. Fraguela
F. Franchetti
R. Garg
M.J. Garzarán

R. Ghiya
M. Girkar
M. Gonzalez
A. Gotsman
J. Guo
S. Hack
J. Hoeflinger
A. Kejariwal
G. Kondrak
D. Koppelman
S. Krishnamoorthy
K. Laufer
O. Lhotak
X. Martorell
L. Meadows
J. Mellor-Crummey
S. Midkiff
R. Niewiadomski
D. Nikolopoulos
R. Nishtala
S. Pande
S. Parthasarathy

P. Petersen
C. Pickett
K. Pingali
J. Ramanujam
A. Ramirez
A. Rountev
R. Rugina
P. Sadayappan
E. Salami
R. Schreiber
P. Sdayappan
A. Sidelnik
K. Strauss
Z. Sura
D. Tarditi
X. Tian
P. Unnikrishnan
N. Vasilache
R. Wilhelm
P. Wu
Y. Zheng
P. Zhao

LCPC at Illinois

1989

2007

Keynote Presentation:
NVIDIA CUDA Software and GPU Parallel Computing Architecture

David Kirk, Chief Scientist, nVidia Corp.

Abstract. In the past, graphics processors were special-purpose hardwired application accelerators, suitable only for conventional rasterization-style graphics applications. Modern GPUs are now fully programmable, massively parallel floating point processors. This talk describes NVIDIA's massively multithreaded computing architecture and CUDA software for GPU computing. The architecture is a scalable, highly parallel architecture that delivers high throughput for data-intensive processing. Although not truly general-purpose processors, GPUs can now be used for a wide variety of compute-intensive applications beyond graphics.

Panel I:
How Is Multicore Programming Different from Traditional Parallel Programming?

Panelists:
Arch Robison (Intel)
Călin Caşcaval (IBM Research)
Wen-mei Hwu (University of Illinois at Urbana-Champaign)
Hironori Kasahara (Waseda University, Japan) and
Gudula Rünger (Chemnitz University of Technology, Germany)
Moderator:
Vikram Adve (University of Illinois at Urbana-Champaign)

Panel II:
What Have We Learned After 20 LCPCs?

Panelists:
David Kuck (Intel)
Arvind (MIT)
Monica Lam (Stanford University)
Alexandru Nicolau (University of California Irvine)
Keshav Pingali (University of Texas, Austin)
Burton Smith (Microsoft Research) and
Michael Wolfe (the Portland Group)
Moderator:
David Padua (University of Illinois at Urbana-Champaign)

Table of Contents

Libraries

Run-Time Systems and Performance Analysis

Parallel Compiler Technology II

Languages II

General Compiler Techniques

Compiler-Enhanced Incremental Checkpointing

Greg Bronevetsky[1], Daniel Marques[2],
Keshav Pingali[2], and Radu Rugina[3]

[1] Center for Applied Scientific Computing,
Lawrence Livermore National Laboratory,
Livermore, CA 94551, USA
greg@bronevetsky.com
[2] Department of Computer Sciences,
The University of Texas at Austin,
Austin, TX 78712, USA
daniel@ices.utexas.edu, pingali@cs.utexas.edu
[3] Department of Computer Science,
Cornell University,
Ithaca, NY 14850, USA
rugina@cs.cornell.edu

Abstract. As modern supercomputing systems reach the peta-flop performance range, they grow in both size and complexity. This makes them increasingly vulnerable to failures from a variety of causes. Checkpointing is a popular technique for tolerating such failures in that it allows applications to periodically save their state and restart the computation after a failure. Although a variety of automated system-level checkpointing solutions are currently available to HPC users, manual application-level checkpointing remains by far the most popular approach because of its superior performance. This paper focuses on improving the performance of automated checkpointing via a compiler analysis for incremental checkpointing. This analysis is shown to significantly reduce checkpoint sizes (upto 78%) and to enable asynchronous checkpointing.

1 Introduction

The dramatic growth in supercomputing system capability from the tera-flop to the peta-flop range has resulted in a dramatic increase in system complexity. While efforts have been made to limit the complexity of the Operating System used by these machines, their component counts have continued to grow. Even as systems like BlueGene/L [3] and the upcoming RoadRunner grow to more than 100,000 processors and tens of TBs of RAM, future designs promise to exceed these limits by large margins. While large supercomputers are made from high-quality components, increasing components counts make them vulnerable to faults, including hardware breakdowns [11] and soft errors [6].

Checkpointing is a popular technique for tolerating failures. The state of the application is periodically saved to reliable storage and on failure, the application rolls back to a prior state. However, automated checkpointing can be very

V. Adve, M.J. Garzarán, and P. Petersen (Eds.): LCPC 2007, LNCS 5234, pp. 1–15, 2008.

expensive due to the amount of data saved and the amount of time that the application loses while being blocked. For example, dumping all of RAM on a 128k-processor BlueGene/L supercomputer to a parallel file system would take approximately 20 minutes [9]. Incremental checkpointing [10] is one technique that can reduce the cost of checkpointing. A runtime monitor keeps track of any application writes. If it detects that a given memory region has not been modified between two adjacent checkpoints, this region is omitted from the second checkpoint, thus reducing the amount of data that needs to be saved. Possible monitors that have been explored in the past include virtual memory fault handlers [5], page table dirty bits and cryptographic encoding techniques [4].

When virtual memory fault handlers are used to track application writes, it is possible to further optimize the checkpointing process via a technique called "copy-on-write checkpointing" or more generally, "asynchronous checkpointing". At each checkpoint all pages that need to be checkpointed are marked non-writable and placed on a write-out queue. The application is then allowed to continue executing, while a separate thread asynchronously saves pages on the write-out queue. When the checkpointing thread is finished saving a given page, the page is marked writable. If the application tries to write to a page that hasn't yet been saved, the segmentation fault handler is called, a copy of the page is placed in the write-out queue and the application is allowed to resume execution. The result is that checkpointing is spaced out over a longer period of time, reducing the pressure on the I/O system, while allowing the application to continue executing.

In contrast to prior work, which uses runtime techniques for monitoring application writes, this paper presents a compile-time analysis for tracking such writes. Given an application that has been manually annotated with calls to a checkpoint function, for each array the analysis identifies points in the code such that either

- there exist no writes to the array between the point in the code and the next checkpoint and/or
- there exist no writes to the array between the last checkpoint and the point in the code

When the analysis detects that a given array is not modified between two checkpoints, this array is omitted from the second checkpoint. Furthermore, the analysis enables asynchronous checkpointing by allowing the checkpointing thread to save a given array during the period of time while there are no writes to it. Because the compiler analysis can identify write-free regions that begin before the checkpoint itself, it allows asynchronous checkpointing to begin earlier than is possible with purely runtime solutions. However, because it works at array granularity rather than the page- or word-granularity of runtime monitoring mechanisms, it can be more conservative in its decisions. Furthermore, the analysis makes the assumption that a checkpoint is taken every time the checkpoint function is called, which makes it more complex for users to target a specific checkpointing frequency.

While prior work has looked at compiler analyses for checkpoint optimization [7] [12], it has focused on pure compiler solutions that reduce the amount of data checkpointed. Our work presents a hybrid compiler/runtime approach that uses the compiler to optimize certain portions of an otherwise runtime checkpointing solution. This allows us to both reduce the amount of data being checkpointed as well as support purely runtime techniques such as asynchronous checkpointing.

2 Compiler/Runtime Interface

Our incremental checkpointing system is divided into run-time and compile-time components. The checkpointing runtime may either checkpoint application memory inside of checkpoint calls or include an extra thread that checkpoints asynchronously. Two checkpointing policies are offered. Memory regions that do not contain arrays (a small portion of the code in most scientific applications) are saved in a blocking fashion during calls to checkpoint. Arrays are dealt with in an incremental and possibly asynchronous fashion, as directed by the annotations placed by the compiler. The compiler annotates the source code with calls to the following functions:

- add_array(ptr, size) - Called when an array comes into scope to identify the array's memory region.
- remove_array(ptr) - Called when an array leaves scope. Memory regions that have been added but not removed are treated incrementally by the checkpointing runtime.
- start_chkpt(ptr) - Called to indicate that the array that contains the address ptr will not be written to until the next checkpoint. The runtime may place this array on the write-out queue and begin to asynchronously checkpoint this array.
- end_chkpt(ptr) - Called to indicate that the array that contains the address ptr is about to be written to. The end_chkpt call must block until the checkpointing thread has finished saving the array. It is guaranteed that there exist no writes to the array between any checkpoint and the call to end_chkpt.

Overall, the runtime is allowed to asynchronously checkpoint a given array between calls to start_chkpt and end_chkpt that refer to this array. If start_chkpt is not called for a given array between two adjacent checkpoints, this array may be omitted from the second checkpoint because it is known that it was not written to between the checkpoints.

For a more intuitive idea of how this API is used, consider the transformation in Figure 1. The original code contains two checkpoint calls, with assignments to arrays A and B in between. The code within the . . .'s does not contain any writes to A or B. It is transformed to include calls to start_chkpt and end_chkpt around the writes. Note that while end_chkpt(B) is placed immediately before the write to B, start_chkpt(B) must be placed at the end of B's write loop. This

Original Code	Transformed Code
checkpoint();	checkpoint();
...	...
A[...]=...;	end_chkpt(A);
...	A[...]=...;
for(...) {	start_chkpt(A);
...	...
B[...]=...;	for(...) {
...	...
}	end_chkpt(B);
...	B[...]=...;
checkpoint();	...
	}
	start_chkpt(B);
	...
	checkpoint();

Fig. 1. Transformation example

is because a start_chkpt(B) call inside the loop may be followed by writes to B in subsequent iterations. Placing the call immediately after the loop ensures that this cannot happen.

3   Compiler Analysis

The incremental checkpointing analysis is a dataflow analysis that consists of forward and backward components. The forward component, called the *Dirty Analysis*, identifies the first write to each array after a checkpoint. The backward, called the *Will-Write* analysis, identifies the last write to each array before a checkpoint.

3.1   Basic Analysis

For each array at each node n in a function's control-flow graph(CFG) the analysis maintains two bits of information:

- $mustDirty[n](array)$: True if there *must* exist a write to *array* along *every* path from a checkpoint call to this point in the code; False otherwise. Corresponds to the dataflow information immediately *before* n.
- $mayWillWrite[n](array)$: True if there *may* exist a write to *array* along *some* path from a this point in the code to a checkpoint call; False otherwise. Corresponds to the dataflow information immediately *after* n.

   This information is propagated through the CFG using the dataflow formulas in Figure 2. The Dirty and Will-Write analyses start at the top and bottom of each function's CFG, respectively, in a state where all arrays are considered to be clean (e.g. consistent with the previous, next checkpoint, respectively). They then propagate forward and backward, respectively, through the CFG, setting each array's write bit to $True$ when it encounters a write to this array. When each analysis reaches a `checkpoint` call, it resets the state of all the arrays to $False$. For the Dirty Analysis this is because all dirty arrays will become clean because they are checkpointed. For the WillWrite Analysis this is because at the point immediately before a checkpoint there exist no writes to any arrays until the next checkpoint, which is the checkpoint in question.

$$mustDirty[n](array) = \begin{cases} False & \text{if } n = \text{first node} \\ \bigcap_{m \in pred(n)} mustDirtyAfter[m](array) & \text{otherwise} \end{cases}$$

$$mustDirtyAfter[m](array) = [\![m]\!](mustDirty[m](array), array)$$

$$mayWillWrite[n](array) = \begin{cases} False & \text{if } n = \text{last node} \\ \bigcup_{m \in succ(n)} mayWillWriteBefore[m](array) & \text{otherwise} \end{cases}$$

$$mayWillWriteBefore[m](array) = [\![m]\!](mayWillWrite[m](array), array)$$

Statement m	$[\![m]\!](val, array)$
`array[expr] = expr`	$True$
`checkpoint()`	$False$
other	val

Fig. 2. Dataflow formulas for Dirty and Will-Write analyses

The application source code is annotated with calls to `start_chkpt` and `end_chkpt` using the algorithm in Figure 3. Such calls are added in three situations. First, `end_chkpt (array)` is inserted immediately before node n if n is a write to $array$ and it is not preceded by any other write to $array$ along $some$ path that starts at a call to `checkpoint` and ends with node n. Second, `start_chkpt(array)` is inserted immediately after node n if n is a write to $array$ and there do not exist any more writes to $array$ along any path that starts with n and ends at a `checkpoint` call. Third, a `start_chkpt(array)` is inserted on a CFG branching edge $m \rightarrow n$ if $mayWillWrite[n](array)$ is true at m, but false at n, due to merging of dataflow information at branching point m. This treatment is especially important when an array is being written inside a loop. In this case, $mayWillWrite[n](array)$ is true at all points in the loop body, since the array may be written in subsequent loop iterations. The flag becomes false on the edge that branches out of the loop, and the compiler inserts the `start_chkpt(array)` call on this edge.

Because the Dirty analysis is based on $must\text{-}write$ information, `end_chkpt` calls are conservatively placed as late as possible after a checkpoint. Furthermore, the Will-Write analysis' use of $may\text{-}write$ information conservatively places `start_save` calls as early as possible before a checkpoint.

To provide an intuition of how the analysis works, consider the example in Figure 4. In particular, consider the points in the code where $mustDirty$

foreach (array *array*), foreach (CFG node n) in application

> // if node n is the first write to *array* since the last **checkpoint** call
> if($mustDirty[n](array) = False \wedge mustDirtyAfter[n](array) = True$)
>> place **end_chkpt**(*array*) immediately before n
>
> // if node n is the last write to *array* until the next **checkpoint** call
> if($mayWillWriteBefore[n](array) = True \wedge mayWillWrite[n](array) = False$)
>> place **start_chkpt**(*array*) immediately after n
>
> // if node n follows the last write on a branch where *array* is no longer written
> if($mayWillWriteBefore[n](array) = False \wedge$
>> $\exists m \in pred(n).\ mayWillWrite[m](array) = True$)
>> place **start_chkpt**(*array*) on edge $m \rightarrow n$

Fig. 3. Transformation for inserting calls to **start_chkpt** and **end_chkpt**

and *mayWillWrite* change from *False* to *True*. These are the points where **end_chkpt** and **start_chkpt** calls are inserted.

3.2 Loop-Sensitive Analysis

While the basic analysis performs correct transformations, it has performance problems when it is applied to loops. This can be seen in the transformed code in Figure 4. While **start_chkpt**(B) is placed immediately after the loop that writes to B, **end_chkpt**(B) is placed inside the loop, immediately before the write to B itself. This happens because the placement of **end_chkpt** depends on *must-write* information, instead of the *may-write* information used in placing **start_chkpt**. While this placement is conservative, it becomes problematic in the case where the first post-checkpoint write to an array happens in a small, deeply-nested loop, which are very common in scientific computing. In this case **end_chkpt** will be called during each iteration of the loop, causing a potentially severe overhead.

Original Code	Code with Dirty States	Code with Will-Write States	Transformed Code
checkpoint();	checkpoint(); [A→F,B→F]	checkpoint(); [A→T,B→T]	checkpoint();
...	... [A→F,B→F]	... [A→T,B→T]	...
A[...]=...;	A[...]=...; [A→F,B→F]	A[...]=...; [A→F,B→T]	end_chkpt(A);
...	... [A→T,B→F]	[A→F,B→T]	A[...]=...;
for(...) {	for(...) { [A→T,B→F]	for(...) { [A→F,B→T]	start_chkpt(A);
...	... [A→T,B→F]	... [A→F,B→T]	...
B[...]=...;	B[...]=...; [A→T,B→F]	B[...]=...; [A→F,B→T]	for(...) {
...	... [A→T,B→T]	... [A→F,B→F]	...
}	} [A→T,B→T]	} [A→F,B→T]	end_chkpt(B);
...	... [A→T,B→F]	... [A→F,B→F]	B[...]=...;
checkpoint();	checkpoint(); [A→T,B→F]	checkpoint(); [A→F,B→F]	...
			}
			start_chkpt(B);
			...
			checkpoint();

Fig. 4. Analysis example

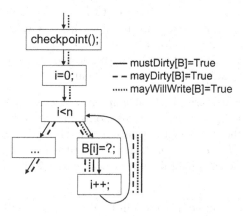

Fig. 5. Dataflow pattern for writes inside loops

To address this problem the above analysis was augmented with a loop-detection heuristic, shown in Figure 5. This heuristic uses may-Dirty information, in addition to the must-Dirty and may-WillWrite information of Section 3 and identifies the patterns of dataflow facts that must hold at the top of the first loop that writes to an array after a checkpoint. Figure 5 contains the CFG of such a loop and identifies the edges in the CFG where the various dataflow facts are $True$. It can be seen that the pattern at node $i < n$ is:

- $mustDirty[i < n](B) = False$
- $mayDirty[i < n](B) = True$
- $mayWillWrite[i < n](B) = True$
- $pred(i < n) > 1$

Furthermore, the CFG edge that points to $i < n$ from outside the loop is the one coming from the predecessor p where $mustDirtyAfter[p](B) = False$. Thus, by placing end_chkpt(B) on this incoming edge we can ensure both that end_chkpt(B) is called before any write to B and that it is not executed in every iteration of the loop.

Since this heuristic only applies to loops, it does not place end_chkpt(A) before the write to A in Figure 1. As such, we need to use both rules to ensure that end_chkpt is placed conservatively. However, if both rules are used then the example in Figure 1 will get two end_chkpt(B) calls: one before B's write loop and one before the write itself, negating the purpose of the loop-sensitive placement strategy. To prevent this from happening we propose an extra *EndChkpt-Placed* analysis that prevents end_chkpt(array) from being placed at a given node if there already exists an end_chkpt(array) on every path from any checkpoint call to the node. *EndChkpt-Placed* is a forward analysis that is executed as a separate pass from the Dirty and Will-Write passes. It maintains a bit of information for every array at every CFG node. $mustEndChkptPlaced[n](array)$ is set to $True$ if end_chkpt(array) is to be placed immediately before node n. It is set to $False$ if start_chkpt(array) is to be inserted at n. The later rule ensures that the "exclusion-zone" of a given insertion of end_chkpt(array) doesn't last past the next checkpoint call.

To implement this rule the loop-sensitive analysis maintains for each CFG node n the following additional dataflow information:

– $mayDirty[n](array)$: True if there *may* exist a write to $array$ along *some* path from a checkpoint call to this point in the code; False otherwise. Corresponds to the dataflow information immediately *before* n.
– $mustEndChkptPlaced[n](array)$: true if *all* paths from any checkpoint call to this point in the code contain a point where a end_chkpt(array) call will be placed.

This information is computed as shown in Figure 6. The modified rules for placing end_chkpt calls are shown in Figure 7 and Figure 8 extends the example in Figure 1 with the new $mustEndChkptPlaced$ information and the new placement of end_chkpt calls.

3.3   Inter-procedural Analysis

We have extended the above analysis with a context-insensitive, flow-sensitive inter-procedural analysis. The inter-procedural analysis works by applying the data-flow analysis from Section 3.2 to the CFG that contains all of the application's functions. When the analysis reaches a function call node for the first time, it computes a summary for this function. This is done by applying the dataflow analysis using the formulas in Figure 6 but with a modified lattice.

In addition to the standard $True$ and $False$, we introduce an additional $Unset$ state that appears below $True$ and $False$ in the lattice. All the dataflow facts for all arrays are initialized to $Unset$ at the start or end of the function (start for the forward analyses and end for the backward analysis). The standard analysis is then executed on the function using the extended lattice, with $Unset$ being treated as $False$ for the purposes of the EndChkpt-Placed analysis. If the state of a given array remains $Unset$ at the end of a given pass, this means that it was not modified by the pass. In the case of the Dirty and Will-Write analyses this means that the array is not written to inside the function. In the case of the EndChkpt-Placed analysis, this means that no end_chkpt calls are placed for this array inside the function. The function summary then is the dataflow facts for each array at the opposite end of the function: end for the forward analyses and start for the backward analysis. Function calls are processed by applying the function summary as a mask on all dataflow state. If $dataFlow[array] = Unset$ in the function summary, $array$'s mapping is not changed in the caller. However, if $dataFlow[array] = True$ or $False$ in the summary, the corresponding dataflow fact for $array$ is changed to $True$ or $False$ in the caller.

$$mayDirty[n](array) = \begin{cases} False & \text{if } n = \text{first node} \\ \bigcup_{m \in pred(n)} mayDirtyAfter[m](array) & \text{otherwise} \end{cases}$$

$$mayDirtyAfter[m](array) = [\![m]\!](mayDirty[m](array), array)$$

$$mustEndChkptPlaced[n](array) =$$

$$\begin{cases} False & \text{if } n = \text{first node} \\ \bigcap_{m \in pred(n)} mustEndChkptPlacedAfter[m](array) & \text{otherwise} \end{cases}$$

$mustEndChkptPlacedAfter[m](array) =$
    if $\neg \; placeStartChkptNode(m, array) \; \wedge$
      $\neg \; \exists l \in pred(m). \; placeStartChkptEdge(l, m, array))$ then
      $False$
    else if $(placeEndChkptNode(m, array) \; \vee$
      $\exists l \in pred(m). \; placeEndChkptEdge(l, m, array))$ then
      $True$
    else $mustEndChkptPlaced[m](array)$

// **end_chkpt(array)** will be placed immediately before node n if
$placeEndChkptNode(n, array) =$
    // node n is the first write to $array$ since the last **checkpoint**
    $(mustDirty[n](array) = False \wedge mustDirtyAfter[n](array) = True)$

// **end_chkpt(array)** will be placed along the edge $m \rightarrow n$ if
$placeEndChkptEdge(m, n, array) =$
    // node n is itself clean but predecessor m is dirty, n contains or is followed
    // by a write and predecessor m is not itself preceded by $end\_chkpt(array)$
    $(mustDirty[n](array) = False \wedge mayDirty[n](array) = True\wedge$
    $mayWillWrite[n](B) = True \wedge mustDirtyAfter[m](array) = False\wedge$
    $mustEndChkptPlaced[m](array) = False)$

// **start_chkpt(array)** will be placed immediately after node n if
$placeStartChkptNode(n, array) =$
    // node n is the last write to $array$ until the next **checkpoint**
    $(mayWillWriteBefore[n](array) = True \; \wedge \; mayWillWrite[n](array) = False)$

// **start_chkpt(array)** will be placed along the edge $m \rightarrow n$ if
$placeStartChkptEdge(m, n, array) =$
    // node n follows the last write to $array$ until the next **checkpoint**
    $(mayWillWriteBefore[n](array) = False \wedge mayWillWrite[m](array) = True)$

Fig. 6. Dataflow formulas for the loop-sensitive extension

foreach (*array*), foreach (CFG node *n*) in application
   if *placeEndChkptNode(n, array)*
      place **end_chkpt**(*array*) immediately before *n*
   if ∃*m* ∈ *pred(n)*. *placeEndChkptEdge(m, n, array)*
      place **end_chkpt(array)** on edge *m* → *n*

Fig. 7. Loop-sensitive transformation for inserting calls to **end_chkpt**

Original Code	Code with Must-EndChkptPlaced States	Transformed Code

checkpoint();
 	
...
 	
A[...]=...;
 	
...
 	
for(...) {
 	
  ...
 	
  B[...]=...;
 	
  ...
 	
}
 	
...
 	
checkpoint();
	checkpoint(); [A→F,B→F]
	
	... [A→F,B→F]
	
	A[...]=...; [A→F,B→F]
	
	[A→T,B→F]
	
	for(...) { [A→T,B→T]
	
	  ... [A→T,B→T]
	
	  B[...]=...; [A→T,B→T]
	
	  ... [A→T,B→T]
	
	} [A→T,B→T]
	
	... [A→T,B→T]
	
	checkpoint(); [A→T,B→T]
		checkpoint();
		
		...
		
		end_chkpt(A);
		
		A[...]=...;
		
		start_chkpt(A);
		
		...
		
		end_chkpt(B);
		
		for(...) {
		
		  ...
		
		  B[...]=...;
		
		  ...
		
		}
		
		start_chkpt(B);
		
		...
		
		checkpoint();

Fig. 8. Transformation example with loop-sensitive optimizations

4 Experimental Evaluation

4.1 Experimental Setup

We have evaluated the effectiveness of the above compiler analysis by implementing it on top of the ROSE [8] source-to-source compiler framework and applying it to the OpenMP versions [1] of the NAS Parallel Benchmarks [2]. We have used these codes in sequential mode and have focused on the codes BT, CG, EP, FT, LU, SP. We have omitted MG from our analysis since it uses dynamic multi-dimensional arrays (arrays of pointers to lower-dimensional arrays), which requires additional complex pointer analyses to identify arrays in the code. In contrast, the other codes use simple contiguous arrays, which require no additional reasoning power. Each NAS code was augmented with a checkpoint call at the top of its main compute loop and one immediately after the loop.

The target applications were executed on problem classes S, W and A (S is the smallest of the three and A the largest), on 4-way 2.4Ghz dual-core Opteron SMPs, with 16GB of RAM per node (Atlas cluster at the Lawrence Livermore National Laboratory). Each run was performed on a dedicated node and all reported results are averages of 10 runs. Each application was set to checkpoint

5 times, with the checkpoints spaced evenly throughout the application's execution. This number was chosen to allow us to sample the different checkpoint sizes that may exist in different parts of the application without forcing the application to take a checkpoint during every single iteration, which would have been unrealistically frequent.

The transformed codes were evaluated with a model checkpointing runtime that implements the API from Section 2 and simulates the costs of a real checkpointer. It performs the same state tracking as a real checkpointer but instead of actually saving application state, it simply sleeps for an appropriate period of time. One side-effect of this is the fact that our checkpointer does not simulate the overheads due to saving variables other than arrays. However, since in the NAS benchmarks such variables make up a tiny fraction of overall state, the resulting measurement error is small. Furthermore, since the model checkpointer can sleep for any amount of time, it can simulate checkpointing performance for a wide variety of storage I/O bandwidths.

The model checkpointer can be run in both a blocking and a non-blocking mode. In blocking mode the checkpointer does not spawn an asynchronous checkpointing thread but instead saves all live state inside the main thread's `checkpoint` calls. The model runtime can simulate both a basic checkpointer, which saves all state and an incremental checkpointer, which only saves the state that has changed since the last checkpoint. In particular, in incremental mode the the model checkpointer simulates the checkpointing of any array for which `start_chkpt` has been called since the last `checkpoint` call. Arrays for which `start_chkpt` has not been called are ignored.

In non-blocking mode, the model checkpointer spawns off an asynchronous checkpointing thread. The thread maintains a write-out queue of memory regions to save and continuously pulls memory regions the queue, sleeping for as long at it takes to save the next memory region to disk at the given I/O bandwidth. When the main thread calls `end_chkpt` for one array, it may be that the checkpointing thread is currently sleeping on another array. To control the amount of waiting time, the model checkpointer breaks arrays up into smaller blocks and simulates checkpointing at block granularity. `start_chkpt(array)` inserts `array`'s blocks at the end of the write-out queue. We also tried spreading the new array's blocks evenly across the queue but did not find a substantial or consistent performance difference between the two policies.

4.2   Incremental Checkpointing

We evaluated the effectiveness of the above analysis for incremental checkpointing by comparing the performance of two configurations of the model checkpointer's blocking mode:

- CHKPT_ALL - simulates the checkpointing of all application arrays inside each `checkpoint` call.
- CHKPT_INCR - same as CHKPT_ALL but omits any arrays for which `start_chkpt` hasn't been called since the last `checkpoint` call.

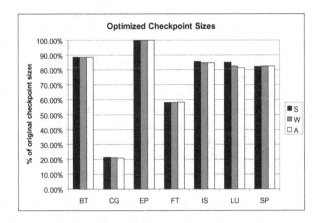

Fig. 9. Checkpoint sizes in CHKPT_INCR as a fraction of checkpoint sizes in CHKPT_ALL

We first compare the checkpoint sizes generated by the two modes. In the context of the NAS codes, which have a initialization phase, followed by a main compute loop, the primary effect of the above analysis is to eliminate write-once arrays from checkpointing. These are the arrays that are written to during the initialization phase and then only read from during the main compute loop. As such, since there do not exist any start_chkpt calls for these arrays during the main compute loop, they are only saved during the first checkpoint and omitted in subsequent checkpoints.

The measured reductions in checkpoint size are shown in Figure 9. It can be seen that even using array granularity, incremental checkpointing can result in a dramatic reduction in checkpoint sizes. Indeed, in CG checkpoints drop to below 22% of their original size, while FT's drop to 60%. Other codes see drops from 0% to 18%. While there are small differences in the effect of incremental checkpointing across different problem sizes, the effect is generally small.

Figure 10 shows the the execution time of an application that uses incremental checkpointing as a percentage of the execution time of one that does not. We show only CG and EP, since the behavior of these codes is similar to that of other codes that have a large or a small checkpoint size reduction, respectively. The x-axis is the I/O bandwidth used in the experiments, ranging from 1 MB/s to 1 GB/s in multiples of 4 and including Infinite bandwidth. This range includes a variety of use-cases, including hard-drives (60MB/s write bandwidth) and 10 Gigabit Ethernet(1GB/s bandwidth). In the case of EP, although there is some difference in performance between the two versions, the effect is at noise level at all bandwidths, with no correlation between execution time and performance. However, for CG, the effect is quite dramatic, ranging from pronounced difference in execution times for low bandwidths, when the cost of checkpointing is important, to a much smaller difference for high bandwidths.

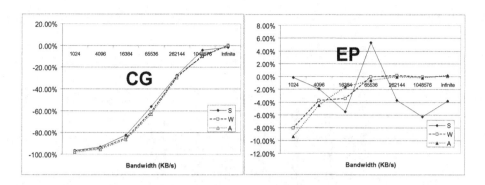

Fig. 10. Relative execution time differences between CHKPT_INCR and CHKPT_ALL

4.3   Asynchronous Checkpointing

We examined the performance characteristics of asynchronous checkpointing by looking at the relationship between the I/O bandwidth and the block size used for queue management. To this end we examined a range of block sizes ranging from 1KB to 64MB in multiples of 4, using the above bandwidth range. For almost all code/input class/bandwidth combinations we found that the execution times formed a bowl shape, an example of which is shown in Figure 11. This Figure shows LU running on input size W. For each I/O bandwidth we can see high execution times for the largest and the smallest batch size, with faster runs for intermediate batch sizes. Large batch sizes have high overhead because of the increased probability that an end_chkpt call for some array will occur in the middle of a long wait for a large block of another array. Small batch sizes are a problem because of the increased overhead associated with synchronizing on and manipulating a large number of memory regions. While this work does not address the problem of picking an optimal batch size for a given code/input class/bandwidth combination, we did find that in general the bottom of the bowl stays flat, with a wide variety of batch sizes offering similarly good performance. This suggests that near-optimal batch sizes can be found for a wide variety of combinations. In our experiments, 64KB batches provided near-optimal performance in all configurations examined.

We evaluated the performance of asynchronous checkpointing by picking the best batch size for each code/input size/bandwidth combination and compared its performance to that of blocking incremental checkpointing (the CHKPT_INCR configuration from above). The result, for input size W, is shown in Figure 4.3. For each application it plots:

$$\frac{(\text{execution time w/ asynchronous checkpointing}) - (\text{execution time w/ blocking checkpointing})}{(\text{execution time w/ blocking checkpointing})}$$

It can be seen that different applications respond very differently to the two algorithms. Whereas CG performs better with asynchronous checkpointing, FT and IS

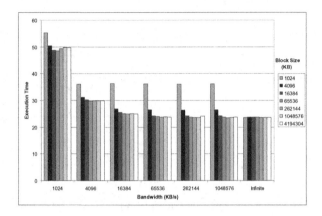

Fig. 11. Execution times for different bandwidths and batch sizes (LU-W)

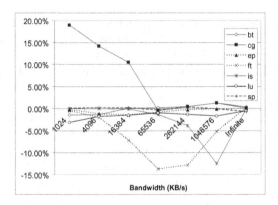

Fig. 12. Relative execution times for asynchronous vs blocking checkpointing (Class W)

tend to perform better with blocking checkpointing. Input class A shows very similar results, while class S exhibits a stronger preference for blocking checkpointing.

While intuitively it may appear that asynchronous checkpointing should always perform better than blocking checkpointing, these experiments show that there are some interference effects that complicate this simple analysis. While the full reason for this effect is still under investigation, it appears that the additional synchronization required to implement asynchronous checkpointing may have a negative performance impact. In particular, each call by the application thread to start_chkpt and end_chkpt requires synchronization with the asynchronous checkpointing thread.

5   Summary

We have presented a novel compiler analysis for optimizing automated checkpointing. Given an application that has been augmented by the user with calls to a **checkpoint** function, the analysis identifies regions in the code that do not have any writes to a given array. This information can be used to reduce the amount of data checkpointed and to asynchronously checkpoint this data in a separate thread. In our experiments with the NAS Parallel Benchmarks we have found that this analysis reduces checkpoint sizes by between 15% and 78% for most of the codes. These checkpoint size reductions were found to have a notable effect on checkpointing performance. Furthermore, we evaluated the performance of compiler-enabled asynchronous checkpointing. Although our experiments showed that asynchronous checkpointing can sometimes be better than blocking checkpointing, we discovered that this is frequently not the case. As such, the choice between asynchronous and blocking checkpointing depends on the application itself.

References

1. http://phase.hpcc.jp/Omni/benchmarks/NPB
2. http://www.nas.nasa.gov/Software/NPB
3. Adiga, N.R., Almasi, G., Almasi, G.S., Aridor, Y., Barik, R., Beece, D., Bellofatto, R., Bhanot, G., Bickford, R., Blumrich, M., Bright, A.A., Brunleroto J.: An overview of the bluegene/l supercomputer. In: IEEE/ACM Supercomputing Conference (2002)
4. Agarwal, S., Garg, R., Gupta, M.S., Moreira, J.: Adaptive incremental checkpointing for massively parallel systems. In: Proceedings of the 18th International Conference on Supercomputing (ICS), pp. 277–286 (2004)
5. Gioiosa, R., Sancho, J.C., Jiang, S., Petrini, F.: Transparent, incremental checkpointing at kernel level: a foundation for fault tolerance for parallel computers. In: Supercomputing (November 2005)
6. Michalak, S.E., Harris, K.W., Hengartner, N.W., Takala, B.E., Wender, S.A.: Predicting the number of fatal soft errors in los alamos national laboratorys asc q supercomputer. IEEE Transactions on Device and Materials Reliability 5(3), 329–335 (2005)
7. Plank, J.S., Beck, M., Kingsley, G.: Compiler-assisted memory exclusion for fast checkpointing. IEEE Technical Committee on Operating Systems and Application Environments 7(4), 10–14 (Winter 1995)
8. Quinlan, D.: Rose: Compiler support for object-oriented frameworks. Parallel Processing Letters 10(2-3), 215–226 (2000)
9. Ross, K.C.R., Moreirra, J., Preiffer, W.: Parallel i/o on the ibm blue gene /l system. Technical report, BlueGene Consortium (2005)
10. Sancho, J.C., Petrini, F., Johnson, G., Fernandez, J., Frachtenberg, E.: On the feasibility of incremental checkpointing for scientific computing. In: 18th International Parallel and Distributed Processing Symposium (IPDPS), p. 58 (2004)
11. Schroeder, B., Gibson, G.A.: A large-scale study of failures in high-performance computing systems. In: Proceedings of the International Conference on Dependable Systems and Networks (DSN) (June 2006)
12. Zhang, K., Pande, S.: Efficient application migration under compiler guidance. In: Proceedings of the Conference on Languages, Compilers, and Tools for Embedded Systems, pp. 10–20 (2005)

Techniques for Efficient Software Checking*

Jing Yu, María Jesús Garzarán, and Marc Snir

University of Illinois at Urbana-Champaign
{jingyu,garzaran,snir}@cs.uiuc.edu

Abstract. Dramatic increases in the number of transistors that can
be integrated on a chip make processors more susceptible to radiation-
induced transient errors. For commodity chips which are cost- and
energy-constrained, we need a flexible and inexpensive technology for
fault detection. Software approaches can play a major role for this sector
of the market because they need little hardware modifications and can
be tailored to fit different requirements of reliability and performance.
However, software approaches add a significant overhead.

In this paper we propose two novel techniques that reduce the overhead of software error checking approaches. The first technique uses
boolean logic to identify code patterns that correspond to outcome tolerant branches. We develop a compiler algorithm that finds those patterns
and removes the unnecessary replicas. In the second technique we evaluate the performance benefit obtained by removing address checks before
load and stores. In addition, we evaluate the overheads that can be removed when the register file is protected in hardware.

Our experimental results show that the first technique improves performance by an average 7% for three of the SPEC benchmarks. The
second technique can reduce overhead by up-to 50% when the most aggressive optimization is applied.

1 Introduction

Dramatic increases in the number of transistors that can be integrated on a
chip will deliver great performance gains. However, it will also expose a major
roadblock, namely the poor reliability of the hardware. Indeed, in the near-future
environment of low power, low voltage, relatively high frequency, and very small
feature size, processors will be more susceptible to transient errors. Transient
faults, also known as soft errors are due to impacts from high-energy particles
that change the logic values of latches or logic structures [1,2,3,4].

In this new environment, we believe that a Software Checking System has a
fundamental role in providing fault detection and recovery. It is possible that
high-end architectures will include several hardware-intensive fault-tolerant techniques that are currently supported by IBM mainframes [5], HP NonStop [6] or
mission-critical computers [7]. However, commodity multicore chips will likely be

* This material is based upon work supported by the National Science Foundation
under the CSR-AES program Award No. 0615273.

V. Adve, M.J. Garzarán, and P. Petersen (Eds.): LCPC 2007, LNCS 5234, pp. 16–31, 2008.
© Springer-Verlag Berlin Heidelberg 2008

too cost- and energy-constrained to include such hardware. Instead, we believe that they will likely include only relatively simple hardware primitives, such as parity for certain processor buses and structures, error correction codes (ECC) and scrubbing in the memory hierarchy [8] and low-cost support for memory checkpointing and rollback (e.g., ReVive [9] or SafetyNet [10]). Then they will rely on flexible and inexpensive software technology for error protection.

Current software approaches address the problem by replicating the instructions and adding checking instructions to compare the results, but they add a significant overhead. In this paper we propose two novel techniques to reduce the overhead of the software error checking approaches. The first technique is based on the fact that programs already have redundancy, and if the compiler can determine the programs sections where such redundancy exists, it can avoid the replication and later checking. We use boolean logic to identify a code pattern that corresponds to outcome tolerant branches and develop a compiler algorithm that automatically finds those patterns and removes the unnecessary replicas. The second technique is based on the observation that faults that corrupt the application tend to quickly generate other noisy errors such as segmentation faults [11]. Thus, we can reduce replication of the instructions that tend to generate these type of errors, trading reliability for performance. In this paper we remove the checks of the memory addresses and discuss situations where removing these checks affect little to the fault coverage. This occurs when a check of a variable is covered by a later check to the same variable, and thus errors in the first check will be detected by the later checks; and in pointer-chasing, when the data loaded by a load is used immediately by another load. Finally, We also consider the situation where the register file is protected with parity or ECC, such as Intel Itanium [12], Sun UltraSPARC [13] and IBM Power4-6 [14]. We call them register safe platforms.

We have implemented the baseline replication and the proposed techniques using the LLVM Compiler Infrastructure [15] and run experiments on a Pentium 4 using Spec benchmarks. Our results show that the boolean logic technique achieves 7% performance speedup on three benchmarks, and 1.6% on average. If we do not check load addresses, the performance is improved by 20.2%. If we do not check addresses of both load and store, the performance is improved by 24.8%. On platforms where registers are protected in hardware, we can combine these techniques and obtain an average speedup of 35.2% and 40.8%, respectively, and decrease the software checking overhead by 44.9% and 50%, respectively. Our fault injection experiments show that removing address checks before loads only increases Silent Data Corruption (SDC) from 0.27% to 0.35%, and removing address checks for loads and stores raises SDC to 1.11%.

The rest of the paper is organized as follows. Section 2 presents the background and the baseline software checking; Section 3 describes the techniques to detect outcome tolerant branches; Section 4 describes the removal of address checks; Section 5 discusses the benefits of having a register file that is checked in hardware; Section 6 presents our experimental results; Section 7 presents related work, and finally Section 8 concludes the paper.

2   Background and Baseline Software Checking

The use of software approaches for fault tolerance has received significant attention in the research domain. Software techniques such as SWIFT [16] replicate the instructions of the original program and interleave the original instructions and their replicas in the same thread. Memory does not need to be replicated because the memory hierarchy is protected with ECC and scrubbing. Stores, branches, function calls and returns are considered "synchronization" points and checking instructions are inserted before these instructions to validate certain values. Before a store, checking instructions verify that the correct data is stored to the correct memory location. Before a branch, checking instructions verify that the branch takes the appropriate path. Before a function call checking instructions verify the input operands by comparing them against their replica. Before a function return, checking instructions verify the return value by comparing the return register and its replica.

Stores are executed only once, but loads are replicated because the loaded data can be corrupted. However, uncachable loads, such as those from external devices, and loads in a multithreaded program may return different values when executing two consecutive loads to the same memory address; so rather than replicating the load, checking instructions are also added before loads to verify that the address of the load matches its replica. After that verification, the loaded value can be copied to another register [16,17,18]. Thus, since loads are not replicated, they are also considered "synchronization" points. An example with the original and its corresponding replicated code is shown in Figure 1-(a) and (b), respectively. The replicated code contains additional instructions and uses additional registers marked with a '. The additional instructions are shown in bold and numbered. Instructions 1 and 2 check that the load is loading from the correct address, instruction 3 copies the value in r3 to r3', instruction 4 replicates the addition, and instruction 5-8 check that the store writes the correct data to the correct memory address.

```
                          cmp r6, r6'    (1)
                          jne faultDet   (2)
       ld r3=[r6]         ld r3=[r6]                ld r3=[r6]
                          mov r3'=r3     (3)

       ....               ....                      ....
       add r4= r3,1       add r4= r3,1              add r4= r3,1
                          add r4'=r3',1  (4)        add r4'=r3,1   (4)

                          ....                      ....
                          cmp r4, r4'    (5)        cmp r4, r4'    (5)
                          jne faultDet   (6)        jne faultDet   (6)
                          cmp r6, r6'    (7)
                          jne faultDet   (8)
       store [r6]=r4      store [r6]=r4             store [r6]=r4

    (a) Original code     (b) Replicated code       (c) Safe registers
```

Fig. 1. Example of baseline software replication and checking

3 Use of Boolean Logic to Find Outcome Tolerant Branches

In this Section we explain how to use boolean logic to reduce the amount of replicated instructions. We first do an overview (Section 3.1) and then explain the compiler algorithm (Section 3.2).

3.1 Overview

Our technique is based on the fact that programs have redundancy. For instance, Wang et al. [19] performed fault injection experiments and found that about 40% of all the dynamic conditional branches are outcome tolerant. These are branches that, despite an error, converge to the correct point of execution. These branches are outcome-tolerant due to redundancies introduced by the compiler or the programmer. An example of outcome-tolerant branch appears in a structure such as if (A || B || C) then X else Y. In this case if A is erroneously computed to be true, but B or C are actually true, this branch is outcome tolerant, since the code converges to the correct path. The control flow graph of this structure is shown in Figure 2-(a).

The state-of-the-art approach to check for errors is to replicate branches as shown in Figure 2-(b), where the circles correspond to the branch replicas. However, we can reduce overheads by removing the comparison replica when the branch correctly branches to X. If the original comparison in A is true we need to execute the comparison replica to verify that the code correctly branches to X. However, if A is false, we can skip the execution of the A replica and move to check B. We will only need to execute the A replica if both B and C are also false. The resulting control flow graph is shown in Figure 2-(c). In situations where A and B are false, but C is true, we can save a few comparisons.

Outcome tolerant branches also appear in code structures such as if (A & B & C) then X else Y, and in general in all the code structures that contain one or more shortcut paths in the control flow graph. A basic *shortcut path* is edge(A->X) in Figure 3-(a), where both A and its child point to the same block. However, most shortcut paths are more complex. For instance, in Figure 3-(b), block A points to the same block pointed by its grandchild (not its direct

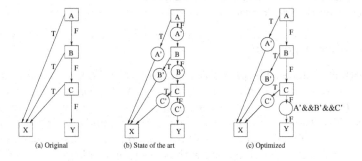

(a) Original   (b) State of the art   (c) Optimized

Fig. 2. Eliminating replicated predicate evaluation

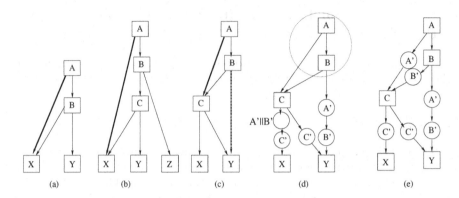

Fig. 3. Shortcut graphs and optimizations

child). Thus, the optimizer should move A' from edge(A->B) to edge(B->Z) and edge(C->Y). The example in Figure 3-(c) can be optimized in two different ways. If A and B are considered as a whole unit, edge(B->Y) is the shortcut path, and the graph can be optimized as shown in Figure 3-(d); otherwise, it can be optimized as shown in Figure 3-(e).

Detecting the existence of a shortcut path is not sufficient to determine that there is an outcome tolerant branch. The reason is that one of the blocks involved in the shortcut can modify a variable that is later used by instructions outside the block. That block needs to be replicated or the error could propagate outside the block. Next we show two examples:

(a) if (*m > 0) && (m < N) then X else Y
(b) if (t=(*m > 0)) && (m < N) then X else Y

In the example in (a), if (*m>0) is mistakenly computed as True, but (m<N) is False, we can safely ignore the error on (*m>0) and take the Y path. However, if the error occurs to the example in (b), and t is used in Y, ignoring the error will result in a wrong value for t being propagated to Y, which may end up corrupting the system. To avoid this type of errors our compiler algorithm only considers blocks that are involved in a shortcut path and produce values that are only used by the block itself.

3.2   Compiler Algorithm

Our algorithm analyzes the control flow graph of the original program and extracts the shortcut paths and the related blocks. A *shortcut graph* always has a head node (block A in all the examples in Figure 3), one or more intermediate nodes (like B and C), two or more leaves (like X and Y), and one or more shortcut paths. Notice that in this paper we call a *block* to a single basic block or a list of basic blocks connected one by one with edges of unconditional branches.

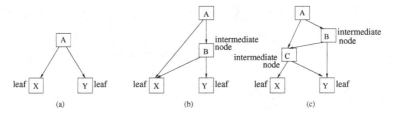

Fig. 4. Constructing potential shortcut graphs

Our algorithm has two phases: first a search of all potential shortcut graphs, and second, the optimization and appropriate placement of the replicas.

Shortcut Graphs Search. The searching process starts by classifying each block as an intermediate node or a leaf, and building an intermediate node set and a leaf set. A block is called "intermediate node" if it ends with a conditional branch and does not contain side effects (does not contain a function call, a memory write or generates a value used by another block). In addition, to avoid being trapped in loops, we require that none of the outgoing edges of an intermediate node is a loop backward edge. If the node does not classify as intermediate node, then it is considered a "leaf", meaning that this block can be at the most an ending node in a shortcut graph. At the same time we build the intermediate and leaf sets, we also build a separate head node set. A block is called "head node" if it ends with a conditional branch and none of the outgoing edges is backwards, no matter it has side effects or not. Thus the head node set contains all intermediate nodes and some of the leaves.

After building the intermediate node set, the leaf set, and the head node set the shortcut graphs are built from bottom to up by scanning the head node set repeatedly. We start by initializing an empty set "graph-head-set", which will contain temporary graph head nodes. For any node(A) in the head node set, we check its two children (see Figure 4):

1. If the two children are leaves, this node is added to the graph-head-set (Figure 4-(a)).
2. If one child is a leaf(X) and the other child is an intermediate node(B) and node(B) is already in the graph-head-set, node(B) is replaced by the current node(A) in the graph-head-set (Figure 4-(b)). We also check if the leaf(X) is a child or grandchild of node(B), in which case a shortcut path for node (A) is marked.
3. If the two children are both intermediate nodes((B) and (C)) and both are in the graph-head-set, nodes (B) and (C) are replaced by node(A) in the graph-head-set (Figure 4-(c)). We also check if (A) introduces new shortcut paths.

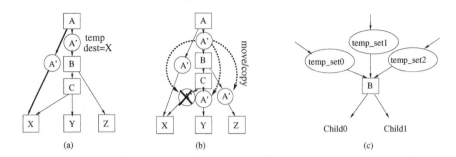

Fig. 5. Optimizing shortcut graphs

The scan continues until all the nodes in the head node set have been visited. Then, a node in the graph-head-set represents a graph led by this node together with the shortcut paths found. A final pass traverses the graph-head-set and removes those heads that do not contain any shortcut path.

Optimization. After the shortcut paths are found we start applying the optimization, but we first check when it is legal to perform it. In Figure 2-(b), our optimization will move the replica A' from edge(A->B) to edge(C->Y). However, this is only legal if A dominates C. Otherwise A' may use undefined values in the new position. Thus to apply our optimization phase we first verify the domination relationship of all shortcut paths.

The goal of our optimization pass is to move replicas of the non-shortcut path down to the edge/s between the last child and the leaf/leaves. Next, we explain how this algorithm proceeds using the example in Figure 5. For each shortcut graph in the graph-head-set the algorithm finds all the shortcut paths (edge(A->X) in Figure 5-(a)), marks the replica (A') on the other path as temporary (temp), and records the destination of the shortcut path (X). Next the optimization pass scans all the intermediate nodes in the shortcut graph in a top-down fashion, and moves temporary replicas from the incoming edges to all the outgoing ones, except to those where the recorded destination of the replica and the destination of the intermediate node that we are processing are the same (an example is shown in Figure 5-(b)). Notice that when an intermediate node has multiple incoming edges (as shown in Figure 5-(c)) we only move the replicas that appear on all the incoming edges. Also notice that this optimization pass processes nodes top-down, and it does not treat multiple nodes as a single unit. Thus, for the example in Figure 3-(c), the optimized version after this pass will be the one shown in Figure 3-(e).

Finally note that A, B and C can contain computations like (s+1) == 5. In this case, if the computations are only used to determine the outcome of the branch, the computation replicas are also eliminated when the branch replica does not need to execute.

4   Removal of Address Checks

Recent experiments have shown that faults produce not only data corruption, but also events that are atypical of steady state operation and that can be used as a warning that something is wrong [11]. Thus, we can reduce the overhead of the software approaches and trade reliability for performance by reducing the replication, hoping that the error will manifest with these atypical events.

In this Section we consider the removal of address checks before load and store instructions. Errors in the registers containing memory addresses may manifest as segmentation faults. However, any fault-tolerant system must also include support for roll-back to a safe state and thus, on a segmentation fault we can roll-back and re-execute, and only communicate the error to the user if it appears again. However, by doing this the system will be vulnerable to errors, since some of these faulty addresses will access a legal space and the operating system will not be able to detect the error. Thus, this technique will decrease error coverage. Next, we discuss two techniques that the compiler can use to determine which load and store instructions are most suitable for address check removal.

Address checks can be removed when there are later checks checking the same variable. For example, in Figure 1-(b), checking instructions (1-2) and (7-8) are checking the register r6. This makes the first check (1-2) unnecessary, because if an error occurs to r6 it will manifest as a segmentation fault or will be eventually detected by the checking instructions (7-8). We have observed many of these checks in the SPEC benchmarks due to the register indirect addressing mode, since the same register is used to access two fields of a structure, or because two array accesses share a common index. Removing these replicated checks can significantly reduce the software overhead.

Address checks can also be removed when the probability of error to the loaded value is small. This case appears in pointer chasing, where the data loaded from memory is used as the address for a subsequent load. An example is shown in Figure 6-(a) and (b). In this case, since the processor will issue the second load as soon as the first one completes, the probability of error is very small. In some cases, however, the value loaded by the first load is not exactly the one used by the next load, if not that it may be first modified by an **add** instruction. This occurs when accessing an element of a structure that is different from the first one. In this case, the probability of error is higher, and the checking instructions will also determine if an error occurred during the computation of the addition. An example is shown in Figure 6-(c) and (d).

ld r2=[r1]	ld r2=[r1]	ld r2=[r1]	ld r2=[r1]
	~~check r2~~	add r4=r2,16	add r4=r2,16
ld r3=[r2]	ld r3=[r2]	**check r4**	**check r4**
		ld r3=[r4]	ld r3=[r4]
(a)	(b)	(c)	(d)

Fig. 6. Address check removal for pointer chasing

In this paper we evaluate the removal of the address checks for only the loads, or for both loads and stores. Thus, our results are an upper bound on the performance benefit that we can obtain and the reliability that we can lose. In the future we plan to write a data flow analysis to identify the checks that are safe to remove, as explained above.

5   Register Safe Platforms

In this Section we consider the situation where the register file is hardware protected with parity or ECC, or other cost-effective mechanisms as the ones proposed by [20,21,22,23]. In fact, the register file of the Intel Itanium [12], Sun UltraSPARC [13] and IBM Power4-6 [14] are already protected by parity or ECC. However, the ALUs and other portions of the processor are not protected, so arithmetic and logic operations can return wrong results. Thus, all the instructions that imply ALU operations need to be replicated; however, memory operations such as load and stores are safe. As a result, a register that is defined by a load does not need to be replicated, saving the instruction to perform the copy and the additional register. An example is shown in Figure 1. The replicated code in Figure 1-(b) can be simplified as shown in Figure 1-(c). Register r3' is not necessary because registers and memory are safe, and instruction 4 can use directly the contents from register r3. Instructions 1, 2, 7 and 8 can be removed if we assume register r6 has been defined by a load. Instructions 5 and 6 cannot be removed because register r4 is defined by an addition, and we need to validate the results of the addition.

6   Evaluation

In this Section we evaluate our proposed techniques. We first discuss our environmental setup (Section 6.1), analyze our techniques statically (Section 6.2), evaluate performance (Section 6.3), and measure reliability (Section 6.4).

6.1   Environmental Setup

We use LLVM [15] as our compiler infrastructure to generate redundant codes. Replicated and checking instructions are added at the intermediate level, right after all the static optimizations have been done. We replicate all the integer and floating point instructions. Previous implementations have replicated instructions at the backend, right before register allocation [16,24] or via dynamic binary translation [25]. However, the advantages of working at the intermediate level are: i) the redundant code can be easily ported to other platforms, ii) we do not need to fully understand the assembly code for that platform, and iii) at the intermediate level we see a simple memory access model rather than complex one of the x86 ISA. To prevent optimizations done by the backend generator such as common subexpression elimination and instruction combination, we tag the replicated instructions, and the backend optimizations are applied separately to the tag and the untag instructions.

For the evaluation we use SPEC CINT2000 and the C codes from SPEC CFP 2000, running with the ref inputs. Experiments are done on a 3.6GHz INTEL Pentium 4 with 2GB of RAM running RedHat9 Linux.

6.2 Static Analysis

In this Section we characterize load addresses depending on whether the register is checked by a later checking instruction (Covered), or if the register used by the load was just loaded from memory (Loaded), as in the pointer chasing example of Section 4. All the remaining load addresses are classified as (Other). The breakdown is shown in Figure 7. On average more than 40% load addresses have nearby later checks on the same value. About 20% of the loads use registers whose contents where just loaded from memory. As we have discussed in Section 4, the probability of error of any of these addresses is very small, because the processor will likely issue the second load as soon as the first one completes. Also, if we assume a register safe platform these checks are unnecessary. For the remaining 40% of the addresses, an error in the most significant bits will be detected as a form of segmentation faults, but an error in the least significant ones can cause a silent error.

6.3 Performance

Figure 8 shows the performance speedup obtained when using boolean logic to eliminate replication and checks on outcome tolerant branches (Section 3). Three benchmarks (gzip, vpr, and perlbmk) achieve 7% performance gains, though the average speedup is 1.6% through all tested benchmarks. Notice that there is also a negative impact on vortex, where we observe more load/store instructions after the optimization, meaning that this optimization introduces additional register spills that hurt the benefit of less dynamic instructions.

Figure 9 evaluates the performance benefit of our second technique (Section 4): baseline Fully Replicated(FullRep), No checks for Address of Loads(NAL), No checks for Address of Load and Store(NALS), and No checks when the Register file is safe (R). The Fully Replicated code(FullRep) is on average 2.38 times

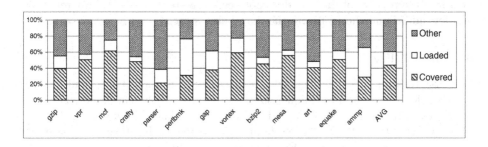

Fig. 7. Characterization of load addresses

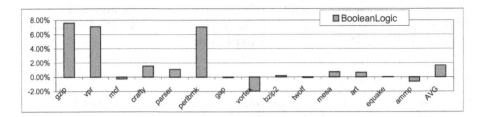

Fig. 8. Performance speedup with boolean logic optimization compared to baseline replication

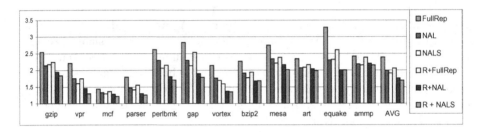

Fig. 9. Performance of the different optimizations normalized against the original non-replicated code

slower than the original code. This large overhead is due to high register pressure and additional instructions. On average, register safe optimization (R) runs 16.0% faster than the (FullRep).

After we remove checks for address of loads (NAL), we get an average 20.2% speedup over the baseline Fully Prelicated (FullRep). If we further remove checks for address of stores (NALS), we improve 4.6% more. And if the register is protected in hardware and we combine (NAL) or (NALS) with (R), we can obtain an average speedup of 35.2% and 40.8% respectively, what will reduce the the software checking overhead by 44.9% and 50%, respectively. Notice that with (NALS) all address checks before loads and stores are removed, so the performance benefit of (R+NALS) versus (NALS) is due to the reduced register pressure (the register of the load does not need to be replicated) and the removal of a few additional checks before the data being stored.

6.4 Reliability

Our first technique is very conservative and should not affect the fault coverage. But for the second technique, since we remove all the checks for memory addresses, memory can be corrupted. In order to evaluate the loss of fault coverage, we use Pin [26] and inject faults to the binary file (excluding system libraries). We assume a Single Event Upset(SEU) fault model, so only one bit fault is injected during the execution of the program. In total 300 faults are injected for each program. Although both integer and floating point registers

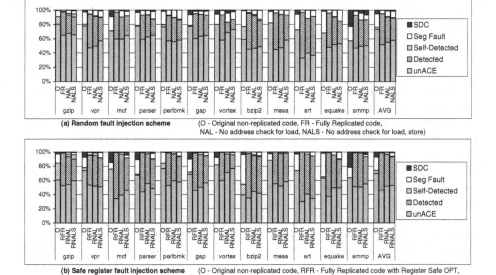

(a) **Random fault injection scheme**   (O - Original non-replicated code, FR - Fully Replicated code, NAL - No address check for load, NALS - No address check for load, store)

(b) **Safe register fault injection scheme**   (O - Original non-replicated code, RFR - Fully Replicated code with Register Safe OPT, RNAL - No address check for load with Register Safe OPT, RNALS - No address check for load, store with Resiter Safe OPT)

Fig. 10. Fault-detection rates break down

can be corrupted, in order to magnify the impact of the errors we only inject fault to the 8 32-bit integer registers and the status flags EFLAGS. When we consider that the register file is not protected in hardware we mimic the fault distribution by randomly selecting a dynamic instruction and flipping a random bit in a random register (we call this scheme "random fault injection"). When the register file is protected in hardware, we do the same, but flip the random bit from its "output". The output can be in a register or in memory if it has been spilled. In this scheme, memory load instructions are avoided (we call this scheme "safe register fault injection").

After injecting an error into the binary, the program is run to completion (unless it aborts) and its output is compared to a correct output. Depending on the result the error will be categorized as: (unACE), the bit is unnecessary for Architectural Correct Execution [27]; (Detected), the error is detected by our checking code; (Self-Detected), the error is detected by the program assertions; (Seg Fault), the error manifests as an exception or a segmentation fault; (SDC), Silent Data Corruption, when the program finishes normally but the produced output is incorrect. (SDC) is the first type of errors we want to prevent. Then, we also want to minimize (self-Detected) errors and (Seg Fault), because it is usually hard to determine if the error is due to a program bug or a soft error. But with proper support, if we can roll-back and re-execute, these faults can be recovered, so they are less harmful.

Figure 10-(a) and (b) show the experimental results for random fault injection and safe register fault injection, respectively. The fault detection rates for these two schemes are very similar. Notice that the original program (O) has on average 75% (unACE) and less than 10% (SDC), which means that the software itself has a certain fault maskability. With the safe register scheme more faults result in SDC than with the random scheme (8.5% over 5%) and less Seg Fault (15.6% over 17%). The reason is that the random scheme is more likely to pick up a dynamic dead register or a register that holds the index for addresses.

After the program is replicated (FR), most (Seg Fault), (Self-Detected) and (SDC) go to the (Detected) category. (SDC) errors appear because some faults are injected before the value is used but after is checked. If we remove checks for addresses, reliability does not drop much. Under random injection scheme, if we remove checks for load addresses (NAL), comparing to (FR), (SDC) increases from 0.36% to 1.08%, (Seg Fault) increases from 4.47% to 8.05%. If we also remove checks for store addresses (NALS), (SDC) rises to 1.44%, and (Seg Fault) rises to 9.02%. Under safe register injection scheme, removing checks for load addresses increases (SDC) from 0.27% to 0.38%, increase (Seg Fault) from 2.66% to 4.99%. Removing checks for store addresses further results in (SDC) of 1.11%, and (Seg Fault) of 4.99%. In other words, when normalized to the original program, under the safe register scheme removing checks for addresses of load only incurs an extra 1.3% (SDC), while removing checks for all addresses incurs 9.8%(SDC). Given that we almost decrease the performance overhead by half, this loss of fault coverage seems acceptable.

7   Related Work

Previous work on compiler instrumentation for fault tolerance focuses on replication and checking. There have been previous works on software checking optimization. For example, SWIFT [16] merges checks before branches into control flow signature checks, and removes checks for blocks that do not have stores. In this paper, we propose a new area for optimization: when the code structure itself can mask errors and the compiler can determine those programs sections, replication and later checking can be avoided.

Some previous works provide ways to trade reliability for performance. For example, the work by Oh and McCluskey [28] selectively duplicates procedure calls instead of replicating instructions inside them. This way error detection latency is sacrificed for less power consumption. But for each procedure, either all the instructions in the procedure or the call needs to be replicated. PROFiT [29] and Spot [25] divide program into regions and pick up only important regions to do software replication and checking. Spot provides very flexible selection granularity, ranging from a few blocks to a whole procedure. However, in Spot making a good selection requires knowledge of fault mask probability and replication overhead for each region. Jonathan Chang et. al [20] propose to protect a portion of the register file based on a profile of register life time and usage. For different platforms or different programs, the protected portion may be different. In this paper, we provide a fine and simple leverage control: we choose to remove checks for addresses of load or stores. With static compiler analysis, this technique can be applied independently of the target platform. Furthermore, we can combine this technique with previous ones to trade fault coverage with performance.

Previous works on compiler instrumentation for fault-tolerance implement their techniques at the source level [30], compiler backend [16,24,31,29,32], or runtime binary level [25]. However, our techniques are implemented at the intermediate level, which makes it portable across platforms and friendly to users who are not expert on the target ISA.

8 Conclusion

This paper makes several contributions. First, we identify a code pattern that corresponds to outcome tolerant branches, and develop a compiler algorithm that finds these patterns, avoiding unnecessary replication and checking. Second, we evaluate the removal of address checks for loads and stores, and analyze situations where these checks can be removed with little loss of fault coverage. We also identify the check and replicated registers that can be removed on a register safe platform.

Optimizing outcome tolerant branches obtains 7% performance speedup for 3 benchmarks, and an average of 1.6% for all, while keeping the same level of reliability. We also find that on register safe platforms removing the checks for the addresses of load reduce the replication overhead by 44.9%, and only increases SDC (Silent Data Corruption) rate from 0.27% to 0.38%. Also, if 1.11% SDC rate is acceptable, we can furthermore reduce the replication overhead by 50% by also removing checks for the store addresses.

References

1. Constantinescu, C.: Impact of Deep Submicron Technology on Dependability of VLSI Circuits. In: Proc. of the International Conf. on Dependable Systems and Networks, pp. 205–209 (2002)
2. Hazucha, P., Karnik, T., Walstra, S., Bloechel, B., Tschanz, J.W., Maiz, J., Soumyanath, K., Dermer, G., Narendra, S., De, V., Borkar, S.: Measurements and Analysis of SER-tolerant Latch in a 90-nm dual-V/sub T/ CMOS Process. IEEE Journal of Solid-State Circuits 39(9), 1536–1543 (2004)
3. Karnik, T., Hazucha, P.: Characterization of Soft Errors Caused by Single Event Upsets in CMOS Processes. IEEE Transactions on Dependable and Secure Computing 1(2), 128–143 (2004)
4. Shivakumar, P., Kistler, M., Keckler, S., Burger, D., Alvisi, L.: Modeling the Effect of Technology Trends on the Soft Error Rate of Combinational Logic. In: Proc. of the International Conf. on Dependable Systems and Networks, pp. 289–398 (2002)
5. Slegel, T., Averill, R., Check, M., Giamei, B., Krumm, B., Krygowski, C., Li, W., Liptay, J., MacDougall, J., McPherson, T., Navarro, J., Schwarz, E., Shum, K., Webb, C.: IBM's S/390 G5 Microprocessor Design. IEEE Micro 19(2), 12–23 (1999)
6. McEvoy, D.: The architecture of tandem's nonstop system. In: ACM 1981: Proceedings of the ACM 1981 conference, p. 245. ACM Press, New York (1981)

7. Yeh, Y.: Triple-triple Redundant 777 Primary Flight Computer. In: Proc. of the IEEE Aerospace Applications Conference, pp. 293–307 (1996)
8. Mukherjee, S., Emer, J., Fossum, T., Reinhardt, S.: Cache Scrubbing in Microprocessors: Myth or Necessity? In: Proc. of the Pacific RIM International Symposium on Dependable Computing, pp. 37–42 (2004)
9. Prvulovic, M., Zhang, Z., Torrellas, J.: ReVive: Cost-Effective Architectural Support for Rollback Recovery in Shared-Memory Multiprocessors. In: Proc. of the International Symposium on Computer Architecture (ISCA) (2002)
10. Sorin, D., Martin, M., Hill, M., Wood, D.: SafetyNet: Improving the Availability of Shared Memory Multiprocessors with Global Checkpoint/Recovery. In: Proc. of the International Symposium on Computer Architecture (ISCA) (2002)
11. Wang, N.J., Patel, S.J.: ReStore: Symptom Based Soft Error Detection in Microprocessors. In: Proc. of the International Conference on Dependable Systems and Network (DSN), pp. 30–39 (2005)
12. McNairy, C., Bhatia, R.: Montecito: A Dual-core, Dual-thread Itanium Processor. IEEE Micro 25(2), 10–20 (2005)
13. Kongetira, P., Aingaran, K., Olukotun, K.: Niagara: A 32-way multithreaded sparc processor. IEEE Micro 25(2), 21–29 (2005)
14. Bossen, D., Tendler, J., Reick, K.: Power4 system design for high reliability. IEEE Micro 22(2), 16–24 (2002)
15. Lattner, C., Adve, V.: The LLVM Compiler Framework and Infrastructure Tutorial. In: Eigenmann, R., Li, Z., Midkiff, S.P. (eds.) LCPC 2004. LNCS, vol. 3602. Springer, Heidelberg (2005)
16. Reis, G.A., Chang, J., Vachharajani, N., Rangan, R., August, D.I.: SWIFT: Software Implemented Fault Tolerance. In: Proc. of the International Symposium on Code Generation and Optimization (CGO) (2005)
17. Mukherjee, S.S., Kontz, M., Reinhardt, S.K.: Detailed Design and Evaluation of Redundant Multithreading Alternatives. In: Proc. of International Symposium on Computer Architecture, Washington, DC, USA, pp. 99–110. IEEE Computer Society, Los Alamitos (2002)
18. Reinhardt, S.K., Mukherjee, S.S.: Transient Fault Detection via Simultaneous Multithreading. In: Proc. of International Symposium on Computer Architecture, pp. 25–36. ACM Press, New York (2000)
19. Wang, N., Fertig, M., Patel, S.: Y-Branches: When You Come to a Fork in the Road, Take It. In: Proc. of the International Conference on Parallel Architectures and Compilation Techniques (PACT) (2003)
20. Chang, J., Reis, G.A., Vachharajani, N., Rangan, R., August, D.: Non-uniform fault tolerance. In: Proceedings of the 2nd Workshop on Architectural Reliability (WAR) (2006)
21. Gaisler, J.: Evaluation of a 32-bit microprocessor with built-in concurrent error detection. In: FTCS 1997: Proceedings of the 27th International Symposium on Fault-Tolerant Computing (FTCS 1997), Washington, DC, USA, p. 42. IEEE Computer Society, Los Alamitos (1997)
22. Montesinos, P., Liu, W., Torrellas, J.: Shield: Cost-Effective Soft-Error Protection for Register Files. In: Third IBM TJ Watson Conference on Interaction between Architecture, Circuits and Compilers (PAC 2006) (2006)
23. Hu, J., Wang, S., Ziavras, S.G.: In-register duplication: Exploiting narrow-width value for improving register file reliability. In: DSN 2006: Proceedings of the International Conference on Dependable Systems and Networks (DSN 2006), Washington, DC, USA, pp. 281–290. IEEE Computer Society, Los Alamitos (2006)

24. Reis, G.A., Chang, J., Vachharajani, N., Rangan, R., August, D.I., Mukherjee, S.S.: Design and Evaluation of Hybrid Fault-Detection Systems. In: Proc. of the International International Symposium on Computer Architecture (ISCA) (2005)

25. Reis, G.A., Chang, J., August, D.I., Cohn, R., Mukherjee, S.S.: Configurable Transient Fault Detection via Dynamic Binary Translation. In: Proceedings of the 2nd Workshop on Architectural Reliability (WAR) (2006)

26. Luk, C., Cohn, R., Muth, R., Patil, H., Klauser, A., Lowney, G., Wallace, S., Reddi, V.J., Hazelwood, K.: Pin: Building Customized Program Analysis Tools with Dynamic Instrumentation. In: Proc. of the International Conference on Programming Language Design and Implementation (PLDI) (2005)

27. Mukherjee, S.S., Weaver, C., Emer, J., Reinhardt, S.K., Austin, T.: A Systematic Methodology to Compute the Architectural Vulnerability Factors for a High-Performance Microprocessor. In: MICRO 36: Proceedings of the 36th annual IEEE/ACM International Symposium on Microarchitecture, Washington, DC, USA, p. 29. IEEE Computer Society, Los Alamitos (2003)

28. Oh, N., McCluskey, E.J.: Low Energy Error Detection Technique Using Procedure Call Duplication. In: Proc. of the International Conference on Dependable Systems and Network (DSN) (2001)

29. Reis, G.A., Chang, J., Vachharajani, N., Rangan, R., August, D.I., Mukherjee, S.S.: Software-controlled fault tolerance. ACM Trans. Archit. Code Optim. 2(4), 366–396 (2005)

30. Rebaudengo, M., Reorda, M.S., Violante, M., Torchiano, M.: A Source-to-Source Compiler for Generating Dependable Software. In: IEEE International Workshop on Source Code Analysis and Manipulation (SCAM), pp. 35–44 (2001)

31. Oh, N., Shirvani, P., McCluskey, E.J.: Error Detection by Duplicated Instructions in Super-scalar Processors. IEEE Transactions on Reliability 51(1), 63–75 (2002)

32. Chang, J., Reis, G.A., August, D.I.: Automatic Instruction-Level Software-Only Recovery. In: DSN 2006: Proceedings of the International Conference on Dependable Systems and Networks (DSN 2006), Washington, DC, USA, pp. 83–92. IEEE Computer Society, Los Alamitos (2006)

Revisiting SIMD Programming

Anton Lokhmotov[1,*], Benedict R. Gaster[2],
Alan Mycroft[1], Neil Hickey[2], and David Stuttard[2]

[1] Computer Laboratory, University of Cambridge
15 JJ Thomson Avenue, Cambridge, CB3 0FD, UK
[2] ClearSpeed Technology
3110 Great Western Court, Bristol, BS34 8HP, UK

Abstract. Massively parallel SIMD array architectures are making their way into embedded processors. In these architectures, a number of identical processing elements having small private storage and using asynchronous I/O for accessing large shared memory executes the same instruction in lockstep.

In this paper, we outline a simple extension to the C language, called C^n, used for programming a commercial SIMD array architecture. The design of C^n is based on the concept of the SIMD array type architecture and revisits first principles of designing efficient and portable parallel programming languages. C^n has a low level of abstraction and can also be seen as an intermediate language in the compilation from higher level parallel languages to machine code.

1 Introduction

Massively parallel SIMD array architectures are no longer merely the province of large supercomputer systems but are making their way into embedded processors. What seemed a cautious extrapolation a decade ago ("even a parallel SIMD coprocessor embedded in a single-user workstation may not be such a far-fetched idea" [1]) has now become a reality.

In the 40 years since the design of Illiac IV [2], the first large-scale array computer consisting of 64 processing elements (PEs), the progress of VLSI technology allows to pack even more PEs into a single-chip microprocessor that in most respects can be considered "embedded". For example, ClearSpeed's CSX600 array processor consisting of 96 PEs has excellent performance per unit power by delivering more than 3 GFLOPS per watt [3].

The CSX is a SIMD array architecture with a control unit and a number of processing elements, with each PE having relatively small private storage and using asynchronous I/O mechanisms to access large shared memory.

In this paper, we describe a data-parallel extension to the C language, called C^n, for programming the CSX architecture. In C^n, parallelism is mainly expressed at the type level rather than at the code level. Essentially, C^n introduces a new multiplicity type qualifier **poly** which implies that each PE has its own copy of a value of that type. For example, the definition **poly int** x; implies that, on the CSX600 with 96 PEs, there

---

* This author gratefully acknowledges the financial support by a TNK-BP Cambridge Kapitza Scholarship and by an Overseas Research Students Award.

V. Adve, M.J. Garzarán, and P. Petersen (Eds.): LCPC 2007, LNCS 5234, pp. 32–46, 2008.

exist 96 copies of integer variable x, each having the same address within its PE's local storage.

The multiplicity is also manifested in conditional statements. For example, the following code assigns zero to (a copy of) x on every even PE (the runtime function get_penum() returns the ordinal number of a PE):

```
if (get_penum()%2 == 0) X = 0;
```

On every odd PE, the assignment is not executed (this is equivalent to issuing a NOP instruction, as the SIMD array operates in lock-step).

We describe designing C^n as an efficient *and* portable language. Efficiency and portability often conflict with each other (especially in parallel languages [4]). We argue that the CSX architecture (§2) is representative of its class and thus can be considered as a *SIMD array type architecture* (§3). Core C^n operations (§4) can be thought of as cheap (in the spirit of C), while more expensive operations are relegated to the standard library. We compare and contrast C^n design decisions with similar approaches (§5), and then argue that C^n can be seen as an *intermediate* language in the compilation from higher level parallel languages (§6). We briefly discuss the C^n compiler implementation (§7) and outline future work in conclusion (§8).

2 CSX Architecture

This section outlines ClearSpeed's CSX architecture [3], which largely honours the classical SIMD array organisation pioneered by the Solomon/Illiac IV designs [5], albeit embodied in a single chip.

2.1 CSX Family

The CSX architecture is a family of processors based on ClearSpeed's multi-threaded array processor (MTAP) core. The architecture has been developed for high rate processing. CSX processors can be used as application accelerators, alongside general-purpose processors such as those from Intel and AMD.

The MTAP consists of execution units and a control unit. One part of the processor forms the *mono* execution unit, dedicated to processing scalar (or mono) data. Another part forms the *poly* execution unit, which processes parallel (or poly) data, and may consist of tens, hundreds or even thousands of identical processing element (PE) cores. This array of PE cores operates in a synchronous, Single Instruction Multiple Data (SIMD) manner, where every enabled PE core executes the same instruction on its local data.

The control unit fetches instructions from a *single* instruction stream, decodes and dispatches them to the execution units or I/O controllers. Instructions for the mono and poly execution units are handled similarly, except for conditional execution. The mono unit uses conditional jumps to branch around code like a standard RISC architecture. This affects both mono and poly operations. The poly unit uses an *enable register* to control execution of each PE. If one or more of the bits of that PE enable register is zero, then the PE core is *disabled* and most instructions it receives will be ignored. The enable register is a stack, and a new bit, specifying the result of a test, can be pushed onto the top of the stack allowing nested predicated execution. The bit can later be popped from the top of the stack to remove the effect of that condition. This makes handling nested conditions and loops efficient.

In order to provide fast access to the data being processed, each PE core has its own local memory and register file. Each PE core can directly access only its own storage. (Instructions for the poly execution unit having a mono register operand indirectly access the mono register file, as a mono value gets broadcast to each PE.) Data is transferred between PE (poly) memory and the poly register file via load/store instructions. The mono unit has direct access to main (mono) memory. It also uses load/store instructions to transfer data between mono memory and the mono register file. Programmed I/O (PIO) extends the load/store model: it is used for transfers of data between mono memory and poly memory.

2.2 CSX600 Processor

The CSX600 is the first product in the CSX family. The processor is optimised for intensive double-precision floating-point computations, providing sustained 33 GFLOPS of performance on DGEMM (double precision matrix multiply), while dissipating an average of 10 watts. The poly execution unit is a linear array of 96 PE cores, with 6KB SRAM and a superscalar 64-bit FPU on each PE core. The PE cores are able to communicate with each other via what is known as *swazzle path* that connects each PE with its left and right neighbours. Further details can be found in white papers [3].

2.3 Acceleration Example

A C^n implementation of Monte-Carlo simulations for computing European option pricing with double precision performs 100,000 Monte-Carlo simulations at the rate of 206.5M samples per second on a ClearSpeed Advance board having two CSX600 chips. In comparison, an optimised C program using the Intel Math Kernel Library (MKL) and compiled with the Intel C Compiler achieves the rate of 40.5M samples per second on a 2.33GHz dual-core Intel Xeon (Woodcrest, HP DL380 G5 system). Combining both the Intel processor and the ClearSpeed board achieves the rate of 240M samples per second, which is almost 6 times the performance of the host processor alone.

3 C^n Design Goals and Choices

The key design goals of C^n were efficiency and portability. We first discuss these goals in a broader context of programming languages for sequential and parallel computers (§3.1), and then discuss how they affected the design choices of C^n (§3.2).

3.1   Efficiency and Portability

Program efficiency and portability are two common tenets of high-level programming languages. Efficiency means that it is possible to write a compiler generating code that is "almost" as fast as code written in assembly. Portability means that software can be adapted to run on different target systems.

Languages like C have been successful largely because of their efficiency and portability on von Neumann machines, having a single processor and uniform random access memory. Efficiency comes from the programmer's clear understanding of the performance implications of algorithm selection and coding style. Portability is achieved because languages like C hide most features of physical machines, such as instruction set, addressing modes, register file, *etc.* Moreover, the hidden features apparently have a negligible effect on performance, so porting often maintains efficiency [4].

Efficiency and portability are even more desired when programming parallel systems. Performance is the most compelling argument for parallel computing; and given the amount of human effort required to develop an efficient parallel program, the resulting program should better have a long useful life [6].

In the world of parallelism, however, no single model accurately abstracts the variability of parallel systems. While it is possible, for example, to program distributed memory machines using a shared memory model, programmers having limited control over data distribution and communication are unlikely to write efficient programs. So in this world, sadly, efficiency and portability are no longer close friends.

Snyder introduced [7] the notion of a *type architecture*—a machine model abstracting the performance-important features of a family of physical machines, in the same way as the RAM model abstracts von Neumann machines. He proposed the Candidate Type Architecture (CTA) which effectively abstracts MIMD machines (multicomputers) with unspecified interconnect topology. The key CTA abstraction is that accessing another processor's memory is significantly more expensive than accessing local memory (typically by 2–5 orders of magnitude) [4].

3.2 C^n as a Language for the SIMD Array Type Architecture

Our key observation is that the CSX architecture can be considered a *SIMD array type architecture* (SATA), as it respects classical organisation and has typical costs of communicating data between main (mono) and local (poly) memory. Designing a core language based on the type-architecture facilities should provide both efficiency and portability [7]. To match the programmer's intuition, core language operations are cheap, while operations relegated to the standard library are more expensive. For example, arithmetic operations are cheap, while reduction operations (using the inter-PE communication) are somewhat more expensive, albeit still cheaper than data transfer operations between mono and poly memories.

Efficiency mandates only providing language constructs that can be reliably implemented on the SATA using standard compiler technology. History shows that languages that are difficult to implement are also rarely successful (HPF is a dismal example [8]).

Portability is important because the CSX architecture family (§2.1) does not fix the PE array size. Also, as the number of PE cores increases, other (than linear) interconnect topologies could be introduced.

Designing C^n as a C extension provides a known starting point for a large community of C programmers. In addition, software development tools can be written by making (small) modifications to existing ones, rather than from scratch.

4 C^n Outline

In this section we outline the most salient features of C^n. We give further rationale behind some design decisions in §5.

4.1   Types

C^n extends C with two additional keywords that can be used as part of the declaration qualifier for declarators, *i.e.* logically amend the type system [9]. These keywords are *multiplicity qualifiers* and allow the programmer to specify a memory space in which a declared object resides. The new keywords are:

- **mono**: for declaring an object in the mono domain (*i.e.* one copy exists in main memory);
- **poly**: for declaring an object in the poly domain (*i.e.* one copy per PE in its local memory).

The default multiplicity is **mono**. Wherever a multiplicity qualifier may be used, an implicit **mono** is assumed, unless an explicit **poly** is provided. A consequence of this is that all C programs are valid C^n programs, with the same semantics. Thus, C^n is a superset of C (but see §5.2).

Basic types. C^n supports the same basic types as C. They can be used together with a multiplicity qualifier to produce declarations (only one of the qualifiers can be used in a basic type declaration). Some example declarations follow:

```
poly int i; // multiple copies in PE local (poly) memory
mono unsigned cu; // a single copy in main (mono) memory
unsigned long cs; // a single copy in main (mono) memory
```

Pointer types. The pointer types in C^n follow similar rules to those in C. Pointer declarations consist of a base type and a pointer. The declaration on the left of the asterisk represents the base type (the type of the object that the pointer points to). The declaration on the right of the asterisk represents the pointer object itself. It is possible to specify the multiplicity of either of these entities in the same way as **const** and **volatile** work in C. For example:

```
poly int * poly sam; // poly pointer to poly int
poly int * frodo;     // mono pointer to poly int
int * poly bilbo;     // poly pointer to mono int
```

Thus, there are four different ways of declaring pointers with multiplicity qualifiers:

- mono pointer to mono object (*e.g.* **mono int * mono**);
- mono pointer to poly object (*e.g.* **poly int * mono**);
- poly pointer to mono data (*e.g.* **mono int * poly**);
- poly pointer to poly data (*e.g.* **poly int * poly**).

Note that in the case of a poly pointer, multiple copies of the pointer exist, potentially pointing to different locations.

As in C, pointers are used to access memory. The compiler allocates named poly objects to the same address within each PE local memory. Thus, taking the address of a named object (whether mono or poly) always yields a mono pointer.

Array types. The syntax for array declaration in C^n is similar to that in C. It is possible to use a multiplicity qualifier in an array declaration. Consider the declaration `poly int` A[42];. The multiplicity qualifier applies only to the base type of the array (*i.e.* to the type of array elements). This declaration will reserve a poly space for 42 integers at the same location on each PE. Similar to C, we can say that the array name is coerced to the address of its first element, which is a mono pointer to poly object (*e.g.* `poly int * mono`).

There are some additional restrictions when dealing with arrays, specifically with array subscripting, discussed in §4.3.

Aggregate types. Similar to C, C^n distinguishes between declaration and definition of objects. A declaration is where an object type is specified but no object of that type is created, *e.g.* a struct type declaration. A definition is where an object of a particular type is created, *e.g.* a variable definition. Structs and unions in C^n match their C equivalents, the only difference being the type of fields one can specify inside a struct or union type declaration.

Standard C allows essentially any declaration as a field, with the exception of storage class qualifiers. C^n allows the same with the additional restriction that fields cannot have multiplicity qualifiers. This is because a struct type declaration just specifies the structure of memory. Memory is not allocated until an instance of that struct type is created. Thus, putting a poly field in a struct declaration and then defining an instance of that struct in the mono domain would result in having contradictory multiplicity specifications. (Similarly for a mono field in a struct instance defined in the poly domain.) For example:

```
// legal struct declaration
struct _A {
    int a;
    float b;
};
poly struct _A kaiser;

// illegal struct declaration
struct _B {
    poly int a;    // illegal use of multiplicity
    mono float b;  // illegal use of multiplicity
};
mono struct _B king;  // where should king.a go?
poly struct _B tsar;  // where should tsar.b go?
```

Multiplicity qualifiers, however, can be used on the base type of pointers (otherwise pointers to poly data could not be declared as fields). For example:

```
union _C { // define a union
    poly int * a;
    mono int * poly * b;
};
poly union _C fred;
mono union _C barney;
```

In the declaration of fred, the field a is created as a poly pointer to a poly int (**poly int * poly**) and b is created as a poly pointer to a poly pointer to a mono int (**mono int * poly * poly**). In the declaration of barney, a is created as a mono pointer to a poly int (**poly int * mono**) and b is created as a mono pointer to a poly pointer to a mono int (**mono int * poly * mono**).

4.2 Expressions

C^n supports all the operators of C. Mono and poly objects can usually be used interchangeably in expressions (but see §4.3 for exceptions).

Note that the result of any expression involving a mono and a poly object invariably has a poly type. Thus, mono objects are promoted to the poly domain in mixed expressions. In the following example,

```
poly int x; int y; x = x + y;
```

where y is promoted to **poly int** before being added to (every copy of) x. (Technically, the promotion is done by broadcasting values from the mono register file to the poly execution unit.)

4.3 Assignment Statements

Assignment within a domain (*i.e.* poly to poly, or mono to mono) is always legal and has the obvious behaviour.

A mono value can also be assigned to a poly variable. In this case the same value is assigned to every copy of the variable on each PE. For example, **poly int** x = 1; results in (every copy of) x having the value of 1. (Again, the architecture supports such assignments by broadcasting the mono value to the poly unit.)

It is not obvious, however, what should happen when assigning a poly to a mono, *i.e.* when taking data from multiple copies of the poly variable and storing it in the single mono variable. Therefore direct assignment from the poly domain to the mono domain is disallowed in C^n.

Note that certain C^n expressions are disallowed, as otherwise they would require an implicit data transfer from mono to poly memory. One such expression is dereferencing of a poly pointer to mono data (*e.g.* **mono int * poly**). Attempting to dereference such a pointer would result in poly data, but the data is stored in the mono domain and would therefore need to be copied to poly memory. Since broadcasting can only send a single mono value to the poly unit at a time, such a copy would involve expensive programmed I/O mechanisms. Therefore, allowing such dereferencing would conflict with the design goal that the core language operations should be cheap. Thus, the compiler reports dereferencing a poly pointer to mono data as an error.

Since, following C, C^n treats x[i] as equivalent to *(x + i), it follows that indexing a mono array with a poly expression is also forbidden, because it would implicitly dereference a poly pointer to mono data.

In all the cases when data transfers between mono and poly memories are required, the programmer has to use memory copy routines from the standard C^n library.

4.4   Reduction Operations

Many parallel algorithms require reducing a vector of values to a single scalar value. In addition to the core operations defined above, the C^n standard library provides sum, times, and bit-wise operations defined for basic types for reducing a poly value into a mono value. For example, on an array of n PEs,

```
poly float x; mono float y; ...
y = reduce_mono_sum(x);
```

means

```
y = x(0) + x(1) + ... + x(n-1);
```

where x(i) refers to the value of x on ith PE.

For some algorithms another form of reduction is useful: logically, a poly value is reduced to an intermediate mono value which is then broadcast into a result poly value. Thus,

```
poly float x, z; ...
z = reduce_poly_sum(x);
```

means

```
z(0) = ... = z(n-1) = x(0) + x(1) + ... + x(n-1);
```

Both forms can be efficiently implemented on the CSX using the inter-PE swazzle path. The order in which the result is evaluated is unspecified.

4.5   Control Statements

The basic control flow constructs in C^n are the same as in C. Conditional expressions, however, can be of mono or poly domain. Consider the **if** statement:

```
if(expression) { statement-list }
```

A mono expression for the condition affects both the mono and poly execution units. If the expression is false, the statement list will be skipped entirely, and execution will continue after the **if** statement.

A poly expression for the condition can be true on some PEs and false on others. This is where the PE enable state (described in §2.1) comes in: all the PEs for which the condition is false are disabled for the duration of executing the statement list. The statement list is executed (even if all PEs are disabled by the condition), but any poly statements (*e.g.* assignments to poly variables) have an affect only on the enabled PEs. Mono statements inside a poly **if**, however, get executed irrespective of the conditions. Consider the following example:

```
poly int foo = 0; mono int bar = 1;
if(get_penum()%2 == 0) { // disable all odd PEs
  foo = 1; // foo is 1 on even and 0 on odd PEs
  bar = 2; // bar is 2
}
```

Effectively, a poly condition is invisible to any mono code inside that **if** statement.[1] This language design choice may seem counterintuitive and is indeed a controversial point in the design of SIMD languages, to which we return in §5.2.

A poly condition in an **if..else** statement implies that for the **if**-clause all the PEs on which the condition evaluates to true are enabled, and the others are disabled. Then, for the **else**-clause, the enable state of all the PEs is inverted: those PEs that were enabled by the condition are disabled and vice-versa.

Conditional statements can be nested just as in C. Poly statements are only executed on PEs when all the nested conditional expressions evaluate to true.

These rules, of course, dictate different compilation of conditional statements. Mono conditional statements result in generating branch instructions, while poly conditional statements result in generating poly instructions enabling and disabling PEs (enable stack operations on the CSX; see §7 for more details).

Similar principles apply to loop constructs **for**, **while** and **do..while**. A loop with a poly control expression executes until the loop condition is false on every PE. Note that a poly loop can iterate zero times, so in that case, unlike the **if** statement, even mono statements in its body will not be executed.

4.6   Functions

Multiplicity qualifiers can be specified for the return type of a function, as well as the types of any arguments. We refer to a function as being mono or poly according to whether its return type is mono or poly.

A return statement from a mono function behaves exactly as expected by transferring control to the point after the call statement. A poly function does not actually return control until the end of the function body. A return from a poly function works by disabling the PEs which execute it. Other PEs execute the rest of the function code. When the function returns, all PEs have their enable state restored to what it was on entry. Note that all mono code in the function is always executed (unless branched over by mono conditional statements).

5 C^n Design Rationale

5.1   Low-Level Abstraction

Early SIMD programming languages for the Illiac IV computer included Glypnir [10], with syntax based on Algol 60, and CFD [11], based on Fortran. The main design goal of these languages was "to produce a useful, reliable, and efficient programming

---

[1] It way be worth noting that the block structure of code is still relevant. So, for example, any mono declarations within the body of a poly conditional statement are local to that body.

tool with a high probability of success" [10]. Given the state of compiler technology in the early 1970s, the languages could not *both* be machine independent *and* satisfy this goal.[2] In addition to explicit means for specifying storage allocation and program control as in C^n, these languages even provided means for accessing subwords and registers.

Many vector processing languages have appeared since then, providing higher levels of abstraction for array-based operations (*e.g.* Actus [12], Vector C [13], High Performance Fortran [8], *etc.*). Unfortunately, such languages present greater complexity for the implementors because of data alignment, storage allocation and communication issues on SIMD machines (*e.g.* see [14,15]).

C^n builds on the C strength of "solving" most implementation efficiency problems by leaving them to the programmers. While not the most desirable solution, it relieves the programmers from solving the same problems using assembly language. In §6 we argue that C^n can be seen as an intermediate representation for compiling from higher level parallel languages.

5.2 C^n and Other SIMD Dialects of C

C^n is by no means the first C dialect for SIMD programming. Notable examples include C* [16] for programming the Connection Machine models, MPL [17] for the MasPar models, and 1DC (one-dimensional C) [18] for the IMAP models.

All these languages intentionally reflect their respective architectures. The unifying theme is the use of a keyword to specify multiple instance variables (`poly` in C*, `plural` in MPL, `sep` in 1DC). The language differences stem from the differences between the architectures and design goals.

Communication. While the `poly` keyword implies the physical data distribution, C* enshrines the viewpoint that no parallel version of C can abandon the uniform address space model without giving up its claim to be a superset of C. Uniform memory means that a PE can have a pointer p into the memory of another PE. For example, the statement `*p = x;` means "send message x to a location pointed to by p". Thus, C* relies on pointers for interprocessor communication.

This C* feature is underpinned by Connection Machine's key capability allowing any PE to establish a connection with any other PE in the machine (via the global routing mechanism or local meshes). Still, the programmer relies on the compiler writer's ability to implement pointer-based communication efficiently. Perhaps, this is the reason why, in contrast, MasPar's MPL provides explicit communication operators, although the MasPar has connection capabilities similar to the Connection Machine.

The IMAP architectures have a linear nearest neighbour interconnect, as does the CSX. 1DC supports special operators for nearest neighbour communication, while C^n relegates communication functions to the C^n standard library.

Dereferencing pointers. Even rejecting the pointer-based communication in C* does not mean that the compiler will be able to optimise poorly written code; in particular,

---

[2] Indeed, the compiler for Tranquil—the first Illiac IV language—was abandoned because of implementation difficulties and lack of resources [10].

code that makes a heavy use of costly DMA transfers between mono and poly memories. The C^n ban on dereferencing poly pointers to mono data (which would transfer only several bytes at a time) aims to shut the door in front of the abusing programmers. In contrast, MPL does not sacrifice convenience for efficiency and allows all pointer operations.

Poly conditional statements. In §4.5, we discussed the behaviour of poly **if** statements in C^n: even if the poly condition is false on every PE, the statement list is executed regardless, including all mono statements in the list. This model of execution is easy to implement on the CSX by inserting operations on the hardware enable stack (see §7). The same model was used in MPL [19].

The designers of C* followed the other route by adopting the "Rule of Local Support" [16, §6.2]: if the poly condition is false on every PE, then the statement list is not executed at all. The Rule of Local Support required extra implementation trouble but preserved the usual model of a **while** loop in terms of **if** and **goto** statements. The C* designers, nevertheless, admitted that their rule occasionally also caused inconvenience and confusion.

Deciding on whether to preserve or to change the semantics of familiar statements when extending a sequential language for parallelism is hard, and may even drive the designers to a thought that designing a language from scratch is a better idea (*e.g.* see the history of ZPL [4]). In the case of **if** statements, the solution does not need to be that radical and could merely come as using different keywords in a more general language supporting both execution models (for example, **ifp** for the C^n/MPL model and **ifm** for the C* model).

6 C^n as Intermediate Language

SIMD array supercomputers went out of fashion in the early 1990s when clusters of commodity computers proved to be more cost effective. Ironically, vector-style instructions reemerged in commodity processors under the name of SIMD (or multimedia) extensions, such as Intel MMX/SSE and PowerPC AltiVec.

The principal difference between "real" (array) SIMD and vector extensions is that the latter operate on data in long registers and do not have local memory attached to each PE as in SIMD arrays. In terms of the C^n language, this means that it would be inefficient (if not impossible) to use pointers to poly data when programming in C^n for vector extensions. This is because it would not be straightforward to compile C^n programs expressing memory operations that are not supported by the hardware.

We argue, however, that the C^n language can be regarded as a "portable assembly" language for both SIMD and vector architectures. Given an architecture description, high-level languages providing more abstract array-based operations can be translated to C^n and then efficiently mapped to machine code by the C^n compiler.

For example, consider a Fortran 90 style statement B[0:959] = A[0:959]+42; where A[] and B[] are arrays of floats. This statement loads 960 values from A, adds 42 to each, and stores 960 results to B. Suppose that the target architecture is a vector machine with 96 elements per vector register, hence the statement parallelism needs to be folded 10 times to fit the hardware by *strip mining* [20,15].

For a vector machine, the declaration **poly float** va, vb; can be thought of as defining two vector registers in a similar way as **vector float** vc; can be used to define a (4-element) vector in the AltiVec API [21]. The vector statement can then be strip-mined *horizontally* [15], resulting in:

```
const poly int me = get_penum(); // get PE number
mono float * poly pa = A + me;
mono float * poly pb = B + me;
for(int i = 0; i < 10; i++, pa += 96, pb += 96) {
  va  = *pa; // load 96-element vector
  vb  = va + 42;
  *pb = vb; // store 96-element vector
}
```

(Note that here we have lifted the C^n ban on dereferencing poly pointers to mono data, which is the artefact of distributed memory SIMD arrays.)

The same strategy works on a SIMD machine having 96 PEs: 10 vector indirect loads (one on each iteration) are replaced with 10 DMA transfers from mono to poly memory, 10 vector stores with 10 DMA transfers from poly to mono memory; each transfer moves a single float to/from a PE. It is more efficient, however, to strip-mine *vertically* [15], which in pseudo-vector notation can be written as:

```
poly float pA[10], pB[10];
pA[0:9] = A[10*me:10*me+9]; // DMA mono to poly
pB[0:9] = pA[0:9] + 42;
B[10*me:10*me+9] = pB[0:9]; // DMA poly to mono
```

This requires only two DMA transfers of 10 floats each. Given high DMA start-up costs, vertical strip-mining is several times more efficient. Hence, the compiler should favour the second form on SIMD machines. (This is a trivial example of the decisions we referred to in §5.1 that the compiler needs to make to efficiently compile high-level vector abstractions).

To summarise, C^n code can be seen as an intermediate language, from which target code can be generated. Once a C^n compiler is written and well-tuned, the quality of target code should principally depend on the ability of the (machine-description driven) front-end to generate efficient intermediate code from a higher level parallel language. Even if the front-end generates suboptimal intermediate code, the performance-conscious programmer still has a fallback to the intermediate language, rather than to assembly.

C^n has already been targeted from a subset of OpenMP [22]. We believe that C^n can also be targeted from high-level data parallel libraries such as MSR Accelerator [23] and memory hierarchy oriented languages such as Stanford Sequoia [24].

7 C^n Compiler Implementation

ClearSpeed has developed a C^n optimising compiler for the CSX architecture using the CoSy compiler development framework [25]. Small modifications to the front-end were needed to support the multiplicity qualifiers in the source code. Each type is supplemented with a flag indicating whether it is mono or poly. A special phase was written to recognise poly conditional statements and transform them into a form of predicated execution. For example, assuming that both x and y are in the poly domain,

```
if (y > 0) {
   x = y;
}
```

becomes

```
enablestate = push(y > 0, enablestate);
x ?= y;
enablestate = pop(enablestate);
```

where the predicated assignment operator ?= assigns its *rhs* expression to the *lhs* location only on those PEs where all the bits of the hardware enable stack (represented by the variable enablestate) are 1.

Predicated execution requires careful rethinking of standard optimisations. For example, the standard register allocation algorithm via coloring has to recognise that liveness of a virtual poly register is not simply implied by its def-use chain but is also a function of the enable state. This is not, however, a new problem (*e.g.* see [26]).

7.1 C^n Compiler Performance

ClearSpeed has developed a number of interesting applications in C^n, including functions from the molecular dynamics simulation package AMBER, Monte-Carlo option pricing simulations, implementations of 2D and 3D FFTs, and others.

The C^n design choice of only including features that can be efficiently implemented using standard compiler technology pays off handsomely, since the implementors can concentrate their efforts on optimisations that the programmer expects the compiler to get right. For example, Fig. 1 shows on 20 benchmarks the performance improvement achieved by the version 3.0 of the C^n compiler over the version 2.51.

Much of the improvement comes from the work on the register allocator and other optimisations becoming aware of poly variables. Particular optimisations, *e.g.* loop-invariant code motion, have proved to benefit from the target processor's ability to issue *forced* poly instructions which are executed regardless of the enable state.

Code for the amber benchmark generated by the current version of the compiler performs within 20% of hand-coded assembly. (No other similar data is available for comparison, because it makes little sense to re-implement assembly programs in C^n, other than to improve portability.)

8 Future Work and Conclusion

Programming in C^n tends to require the programmer to restructure programs to expose the parallelism lost when writing in a sequential language. Essentially, the C^n programmer indicates a parallel loop. We believe it is possible to ease the programmer's task of annotating sequential C programs (but expressing parallel algorithms) with the **poly** qualifier, if the programmer can assert certain properties.

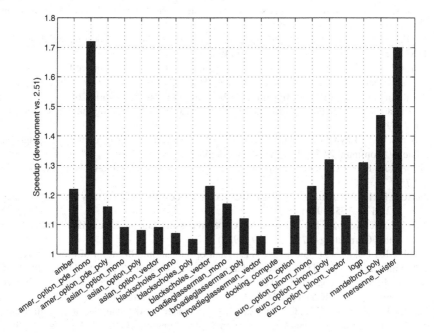

Fig. 1. Performance improvement of code generated by the compiler version 3.0 over code generated by the compiler version 2.51

We are developing an auto-parallelising compiler module converting C code to valid C^n code using programmer's annotations based on the concept of delayed writes [27]. The resulting C^n code is then fed into the optimisation and code generation phases of the C^n compiler.

ClearSpeed has developed a set of production quality tools targeting the CSX array architecture, including an optimising compiler, assembler, linker and debugger, that make software development in C^n a viable alternative to hand-coding in assembly as loss in performance is far outweighed by the advantages of high-level language programming.

References

1. Parhami, B.: SIMD machines: do they have a significant future? SIGARCH Comput. Archit. News 23(4), 19–22 (1995)
2. Barnes, G.H., Brown, R.M., Kato, M., Kuck, D.J., Slotnick, D.L., Stokes, R.A.: The Illiac IV computer. IEEE Trans. Computers C-17(8), 746–757 (1968)
3. ClearSpeed Technology: The CSX architecture, http://www.clearspeed.com/
4. Snyder, L.: The design and development of ZPL. In: Proc. of the third ACM SIGPLAN conference on History of programming languages (HOPL III), pp. 8–1–8–37. ACM Press, New York (2007)
5. Slotnick, D.: The conception and development of parallel processors—a personal memoir. IEEE Annals of the History of Computing 4(1), 20–30 (1982)

6. Wilkes, M.V.: The lure of parallelism and its problems. In: Computer Perspectives. Morgan Kaufmann, San Francisco (1995)
7. Snyder, L.: Type architecture, shared memory and the corollary of modest potential. Annual Review of Computer Science 1, 289–317 (1986)
8. Kennedy, K., Koelbel, C., Zima, H.: The rise and fall of High Performance Fortran: an historical object lesson. In: Proc. of the third ACM SIGPLAN conference on History of programming languages (HOPL III), pp. 7-1–7-22. ACM Press, New York (2007)
9. American National Standards Institute: ANSI/ISO/IEC 9899-1999: Programming Languages – C (1999)
10. Lawrie, D.H., Layman, T., Baer, D., Randal, J.M.: Glypnir—a programming language for Illiac IV. Commun. ACM 18(3), 157–164 (1975)
11. Stevens Jr., K.: CFD—a Fortran-like language for the Illiac IV. SIGPLAN Not. 10(3), 72–76 (1975)
12. Perrott, R.H.: A language for array and vector processors. ACM Trans. Program. Lang. Syst. 1(2), 177–195 (1979)
13. Li, K.C., Schwetman, H.: Vector C: a vector processing language. Journal of Parallel and Distributed Computing 2(2), 132–169 (1985)
14. Knobe, K., Lukas, J.D., Steele Jr., G.L.: Data optimization: allocation of arrays to reduce communication on SIMD machines. J. Parallel Distrib. Comput. 8(2), 102–118 (1990)
15. Weiss, M.: Strip mining on SIMD architectures. In: Proc. of the 5th International Conference on Supercomputing (ICS), pp. 234–243. ACM Press, New York (1991)
16. Rose, J.R., Steele Jr., G.L.: C*: An extended C language for data parallel programming. In: Proc. of the 2nd International Conference on Supercomputing (ICS), vol. 2, pp. 2–16 (1987)
17. MasPar Computer Corporation: MasPar Programming Language (ANSI C compatible MPL) Reference Manual (1992)
18. Kyo, S., Okazaki, S., Arai, T.: An integrated memory array processor for embedded image recognition systems. IEEE Trans. Computers 56(5), 622–634 (2007)
19. Christy, P.: Software to support massively parallel computing on the MasPar MP-1. In: Proc. of the 35th IEEE Computer Society International Conference (Compcon Spring), pp. 29–33 (1990)
20. Allen, R., Kennedy, K.: Optimizing Compilers for Modern Architectures. Morgan Kaufmann, San Francisco (2002)
21. Freescale Semiconductor: AltiVec technology programming interface manual (1999)
22. Bradley, C., Gaster, B.R.: Exploiting loop-level parallelism for SIMD arrays using OpenMP. In: Proc. of the 3rd International Workshop on OpenMP (IWOPM) (2007)
23. Tarditi, D., Puri, S., Oglesby, J.: Accelerator: using data parallelism to program GPUs for general-purpose uses. In: Proc. of the 12th International Conference on Architectural Support for Programming Languages and Operating Systems (ASPLOS-XII), pp. 325–335. ACM Press, New York (2006)
24. Fatahalian, K., Horn, D.R., Knight, T.J., Leem, L., Houston, M., Park, J.Y., Erez, M., Ren, M., Aiken, A., Dally, W.J., Hanrahan, P.: Sequoia: programming the memory hierarchy. In: Proc. of the 2006 ACM/IEEE Conference on Supercomputing (SC), pp. 83–92. ACM Press, New York (2006)
25. ACE Associated Compiler Experts: The CoSy compiler development system, http://www.ace.nl/
26. Kim, H.: Region-based register allocation for EPIC architectures. PhD thesis, Department of Computer Science, New York University (2001)
27. Lokhmotov, A., Mycroft, A., Richards, A.: Delayed side-effects ease multi-core programming. In: Kermarrec, A.-M., Bougé, L., Priol, T. (eds.) Euro-Par 2007. LNCS, vol. 4641. Springer, Heidelberg (2007)

Multidimensional Blocking in UPC

Christopher Barton[1], Călin Caşcaval[2], George Almasi[2], Rahul Garg[1],
José Nelson Amaral[1], and Montse Farreras[3]

[1] University of Alberta, Edmonton, Canada
[2] IBM T.J. Watson Research Center
[3] Universitat Politècnica de Catalunya
Barcelona Supercomputing Center

Abstract. Partitioned Global Address Space (PGAS) languages offer an attractive, high-productivity programming model for programming large-scale parallel machines. PGAS languages, such as Unified Parallel C (UPC), combine the simplicity of shared-memory programming with the efficiency of the message-passing paradigm by allowing users control over the data layout. PGAS languages distinguish between private, shared-local, and shared-remote memory, with shared-remote accesses typically much more expensive than shared-local and private accesses, especially on distributed memory machines where shared-remote access implies communication over a network.

In this paper we present a simple extension to the UPC language that allows the programmer to block shared arrays in multiple dimensions. We claim that this extension allows for better control of locality, and therefore performance, in the language.

We describe an analysis that allows the compiler to distinguish between local shared array accesses and remote shared array accesses. Local shared array accesses are then transformed into direct memory accesses by the compiler, saving the overhead of a locality check at runtime. We present results to show that locality analysis is able to significantly reduce the number of shared accesses.

1 Introduction

Partitioned Global Address Space (PGAS) languages, such as UPC [14], Co-Array Fortran [10], and Titanium [16], extend existing languages (C, Fortran and Java, respectively) with constructs to express parallelism and data distributions. They are based on languages that have a large user base and therefore there is a small learning curve to move codes to these new languages.

We have implemented several parallel algorithms — stencil computation and linear algebra operations such as matrix-vector and Cholesky factorization — in the UPC programming language. During this effort we identified several issues with the current language definition, such as: rudimentary support for data distributions (shared arrays can be distributed only block cyclic), flat threading model (no ability to support subsets of threads), and shortcomings in the collective definition (no collectives on subsets of threads, no shared data allowed as target for collective operations, no concurrent participation of a thread in multiple collectives). In addition, while implementing a compiler and runtime system we found that naively translating all shared accesses to runtime

V. Adve, M.J. Garzarán, and P. Petersen (Eds.): LCPC 2007, LNCS 5234, pp. 47–62, 2008.

calls is prohibitively expensive. While the language supports block transfers and cast operations that could alleviate some of the performance issues, it is more convenient to address these problems through compiler optimizations.

Tackling some of these issues, this paper makes the following contributions:

– propose a new data distribution directive, called multidimensional blocking, that allows the programmer to specify n-dimensional tiles for shared data (see Section 2);
– describe a compile-time algorithm to determine the locality of shared array elements and replace references that can be proven to be locally owned by the executing thread with direct memory accesses. This optimization reduces the overhead of shared memory accesses and thus brings single thread performance relatively close to serial implementations, thereby allowing the use of a scalable, heavier, runtime implementation that supports large clusters of SMP machines (see Section 3);
– present several benchmarks that demonstrate the benefits of the multidimensional blocking features and the performance results of the locality analysis; these performance results were obtained on a cluster of SMP machines, which demonstrates that the flat threading model can be mitigated through knowledge in the compiler of the machine architecture (Section 5).

2   Multidimensional Blocking of UPC Arrays

In this section we propose an extension to the UPC language syntax to provide additional control over data distribution: tiled (or *multiblocked*) arrays. Tiled data structures are used to enhance locality (and therefore performance) in a wide range of HPC applications [2]. Multiblocked arrays can help UPC programmers to better express these types of applications, allowing the language to fulfill its promise of allowing both high productivity and high performance. Also, having this data structure available in UPC facilitates using library routines, such as BLAS [4], in C or Fortran that already make use of tiled data structures.

Consider a simple stencil computation on a 2 dimensional array that calculates the average of the four immediate neighbors of each element.

```
1  shared double A[M][N];
2  ...
3  for (i=1..M-2,j=1..N-2)
4    B[i][j] = 0.25*(A[i-1][j]+A[i+1][j]+A[i][j-1]+A[i][j+1]);
```

Since it has no data dependencies, this loop can be executed in parallel. However, the naive declaration of A above yields suboptimal execution, because e.g. A[i-1][j] will likely not be on the same UPC thread as A[i][j] and may require inter-node communication to get to. A somewhat better solution allowed by UPC is a striped 2D array distribution:

```
shared double [M*b] A[M][N];
```

$M \times b$ is the *blocking factor* of the array; that is, the array is allocated in contiguous blocks of this size. This however, limits parallelism to $\frac{N}{b}$ processors and causes $O(\frac{1}{b})$ remote array accesses. By contrast, a tiled layout provides $\frac{M \times N}{b^2}$ parallelism and $O(\frac{1}{b^2})$ of the accesses are remote. Typical MPI implementations of stencil computation tile the array and exchange "border regions" between neighbors before each iteration. This approach is also possible in UPC:

```
struct block { double tile[b][b]; };
shared block A[M/b][N/b];
```

However, the declaration above complicates the source code because two levels of indexing are needed for each access. We cannot pretend that A is a simple array anymore. We propose a language extension that can declare a tiled layout for a shared array, as follows:

```
shared <type> [b0][b1]...[bn] A[d0][d1] ... [dn];
```

Array A is an n-dimensional tiled (or "multi-blocked") array with each tile being an array of dimensions $[b0][b1]...[bn]$. Tiles are understood to be contiguous in memory.

2.1 UPC Array Layout

To describe the layout of multiblocked arrays in UPC, we first need to discuss conventional shared arrays. A UPC array declared as below:

```
shared [b] <type> A[d0][d1]...[dn];
```

is distributed in memory in a block-cyclic manner with blocking factor b. Given an array index $\mathbf{v} = v_0, v_1, ...v_{n-1}$, to locate element $A[\mathbf{v}]$ we first calculate the linearized row-major index (as we would in C):

$$L(\mathbf{v}) = v_0 \times \prod_{j=1}^{n-1} d_j + v_1 \times \prod_{j=2}^{n-1} d_j + ... + v_{n-1} \qquad (1)$$

Block-cyclic layout is based on this linearized index. We calculate the UPC *thread* on which array element $A[\mathbf{v}]$ resides. Within the local storage of this thread the array is kept as a collection of blocks. The *course* of an array location is the block number in which the element resides; the *phase* is its location within the block.

$$\begin{cases} thread(A, \mathbf{v}) & ::= \left\lfloor \frac{L(\mathbf{v})}{b} \right\rfloor \bmod \mathcal{T} \\ phase(A, \mathbf{v}) & ::= L(\mathbf{v}) \bmod b \\ course(A, \mathbf{v}) & ::= \left\lfloor \frac{L(\mathbf{v})}{b \times \mathcal{T}} \right\rfloor \end{cases}$$

Multiblocked arrays: The goal is to extend UPC syntax to declare tiled arrays while minimizing the impact on language semantics. The internal representation of multiblocked arrays should not differ too much from that of standard UPC arrays. Consider a multiblocked array A with dimensions $D = \{d_0, d_1, ...d_n\}$ and blocking factors $B = \{b_0, b_1, ...b_n\}$. This array would be allocated in $k = \prod_{i=0}^{n-1} \left\lceil \frac{d_i}{b_i} \right\rceil$ blocks (or tiles) of $b = \prod_{i=0}^{n-1} b_i$ elements. We continue to use the concepts of *thread*, *course* and *phase* to find array elements. However, for multiblocked arrays two linearized indices must be computed: one to find the block and another to find an element's location within a block. Note the similarity of Equations 2 and 3 to Equation 1:

$$L_{in-block}(\mathbf{v}) = \sum_{k=0}^{n-1} ((v_k \bmod b_k) \times \prod_{j=k+1}^{n-1} b_j) \qquad (2)$$

$$L(\mathbf{v}) \quad = \sum_{k=0}^{n-1} (\left\lfloor \frac{v_k}{b_k} \right\rfloor \times \prod_{j=k+1}^{n-1} \left\lceil \frac{d_j}{b_j} \right\rceil) \qquad (3)$$

The *phase* of a multiblocked array element is its linearized in-block index. The *course* and *thread* are calculated with a cyclic distribution of the block index, as in the case of regular UPC arrays.

$$\begin{cases} thread(A, \mathbf{v}) & ::= \left\lfloor \frac{L(\mathbf{v})}{\prod_{i=0}^{n-1} b_i} \right\rfloor \bmod \mathcal{T} \\ phase(A, \mathbf{v}) & ::= L_{in-block}(\mathbf{v}) \\ course(A, \mathbf{v}) & ::= \left\lfloor \frac{L(\mathbf{v})}{\prod_{i=0}^{n-1} b_i \times \mathcal{T}} \right\rfloor \end{cases} \qquad (4)$$

Array sizes that are non-multiples of blocking factors: The blocking factors of multiblocked arrays are not required to divide their respective dimensions, just as blocking factors of regular UPC arrays are not required to divide the array's dimension(s). Such arrays are padded in every dimension to allow for correct index calculation.

2.2   Multiblocked Arrays and UPC Pointer Arithmetic

The address of any UPC array element (even remote ones) can be taken with the upc_addressof function or with the familiar & operator. The result is called a *pointer-to-shared*, and it is a reference to a memory location somewhere within the space of the running UPC application. In our implementation a pointer-to-shared identifies the base array as well as the thread, course and phase of an element in that array.

UPC pointers-to-shared behave much like pointers in C. They can be incremented, dereferenced, compared etc. The familiar pointer operators (*, &, ++) are available. A series of increments on a pointer-to-shared will cause it to traverse a UPC shared array in row-major order.

Pointers-to-shared can also used to point to multiblocked arrays. Users can expect pointer arithmetic and operators to work on multiblocked arrays just like on regular UPC shared arrays.

Affinity, casting and dynamic allocation of multiblocked arrays: Multiblocked arrays can support affinity tests (similar to the upc_threadof function) and type casts the same way regular UPC arrays do.

Dynamic allocation of UPC shared arrays can also be extended to multiblocked arrays. UPC primitives like upc_all_alloc always return shared variables of type shared void *; multiblocked arrays can be allocated with such primitives as long as they are cast to the proper type.

2.3 Implementation Issues

Pointers and dynamic allocation of arrays: Our current implementation supports only statically allocated multiblocked arrays. Dynamically allocated multiblocked arrays could be obtained by casting dynamically allocated data to a shared multiblocked type, making dynamic multiblocked arrays a function of correct casting and multiblocked pointer arithmetic. While correct multiblocked pointer arithmetic is not conceptually difficult, implementation is not simple: to traverse a multiblocked array correctly, a pointer-to-shared will have to have access to all blocking factors of the shared type.

Processor tiling: Another limitation of the current implementation is related to the cyclic distribution of blocks over UPC threads. An alternative would be to specify a processor grid to distribute blocks over. Equation 3 would have to be suitably modified to take thread distribution into consideration. We have not implemented this yet in the UPC runtime system, although performance results presented later in the paper clearly show the need for it.

Hybrid memory layout: Our UPC runtime implementation is capable of running in mixed multithreaded/multinode environments. In such an environment locality is interpreted on a per-node basis, but array layouts have to be on a per-UPC-thread basis to be compatible with the specification. This is true both for regular and multiblocked arrays.

3 Locality Analysis for Multi-dimensional Blocking Factors

This section describes a compile-time analysis for multi-dimensional blocking factors in UPC shared arrays. The analysis considers loop nests that contain accesses to UPC shared arrays and finds shared array references that are provably local (on the same UPC thread) or shared local (on the same node in shared memory, but on different UPC threads). All other shared array references are potentially remote (reachable only via inter-node communication).

The analysis enables the compiler to refactor the loop nest to separate local and remote accesses. Local and shared local accesses cause the compiler to generate simple memory references; remote variable accesses are resolved through the runtime with a significant remote access overhead. We consider locality analysis crucial to obtaining good performance with UPC.

In Figure 1 we present a loop nest that will be used as an example for our analysis. In this form the shared array element in the affinity test — the last parameter in the upc_forall statement — is formed by the current loop-nest index, while the single element referenced in the loop body has a displacement, with respect to the affinity expression, specified by the distance vector $\mathbf{k} = [k_0, k_1, \ldots, k_{n-1}]$. Any loop nest in which the index for each dimension, both in the affinity test and in the array reference, is an affine expression containing only the index in the corresponding dimension can be transformed to this cannonical form.[1] Table 1 summarizes the notation used throughout

---

[1] An example of a loop nest that cannot be transformed to this cannonical form is a two-level nest accessing a two-dimensional array in which either the affinity test or the reference contains an expression such as A$[v_0 + v_1]$$[v_1]$.

```
shared [b₀][b₁]⋯[b_{k-1}] int A[d₀][d₁]⋯[d_{k-1}];
for(v₀=0 ;  v₀ < d₀ - k₀ ;  v₀++)
   for(v₁=0 ;  v₁ < d₁ - k₁ ;  v₁++){
      ...
      upc_forall(v_{n-1}=0 ; v_{n-1} < d_{n-1} - k_{n-1} ; v_{n-1}++ ; &A[v₀][v₁]...[v_{n-1}])
            A[v₀ + k₀][v₁ + k₁]...[v_{n-1} + k_{n-1}]  =  v₀ * v₁ * ... * v_{n-1};
}
```

Fig. 1. Multi-level loop nest that accesses a multi-dimensional array in UPC

Table 1. Expressions used to compute the node ID that each element $A[\mathbf{v}]$ of array A belongs to

Ref	Expression	Description
1	n	number of dimensions
2	b_i	blocking factor in dimension i
3	d_i	array size in dimension i
4	v_i	position index in dimension i
5	$\mathbf{v} = [v_0, v_1, \ldots, v_{n-1}]$	Index of an array element
6	$\mathcal{T}$	number of threads
7	t	number of threads per node
8	$\mathcal{B}_i = \lfloor \frac{v_i}{b_i} \rfloor$	Block index in dimension i
9	$L(\mathbf{v}) = \sum_{i=0}^{n-1} \mathcal{B}_i \times \prod_{j=i+1}^{n-1} \lceil \frac{d_j}{b_j} \rceil$	Linearized block index
10	$L'(\mathbf{v}) = L(\mathbf{v}) \% \mathcal{T}$	Normalized linearized block index
11	$\mathcal{N}(\mathbf{v}) = \lfloor \frac{L'(\mathbf{v})}{t} \rfloor$	Node ID
12	$\mathcal{O}(\mathbf{v}) = L(\mathbf{v}) \% t$	Block offset within a node

this section and the expressions used by the locality analysis to compute the locality of array elements. The goal of the locality analysis is to compute symbolically the node ID of each shared reference in the loop and compare it to the node ID of the affinity expression. All references having a node ID equal to the affinity expression's node ID are local.

Locality analysis is done on the n-dimensional blocks of the multiblocked arrays present in the loop. For conventional UPC shared arrays declared with a blocking factor b, the analysis uses blocking factors of 1 in all dimensions except the last dimension, where b is used. The insight of the analysis is that a block shifted by a displacement vector $\mathbf{k}$ can span at most two threads along each dimension. Therefore locality can only change in one place in this dimension. We call this place the cut.

Once the cut is determined, our analysis tests the locality of the elements at the 2^n corners of the block. If a corner is found to be local, all the elements in the region from the corner up to the cuts in each dimension are also local.

Definition 1. *The value of a cut in dimension i, Cut_i, is the distance, measured in number of elements, between the corner of a block and the first transition between nodes on that dimension.*

Consider the two-level loop nest that accesses a two-dimensional blocked array shown in Figure 2. The layout of the array used in the loop is shown to the right of the code.

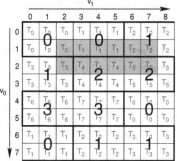

```
1  /* 8 threads and 2 threads/node */
2
3  shared [2][3] int A[8][8];
4
5  for(v0=0; v0<7 ; v0++){
6    upc_forall(v1=0; v1<6 ; v1++; &A[v0][v1]){
7      A[v0+1][v1+2] = v0*v1 ;
8    }
9  }
```

Fig. 2. A two-dimensional array node example

Thin lines separate the elements of the array. Large bold numbers inside each block of 2×3 elements denote the node ID to which the block is mapped. Thick lines separate nodes from each other. The grey area in the array represents all elements that are referenced by iterations of the forall loop that are affine with &A[0][0]; cuts in this iteration space are determined by the thick lines (node boundaries).

Finding the cuts: In general, for dimensions $i = 0$ to $n - 2$ the value of the cut in that dimension is given by the following expression.

$$\mathrm{Cut}_i = b_i - k_i \mathbin{\%} b_i \tag{5}$$

Thus in the example $\mathrm{Cut}_0 = 1$, which means that the only possible change of locality value happens between the first and second row of the block being accessed.

The cuts in the last dimension of the array are not necessarily the same for each corner. In Figure 2, for the top corners the cut is 4 but for the bottom corners the cut is 1. This happens when there are multiple colocated UPC threads in a node (in a hybrid setup); because the blocks in a node may "wrap around" the rows in the array.

Thus the analysis has to compute two separate values for the last cut: one for the upper corners and a second one for the lower corners. Upper and Lower refers to the last dimension in a multi-dimensional array. Let $\mathbf{k}' = [k_0 + b_0 - 1, k_1, \ldots, k_{n-1}]$. The expression for the last cut in the upper corner is as follows:

$$\mathrm{Cut}_{n-1}^{\mathrm{Upper}} = (t - \mathcal{O}(\mathbf{k})) \times b_{n-1} - k_{n-1} \mathbin{\%} b_{n-1} \tag{6}$$

$$\mathrm{Cut}_{n-1}^{\mathrm{Lower}} = (t - \mathcal{O}(\mathbf{k}')) \times b_{n-1} - k_{n-1} \mathbin{\%} b_{n-1} \tag{7}$$

where t is the number of threads per node.

When there is a single thread per node (*i.e.* $t = 1$), the normalized linearized block index is zero, and thus equations 6 and 7 simplify to equation 5.

Axiom 3.0.1. *Given an* upc_forall *loop with affinity test* AffTest $= A(\mathbf{v})$ *and a shared array reference* Ref $= A(\mathbf{v} + \mathbf{k})$, *this reference is local if and only if* $\mathcal{N}(\mathrm{AffTest}) = \mathcal{N}(\mathrm{Ref})$

Theorem 1. *Let A be an n-dimensional shared array with dimensions $d_0, d_1, \ldots, d_{n-1}$ and with blocking dimensions $b_0, b_1, \ldots, b_{n-1}$. Let $\mathbf{w} = v_0, v_1, \ldots, v_p, \ldots, v_{n-1}$ and $\mathbf{y} = v_0, v_1, \ldots, v_p + 1, \ldots v_{n-1}$ be two vectors such that $A(\mathbf{w})$ and $A(\mathbf{y})$ are elements of A. Let $B_{\mathrm{Off}} = \mathcal{O}(v_0, v_1, \ldots, 0)$ be the block offset for the first element in the block in dimension $n - 1$. Let*

$$v_i' = \begin{cases} v_i \, \% \, b_i - k_i \, \% \, b_i & \text{if } i \neq n - 1 \\ (v_i + B_{\mathrm{Off}} \times b_i) \, \% \, (b_i \times t) & \text{Otherwise.} \end{cases} \tag{8}$$

if $v_p' \neq \mathrm{Cut}_p - 1$ then $\mathcal{N}(\mathbf{w}) = \mathcal{N}(\mathbf{y})$.

Proof. We only present the proof for the case $p \neq n - 1$ here. The proof for the case $p = n - 1$ follows a similar reasoning but is more involved because it has to take into account the block offset for the first element in dimension $n - 1$.

From the expressions in Table 1 the expression for the node id of elements $\mathbf{w}$ and $\mathbf{y}$ are given by:

$$\mathcal{N}(\mathbf{w}) = \left\lfloor \frac{L(\mathbf{w}) \, \% \, \mathcal{T}}{t} \right\rfloor \text{ and } \mathcal{N}(\mathbf{y}) = \left\lfloor \frac{L(\mathbf{y}) \, \% \, \mathcal{T}}{t} \right\rfloor \tag{9}$$

The linearized block index for $\mathbf{w}$ and $\mathbf{y}$ can be written as:

$$L(\mathbf{w}) = \sum_{i=0}^{n-1} \left\lfloor \frac{v_i}{b_i} \right\rfloor \times \prod_{j=i+1}^{n-1} \left\lceil \frac{d_j}{b_j} \right\rceil \tag{10}$$

$$L(\mathbf{y}) = L(\mathbf{w}) + \left(\left\lfloor \frac{v_p + 1}{b_p} \right\rfloor - \left\lfloor \frac{v_p}{b_p} \right\rfloor \right) \times \prod_{j=p+1}^{n-1} \left\lceil \frac{d_j}{b_j} \right\rceil \tag{11}$$

From equations 5 and 8:

$$v_p' = \mathrm{Cut}_p - 1 \tag{12}$$

$$v_p \, \% \, b_p - k_p \, \% \, b_p = b_p - k_p \, \% \, b_p - 1 \tag{13}$$

From equation 13, the condition $v_p' \neq \mathrm{Cut}_p - 1$ implies that $v_p \, \% \, b_p \neq b_p - 1$, which implies that $v_p \, \% \, b_p \leq b_p - 2$. Therefore:

$$\left\lfloor \frac{v_p + 1}{b_p} \right\rfloor = \left\lfloor \frac{v_p}{b_p} \right\rfloor \tag{14}$$

Substituting this result in equation 11 results that $L(\mathbf{y}) = L(\mathbf{w})$ and therefore $N(\mathbf{w}) = N(\mathbf{y})$.

Theorem 1 is the theoretical foundation of locality analysis based on corners and cuts. It establishes that the only place within a block where the node ID may change is at the cut. The key is that the elements $A(\mathbf{w})$ and $A(\mathbf{y})$ are adjacent elements of A.

4   Identifying Local Shared Accesses

In this section we present an algorithm that splits a loop nest into a number of smaller regions in the iteration space, such that in each region, each shared reference is known to be local or known to be remote. In a region, if a shared reference is determined to be local then the reference is privatized otherwise a call to the runtime is inserted.

To determine such regions, our analysis reasons about the positions of various shared references occuring in the loop nest relative to the affinity test expression. For each region, we keep track of a *position* relative to the affinity test shared reference. For each shared reference in the region, we also keep track of position of each reference relative to the region.

We start with the original loop nest as a single region. This region is analyzed and the cuts are computed. The region is then split according to the cuts generated. The new generated regions are again analyzed and split recursively until no more cuts are required. When all of the regions have been generated, we use the position of the region, and the position of the shared reference within the region to determine if it is local or remote. All shared references that are local are privatized. Figure 3 provides a sample

```
1  shared [5][5] int A[20][20];
2  int main() {
3    int i,j;
4    for (i=0; i < 19; i++)
5      upc_forall(j=0; j < 20; j++; &A[i][j]) {
6        A[i+1][j] = MYTHREAD;
7      }
8  }
```

Fig. 3. Example upc_forall loop containing a shared reference

loop nest containing a upc_forall loop and a shared array access. We will assume the example is compiled for a machine containing 2 nodes and will run with 8 UPC threads, creating a thread group size of 4. In this scenario, the shared array access on Line 6 will be local for the first four rows of every block owned by a thread T and remote for the remaining row. The LOCALITYANALYSIS algorithm in Figure 4 begins by collecting all top-level loop nests that contain a candidate upc_forall loop. To be a candidate for locality analysis, a upc_forall loop must be normalized (lower bound begins at 0 and the increment is 1) and must use a pointer-to-shared argument for the affinity test. The algorithm then proceeds to analyze each loop nest independently (Step 2).

Phase 1 of the per-loopnest analysis algorithm finds and collects the upc_forall loop l_{forall}. The affinity statement used in l_{forall}, A_{stmt} is also obtained. Finally the COLLECTSHAREDREFERENCES procedure collects all candidate shared references in the specified upc_forall loop. In order to be a candidate for locality analysis, a shared reference must have the same blocking factor as the shared reference used in the affinity test. The compiler must also be able to compute the *displacement vector* $k = ref_{shared} - affinityStatement$ for the shared reference, the vectorized difference between the indices of the reference and of the affinity statement.

In the example in Figure 3 the loop nest on Line 4 is collected as a candidate for locality analysis. The shared reference on Line 6 is collected as a candidate for locality analysis; the computed displacement vector is [1,0].

Phase 2 of the algorithm restructures the loop nest by splitting the iteration space of each loop into *regions* where the locality of shared references is known. Each region has

```
LOCALITYANALYSIS(Procedurep)
1. NestSet ← GATHERFORALLLOOPNESTS(p)
2. foreach loop nest L in NestSet
Phase 1 - Gather Candidate Shared References
3.        l_forall ← upc_forall loop found in loop nest L
4.        nestDepth ← depth of L
5.        A_stmt ← Affinity statement used in l_forall
6.        SharedRefList ← COLLECTSHAREDREFERENCES(l_forall, A_stmt)
Phase 2 - Restructure Loop Nest
7.        FirstRegion ← INITIALIZEREGION(L)
8.        L_R ← FirstRegion
9.        while L_R not empty
10.            R ← Pop head of L_R
11.            CutList ← GENERATECUTLIST(R, SharedRefList)
12.            nestLevel ← R.nestLevel
13.            if nestLevel < nestDepth − 1
14.                L_R ← L_R ∪ GENERATENEWREGIONS(R, CutList)
15.            else
16.                L_R^final ← L_R^final ∪ GENERATENEWREGIONS(R, CutList)
17.            endif
18.        end while
Phase 3 - Identify Local Accesses and Privatize
19.        foreach R in L_R^final
20.            foreach ref_shared in SharedRefList
21.                refPosition ← COMPUTEPOSITION(ref_shared, R)
22.                nodeId ← COMPUTENODEID(ref_shared, refPosition)
23.                if nodeId = 0
24.                    PRIVATIZESHAREDREFERENCE(ref_shared)
25. endfor
```

Fig. 4. Locality analysis for UPC shared references

a *statement list* associated with it, i.e. the lexicographically ordered list of statements as they appear in the program. Each region is also associated with a *position* in the iteration space of the loops containing the region.

In the example in Figure 3 the first region, R_0 contains the statements on Lines 5 to 7. The position of R_0 is 0, since the iteration space of the outermost loop contains the location 0. Once initialized, the region is placed into a list of regions, $\mathcal{L}_R$ (Step 8).

The algorithm iterates through all regions in $\mathcal{L}_R$. For each region, a list of cuts is computed based on the shared references collected in Phase 1. The cut represents the transition between a local access and a remote access in the given region. The GENERATECUTLIST algorithm first determines the loop-variant induction variable iv in R that is used in ref_{shared}. The use of iv identifies the dimension in which to obtain the blocking factor and displacement when computing the cut. Depending on the dimension of the induction variable, either Equation 5 or Equations 6 and 7 are used to compute the cuts.

GENERATECUTLIST sorts all cuts in ascending order. Duplicate cuts and cuts outside the iteration space of the region ($Cut = 0$ or $Cut \geq b$) are discarded. Finally, the current region is cut into multiple iteration ranges, based on the cut list, using the GENERATENEWREGION algorithm. Newly created regions are separated by an if statement containing a *cut expression* of the form $iv\%b < Cut$ (the modulo is necessary since a cut is always in the middle of a block).

Step 13 determines if the region R is located in the innermost loop in the current loop nest (*i.e.* there are no other loops inside of R). If R contains innermost statements the regions generated by GENERATENEWREGIONS are placed in a separate list of final regions. $\mathcal{L}_R^{final}$. This ensures that at the end of Phase 2, the loop nest has been refactored into several iteration ranges and final statement lists (representing the innermost loops) are collected for use in Phase 3.

```
1  shared  [5][5]  int  A[20][20];
2
3  int  main () {
4      int  i,j;
5      for  (i=0;  i < 19;  i++)
6          if  ((i % 5) < 4) {
7              upc_forall (j=0;  j < 20;  j++;
8                          &A[i][j]) {
9                  A[i+1][j] = MYTHREAD;
10             }
11         }
12         else {
13             upc_forall (j=0;  j < 20;  j++;
14                         &A[i][j]) {
15                 A[i+1][j] = MYTHREAD;
16             }
17         }
18 }
```

Fig. 5. Example after first cut

```
1  shared  [5][5]  int  A[20][20];
2  int  main () {
3      int  i,j;
4      for  (i=0;  i < 19;  i++)
5          if  ((i % 5) < 4) {
6              upc_forall (j=0;  j < 20;  j++;
7                          &A[i][j]) {
8                  offset = ComputeOffset(i,j);
9                  base_A+offset = MYTHREAD;
10             }
11         }
12         else {
13             upc_forall (j=0;  j < 20;  j++;
14                         &A[i][j]) {
15                 A[i+1][j] = MYTHREAD;
16             }
17         }
18 }
```

Fig. 6. Example after final code generation

The second phase iterates through the example in Figure 3 three times. The first region, R_0 and the $CutList = 4$, calculated by GENERATECUTLIST are passed in and the intermediate code shown in Figure 5 is generated. GENERATENEWREGIONS inserts the **if** ((i \% 5) < 4) branch and replicates the statements in region R_0. Two new regions, R_1 containing statements between lines 8 to 10 and R_2, containing lines 14 to 16, are created and added to the $NewList$. The respective positions associated with R_1 and R_2 are [0] and [4], respectively.

The new regions, R_1 and R_2 are popped off of the region list $\mathcal{L}_R$ in order. Neither region requires any cuts. GENERATENEWREGIONS copies R_1 and R_2 into R_3 and R_4 respectively. Since R_1 and R_2 represent the innermost loops in the nest, the new regions R_3 and R_4 will be placed into the final regions list (Step 16 in Figure 4). The position of region R_3 is [0,0] and the position of region R_4 is [4,0].

Phase 3 of the algorithm uses the position information stored in each of the final regions to compute the position of each shared reference in that region (Step 21). This information is then used to compute the node ID of the shared reference using the equations presented in Section 3 (Step 22). All shared references with a node ID of 0 are local and are privatized (Step 24). The shared reference $ref_{shared}^{R_3}$ located in R_3 is computed to have a position of $[1, 0]$ based on the position of $R_3, [0, 0]$, and the displacement vector of ref_{shared}, $[1, 0]$. The node ID for this position is 0 and thus $ref_{shared}^{R_3}$ is local. The shared reference $ref_{shared}^{R_4}$ is computed to have a position of $[5, 0]$ using the position for region R_4, $[4, 0]$. The node ID for this position is 1, and thus this reference is remote. Figure 6 shows the final code that is generated.

5   Experimental Evaluation

In this section we propose to evaluate the claims we have made in the paper: namely the usefulness of multiblocking and locality analysis. For our evaluation platform we used 4 nodes of an IBM Squadron™cluster. Each node has 8 SMP Power5 processors running at 1.9 GHz and 16 GBytes of memory.

Cholesky factorization and Matrix multiply: Cholesky factorization was written to showcase multi-blocked arrays. The tiled layout allows our implementation to take direct advantage of the ESSL [5] library. The code is patterned after the LAPACK [4] dpotrf implementation and adds up to 53 lines of text. To illustrate the compactness of the code, we reproduce one of the two subroutines used, distributed symmetric rank-k update, below.

```
1  void update_mb (shared double [B][B] A[N][N], int col0, int col1) {
2     double a_local[B*B], b_local[B*B];
3     upc_forall (int ii=col1; ii<N; ii+=B; continue)
4       upc_forall (int jj=col1; jj<ii+B; jj+=B; &A[ii][jj]) {
5         upc_memget (a_local, &A[ii][col0], sizeof(double)*B*B);
6         upc_memget (b_local, &A[jj][col0], sizeof(double)*B*B);
7         dgemm ("T", "N", &n, &m, &p, &alpha, b_local, &B, a_local,
8                &B, &beta, (void *)&A[ii][jj], &B);
9       }
10 }
```

The matrix multiply benchmark is written in a very similar fashion. It amounts to little more than a (serial) k loop around the update function above with slightly different loop bounds and three shared array arguments A, B and C instead of only one. It amounts to 20 lines of code. Without question, multiblocking allows compact code representation. The benchmark numbers presented in Figures 7 show mediocre scaling and performance "hiccups", which we attribute to communication overhead and poor communication patterns. Clearly, multiblocking syntax needs to be extended with a distribution directive. Also, the UPC language could use better collective communication primitives; but that is in the scope of a future paper.

Dense matrix-vector multiplication: This benchmark multiplies a two-dimensional shared matrix with a one-dimensional shared vector and places the result in a one-dimensional shared vector. The objective of this benchmark is to measure the speed difference between compiler-privatized and unprivatized accesses.

The matrix, declared of size 14400×14400, the vector as well the result vector are all blocked using single dimensional blocking. The blocking factors are equivalent to the [*] declarations. Since the vector is shared, the entire vector is first copied into a

Cholesky Performance (GFlops)	1 node	2 nodes	3 nodes	4 nodes
1 TPN	5.37	10.11	15.43	19.63
2 TPN	9.62	16.19	28.64	35.41
4 TPN	14.98	23.03	45.43	59.14
6 TPN	18.73	35.29	52.57	57.8
8 TPN	26.65	23.55	59.83	74.14

Matrix Multiply Performance (GFlops)	1 node	2 nodes	3 nodes	4 nodes
1 TPN	5.94	11.30	16.17	22.24
2 TPN	11.76	21.41	29.82	42.20
4 TPN	23.24	39.18	51.05	73.44
6 TPN	31.19	54.51	66.17	89.55
8 TPN	44.20	63.24	79.00	99.71

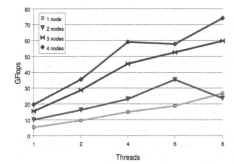
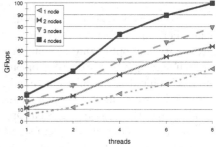

Fig. 7. Performance of multiblocked Cholesky and matrix multiply as a function of participating nodes and threads per node (TPN). Theoretical peak: $6.9\ GFlops \times threads \times nodes$.

Matrix-vector multiply

Naive	1 node	2 nodes	3 nodes	4 nodes
1 TPN	27.55	16.57	14.13	9.21
2 TPN	16.57	8.59	7.22	4.32
4 TPN	8.57	4.3	3.63	2.18
6 TPN	7.2	3.62	2.43	1.89
8 TPN	4.33	2.2	1.96	1.28

Opt.	1 node	2 nodes	3 nodes	4 nodes
1 TPN	2.08	1.22	0.78	0.6
2 TPN	1.7	0.85	0.63	0.43
4 TPN	0.85	0.44	0.33	0.23
6 TPN	0.65	0.35	0.25	0.19
8 TPN	0.44	0.23	0.22	0.17

Stencil benchmark

Naive	1 node	2 nodes	3 nodes	4 nodes
1 thread	35.64	24.59	19.04	13.41
2 threads	18.85	13.56	9.82	7.9
4 threads	9.8	13.64	5.58	8.9
6 threads	10.85	8.98	7.53	6.12
8 threads	4.9	5.58	9.52	3.66

Opt.	1 node	2 nodes	3 nodes	4 nodes
1 thread	0.30	1.10	1.41	0.74
2 threads	0.73	0.72	0.75	1.06
4 threads	0.44	1.19	0.39	0.84
6 threads	0.32	0.30	1.11	0.75
8 threads	0.22	0.63	1.07	1.02

Fig. 8. Runtime in seconds for the matrix-vector multiplication benchmark (left) and for the stencil benchmark (right). The tables on the top show naive execution times; the tables on the bottom reflect compiler-optimized runtimes.

local buffer using upc_memget. The matrix-vector multiplication itself is a simple 2 level nest with the outer loop being upc_forall . The address of the result vector element is used as the affinity test expression.

Results presented in Figure 8 (left side) confirm that compiler-privatized accesses are about an order of magnitude faster than unprivatized accesses.

5-point Stencil: This benchmark computes the average of a 4 immediate neighbors and the point itself at every point in a 2 dimensional matrix and stores the result in a different matrix of same size. The benchmark requires one original data matrix and one result matrix. 2-d blocking was used to maximize the locality. The matrix size used for the experiments was 5760×5760. Results, presented in Figure 8 (right side), show that in this case, too, run time is substantially reduced by privatization.

6   Related Work

There is a significant body of work on data distributions in the context of High Performance Fortran (HPF) and other data parallel languages. Numerous researchers have tackled the issue of optimizing communication on distributed memory architectures by either finding an appropriate distribution onto processors [1,9] or by determining a computation schedule that minimizes the number of message transfers [7,12]. By contrast to these works, we do not try to optimize the communication, but rather allow the programmer to specify at very high level an appropriate distribution and then eliminate the need for communication all together using compiler analysis. We do not attempt to restructure or improve the data placement of threads to processors in order to minimize communication. While these optimizations are certainly possible in our compiler, we leave them as future work.

The locality analysis presented in this paper is also similar to array privatization [13,11]. However, array privatization relies on the compiler to provide local copies and/or copy-in and copy-out semantics for all privatized elements. In our approach, once ownership is determined, private elements are directly accessed. In future work we will determine if there is sufficient reuse in UPC programs to overcome the cost of copying array elements into private memory.

Tiled and block distributions are useful for many linear algebra and scientific codes [2]. HPF-1 provided the ability to choose a data distribution independently in each dimesion if desired. Beside HPF, several other languages, such as ZPL [3] and X10 [15] provide them as standard distributions supported by the language. In addition, libraries such as the Hierarichical Tiled Arrays library [2] provide tiled distributions for data decomposition. ScaLAPACK [6], a widely used parallel library provides a 2 dimensional block-cyclic distribution for matrices which allows the placement of blocks over a 2-dimensional processor grid. The distribution used by ScaLAPACK is therefore more general than the distribution presented in the this paper.

7   Conclusions and Future Work

In this paper we presented a language extension for UPC shared arrays that provides fine control over array data layout. This extensions allows the programmer to obtain better performance while simplifying the expression of computations, in particular matrix computations. An added benefit is the ability to integrate existing libraries written in C and Fortran, which require specific memory layouts. We also presented a compile-time analysis and optimization of shared memory accesses. Using this analysis, the compiler is able to reduce the overheads introduced by the runtime system.

A number of issues still remain to be resolved, both in the UPC language and more importantly in our implementation. For multiblocked arrays, we believe that adding processor tiling will increase the programmer's ability to write codes that scale to large numbers of processors. Defining a set of collectives that are optimized for the UPC programming model will also address several scalability issues, such as the ones occuring in the LU Factorization and the High Performance Linpack kernel [8].

Our current compiler implementation suffers from several shortcomings. In particular, several loop optimizations are disabled in the presence of upc_forall loops. These limitations are reflected in the results presented in this paper, where the baseline C compiler offers a higher single thread performance compared to the UPC compiler.

Acknowledgements

This material is based upon work supported in part by the Defense Advanced Research Projects Agency under its Agreement No. HR0011-07-9-0002. This work has also been supported by the Ministry of Education of Spain under contract TIN2007-60625. We also want to thank Philip Luk and Ettore Tiotto for their help with the IBM xlUPC compiler.

References

1. Ayguade, E., Garcia, J., Girones, M., Labarta, J., Torres, J., Valero, M.: Detecting and using affinity in an automatic data distribution tool. In: Languages and Compilers for Parallel Computing, pp. 61–75 (1994)
2. Bikshandi, G., Guo, J., Hoeflinger, D., Almási, G., Fraguela, B.B., Garzarán, M.J., Padua, D.A., von Praun, C.: Programming for parallelism and locality with hierarchically tiled arrays. In: PPOPP, pp. 48–57 (2006)
3. Chamberlain, B.L., Choi, S.-E., Lewis, E.C., Lin, C., Snyder, L., Weathersby, D.: ZPL: A machine independent programming language for parallel computers. Software Engineering 26(3), 197–211 (2000)
4. Dongarra, J.J., Du Croz, J., Hammarling, S., Hanson, R.J.: An extended set of FORTRAN Basic Linear Algebra Subprograms. ACM Transactions on Mathematical Software 14(1), 1–17 (1988)
5. ESSL User Guide,
   http://www-03.ibm.com/systems/p/software/essl.html
6. Blackford, L.S., et al.: ScaLAPACK: a linear algebra library for message-passing computers. In: Proceedings of the Eighth SIAM Conference on Parallel Processing for Scientific Computing (Minneapolis, MN, 1997) (electronic), Philadelphia, PA, USA, p. 15. Society for Industrial and Applied Mathematics (1997)
7. Gupta, M., Schonberg, E., Srinivasan, H.: A unified framework for optimizing communication in data-parallel programs. IEEE Transactions on Parallel and Distributed Systems 7(7), 689–704 (1996)
8. HPL Algorithm description,
   http://www.netlib.org/benchmark/hpl/algorithm.html
9. Kremer, U.: Automatic data layout for distributed memory machines. Technical Report TR96-261, 14 (1996)

10. Numrich, R.W., Reid, J.: Co-array fortran for parallel programming. ACM Fortran Forum 17(2), 1–31 (1998)
11. Paek, Y., Navarro, A.G., Zapata, E.L., Padua, D.A.: Parallelization of benchmarks for scalable shared-memory multiprocessors. In: IEEE PACT, p. 401 (1998)
12. Ponnusamy, R., Saltz, J.H., Choudhary, A.N., Hwang, Y.-S., Fox, G.: Runtime support and compilation methods for user-specified irregular data distributions. IEEE Transactions on Parallel and Distributed Systems 6(8), 815–831 (1995)
13. Tu, P., Padua, D.A.: Automatic array privatization. In: Compiler Optimizations for Scalable Parallel Systems Languages, pp. 247–284 (2001)
14. UPC Language Specification, V1.2 (May 2005)
15. The X10 programming language (2004), http://x10.sourceforge.net
16. Yelick, K., Semenzato, L., Pike, G., Miyamoto, C., Liblit, B., Krishnamurthy, A., Hilfinger, P., Graham, S., Gay, D., Colella, P., Aiken, A.: Titanium: A high-performance java dialect. Concurrency: Practice and Experience 10(11-13) (September-November 1998)

An Experimental Evaluation of the New OpenMP Tasking Model

Eduard Ayguadé[1], Alejandro Duran[1], Jay Hoeflinger[2], Federico Massaioli[3],
and Xavier Teruel[1]

[1] BSC-UPC
[2] Intel
[3] CASPUR

Abstract. The OpenMP standard was conceived to parallelize dense array-based applications, and it has achieved much success with that. Recently, a novel tasking proposal to handle unstructured parallelism in OpenMP has been submitted to the OpenMP 3.0 Language Committee. We tested its expressiveness and flexibility, using it to parallelize a number of examples from a variety of different application areas. Furthermore, we checked whether the model can be implemented efficiently, evaluating the performance of an experimental implementation of the tasking proposal on an SGI Altix 4700, and comparing it to the performance achieved with Intel's Workqueueing model and other worksharing alternatives currently available in OpenMP 2.5. We conclude that the new OpenMP tasks allow the expression of parallelism for a broad range of applications and that they will not hamper application performance.

1 Introduction

OpenMP grew out of the need to standardize the directive languages of several vendors in the 1990s. It was structured around parallel loops and was meant to handle dense numerical applications. The simplicity of its original interface, the use of a shared memory model, and the fact that the parallelism of a program is expressed in directives that are loosely-coupled to the code, all have helped OpenMP become well-accepted today. However, the sophistication of parallel programmers has grown in the last 10 years since OpenMP was introduced, and the complexity of their applications is increasing. Therefore, OpenMP is in the process of adding a tasking model to address this new programming landscape. The new directives allow the user to identify units of independent work, leaving the decisions of how and when to execute them to the runtime system.

In this paper, we have attempted to evaluate this new tasking model. We wanted to know how the new tasking model compared to traditional OpenMP worksharing and the existing Intel workqueueing model, both in terms of expressivity and performance. In order to evaluate expressivity, we have parallelized a number of problems across a wide range of application domains, using the tasking proposal. Performance evaluation has been done on a prototype implementation

V. Adve, M.J. Garzarán, and P. Petersen (Eds.): LCPC 2007, LNCS 5234, pp. 63–77, 2008.

```
1   #pragma omp parallel private (p)
2   {
3       #pragma omp for
4       for (i=0; i< n_lists; i++) {
5           p = listheads[i];
6           while(p) {
7               #pragma omp task
8                   process(p)
9               p=next(p);
10          }
11      }
12  }
```

```
1  void traverse(node *p, bool post)
2  {
3      if (p->left)
4          #pragma omp task
5              traverse(p->left, post);
6      if (p->right)
7          #pragma omp task
8              traverse(p->right, post);
9      if (post) { /* postorder! */
10         #pragma omp taskwait
11     }
12     process(p);
13 }
```

Fig. 1. Parallel pointer chasing on multiple lists using task

Fig. 2. Parallel depth-first tree traversal

of the tasking model. Performance results must be treated as preliminary, although we have validated the performance of our implementation against the performance of the commercial Intel workqueueing model implementation[1].

2 Motivation and Related Work

The task parallelism proposal under consideration by the OpenMP Language committee [2] gives programmers a way to express patterns of concurrency that do not match the worksharing constructs defined in the current OpenMP 2.5 specification.The proposal addresses common operations like complex, possibly recursive, data structure traversal, and situations which could easily cause load imbalance. The efficient parallelization of these algorithms using the 2.5 OpenMP standard is not impossible, but requires extensive program changes, such as run-time data structure transformations. This implies significant hand coding and run-time overhead, reducing the productivity that is typical of OpenMP programming[3].

Figure 1 illustrates the use of the new omp task[1] construct from the proposal. It creates a new flow of execution, corresponding to the construct's structured block. This flow of execution is concurrent to the rest of the work in the parallel region, but its execution can be performed only by a thread from the current team. Notice that this behavior is different from that of worksharing constructs, which are cooperatively executed by the existing team of threads. Execution of the task region does not necessarily start immediately, but can be deferred until the runtime schedules it.

The p pointer variable used inside the tasks in Figure 1 is implicitly determined *firstprivate*, i.e. copy constructed at task creation from the original copies used by each thread to iterate through the lists. This default was adopted in the proposal to balance performance, safety of use, and convenience for the programmer. It can be altered using the standard OpenMP data scoping clauses.

---

[1] This paper will express all code in C/C++, but the tasking proposal includes the equivalent directives in Fortran.

The new `#pragma omp taskwait` construct used in Figure 1 suspends the current execution flow until all tasks it generated have been completed. The semantics of the existing `barrier` construct is extended to synchronize for completion of all generated tasks in the team.

For a programming language extension to be successful, it has to be useful, and must be checked for expressiveness and productivity. Are the directives able to describe explicit concurrency in the problem? Do data scoping rules, defaults and clauses match the real programmers' needs? Do common use cases exist that the extension does not fulfill, forcing the programmer to add lines of code to fill the gap? The two examples above, while illustrative, involve very basic algorithms. They cannot be considered representative of a real application kernel.

In principle, the more concurrency that can be expressed in the source code, the more the compiler is able to deliver parallelism. However, factors like subtle side effects of data scoping, or even missing features, could hamper the actual level of parallelism which can be achieved at run-time. Moreover, parallelism *per se* does not automatically imply good performance. The semantics of a directive or clause can have unforeseen impact on object code or runtime overheads. In a language extension process, this aspect should also be checked thoroughly, with respect to the existing standard and to competing models.

The suitability of the current OpenMP standard to express irregular forms of parallelism was already investigated in the fields of dense linear algebra [4,5], adaptive mesh refinement [6], and agent-based models [7].

The Intel *workqueueing* model [8] was the first attempt to add dynamic task generation to OpenMP. The model, available as a proprietary extension in Intel compilers, allows hierarchical generation of tasks by the nesting of `taskq` constructs. Synchronization of descendant tasks is controlled by means of the default barrier at the end of `taskq` constructs. The implementation exhibits some overhead problems [7] and other performance issues [9].

In our choice of the application kernels to test drive the OpenMP tasking proposal, we were also inspired by the classification of different application domains proposed in [10], which addresses a much broader range of computations than traditional in the HPC field.

3   Programming with OpenMP Tasks

In this section we describe all the problems we have parallelized with the new task proposal. We have worked on applications across a wide range of domains (linear algebra, sparse algebra, servers, branch and bound, etc) to test the expressiveness of the proposal. Some of the applications (*multisort*, *fft* and *queens*) are originally from the Cilk project[11], some others (*pairwise alignment*, *connected components* and *floorplan*) come from the Application Kernel Matrix project from Cray[12] and two (*sparseLU* and *user interface*) have been developed by us. These kernels were not chosen because they were the best representatives of their class but because they represented a challenge for the current 2.5 OpenMP standard and were publicly available.

We have divided them into three categories. First were those applications that could already be easily parallelized with current OpenMP worksharing but where the use of tasks allows the expression of additional parallelism. Second were those applications which require the use of nested parallelism to be parallelized by the current standard. Nested parallelism is an optional feature and it is not always well supported. Third were those applications which would require a great amount of effort by the programmer to parallelize with OpenMP 2.5 (e.g. by programming their own tasks).

3.1   Worksharing Versus Tasking

SparseLU. The sparseLU kernel computes an LU matrix factorization. The matrix is organized in blocks that may not be allocated. Due to the sparseness of the matrix, a lot of imbalance exists. This is particularly true for the the *bmod phase* (see Figure 3). SparseLU can be parallelized with the current worksharing directives (using an OpenMP *for* with dynamic scheduling for loops on lines 10, 15 and 21 or 23). For the *bmod phase* we have two options: parallelize the outer (line 21) or the inner loop (line 23). If the outer loop is parallelized, the overhead is lower but the imbalance is greater. On the other hand, if the inner loop is parallelized the iterations are smaller which allows a dynamic schedule to have better balance but the overhead of the worksharing is much higher.

```
 1 int sparseLU() {
 2     int ii, jj, kk;
 3 #pragma omp parallel
 4 #pragma omp single nowait
 5     for (kk=0; kk<NB; kk++) {
 6         lu0(A[kk][kk]);
 7         /* fwd phase */
 8         for (jj=kk+1; jj<NB; jj++)
 9             if (A[kk][jj] != NULL)
10                 #pragma omp task
11                     fwd(A[kk][kk], A[kk][jj]);
12         /* bdiv phase */
13         for (ii=kk+1; ii<NB; ii++)
14             if (A[ii][kk] != NULL)
15                 #pragma omp task
16                     bdiv(A[kk][kk], A[ii][kk]);
17         #pragma omp taskwait
18         /* bmod phase */
19         for (ii=kk+1; ii<NB; ii++)
20             if (A[ii][kk] != NULL)
21                 for (jj=kk+1; jj<NB; jj++)
22                     if (A[kk][jj] != NULL)
23                         #pragma omp task
24                         {
25                             if (A[ii][jj]==NULL) A[ii][jj]=allocate_clean_block();
26                             bmod(A[ii][kk], A[kk][jj], A[ii][jj]);
27                         }
28         #pragma omp taskwait
29     }
30 }
```

Fig. 3. Main code of SparseLU with OpenMP tasks

Using tasks, first we only create work for non-empty matrix blocks. We also create smaller units of work in the bmod phase with an overhead similar to the outer loop parallelization. This reduces the load imbalance problems.

It is interesting to note that, if the proposed extension included mechanisms to express dependencies among tasks, it would be possible to express additional parallelism that exists between tasks created in lines 12 and 17 and tasks created in line 25. Also it would be possible to express the parallelism that exists across consecutive iterations of the *kk* loop.

Protein pairwise alignment. This application aligns all protein sequences from an input file against every other sequence. The alignments are scored and the best score for each pair is output as a result. The scoring method is a full dynamic programming algorithm. It uses a weight matrix to score mismatches, and assigns penalties for opening and extending gaps. It uses the recursive Myers and Miller algorithm to align sequences.

The outermost loop can be parallelized, but the loop is heavily unbalanced, although this can be partially mitigated with dynamic scheduling. Another problem is that the number of iterations is too small to generate enough work when the number of threads is large. Also, the loops of the different passes (forward pass, reverse pass, diff and tracepath) can also be parallelized but this parallelization is much finer so it has higher overhead.

We used OpenMP tasks to exploit the inner loop in conjunction with the outer loop. Note that the tasks are nested inside an OpenMP *for* worksharing construct. This breaks iterations into smaller pieces, thus increasing the amount of parallel work but at lower cost than an inner loop parallelization because they can be excuted inmediately.

```
1  #pragma omp for
2  for ( si = 0;  si < nseqs;  si++) {
3      len1 = compute_sequence_length( si +1);
4
5      /* compare to the other sequences */
6      for ( sj = si + 1;  sj < nseqs;  sj++) {
7          #pragma omp task
8          {
9              len2 = compute_sequence_length( sj +1);
10             compute_score_penalties ( ... );
11             forward_pass ( ... );
12             reverse_pass ( ... );
13             diff ( ... );
14             mm_score = tracepath ( ... );
15             if ( len1 == 0 || len2 == 0) mm_score  = 0.0;
16             else                          mm_score /= (double) MIN( len1 , len2 );
17
18             #pragma omp critical
19             print_score ();
20         }
21     }
22 }
```

Fig. 4. Main code of the pairwise aligment with tasks

3.2   Nested Parallelism Versus Tasking

Floorplan. The Floorplan kernel computes the optimal floorplan distribution of
a number of cells. The algorithm is a recursive branch and bound algorithm. The
parallelization is straight forward (see figure 5). We hierarchically generate tasks
for each branch of the solution space. But this parallelization has one caveat. In
these kind of algorithms (and others as well) the programmer needs to copy the
partial solution up to the moment to the new parallel branches (i.e. tasks). Due
to the nature of C arrays and pointers, the size of it becomes unknown across
function calls and the data scoping clauses are unable to perform a copy on their
own. To ensure that the original state does not disappear before it is copied, a
task barrier is added at the end of the function. Other possible solutions would
be to copy the array into the parent task stack and then capture its value or
allocate it in heap memory and free it at the end of the child task. In all these
solutions, the programmer must take special care.

Multisort, FFT and Strassen. Multisort is a variation of the ordinary merge-
sort. It sorts a random permutation of n 32-bit numbers with a fast parallel
sorting algorithm by dividing an array of elements in half, sorting each half

```
1 void add_cell(int id, coor FOOTPRINT, ibrd BOARD, struct cell *CELLS) {
2    int  i, j, nn, area;  ibrd board;  coor footprint, NWS[DMAX];
3
4    for (i = 0; i < CELLS[id].n; i++) {
5         nn = compute_possible_locations(id, i, NWS, CELLS);
6 /* for all possible locations */
7         for (j = 0; j < nn; j++) {
8 #pragma omp task private(board, footprint, area) \
9              shared(FOOTPRINT,BOARD,CELLS)
10 {       /* copy parent state */
11          struct cell cells[N+1];
12          memcpy(cells,CELLS, sizeof(struct cell)*(N+1));
13       memcpy(board, BOARD, sizeof(ibrd));
14
15       compute_cell_extent(cells,id,NWS,j);
16
17          /* if the cell cannot be layed down, prune search */
18          if (! lay_down(id, board, cells)) {
19             goto _end;
20          }
21       area = compute_new_footprint(footprint,FOOTPRINT,cells[id]);
22
23       /* if last cell */
24          if (cells[id].next == 0) {
25             if (area < MIN_AREA)
26             #pragma omp critical
27                if (area < MIN_AREA)   save_best_solution();
28          } else if (area < MIN_AREA)
29       /* only continue if area is smaller to best area, otherwise prune */
30             add_cell(cells[id].next, footprint, board,cells);
31 _end:;
32 }
33       }
34    }
35    #pragma omp taskwait
36 }
```

Fig. 5. C code for the Floorplan kernel with OpenMP tasks

recursively, and then merging the sorted halves with a parallel divide-and-conquer method rather than the conventional serial merge. When the array is too small, a serial quicksort is used so the task granularity is not too small. To avoid the overhead of quicksort, an insertion sort is used for arrays below a threshold of 20 elements.

The parallelization with tasks is straight forward and makes use of a few **task** and **taskgroup** directives (see figure 6), the latter being the structured form of the **taskwait** construct introduced in section 2.

FFT computes the one-dimensional Fast Fourier Transform of a vector of n complex values using the Cooley-Tukey algorithm. Strassen's algorithm for multiplication of large dense matrices uses hierarchical decomposition of a matrix. The structure of the parallelization of these two kernels is almost identical to the one used in multisort, so we will omit it.

N Queens problem. This program, which uses a backtracking search algorithm, computes all solutions of the n-queens problem, whose objective is to find a placement for n queens on an n x n chessboard such that none of the queens attacks any other.

In this application, tasks are nested dynamically inside each other. As in the case of floorplan, the state needs to be copied into the newly created tasks so we need to introduce additional synchronizations (in the form of **taskgroup**) in order for the original state to be alive when the tasks start so they can copy it.

```
1 void sort (ELM *low, ELM *tmp, long size) {
2    if (size < quick_size) {
3        /* quicksort when reach size threshold */
4        quicksort(low, low + size - 1);
5        return;
6    }
7    quarter = size / 4;
8
9    A = low; tmpA = tmp;
10   B = A + quarter; tmpB = tmpA + quarter;
11   C = B + quarter; tmpC = tmpB + quarter;
12   D = C + quarter; tmpD = tmpC + quarter;
13
14   #pragma omp taskgroup {
15       #pragma omp task
16       sort(A, tmpA, quarter);
17       #pragma omp task
18       sort(B, tmpB, quarter);
19       #pragma omp task
20       sort(C, tmpC, quarter);
21       #pragma omp task
22       sort(D, tmpD, size - 3 * quarter);
23   }
24   #pragma omp taskgroup {
25       #pragma omp task
26       merge(A, A+quarter -1, B, B+quarter -1, tmpA);
27       #pragma omp task
28       merge(C, C+quarter -1, D, low+size -1, tmpC);
29   }
30   merge(tmpA, tmpC-1, tmpC, tmpA+size -1, A);
31 }
```

Fig. 6. Sort function using OpenMP tasks

Another issue is the need to count all the solutions found by different tasks. One approach is to surround the accumulation with a critical directive but this would cause a lot of contention. To avoid it, we used **threadprivate** variables that are reduced within a **critical** directive to the global variable at the end of the parallel region.

Concom (Connected Components). The concom program finds all the connected components of a graph. It uses a depth first search starting from all the nodes of the graph. Every node visited is marked and not visited again.

The parallelization with tasks involves just four directives: a parallel directive, a single directive, a task directive and a critical directive. This is a clear example of how well tasks map into tree-like traversals.

3.3   Almost Impossible in OpenMP 2.5

Web server. We used tasks to parallelize a small web server called Boa. In this application, there is a lot of parallelism, as each client request to the server can be processed in parallel with minimal synchronizations (only update of log files and statistical counters). The unstructured nature of the requests makes it very difficult to parallelize without using tasks.

On the other hand, obtaining a parallel version with tasks requires just a handful of directives, as shown in figure 8. Basically, each time a request is ready, a new task is created for it.

```
1 void CC (int i, int cc) {
2     int j, n;
3     /* if node has not been visited */
4     if (!visited[i]) {
5         /* add node to current component */
6         add_to_component(i, cc); /* omp critical inside */
7
8         /* add each neighbor's subtree to the current component */
9         for (j = 0; j < nodes[i].n; j++) {
10            n = nodes[i].neighbor[j];
11        #pragma omp task
12            CC(n, cc);
13        }
14    }
15 }
16
17 void main () {
18     init_graph();
19     cc = 0;
20     /* for all nodes ... unvisited nodes start a new component */
21     for (i = 0; i < NN; i++)
22         if (!visited[i]) {
23     #pragma omp parallel
24         #pragma omp single
25             CC(i, cc);
26         cc++;
27     }
28
29 }
```

Fig. 7. Connected components code with OpenMP tasks

```
1 #pragma omp parallel
2 #pragma omp single nowait
3 while (!end) {
4     process signals (if any)
5     foreach request from the blocked queue {
6         if ( request dependences are met ) {
7             extract from the blocked queue
8             #pragma omp task
9                 serve_request(request);
10        }
11    }
12    if ( new connection ) {
13        accept_it();
14        #pragma omp task
15            serve_request(new connection);
16    }
17    select();
18 }
```

Fig. 8. Boa webserver main loop with OpenMp tasks

The important performance metric for this application is response time. In the proposed OpenMP tasking model, threads are allowed to switch from the current task to a different one. This task switching is needed to avoid starvation, and prevent overload of internal runtime data structures when the number of generated tasks overwhelms the number of threads in the current team. The implementation is allowed to insert implicit switching points in a task region, wherever it finds appropriate. The taskyield construct inserts an explicit switching point, giving programmers full control. The experimental implementation we used in our tests is not aggressive in inserting implicit switching points. To improve the performance of the Web server, we inserted a taskyield construct inside the serve_request function so that no request is starved.

User Interface. We developed a small kernel that simulates the behavior of user interfaces (UI). In this application, the objective of using parallelism is to obtain a lower response time rather than higher performance (although, of course, higher performance never hurts). Our UI has three possible operations, which are common to most user interfaces: start some work unit, list current ongoing work units and their status, and cancel an existing work unit.

The work units map directly into tasks (as can be seen in Figure 9). The thread executing the single construct will keep executing it indefinitely. To be able to communicate between the interface and the work units, the programmer needs to add new data structures. We found it difficult to free these structures from within the task because it could easily lead to race conditions (e.g. free the structure while listing current work units). We decided to just mark them to be freed by the main thread when it knows that no tasks are using it. In practice, this might not always be possible and complex synchronizations may be needed.

We also used the taskyield directive to avoid starvation.

```
 1 void Work::exec ( ) {
 2   while (!end) {
 3       //do some amount of work
 4       #pragma omp taskyield
 5   }
 6 }
 7
 8 void start_work (...) {
 9   Work *work = new Work(...);
10   list_of_works.push_back(work);
11   #pragma omp task
12   {
13       work->exec();
14       work->die();
15   }
16   gc();
17 }
18
19 void ui () {
20   ...
21   if ( user_input == START_WORK ) start_work (...);
22 }
23
24 void main ( int argc , char **argv ) {
25     #pragma omp parallel
26     #pragma omp single nowait
27         ui();
28 }
```

Fig. 9. Simplified code for a user interface with OpenMP tasks

4   Evaluation

4.1   The Prototype Implementation

In order to test the proposal in terms of expressiveness and performance, we have developed our own implementation of the proposed tasking model. We developed the prototype on top of a research OpenMP compiler (source-to-source restructuring tool) and runtime infrastructure [13].

The implementation uses execution units, that are managed through different execution queues (usually one *global queue* and one *local queue* for each thread used by the application). The library offers different services (fork/join, synchronize, dependence control, environment queries, ...) that can provide the worksharing and structured parallelism expressed by the OpenMP 2.5 standard. We added several services to the library to give support to the task scheme. The most important change in the library was the offering of a new scope of execution that allows the execution of independent units of work that can be deferred, but still bound to the thread team (the concept of *task*, see section 2).

When the library finds a task directive, it is able to decide (according to internal parameters: *maximum depth level* in task hierarchy, *maximum number of tasks* or *maximum number of tasks by thread*) whether to execute it immediately or create a work unit that will be queued and managed through the runtime scheduler. This new feature is provided by adding a new set of queues:

team queues. The scheduler algorithm is modified in order to look for new work in the *local*, *team* and *global* queues respectively.

Once the task is first executed by a thread, and if the task has *suspend/resume* points, we can expect two different behaviors. First, the task could be bound to that thread (so, it can only be executed by that thread) and second, the task is not attached to any thread and can be executed by any other thread of the team. The library offers the possibility to move a task from the *team* queues to the *local* queues. This ability covers the requirements of the `untied` clause of the `task` construct, which allows a task suspended by one thread to be resumed by a different one.

The synchronization construct is provided through *task counters* that keep track of the number of tasks which were created in the current scope (the current scope can be a `task` or `taskgroup` construct). Each task has in its own structure with a *successor* field that points to the counter it must decrement.

4.2 Evaluation Methodology

We have already shown the flexibility of the new tasking proposal, but what about its performance? To determine this, we have evaluated the performance of the runtime prototype against other options.

We have run all the previous benchmarks but we do not include the results for the webserver (due to a lack of the proper network environment) and the simple-ui (because it has an interactive behavior). For each application we have tried each possible OpenMP version: a single level of parallelism (labeled OpenMP worksharing), multiple levels of parallelism (labeled OpenMP nested) and with OpenMP tasks. For those applications that could be parallelized with Intel's taskqueues, we also evaluated them with taskqueues.

Table 1 summarizes the different input parameters and the experiments run for each application.

Table 1. Input parameters for each application

Application	Input parameters	Experiments
strassen	Matrix size of 1280x1280	nested, tasks, taskqueues
multisort	Array of 32M of integers	nested, tasks, taskqueues
fft	Array of 32M of complex numbers	nested, tasks, taskqueues
queens	Size of the board is 14x14.	nested, tasks, taskqueues
alignment	100 sequences	worksharing, nested, tasks
floorplan	20 cells	nested, tasks, taskqueues
concom	500000 graph nodes, 100000 edges	nested, tasks, taskqueues
sparseLU	Sparse matrix of 50 blocks of 100x100	worksharing, nested, tasks, taskqueues

We compiled the codes with taskqueues and nested parellelism with Intel's icc compiler version 9.1 at the default optimization level. The versions using tasks use our OpenMP source-to-source compiler and runtime prototype implementation, using icc as the backend compiler. The speedup of all versions is computed, using as a baseline the serial version of each kernel. We used Intel's icc compiler to compile the serial version.

All the benchmarks have been evaluated on an SGI Altix 4700 with 128 processors, although they were run on a cpuset comprising a subset of the machine to avoid interference with other running applications.

4.3   Results

In figure 10 we show the speedup for all the kernels (except the *concom*) with the different evaluated versions: OpenMP worksharing, OpenMP nested, OpenMP tasks and Intel's taskqueues. We do not show the results of the *concom* kernel because the slowdowns prevented us from running the experiments due to time constraints. These slowdowns were not only affecting the OpenMP task version but also the OpenMP nested and Intel's taskqueues. The main reason behind the slowdown is granularity. The tasks (or parallel regions in the nested case) are so fine grained that it is impossible to scale without aggregrating them. That is something that currently none of the models supports.

For a small number of threads (up to 4) we see that the versions using the new OpenMP tasks perform about the same as those using current OpenMP (worksharing and nested versions). But, as we increase the number of processors the task version scales much better, always improving over the other versions except for the *multisort* kernel, which has the same performance. These improvements are due to different factors, depending on the kernel: better load balance (*sparseLU, alignment, queens, fft, strassen* and *floorplan*), greater amount of parallel work (*alignment* and *sparseLU*) and less overhead (*alignment*). Overall, we can see that the new task proposal has the potential to benefit a wide range of application domains.

When we compare how the current prototype performs against a well established implementation of tasking, Intel's taskqueue, we can see that in most of the kernels the obtained speedup is almost the same and in a few cases (*sparseLU* and *floorplan*), even better. Only in two of them (*fft* and *strassen*) does taskqueue perform better, and even then, not by a large amount.

Taking into account that the prototype implementation has not been well tuned, we think that the results show that the new model will allow codes to obtain at least the performance of Intel's taskqueue and is even more flexible.

5   Suggestions for Future Work

While the performance and flexibility of the new OpenMP tasking model seem good, there is still room for improvement. We offer these suggestions for ways to improve the usability and performance of the model, based on our experience with the applications described in this paper.

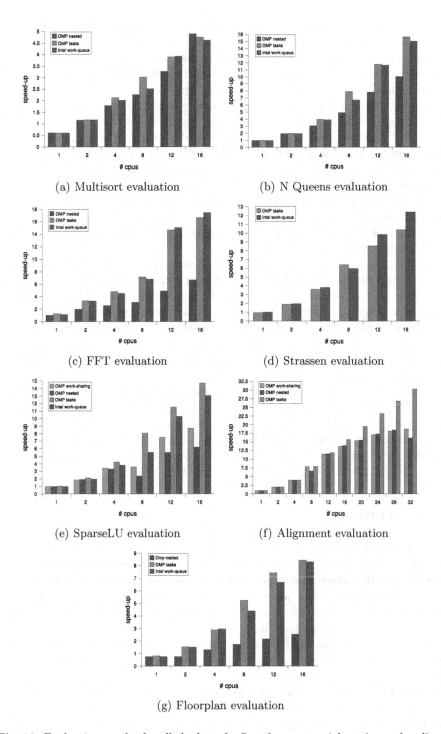

(a) Multisort evaluation

(b) N Queens evaluation

(c) FFT evaluation

(d) Strassen evaluation

(e) SparseLU evaluation

(f) Alignment evaluation

(g) Floorplan evaluation

Fig. 10. Evaluation results for all the kernels. Speedups use serial version as baseline.

One problem we encountered consistently in our programming was the need to capture the value of a data structure when all we had was a pointer to it. If a pointer is used in a `firstprivate` directive, only the pointer is captured. In order to capture the data structure pointed-at, the user must program it by hand inside the task, including proper synchronization, to make sure that the data is not freed or popped off the stack before it is copied. Support for this in the language would improve the usability of the tasking model.

In the N Queens problem, we could have used a reduction operation for tasks. In other words, we could have used a way to automatically make tasks contribute values to a shared variable. It can be programmed explicitly using threadprivate variables, but a reduction clause would save programming effort.

The `taskgroup` and `taskwait` constructions provide useful task synchronization, but are cumbersome for programming some types of applications, such as a multi-stage pipeline. A pipeline could be implemented by giving names to tasks, and waiting for other tasks by name.

We anticipate much research in the area of improving the runtime library. One research direction that would surely yield improvements is working on the task scheduler, as it can significantly affect application performance. Another interesting idea would be to find the impact of granularity on application performance and develop ways, either explicitly or implicitly, to increase the granularity of the tasks (for example by aggregating them) so they could be applied to applications with finer parallelism (e.g. the connected components problem) or reduce the overhead in other applications.

Of course, we have not explored all possible application domains, so other issues may remain to be found. Therefore, it is important to continue the assesment of the proposal by looking at new applications and particularly at Fortran codes, where optimizations could be affected differently by the tasking model. Another interesting dimension to assess in the future is the point of view of novice programmers and their learning curve with the model.

6   Conclusions

This paper had two objectives: first, test the expressiveness of the new OpenMP tasks proposal. Second, verify that the model does not introduce hidden factors that hamper the actual level of parallelism which can be achieved at runtime.

We have shown that the new proposal allows the programmer to express the parallelism of a wide range of applications from very different domains (linear algebra, server applications, backtracking, etc). Furthermore, we have found different issues that OpenMP language designers may want to consider in the future to further improve the expressiveness of the language and simplify the programming effort in some scenarios.

Using these applications we have seen the new proposal matches other tasking proposals in terms of performance and that it surpasses alternative implementations with the current 2.5 OpenMP elements. While these results are not conclusive, as they certainly have not explored exhaustively all possibilities, they provide a strong indication that the model can be implemented without incurring significant overheads. We have also detected two areas where runtime improvements would benefit the applications (i.e. task scheduling and granularity).

In summary, we think that while the new OpenMP task proposal can be improved, it provides a solid basis for the development of applications containing irregular parallelism.

Acknowledgments

The Nanos group at BSC-UPC has been supported by the Ministry of Education of Spain under contract TIN2007-60625, and the European Commission in the context of the SARC integrated project #27648 (FP6).

References

1. Intel Corporation. Intel(R) C++ Compiler Documentation (May 2006)
2. Ayguadé, E., Copty, N., Duran, A., Hoeflinger, J., Lin, Y., Massaioli, F., Unnikrishnan, P., Zhang, G.: A Proposal for Task Parallelism in OpenMP. In: Chapman, B.M., Zheng, W., Gao, G.R., Sato, M., Ayguadé, E., Wang, D. (eds.) IWOMP 2007. LNCS, vol. 4935. Springer, Heidelberg (2008)
3. Hochstein, L., et al.: Parallel Programmer Productivity: A Case Study of Novice Parallel Programmers. In: SuperComputing 2005 (November 2005)
4. Salvini, S.: Unlocking the Power of OpenMP. In: 5th European Workshop on OpenMP (EWOMP 2003) (September 2003) (Invited)
5. Kurzak, J., Dongarra, J.: Implementing Linear Algebra Routines on Multi-Core Processors with Pipelining and a Look Ahead. LAPACK Working Note 178, Dept. of Computer Science, University of Tennessee (September 2006)
6. Blikberg, R., Sørevik, T.: Load balancing and OpenMP implementation of nested parallelism. Parallel Computing 31(10-12), 984–998 (2005)
7. Massaioli, F., Castiglione, F., Bernaschi, M.: OpenMP parallelization of agent-based models. Parallel Computing 31(10-12), 1066–1081 (2005)
8. Shah, S., Haab, G., Petersen, P., Throop, J.: Flexible control structures for parallellism in OpenMP. In: 1st European Workshop on OpenMP (September 1999)
9. Van Zee, F.G., Bientinesi, P., Low, T.M., van de Geijn, R.A.: Scalable Parallelization of FLAME Code via the Workqueuing Model. ACM Trans. Math. Soft. (submitted, 2006)
10. Asanovic, K., et al.: The Landscape of Parallel Computing Research: A View from Berkeley. Technical Report UCB/EECS-2006-183, Electrical Engineering and Computer Science Depts., University of California at Berkeley (December 2006)
11. Frigo, M., Leiserson, C.E., Randall, K.H.: The implementation of the Cilk-5 multithreaded language. In: PLDI 1998: Proceedings of the ACM SIGPLAN 1998 conference on Programming language design and implementation, pp. 212–223. ACM Press, New York (1998)
12. Chamberlain, B., Feo, J., Lewis, J., Mizell, D.: An application kernel matrix for studying the productivity of parallel programming languages. In: W3S Workshop - 26th International Conference on Software Engineering, pp. 37–41 (May 2004)
13. Balart, J., Duran, A., Gonzàlez, M., Martorell, X., Ayguadé, E., Labarta, J.: Nanos mercurium: a research compiler for openmp. In: Proceedings of the European Workshop on OpenMP 2004 (October 2004)

Language Extensions in Support of Compiler Parallelization

Jun Shirako[1,2], Hironori Kasahara[1,3], and Vivek Sarkar[4]

[1] Dept. of Computer Science, Waseda University
[2] Japan Society for the Promotion of Science, Research Fellow
[3] Advanced Chip Multiprocessor Research Institute, Waseda University
[4] Department of Computer Science, Rice University
{shirako,kasahara}@oscar.elec.waseda.ac.jp, vsarkar@rice.edu

Abstract. In this paper, we propose an approach to automatic compiler parallelization based on language extensions that is applicable to a broader range of program structures and application domains than in past work. As a complement to ongoing work on high productivity languages for explicit parallelism, the basic idea in this paper is to make sequential languages more amenable to compiler parallelization by adding enforceable declarations and annotations. Specifically, we propose the addition of annotations and declarations related to multidimensional arrays, points, regions, array views, parameter intents, array and object privatization, pure methods, absence of exceptions, and gather/reduce computations. In many cases, these extensions are also motivated by best practices in software engineering, and can also contribute to performance improvements in sequential code. A detailed case study of the Java Grande Forum benchmark suite illustrates the obstacles to compiler parallelization in current object-oriented languages, and shows that the extensions proposed in this paper can be effective in enabling compiler parallelization. The results in this paper motivate future work on building an automatically parallelizing compiler for the language extensions proposed in this paper.

1 Introduction

It is now well established that parallel computing is moving into the mainstream with a rapid increase in the adoption of multicore processors. Unlike previous generations of mainstream hardware evolution, this shift will have a major impact on existing and future software. A highly desirable solution to the multicore software productivity problem is to automatically parallelize sequential programs. Past work on automatic parallelization has focused on Fortran and C programs with a large body of work on data dependence tests [1,25,18,9] and research compilers such as Polaris [7,19], SUIF [10], PTRAN [21] and the D System [12]. However, it is widely acknowledged that these techniques have limited effectiveness for programs written in modern object-oriented languages such as Java.

V. Adve, M.J. Garzarán, and P. Petersen (Eds.): LCPC 2007, LNCS 5234, pp. 78–94, 2008.

In this paper, we propose an approach to compiler parallelization based on language extensions that is applicable to a broader range of program structures and application domains than in past work. As a complement to ongoing work on high productivity languages for explicit parallelism, the basic idea in this paper is to make sequential languages more amenable to compiler parallelization by adding enforceable declarations and annotations. In many cases, these extensions are also motivated by best practices in software engineering, and can also contribute to performance improvements in sequential code.

A detailed case study of the Java Grande Forum benchmarks [22,13] confirms that the extensions proposed in this paper can be effective in enabling compiler parallelization. Experimental results were obtained on a 16-way Power6 SMP to compare the performance of four versions of each benchmark: 1) sequential Java, 2) sequential X10, 3) hand-parallelized X10, 4) parallel Java. Averaged over ten JGF Section 2 and 3 benchmarks, the parallel X10 version was 11.9× faster than the sequential X10 version, which in turn was 1.2× faster than the sequential Java version (Figure 1). An important side benefit of the annotations used for parallelization is that they can also speed up code due to elimination of runtime checks. For the eight benchmarks for which parallel Java versions were available, the parallel Java version was an average of 1.3× faster than the parallel X10 version (Figure 2). However, for two of the eight benchmarks, the parallel Java version used a different algorithm from the sequential Java version, and resulted in super-linear speedups. When the sequential and parallel X10 versions for the two benchmarks were modified to be consistent with the new algorithms, the parallel Java and X10 versions delivered the same performance on average (Figure 3).

The rest of the paper is organized as follows. Section 2 describes the language extensions (annotations and declarations) proposed in this paper. Section 3 summarizes the results of the case study including experimental results, and Section 5 contains our conclusions.

2 Language Extensions

While modern object-oriented languages such as Java have improved programming productivity and code reuse through extensive use of object encapsulation and exceptions, these same features have made it more challenging for automatically parallelizing compilers relative to Fortran programs where data structures and control flow are more statically predictable. In this section, we propose a set of declarations and annotations that enable compilers to perform automatic parallelization more effectively for these languages. Unlike annotations that explicitly manage parallelism as in OpenMP [6], our approach is geared toward enforceable declarations and annotations that can be expressed and understood in the context of sequential programs, and that should be useful from a software engineering viewpoint because of their ability to reduce common programming errors. Another difference from OpenMP is that the correctness of all our proposed annotations and declarations is enforced by the language system *i.e.,* they are all checked statically or dynamically, as outlined below.

2.1 Multidimensional Arrays, Regions, Points

Multidimensional arrays in Java are defined and implemented as nested unidimensional arrays. While this provides many conveniences for guaranteeing safety in a virtual machine environment (e.g., subarrays can be passed as parameters without exposing any unsafe pointer arithmetic), it also creates several obstacles to compiler optimization and parallelization. For example, a compiler cannot automatically conclude that A[i][j] and A[i+1][j] refer to distinct locations since the nested array model allows for the possibility that A[i] and A[i+1] point to the same subarray. Instead, we propose the use of object-oriented multidimensional arrays as in X10 [3], in which a compiler is guaranteed that A[i,j] and A[i+1,j] refer to distinct locations. *Array Views* (Section 2.2) make it possible to safely work with subarrays of multidimensional arrays without introducing unsafe pointer arithmetic.

A related issue is that induction variable analysis can be challenging in cases when an iterator is used or an integer variable is incremented by a step value that is not a compile-time constant as illustrated in the following common idiom from a DAXPY-like computation:

```
iy = 0; if (incy < 0) iy = (-n+1)*incy;
for (i = 0;i < n; i++) {
  dy[iy +dy_off] += . . .;  iy += incy;
}
```

In the above example, it is not easy for compilers to establish that $incy \neq 0$ and that there are no loop-carried dependences on the dy array.

To simplify analysis in such cases, we recommend the use of *regions* and *points* as proposed in ZPL [23] and X10, with extensions to support two kinds of region constructors based on triple notation, [<start-expr> : <end-expr> : <step-expr>] and [<start-expr> ; <count-expr> ; <step-expr>], both of which are defined to throw a ZeroStepException if invoked with a zero-valued step expression. The use of high level regions and points distinguishes our approach from past work on annotations of arrays for safe parallelization [16].

A key property of regions and points is that they can be used to define both loops and arrays in a program. The above DAXPY-like example can then be rewritten as follows:

```
iy = 0; if (incy < 0) iy = (-n+1)*incy;
// Example of [<start-expr>;<count-expr>;<step-expr>] region
for (point p : [iy ; n ; incy] ) {
  dy[p] += . . .;
}
```

In this case, the compiler will know that $incy \neq 0$ when the loop is executed, and that all dy[p] accesses are distinct.

2.2 Array Views

As indicated in the previous section, it is easier for a compiler to parallelize code written with multidimensional arrays rather than nested arrays. However, this raises the need for the programmer to work with subarrays of multidimensional arrays without resorting to unsafe pointer arithmetic. Our solution is the use of *array views*. An array view can be created by invoking a standard library method, `view( <start-point-expr>, <region-expr>)`, on any array expression (which itself may be a view). Consider the following code fragment with array views:

```
// Allocate a two-dimensional M*N array
double[.] A = new double[[1:M,1:N]];
. . .
A[i,j] = 99;
. . .
// Allocate a one-dimensional view on A for row i
double[.] R = A.view([i,1], [1:N]);
. . .
temp = R[j]; // R[j] = 99, the value stored in A[i,j]
```

In the above example, R can be used like any one-dimensional array but accesses to R are aliased with accesses to A as specified by the region in the call to `A.view()`. A `ViewOutOfBoundsException` is thrown if a view cannot be created with the specified point and region. All accesses to R can only be performed with points (subscripts) that belong to the region specified when creating the view.

Views can also be created with an optional *intent* parameter that must have a value from a standard *enum*, {In, Out, InOut}. The default value is InOut which indicates that the view can be used to read and write array elements. In and Out intents are used to specify read-only and write-only constraints on the array views. Read-only views can be very helpful in simplifying compiler parallelization and optimization by identifying heap locations that are guaranteed to be immutable for some subset of the program's lifetime [17]. The runtime system guarantees that each array element has the same intent in all views containing the element. If an attempt is made to create a view that conflicts with the intent specified by a previous view, then a `ViewIntentException` is thrown.

2.3   Annotations on Method Parameters

We propose the use of a `disjoint` annotation to assert that all mutable (non-value) reference parameters in a method must be disjoint. (The *this* pointer is also treated as a parameter in the definition of the `disjoint` annotation.) If a disjoint method is called with two actual parameters that overlap, a `ParameterOverlap-Exception` is thrown at runtime. Declaring a method as disjoint can help optimization and parallelization of code within the method by assisting the compiler's alias analysis. This benefit comes at the cost of runtime tests that the compiler must insert on method entry, though the cost will be less in a strongly typed language like Java or X10 compared to a weakly typed language like C since runtime tests are not needed for parameters with non-compatible types in X10 but would be necessary in C due to its pointer addressing and cast operators. This is also why we expect it to be more effective for X10 than the `noalias` and `restricted` proposals that have been made in the past for C.

In addition to the `disjoint` annotation, we also propose the use of `in`, `out`, and `inout` intent annotations on method parameters as in Fortran. For object/array references, these annotations apply only to the object/array that is the immediate target of the reference.

2.4   Array and Object Privatization

It is well known that *privatization analysis* is a key enabling technique for compiler parallelization. For modern object-oriented languages with dynamically allocated objects and arrays, the effectiveness of privatization analysis is often bounded by the effectiveness of *escape analysis* [4]. We propose a `retained` type modifier[1] for declarations of local variables and parameters with reference types which asserts that the scope in which the local/parameter is declared will not cause any reference in a retained variable to escape. We also permit the `retained` modifier on declarations of methods with a non-value reference return type, in which case it ensures that the `this` pointer does not escape the method invocation.

The following loop from the MonteCarlo benchmark illustrates the use of the retained modifier to declare that each `ps` object is private to a single loop iteration.

```
results = new Vector(nRunsMC);
for( int iRun=0; iRun < nRunsMC; iRun++ ) {
    // ps object is local to a single loop iteration
    retained PriceStock ps = new PriceStock();
    // All methods invoked on ps must be declared as "retained"
    ps.setInitAllTasks((ToInitAllTasks) initAllTasks);
    ps.setTask((x10.lang.Object) tasks.elementAt(iRun));
    ps.run();
    results.addElement(ps.getResult());
} // for
```

To enable automatic parallelization, the compiler will also need information that indicates that results.addElement() is a reduction-style operator (associative and commutative). We discuss later in Section 2.7 how this information can be communicated using a `gather` clause.

2.5   Pure Annotation for Side-Effect-Free Methods

The return value (or exception value) and all parameters of a method annotated as `pure` must have *value types i.e.,* they must be immutable after initialization. Pure methods can call other pure methods and only allocate/read/write mutable heap locations whose lifetimes are contained within the method's lifetime (as defined with the `retained` type modifier). Therefore, if two calls are made to the same pure method with the same value parameters, they are guaranteed

---

[1] The `retained` name chosen because other candidates like "private" and "local" are overloaded with other meanings in Java.

to result in the same return value (or exception value). The only situation in which the two calls may not have the same outcome is if one of the calls triggers a nonfunctional error such as OutOfMemoryError. This definition of method purity is similar to the definition of "moderately pure" methods in [26]. The correctness of all **pure** annotations is enforced statically in our proposed approach, analogous to the static enforcement of immutability of value types in the X10 language [3].

2.6 Annotations Related to Exceptions

We propose the following set of declarations and annotations that can be used to establish the absence of runtime exceptions. All type declarations are assumed to be checked statically, but dynamic cast operations can be used to support type conversion with runtime checks. Some of the type declarations are based on the theory of *dependent types* (*e.g.*, see [11]) as embodied in version 1.01 of the X10 language [20].

- **Null Pointer exceptions:** A simple way to guarantee the absence of a NullPointerException for a specific operation is to declare the type of the underlying object/array reference to be *non-null*. As an example, the Java language permits null-valued references by default, with a proposal in JSR 305 [15] to introduce an @NonNull annotation to declare selected references as non-null. In contrast, the X10 language requires that all references be non-null by default and provides a special *nullable* type constructor that can be applied to any reference type. Though the results in our paper can be used with either default convention, we will use the X10 approach in all examples in this paper.
- **Array Index Out of Bounds exceptions:** A simple way to guarantee the absence of an IndexOutOfBoundsExecption for an array access is to ensure that the array access is performed in a loop that is defined to iterate over the array's region *e.g.*,

```
for (point p : A.region) A[p] = ... ; //Iterate over A.region
```

This idea can be extended by iterating over a region that is guaranteed to be a subset of the array's region, as in the following example (assuming && represents region intersection):

```
// Iterate over a subset of A.region
for (point p : A.region && region2) A[p] = ... ;
```

When working with multiple arrays, dependent types can be use to establish that multiple arrays have the same underlying region *e.g.*,

```
final region R1 = ...;
// A and B can only point to arrays with region = R1
final double[:region=R1] A = ...;
final double[:region=R1] B = ...;
for (point p : R1 ) A[p] = F(B[p]) ; // F is a pure method
```

In the above example, the compiler knows from the dependent type declarations (and from the fact that the loop iterates over region R1) that array accesses A[p] and B[p] cannot throw an exception.

Dependent types can also be used on point declarations to ensure the absence of IndexOutOfBoundsException's as in the access to A[p] in the following example:

```
final region R1 = ...;
final double[:region=R1] A = ...;
// p can only take values in region R1
point(:region=R1) p = ...;
double d = A[p];
```

– **Zero Divide/Step exceptions:** A simple way to guarantee the absence of a DivideByZeroException or a ZeroStepException for a specific operation is to declare the type of the underlying integer expression to be *nonzero* using dependent types as follows:

```
int(:nonzero) n = ...; // n's value must be nonzero
int q = m / n; // No DivideByZeroException
region R3 = [low : high : n]; // No ZeroStepException
```

– **ExceptionFree annotation:** A code region annotated as ExceptionFree is guaranteed to not throw any user-defined or runtime exception. As with pure methods, it is possible that a region of code annotated as ExceptionFree may encounter a nonfunctional error such as an OutOfMemoryError. The compiler checks all operations in the annotated code region to ensure that they are statically guaranteed to not throw an exception (by using the declarations and annotations outlined above).

2.7   Gather Computations and Reductions in Loops

A common requirement in parallel programs is the ability to either *gather* or *reduce* values generated in each loop iteration into (respectively) a collection or aggregate value. There has been a large body of past work on compiler analyses for automatically detecting gather and reduction idioms in loops and arrays *e.g.,* [14,8], but the presence of potentially aliased objects and large numbers of virtual calls render these techniques ineffective for object-oriented programs. Instead, we propose an extension to counted pointwise for loops that enables the programmer to specify the *gather* and *reduce* operators explicitly in a sequential program in a way that simplifies the compiler's task of automatic parallelization. Specifically, we extend the for loop with an optional gather clause as follows:

```
for ( ... ) { <body-stmts> gather <gather-stmt> }
```

A unique capability of the gather statement is that it is permitted to read private (retained) variables in the loop body that have primitive or value types, including the index/point variables that control the execution of the counted for loop. The design of gather clause is similar to the inlet feature in Cilk [24], which represents a post-processing of each parallel thread. Informally, the semantics of a for loop with a gather clause can be summarized as follows:

1. Identify `retained` variables in `<body-stmt>` with primitive or value types that are also accessed in `<gather-stmt>`. We refer to these as *gather* variables.
2. Execute all iterations of the `for` loop sequentially as usual, but store the values of *all* gather variables at the end of each iteration.
3. Execute `<gather-stmt>` once for each iteration of the `for` loop in a nondeterministic order (analogous to the nondeterminism inherent in iterating over an unordered collection in Java).
4. During execution of an instance of `<gather-stmt>` in Step 3, resolve read accesses to gather variables by returning the corresponding instances stored in Step 2.

We use the loop from the MonteCarlo benchmark discussed earlier to illustrate the use of the gather clause to specify the gather statement:

```
results = new Vector(nRunsMC);
for( point p[iRun] : [0 : nRunsMC-1] ) {
    // ps object is local to a single loop iteration
    retained PriceStock ps = new PriceStock();
    // All methods invoked on ps must be declared as "retained"
    ps.setInitAllTasks((ToInitAllTasks) initAllTasks);
    ps.setTask((x10.lang.Object) tasks.elementAt(iRun));
    ps.run();
    retained ToResult R = ps.getResult(); // must be a value type
    gather {
        // Invoked once for each iteration of the for loop
        results.addElement(R));
    }
}
```

3   Case Study: Java Grande Forum Benchmarks

In this section, we present the results of a case study that we undertook to validate the utility of the language annotations and extensions introduced in the previous section for compiler parallelization. The case study was undertaken on the Java Grande Forum (JGF) benchmark suite [22] because this suite includes both sequential and parallel (multithreaded) Java versions of the same benchmarks. We converted the sequential Java versions into sequential X10 versions, and then studied which annotations were necessary to enable automatic parallelization. A summary of the results can be found in Table 1, with discussion of the LUFact and Euler benchmarks in the following subsections. Performance results for sequential and parallel versions of the Java and X10 programs are presented later in Section 4.

3.1   LUFact

This benchmark solves a $N \times N$ linear system using LU factorization followed by a triangular solve. The kernel computation of the sequential Java version is as follows:

Table 1. Annotations required to enable parallelization of Java Grande Forum benchmarks

	Series	Sparse*	SOR	Crypt	LUFact	FFT	Euler	MolDyn	Ray*	Monte*
Multi-dim arrays	×		×		×		×			
Regions, Points	×	×	×		×		×	×		
Array views		×			×					
In/Out/InOut					×					
Disjoint		×		×		×				
Retained						×			×	×
Pure method	×					×				
NonNull	×	×	×	×	×	×	×	×	×	×
Region Dep-type		×		×	×	×			×	
Nonzero						×				
Exception free	×				×	×		×	×	×
Reduction		×						×	×	×

* Sparse: SparseMatmult, Ray: RayTracer, Monte: MonteCarlo

```
for (k = 0; k < nm1; k++) {
  col_k = a[k];
  l = idamax(n-k, col_k, k, 1) + k;
  ...
  for (j = kp1; j < n; j++) {
    col_j = a[j];
    t = col_j[l];
    if (l != k) { col_j[l] = col_j[k]; col_j[k] = t; }
    daxpy(n-(kp1), t, col_k, kp1, 1, col_j, kp1, 1);
  }
}
```

It is well known that all iterations of the inner j-loop can logically be executed in parallel, however there are numerous obstacles that make it challenging or intractable for a parallelizing compiler to discover this fact automatically. First, most compilers will have to conservatively assume that references to col_j from distinct iterations could potentially be aliased to the same subarray. Second, it will be hard for a compiler to statically establish that no array element access in the loop will throw an ArrayIndexOutOfBoundsException, especially the col_j[l] access with subscript l that is the return value of the call to function idamax. Third, a compiler will need to establish that the call to daxpy will not inhibit parallel execution of the j loop.

Now, consider the scenario in which the sequential code is written as follows using some of the language extensions proposed in this paper:

```
for (point k : [0:nm1-1] && a.region.rank(0) && a.region.rank(1)) {
  final double[.] col_k = a.view([k,0], [0:nm-1], IN);
  point (:region=a.region.rank(1)) l =
    (point (:region=a.region.rank(1))) idamax(n-k, col_k, k, 1) + k;
  ...
```

```
for (point j : [kp1:n-1] && a.region.rank(0)) {
    final double[.] col_j = a.view([j,0], [0:nm-1], OUT);
    t = a[j, l];
    if (l != k) {  a[j, l] = a[j, k];  a[j, k] = t;  }
    daxpy(n-(kp1), t, col_k, kp1, 1, col_j, kp1, 1);
  }
}
```

As indicated in Table 1, the following annotations are sufficient to enable compiler parallelization for the LUFact benchmark:

- **Multi-dimensional arrays, Regions and Points, Array views:** In this example, array a is allocated as a two-dimensional array, and the use of multidimensional array views ensures that references to col_j from distinct iterations are guaranteed to point to distinct subarrays.
- **In/Out intents:** The use of an IN intent for col_k and an OUT intent for col_j ensures that accesses to the two subarrays will not inhibit parallelism.
- **NonNull:** Unlike Java, the default in X10 is that all object references are non-null by default, thereby ensuring that NullPointerException's cannot inhibit parallelism in this loop.
- **Region dependent types:** The use of a dependent type with a region constraint in the declaration of variable l ensures that all uses of l as a subscript in the second dimension (dimension 1) of array a must be in bounds — the cast operator effectively serves as a runtime check on the return value from function idamax.
- **Exception free:** Finally, an exception-free annotation on the **daxpy** method declaration (not shown above) assists the compiler in establishing that no exceptions can inhibit parallelization of the j loop.

With these extensions, it becomes entirely tractable for a compiler to automatically determine that iterations of the j loop can be executed in parallel.

3.2 Euler

The Euler benchmark solves a set of equations using a fourth order Runge Kutta method. It has many loops that can only be parallelized if the compiler knows that certain objects being accessed are private to each loop iteration. For example, consider the following i loop in method calculateDummyCells:

```
private void calculateDummyCells(double localpg[][],
    double localtg[][], Statevector localug[][]) {  ...
  Vector2 tan = new Vector2();
  ...
  for (i = 1; i < imax; ++i) {
    tan.ihat = xnode[i][0] - xnode[i-1][0];
    tan.jhat = ynode[i][0] - ynode[i-1][0];
    ...  scrap = tan.magnitude();  ...
  }
  ...
}
```

In the sequential version, a single instance of the tan object is allocated and reused across all iterations of the i loop. However, a closer examination reveals that each iteration could use a private copy of the tan object, thereby removing one of the obstacles to parallelization of the i loop.

We now consider the following alternate sequential version written using some of the language extensions proposed in this paper:

```
private disjoint void calculateDummyCells(double[.] localpg,
    double[.] localtg, Statevector[.] localug) {  ...
  for (point i : [1:imax-1] && xnode.region.rank(1) && ...) {
    retained Vector2 tan = new Vector2();
    tan.ihat = xnode[i, 0] - xnode[i-1, 0];
    tan.jhat = ynode[i, 0] - ynode[i-1, 0];
    ...  scrap = tan.magnitude();  ...
  }
  ...
}
```

As indicated in Table 1, the following annotations are sufficient to enable compiler parallelization for the Euler benchmark:

– **Multi-dimensional arrays, Regions and Points:** As with LUFact, the use of multidimensional arrays, regions and points enables a compiler to ensure that distinct iterations of the i loop are guaranteed to access distinct subarrays of xnode and ynode without ArrayIndexOutOfBoundsException.
– **Disjoint:** The disjoint annotation on method calculateDummyCells ensures that references localpg and localtg must point to distinct arrays.
– **Retained:** The retained annotation on the declaration of variable tan can be used by the compiler to determine that there are no loop-carried dependences on that variable.
– **NonNull:** As with LUFact, the fact that all object references are non-null by default ensures that NullPointerException's cannot inhibit parallelism in this loop.

4   Experimental Results

We then compared the performance of four versions of the Java Grande Forum (JGF) benchmarks:

1. **Sequential Java:** This set consists of six Section 2 benchmarks (Crypt, FFT, LUFact, Series, SOR, SparseMatmult) and four Section 3 benchmarks (Euler, MolDyn, MonteCarlo, RayTracer) taken from version v2.0 of the JGF benchmark release [13][2].
2. **Sequential X10:** Since the sequential subset of X10 overlaps significantly with the sequential subset of Java, this version is quite close to the Sequential

---

[2] Section 1 was excluded because it only contains microbenchmarks for low-level operations.

Java version in most cases. As in [2] we use a "lightweight" X10 version with regular Java arrays to avoid the large overheads incurred on X10 arrays in the current X10 implementation. However, all the other characteristics of X10 (*e.g.*, non-null used as the default type declaration, forbidden use of non-final static fields, etc.) are preserved faithfully in the Sequential X10 versions.

3. **Hand Parallelized X10:** This version emulates by hand the parallel versions that can be obtained by a compiler, assuming that annotations are added to the sequential X10 versions as outlined in Table 1.

4. **Parallel Java:** This is the threadv1.0 version of the JGF benchmarks [13], which contains multithreaded versions of five of the six Section 2 benchmarks and three of the four Section 3 benchmarks. The unimplemented benchmarks are FFT and Euler. Further, the threaded versions of two of the Section 2 benchmarks, SOR and SparseMatmult, were implemented using a different underlying algorithm from the sequential versions in v2.0.

All performance results were obtained using the following system settings:

- The target system is a p570 16-way Power6 4.7GHz SMP server with 186GB main memory running AIX5.3 J. In addition, each dual-core chip can access 32MB L3 cache per chip and 4MB L2 cache per core. The size of the L1 instruction cache is 64KB and data cache is 64KB.
- For all runs, SMT was turned off and a large page size of 16GB was used. The sequential Java and X10 versions used only 1 processor, where as the parallel Java and X10 versions used all 16 processors.
- The execution environment used for all Java runs is IBM's J9 VM (build 2.4, J2RE 1.6.0) with the following options, `-Xjit:count=0,optLevel=veryHot, ignoreIEEE -Xms1000M -Xmx1000M`.
- The execution environment used for all X10 runs was version 1.0.0. of the X10 compiler and runtime, combined with the same JVM as above, IBM's J9 VM (build 2.4, J2RE 1.6.0), but with additional options to skip null pointer and array bounds checks in X10 programs in accordance with the annotation in the X10 source program. The `INIT_THREADS_PER_PLACE` parameter was set to 1 and 16 for the sequential and parallel X10 runs respectively. (`MAX_NUMBER_OF_PLACES` was set to 1 in both cases.)
- The X10 runtime was also augmented with a special *one-way* synchronization mechanism to enable fine-grained producer-consumer implementations of X10's `finish` and `next` operations.
- For all runs, the main program was extended with a three-iteration loop within the same Java process, and the best of the three times was reported in each case. This configuration was deliberately chosen to reduce/eliminate the impact of JIT compilation time in the performance comparisons.

4.1   Sequential and Parallel Versions of X10

Figure 1 shows the speedup ratio of the serial and parallel X10 versions relative to the sequential Java version (JGF v2.0) for all ten benchmarks. An interesting

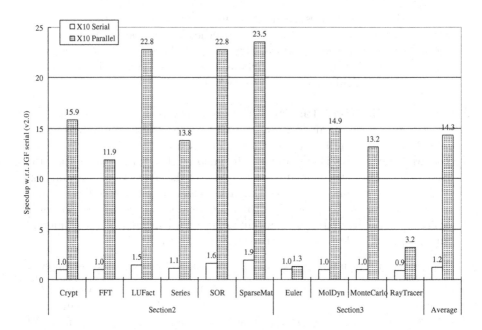

Fig. 1. Performance of Sequential and Parallel versions of X10 relative to Sequential Java

observation is that the sequential X10 version often runs faster than the sequential Java version. This is due to the annotations in the X10 program which enabled null checks and array bounds checks to be skipped. On average, the sequential X10 version was 1.2× faster than the sequential Java version, and the parallel X10 version was 11.9× faster than the sequential X10 version.

The sources of large speedups for SOR and LUFact were as follows. SOR's pipeline parallelism (faithful to the sequential version) was implemented using tightly-coupled one-way synchronizations which were added to the X10 runtime. The annotations for LUFact enabled a SPMD parallelization by following classical SPMDization techniques such as the approach outlined in [5].

The speedup was lowest for two benchmarks, *Euler* and *Raytracer*. The challenge in *Euler* is that it consists of a large number of small parallel loops which could probably benefit from more aggressive loop fusion and SPMD parallelization transformations than what was considered in our hand-parallelized experiments. The challenge in *Raytracer* is the classic trade-off between load balance (which prefers cyclic-style execution of the parallel loop) and locality (which prefers a block-style execution of the parallel loop).

4.2   Comparison with Parallel Java Versions

In this section, we extend results from the previous section by including results for Parallel Java executions as well. As mentioned earlier, Parallel Java versions (threadv1.0) are available for 8 of the 10 benchmarks. Results for these 8

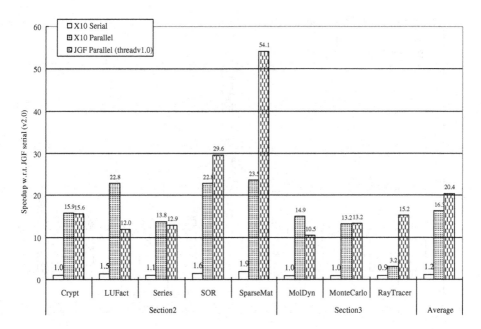

Fig. 2. Performance of Sequential and Parallel versions of X10 and Parallel Java relative to Sequential Java

benchmarks are shown in Figure 2. The two benchmarks for which the Parallel Java versions significantly out-performed the Parallel X10 versions were SOR and SparseMatmult. On closer inspection, we discovered that the underlying sequential algorithm was modified in both parallel versions (relative to the v2.0 sequential Java versions).

For SOR, the threadv1.0 parallel Java version uses a "red-black" scheduling of loop iteration to expose doall parallelism, even though this transformation results in different outputs compared to the sequential Java version. In contrast, the parallel X10 version contains pipeline parallelism that we expect can be automatically extracted from the sequential X10 version, and in fact returns the same output as the sequential X10 version.

For SparseMatmult, the thread v1.0 parallel Java version inserts an algorithmic step to sort non zero elements by their row value, so that the kernel computation can be executed as simple doall loop. Unfortunately, this additional step isn't included in the execution time measurement for the Parallel Java case.

To take into account the algorithmic changes in the Parallel Java versions, Figure 3 show an alternate version of Figure 2 in which the algorithms used for the sequential and parallel X10 versions are modified to match the algorithm used in the parallel Java versions. With the algorithmic changes, we see that the performance of the parallel Java and X10 versions are now evenly matched in the average case.

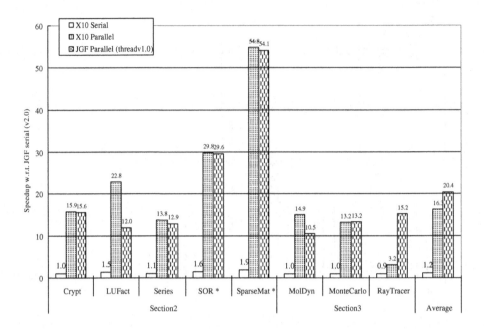

Fig. 3. Performance of Sequential and Parallel versions of X10 and Parallel Java relative to Sequential Java, with alternate Parallel X10 versions for SOR and SparseMatmult

5 Conclusions and Future Work

In this paper, we proposed a set of language extensions (enforced annotations and declarations) designed with a view to making modern object oriented languages more amenable to compiler parallelization. Many of the proposed extensions are motivated by best practices in software engineering for sequential programs. This is in contrast to the OpenMP approach where the annotations are geared towards explicit parallel programming and the correctness of user pragmas is not enforced by the language system.

We also performed a detailed case study of the Java Grande Forum benchmarks to confirm that the extensions proposed in this paper are effective in enabling compiler parallelization. Experimental results obtained on a 16-way Power6 SMP showed that the use of these language extensions can improve sequential execution time by 20% on average, and that a hand-simulation of automatically parallelized X10 programs can deliver speedup by matching the performance of the multithreaded Java versions of the JGF benchmarks.

The main topic for future work is to build an automatically parallelizing compiler which exploits the language extensions proposed in this paper. Another topic is to extend the definition of the language extensions to apply to explicitly parallel code *e.g.,* defining array views in the presence of distributions, and defining the semantics of in/out/inout intents for array views in the presence of concurrent array operations.

Acknowledgments

We are grateful to all X10 team members for their contributions to the X10 software used in this paper. We would like to especially acknowledge Vijay Saraswat's work on the design and implementation of dependent types in the current X10 implementation, and Chris Donawa and Allan Kielstra's implementation of experimental options for X10 in IBM's J9 virtual machine. While at IBM, Vivek Sarkar's work on X10 was supported in part by the Defense Advanced Research Projects Agency (DARPA) under its Agreement No. HR0011-07-9-0002. Finally we would like to thank Doug Lea, John Mellor-Crummey and Igor Peshansky for their feedback on this paper.

References

1. Allen, R., Kennedy, K.: Optimizaing Compilers for Modern Architectures. Morgan Kaufmann Publishers, San Francisco (2001)
2. Barik, R., Cave, V., Donawa, C., Kielstra, A., Peshansky, I., Sarkar, V.: Experiences with an smp implementation for x10 based on the java concurrency utilities. In: Workshop on Programming Models for Ubiquitous Parallelism (PMUP), held in conjunction with PACT 2006 (September 2006)
3. Charles, P., Donawa, C., Ebcioglu, K., Grothoff, C., Kielstra, A., von Praun, C., Saraswat, V., Sarkar, V.: X10: an object-oriented approach to non-uniform cluster computing. In: Proceedings of OOPSLA 2005, pp. 519–538. ACM Press, New York (2005)
4. Choi, J.-D., Gupta, M., Serrano, M.J., Sreedhar, V.C., Midkiff, S.P.: Stack allocation and synchronization optimizations for java using escape analysis. ACM Trans. Program. Lang. Syst. 25(6), 876–910 (2003)
5. Cytron, R., Lipkis, J., Schonberg, E.: A compiler-assisted approach to spmd execution. In: Supercomputing 1990: Proceedings of the 1990 ACM/IEEE conference on Supercomputing, Washington, DC, USA, pp. 398–406. IEEE Computer Society, Los Alamitos (1990)
6. Dagum, L., Menon, R.: OpenMP: An industry standard API for shared memory programming. IEEE Computational Science & Engineering (1998)
7. Eigenmann, R., Hoeflinger, J., Padua, D.: On the automatic parallelization of the perfect benchmarks. IEEE Trans. on parallel and distributed systems 9(1) (January 1998)
8. Gerlek, M.P., Stoltz, E., Wolfe, M.: Beyond induction variables: detecting and classifying sequences using a demand-driven ssa form. ACM Trans. Program. Lang. Syst. 17(1), 85–122 (1995)
9. Haghighat, M.R., Polychronopoulos, C.D.: Symbolic analysis for parallelizing compilers. Kluwer Academic Publishers, Dordrecht (1995)
10. Hall, M.W., Anderson, J.M., Amarasinghe, S.P., Murphy, B.R., Liao, S., Bugnion, E., Lam, M.S.: Maximizing multiprocessor performance with the SUIF compiler. IEEE Computer (1996)
11. Harper, R., Mitchell, J.C., Moggi, E.: Higher-order modules and the phase distinction. In: POPL 1990: Proceedings of the 17th ACM SIGPLAN-SIGACT symposium on Principles of programming languages, pp. 341–354. ACM Press, New York (1990)

12. Hiranandani, S., Kennedy, K., Tseng, C.-W.: Preliminary experiences with the fortran d compiler. In: Proc. of Supercomputing 1993 (1993)
13. The Java Grande Forum benchmark suite, http://www.epcc.ed.ac.uk/javagrande
14. Jouvelot, P., Dehbonei, B.: A unified semantic approach for the vectorization and parallelization of generalized reductions. In: ICS 1989: Proceedings of the 3rd international conference on Supercomputing, pp. 186–194. ACM Press, New York (1989)
15. Jsr 305: Annotations for software defect detection, http://jcp.org/en/jsr/detail?id=305
16. Moreira, J.E., Midkiff, S.P., Gupta, M.: Supporting multidimensional arrays in java. Concurrency and Computation Practice & Experience (CCPE) 15(3:5), 317–340 (2003)
17. Pechtchanski, I., Sarkar, V.: Immutability Specification and its Applications. Concurrency and Computation Practice & Experience (CCPE) 17(5:6) (April 2005)
18. Pugh, W.: The omega test: A fast and practical integer programming algorithm for dependence analysis. In: Proc. of Super Computing 1991 (1991)
19. Rauchwerger, L., Amato, N.M., Padua, D.A.: Run-time methods for parallelizing partially parallel loops. In: Proceedings of the 9th ACM International Conference on Supercomputing, Barcelona, Spain, pp. 137–146 (July 1995)
20. Saraswat, V.: Report on the experimental language x10 version 1.01, http://x10.sourceforge.net/docs/x10-101.pdf
21. Sarkar, V.: The PTRAN Parallel Programming System. In: Szymanski, B. (ed.) Parallel Functional Programming Languages and Compilers. ACM Press Frontier Series, pp. 309–391. ACM Press, New York (1991)
22. Smith, L.A., Bull, J.M., Obdrzálek, J.: A parallel java grande benchmark suite. In: Supercomputing 2001: Proceedings of the 2001 ACM/IEEE conference on Supercomputing (CDROM), p. 8. ACM Press, New York (2001)
23. Snyder, L.: The design and development of zpl. In: HOPL III: Proceedings of the third ACM SIGPLAN conference on History of programming languages, pp. 8–1–8–37. ACM Press, New York (2007)
24. MIT laboratory for computer science Supercomputing technologies group. Cilk 5.3.2 reference manual, http://supertech.csail.mit.edu/cilk/manual-5.3.2.pdf
25. Wolfe, M.: High Performance Compilers for Parallel Computing. Addison-Wesley Publishing Company, Reading (1996)
26. Xu, H., Pickett, C.J.F., Verbrugge, C.: Dynamic purity analysis for java programs. In: PASTE 2007: Proceedings of the 7th ACM SIGPLAN-SIGSOFT workshop on Program analysis for software tools and engineering, pp. 75–82. ACM Press, New York (2007)

Concurrency Analysis for Shared Memory Programs with Textually Unaligned Barriers

Yuan Zhang[1], Evelyn Duesterwald[2], and Guang R. Gao[1]

[1] University of Delaware, Newark, DE
{zhangy,ggao}@capsl.udel.edu
[2] IBM T.J.Watson Research Center, Hawthorne, NY
duester@us.ibm.com

Concurrency analysis is a static analysis technique that determines whether two statements or operations in a shared memory program may be executed by different threads concurrently. Concurrency relationships can be derived from the partial ordering among statements imposed by synchronization constructs. Thus, analyzing barrier synchronization is at the core of concurrency analyses for many parallel programming models. Previous concurrency analyses for programs with barriers commonly assumed that barriers are named or textually aligned. This assumption may not hold for popular parallel programming models, such as OpenMP, where barriers are unnamed and can be placed anywhere in a parallel region, i.e., they may be textually unaligned. We present in this paper the first interprocedural concurrency analysis that can handle OpenMP, and, in general, programs with unnamed and textually unaligned barriers. We have implemented our analysis for OpenMP programs written in C and have evaluated the analysis on programs from the NPB and SpecOMP2001 benchmark suites.

1 Introduction

Concurrency analysis is a static analysis technique that determines whether two statements or operations in a shared memory program may be executed by different threads concurrently. Concurrency analysis has various important applications, such as statically detecting data races [6,10], improving the accuracy of various data flow analyses [16], and improving program understanding. In general, precise interprocedural concurrency analysis in the presence of synchronization constraints is undecidable [15], and a precise intraprocedural concurrency analysis is NP-hard [18]. Therefore, a practical solution is to make a conservative estimate of all possible concurrency relationships, such that two statements that are not determined to be concurrent cannot execute in parallel in any execution of the program. If two statements are determined to be concurrent, they *may* execute concurrently.

In this paper we present a new interprocedural concurrency analysis that can handle parallel programming models with unnamed and textually unaligned barriers. We present our analysis in the context of the OpenMP programming model but our approach is also applicable to other SPMD (Single Program Multiple Data) parallel programming models.

V. Adve, M.J. Garzarán, and P. Petersen (Eds.): LCPC 2007, LNCS 5234, pp. 95–109, 2008.
© Springer-Verlag Berlin Heidelberg 2008

OpenMP is a standardized set of language extensions (i.e., pragmas) and APIs for writing shared memory parallel applications in C/C++ and FORTRAN. Parallelism in an OpenMP program is expressed using the `parallel` construct. Program execution starts with a single thread called the *master thread*. When control reaches a `parallel` construct, a set of threads, called a *thread team*, is generated, and each thread in the team, including the master thread, executes a copy of the parallel region. At the end of the parallel region the thread team synchronizes and all threads except for the master thread terminate. The execution of the parallel region can be distributed within the thread team by work-sharing constructs (e.g., `for`, `sections` and `single`).

Synchronization is enforced mainly by global barriers and mutual exclusion (i.e., `critical` constructs and lock/unlock library calls). When a thread reaches a barrier it cannot proceed until all other threads have arrived at a barrier. In OpenMP, barriers are unnamed and they may be textually unaligned. Thus, threads may synchronize by executing a set of textually distinct barrier statements. Textually unaligned barriers make it difficult to reason about the synchronization structure in the program. Some parallel languages, therefore, require barriers to be textually aligned [19]. Textually unaligned barriers also hinder concurrency analysis because understanding which barrier statements form a common synchronization point is a prerequisite to analyzing the ordering constraints imposed by them. Our analysis is the first interprocedural concurrency analysis that can handle barriers in OpenMP and, in general, programs with unnamed and textually unaligned barriers. Figure 1 shows an OpenMP example program with a parallel region.

Barriers structure the execution of a parallel region into a series of synchronized execution phases, such that threads synchronize on barriers only at the beginning and at the end of each phase. Computing these execution phases for each parallel region provides the basic skeleton for ordering relationships among statements. Statements from different execution phases cannot execute concurrently. Thus, only statements within the same phase need to be examined for computing the concurrency relation.

To illustrate the concept of execution phases consider the sample program shown in Figure 1. The first execution phase, denoted as $(begin, \{b_1, b_2\})$, starts at the beginning of the parallel region and extends up to barriers b_1 and b_2. Note that barriers b_1 and b_2 establish a common synchronization point, i.e., they *match*. The next barrier synchronization point is at barriers $\{b_3, b_4\}$. Hence, the next execution phase is $(\{b_1, b_2\}, \{b_3, b_4\})$.

It is easy to see that statements from two different execution phases are ordered by barriers and thus cannot be concurrent. On the other hand, two statements from the same execution phase may be concurrent, such as S_1 and S_3 in Figure 1. However, barriers are not the only constructs that need to be considered to determine execution phases. Additional ordering constraints may be imposed by control constructs. Consider statements S_9 and S_{11} in Figure 1, which are on different branches of the conditional statement with predicate C_4. Since all threads agree on the value of predicate C_4 (i.e., the predicate is *single-valued*),

```
main()
{
    int my_ID, num, i, y, sum = 0;
    ......
    #pragma omp parallel private(my_ID, num, y)
    {
        my_ID = omp_get_thread_num();
C1:     if(my_ID > 2){
S1:         i = 0;
            #pragma omp barrier // b1
S2:         y = i + 1;
        } else {
S3:         i = 1;
            #pragma omp barrier // b2
S4:         y = i - 1;
        }
P1:     sum += my_ID;
C2:     if( my_ID == 0){
S5:         ......
            #pragma omp barrier // b3
S6:         ......
        }
```

```
C3:     if( my_ID != 0){
S7:         ......
            #pragma omp barrier // b4
S8:         ......
        }
P2:     num = omp_get_num_threads();
C4:     if(num > 2){
S9:         ......
            #pragma omp barrier // b5
S10:        ......
        } else {
S11:        ......
            #pragma omp barrier // b6
S12:        ......
        }
C5:     if(my_ID == 0)
            printf("i = %d\n", i);
    } // end of parallel
} // end of main
```

Fig. 1. Example OpenMP program. The OpenMP library function calls *omp_get_thread_number()* and *omp_get_num_threads()* return the thread identifier of the calling thread and the total number of threads in the current team, respectively.

statements S_9 and S_{11} can never be executed together in one execution, hence they cannot be concurrent. On the contrary, predicate C_1 is evaluated differently by different threads (i.e., the predicate is *multi-valued*), so that statements on the two branches may execute concurrently. Thus, another key issue in understanding the concurrency constraints is determining whether a control predicate is single- or multi-valued.

In this paper, we propose an interprocedural concurrency analysis technique that addresses the above ordering constraints imposed by synchronization and control constructs. Our analysis computes for each statement s the set of statements that may execute concurrently with s. The analysis proceeds in four major steps:

Step 1: CFG construction: The first step consists of constructing a control flow graph (CFG) that correctly models the various OpenMP constructs.

Step 2: Barrier matching: As a prerequisite to computing execution phases we need to understand which barrier statements synchronize together, i.e, which barrier statements *match*. We solve this problem as an extension to barrier matching analysis [20]. Barrier matching verifies that barriers in an SPMD program are free of synchronization errors. For verified programs, a *barrier matching function* is computed that maps each barrier statement s to the set of barrier statement that synchronize with s in at least one execution. Barrier matching was previously described for MPI programs and we have extended it to handle OpenMP programs. The computed barrier matching function is an input to the next step.

Step 3: Phase partition and aggregation: In this step, we first partition the program into a set of static execution *phases*. A *phase* (b_i, b_j) consists of a set of basic blocks that lie on a barrier-free path between barrier b_i and b_j in the CFG. We then aggregate phases (b_p, b_q) and (b_m, b_n) if b_p matches b_m, and b_q matches b_n. A dynamic execution phase at runtime is an instance of an aggregated static execution phase.

Step 4: Concurrency relation calculation: We first conservatively assume that statements from the same execution phase may be concurrent but statements from different phases are ordered and non-concurrent. We then apply a set of ordering rules that reflect the concurrency constraints from other OpenMP synchronization and work-sharing constructs to iteratively refine the concurrency relation.

We have implemented the analysis for OpenMP programs written in C and evaluated it on programs from the NPB [5] and SpecOMP2001 [17] benchmark suites. Our evaluation shows that our concurrency analysis is sufficiently accurate with the average size of a concurrency set for a statement being less than 6% of total statements in all but one program.

The rest of the paper is organized as follows. We first present related work in Section 2. The control flow graph is presented in Section 3. In Section 4 we first review the barrier matching technique and then present extensions to handle multi-valued expressions in OpenMP and structurally incorrect programs. Phase partition and aggregation is presented in Section 5, and the concurrency relation calculation is presented in Section 6. We present experimental results in Section 7, and finally conclude in Section 8.

2   Related Work

A number of researchers have looked at concurrency analysis for programs with barriers. Lin [10] proposed a concurrency analysis technique (called non-concurrency analysis) for OpenMP programs based on phase partitioning. Lin's analysis differs from our concurrency analysis in two main aspects. First, Lin's method is intraprocedural and cannot compute non-concurrency relationship across procedure calls. Second, Lin's method cannot account for synchronization across textually unaligned barriers. The analysis does not recognize that textually unaligned barriers may in fact synchronize together, resulting in spurious non-concurrency relationships. For instance, Lin's technique would wrongfully conclude that S_1 and S_3 in Figure 1 are non-concurrent.

Jeremiassen and Eggers [7] present a concurrency analysis technique that, similar to our analysis, first partitions the program into phases, then aggregates some phases together. Their analysis avoids the problem of having to identify whether textually unaligned barriers synchronize together by assuming that barriers are named through barrier variables. Barrier statements that refer to the same barrier are assumed to be matched. Their technique also does not account for concurrency constraints imposed by control constructs with a single-valued predicate. For instance, in Figure 1 their analysis would conclude that S_9 and S_{11} are concurrent.

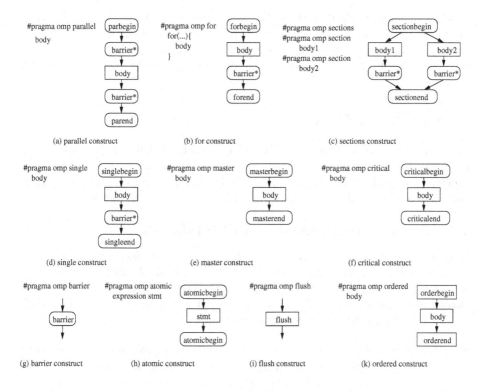

Fig. 2. Control flow graph construction

Kamil and Yelick [8] proposed a concurrency analysis method for the Titanium language [19] in which synchronization across textually unaligned barriers is not allowed.

There also has been a lot of work on concurrency analysis for other parallel programming languages, such as Ada and Java [3,2,6,11,13] in which synchronization is mainly enforced by event-driven constructs like post-wait/wait-notify. Agarwal et.al. [1] presents a may-happen-in-parallel analysis for X10 programs.

3 Step 1: Control Flow Graph Construction

The control flow graph for an OpenMP program is an extension of the control flow graph for a sequential program. Figure 2 illustrates the graph construction for each OpenMP construct. *Begin* and *end* nodes are inserted for each OpenMP directive with a construct body. To model the `sections` construct, we insert a control flow edge from the *begin* node to the first statement node of each section in the construct, and a control flow edge from the last statement node of each section to the *end* node of the `sections` construct. Constructs without a body statement (e.g., `barrier` and `flush`) are represented by a single block.

There is an implicit barrier at the end of the work-sharing constructs `for`, `sections` and `single`, unless the `nowait` clause is specified. Implicit barriers are depicted as `barrier*` in Figure 2. Similarly, there is an implicit barrier at the beginning of a parallel region, and an implicit barrier at the end of a parallel region.

4   Step 2: Barrier Matching

The second step in our concurrency analysis consists of identifying the matching barrier statements that synchronize together. Barrier matching analysis [20] was previously described for MPI programs. In this section we first review the MPI barrier matching analysis and then show how to extend it to handle OpenMP.

4.1   Review of Barrier Matching for MPI Programs

Barrier matching is an analysis and verification technique to detect stall conditions caused by barriers. When the program is verified, the analysis computes a barrier matching function that maps each barrier statement s to the set of barrier statements that synchronize with s in at least one execution. The MPI barrier matching analysis proceeds in three main steps:

Multi-valued Expression Analysis: In SPMD-style programs all threads execute the same program but they may take different program paths. The ability to determine which program paths may be executed concurrently requires an analysis of the *multi-valued* expressions in the program. An expression is called multi-valued if it evaluates differently in different threads. If used as a control predicate, multi-valued expressions split threads into different program paths that are executed concurrently by different threads. An example of a multi-valued expression is my_ID shown in Figure 3(a). Conversely, an expression that has the same value in all threads is called *single-valued*. SPMD programming paradigms like MPI or OpenMP usually contain multi-valued seed expressions, such as library calls that return the unique thread identifier. All other multi-valued expressions in the program are directly or indirectly dependent on these multi-valued seed expressions.

The interprocedural multi-valued analysis is solved as a forward slicing problem based on a revised program dependence graph. The revised program dependence graph contains nodes to represent statements that are connected through data dependence edges and so called ϕ-edges. ϕ-edges are based on the notion of ϕ-nodes in Static Single Assignment (SSA) form [4]. In SSA, a ϕ-node is inserted at a join node where multiple definitions of a variable merge. The predicate that controls the join node is called a ϕ-gate. A ϕ-edge connects a ϕ-gate with the corresponding ϕ-node. Multi-valued expressions result as those expressions that are reachable from a multi-valued seed expression along either data-dependence or ϕ-edges in the revised program dependence graph.

Figure 3(c) illustrates the revised program dependence graph and multi-valued expression analysis for the MPI program shown in Figure 3(a). It is important

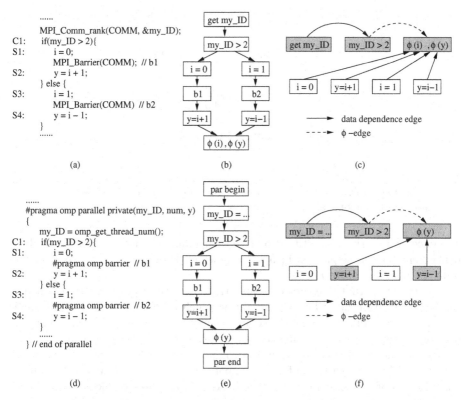

Fig. 3. An MPI program (a), its CFG (b), and its revised program dependence graph (c). An OpenMP program (d), its CFG (e), and its revised program dependence graph (f). The multi-valued expression slices are shown as shaded nodes in (c) and (f).

to note that variables i and y are single-valued for the executing threads inside the conditional statement but they become multi-valued after the conditional paths merge at the ϕ-node.

Barrier Expressions: A barrier expression at a node n in the CFG represents the sequences of barriers that may execute along any paths from the beginning of the program to node n. Barrier expressions are regular expressions with barrier statements and function labels as terminal symbols, and three operators: concatenation ($\cdot$), alternation ($|$) and quantification ($*$), which represents barriers in a sequence, in a condition, and in a loop, respectively. For example, the barrier expression for Figure 3(a) is $(b_1| b_2)$. A barrier expression is usually represented by a barrier expression tree. Figure 4 shows the barrier expression tree for the program shown in Figure 1.

Barrier matching: The final step combines the results of the previous two steps to detect potential stall conditions caused by barriers. Recall that multi-valued predicates create concurrent paths. Thus, a barrier subtree whose root is an alternation with a multi-valued predicate describes two concurrent barrier

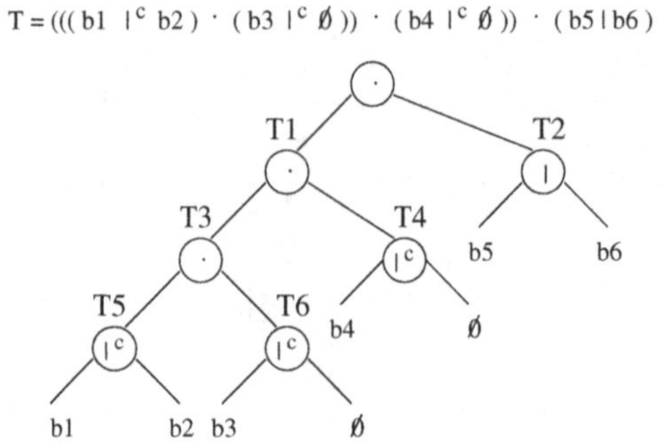

$$T = (((\, b1 \ \mid^c b2 \,) \cdot (\, b3 \ \mid^c \emptyset \,)) \cdot (\, b4 \ \mid^c \emptyset \,)) \cdot (\, b5 \mid b6 \,)$$

Fig. 4. The barrier expression tree for the program in Figure 1. The symbol $\mid^c$ denotes alternation with a multi-valued predicate.

sequences. Similarly, a quantification tree with a multi-valued predicate describes concurrent barrier sequences in a loop in which threads concurrently execute different numbers of iterations.

A barrier tree that does not contain either concurrent alternation or concurrent quantification describes a program in which all threads execute the same sequence of barriers (although the sequence may be different across different executions of the program). Such a tree is obviously free of barrier synchronization errors. A concurrent quantification tree signals a synchronization error because concurrent threads execute different numbers of loop iterations and hence different numbers of barriers. Therefore, the barrier verification problem comes down to checking that all concurrent alternation subtrees in the program's barrier tree are well-matched, i.e., the two alternation subtrees always produce barrier sequences of the same length. The barrier matching analysis implements this check by a counting algorithm that traverses the two subtrees of each concurrent alternation tree. Details of the counting algorithm can be found in [20].

After verifying a concurrent alternation barrier tree, the analysis computes the barrier matching function by ordering the leave nodes from each of its two subtrees in a depth-first order, and then matching barriers in the same position of the two ordered sequences.

4.2   Multi-valued Expressions Analysis for OpenMP Programs

In order to use barrier matching for our concurrency analysis, we developed an extension of the multi-valued expressions analysis for shared variables. In MPI programs all variables are local to the executing thread. In OpenMP programs, on the other hand, variables are either shared or private. Private variables are stored in thread private memory and observable only by the executing thread. Private variables in OpenMP can therefore be handled in the same way as variables in MPI programs. Shared variables in OpenMP programs are stored in global memory and observable by all threads simultaneously. The order of a sequence of shared variables reads and writes that is observed by a thread is not only determined by the program order, but also influenced by the memory consistency model. The memory consistency model also complicates the multi-valued expressions analysis by making some expressions that are not dependent on the seed expression multi-valued.

To simplify the presentation we first assume the sequential consistency model (SC model) [9]. The SC model requires that the result of the execution is the same as if the operations of all the threads were executed in some sequence, and the operations of each individual thread occur in the order specified by the program. All threads observe the same sequence of operations. For instance, consider the program fragment in Figure 5(a), in which variable i is shared, and variable x is private. Figure 5(b) illustrates one of the possible execution sequences with two threads under the SC model. Thread 1 reads $i = 0$ in statement S_3 due to the preceding write operation issued by thread 2, while thread 2 reads $i = 1$ in statement S_3. In this example the shared variable i is multi-valued even if it is not dependent on the seed expression. Therefore, we need to extend the multi-valued expressions analysis for shared variables under the SC model by incorporating all read operations on shared variables as multi-valued, and no further slicing for shared variables is needed.

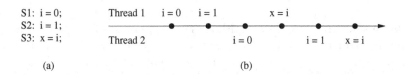

(a)   (b)

Fig. 5. (a) Example program (b) An execution sequence under the SC model

OpenMP provides a relaxed memory consistency model, under which a thread may have its own temporary view of memory which is not required to be consistent with global memory at all times. As a consequence, different threads may observe different sequences of shared memory operations, and the shared variable i in Figure 5(a) may be single-valued in some executions. However, since the execution sequence illustrated in Figure 5(b) is also a valid execution under OpenMP's relaxed memory model, we still need to conservatively incorporate all read operations on shared variables as multi-valued.

Consider again our sample program shown in Figure 3(d). Since variable i is shared, we treat two reads on i at S_1 and S_3 as multi-valued. We then apply the interprocedural forward slicing algorithm used in the original MPI analysis to compute multi-valued expressions for private variables in OpenMP. Figure 3(f) shows the resulting multi-valued expressions as the set of shaded nodes in the graph.

As in the original MPI multi-valued expression analysis, we assume OpenMP and other library calls are annotated as either single- or multi-valued. Arrays are treated as scalar variables and pointers are conservatively handled by treating every pointer dereference and every variable whose address is taken as multi-valued.

4.3 Barrier Trees and Barrier Matching for OpenMP Programs

Once the multi-valued expressions have been computed, barrier tree construction and barrier matching for OpenMP programs proceed as described for MPI programs. Figure 4 shows the barrier expression tree for the program shown in Figure 1. Barrier matching checks the three concurrent alternation subtrees T_5, T_6 and T_4. The analysis verifies subtree T_5 as correct and reports that barriers b_1 and b_2 match. However, the other subtrees T_6 and T_4 cannot be statically verified and the analysis would report a potential error, warning that the subtrees are structurally incorrect.

4.4 Handling Structurally Incorrect Programs

Barrier matching analysis produces a barrier matching function only for verified programs. As a static analysis, barrier matching is conservative and may therefore reject a program, although the program produces no synchronization errors at runtime. Programs that will always be rejected are so called *structurally incorrect* programs. Informally, structural correctness means that a program property holds for a program if it holds for every structural component of the program, (i.e., every statement, expression, compound statement, etc.). In other words, a structurally incorrect program contains a component that, if looked at in isolation, has a synchronization error, although in the context of the entire program no runtime error may result. Figure 1 is an example of a structurally incorrect program because it contains two structural components, the conditionals C_2 and C_3 that, if looked at in isolation, are incorrect. Thus, the overall program is deemed incorrect although no runtime synchronization error would result because C_3 is the logical complement of C_2. As reported in the previous section, barrier matching analysis reports a potential error for each of the two conditional components.

We discuss in this section modifications to compute partial barrier matching information for programs whose synchronization structure is dynamically correct (i.e., the program terminates) even if they cannot be statically verified. Our approach to handling structural incorrectness is to isolate the program region that cannot be statically verified, and to partition the program into structurally correct and structurally incorrect regions. Based on this partition we can apply barrier matching and, in turn, our concurrency analysis for the structurally correct components of the program. For the structurally incorrect regions we conservatively assume that all statements may execute concurrently.

When barrier matching encounters a program with a structurally incorrect component p, a synchronization error is detected when processing the root of the barrier expression subtree that represents p. We refer to such structural component as an error component. For example, the barrier tree in Figure 4, contains two error components T_4 and T_6.

Based on these error components we define two well-matched regions of a structurally incorrect program. The first well-matched region consists of any sequence of statements along an error-component-free path in the CFG that starts at the program entry and terminates at a program point immediately preceding an error component. Similarly, the second well-matched region consists of any sequence of statements along an error-component-free path in the CFG that starts at a program point immediately following an error component and terminates at program exit. We define the "structurally incorrect region" as the remainder of the program, that is, any statement that is not included in one of the above well-matched regions. We conservatively treat all statements in the structurally incorrect region as concurrent and compute barrier matching functions for the structurally correct regions.

Consider again our example in Figure 4 and recall that barrier matching reports two error components T_4 and T_6. The two well-matched regions of the program in Figure 1 are defined as follows. The first region starts at program entry and terminates at program point P_1 in Figure 1 which immediately precedes the error component T_6. The second region starts at program point P_2 which immediately follows the error component T_4 and extends up to program exit. All statements between P_1 and P_2 are assumed to be concurrent.

5   Step 3: Phase Partition and Aggregation

The third step of the OpenMP concurrency analysis uses the computed barrier matching function to divide the program into a set of static phases. A static phase (b_i, b_j) consists of a sequence of basic blocks along all barrier-free paths in the CFG that start at the barrier statement b_i and end at the barrier statement b_j. Note that b_i and b_j may refer to the same barrier statement.

The phase partition method proceeds as proposed by Jeremiassen and Eggers [7]. First we assume each barrier statement b_i corresponds to a new global variable V_{b_i}. We then treat each barrier statement as a use of its corresponding barrier variable, followed by definitions of all barrier variables in the program. The problem of phase partition is then reduced to computing live barrier variables in the program. Recall that a variable v is live at program point p if the value of v at p is used before being re-defined along some path in the control flow graph starting at p. Precise interprocedural live analysis has been described in [12]. Let $Live(b)$ denote the set of barrier variables live at the barrier b. The set of static phases in an OpenMP program is then summarized as:

$$\{(b_i, b_j)|V_{b_j} \in Live(b_i), \ for \ all \ i \ and \ j\}$$

In order to determine to which phases a basic block u belongs, we need to reverse the control flow edges in the CFG and calculate live barrier variables for each basic block again. Let $LiveR(u)$ denote the set of live barrier variables at basic block u in the reversed CFG. The phases to which block u belongs are:

$$\{(b_i, b_j)|b_i \in LiveR(u) \wedge b_j \in Live(u)\}$$

According to the barrier matching information, we then aggregate phases (b_m, b_n) and (b_p, b_q) if barriers b_m matches b_p and b_n matches b_q. A dynamic execution phase is an instance of an aggregated phase at runtime.

6   Step 4: Concurrency Relation Calculation

The final step of our concurrency analysis consists of calculating the concurrency relation among basic blocks. Since basic blocks from different aggregated phases are separated by barriers, no two blocks in different phases can be executed concurrently. We can therefore establish a first safe approximation of the concurrency relation in the program by assuming that all blocks from the same aggregated phase may be concurrent. However, this first approximation is overly conservative and does not take concurrency constraints from certain OpenMP constructs into account. We have developed the following set of concurrency rules that address these constraints to refine the initial concurrency approximation.

1. **(Concurrency Rule)** Any two (possibly identical) basic blocks from the same aggregated phase are concurrent. The set of concurrency relationships obtained from this rule is denoted as CR.
2. **(Non-concurrency Rules)**
   (a) Any two basic blocks from a `master` construct under the same parallel region are not concurrent because they are executed serially by the master thread.
   (b) Any two basic blocks from `critical` constructs with the same name (or from within the lock regions, enclosed by the omp_set_lock() and omp_unset_lock() library calls, that are controlled by the same lock variable) are not concurrent because they are executed mutually exclusively. Note that we treat two potentially aliased lock variables as different.
   (c) Two blocks in the same `ordered` construct are not concurrent because the `ordered` construct body within a loop is executed in the order of loop iterations.
   (d) Two blocks from the same `single` construct that is not enclosed by a sequential loop are not concurrent. Note that OpenMP requires a `single` construct body to be executed by one thread in the team, but it does not specify which thread. Therefore two instances of a `single` construct inside a sequential loop might be executed by two different threads concurrently.
   The set of non-concurrency relationships obtained from the non-concurrency rules is denoted as NCR.

Finally, the concurrency relation among basic blocks results as $CR - NCR$.

Returning to our sample program in Figure 1. S_1 and S_3 are concurrent because they are in the same aggregated phase $(start, \{b_1, b_2\})$. The same holds for S_2 and S_4. However, S_9 and S_{11} are not concurrent because barrier b_5 does not match barrier b_6 (due to the single-valued predicate C_4) thus S_9 and S_{11} are in different phases.

7   Experimental Evaluations

We have implemented the concurrency analysis for OpenMP/C programs on top of the open-source CDT (C Development Tool) in Eclipse. The Eclipse CDT

Table 1. Experimental results

Benchmark	FT	IS	LU	MG	SP	quake
Source	NPB2.3-C	NPB3.2	NPB2.3-C	NPB2.3-C	NPB2.3-C	SpecOMP2001
# Souce Lines	1162	629	3471	1264	2991	1591
# Blocks	682	278	2132	909	2503	1191
# Procedures	17	9	18	15	22	27
# Barriers	13	5	30	28	67	13
OpenMP constructs	single master for critical	for	for single critical master flush	single for critical	for master	for
# Aggr. phases	29	11	41	103	223	24
Max. concurrency set size	101	59	83	256	130	33
Relative max. concurrency set size	14.8%	21.2%	3.9%	28.1%	5.2%	2.8%
Avg. concurrency set size	40	36	23	50	52	15
Relative avg. concurrency set size	5.9%	12.9%	1.1%	5.5%	2.1%	1.3%

constructs Abstract Syntax Trees for C programs. We evaluated the effectiveness of our OpenMP concurrency analysis on a set of OpenMP programs from the NPB (Nas Parallel Benchmarks) and SpecOMP2001 benchmark suites, as shown in Table 1.

FT (3-D FFT), LU (LU solver), MG (Multigrid), and SP (Pentadiagonal solver) are derived from the serial Fortran versions of NPB2.3-serial by the Omni OpenMP compiler project [14]. IS (Integer sort) is an OpenMP C benchmark from NPB3.2. Quake from SpecOMP2001 benchmark suite simulates seismic wave propagation in large basins.

The top part of Table 1 lists several characteristics of the benchmark programs such as the number of source lines, the number of barriers, either explicit or implicit, and the various OpenMP constructs used in each benchmark.

The results of the concurrency analysis are shown in the bottom part of the table. As an intermediate result, the table lists the number of aggregated phases that have been computed. To estimate the accuracy of our concurrency analysis we computed the average and maximum set size among the concurrency sets for all nodes in the CFG. Our CFG is based on the CDT and includes statement level block nodes. Set sizes would be smaller if statements would be composed into basic block nodes. The table shows the absolute set size and the relative size which is the percentage of the total number of nodes in the CFG. Recall that the concurrency set of a block b consists of a set of blocks that might execute concurrently with b in at least one execution. A concurrency set is usually a superset of the real concurrency relation. Therefore the smaller the concurrency set, the less conservative our concurrency analysis is. Table 1 indicates that our analysis is not overly conservative since the size of the average concurrency set is less than 6% of the total blocks for all benchmarks except IS, for which the average concurrency set is 12.9% of the total number of blocks in the program.

8   Conclusions

In this paper we present the first interprocedural concurrency analysis that can handle OpenMP and, in general, shared memory programs with unnamed and textually unaligned barriers. Our approach is built on the barrier matching technique that has previously been described to verify barrier synchronization in MPI. We extended barrier matching to handle shared variables and OpenMP. We have implemented our analysis for OpenMP C programs and evaluated the effectiveness of our analysis using benchmarks from the NPB and SpecOMP2001 benchmark suites. The experimental results confirm that our analysis is not overly conservative. We are currently exploring the use of our concurrency analysis in combination with a dynamic data race detection tool by limiting the instrumentation points that have to be considered during dynamic checking. Other potential uses are in combination with performance tools to point the user to areas with low levels of concurrency.

Acknowledgement

This work is, in part, based upon work supported by the Defense Advanced Research Projects Agency under its Agreement No. HR0011-07-9-0002.

References

1. Agarwal, S., Barik, R., Sarkar, V., Shyamasundar, R.K.: May-happen-in-parallel analysis of x10 programs. In: PPoPP 2007: Proceedings of the 12th ACM SIGPLAN Symposium on Principles and Practice of Parallel Programming, pp. 183–193. ACM Press, New York (2007)
2. Callahan, D., Kennedy, K., Subhlok, J.: Analysis of event synchronization in a parallel programming tool. In: PPOPP 1990: Proceedings of the Second ACM SIGPLAN Symposium on Principles and Practice of Parallel Programming, pp. 21–30 (1990)
3. Callahan, D., Sublok, J.: Static analysis of low-level synchronization. In: PADD 1988: Proceedings of the 1988 ACM SIGPLAN and SIGOPS Workshop on Parallel and Distributed Debugging, pp. 100–111 (1988)
4. Cytron, R., Ferrante, J., Rosen, B.K., Wegman, M.N., Zadeck, F.K.: Efficiently computing static single assignment form and the control dependence graph. ACM Trans. Program. Lang. Syst. 13(4), 451–490 (1991)
5. NASA Advanced Supercomputing Divsion. Nas parallel benchmarks, http://www.nas.nasa.gov/Software/NPB/
6. Duesterwald, E., Soffa, M.L.: Concurrency analysis in the presence of procedures using a dataflow framework. In: TAV4: Proceedings of the Symposium on Testing, Analysis, and Verification, pp. 36–48 (1991)

7. Jeremiassen, T., Eggers, S.: Static analysis of barrier synchronization in explicitly parallel systems. In: Proceedings of the International Conference on Parallel Architectures and Compilation Techniques (PACT), Montreal, Canada (1994)
8. Kamil, A.A., Yelick, K.A.: Concurrency analysis for parallel programs with textually aligned barriers. Technical Report UCB/EECS-2006-41, EECS Department, University of California, Berkeley (April 2006)
9. Lamport, L.: How to make a multiprocessor computer that correctly executes multiprocess programs. IEEE Trans. Computers 28(9), 690–691 (1979)
10. Lin, Y.: Static nonconcurrency analysis of openmp programs. In: First International Workshop on OpenMP (2005)
11. Masticola, S.P., Ryder, B.G.: Non-concurrency analysis. In: PPOPP 1993: Proceedings of the Fourth ACM SIGPLAN Symposium on Principles and Practice of Parallel Programming, pp. 129–138 (1993)
12. Myers, E.M.: A precise inter-procedural data flow algorithm. In: POPL 1981: Proceedings of the 8th ACM SIGPLAN-SIGACT Symposium on Principles of Programming Languages, pp. 219–230. ACM Press, New York (1981)
13. Naumovich, G., Avrunin, G.S., Clarke, L.A.: An efficient algorithm for computing mhp information for concurrent java programs. In: ESEC/FSE- 7: Proceedings of the 7th European Software Engineering Conference held jointly with the 7th ACM SIGSOFT International Symposium on Foundations of Software Engineering, pp. 338–354 (1999)
14. Omni OpenMP Compiler Project. Omni OpenMP Compiler, http://phase.hpcc.jp/Omni/home.html
15. Ramalingam, G.: Context-sensitive synchronization-sensitive analysis is undecidable. ACM Transactions on Programming languages and Systems (TOPLAS) 22(2), 416–430 (2000)
16. Sreedhar, V., Zhang, Y., Gao, G.: A new framework for analysis and optimization of shared memory parallel programs. Technical Report CAPSL- TM-063, University of Delaware, Newark, DE (2005)
17. Standard Performance Evaluation Corporation. SPEC OMP (OpenMP benchmark suite), http://www.spec.org/omp/
18. Taylor, R.N.: Complexity of analyzing the synchronization structure of concurrent programs (1983)
19. Yelick, K., Semenzato, L., Pike, G., Miyamoto, C., Liblit, B., Krishnamurthy, A., Hilfinger, P., Graham, S., Gay, D., Colella, P., Aiken, A.: Titanium: A high-performance Java dialect. In: ACM (ed.) ACM 1998 Workshop on Java for High-Performance Network Computing ACM Press, New York (1998)
20. Zhang, Y., Duesterwald, E.: Barrier matching for programs with textu- ally unaligned barriers. In: PPoPP 2007: Proceedings of the 12th ACM SIGPLAN Symposium on Principles and Practice of Parallel Programming, pp. 194–204 (2007)

Iteration Disambiguation for Parallelism Identification in Time-Sliced Applications

Shane Ryoo, Christopher I. Rodrigues, and Wen-mei W. Hwu

Center for Reliable and High-Performance Computing and
Department of Electrical and Computer Engineering
University of Illinois at Urbana-Champaign
{sryoo,cirodrig,hwu}@crhc.uiuc.edu

Abstract. Media and scientific simulation applications have a large amount of parallelism that can be exploited in contemporary multi-core microprocessors. However, traditional pointer and array analysis techniques often fall short in automatically identifying this parallelism. This is due to the allocation and referencing patterns of time-slicing algorithms, where information flows from one time slice to the next. In these, an object is allocated within a loop and written to, with source data obtained from objects created in previous iterations of the loop. The objects are typically allocated at the same static call site through the same call chain in the call graph, making them indistinguishable by traditional heap-sensitive analysis techniques that use call chains to distinguish heap objects. As a result, the compiler cannot separate the source and destination objects within each time slice of the algorithm. In this work we discuss an analysis that quickly identifies these objects through a partially flow-sensitive technique called iteration disambiguation. This is done through a relatively simple aging mechanism. We show that this analysis can distinguish objects allocated in different time slices across a wide range of benchmark applications within tens of seconds even for complete media applications. We will also discuss the obstacles to automatically identifying the remaining parallelism in studied applications and propose methods to address them.

1 Introduction

The pressure of finding exploitable coarse-grained parallelism has increased with the ubiquity of multi-core processors in contemporary desktop systems. Two domains with high parallelism and continuing demands for performance are media and scientific simulation. These often operate on very regular arrays with relatively simple pointer usage, which implies that compilers may be able to identify coarse-grained parallelism in these applications. Recent work has shown that contemporary analyses are capable of exposing a large degree of parallelism in media applications written in C [14].

However, there are still obstacles to be overcome in analyzing the pointer behavior of these applications. A significant percentage of these applications are based on time-sliced algorithms, with information flowing from one time slice

V. Adve, M.J. Garzarán, and P. Petersen (Eds.): LCPC 2007, LNCS 5234, pp. 110–124, 2008.
© Springer-Verlag Berlin Heidelberg 2008

to the next. The code of these applications typically consists of a large loop, often with multiple levels of function calls in the loop body, where each iteration corresponds to a time slice. Results from a previous iteration(s) are used for computation in the current iteration. While there are typically dependences between iterations, there is usually an ample amount of coarse-grained parallelism within each iteration, or time slice, of the algorithm. For example, in video encoding applications, there is commonly a dependence between the processing of consecutive video frames, a fundamental time slice of video processing. However, there is significant parallelism within the video frame, where thousands of sub-pictures can be processed in parallel.

From our experience, time-sliced algorithms typically operate by reading from data objects that are written in the previous time slice, performing substantial computation, and writing to data objects that will be used by the next time slice. The primary step of parallelizing the computation of the time slice lies in the disambiguation between the input and output objects of the time slice. This proves to be a challenging task for memory disambiguation systems today. The difficulty lies in the fact that the code is cyclic in nature. The output objects of an iteration must become the input of the next iteration. That is, the input and output objects are coupled by either a copying action or a pointer swapping operation during the transition from one time slice to the next. Without specialized flow sensitivity, a memory disambiguation system will conclude that the input and output objects cannot be distinguished from each other.

Three different coding styles exist for transitioning output objects to input objects in time-sliced algorithms:

1. **Fixed purpose:** The data objects operated on are allocated in an acyclic portion of the program and designated specifically as input and output structures. At the end of an iteration, the data in the output structure are copied to the input structure for use in the next iteration. Previous parallelism-detection work [14] assumes this coding style.
2. **Swapped buffer**, or double-buffering: Two or more data objects are created in the acyclic portion of the program and pointed to by input(s) and output pointers. At the end of an iteration, the pointer values are rotated.
3. **Iterative allocation:** A new data object is allocated and written during each iteration of the primary program loop and assigned to the output pointer. At the end of the iteration, the output object of the current iteration is assigned to the input pointer in preparation for consumption by the next iteration. Objects that are no longer needed are deallocated.

Many compiler analyses, even some that are flow-sensitive, will see the pointers in the latter two categories as aliasing within the loop. This is true when considering the static code, since the stores in one iteration are writing the objects that will be read in the next iteration. When the dynamic stream of instructions is considered, however, the pointers and any stores and loads from them are independent within a single iteration of the loop. In media and simulation applications, this is where much of the extractable loop-level parallelism lies. The goal of our work is to create a targeted, fast, and scalable analysis that is *cycle-sensitive*, meaning that it can distinguish objects allocated or referenced in cyclic patterns. We will address the third category; the first is adequately disambiguated by traditional points-to analysis and the second can be handled by tracking the independence of the pointers via alias pairs [10] or connection analysis [4].

Figure 1 shows an example of this within a video encoder. At least two related images exist during MPEG-style P-frame encoding: the frame currently being encoded and reconstructed and the frame(s) that was/were previously reconstructed. During motion estimation and compensation, the encoder attempts to achieve a close match to the desired, current image by copying in pieces from the previous reconstructed frame. In terms of memory operations, it reads data from the previous frame and writes it to the current frame. In the reference MPEG-4 encoder [11], these objects can come from the same static call sites and calling contexts and must be disambiguated by determining that they were created in different iterations of a control flow cycle.

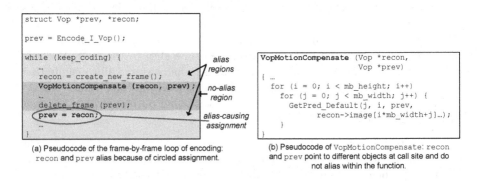

(a) Pseudocode of the frame-by-frame loop of encoding: recon and prev alias because of circled assignment.

(b) Pseudocode of VopMotionCompensate: recon and prev point to different objects at call site and do not alias within the function.

Fig. 1. An example of cycle-sensitivity enabling parallelism

In the loop shown in Figure 1(a), the pointers `prev` and `recon` will point to the same object at the circled assignment. Within the middle shaded region, however, the two pointers will always point to different objects, since `recon` is allocated in the current loop iteration and `prev` is not. Thus, loops within this region, such as those within `VopMotionCompensate` as shown in Figure 1(b), can have their iterations executed in parallel. The goal of our analysis, *iteration disambiguation*, is to distinguish the most recently allocated object from older objects that are allocated at the same site. This and similar cases require an interprocedural analysis to be effective because the objects and loops involved nearly always span numerous functions and loop scopes.

We first cover related work in Section 2. We then describe the analysis in Section 3. Section 4 shows analysis results for several benchmark programs. We conclude with some final comments and future work.

2   Related Work

The intent of iteration disambiguation is to quickly distinguish objects that come from the same static call site and chain, but different iterations of a control flow loop. It is designed as an extension of a more general pointer analysis system. By doing this, the analysis is able to capture cases which general analyses are incapable of distinguishing or cannot accomplish in an inexpensive manner. For an overview of previous work in pointer analysis, we refer to [8].

The closest existing work to iteration disambiguation, in terms of disambiguation results, is connection analysis, as proposed by Ghiya and Hendren [4]. It attempts to overcome the limitation of basic points-to analysis and naming schemes by using a storeless model [3] to determine the sets of interacting, or connected, pointers that may alias. At each program point and for each calling context, the analysis maintains the sets of connected local and global pointer variables. Each pointer's connection set approximates the set of other pointers with which it may alias. Connections are removed, or "killed", for a pointer when it is assigned, and replaced with the connection information of the right-hand expression, if any. At a given program point, disjoint connection sets for two pointers indicates that they have not interacted in any way and do not conflict. Interprocedural analysis is handled by exhaustive inlining.

Connection analysis distinguishes new and old objects in a loop by making a newly-allocated object be initially unconnected to anything else. The basic example shown in Figure 1 can be disambiguated by connection analysis because the assignment to the variable recon kills recon's connection to previous objects. However, control flow within the loop body can foil connection analysis. When a variable is assigned on only some paths through a loop, its connections are not killed on the other paths. This leads to pointer aliasing of the variable and its connected variables after the paths merge. This case has been observed in video encoders and obscures parallelism in those applications.

Shape analysis is a flow-sensitive analysis which attempts to analyze the pattern of pointer usage to express relationships between different instances of the same abstract heap object, examples of which are presented in [5,6,15]. This can improve pointer disambiguation for recursive data structures. Generally, the possible types of structures must be known a priori to the analysis, with the exception of [6]. The purpose of this work is not to identify the relationship between instances of recursive structures, but to disambiguate "top-level" pointers retained in local or global variables that refer to objects created in different iterations of a control flow cycle. Shape analysis generally does not focus on this aspect of pointer behavior.

Two independently developed may-alias points-to analyses [16,17] can distinguish different elements of an array where array elements are initialized in a loop using a monotonically increasing variable to index the array. In their analyses, there can be no data transfer between the array elements, whereas the objects targeted by iteration disambiguation are coupled through copying or pointer assignment at the end of loop iterations. Their work is complementary to ours and can be combined to provide greater precision.

3   Analysis

This section describes iteration disambiguation, a dataflow algorithm that distinguishes objects allocated in different iterations of a cycle at compile-time. It does this by marking objects' references with different *ages*. Intuitively, if one considers a loop body as a code segment observed during dynamic execution, the objects created outside of the segment or in previous instances of the segment are distinct from any objects created in the examined segment.

3.1   Example

Figure 2(a) shows the control flow graph for a simple example of an iteration disambiguation opportunity, while Figure 2(b) shows an unrolled version of the loop to clarify the relationship between pointers a and b within each outer loop iteration. We define two memory objects A and B by their static allocation sites. Since object B lies within a loop, its instances are given subscripts to indicate the iteration of the loop in which they were allocated.

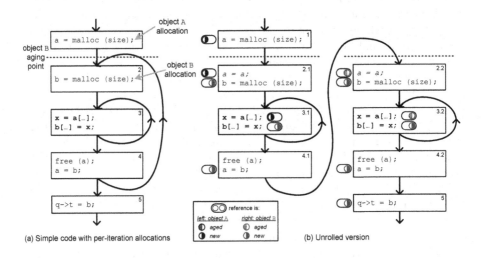

Fig. 2. Iteration disambiguation example

In the first iteration of the loop in Figure 2(b), pointer a points to object A, while pointer b points to object B_1, created in block 2.1. These two pointers do not alias within block 3.1 but do in block 4.1. There is a similar situation in block 3.2, except that in this case a points to object B_1, created in block 2.1, while b points to object B_2, created in block 2.2. Additional iterations of the loop would be similar to the second iteration. Although b aliases with a within instances of block 4, the two do not alias within any instance of block 3: a points to A or B_{n-1}, while b points to B_n. The compiler can determine that loads are independent from stores within the smaller loop in block 3 and can combine this with array index analysis to determine that parallel execution is safe for those loop iterations.

Another way of looking at this relationship is that object B_n is a separate points-to object from previously created objects. We call the B_n object *new*, while B_{n-1} and older objects are lumped together as *aged*. Objects become aged at *aging points*, which are ideally just before a new object is created. Between the *aging points* for an object, or between an aging point and the end of the program, two pointers that point to these two objects cannot alias for any n.

3.2   Algorithm

Our algorithm operates on non-address-taken local variables in the program's control flow graph. A pointer analysis, run prior to the algorithm, annotates variables with sets of objects they may point to. Points-to sets are represented as a set of abstract object IDs, where each ID stands for an unknown number of dynamic objects that exist at runtime. Intuitively, the analysis distinguishes **new** references to an abstract object created within the body of a loop from **aged** ones that must have been created prior to entering the loop or within a prior iteration of the loop. References are **ambiguous** when it becomes unclear whether they refer to **aged** or **new** objects. As long as the ages of two references are distinct and unambiguous, they refer to independent dynamic objects within the scope of an iteration of the most deeply nested loop that contains both references and the allocation for that object. The algorithm is described for a single abstract object with a unique allocation site and calling context. When analyzing multiple objects, analyses of separate abstract objects do not interact. The compiler may choose the objects which are potentially profitable; at this time every heap object allocated within a cycle is analyzed.

The analysis uses *aging points* in the control flow graph to delineate the scope over which a reference is considered **new**. A reference becomes **aged** when it crosses an aging point. Aging points are placed at the entry point of each loop and function containing the allocation. Placing aging points at the beginning of loop iterations ensures that all **new** references within the loop are to objects created in the current loop iteration. New references outside the loop point to objects created in the last loop iteration. Aging at function entry points is necessary for recursive function calls.

Recursive functions require additional consideration. A **new** reference becomes **aged** at the entrance of a recursive function that may allocate it, and could be returned from the function. This is effectively traveling backwards across an aging point, creating a situation where the same reference is both **aged** and **new** in the same region. We avoid this error by conservatively marking an **aged** return value of a recursive function **ambiguous** when it is passed to callers which are also in the recursion. [1]

---

[1] If a function could have multiple return values, the same situation can occur without recursion. We analyze low-level code that places a function's return data on the stack unless it fits in a single register. Our conservative handling of memory locations yields correct results for multiple return values on the stack.

The example in Figure 2 obtained the **aged** reference via a local variable that was live across the back edge of the loop. However, many programs retain pointers to older objects in lists or other non-local data structures and load them for use. In order to detect these pointers as **new**, the analysis must determine that the load occurs before any **new** references are stored to non-local memory. Once non-local memory contains a **new** reference, the abstract object is labeled **escaped** until control flow reaches the next aging point. Loads of an **escaped** object return references that are **ambiguous** instead of **aged**. Effectively, non-local memory is an implicit variable that is either ambiguous (**escaped**) or aged (not **escaped**). Escaped reference analysis runs concurrently with propagation of **new** and **aged** reference markings.

Setup. There are several items that need to be performed prior to executing the dataflow algorithm:

1. A heap-sensitive pointer analysis is run to identify dynamically-allocated objects, distinguished by call site and calling context [2], and find which variables may reference the object(s). Figure 3(a) shows a code example with initial flow-insensitive pointer analysis information.
2. SSA notation is constructed for each function in the program, with μ-functions[2] at loop entry points. Although constructing SSA notation prior to pointer analysis can improve the resolution of the input information via partial flow-sensitivity [7], this is not necessary for the algorithm to function correctly.
3. Aging points are marked, for each abstract object, at the entry of each loop or function containing an allocation of the object. This is a bottom-up propagation and visits strongly connected components in the program callgraph only once. In loops, μ-functions that assign references to objects created within the loops are aging points. The input parameters to a function that may create the object are also marked as aging points.
4. A dataflow predicate, representing age, is initialized for each pointed-to object on each pointer assignment, including SSA's μ- and ϕ-functions, and function parameter. The latter are treated as implicit copy operations during interprocedural propagation. We initialize these predicates as follows:
   - Pointer variables which receive the return address of the allocation call are marked with **new** versions of the references.
   - The destination of μ-functions are marked **aged** for an object if the corresponding loop contains an allocation of the object.
   - Destinations of loads that retrieve a reference from memory are optimistically marked **aged**. Unlike the previous two cases, this initialized value may change during propagation of dataflow.
   - All other pointer assignments are marked **unknown**.
   Figure 3(b) shows the results of SSA construction, marking of aging points, and initialization of dataflow predicates for the example in Figure 3(a).

---

[2] μ-functions were proposed for the Gated Single Assignment notation [1]. Unlike that work, it is not necessary to know which references are propagated from the loop backedges; we use the form simply to mark entries of loops.

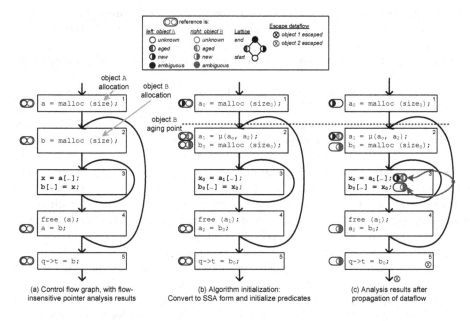

Fig. 3. Iteration disambiguation dataflow

Propagation. Figure 3(c) shows the results of dataflow propagation for the given example. Conceptually, the algorithm marks a reference returned by an allocation routine as **new**. This dataflow predicate propagates forward through the def-use chain until it reaches an aging point, after which it becomes **aged**. This **aged** reference is also propagated forward. If **aged** and **new** references for the same object meet at control flow merges other than aging points, the result becomes **ambiguous**. Separate abstract objects do not interact in any way; for example, propagation from a_0 to a_1 remains **new** for object A because there is only an aging point for object B for that transition.

As mentioned previously, we desire that the analysis capture cases where older object references are loaded from non-local memory. For this, the analysis identifies regions of the program where **new** or **ambiguous** references have **escaped** to non-local memory. References loaded from memory outside this region are guaranteed to be **aged**, but those loaded within the region are **ambiguous** because a potentially **new** reference has been placed in memory.

Propagation of age markings for object references and detection of escaped references proceed concurrently. All propagation is done in the forward direction. Age markings propagate via SSA def-use chains, while escape markings propagate along intra- and inter-procedural control flow paths. Age propagation uses a three-stage lattice of values, depicted in the legend in Figure 3. The least value of the lattice is **unknown**. The other lattice values are **aged**, **new**, and **ambiguous**. The join or union of an **aged** and a **new** reference is **ambiguous**, which means that the compiler cannot tell the iteration relationship of the reference relative to other object references in the loop. The contents of memory are **ambiguous** where an object has escaped; elsewhere, memory only contains aged references. Age and escape markings increase monotonically over the course of the analysis. The analysis provides a measure of flow-sensitivity if the base pointer analysis did not support it: references that remain unknown at analysis termination are not realizable.

Age markings propagate unchanged through assignment and address arithmetic. The union of the ages is taken for references passed in to ϕ-functions or to input parameters of functions that do not contain an allocation call. New and ambiguous ages do not propagate through aging points. Function return values are handled differently depending on whether the caller and callee lie in a recursive callgraph cycle. For the nonrecursive case, return values are simply propagated to the caller. For the recursive case, aged returns are converted to ambiguous. This is necessary to preserve correctness; since the call itself is not an aging point but the callee may contain aging points, a new reference passed into the recursive call may be returned as aged while other references in the caller to the same dynamic object would remain new.

Propagation proceeds analogously for escaped markings. The union of escaped markings is taken at control flow merge points. Escaped markings are not propagated past aging points since all references in memory become aged at those points. At the return point of a call where the caller and callee lie in a recursive cycle, memory is conservatively marked escaped.

Age and escaped reference markings influence one another through load and store instructions. Stores may cause a new or ambiguous reference to escape past the bounds that can be tracked via SSA. For our implementation, this occurs when a pointer is stored to a heap object, global variable, or local variable which is address-taken. At that store instruction, the analysis sets an escaped marking which propagates forward through the program. The region where this escape dataflow predicate is set is called the *escaped region*.

The analysis optimistically assumes during setup that loaded references are aged. If a loaded reference is found to be in the escaped region, the analysis must correct the reference's marking to ambiguous and propagate that information forward through def-use chains. Conceptually, the compiler cannot determine whether the reference was the most recent allocation or an earlier one, since a new reference has been placed in memory. An example of an escaped reference is shown in the bottom block of Figure 3(c). Aged references do not escape because the default state of references loaded from memory is aged.

Iteration disambiguation preserves context-sensitivity provided by the base pointer analysis. The calling context is encoded for each object. When the analysis propagates object references returned from functions, the contexts are examined and objects with mismatched contexts are filtered out. The analysis also performs filtering to prevent the escaped dataflow from propagating to some unrealizable call paths: references can escape within a function call only if they were created in that function or passed in as an input parameter. Our implementation currently is overly conservative for escaped dataflow when a reference is an input parameter which doesn't escape on some call paths. Handling this case requires an analysis to determine which input parameters may escape, and the case has not been prominent in studied applications.

3.3   Properties and Limitations

The iteration disambiguation algorithm explained here is only able to distinguish the object from the current/youngest iteration of a cycle from objects allocated during previous iterations. In other terms, the analysis is k-limited [9] to two ages. The benefit of this is that the analysis is relatively simple and can be formulated as an interprocedural, monotonic dataflow problem. In general only the most recently allocated object is written, while older ones are read-only, so a single age delineation is sufficient to identify parallelism.

The profitability of iteration disambiguation depends on how long a **new** object stays in a local variable and is operated on before escaping. In studied media and simulation applications, **new** references are often created at the top of loop bodies and escape towards the bottom of the loop after significant computation is performed. This exposes the available parallelism within the primary computation loops. However, is not uncommon for a reference to escape immediately on allocation and not be retained in a local variable, which prevents benefit from iteration disambiguation. The common case for this is sub-objects which are linked into an aggregate object, such as separate color planes of an image. Possible methods for resolving these objects are discussed in the next section.

The presented algorithm's effectiveness is also inversely tied to the distance between the aging points and the allocation of the object, since all objects between the aging locations and the allocation are **aged**. These cases might be disambiguable if the aging point were relocated, but this causes more complexity in utilizing the analysis results.

4   Experiments

This section presents empirical results that show that iteration disambiguation generally takes a small amount of time and can identify the distinction between cyclic objects. We covered two categories of benchmarks. For the first, we chose programs from SPEC CPU 2000 and 2006, excluding those from 2000 that have newer versions or equivalents in 2006, and those that the current version of our compiler cannot compile correctly, notably gcc and perl. For the second category, we used several applications from MediaBench I as well as a few independent ones. Our intent with the broad selection is to show that the analysis can disambiguate references in application domains other than media and scientific simulation. We use Fulcra [12] as our base pointer analysis.

4.1   Analysis Statistics

Figure 4 shows analysis statistics for the benchmark programs analyzed. The bars represent iteration disambiguation's time to analyze, annotate, and count statistics

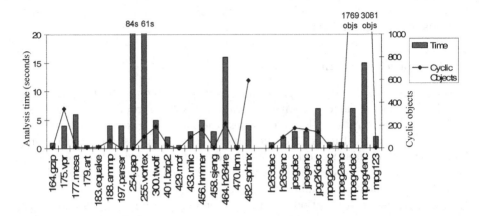

Fig. 4. Iteration disambiguation analysis time and object count

in seconds, on a 1.8 GHz Athlon 64. The dots connected by lines represent the number of distinct cyclic objects, distinguishable by call site and calling contexts. The number of heap objects is dependent on the degree of cloning (replication per call site and path) [13] performed by the base pointer analysis. For example, the MPEG-4 decoder and encoder applications have a large number of nested allocation functions which create the large number of objects seen in the figure. The "lowest-level" objects tend to be replicated the most, which affects some of our metrics.

In general the analysis is fast; for most programs, which have few cyclic objects, the analysis takes only a few seconds. Even for programs with many cyclic objects, such as 464.h264ref and mpeg4enc, the analysis runs within 16 seconds. The majority of analysis time is spent in the setup phase and the time for propagation of age markings and escaped dataflow is usually insignificant. The primary outliers are two SPEC CPU2000 benchmarks, 254.gap and 255.vortex. These benchmarks are over twice as large as the majority of the benchmarks in the program, with a correspondingly higher setup time. The larger size also increases the amount of code that escaped reference dataflow must propagate through. Finally, they have an unusually high number of references relative to the size of the codes. Unlike the other benchmarks, the time for age propagation and escaped reference dataflow is on the same order as setup time.

4.2   Object Classifications

There are two special object classifications which are exposed by the analysis. First, some objects allocated within cycles are used as temporary storage and are deallocated within the same iteration. These cases are interesting because they represent privatization opportunies. In iteration disambiguation, these objects are recognizable since only **new** references are used to load data from or store data to them. The percentage of only-new objects is shown in Figure 5. Benchmarks that have no cyclic objects are omitted.

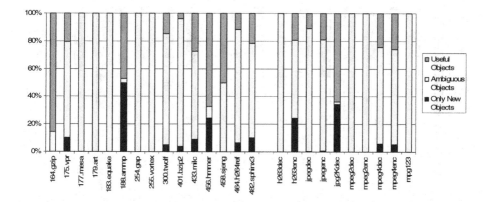

Fig. 5. Iteration disambiguation results: proportion of only new and ambiguous objects

Second, for some cyclic objects, there are either no **new** markings or no **aged** markings. For these objects, iteration disambiguation has no useful effect. We term these *ambiguous objects*. In programs with inherent parallelism, these objects are commonly multidimensional arrays and sub-structures, which require complementary analyses when detecting parallelism. As mentioned previously, these lower-level objects are a significant portion of the total object count due to heap cloning, and thus increase the apparent number of ambiguous objects beyond a static count of call sites when heap cloning has an effect. Even excluding this effect, direct inspection of several of the applications has shown that the majority of the heap objects are ambiguous.

4.3   Analysis Results

Prior to discussing the analysis results, we break the categories of **aged** and **ambiguous** references into subcategories to gain a better understanding of the results and program properties. They are:

- **Loop Aged**: The reference was passed via a local variable across the back-edge of a loop, or entered a recursive function that may allocate the object.
- **Loaded Aged**: The reference's source is loaded from memory in a region where a **new** or **ambiguous** reference has not escaped.
- **Merge Ambiguous**: The age of the reference is ambiguous due to a control flow or procedure call merge in which new and aged references of an object merge via dataflow, such as for conditional allocations.
- **Escape Ambiguous**: The age of the reference is ambiguous because it was obtained via a load in a code region where a **new** or **ambiguous** reference has escaped. We also include aged references returned from a recursive function to callers within the recursion in this category.
- **Combination Ambiguous**: This represents a merge of an escape-ambiguous reference with other types of references.

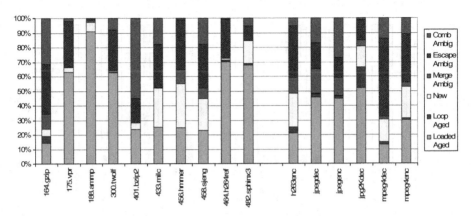

Fig. 6. Iteration disambiguation results: percentages of reference types

Figure 6 shows statistics of the results of iteration disambiguation. Results are shown as a percentage of the total static, heap-referencing memory operations, in an assembly-like representation, for each program. When a memory operation may access multiple cyclic objects, an equal fraction is assigned to each object. References to objects that are only **new** have been omitted because they inflate the apparent utility of the analysis. A significant percentage of both **new** and **aged** references indicates likely independence of operations within a loop body. Applications that have no useful cyclic objects have been omitted.

Although a more appropriate test of this analysis would be to show the amount of parallelism exposed by the analysis, we do not attempt this for this work. The objects of interest in many time-sliced applications are children objects of the top-level objects that iteration disambiguation can operate on, and are identified as ambiguous objects. We currently do not have an analysis to prove that children are unique to a parent object, so the amount of extractable parallelism is small. In the future we hope to show the difference in application performance when the additional analyses are integrated into our framework.

The high percentage of escape and combination ambiguous references indicate that many static operations on heap objects use references that have been stored to and then loaded back from memory prior to an aging point. This is expected for programs that build up large aggregate structures and then operate on them, such as the larger SPEC CPU benchmarks. Despite the fact that ambiguous objects tend to make up the majority of objects, they do not always dominate the references because of fractional counting per memory operation. We observed a tendency for operations to be one type of reference, because the objects they reference usually have similar usage patterns.

Media programs have a high percentage of ambiguous references because the majority of operations work on data substructures linked to top-level structures. As previously mentioned, escaped references are often multidimensional arrays and can be addressed with the appropriate analysis. Another case that is missed by iteration disambiguation is sub-structures of a cyclic object linked into an aggregate structure. We are currently developing a complementary analysis to address this shortcoming.

One interesting case is 464.h264ref, which is a video encoder application and thus expected to do well with iteration disambiguation. However, it has a smaller percentage of new references than most applications. The reason is the common use of an exit-upon-error function, which both calls and is called by many of the allocation and free functions used in the application. This creates a large recursion in the call graph, which has the effect of aging new references rapidly. In addition, we discovered that approximately half of the loaded aged references become escape ambiguous if the analysis does not prevent dataflow propagation through unrealizable paths, such as calls to exit().

5   Conclusions and Future Work

This paper discusses iteration disambiguation, an analysis that distinguishes high-level, dynamically-allocated, cyclic objects in programs. This cyclic relationship is common in media and simulation applications, and the appropriate analysis is necessary for automatic detection and extraction of parallelism. We show that we can disambiguate a significant percentage of references in a subset of the presented applications. We also explain some of the reasons why the analysis was not able to disambiguate more references in cases where we would expect a compiler to be able to identify parallelism.

For future work, we will be developing complementary analyses which will enable a compiler to automatically identify parallelism within programs that are amenable to parallel execution. These include array analyses, analyses that identify structure relationships such as trees, and value flow and constraint analyses.

Acknowledgment

This work would not have been possible without the work performed by Erik Nystrom and Sara Sadeghi Baghsorkhi on the Fulcra pointer analysis. We thank Bolei Guo for his advice and the anonymous reviewers for their feedback. We also acknowledge the support of the Gigascale Systems Research Center, funded under the Focus Center Research Program, a Semiconductor Research Corporation program.

References

1. Ballance, R., Maccabe, A., Ottenstein, K.: The Program Dependence Web: A representation supporting control-, data-, and demand-driven interpretation of imperative languages. In: Proceedings of the ACM SIGPLAN 1990 Conference on Programming Language Design and Implementation, pp. 257–271 (1990)
2. Choi, J.D., Burke, M.G., Carini, P.: Efficient flow-sensitive interprocedural computation of pointer-induced aliases and side effects. In: Proceedings of the 20th ACM Symposium on Principles of Programming Languages, pp. 232–245 (January 1993)

3. Deutsch, A.: A storeless model of aliasing and its abstractions using finite representations of right-regular equivalence relations. In: Proceedings of the 1992 International Conference on Computer Languages, pp. 2–13 (April 1992)

4. Ghiya, R., Hendren, L.J.: Connection analysis: A practical interprocedural heap analysis for C. In: Proceedings of the Eighth Workshop on Languages and Compilers for Parallel Computing, pp. 515–533 (August 1995)

5. Ghiya, R., Hendren, L.J.: Is it a tree, a DAG, or a cyclic graph? A shape analysis for heap-directed pointers in C. In: Proceedings of the 23rd ACM Symposium on Principles of Programming Languages, pp. 1–15 (1996)

6. Guo, B., Vachharajani, N., August, D.I.: Shape analysis with inductive recursion synthesis. In: Proceedings of the ACM SIGPLAN 2007 Conference on Programming Language Design and Implementation (June 2007)

7. Hasti, R., Horwitz, S.: Using static single assignment form to improve owinsensitive pointer analysis. In: Proceedings of the ACM SIGPLAN 1998 Conference on Programming Language Design and Implementation, pp. 97–105 (June 1998)

8. Hind, M.: Pointer analysis: Haven't we solved this problem yet? In: Proceedings of the 2001 ACM SIGPLAN-SIGSOFT Workshop on Program Analysis for Software Tools and Engineering, pp. 54–61 (2001)

9. Jones, N.D., Muchnick, S.S.: Flow analysis and optimization of LISP-like structures. In: Proceedings of the 6th ACM SIGPLAN Symposium on Principles of Programming Languages, pp. 244–256 (1981)

10. Landi, W., Ryder, B.G.: A safe approximate algorithm for interprocedural pointer aliasing. In: Proceedings of the ACM SIGPLAN 1992 Conference on Programming Language Design and Implementation, pp. 235–248 (June 1992)

11. MPEG Industry Forum, http://www.mpegif.org/

12. Nystrom, E.M.: FULCRA Pointer Analysis Framework. PhD thesis, University of Illinois at Urbana-Champaign (2005)

13. Nystrom, E.M., Kim, H.-S., Hwu, W.W.: Importance of heap specialization in pointer analysis. In: Proceedings of ACM-SIGPLAN-SIGSOFT Workshop on Program Analysis for Software Tools and Engineering, pp. 43–48 (June 2004)

14. Ryoo, S., Ueng, S.-Z., Rodrigues, C.I., Kidd, R.E., Frank, M.I., Hwu, W.W.: Automatic discovery of coarse-grained parallelism in media applications. Transactions on High-Performance Embedded Architectures and Compilers 1(1), 194–213 (2007)

15. Sagiv, M., Reps, T., Wilhelm, R.: Solving shape-analysis problems in languages with destructive updating. In: Proceedings of the ACM Symposium on Programming Languages, pp. 16–31 (January 1996)

16. Venet, A.: A scalable nonuniform pointer analysis for embedded programs. In: Proceedings of the International Static Analysis Symposium, pp. 149–164 (2004)

17. Wu, P., Feautrier, P., Padua, D., Sura, Z.: Instance-wise points-to analysis for loop-based dependence testing. In: Proceedings of the 16th International Conference on Supercomputing, pp. 262–273 (2002)

A Novel Asynchronous Software Cache Implementation for the Cell-BE Processor

Jairo Balart[1], Marc Gonzalez[1], Xavier Martorell[1], Eduard Ayguade[1], Zehra Sura[2], Tong Chen[2], Tao Zhang[2], Kevin O'Brien[2], and Kathryn O'Brien[2]

[1] Barcelona Supercomputing Center (BSC), Technical University of Catalunya (UPC)
[2] IBM TJ Watson Research Center
{jairo.balart,marc.gonzalez,xavier.martorell,
eduard.ayguade}@bsc.es,
{zsura,chentong,taozhang,caomhin,kmob}@us.ibm.com

Abstract. This paper describes the implementation of a runtime library for asynchronous communication in the Cell BE processor. The runtime library implementation provides with several services that allow the compiler to generate code, maximizing the chances for overlapping communication and computation. The library implementation is organized as a Software Cache and the main services correspond to mechanisms for data look up, data placement and replacement, data write back, memory synchronization and address translation. The implementation guarantees that all those services can be totally uncoupled when dealing with memory references. Therefore this provides opportunities to the compiler to organize the generated code in order to overlap as much as possible computation with communication. The paper also describes the necessary mechanism to overlap the communication related to write back operations with actual computation. The paper includes the description of the compiler basic algorithms and optimizations for code generation. The system is evaluated measuring bandwidth and global updates ratios, with two benchmarks from the HPCC benchmark suite: Stream and Random Access.

1 Introduction

In a system where software is responsible for data transfers between certain memory regions, it is desirable to assist the programmer by automatically managing some or all of these transfers in system software. For asynchronous data transfers, it is possible to overlap the memory access time with computation time by initiating the data transfer request in advance, i.e. before computation reaches the point when it needs to use the data requested. The placement of such memory access calls in the code is important since it can change the amount of overlap between data communication and computation, and thus affect the overall performance of the application. In this work, we target a Cell BE system to explore our approach to automatically managing asynchronous data transfers. Our technique implements a software caching mechanism that works differently from traditional hardware caching mechanisms, with the goal being to facilitate the decoupling of the multiple steps involved in a memory access

V. Adve, M.J. Garzarán, and P. Petersen (Eds.): LCPC 2007, LNCS 5234, pp. 125–140, 2008.
© Springer-Verlag Berlin Heidelberg 2008

(including address calculation, cache placement, and data transfer) as well as the actual use of the data. Software caching is not a novel proposal since it has been extensively used in specific domains, like embedded processors [4][5][6].

Our target platform, the Cell BE architecture [2], has nine processing cores on a single chip: one 64-bit Power Processing Element (PPE core) and eight Synergistic Processing Elements (SPE cores) that use 18-bit addresses to access a 256K Local Store. The PPE core accesses system memory using a traditional cache-coherent memory hierarchy. The SPE cores access system memory via a DMA engine connected to a high bandwidth bus, relying on software to explicitly initiate DMA requests for data transfer. The DMA engine can support up to 16 concurrent requests of up to 16K, and bandwidth between the DMA engine and the bus is 8 bytes per cycle in each direction. Each SPE uses its Local Store to buffer data transferred to and from system memory. The bus interface allows issuing asynchronous DMA transfer requests, and provides synchronization calls to check or wait for previously issued DMA requests to complete.

The rest of this paper is organized as follows. In Section 2, we motivate the use of a novel software cache organization for automatically managing asynchronous data transfers. In Section 3, we detail the structure and implementation of this software cache mechanism. In Section 4, we describe the compiler support needed to enable effective use of the runtime software cache services. In Section 5, we evaluate basic performance of our software caching technique using the Stream and Random Access benchmarks from the HPCC benchmark suite. In Section 6 we present some concluding remarks.

2 Motivation

The particular memory model in the Cell BE processor poses several difficulties for generating efficient code for the SPEs. The fact that each SPE owns a proper address space within the Local Storage, plus the limitation on its size, 256Kb shared by data and code, causes the performance being very sensible on how the communications are scheduled along the computation. Overlapping computation with communication becomes a crucial optimization.

When the access patterns in the computation can be easily predicted, static buffers can be introduced by the compiler, double-buffering techniques can be exploited at runtime, usually involving loop tiling techniques [1][7]. In the presence of pointer-based accesses, the compiler is no longer able to transform the code in order to overlap communication and computation. Usually, this kind of access is treated by a runtime library implementing a software cache [1]. The resulting code is difficult to be efficient as every memory reference in the code has to be monitored in order to ensure that the data is present in the Local Store, before any access to it takes place. This is usually implemented through the instrumentation of every memory reference with a runtime call responsible for the monitoring, where many checks have to occur. A general protocol to treat a single memory reference could include the following steps:

1. Check if the data is already present in local storage
2. In case not present, decide where to place it and ...
3. If out of space, decide what to send out from Local Storage

4. If necessary, perform DMA operations
5. If necessary synchronize with DMA
6. Translate from virtual address space to Local Storage address space
7. Perform memory access

Under that execution model, the chances for overlapping computation with communication are quite limited. Besides, the memory references instrumentation incurs in unacceptable overheads. The motivation of this paper is to describe what should be the main features within a software cache implementation that maximizes the chances for overlapping computation and communication, and minimizes overhead related to the memory references instrumentation.

Following the previous scheme, the overlap of communication with computation it can only be implemented by uncoupling the DMA synchronization (step 5) from the previous runtime checks (steps 1 to 4). If the runtime were to support such uncoupling, then it could be possible to reorganize the code, placing some amount of computation between step 4 and step 5 of every reference. Notice that this optimization is conditioned by the computation, in the sense that it might happen that data dependences do not allow the code reorganization. Although that, decoupling steps 4 and 5 still can offer some important benefits. It is also possible to mix the 1, 2, 3, and 4 steps of two or more memory references and group all the DMA synchronization in one single step. That would translate on some overlapping between cache management code and data communication, reducing the overhead impact. But such overlapping needs of some specific features within the implementation of steps 1, 2 and 3. It is necessary that no conflict appears between steps 1, 2 and 3 of every memory reference treated before the synchronization step. That is, the placement and replacement mechanisms must not assign the same cache line for two different memory references. This is one point of motivation of the work in this paper: the implementation of a software cache that enhances the chances for the overlapping of computation (whether it is cache control code or application code) and data communication, by uncoupling steps 4 and 5 and reducing the cache conflicts to capacity conflicts.

Because of the limited size of the Local Storage, it is necessary to provide the cache implementation with a write back mechanism to send out data to main memory. The write back mechanism involves a DMA operation moving data from the Local Storage to main memory, and requires the SPE to synchronize with the DMA engine before the flushed cache line is being reused. Deciding the moment to initiate the DMA operation becomes an important issue to increase performance. If the write back mechanism is invoked just when a modified cache line has to be replaced, then the SPE is going to be blocked until the associated DMA operation ends. The implementation described in this paper introduces two mechanisms to minimize as much as possible the number of lost cycles waiting for a DMA operation to complete (related to a flush operation). First, a mechanism to foresee future flush operations, based on information about what cache lines are referenced by the code, and detecting the precise moment where a cache line becomes unreferenced. Second, a specific replacement policy that delays as much as possible the next assignment for a flushed cache line, thus giving time to the flush operation to complete, and avoid lost cycles dedicated to synchronization at the moment of reuse.

3 Software Cache Implementation

The software cache is described according to the cache parameters, cache structures and the main services: look up, placement/replacement policies, write back, communication/synchronization and address translation.

3.1 Cache Parameters

The main cache parameters are the following: capacity, size of cache line and associativity level. For the rest of this document C stands for capacity, L stands for the cache line size, S stands for the level of associativity and N=C/L stands for the number of cache lines.

3.2 Cache Structures

The cache is composed mainly by three structures. Two list-based structures, where the cache lines can be placed depending on their state and attributes value. These are the *Directory* and the *Unused Cache Lines* lists. A third structure under a table shape, basically used for look up and translation operations: the *Look Up and Translating* table.

- The *Directory* list holds all the cache lines that are resident in the cache.
- The *Unused Cache Lines* list holds all cache lines that are no longer in use by the computation. The notion of being under use is defined by the existence of any memory reference in the computation that references the in-use cache line. The cache implementation is able to keep track of what cache lines are being referenced, and what are not.
- The *Look Up and Translating* table holds information for optimizing the look up mechanism and for implementing the translation from the virtual address space to the Local Storage address space.

3.2.1 Directory

The *Directory* is composed of S lists. Cache lines in the *Directory* are stored in a double –linked list form. There is no limitation on the number of cache lines that can be placed in any of the S lists. That makes the cache implementation a full-associative cache. Basically the S lists are used as a hash structure to speed up the look up process.

3.2.2 Unused Cache Lines List

This list holds the cache lines that were previously used by the computation, but that at a given moment they were no longer in use. The main role for this structure is related to the placement/replacement policy. Cache lines placed in this list become the immediate candidates for replacement, thus placement for other incoming cache lines required by the computation. The cache lines are stored in a double-linked list form.

3.2.3 Look up and Translating Table

This structure is organized as a table, where each row is assigned to a particular memory reference in the computation. A row contains three values used for the look up and translation mechanisms: the base address of the cache line in the Local Storage address space, the base address of the correspondent cache line in the virtual address space and a pointer to the structure representing the cache being used by the memory reference.

3.2.4 Cache Line State and Attributes

For every cache line, the implementation records information about the cache line state and other attributes, necessary to control the placement/replacement, write back, look up, and translation mechanisms.

The state of a cache line is determined by the fact any memory reference in the computation referencing the cache line. The implementation keeps track of what cache lines are under use, by maintaining a reference counter associated to each cache line. The reference counter is incremented/decremented appropriately during the *Look Up* mechanism. Therefore, the state of a cache line can take two different values: USED or UNUSED. Besides the cache line state, there are other attributes:

- CLEAN: the cache line has been only used for READ memory operations. The data stored in the cache line has not been modified.
- DIRTY: the cache line has been used for WRITE and/or READ memory operations. The data stored in the cache line has been modified.
- FLUSHED: the cache line has already been flushed to main memory.
- LOCKED: the cache line is excluded from the replacement policy, which means that a cache line holding this attribute can not be replaced.
- PARTITIONED: the data transfer from/to main memory involves a different amount of data than the actual cache line size. The total number of bytes to be transferred is obtained by dividing the cache line size by a factor of 32.

The implementation also records the mapping between the cache line in the Local Storage, and its associated cache line in virtual memory.

3.3 Look up

The *Look Up* mechanism is divided in two different phases. First phase takes place within the computation code, second phase occurs inside the cache runtime system. For the first phase of look up, it is necessary some coordination with the compiler support. For each memory reference the implementation keeps track about the base address for the cache line being accessed. This information is stored in the *Look Up and Translating* table. Each time a new instance of a memory reference occurs, the implementation checks if the referenced cache line has changed. If this happens, then the second phase for the look up is invoked. Detecting if the cache line has changed is as simple as performing an AND operation between the memory address generated in the memory reference, and a particular mask value (in C syntax: ~(L-1)), plus a comparison with the value in the *Look Up and Translating* table. It is under the compiler responsibility to assign an entry in the *Look Up and Translating* table for each memory reference in the code. Section 4.2 is giving the detailed description on how this is implemented.

The second phase of the *Look Up* mechanism accesses the cache *Directory* looking for the new required cache line. Only one of the S lists has to be selected to perform the search. This is done through a hash function applied to the base address of the cache line. The implementation ignores the offset bits, and takes all other most significant bits. Then applies an S-modulo operation and determines one of the S lists. The *Look Up* continues with the list traversal, and if the cache line is found, a hit is reported. In case not, the placement/replacement mechanisms are invoked, and the necessary DMA operations are programmed.

During the *Look Up* process, the reference counters for the two cache lines that are going to be involved are incremented/decremented. For the cache line that is no longer referenced by the memory reference, the counter is decremented. For the new referenced cache line, the counter is incremented, no matter the *Look Up* ended with a hit or miss.

At the end of the *Look Up* process the *Look Up and Translating* table is updated. The row assigned to the memory reference the *Look Up* operation was treating is appropriately filled: base address of the cache line in the Local Storage, base address of the cache line in virtual memory and a pointer to the structure representing the cache line.

3.4 Write Back

The Write Back mechanism only applies for modified cache lines, that is, those lines that hold the DIRTY attribute. The write back is activated when the reference counter of a modified cache line reaches the zero value. This event is interpreted by the implementation as a hint of future possible uses of the cache line. Particularly, the event is interpreted as if the cache line is not going to be referenced by the computation up to its completion. Therefore, this point becomes a good opportunity to go in advance to the needs of the computation and program the flush of the cache line, under an asynchronous scheme. Notice that this is giving, but not ensuring, time to the implementation to overlap communication and computation. Of course, it is necessary at some point to synchronize with the DMA operation. In order to do so, the implementation records the TAG used in the DMA operation, and delays the synchronization until the next use of the cache line, when ever the replacement policy determines the next reuse to happen.

3.5 Placement / Replacement

The Placement/Replacement mechanisms are executed during the second phase of *Look Up*. The replacement policy relies on the reference counter and the *Unused Cache Lines* list. When the cache line reference counter equals zero, the cache line is placed on the *Unused Cache Lines* list as the LAST of the list, and as stated in previous section, if the line was modified, a flush operation is immediately programmed. Notice that the cache line is not extracted from the *Directory*.

The *Unused Cache Lines* list contains the cache lines candidates for replacement actions. When new data has to be brought in the cache, a cache line has to be selected.

If the *Unused Cache Lines* list is not empty, the implementation selects the FIRST in the list. If the line is holding the FLUSHING attribute, the tag that was recorded during write back execution is used to synchronize with the DMA engine. After that, a DMA operation is programmed under an asynchronous scheme to bring in the data, relying on the compiler for placing in the computation code the necessary synchronization statement. Notice that selecting the FIRST element in the list, while unused cache lines are placed as LAST, is what separates as much as possible the DMA operation associated to a flushed cache line, and its next reuse. Hence, delaying as much as possible the execution of the necessary synchronization with the DMA engine and avoiding unnecessary stalls in the SPE.

If the *Unused cache Lines* list is empty, then the replacement policy traverses the *Directory* from set 0 to S-1, and selects the line that first entered in the cache. This is implemented through the assignment of a number that is incremented each time a cache line is brought in. The minimum number within all resident cache lines determines the cache line to be replaced. If the replaced line was modified, the line is flushed to main memory under a synchronous scheme. After that, the data is brought in through an asynchronous DMA operation, and relying on the compiler to introduce the necessary synchronization statement. Notice that an appropriate relation between the number of cache lines and the number of memory references might perfectly avoid this kind of replacement, since it can be ensured that the list of unused cache lines is never going to be empty (see section 4.6).

Initially, all cache lines are stored in both the *Directory* and the *Unused Cache Lines* list, with the counter reference equaling zero.

3.6   Communications and Synchronization

The implementation distinguishes between DMA transfers related to write back operations and DMA transfers responsible for bringing data into the cache. For the former case, a set of 15 tags are reserved, for the latter another different 15 tags. For both cases tags are assigned in a round robin fashion, which means after 15 DMA operations tags start being reused.

All DMA operations assigned to the same tag, are executed always one after the other. This is achieved through the use of fenced DMA operations that forbids the memory flow controller to reorder any DMA operations associated to the same tag. This becomes necessary for treating the following situation: suppose a modified cache line is no longer in use, so it is flushed to main memory, and placed in the *Unused Cache Lines* list. Then the code being executed references again the data in the cache line, and since it was not extracted from the *Directory*, no miss is produced, but it is necessary to extract the cache line from the *Unused Cache Lines* list. The cache line might or might not be modified, but at some point the cache line will be no longer in use. In the case the cache line was modified it will be flushed again. It is mandatory for memory consistency that the two flush operations get never reordered. To ensure that, the implementation reuses the same tag for both flush operations, and introduces a "memory fence" between them.

All DMA operations are always programmed under an asynchronous scheme, unless those associated to a replacement that found empty the *Unused Cache Lines* list. Those related to flush operations, synchronize at the next reuse of the flushed cache line. Those related to bring data into the cache get synchronized by specific statements introduced by the compiler. It is important to mention that this is what allows the compiler to try to maximize the overlap between communication and communication. Section 4 describes the necessary compiler support to achieve the communication/computation overlapping.

3.7 Address Translation

To perform the translation from the virtual address space to the Local Storage address space the data in the *Look Up and Translating* table is enough. Each memory reference has been assigned with a row in the *Look Up and Translating* table. In that row, the base address for the cache line in the Local Storage can be obtained. Translation is as simple as computing the offset of the access and add the offset to the base address of the cache line in the Local Storage. The offset computation can be done through an AND operation between the generated address in the memory reference and a bit mask according to the size of the cache line (e.g: ~(L-1)).

4   Compiler Code Generation

This section describes the compiler support and code generation for transforming programs to SPE executables relying on the software cache described in the previous section. In this paper we describe the compiler support that is required to target the execution of loops.

4.1 Basic Runtime Services

This section describes the main runtime available services which the compiler should target while generating code.

- _LOOKUP: runtime service performing the phase 1 in the *Look Up* mechanism.
- _MMAP: runtime service executing phase 2 in the *Look Up* mechanism. In case a miss is produced, then the placement/replacement mechanisms are executed, the reference counters are incremented/decremented, and the all necessary DMA operations are performed asynchronously. In case the replacement algorithm indicates the use of a previously flushed cache line, synchronization with the DMA engine occurs.
- _MEM_BARRIER: runtime service that forces the synchronization with the DMA engine. It is a blocking runtime service.
- _LD, _ST: runtime services responsible for the address translation between the virtual address space and the Local Storage address space. Include arithmetic pointer operations such as the computation of the offset in the access to the cache line base address in virtual memory, and the computation of the actual Local Storage address by adding the offset to the base address of the cache line in the Local Storage.

4.2 Code Generation

This section describes the basic algorithms and optimizations related to code generation.

4.2.1 Assign Identifiers to Memory References

The first step for the compiler is to assign a numerical identifier to each different memory reference in the code. This identifier is going to be used at runtime to link each memory reference to the runtime structure supporting the *Look Up* (phase one), and the translating mechanisms. The runtime structure corresponds to one entry in the *Look Up and Translating* table.

```
for (i=0;i<NUM_ITERS;i++) {
    v1[i] = v2[i];
    v3[v1[i]]++;
}
```

Fig. 1. Example of C code for code generation

For the example shown in Figure 1, three different memory references can be distinguished: *v1[]* , *v2[]* and *v3[]* . The compiler would fro example associate identifiers 0, 1, 2 to memory references to *v1[]* , *v2[]* and *v3[]* respectively.

```
for (i=0;i<NUM_ITERS;i++) {
    if (_LOOKUP(0, ,&v2[i],...)) {
        _MMAP(0,&v2[i],...);
        _MEM_BARRIER(0);
    }
    if (_LOOKUP(1, ,&v1[i],...)) {
        _MMAP(1,&v1[i],...);
        _MEM_BARRIER(1);
    }
    _LD(0,&v2[i],_int_tmp00);
    _ST(1,&v1[i],_int_tmp00);
    if (_LOOKUP(2, ,&v3[_int_tmp00],...)) {
        _MMAP(2,&v3[_int_tmp00],...);
        _MEM_BARRIER(2);
    }
    _LD(2,&v3[_int_tmp00],_int_tmp01);
    _int_tmp01++;
    _ST(2,&v3[_int_tmp00],_int_tmp01);
}
```

Fig. 2. Initial code transformation

4.2.2 Basic Code Generation

For every memory reference, the compiler has to inject code to check if the data needed by the computation is in the Local Storage. The compiler injects a _LOOKUP operation for every memory reference, and a conditional statement depending on the output of the _LOOKUP operation. Figure 2 shows the transformed code for the example in figure 1. All _MMAP operations are controlled by a _LOOKUP operation, relying on the runtime structures pointed out by the assigned identifier according to what has been described in the previous section. Right at the end on the conditional branch, the compiler injects a _MEM_BARRIER operation that enforces the synchronization with the DMA engine.

```
_lb_01 = 0; _ub_01 = NELEM;
_work_01 = (_lb_01 < _ub_01);
while (_work_01) {
   _start_01 = _lb_01;
   _LOOKUP(0, ,&v2[i],...,_lookpu_01);
   if (_lookup_01) _MMAP(0, &v2[_start_01], ..., LOCK);
   _LOOKUP(1, ,&v1[i],...,_lookup_01);
   if (_lookup_01) _MMAP(1, &v1[_start_01], ..., LOCK);
   _next_iters_01 = LS_PAGE_SIZE;
   _NEXT_MISS(0, &v2[_start_01], float, sizeof(float), _next_iters_01);
   _NEXT_MISS(1, &v1[_start_01], float, sizeof(float), _next_iters_01);
   _end_01 = _start_01 + _next_iters_01;
   if (_end_01>_ub_01) _end_01 = _ub_01;
   _lb_01 = _end_01;
   _work_01 = (_lb_01 < _ub_01);
   _MEM_BARRIER();
   for (int i = _start_01; i < _end_01; i=i+1) {
      _LD(0,&v2[i],_int_tmp00);
      _ST(1,&v1[i],_int_tmp00);
      if (_LOOKUP(2, &v3[_int_tmp00],...)) {
         _MMAP(2,&v3[_int_tmp00],...);
         _MEM_BARRIER(2);
      }
      _LD(2,&v3[_int_tmp00],_int_tmp01);
      _int_tmp01++;
      _ST(2,&v3[_int_tmp00],_int_tmp01);
   }
}
```

Fig. 3. Code transformation for stride accesses

This preliminary version of the transformed code does not allow any overlap between computation and communication. It contains unnecessary conditional statements that for sure are not going to be optimal. Besides, it does not take into account the different type of accesses in the code, distinguishing between strided accesses and pointer-based accesses. But before describing any optimization technique, it is necessary to outline what are the limitations that condition the compiler transformations. Since the main target of the compiler is to enhance the overlapping of computation (whether cache control code or original computation in the code) it is reasonable to try to reorganize the preliminary code in order to group _MMAP operations, making them to be executed at runtime right one after the other. Notice that such grouping makes all the communication performed within a _MMAP operation, be overlapped with the execution of the following _MMAP operations. In the example, the if statements corresponding to the accesses to *v1[i]* and *v2[i]* could be joined. One if statement should include the two _MMAP operations, and only one _MEM_BARRIER. Generally, the compiler is only limited by the fact that grouping the _MMAP operations must be done taking to account the possibility of conflicts within the grouped _MMAPs. A conflict may appear along the execution of several _MMAP operations if two of them require the same cache line to bring data in the Local Storage. A conflict is not acceptable to appear before the data of the conflicting _MMAP operations has been accessed. That is, between the execution of a particular _MMAP operation and the _LD/_ST operations with the same identifier, it is not acceptable to place a number of _MMAP operations that can cause a conflict. Since the cache implementation follows a full-associative scheme, conflicts may only appear as capacity conflicts. This determines the limits on the grouping: the compiler can not group _MMAP operations if doing so is causing that between a _LD/_ST operation and the corresponding _MMAP operation (indicated by the identifier associated to _MMAP and

_LD/_ST operations) N _MMAP operations are executed, where N stands for the number of cache lines. Formally, we define the distance of a _MMAP operation as *the maximum number of _MMAP operations between the _MMAP and the _LD/_ST operations with the same identifier.* The compiler is now free of reorganizing the code, grouping _MMAP operations, as long as it keeps every _MMAP distance in the range of [0..N].

4.3   Optimization for Strided Accesses

Strided accesses offer the possibility of reducing the number of the _MMAP operations that need to be performed during the execution of the loop. The basis for such optimization is that the runtime can be provided with a service that computes how many accesses are going to be produced along a cache line, given the starting address and the stride. This information can be used to partition the iteration space in different chunks, defining the initial iteration of each chunk, a change of cache line (actually a miss) in a strided memory access.

Figure 3 shows the compiler code for the example code in Figure 1. Notice that the original loop, has been embedded in an outer *while* loop. The *while* loop iterates along the chunks of iterations, and the inner loop iterates along the actual iteration space. The use of the runtime service _NEXT_MISS computes the number of iterations that can be performed without having a miss on that access, given an initial address and a stride. For every strided access, the _NEXT_MISS service is invoked, and the minimum of these values defines the number of iterations for the next chunk. In the example, the two stride accesses are treated with two _MMAP operations that are going to overlap the communication of the first one with the cache control code of the second one.

Notice the attribute LOCK provided to the runtime system _MMAP, that ensures that the mapped cache line is going to be excluded from the replacement policies. This causes the runtime to treat the memory references in the inner loop, with a different distance boundary, since now the compiler has to assume 2 less available cache lines in the overall cache capacity. A _MEM_BARRIER is placed right before the inner loop execution ensuring that the data is resent before the next chunk of iterations is executed. This synchronization only involves incoming data to the Local Storage. Write back operations executed along the _MMAP runtime service corresponding to the *v1[i]* access operation, are synchronized whenever the cache lines associated to this access are being reused.

4.4   Optimization for Non-strided Accesses

Non-strided accesses become an important source of overhead, since they do not usually spatial locality. Therefore, overlapping computation and communication for this type of access should be highly desirable. Figure 4 shows the compiler transformation for this kind of access, corresponding to the *v3[v1[i]]* access in the example in Figure 1. Only the innermost loop where the non-stride access is placed is showed. The loop has been unrolled 2 times, offering the possibility of grouping the 2 _MMAP operations associated to that access. The 2 factor has been only used as example, since the limit on the unrolling factor is going to be determined by the number

```
for (int i = _start_01; i < _end_01; i=i+2) {
  _LD(0,&v2[i],_int_tmp00);
  _ST(1,&v1[i],_int_tmp00);
  _LD(0,&v2[i+1],_int_tmp02);
  _ST(1,&v1[i+1],_int_tmp02);
  _LOOKUP(2, &v3[_int_tmp00],..., _lookup_01)
  _LOOKUP(2, &v3[_int_tmp02],..., _lookup_01)
  if (_look_up_01) {
    _MMAP(2,&v3[_int_tmp00],...);
    _MMAP(3,&v3[_int_tmp02],...);
    _MEM_BARRIER(2);
  }
  _LD(2,&v3[_int_tmp00],_int_tmp01);
  _int_tmp01++;
  _ST(2,&v3[_int_tmp00],_int_tmp01);

  _LD(3,&v3[_int_tmp02],_int_tmp03);
  _int_tmp03++;
  _ST(3,&v3[_int_tmp02],_int_tmp03);
\
```

Fig. 4. Code transformation for non-stride accesses

of cache lines, minus 2 (two cache lines have been locked for v1 and v2 accesses), as the distance boundary has to be preserved for all _MMAP operations. Notice that the compiler has to assign different identifiers for both accesses to v3 vector, since they define two different memory references.

4.5 Setting the Cache Line Size

Depending on the number of memory references detected in the code, the cache line size has to be adapted to avoid unnecessary capacity conflicts within the execution of a loop iteration. If the number of references exceeds the number of cache lines, then conflicts are quite probable to appear. Therefore, the compiler has to select a cache line size that ensures that the number of available cache lines is greater or equal that the number of memory references.

5 Evaluation

The software cache implementation has been tested with two benchmarks from the HPCC benchmark suite [3]: Stream and Random Access. The Stream benchmark measures bandwidth ratios. It is composed by four synthetic kernels that measure sustainable memory bandwidth (in GB/s) and the corresponding computation rate for simple vector codes. The Random Access benchmark is composed by one kernel that operates on a single vector data type. The benchmark computes Global Updates per Second (GUPS). GUPS are calculated by identifying the number of memory locations that can be randomly updated in one second, divided by 1 billion (1e9). The term "randomly" means that there is little relationship between one address to be updated and the next, except that they occur in the space of 1/2 the total system memory.

All the measures were taken in a Cell BE-based blade machine with two Cell Broadband Engine processors at 3.2 GHz (SMT enabled), with 1 GB XDR RAM (512 MB each processor), running Linux Fedora Core 6 (Linux Kernel 2.6.20-CBE).

The software cache implementation was configured with the following cache parameters: 64Kb of capacity, 1024 sets and a varying cache line size ranging from 128 bytes up to 4096 bytes.

5.1 Stream Benchmark

Figure 5 shows the comparison between three different implementations, differing in the way the communications are managed. The Synchronous version forces a DMA synchronization after every DMA operation is programmed. This version corresponds to an implementation that would not allow for any overlapping between computation and communication. The Synchronous Flush version, allows for having asynchronous data communication from main memory to the Local Storage, but implements the flush operations (transfers from Local Storage to main memory) under a synchronous scheme. This version is not using the reference counter for cache lines, as a hint for determining the moment where a cache line has to be flushed before any reuse of it is required. Finally, the Asynchronous version, implements the software cache described in this paper, trying to maximize the overlapping of computation and communication.

For every version, the performance of each kernel (Copy, Scale, Add and Triad) is shown varying the size of the cache line (128, 256, 512, 1024, 2048 and 4096 bytes, from left to right). The results correspond to the obtained performance while executing with 8 SPEs. For brevity, the results executing with 1, 2 and 4 SPEs have been omitted as they were showing a very similar behavior. Clearly, and as it could be expected, every version significantly improves as long as the cache line size is increased. The comparison of the three versions allows for measuring the capabilities of the software cache implementation to overlap computation and communication. The results for the Synchronous version are taken as a baseline to be improved by the two other versions. The performance for the 128 bytes executions show how the different kernels behave while being dominated by the DMA operations.

The Synchronous version reaches 1.26 Gb/sec in average for the 4 kernels, the Synchronous Flush version reaches 1.75 Gb/sec, and finally the Asynchronous version reaches 2.10 Gb/sec. This corresponds to a speed up about 1.66. Similar behavior is observed when the cache line is increased from 128 up to 2048, reaching the best performance with a 2048 cache line size: 9.17 Gb/sec for Synchronous, 10.46 for

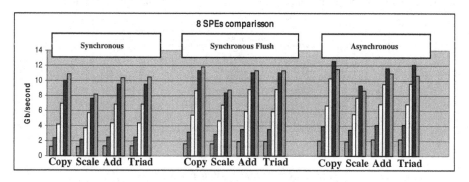

Fig. 5. Code transformation for non-stride accesses

Synchronous Flush and 11.38 for Asynchronous. This corresponds to a speed up about 1.24. Notice that when the cache line size is 4096, the increment of performance is not sustained. For the moment, it is not clear the reason of that behavior, so this needs more study.

5.2 Random Access Benchmark

The Random Access benchmark is used for evaluate the overlapping of computation and communication when the parallel code includes pointer-based memory accesses. Four different versions of the benchmark have been evaluated, depending on the unroll factor in the loop computation. Figure 6 shows the core of the computation. The unroll factor determines how many DMA transfers can be overlapped for the memory references to variable *Table*, according to the transformation described in section 4.5. For a 2 unroll factor, 2 _MMAP operations can be executed one immediate after the other. An unroll factor of 4 allows for overlapping 4 _MMAP operations, a factor of 8 allows for overlapping 8 _MMAP operations.

```
for (i=0; i<NUPDATE/128; i++) {
  for (j=0; j<128; j++) {
      ran[j] = (ran[j] << 1) ^ ((s64Int) ran[j] < 0 ? POLY : 0);
      Table[ran[j] & (TableSize-1)] ^= ran[j];
  }
}
```

Fig. 6. Source code for Random Access benchmark

Figure 7 shows the results executing with 1 and 8 SPEs. The cache line size has been set to 4096, but the access to the *Table* variable it is performed with he _PARTITIONED_ attribute, which makes every DMA transfer just involve 4096/32 = 128 bytes of data. This shows the ability of the software cache implementation to deal with both strided accesses and non strided accesses. The base line measurement corresponds to the version with no loop unrolling. The Y axis measures GUPS (Giga Updates per Second). The 1-SPE version significantly improves while the unrolling factor is increased. Improvements are about 30%, 56% and 73% with 2, 4 and 8 unroll factors respectively. Similar improvements are observed in the 8-SPE version.

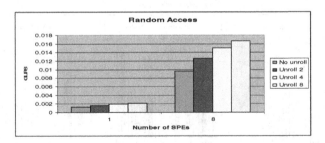

Fig. 7. Performance for Random Access

Although the difference in performance between the non-unrolled and the 8-urolled versions, we have detected a limiting factor due to the relation between the execution time for the _MMAP runtime service, and the DMA time for small data transfers (e.g.: 128 bytes). Small transfers perform very fast in the Cell-BE so they do not offer many chances for overlapping unless the execution time for the _MMAP service is such that can be fitted several times in one DMA transfer. The measurement for the Random Access show that our implementation is limited to the overlapping of 8 _MMAP operations for small DMA transfers. This suggests further study on how to optimize the _MMAP mechanism.

6 Conclusions

This paper describes the main features that have to be included in the implementation of a software cache implementation for the Cell BE processor, in order to maximize the chances for overlapping computation and communication.

It has been proved that a full-associative scheme offers better chances for overlapping computation and communication. It also has been pointed out the necessity of providing with mechanisms to detect the precise moment to initiate write back operations. This translates to overlapping the data transfer from the cache to main memory with actual computation, since the implementation guarantees that the necessary synchronization associated to the write back operation is going to be produced at next reuse of the flushed cache line. Besides, this is accompanied with a replacement policy that tends to increase the time between a use / reuse of the same cache line. Thus, delaying as much as possible the synchronization point and giving the hardware the necessary time to complete the data transfer.

The implementation has been evaluated with two benchmarks in the HPCC suite: Stream and Random Access. For both benchmarks, improvements are significant, ranging from 1.25 and 1.66 of speed up.

Acknowledgement

This work has been supported by the Ministry of Education of Spain under contract TIN2007-60625, and IBM in the context of the SOW Cell project. We would like also to acknowledge the Barcelona Supercomputing Center for letting us access to its Cell BE-based blades, provided by IBM through the SUR Program.

References

1. Eichenberger, A.E., O'Brien, K., O'Brien, K., Wu, P., Chen, T., Oden, P.H., Prener, D.A., Shepherd, J.C., So, B., Sura, Z.: Optimizing Compiler for a Cell Processor. In: 14th Parallel Architectures and Compilation Techniques, Saint Louis (Missouri) (September 2005)
2. Kistler, M., Perrone, M., Petrini, F.: Cell Multiprocessor Communication Network: Built for Speed. IEEE Micro 26(3), 10–23 (2006)

3. Luszczek, P., Bailey, D., Dongarra, J., Kepner, J., Lucas, R., Rabenseifner, R., Takahashi, D.: The HPC Challenge (HPCC) Benchmark Suite. In: SC 2006 Conference Tutorial. IEEE, Los Alamitos (2006)
4. Wang, Q., Zhang, W., Zang, B.: Optimizing Software Cache Performance of Packet Processing Applications. In: LCTES 2007 (2007)
5. Dai, J., Li, L., Huang, B.: Pipelined Execution of Critical Sections Using Software-Controlled Caching in Network Processors. In: Proceedings of the International Symposium on Code Generation and Optimization table of contents, pp. 312–324 (2007), ISBN:0-7695-2764-7
6. Ravindran, R., Chu, M., Mahlke, S.: Compiler Managed Partitioned Data Caches for Low Power. In: LCTES 2007 (2007)
7. Chen, T., Sura, Z., O'Brien, K., O'Brien, K.: Optimizing the use of static buffers for DMA on a Cell chip. In: 19th International Workshop on Languages and Compilers for Parallel Computing, New Orleans, Louisiana, November 2-4 (2006)

Pillar: A Parallel Implementation Language

Todd Anderson, Neal Glew, Peng Guo, Brian T. Lewis, Wei Liu, Zhanglin Liu,
Leaf Petersen, Mohan Rajagopalan, James M. Stichnoth, Gansha Wu, and Dan Zhang

Microprocessor Technology Lab, Intel Corporation

Abstract. As parallelism in microprocessors becomes mainstream, new programming languages and environments are emerging to meet the challenges of parallel programming. To support research on these languages, we are developing a low-level language infrastructure called *Pillar* (derived from Parallel Implementation Language). Although Pillar programs are intended to be automatically generated from source programs in each parallel language, Pillar programs can also be written by expert programmers. The language is defined as a small set of extensions to C. As a result, Pillar is familiar to C programmers, but more importantly, it is practical to reuse an existing optimizing compiler like gcc [1] or Open64 [2] to implement a Pillar compiler.

Pillar's concurrency features include constructs for threading, synchronization, and explicit data-parallel operations. The threading constructs focus on creating new threads only when hardware resources are idle, and otherwise executing parallel work within existing threads, thus minimizing thread creation overhead. In addition to the usual synchronization constructs, Pillar includes transactional memory. Its sequential features include stack walking, second-class continuations, support for precise garbage collection, tail calls, and seamless integration of Pillar and legacy code. This paper describes the design and implementation of the Pillar software stack, including the language, compiler, runtime, and *high-level converters* (that translate high-level language programs into Pillar programs). It also reports on early experience with three high-level languages that target Pillar.

1 Introduction

Industry and academia are reacting to increasing levels of hardware concurrency in mainstream microprocessors with new languages that make parallel programming accessible to a wider range of programmers. Some of these languages are domain-specific while others are more general, but successful languages of either variety will share key features: language constructs that allow easy extraction of high levels of concurrency, a highly-scalable runtime that efficiently maps concurrency onto available hardware resources, a rich set of synchronization constructs like futures and transactions, and managed features from modern languages such as garbage collection and exceptions. In addition, these languages will demand good sequential performance from an optimizing compiler. Implementing such a language will require a sizable compiler and runtime, possibly millions of lines of code.

To reduce this burden and to encourage experimentation with parallel languages, we are developing a language infrastructure called Pillar (derived from Parallel Implementation Language). We believe that key parts of the compilers and runtimes for these

V. Adve, M.J. Garzarán, and P. Petersen (Eds.): LCPC 2007, LNCS 5234, pp. 141–155, 2008.

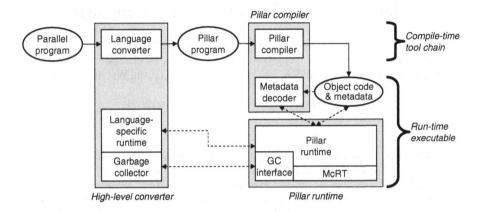

Fig. 1. The Pillar architecture and software stack

languages will have strong similarities. Pillar factors out these similarities and provides a single set of components to ease the implementation and optimization of a compiler and its runtime for any parallel language. The core idea of Pillar is to define a low-level language and runtime that can be used to express the sequential and concurrency features of higher-level parallel languages. The Pillar infrastructure consists of three main components: the Pillar language, a Pillar compiler, and the Pillar runtime.

To implement a parallel language using Pillar, a programmer first creates a *high-level converter* (see Fig. 1). This converter translates programs written in the parallel language into the Pillar language. Its main task is to convert constructs of the parallel language into Pillar constructs. The Pillar language is based on C and includes a set of modern sequential and parallel features (see Section 2). Since the Pillar compiler handles the tasks of code generation and traditional compiler optimizations, creating a high-level converter is significantly easier than creating a new parallel language compiler from scratch.

The second step is to create a runtime for the high-level language that provides the specialized support needed for that language's features. We call this runtime the language-specific runtime (LSR) to distinguish it from the Pillar runtime. The LSR could be written in Pillar and make use of Pillar constructs, or could be written in a language such as C traditionally used for runtime implementation. In either case, the Pillar code generated by the converter can easily call the LSR where necessary. The LSR can also make use of Pillar's runtime that, in addition to supporting the Pillar implementation, provides a set of services for high-level languages such as stack walking and garbage collection (GC) support. The Pillar runtime is layered on top of McRT, the Multi-Core RunTime [3], which provides scheduling, synchronization, and software transactional memory services.

Once the converter and LSR are written, complete executables can be formed by compiling the converted Pillar code with the Pillar compiler to produce object code, and then linking this with the LSR, the Pillar runtime, and McRT. The Pillar compiler produces both object code and associated metadata. This metadata is used by the Pillar runtime to provide services such as stack walking and root-set enumeration, and because of it, the code is said to be *managed*. (Pillar also supports integration with non-Pillar code, such as legacy code, which is said to be *unmanaged*.) The Pillar compiler controls the metadata format, and provides its own *metadata decoder* library to interpret it to the Pillar runtime. The metadata and decoder are also linked into the executable.

The design and implementation of Pillar is still in its early phases, and currently has a few key limitations: most notably, a cache-coherent shared-memory hardware model. Another consequence is that we are not yet in a position to do meaningful performance analysis, so this paper does not present any performance results. We intend to address these issues in the future, and we also hope to increase the range of high-level languages that can target Pillar.

The following sections focus on the Pillar language, compiler, and runtime.

2   The Pillar Language

The Pillar language has several key design principles. First, it is a compiler target language, with the goal of mapping any parallel language onto Pillar while maintaining that language's semantics. As such, Pillar cannot include features that vary across high-level languages, like object models and type-safety rules. C++, C#, and Java, for example, are too high-level to be effective target languages, as their object models and type-safety rules are not appropriate for many languages. Therefore, of necessity, Pillar is a fairly low-level language. Although most Pillar programs will be automatically generated, expert programmers must be able to directly create Pillar programs. As a result, assembly and bytecode languages are too low-level since they are difficult even for experts to use. Although inspired by C-- [4,5], we decided to define Pillar as *a set of extensions to C* because then we could utilize existing optimizing C compilers to get quality implementations of Pillar quickly.

Since the Pillar language is based on C, type safety properties of the source parallel language must be enforced by the high-level converter. For example, array bounds checks might be implemented in Pillar using a combination of explicit tests and conditional branches. Similarly, null-dereference checks, divide-by-zero checks, enforcing data privacy, and restricting undesired data accesses must be done at a level above the Pillar language by the high-level converter. One notable exception is that we are working on annotations to express immutability and disambiguation of memory references.

Second, Pillar must provide support for key sequential features of modern programming languages. Examples include garbage collection (specifically, the ability to identify live roots on stack frames), stack walking (e.g., for exception propagation), proper tail calls (important when compiling functional languages), second-class continuations (e.g., for exception propagation and backtracking), and the ability to make calls between managed Pillar code and unmanaged legacy code.

Third, Pillar must also support key concurrency features of parallel languages, such as parallel thread creation, transactions, data-parallel operations, and futures. Fig. 2 summarizes the syntax of the Pillar features added to the C language. These features are described in the following sections.

Sequential constructs		Concurrency constructs	
Feature	Syntax example	Feature	Syntax example
Second-class continuations	`continuation k(a, b, c): cut to k(x, y, z);`	Pcall	`pcall(aff) foo(a, b, c);`
		Prscall	`prscall(aff) foo(a, b, c);`
Alternate control flow	`foo() also cuts to k1, k2; foo() also unwinds to k3, k4; foo() never returns;`	Futures	`fcall(aff, &st) foo(a, b, c); ftouch(&st); fwait(&st);`
Tail call	`tailcall foo();`	Trans-actions	`TRANSACTION(k) {`
Spans	`span TAG value { ⋯ }`		`⋯`

Virtual stack and destructors	`VSE(k) { ⋯`
	`    continuation k(target):`
	`        ⋯`
	`        cut to target;`
	`}`
			`continuation k(reason):`
			`    if (reason==RETRY)`
			`        ⋯`
			`    else if (reason==ABORT)`
			`        ⋯`

GC references	`ref obj;`		`}`

Managed/ unmanaged calls	`#pragma managed(off)`
	`#include <stdio.h>`
	`#pragma managed(on)`
	`⋯`
	`printf(⋯);`		

Fig. 2. Pillar syntactic elements

2.1 Sequential Features

Second-class continuations: This mechanism is used to jump back to a point in an older stack frame and discard intervening stack frames, similar to C's setjmp/longjmp mechanism. The point in the older stack frame is called a continuation, and is declared by the `continuation` keyword; the jumping operation is called a cut and allows multiple arguments to be passed to the target continuation. For any function call in Pillar, if the target function might ultimately cut to some continuation defined in the calling function rather than returning normally, then the function call must be annotated with all such continuations (these can be thought of as all alternate return points) so that the compiler can insert additional control flow edges to keep optimizations safe.

Virtual stack elements: A `VSE` (virtual stack element) declaration associates a cleanup task with a block of code. The "virtual stack" terminology is explained in Section 5.2. This cleanup task is executed whenever a cut attempts to jump out of the region of code associated with the VSE. This mechanism solves a problem with traditional stack cutting (such as in C−−) where cuts do not compose well with many other operations. For example, suppose that code executing within a transaction cuts to some stack frame outside the transaction. The underlying transactional memory system would not get notified and this is sure to cause problems during subsequent execution. By using a VSE per transaction, the transactional memory system in Pillar is notified when a cut attempts to bypass it and can run code to abort or restart the transaction. Since cuts in Pillar compose well with all the features of Pillar, we call them *composable cuts*.

Stack walking: The Pillar language itself has no keywords for stack walking, but the Pillar runtime provides an interface for iterating over the stack frames of a particular thread. Pillar has the `also unwinds to` annotation on a function call for providing a list of continuations that can be accessed during a stack walk. This is useful for implementing exception propagation using stack walking, as is typical in C++, Java, and C# implementations.

Spans: Spans are a mechanism for associating specific metadata with call sites within a syntactic region of code, which can be looked up during stack walking.

Root-set enumeration: Pillar adds a primitive type called `ref` that is used for declaring local variables that should be reported as roots to the garbage collector. During stack walking these roots can be enumerated. The `ref` type may also contain additional parameters that describe how the garbage collector should treat the reference: e.g., as a direct object pointer versus an interior pointer, as a weak root, or as a tagged union that conditionally contains a root. These parameters have meaning only to the garbage collector, and are not interpreted by Pillar or its runtime. If `ref`s escape to unmanaged code, they must be wrapped and enumerated specially, similar to what is done in Java for JNI object handles.

Tail calls: The `tailcall` keyword before a function call specifies a proper tail call: the current stack frame is destroyed and replaced with the callee's new frame.

Calls between managed and unmanaged code: All Pillar function declarations are implicitly tagged with the *pillar* attribute. The Pillar compiler also understands a special pragma that suppresses the *pillar* attribute on function declarations; this pragma is used when including standard C header files or defining non-Pillar functions.[1] Calling conventions and other interfacing depend on the presence or absence of the *pillar* attribute in both the caller and callee, and the Pillar compiler generates calls accordingly.

Note that spans, second-class continuations, and stack walking are C-- constructs and are described in more detail in the C-- specification [6].

2.2 Concurrency Features

Pillar currently provides three mechanisms for creating new logical threads: `pcall`, `prscall`, and `fcall`. Adding the `pcall` keyword in front of a call to a function with a void return type creates a new child thread, whose entry point is the target function. Execution in the original parent thread continues immediately with the statement following the `pcall`. Any synchronization or transfer of results between the two threads should use global variables or parameters passed to the `pcall` target function.

The `prscall` keyword is semantically identical to `pcall`, but implements a *parallel-ready sequential call* [7]. Prscalls allow programs to specify potential parallelism without incurring the overhead of spawning parallel threads if all processors are already busy. A `prscall` initially starts running the child thread as a sequential call (the parent is suspended). However, if a processor becomes free, it can start executing the parent in parallel with the child. Thus, `prscalls` are nearly as cheap as normal procedure calls, but take advantage of free processors when they become available.

---

[1] One particularly pleasing outcome of this syntax is that managed Pillar code and unmanaged C code can coexist within the same source files.

The fcall construct can be used to parallelize programs that have certain serializable semantics. The fcall annotation indicates that the call may be executed concurrently with its continuation, while allowing the call to be eagerly or lazily serialized if the compiler or runtime deems it unprofitable to parallelize it. The st parameter to the fcall is a synchronization variable, called a future, that indicates the status of the call: *empty* indicates that the call has not yet been started, *busy* indicates that the call is currently being computed, and *full* indicates that the call has completed. Two forcing operations are provided for futures: ftouch and fwait. If the future is full, both return immediately; if the future is empty, both cause the call to be run sequentially in the forcing thread; if the future is busy, fwait blocks until the call completes while ftouch returns immediately. The serializability requirement holds if, for each future, its first ftouch or fwait can be safely replaced by a call to the future's target function.

Both prscall and fcall are geared toward an execution environment where programs have a great deal of available fine-grain concurrency, with the expectation that the vast majority of calls can be executed sequentially within their parents' context instead of creating and destroying a separate thread.

These three keywords take an additional *affinity* parameter [8] that helps the scheduler place related threads close to each other to, e.g., improve memory locality.

Pillar provides support for transactions. A syntactic block of code is marked as a transaction, and transaction blocks may be nested. Within the transaction block, transactional memory accesses are specially annotated, and a continuation is specified as the "handler" for those situations where the underlying transactional memory system needs the program to respond to situations like a data conflict or a user retry.

The concurrency constructs described so far relate to lightweight thread-level parallelism. To support data parallelism, we intend to add Ct primitives [9] to Pillar. These primitives express a variety of nested data-parallel operations, and their semantics allow the compiler to combine and optimize multiple such operations.

3   Compiler and Runtime Architecture

The design of the Pillar language and runtime has several consequences for the Pillar compiler's code generation. In this section, we discuss some of the key interactions between the compiler-generated code and the runtime before getting into more detailed discussion of the compiler and the runtime in the following sections.

We assume that threads are scheduled cooperatively: that they periodically yield control to each other by executing yield check operations. Our experience shows that cooperative preemption offers several performance advantages over traditional preemptive scheduling in multi-core platforms [3]. The Pillar compiler is expected to generate a yield check at each method entry and backward branch, a well-known technique that ensures yielding within a bounded time. In addition to timeslice management, cooperative preemption is used on a running thread to get race-free access to a target thread's stack, for operations like root-set enumeration and prscall continuation stealing.

As we explain in Section 5, our prscall design allows threads to run out of stack space. This requires compiled code to perform an explicit limit check in the method

Compiler phase	Pillar changes	Percentage of compiler code	GC-related Pillar changes
Front-end	5 Kloc	1.2%	5.8%
Middle-end	6 Kloc	0.5%	1.2%
Back-end	11 Kloc	4.2%	20.7%
Total	22 Kloc	1.3%	12.0%

Fig. 3. Compiler modification statistics

prolog, jumping to a special stack extension routine if there is insufficient space for this method's stack frame. This strategy for inserting such copious limit and yield checks is likely to have a noticeable performance impact; future research will focus on mitigating these costs.

Stack walking operations like span lookup, root-set enumeration, and single-frame unwinding require the compiler to generate additional metadata for each call site. One approach would be to dictate a particular metadata format that a Pillar compiler must adhere to. Another approach, which we adopted, is to let the Pillar compiler decide on its own metadata format, and to specify a runtime interface for metadata-based operations. This means that the Pillar compiler also needs to provide its own library of metadata-decoding operations to be linked into Pillar applications, and the Pillar runtime calls those routines as necessary. We favor this latter approach because it gives the compiler more flexibility in generating optimized code.

4   The Pillar Compiler

We implemented our prototype Pillar compiler by modifying Intel's product C compiler. The compiler consists of a front-end, middle-end, and back-end, all of which we modified to support Pillar. Fig. 3 shows the number of lines of source code (LOC) changed or added, as well as the percentage of those source lines compared to those of the original code base. The front-end modifications are relatively small, limited to recognizing new Pillar lexical and syntax elements and translating them into the high-level intermediate representation (IR). In the middle- and back-end, our changes included adding new attributes and nodes to the existing IR and propagating them through compilation phases, as well as generating additional metadata required at run time. In addition, we added new internal data structures to accommodate Pillar constructs (e.g., continuations) and the necessary new analyses and phases (e.g., GC-related analysis).

Some Pillar constructs are implemented as simple mappings to Pillar runtime routines. These include some explicit Pillar language constructs, such as `cut to`, `pcall`, `prscall`, and `fcall`, as well as implicit operations such as stack limit checks, stack extension, yield checks, and managed and unmanaged transitions. The compiler may partially or fully inline calls to the runtime routines to improve performance. Fig. 4 gives an example showing how the compiler deals with some of these constructs:

1. The compiler calculates the function's frame size and generates the stack limit check and extension in the prolog (line 5).

2. For cooperative scheduling, the compiler needs to generate the yield check in the prolog and at loop back-edges (line 5 & 11).
3. For Pillar concurrency constructs (`pcall`, `prscall`, and `fcall`), the compiler maps them to corresponding Pillar runtime interface functions (line 9).
4. When calling unmanaged C functions, the compiler automatically generates the transition call to the runtime routine `prtInvokeUnmanaged` (line 10).

Other Pillar constructs required deeper compiler changes. Continuation data structures must be allocated on the stack and initialized at the appropriate time. The continuation code itself must have a *continuation prolog* that fixes up the stack after a cut operation and copies continuation arguments to the right places. Continuations also affect intra-method control flow and register allocation decisions. The VSE and TRANSACTION constructs require control-flow edges into and out of the region being split so that a VSE is always pushed upon entry and popped upon exit (the push and pop operations are implemented as inlinable calls to the Pillar runtime). For every call site, the compiler must generate metadata to support runtime stack walking operations, such as unwinding a single frame, producing span data, and producing the set of live GC references. Tracking live GC references constitutes the most invasive set of changes to a C compiler, as the new `ref` type must be maintained through all IR generation and optimization phases. GC-related changes account for about 20% of the Pillar modifications in the back-end, and a very small fraction of the front-end and middle-end changes.

Some Pillar constructs need special treatment when implementing function inlining. First, the compiler cannot inline functions containing `tailcall`. Second, if the compiler decides to inline a call, and that call site contains explicit or implicit `also cuts to` and `also unwinds to` annotations, then all call sites within the inlined method inherit these annotations. (Implicit `also cuts to` annotations arise from calls inside a VSE or TRANSACTION construct—there is an implicit cut edge to the destructor continuation.) Third, the compiler needs to maintain extra metadata to support intra-frame unwinding, to ensure that the stack trace looks identical regardless of inlining decisions.

Even though some deep compiler changes were required, we are pleased that the changes only amounted to about 1–2% of the code base of a highly-optimizing

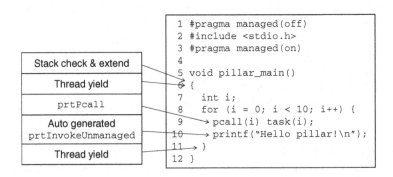

```
1  #pragma managed(off)
2  #include <stdio.h>
3  #pragma managed(on)
4
5  void pillar_main()
6  {
7      int i;
8      for (i = 0; i < 10; i++) {
9          pcall(i) task(i);
10         printf("Hello pillar!\n");
11     }
12 }
```

Stack check & extend

Thread yield

prtPcall

Auto generated
prtInvokeUnmanaged

Thread yield

Fig. 4. A Pillar example

production C compiler, and that they preserved the compiler's traditional optimizations.[2] Of those changes, about 12% overall were related to GC, which is the single most invasive Pillar feature to implement. We believe that Pillar support could be added to other optimizing compilers at a similarly low cost.

One limitation of basing the Pillar compiler on an existing large C compiler is that we are constrained to using Pillar constructs that can be fitted onto C. It would be hard, for example, for us to support struct layout control or multiple return values. The more non-C features we choose to support, the more work we would incur in modifying the compiler to support them. We believe we have chosen a reasonable point in the language design space for Pillar.

5 The Pillar Runtime

The Pillar runtime (PRT) provides services such as stack walking, root-set enumeration, parallel calls, stack management, and virtual stack support to compiled Pillar code and to an LSR. It is built on top of McRT [3], which the PRT relies on primarily for its scheduling and synchronization services, as well as its software transactional memory implementation [10]. The PRT interface is nearly independent of the underlying hardware: its architecture-specific properties include registers in the stack frame information returned by the stack walking support, and the machine word size. The remainder of this section provides some details on how the PRT supports its services.

5.1 Stack Walking and Root-Set Enumeration

The PRT provides support for walking the stack of a thread and enumerating the GC roots in its frames. To do this, PRT functions are called to (cooperatively) suspend the target thread, read the state of its topmost managed frame, then repeatedly step to the next older frame until no frames remain. At each frame, other functions can access that frame's instruction pointer, callee-saved registers, and GC roots. An additional function enumerates any roots that may be present in the thread's VSEs.

Stack walking is complicated by the need to unwind the stack in the presence of interleaved managed and unmanaged frames. The PRT does not presume to understand the layout of unmanaged stack frames, which may vary from compiler to compiler. Instead, it uses the VSE mechanism to mark contiguous regions of the stack corresponding to unmanaged code, and skips over the entire region during unwinding.

5.2 Composable Cuts

The PRT provides the implementation of composable cuts. These operate much like simple cuts but execute any destructor or cleanup operations of intervening VSEs.

Each thread contains a *virtual stack* of VSEs, in which the thread explicitly maintains a pointer to the virtual stack top, and each VSE contains a link to the next VSE on the stack. The continuation data structure also contains a slot for the virtual stack top. The

---

[2] Note, however, that a couple of optimization phases have not yet been made Pillar-safe, and are currently disabled.

PRT provides interfaces to push and pop VSEs. When a continuation is created, the current virtual stack top is stored in the continuation. Later, if a cut is made to this continuation, the PRT compares the current virtual stack top against the value saved in the target continuation. If these are the same, the PRT cuts directly to the target continuation. If they differ, one or more intervening frames require cleanup, and the PRT instead cuts directly to the destructor of the topmost VSE on the virtual stack, passing the original target continuation as an argument. When each VSE destructor is executed, it does its cleanup, removes itself from the virtual stack, then does another cut to the original target continuation passed to the destructor. This sequence continues until the target continuation is reached.

5.3 Prscalls

The Pillar compiler translates a `prscall` into a call to the PRT's prscall interface function. This function pushes a prscall VSE onto the virtual stack, copies arguments, and calls the prscall's child. Thus the child immediately starts executing sequentially. Later, an idle thread looking for work may steal the remainder of the parent's execution (unfortunately also called the parent's "continuation") by setting a continuation-stolen flag and restarting the parent. When the child terminates, it checks the continuation-stolen flag to determine whether to return to the parent or to simply exit because the continuation was stolen.

Our `prscall` design has interesting implications for stack management. When a `prscall` continuation is stolen, the stack becomes split between the parent and child threads, with the parent and child each owning one contiguous half. Since a stack can contain an arbitrary number of active `prscalls`, each of which can be stolen, a stack can become subdivided arbitrarily finely, leaving threads with tiny stacks that will quickly overflow. To deal with this, the Pillar runtime allows a thread to allocate a new "extension" stack (or "stacklet") to hold newer stack frames.

The PRT provides a stack extension wrapper that allocates a new stack (with an initial reference count of one), calls the target function, and deallocates the stack when the function returns. The stack extension wrapper also pushes a VSE whose destructor ensures that the stack will be properly deallocated in the event of a cut operation. To support stack sharing, each full stack contains a reference count word indicating how many threads are using a portion of the stack.

Logically, each `prscall` results in a new thread, regardless of whether the child runs sequentially or in parallel with its parent. When managing locks, those threads should have distinct and persistent thread identifiers, to prevent problems with the same logical thread acquiring a lock in the parent under one thread ID and releasing it under a different ID (the same is true for `pcall` and `fcall`). Each thread's persistent logical ID is stored in thread-local storage, and locking data structures must be modified to use the logical thread ID instead of a low-level thread ID. This logical thread ID is constructed simply as the address of a part of the thread's most recent pcall or prscall VSE. As such, the IDs are unique across all logical threads, and persistent over the lifetimes of the logical threads.

5.4 Fcalls

The Pillar compiler translates an `fcall` into a call to the PRT's future creation function. This function creates a future consisting of a status field (empty/busy/full) and a "thunk" that contains the future's arguments and function pointer, and adds the future to the current processor's future queue. Subsequently, if a call to `ftouch` or `fwait` is made and the future's status is empty, it is immediately executed in the current thread.

At startup, the PRT creates one future pool thread for each logical processor and pins each thread to the corresponding processor. Moreover, the PRT creates a future queue for each future pool thread. A future pool thread tries to run futures from its own queue, but if the queue is empty, it will try to steal futures from other queues to balance system load.

Once the future has been evaluated, the future's thunk portion is no longer needed. To reclaim these, the PRT represents futures using a thunk structure and a separate status structure. These point to each other until the thunk is evaluated, after which the thunk memory is released. The memory for the status structure is under the control of the Pillar program, which may allocate the status structure in places such as the stack, the malloc heap, or the GC heap. We use this two-part structure so that the key part of the future structure may be automatically managed by the GC while minimizing the PRT's knowledge of the existence or implementation of the GC.

6 Experience Using Pillar

This section describes our experience using Pillar to implement three programming languages having a range of different characteristics. These languages are Java, IBM's X10, and an implicitly-parallel functional language.

6.1 Compiling Java to Pillar

As part of our initial efforts, we attempted to validate the overall Pillar design through a simple Java-to-Pillar converter (JPC), leveraging our existing Java execution environment, the Open Runtime Platform (ORP) [11]. Given a trace of the Java classes and methods encountered during the execution of a program, the JPC generates Pillar code for each method from its bytecodes in the method's Java class file.

The resulting code exercises many Pillar features. First, Java variables of reference types are declared using the `ref` primitive type. Second, spans are used to map Pillar functions to Java method identifiers, primarily for the purpose of generating stack traces. They are also used, in conjunction with the `also unwinds to` annotation, to represent exception regions and handlers. Third, when an exception is thrown, ORP uses Pillar runtime functions to walk the stack and find a suitable handler, in the form of an `also unwinds to` continuation. When the continuation is found, ORP simply invokes a `cut to` operation. Fourth, VSEs are used for synchronized methods. Java semantics require that when an exception is thrown past a synchronized method, the lock is released before the exception handler begins. A synchronized method is wrapped inside a VSE whose cleanup releases the lock. Fifth, Java threads are started via the `pcall` construct. Sixth, Pillar's managed/unmanaged transitions are used for implementing JNI calls and other calls into the ORP virtual machine.

Although several Pillar features were not exercised by the JPC, it was still effective in designing and debugging the Pillar software stack, particularly the Pillar compiler that was subjected to hundreds of thousands of lines of JPC-generated code.

6.2   Compiling X10 to Pillar

X10 is a new object-oriented parallel language designed for high-performance computing being developed by IBM as part of the DARPA HPCS program [12]. It is similar to Java but with changes and extensions for high-performance parallel programming. It includes asynchronous threads, multidimensional arrays, transactional memory, futures, a notion of locality (places), and distribution of large data sets.

We selected X10 because it contains a number of parallel constructs not in our other efforts, such as places, data distributions, and clocks. We also want to experiment with thread affinity, data placement, optimizing for locality, and scheduling. X10, unlike our other languages, is a good language in which to do this experimentation.

We currently compile X10 by combining IBM's open-source reference implementation of X10 [13] with the Java-to-Pillar converter. We are able to compile and execute a number of small X10 programs, and this has substantially exercised Pillar beyond that of the Java programs. In the future we will experiment with affinity and data placement.

6.3   Compiling a Concurrent Functional Language

Pillar is also being used as the target of a compiler for a new experimental functional language. Functional languages perform computation in a largely side-effect-free fashion, which means that a great deal of the computational work in a program can be executed concurrently with minimal or no programmer intervention [14,15].

Previous work has compiled functional languages to languages such as C [16], Java byte codes [17,18], and the Microsoft Common Language Runtime (CLR) [19]. These attempts reported benefits such as interoperability, portability, and ease of compiler development. However, they have also noted the mismatches between the functional languages and the different target languages. The inability to control the object model in Java and CLR, the lack of proper tail calls, the restrictions of type safety in Java and CLR, and the inability to do precise garbage collection naturally in C, all substantially complicate compiler development and hurt performance of the final code.

`C--` and Pillar are designed to avoid these problems and provide an easy-to-target platform for functional languages. Like the Java-to-Pillar converter, our experience with the functional language showed Pillar to be an excellent target language. Pillar's lack of a fixed object model, its support for proper tail calls, and its root-set enumeration all made implementing our functional language straightforward. Also, since Pillar is a set of C extensions, we implement most of our lowest IR directly as C preprocessor macros, and generating Pillar from this IR is straightforward. We can include C header files for standard libraries and components (e.g., the garbage collector) coded in C, and Pillar automatically interfaces the Pillar and C code. Pillar's second-class continuations are used to provide a specialized control-flow construct of the language. The stack walking-based exceptions of Java and CLR would be too heavyweight for this purpose, and

C's setjmp/longjmp mechanism is difficult to use correctly and hinders performance. Implementing accurate GC in the converter is as easy as in the Java-to-Pillar converter—simply a matter of marking roots as refs and using the Pillar stack walking and root-set enumeration support.

7 Related Work

The closest language effort to Pillar is C-- [4,5,6]. C-- is intended as a low-level target language for compilers—it has often been described as a "portable assembler". Almost all Pillar features can be expressed in C--, but we designed Pillar to be slightly higher level than C--. Pillar includes, for example, refs and threads instead of (as C-- would) just the mechanisms to implement them. We also designed Pillar as extensions to C, rather than directly using C--, to leverage existing C compilers.

LLVM [20] is another strong and ongoing research effort whose goal is to provide a flexible compiler infrastructure with a common compiler target language. LLVM's design is focused on supporting different compiler optimizations, while Pillar is aimed at simplifying new language implementations, in part by integrating readily into an existing highly-optimizing compiler. Comparing language features, the most important differences between Pillar and LLVM are that LLVM lacks second-class continuations, spans, pcalls, prscalls, and fcalls.

C# and CLI [21,22] are often used as intermediate languages for compiling high-level languages, and early on we considered them as the basis for Pillar. However, they lack second-class continuations, spans, prscalls, and fcalls. Furthermore, they are too restrictive in that they impose a specific object model and type-safety rules.

Pillar uses ideas from or similar to other projects seeking to exploit fine-grained parallelism without creating too many heavyweight threads. Pillar's prscalls are taken directly from Goldstein's parallel-ready sequential calls [7], which were designed to reduce the cost of creating threads yet make effective use of processors that become idle during execution. Also, like Cilk [23] and Lea's Java fork/join framework [24], Pillar uses work stealing to make the most use of available hardware resources and to balance system load. Furthermore, during prscall continuation stealing, Pillar tries to steal the earlier (deeper) continuations as Cilk does, since seizing large amounts of work tends to reduce later stealing costs. Pillar's future implementation differs from the lazy futures of Zhang et al. [25], which are implemented using a lazy-thread creation scheme similar to Pillar's prscalls. Since Pillar supports both prscalls and a separate future pool-based implementation, it will be interesting to compare the performance of both schemes for implementing futures.

8 Summary

We have described the design of the Pillar software infrastructure, consisting of the Pillar language, the Pillar compiler, and the Pillar runtime, as well as the high-level converter that translates programs from a high-level parallel language into Pillar. By defining the Pillar language as a small set of extensions to the C language, we were able to create an optimizing Pillar compiler by modifying only 1–2% of an existing optimizing C compiler. Pillar's thread-creation constructs, designed for a high-level converter that can find a great deal of concurrency opportunities, are optimized for sequential execution to minimize thread creation and destruction costs. Pillar's sequential constructs, many of which are taken from C--, have proven to be a good target for languages with modern features, such as Java and functional languages.

Our future work includes adding support for nested data parallel operations [9] to efficiently allow parallel operations over collections of data. In addition, although we currently assume a shared global address space, we plan to investigate Pillar support for distributed address spaces and message passing.

We are still in the early stages of using Pillar, but our experience to date is positive—it has simplified our implementation of high-level parallel languages, and we expect it to significantly aid experimentation with new parallel language features and implementation techniques.

Acknowledgements

We have engaged in many hours of discussions with Norman Ramsey and John Dias of Harvard University, and Simon Peyton Jones of Microsoft Research, on issues regarding Pillar and C--. These discussions have been instrumental in focusing the design of Pillar. We also thank the reviewers for their feedback on this paper.

References

1. GNU: The GNU Compiler Collection, http://gcc.gnu.org/
2. Open64: The Open Research Compiler, http://www.open64.net/
3. Saha, B., Adl-Tabatabai, A., Ghuloum, A., Rajagopalan, M., Hudson, R., Petersen, L., Menon, V., Murphy, B., Shpeisman, T., Sprangle, E., Rohillah, A., Carmean, D., Fang, J.: Enabling Scalability and Performance in a Large Scale CMP Environment. In: EuroSys (March 2007)
4. Peyton Jones, S., Nordin, T., Oliva, D.: C–: A portable assembly language. In: Implementing Functional Languages 1997 (1997)
5. Peyton Jones, S., Ramsey, N.: A single intermediate language that supports multiple implementations of exceptions. In: Proceedings of the SIGPLAN 2000 Conference on Programming Language Design and Implementation (June 2000)
6. Ramsey, N., Peyton Jones, S., Lindig, C.: The C– language specification, version 2.0 (February 2005), http://cminusminus.org/papers.html
7. Goldstein, S.C., Schauser, K.E., Culler, D.E.: Lazy threads: implementing a fast parallel call. Journal of Parallel and Distributed Computing 37(1), 5–20 (1996)
8. Rajagopalan, M., Lewis, B.T., Anderson, T.A.: Thread Scheduling for Multi-Core Platforms. In: HotOS 2007: Proceedings of the Eleventh Workshop on Hot Topics in Operating Systems (May 2007)
9. Ghuloum, A., Sprangle, E., Fang, J.: Flexible Parallel Programming for Tera-scale Architectures with Ct (2007), http://www.intel.com/research/platform/terascale/TeraScale_whitepaper.pdf

10. Saha, B., Adl-Tabatabai, A.R., Hudson, R.L., Minh, C.C., Hertzberg, B.: McRT-STM: a high performance software transactional memory system for a multi-core runtime. In: PPoPP 2006: Proceedings of the eleventh ACM SIGPLAN symposium on Principles and practice of parallel programming, pp. 187–197. ACM Press, New York (2006)

11. Cierniak, M., Eng, M., Glew, N., Lewis, B., Stichnoth, J.: Open Runtime Platform: A Flexible High-Performance Managed Runtime Environment. Intel Technology Journal 7(1) (February 2003), http://www.intel.com/technology/itj/archive/2003.htm

12. Charles, P., Grothoff, C., Saraswat, V., Donawa, C., Kielstra, A., Ebcioglu, K., von Praun, C., Sarkar, V.: X10: An Object-Oriented Approach to Non-Uniform Cluster Computing. In: OOPSLA 2005: Proceedings of the 20th Annual ACM SIGPLAN Conference on Object Oriented Programming, Systems, Languages, and Applications, pp. 519–538. ACM Press, New York (2005)

13. IBM: The Experimental Concurrent Programming Language X10. SourceForge (2007), http://x10.sourceforge.net/x10home.shtml

14. Harris, T., Marlow, S., Peyton Jones, S.: Haskell on a shared-memory multiprocessor. In: Haskell 2005: Proceedings of the 2005 ACM SIGPLAN workshop on Haskell, pp. 49–61. ACM Press, New York (2005)

15. Hicks, J., Chiou, D., Ang, B.S.: Arvind: Performance studies of Id on the Monsoon Dataflow System. Journal of Parallel and Distributed Computing 18(3), 273–300 (1993)

16. Tarditi, D., Lee, P., Acharya, A.: No assembly required: compiling standard ML to C. ACM Letters on Programming Languages and Systems 1(2), 161–177 (1992)

17. Benton, N., Kennedy, A., Russell, G.: Compiling standard ML to Java bytecodes. In: ICFP 1998: Proceedings of the third ACM SIGPLAN international conference on Functional programming, pp. 129–140. ACM Press, New York (1998)

18. Serpette, B.P., Serrano, M.: Compiling Scheme to JVM bytecode: a performance study. In: ICFP 2002: Proceedings of the seventh ACM SIGPLAN international conference on Functional programming, pp. 259–270. ACM Press, New York (2002)

19. Benton, N., Kennedy, A., Russo, C.V.: Adventures in interoperability: the sml.net experience. In: PPDP 2004: Proceedings of the 6th ACM SIGPLAN international conference on Principles and practice of declarative programming, pp. 215–226. ACM Press, New York (2004)

20. Lattner, C., Adve, V.: LLVM: A Compilation Framework for Lifelong Program Analysis & Transformation. In: Proceedings of the 2004 International Symposium on Code Generation and Optimization (CGO 2004), Palo Alto, California (March 2004)

21. ECMA: Common Language Infrastructure. ECMA (2002), http://www.ecma-international.org/publications/Standards/ecma-335.htm

22. ISO: ISO/IEC 23270 (C$^{\#}$). ISO/IEC standard (2003)

23. Blumofe, R.D., Joerg, C.F., Kuszmaul, B.C., Leiserson, C.E., Randall, K.H., Zhou, Y.: Cilk: An Efficient Multithreaded Runtime System. Journal of Parallel and Distributed Computing 37(1), 55–69 (1996)

24. Lea, D.: A Java Fork/Join Framework. In: Proceedings of the ACM 2000 Java Grande Conference, pp. 36–43. ACM Press, New York (2000)

25. Zhang, L., Krintz, C., Soman, S.: Efficient Support of Fine-grained Futures in Java. In: PDCS 2006: IASTED International Conference on Parallel and Distributed Computing and Systems (November 2006)

Associative Parallel Containers in STAPL⋆

Gabriel Tanase, Chidambareswaran Raman, Mauro Bianco, Nancy M. Amato, and Lawrence Rauchwerger

Parasol Lab, Dept. of Computer Science, Texas A&M University
{gabrielt,chids,bmm,amato,rwerger}@cs.tamu.edu

Abstract. The Standard Template Adaptive Parallel Library (STAPL) is a parallel programming framework that extends C++ and STL with support for parallelism. STAPL provides a collection of parallel data structures (pContainers) and algorithms (pAlgorithms) and a generic methodology for extending them to provide customized functionality. STAPL pContainers are thread-safe, concurrent objects, i.e., shared objects that provide parallel methods that can be invoked concurrently. They also provide appropriate interfaces that can be used by generic pAlgorithms. In this work, we present the design and implementation of the STAPL associative pContainers: pMap, pSet, pMultiMap, pMultiSet, pHashMap, and pHashSet. These containers provide optimal insert, search, and delete operations for a distributed collection of elements based on keys. Their methods include counterparts of the methods provided by the STL associative containers, and also some asynchronous (non-blocking) variants that can provide improved performance in parallel. We evaluate the performance of the STAPL associative pContainers on an IBM Power5 cluster, an IBM Power3 cluster, and on a linux-based Opteron cluster, and show that the new pContainer asynchronous methods, generic pAlgorithms (e.g., pfind) and a sort application based on associative pContainers, all provide good scalability on more than 10^3 processors.

1 Introduction

Parallel programming is becoming mainstream due to the increased availability of multiprocessor and multicore architectures and the need to solve larger and more complex problems. To help programmers address the difficulties of parallel programming, we are developing the Standard Template Adaptive Parallel Library (STAPL) [1,21,23]. STAPL is a parallel C++ library with functionality similar to STL, the ANSI adopted C++ Standard Template Library [18]. STL is a collection of basic algorithms, containers and iterators that can be used as high-level building blocks for sequential applications. Similar to STL, STAPL provides a collection of parallel algorithms (pAlgorithms), parallel containers (pContainers), and views to abstract the data access in pContainers. These are the building blocks for writing parallel programs. An important goal of STAPL

⋆ This work supported in part by NSF (EIA-0103742, ACR-0081510, ACR-0113971, CCR-0113974, EIA-9810937, ACI-0326350, CRI-0551685), the DOE and HP.

V. Adve, M.J. Garzarán, and P. Petersen (Eds.): LCPC 2007, LNCS 5234, pp. 156–171, 2008.

is to provide a high productivity development environment for applications that can execute efficiently on a wide spectrum of parallel and distributed systems.

Contribution. In this work, we present the STAPL *associative* pContainers, a set of data structures intended to be used as parallel counterparts of the STL associative containers. The STAPL associative pContainers provide interfaces for the efficient storage and retrieval of their distributed data based on keys. The STAPL associative pContainers are thread-safe, concurrent objects, i.e., shared objects that provide parallel methods that can be invoked concurrently. They also provide appropriate interfaces (views) that can be used to access their distributed elements efficiently in parallel by generic pAlgorithms. The methods of the STAPL associative containers include counterparts of the methods provided by the STL associative containers, insert, erase, and find, and also some asynchronous (non-blocking) variants, insert_async and erase_async, that can provide improved performance in parallel.

We present the design and implementation of the STAPL associative pContainers: pMap, pSet, pMultiMap, pMultiSet, pHashMap, and pHashSet. We provide a unified framework for constructing thread-safe, distributed and shared STAPL associative pContainers from their corresponding STL counterparts. Our performance evaluation on an IBM Power5 cluster, a large IBM Power3 cluster and on a linux-based Opteron cluster show that the new pContainer asynchronous methods, insert_async and erase_async, generic pAlgorithms (e.g., pfind), and a sort application based on an associative pContainer provide good scalability and low overhead relative to their sequential counterparts.

Outline. The rest of this document is structured as follows: we provide an overview of related work in Section 2, give a high level description of the STAPL library in Section 3, introduce the STAPL associative pContainers in Section 4, and present experimental results in Section 5.

2   Related Work

There has been significant research in the field of parallel and concurrent data structures. Much work has focused on providing efficient locking mechanisms and methodologies for transforming existing sequential data structures into concurrent data structures [6,7,8,10,17]. Investigations of concurrent hash tables [7,8,17] and search trees (the most common internal representation for maps and sets) [15,16] explore efficient storage schemes, different lock implementations, and different locking strategies (e.g., critical sections, non-blocking, wait-free [10]), especially in the context of shared memory architectures. In contrast, STAPL associative pContainers are designed for use in both shared and distributed memory environments, and we focus on developing an infrastructure that will efficiently provide a shared memory abstraction for pContainers (called a shared object view in STAPL) by automating aspects relating to the data distribution and management. We use a compositional approach where data structures (sequential or concurrent) can be used as building blocks for implementing pContainers.

There are several parallel languages and libraries that have similar goals as STAPL[2,3,5,9,14,19]. While a large amount of effort has been put into making array-based data structures suitable for parallel programming, associative data structures have not received as much attention. The PSTL (Parallel Standard Template Library) project [12,13] explored the same underlying philosophy as STAPL of extending the C++ STL for parallel programming. PSTL provided distributed associative containers with support for specifying data distributions and local and global iterators for data access. STAPL differs from PSTL by providing an integrated framework for all associative pContainers, which also allows users to customize the default behavior, such as specifying different data distributions. PSTL is not an active project. Intel Threading Building Blocks (TBB) [11] provide thread-safe containers such as vectors, queues and hashmaps for shared memory architectures. The TBB *concurrent_hash_map* maps keys to values and the interface provided resembles that of a typical STL associative container, but with some modifications to support concurrent access. In STAPL all associative containers provide both STL compatible interfaces and additional interfaces optimized for parallelism. While TBB was inspired by STAPL, our work is distinguished from TBB in that we target both shared and distributed memory systems. Chapel is a new programming language developed by Cray that is focused on reducing the complexity of parallel programming [4]. The language proposes a formal approach for containers and data distributions, and provides default data distributions and specifies a methodology for integrating new ones. Also, although Chapel mentions associative domains, it does not appear to support multiple associative containers at this point. Finally, STAPL differs from Chapel and other parallel languages in that it is a library.

3   STAPL Overview

STAPL consists of a set of components that include pContainers, pAlgorithms, views, pRanges, and a runtime system (see Figure 1). pContainers, the distributed counterpart of STL containers, are thread-safe, concurrent objects, i.e., shared objects that provide parallel methods that can be invoked concurrently. While all pContainers provide *sequentially equivalent interfaces* that are compatible with the corresponding STL methods, individual pContainers may introduce additional methods to exploit the performance offered by parallelism and by the runtime system. pContainers have a *data distribution* manager that provides the programmer with a *shared object view* that presents a uniform access interface regardless of the physical location of the data. Thread-safety is guaranteed by providing mechanisms that guarantee all operations leave the pContainer in a consistent state. Important aspects of all STAPL components are *extendability* and *composability*, e.g., the pContainers implemented within the framework allow users to extend and specialize them for performance, and to use pContainers of pContainers. Specialization is one avenue to improve performance in STAPL's layered architecture.

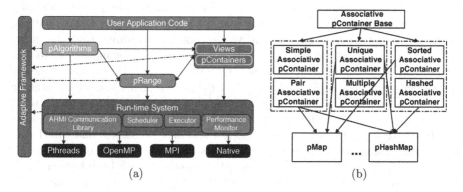

Fig. 1. (a) STAPL components, and (b) associative pContainer hierarchy

pContainer data can be accessed using views which can be seen as generalizations of STL iterators that represent sets of data elements and are not related to the data's physical location. views provide iterators to access individual pContainer elements . Generic parallel algorithms (pAlgorithms) are written in terms of views, similar to how STL algorithms are written in terms of iterators. The pRange is the STAPL concept used to represent a parallel computation. Intuitively, a pRange is a task graph, where each task consists of a work function and a view representing the data on which the work function will be applied. The pRange provides support for specifying data dependencies between tasks that will be enforced during execution.

The runtime system (RTS) and its communication library ARMI (Adaptive Remote Method Invocation [20]) provide the interface to the underlying operating system, native communication library and hardware architecture. ARMI uses the remote method invocation (RMI) communication abstraction to hide the lower level implementations (e.g., MPI, OpenMP, etc.). A remote method invocation in STAPL can be blocking (sync_rmi) or non-blocking (async_rmi). When a sync_rmi is invoked, the calling thread will block until the method executes remotely and returns its results. An async_rmi doesn't specify a return type and the calling thread only initiates the method. The completion of the method happens some time in the future and is handled internally by the RTS. ARMI provides the rmi_fence mechanism to ensure the completion of all previous RMI calls. The asynchronous calls can be aggregated by the RTS in an internal buffer to minimize communication overhead. The buffer size and the aggregation factor impact the performance, and in many cases should be adjusted for the different computational phases of an application. For more details on runtime performance tuning please consult [20,22].

4   Associative pContainers

An associative container provides optimized methods for storing and retrieving data using keys. In STAPL, similar to STL [18], we consider the following six basic associative container concepts: *simple, pair, sorted, hashed, unique* and *multiple*. Simple specifies that the container will store only keys while pair means that the container will store pairs of keys and values. Sorted guarantees that the internal organization allows logarithmic time implementations for insert, delete and find operations, while hashed containers guarantee asymptotic constant time for these operations. In addition, traversing the data of a sorted associative container from begin to end guarantees that the elements are traversed in sorted order. Unique guarantees that all data elements have unique keys, while multi allows for duplicate keys. Each of these concepts specifies properties and interfaces, e.g., simple associative `pContainer` methods have keys in the interface (e.g., sets), while pair associative `pContainers` have methods with both keys and values (e.g., maps), hashed and sorted associative `pContainers` specify complexity requirements, and single or multi specify the semantics of the operations.

Based on this taxonomy, STAPL provides six associative `pContainers` that are compositions of the basic concepts (see Figure 1(b)): `pSet` (simple, sorted, unique), `pMap` (pair, sorted, unique), `pMultiSet` (simple, sorted, multiple), `pMultiMap` (pair, sorted, multiple), `pHashMap` (pair, hashed, unique), and `pHashSet` (simple, hashed, unique). The STAPL associative `pContainers` provide the following generic specification (data types and methods):

- Data Types:
  - `key_type`: the type of the Key
  - `value_type`: the type of the Value (not available for simple)
  - `key_compare`: the type for key comparisons (not available for hashed)
  - `view_type`: the view type
- STL compatible methods:
  - `iterator insert(key[,value])`: insert the (key,value) pair (no value for simple associative). Return iterator pointing to inserted item.
  - `size_t erase(key)`: erases all elements with key equal to k. Return number of erased elements.
  - `iterator find(key)`: Return an iterator pointing to an element with key equal to k or end() if no such element is found.
- New STAPL methods:
  - `void insert_async(key[,value])`, `void erase_async(key)`: non-blocking insert/erase (no `value` for simple associative).
  - `value find_val(key)`: blocking operations returning values (instead of iterators).

All STL equivalent methods require a return type, which in general translates into a synchronous (blocking) method. For this reason, we provide a set of asynchronous methods as part of the associative `pContainer`, e.g., `insert_async` and `erase_async`. These non-blocking methods allow for better communication/computation overlap and enable the STAPL RTS to aggregate messages to reduce the communication overhead.

We also introduce new associative `pContainer` methods that return values instead of iterators. These methods are provided because in STAPL a remote call will be issued when an iterator to a remote element is dereferenced. Hence, if a programmer knows the value will be needed, they should use the method that returns a value rather than the method that returns an iterator.

4.1   Associative pContainer Design and Implementation

The STAPL pContainer framework aims to provide a set of base concepts and a common methodology for the development of thread-safe, concurrent data structures that are extendable and composable. The major concepts in the pContainer framework that provide the support for the properties listed in the previous section are the *global identifier, domain, data distribution, partition, partition_mapping, pContainer component, view* and *pContainerBase*. We define the functionality of these modules in the context of associative pContainers, but they are general and apply to other pContainers.

Global Identifier (GID): In the STAPL pContainer framework, each element is uniquely identified by its GID. This is an important requirement that allows us to provide a shared object view. For a simple associative pContainer the GID associated with each element is a key, whereas it is a (key, m) pair for a multi associative pContainer, where m is an integer used to manage multiplicity.

Domain and Domain Instance: The pContainer *domain* is the universe of possible GIDs that will identify its elements. The domain of the associative pContainer is given by the range of possible keys the pContainer can hold. For example for a pMap over strings the domain can be the set of all possible strings or the set of all possible strings between two boundaries according to some order relation (e.g. lexicographical order). At any instant, there is only a finite set of elements in the container. The GIDs associated with these elements are referred to as the *domain instance* of the pContainer. For example AssociativeDomain<string>('a','k') is a domain comprising all strings that are greater than 'a' and strictly smaller than 'k' according to the lexicographical order. A domain instance corresponding to the previously defined associative domain might be {'a', 'aa', 'abc', 'joe'}. Domain instances are ordered sets to allow their elements to be enumerated or scanned. The enumeration order is specified by implementing two methods: GID get_first_gid() which returns the first GID/index of the set and GID get_next_gid(GID) which returns the GID that immediately follows the one provided as input to the method.

Data Distribution: The Data Distribution is responsible for determining the location where an element associated with a GID is located. A *location* is a component of a parallel machine that has a contiguous memory address space and has associated execution capabilities (e.g., threads). A location can be identified with a process address space. The data distribution manager uses (i) a partition to decide for every key in the domain to which sub-domain it has been allocated, and (ii) a partition-mapper to decide to which location each sub-domain has been allocated.

```
template<class Domain>
class partition_strategy{
  partition_strategy(...);
  //compute the sub-domain
  //to which the GID is associated
  ComponentID map(GID);
}
typedef
  associative_domain<string,
    lexi_compare> Domain;
vector<Domain> doms;
doms.push_back(Domain('a'..'d'));
doms.push_back(Domain('d'..'z'));
partition_strategy(doms);
```

```
1 value associative_pc_base::find(key){
2 Location loc;
3 dist_manager.lookup(key)
4   C_ID = part_strategy.map(key)
5   loc = part_mapper.map(C_ID)
6 if loc is local
7   return component(C_ID).find(key)
8 else
9   return sync_rmi (loc,find(key));
```

(a) Partition Strategy   (b) Implementation of **find()** method

Fig. 2. Interfaces for associative **pContainer** concepts

Partition: The **partition** is a policy class used to specify how a domain is decomposed into sub-domains. The main functionality provided by a **partition** is a mapping from a GID to the *sub-domain* that contains it. Associative **pContainers** are dynamic containers supporting concurrent additions and deletions of elements, thus the corresponding partitioning strategies have to provide functionality to add or delete GIDs to/from the corresponding domain instance or, e.g., to perform repartitions to ensure load balance. The default partition strategy implemented by STAPL sorted associative **pContainers** is a static blocked partition over the key space. Users can provide additional partitions for associative **pContainers** by explicitly enumerating the corresponding sub-domains as illustrated in Figure 2(a). For a hashed associative **pContainer**, the partition can be specified by providing a hash function that will map a key to a sub-domain ID (e.g. **hash(key)%num_subdomains**).

Partition Mapper: A partition is mapped onto a set of locations using a **partition-mapper**, which maps a sub-domain identifier (from 0 to $m-1$) to a location (from 0 to $L-1$). There are two partition mappers currently available in STAPL: **cyclic_mapper**, where sub-domains are distributed cyclically among locations, and **blocked_mapper**, where m/L consecutive sub-domains are mapped to a single location.

pContainer Components: The data corresponding to a sub-domain is stored in *components* within the location where that sub-domain is mapped. The GIDs associated with the stored elements of a component constitute a *sub-domain instance*. There is no data replication. We have implemented the associative **pContainer** components by extending the corresponding sequential container (typically STL containers) with functionality needed to implement domain instances.

Associative pContainer Views: views are defined as the accessors for the data elements stored in the **pContainer**. pAlgorithms in STAPL are written in terms of views, similar to how STL algorithms are written in terms of iterators. A view is defined by an ordered domain of GIDs which is a subset of the domain instance of the pContainer. For all the GIDs of the domain a view provides corresponding iterators that can be used to access the data elements. A view has associated a partition and a partition-mapper to allow parallel processing of the data. The default view provided by a pContainer matches the partition and the mapping of the pContainer data because this view provides the most efficient data access since all the elements in a sub-view are in the same physical location. The views over pMap, pMultiMap, and pHashMap support mutable iterators over data. This allows the value field to be modified. The others (pSet, pMultiSet, and pHashSet) provide read only views with const iterators.

Associative pContainer Base Class: To automate and standardize the process of developing associative pContainers, we designed a common base that is responsible for maintaining the data, the distribution manager, and a default view. The associative pContainer base is generic and uses template parameters and Traits classes to tailor the data structure to the user's needs. Each basic associative concept (simple, pair, unique, multi, sorted, hashed) is implemented as a class derived from the associative pContainer base to provide the specified functionality and enforce the required properties. Each associative pContainer (e.g., pMap), inherits from three corresponding classes as depicted in Figure 1(b).

A typical implementation of a pContainer method is included in Figure 2(b) to illustrate how the pContainer modules interact. The runtime cost of the methods in the associative pContainer interface has three constituents: the time to decide the location and the component where the element is stored, the communication time to get/send the required information, and the time to perform the operation on a component. The time to find the location and the component depends on the partition used. For sorted associative pContainers (pSet, pMap, pMultiSet, and pMultiMap), an optimal search is logarithmic in the number of sub-domains of the partition, while for hashed associative pContainers (pHashSet and pHashMap) it is amortized constant time. The search for location and component IDs is illustrated in Figure 2(b), lines 3-5. The communication time affects only the operations that are executed remotely (Figure 2(d), line 9). For asynchronous operations, this is the time to initiate the RMI call, while for methods that return values it is the time to send the request and to receive the results. The time for performing the operation on the component is logarithmic or amortized constant time for sorted and hashed pContainers, respectively (Figure 2(b), line 7). The memory overhead depends on the partition used. A blocked partition for a sorted pContainer requires space proportional to the number of sub-domains, while for a hashed partition the overhead is constant in each location. Different partitions, with more complex invariants, may incur different computational and memory overheads.

5   Performance Evaluation

In this section, we evaluate the scalability of the parallel methods described in Section 4, we evaluate three generic pAlgorithms, pfind, paccumulate, and pcount, and we consider a simple sorting algorithm as an example of an application based on a STAPL associative pContainer.

5.1 Architectures Used

We evaluated the associative pContainer performance on three architectures. The first system, referred to as P5-CLUSTER, is an IBM HPC cluster consisting of 122 p5-575 nodes, each node with 8 Power5 chips (1.9GHz, 64-bit PowerPC architecture) and 32GB of memory per node. The second system, referred to as P3-CLUSTER, is a 6,656 processor IBM RS/6000 SP system that consists of 416 SMP nodes, each with 16 Power3+ CPUs and where processors on each node have a shared memory pool of between 16 and 64 GB. The third system, referred to as OPTERON-CLUSTER, is a 712-CPU Opteron (2.2 GHz) cluster running the Linux operating system. Processors are organized two on a node with 6GB of memory per node. The nodes are interconnected with a high-speed InfiniBand network. We have used GNU GCC v4 on P5-CLUSTER and OPTERON-CLUSTER and GCC 3.4 on P3-CLUSTER, and the O3 optimization level. All systems are operated by NERSC at Lawrence Berkeley National Laboratory.

5.2 Evaluation of the Associative pContainer Methods

Methodology: We recall from Section 4 that a STAPL associative parallel container provides a set of methods to insert, find and erase elements. We discuss next the performance of the methods and the factors influencing the running time. To evaluate the scalability of individual methods we designed the kernel shown in Figure 3. The figure shows insert_async, but the same kernel is used to evaluate all methods. For a given number of elements N, all P available processors concurrently insert N/P elements. The elements are generated randomly so the resulting data distribution is approximately balanced across the machine. We report the time taken to insert all N elements globally. The measured time includes the cost of an rmi_fence call which is more than a simple barrier. An rmi_fence guarantees that all remote method calls in flight are finished when

```
1  evaluate_performance(N,P){
2      - generate N/P elements in a local vector local_data
3      rmi_fence();              //Barrier
4      tm = stapl::start_timer();    //start timer
5      for(it=local_data.begin(); it != local_data.end(); ++it) {
6          pmap_test.insert_async(*it); //insert N/P elements concurrently
7      }
8      rmi_fence(); //ensure all insert are finished
9      elapsed = stapl::stop_timer(tm); //stop the timer
10     - Reduce elapsed times, getting the max time from all processors.
11     - Report the max time
12     //repeat lines 2-11 for the rest of the methods
```

Fig. 3. Kernel used to evaluate the performance of individual methods provided by associative containers

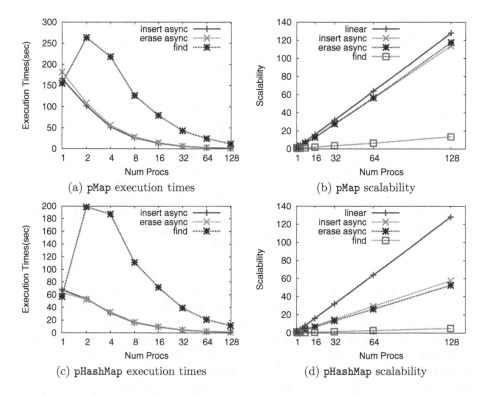

Fig. 4. P5-CLUSTER: Execution times and scalability for (a-b) pMap and (c-d) pHashMap methods with 50 million elements. Results are shown for insert_async, erase_async, and find; the performance of insert and erase is indistinguishable from find.

the method returns. Unless specified, all experiments have been conducted using integer keys. All associative pContainers were evaluated but due to the similarity of the behavior observed and space limitations, we include in this section results only for pMap and pHashMap.

Strong Scaling: In this section we analyze the scalability of the methods using the kernel described in Figure 3. We define scalability as the ratio between the time taken to complete the kernel when using one processor and the time taken when using P processors.

For the strong scaling experiment, the number of elements, N and the number of processors, are chosen differently depending on the architecture. On P5-CLUSTER we used $N = 50$ million elements and the number of processors is varied from 1 to 128. Figure 4 shows the execution times and scalability observed for the pMap and pHashMap methods; since the performance of the synchronous methods (find, insert, and erase) was indistinguishable from each other, only find is shown to simplify the figure. Although the times decrease when increasing the number of processors, the synchronous

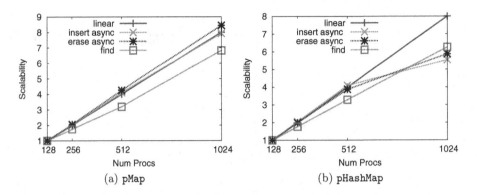

Fig. 5. P3-CLUSTER: Scalability for (a) pMap and (b) pHashMap methods with 400 million elements. Results are shown for insert_async, erase_async, and find; the performance of insert and erase is indistinguishable from find.

methods, insert, erase, and find, show poor scalability. Due to their blocking nature, these methods cannot employ aggregation of messages or overlap communication and computation. In contrast, the asynchronous methods, insert_async and erase_async, exhibit good scalability for both pMap and pHashMap, benefiting from the aggregation and communication/computation overlap support provided by ARMI. Accessing an element in a pMap component requires a number of memory accesses that is logarithmic in the size of the component, while in a pHashMap the number of memory accesses is essentially independent of the size of the component. Hence, since the size of the components decreases as the number of processors increases, the strong scalability of the pMap methods should be higher than for the pHashMap methods. The time for synchronous methods increases from 1 to 2 processors because of the communication overhead, and then shows a steady decline. This is more evident for pHashMap than for pMap since the lower access time for the former makes the communication overhead relatively more significant.

We also evaluated the performance of the pContainer methods on P3-CLUSTER which allows us to study a large number of processors and larger input sizes. In Figure 5 we show results where the pMap and pHashMap methods are executed using 400 million elements and the number of processors varies from 128 to 1024; since the performance of the synchronous methods (find, insert, and erase) was indistinguishable from each other, only find is shown to simplify the figure. The scalability of the pMap asynchronous methods is super-linear, while the pHashMap scalability is sub-linear. The super-linear scalability for the pMap is due to the faster access time for a pMap component as its size decreases, i.e., as the number of processors increases. All synchronous methods show better scalability than on P5-CLUSTER (Figure 4) because the reference point is 128 processors and not 1.

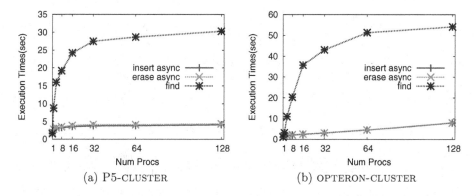

Fig. 6. Execution Times for weak scaling analysis with 1 million elements per processor. Results are shown for `insert_async`, `erase_async`, and `find`; the performance of `insert` and `erase` is indistinguishable from `find`.

Weak Scaling: In this experiment, we modify the input arguments to the test kernel so that each processor concurrently inserts N elements, leading to a total of $N \times P$ operations. We expect the running time to show a slight increase as we increase the number of processors due to the increase in communication overhead. Results for P5-CLUSTER and OPTERON-CLUSTER are shown in Figure 6; since the performance of the synchronous methods (`find`, `insert`, and `erase`) was indistinguishable from each other, only `find` is shown to simplify the figure. We notice an increase in the runtime when going from one (no remote communication) to two processors and the times for the asynchronous methods increase slightly, both as expected. On the OPTERON-CLUSTER the communication is more expensive and the overall running time increases at a faster rate. The synchronous operations do not scale well for small numbers of processors, but improve when the number of processors increases beyond 32. When using more processors, even though the calling thread may be blocked waiting for return values, requests from other threads are served thus improving the rate at which methods are executed by the system.

5.3   Support for Generic Parallel Algorithms

Generic parallel algorithms in STAPL are written in terms of `views`. Associative `pContainers` provide views that can be used to access the data and we study here the performance of generic non-mutating `pAlgorithms` such as `pfind` `pcount`, and `paccumulate` when applied to data in an associative `pContainer`. The `paccumulate` algorithm accumulates in parallel the data in each component followed by a reduction to compute the final result. The `pcount` algorithm is similar but counts the number of data elements that satisfies a given predicate. The `pfind` algorithm finds the iterator corresponding to an input key. Each processor performs a linear search through all elements in its local `pContainer` components and a reduction is performed at the end to return the iterator corresponding to

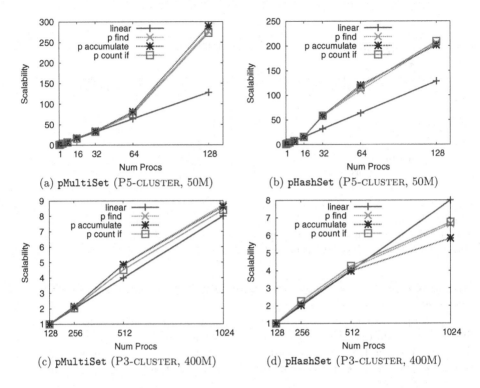

(a) pMultiSet (P5-CLUSTER, 50M)   (b) pHashSet (P5-CLUSTER, 50M)

(c) pMultiSet (P3-CLUSTER, 400M)   (d) pHashSet (P3-CLUSTER, 400M)

Fig. 7. Scalability of generic p_find(), p_count(), and p_accumulate() pAlgorithms on pMultiSet and pHashSet for two architectures and data sizes: (a,b) P5-CLUSTER for 50 million elements, (c,d) P3-CLUSTER for 400 million elements

the first occurrence of the element. We include in Figure 7(a)(b) the scalability of the pAlgorithms on P5-CLUSTER using pMultiSet and pHashSet containers. In Figure 7(c)(d) we show corresponding results on the P3-CLUSTER when using a larger number of processors. The times reported for pfind are for the worst case scenario when the element searched for is not in the pContainer so the entire data space will be scanned. We observe that the algorithms exhibit super-linear speedup. The super-linear speedup is due to the the sequential (STL) containers used in the pContainer components. We performed the following experiment on P5-CLUSTER to verify that our super-linear speedup is justified. We measured sequential std::acumulate on std::multiset and hash_set containers with N=50 million elements and N=50M/128=390625 elements. The running times dropped 217 times for std::multiset and 134 times for hash_set, while the input size was only 128 times smaller.

5.4   Sorting Using Associative pContainers

In this section, we consider a sorting algorithm based on pMultiSet. The algorithm inserts the elements of a view into a pMultiSet which stores the elements

```
p_sort_multiset(INPUT_VIEW view) {
  pair<min, max> = p_min_max_element(view);
  associative_ps = compute_partition_strategy (min, max, P);
  stapl::p_multiset<INPUT_VIEW::data_type> pmultiset(ps);
  - insert in parallel all elements of view into pmultiset;
  - compute prefix sums and align the input view with the
  distribution of the pmultiset
  - copy in parallel from pmultiset back into the input view
  - deallocate the p_multiset
}
```

Fig. 8. Parallel sort using parallel associative containers

in sorted order, followed by a copy of the elements back to the original view; see pseudo-code in Figure 8. We evaluated the scalability of this pAlgorithm on P5-CLUSTER (N=50 million) and P3-CLUSTER (N=400 million) for various number of processors (strong scaling). The input view is defined over a pArray, another pContainer in STAPL[21]. In Figure 9 we see that the algorithm scales fairly well. The sub-linear scalability observed for large number of processors is due to the increased overall communication generated by the main steps of the pAlgorithm (e.g., insert, prefix sums and copy back).

5.5   Overhead of Associative pContainers

One important aspect when introducing a parallel data structure is the run-time overhead added over a corresponding sequential data structure. The run-time overhead depends on the particular container, input sizes, data types, etc. In Table 1 we compare the pMap methods and pAlgorithms on pMultiSet when using one processor with the the corresponding sequential container methods and algorithms. For the parallel STL algorithms the overhead is relative to the sequential STL algorithms executed on the corresponding STL containers. For the parallel sort the comparison is with an equivalent sequential algorithm that is using an std::multiset to sort the elements. We made these measurements on the OPTERON-CLUSTER and the overheads vary between 1.25% and 12.25%. We are working on improving these overheads.

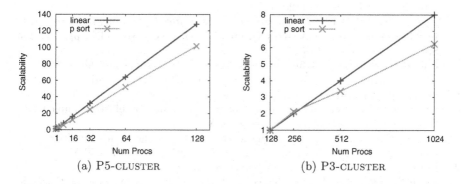

(a) P5-CLUSTER   (b) P3-CLUSTER

Fig. 9. Scalability for parallel sort using parallel associative containers

Table 1. Overhead for pMap methods and pAlgorithms using pMultiSet

	pMap Methods				pAlgorithms			
	insert_ async	erase_ async	find	insert	pfind	paccumulate	pcount	sort assoc
Overhead(%)	7.00	6.39	10.52	8.30	1.25	3.29	3.89	12.25

6 Conclusion

In this paper, we presented the STAPL associative pContainers, a collection of data structures optimized for fast storage and retrieval of data based on keys. We described the design and implementation of these pContainers whose methods include counterparts of the methods provided by the STL associative containers, and also some asynchronous (non-blocking) variants that can provide improved performance in parallel. Our experimental results on a variety of architectures show that STAPL associative pContainers provide good scalability and low overhead relative to STL containers.

References

1. An, P., Jula, A., Rus, S., Saunders, S., Smith, T., Tanase, G., Thomas, N., Amato, N., Rauchwerger, L.: STAPL: A standard template adaptive parallel C++ library. In: Proc. of the International Workshop on Advanced Compiler Technology for High Performance and Embedded Processors (IWACT), Bucharest, Romania (July 2001)
2. Blelloch, G.: Vector Models for Data-Parallel Computing. MIT Press, Cambridge (1990)
3. Blelloch, G.: NESL: A Nested Data-Parallel Language. Technical Report CMU-CS-93-129, Carnegie Mellon University (April 1993)
4. Callahan, D., Chamberlain, B.L., Zima, H.: The cascade high productivity language. In: The Ninth International Workshop on High-Level Parallel Programming Models and Supportive Environments, vol. 26, pp. 52–60 (April 2004)
5. Chan, A., Dehne, F.: CGMgraph/CGMlib: Implementing and testing CGM graph algorithms on PC clusters (2003)
6. Dechev, D., Pirkelbauer, P., Stroustrup, B.: Lock-free dynamically resizable arrays. In: Shvartsman, M.M.A.A. (ed.) OPODIS 2006. LNCS, vol. 4305, pp. 142–156. Springer, Heidelberg (2006)
7. Gao, H., Groote, J., Hesselink, W.: Almost wait-free resizable hashtables. In: Parallel and Distributed Processing Symposium, 2004. Proceedings. 18th International, pp. 26–30 (April 2004)
8. Greenwald, M.: Two-handed emulation: How to build non-blocking implementations of complex data-structures using DCAS (2002)
9. Gregor, D., Lumsdaine, A.: Lifting sequential graph algorithms for distributed-memory parallel computation. SIGPLAN Not. 40(10), 423–437 (2005)
10. Herlihy, M.: A methodology for implementing highly concurrent data structures. In: PPOPP 1990: Proceedings of the second ACM SIGPLAN symposium on Principles & practice of parallel programming, pp. 197–206. ACM Press, New York (1990)

11. Intel. Intel. Reference for Intel Threading Building Blocks, version 1.0 (April 2006)
12. Johnson, E.: Support for Parallel Generic Programming. PhD thesis, Indiana University (1998)
13. Johnson, E., Gannon, D.: HPC++: Experiments with the parallel standard library. In: International Conference on Supercomputing (1997)
14. Kale, L.V., Krishnan, S.: Charm++: a portable concurrent object oriented system based on c++. SIGPLAN Not. 28(10), 91–108 (1993)
15. Kung, H.T., Lehman, P.L.: Concurrent manipulation of binary search trees. ACM Trans. Database Syst. 5(3), 354–382 (1980)
16. Lehman, P.L., Yao, S.B.: Efficient locking for concurrent operations on b-trees. ACM Trans. Database Syst. 6(4), 650–670 (1981)
17. Michael, M.M.: High performance dynamic lock-free hash tables and list-based sets. In: SPAA 2002: Proceedings of the fourteenth annual ACM symposium on Parallel algorithms and architectures, pp. 73–82. ACM Press, New York (2002)
18. Musser, D., Derge, G., Saini, A.: STL Tutorial and Reference Guide, 2nd edn. Addison-Wesley, Reading (2001)
19. Reynders, J.V.W., Hinker, P.J., Cummings, J.C., Atlas, S.R., Banerjee, S., Humphrey, W.F., Karmesin, S.R., Keahey, K., Srikant, M., Tholburn, M.D.: POOMA: A Framework for Scientific Simulations of Paralllel Architectures. In: Wilson, G.V., Lu, P. (eds.) Parallel Programming in C++, ch.14, pp. 547–588. MIT Press, Cambridge (1996)
20. Saunders, S., Rauchwerger, L.: ARMI: An adaptive, platform independent communication library. In: ACM SIGPLAN Symposium on Principles and Practice of Parallel Programming (PPoPP), San Diego, CA (June 2003)
21. Tanase, G., Bianco, M., Amato, N.M., Rauchwerger, L.: The STAPL pArray. In: Proceedings of the 8th MEDEA Workshop, Brasov, Romania, pp. 81–88 (2007)
22. Thomas, N., Saunders, S., Smith, T., Tanase, G., Rauchwerger, L.: ARMI: A high level communication library for STAPL. Parallel Processing Letters 16(2), 261–280 (2006)
23. Thomas, N., Tanase, G., Tkachyshyn, O., Perdue, J., Amato, N.M., Rauchwerger, L.: A framework for adaptive algorithm selection in STAPL. In: Proc. ACM SIGPLAN Symp. Prin. Prac. Par. Prog. (PPoPP), pp. 277–288 (2005)

Explicit Dependence Metadata in an Active Visual Effects Library*

Jay L.T. Cornwall[1], Paul H.J. Kelly[1], Phil Parsonage[2], and Bruno Nicoletti[2]

[1] Imperial College London, UK
[2] The Foundry, UK

Abstract. Developers need to be able to write code using high-level, reusable black-box components. Also essential is confidence that code can be mapped to an efficient implementation on the available hardware, with robust high performance. In this paper we present a prototype component library being developed to deliver this for industrial visual effects applications. Components are based on abstract algorithmic skeletons that provide metadata characterizing data accesses and dependence constraints. Metadata is combined at run-time to build a polytope representation which supports aggressive inter-component loop fusion. We present results for a wavelet-transform-based degraining filter running on multicore PC hardware, demonstrating 3.4x–5.3x speed-ups, improved parallel efficiency and a 30% reduction in memory consumption without compromising the program structure.

1 Introduction

Component-based programming is a software development paradigm in which interoperable and composable components are written, tested and debugged in isolation of one another. They can then be composed into useful programs, perhaps from a library of reusable components. This idea comes so naturally that it has become the primary mode of user interaction in professional video compositing applications, where the user composes effects and video clips into workflows. Elegant design comes at a price, however, and the goals of component-based programming are frequently at odds with performance.

In this paper we explore the barriers to high performance in an industrial visual effect by building a dynamic, self-optimising library from its constituent algorithms. At the heart of our library is the concept of dependence metadata, which enables complex code transformations without expensive dependence analyses. We focus on an effect called degraining [21], produced by our industrial collaborators The Foundry, designed to suppress the random texturing noise introduced by photographic film without compromising an image's clarity. This is achieved by first analysing the grain, or by matching it against a database of grain patterns, and then applying a wavelet-based removal algorithm. The latter is more computationally intensive and thus forms the focus of our work.

---

* This work was partly funded by the EPSRC (ref EP/E002412).

V. Adve, M.J. Garzarán, and P. Petersen (Eds.): LCPC 2007, LNCS 5234, pp. 172–186, 2008.

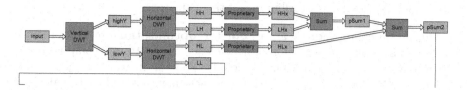

Fig. 1. One iteration of degraining in component form, replicated four times with an appropriate terminator. Dark boxes represent components, while light boxes represent data handles. Handles feed component outputs to other inputs without an intermediate data set necessarily existing, unless the programmer explicitly evaluates the handle.

Figure 1 shows a breakdown of one iteration of the degraining algorithm into components. The complete algorithm chains this graph four times in succession. Our breakdown is faithful to the industrial codebase except that we split summation from the proprietary component, a small improvement in design that our optimising framework allows us to afford. Note that this will artificially inflate our performance gains somewhat, but we believe this to be the most desirable construction; emphasised by the difficulties we encountered in debugging the partially fused implementation. The original algorithm was written in a similar component-based structure; partly to promote reusability and to simplify debugging, and partly due to the difficulty of managing heavily fused code.

From a performance perspective, the optimum structure looks very different. Some knowledge of the dependence structures for each component reveals great redundancy in iteration over intermediate results. Each component is implicitly a whole new iteration. Large data sets carry information from one component to the next, spilling into higher levels of the memory hierarchy, when restructuring transformations could greatly reduce their size. Opportunities for instruction-level parallelism (ILP), an important tool in superscalar architectures, are limited by the barriers between the computations of each component. Crucially, none of these optimisations could be applied directly to the code without greatly disrupting the component-based design. This tension between good design and high performance tends to lead programmers to choose one at the expense of the other.

We argue that these optimisations are crucial for performance and that, with some innovative programming, they can be consistent with good design. Our solution avoids disruption in the original code by promoting a generative approach, in which components are equipped with functionality to create their own implementations. Problem-specific kernel code is left to the programmer as before, while we take control of the loops and collect high-level metadata describing each component's dependence structure. Delayed evaluation reveals component compositions and runtime code generation allows us to produce context-sensitive optimised implementations. The fundamental transformations leading to faster code are made safe and precise by dependence metadata. These are used to build a polytope representation of the loop nests from which optimised code can be instantiated.

In summary, the main contributions of this paper are:

- **Dependence metadata as a tool for optimisation.** In Section 2 we discuss the role and collection of dependence metadata in a component environment through algorithmic skeletons. This information enables precise loop shifting, loop fusion and array contraction without difficult analysis of the implementation.
- **Evaluation of an active visual effects library.** In Section 3 we present a complete active visual effects library built around a polytope code generation framework. We evaluate its performance with a component-based industrial visual effect.

2   System Design

An overview of our design is shown in Figure 2. We have chosen to adopt an offline phase in which optimised code is compiled and linked to the client application. This contrasts with other approaches that maintain client/library separation by moving this phase to runtime. Our approach benefits from requiring no build environment on the end-user system and from having no code generation or compile-time overhead. We lose the ability to specialise to dynamic parameters without pre-tracing every instance of them, but consider this to be a worthwhile trade-off given the large interactive variability of those parameters in our target applications. In practice, we only generate multiple traces when the component graph changes with a parameter (e.g. by disabling or reordering operations).

2.1   Library Front-End

We have designed the front-end to our active library with transparency in mind. The goal is to present an interface to the programmer which matches the existing imperative execution model, while retaining the flexibility to switch to a delayed evaluation mode. Our solution uses proxy functions to build a graph of components connected by abstract data handles at runtime, as shown in Listing 1.1. This code excerpt produces the graph for one iteration of degraining as shown in Figure 1. Run in an imperative mode, the same program would invoke the correct components in sequence and instantiate data handles with real data sets

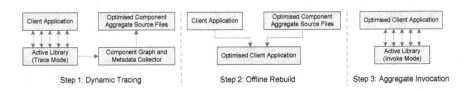

Fig. 2. Stages of the optimisation workflow. The client is run with the library in a trace mode. Optimised aggregate library code is generated and embedded manually into the client application. A second library mode invokes this aggregate code in normal usage.

```
/* Real data sets for reading/writing data. */
Handle input(new Image(width, height, components));
Handle pSum2(new Image(width, height, components));
Handle LL(new Image(width, height, components));

/* Virtual data sets for automatic instantiation. */
Handle highY, lowY, HH, LH, HL, HHx, LHx, HLx, pSum1;

VertDWT(input, highY, lowY, filterHeight, pass);
HorizDWT(highY, HH, LH, filterWidth, pass);
HorizDWT(lowY, HL, LL, filterWidth, pass);

Proprietary(HH, HHx);
Proprietary(LH, LHx);
Proprietary(HL, HLx);

Sum(HHx, LHx, pSum1);
Sum(pSum1, HLx, pSum2);
```

Listing 1.1. Component-based front-end with data sets, handles and proxy functions for a single iteration of degraining.

on-demand. This is useful for generating traces, invoking aggregate code and for debugging the optimisation engine without changing the client application.

Components are constructed through an algorithmic skeleton interface. The goal of skeletons in our library is twofold. Firstly, we need to separate loops from programmer-written kernels so that transformations can be applied to the iteration space. Secondly, we need to extract high-level metadata describing an algorithm's dependence structure in order to determine which transformations can be applied and in what order. We make loose use of the skeleton terminology from Nicolescu and Jonker's work on skeletons in image processing [14] but do not distinguish the numbers of inputs or outputs; instead these parameterise the skeleton.

We place some constraints on the use of skeletons in our library for performance reasons. By controlling the loop structures we can enforce an iteration order and ensure that each element in the output is computed only once. The latter constraint may be relieved through a scatter skeleton but note that this will block loop fusion if the scatter distance is not limited to a subset of the output (i.e. it is not a global operation). The former constraint is somewhat configurable by the algorithm, in being able to choose forwards/backwards and horizontal/vertical iteration parameters. This provides enough flexibility in managing loop-carried dependencies to account for all of the components we have investigated so far, but we plan to explore more complex skeletons in the future.

Figure 3 classifies the three non-proprietary components of degraining as skeletons. Summation matches a simple point skeleton parameterised by two inputs and one output. There are two per-iteration data dependencies from the inputs to a corresponding point in the output. Both the vertical and horizontal DWT match the filter skeleton, parameterised by one input, two outputs and the direction and dimensions of the filter. Dependencies from the input to both outputs cover the filter area. As a result, the dependence structures of the horizontal

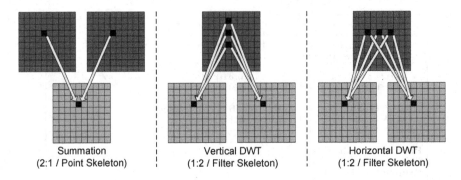

Summation	Vertical DWT	Horizontal DWT
(2:1 / Point Skeleton)	(1:2 / Filter Skeleton)	(1:2 / Filter Skeleton)

Fig. 3. Skeleton classifications for the non-proprietary components of degraining

and vertical DWT components change dynamically with the filter size parameter. Our optimisation engine accounts for this by generating aggregate loops with an iteration space parameterised by this variable.

To illustrate the use of skeletons in our library, Listing 1.2 shows a partial implementation of the vertical DWT component. The component object subclasses an appropriate skeleton. The programmer provides a scalar kernel and an optional vector kernel, expressed in terms of the arrays *in1*, *out1*, and *out2*, and indices y, x and c. Our code generator is free to use whichever implementation it prefers but the current implementation will always choose the vector kernel if it can be used throughout the entire graph; otherwise scalar is chosen. _filterHeight is a parameter to the skeleton that is used inside the kernel and inside the *getRadius* function. The *getRadius* function encodes dependence metadata for the skeleton by defining a windowed access region over the *in1* array, centred over the current iteration point (x, y) – this is discussed in more detail in the following subsection. Thus the metadata is provided by the programmer through a simple overloaded function call in the skeleton.

2.2   Deriving Transformation Parameters from Metadata

We focus on loop fusion and array contraction [2] as potentially beneficial cross-component optimisations to apply to the component graph, as demonstrated in earlier work [18]. In order to apply these transformations safely we must derive two parameters: the loop shift required for fusion and the contracted size of intermediate data sets. Computing these parameters normally requires detailed region and liveness analyses. We aim to demonstrate that explicit dependence metadata can achieve the same result at a much lower cost.

Our metadata is inspired by the THEMIS proposal [12]. THEMIS mapped out a set of properties to describe a procedure's dependence structure. At each point in its iteration domain and for each operand to a procedure, a set of indices which may be read by the procedure is defined. Similarly for the data items which may be written to, further sets are defined. The precise representation of this information is left to the programmer. The authors give an example where

```
class VertDWTSkel : public Filter1DSkeleton {
  void scalarKernel(...) {
    float valT = in1[y-(_filterHeight/2)][x][c];
    float valM = in1[y][x][c];
    float valB = in1[y+(_filterHeight/2)][x][c];
    out1[y][x][c] = (valM-(valL+valR)*0.5f)*0.5f;
    out2[y][x][c] = valM-out1[y][x][c];
  }

  void vectorKernel(...) {
    __m128 valT = in1[y-(_filterHeight/2)][x];
    __m128 valM = in1[y][x];
    __m128 valB = in1[y+(_filterHeight/2)][x];
    out1[y][x] = (valM-(valL+valR)*0.5f)*0.5f;
    out2[y][x] = valM-out1[y][x];
  }

  void getRadius(int *radius) {
    radius[0] = _filterHeight;
    radius[1] = 0;
  }
};
```

Listing 1.2. Partial implementation of the Vertical DWT

affine functions are sufficient to represent dependencies for each iteration relative to the position in the iteration domain. We find that a similar approximation is suitable for all of the components in the degraining algorithm.

We assume that each skeleton's kernel writes once to all points in the output data set(s). This is not the case for our "scatter" skeleton (not used in this algorithm), which potentially overwrites a single point many times, but in that case we simply introduce a larger shift to ensure that we do not read values from the preceding component until they have permanently left the scatter window. Dependence metadata is defined as the dimensions of a window centred over corresponding points in all of the input data sets. For a point skeleton this is simply (1,1). The vertical filter skeleton will have dependence metadata represented by (1,n), where n is the filter height, while the horizontal filter skeleton is similarly characterised by (n,1). This simple scheme is sufficient to enable computation of the transformation parameters for maximal fusion across the entire degraining algorithm.

For a detailed explanation of deriving optimal array contraction parameters see [20]. However, our approach allows these parameters to be derived trivially. Their value is equal to the loop shift of the succeeding component (i.e. precisely the number of iterations that the intermediate data should be held for). We use a small optimisation trick in computing the contracted size by noting that indexing a contracted array requires an expensive modulus operation. However, by padding the contracted size to the nearest power-of-two, cheap bitwise operations can be substituted for modulus arithmetic.

Finally, we put all of this together with a simple propagative algorithm that walks the component graph, computing loop shifts and contracted data set sizes from the *getRadius* dependence metadata and the input transformation parameters to each component.

2.3 Code Generation

Our code generation scheme is slightly unusual. While it would be trivial to generate some text representing the shifted loops, fusion is a difficult transformation to apply. By recognising loop fusion as an iteration space scanning problem – that is, to consolidate kernels in common slices of a domain – we leverage the polytope model for a solution. Polytopes are a mathematical formulation of a loop nest, its statements and their dependence. Loop fusion in this model is trivially solved by overlapping multiple polytopes.

We make use of the CLooG (Chunky Loop Generator) library [3] to achieve this. CLooG is a loop generation tool based on the polytope model. It devises an iteration scheme to visit all of the integral points in a polyhedron under a system of scheduling constraints. Of the many possible loop nests that arise, CLooG picks the one most optimised in control flow. A side effect of this choice is that loop unrolling and fusion are applied implicitly in the polyhedral scanning process. CLooG will not perform enabling transformations, such as loop shifting, by itself. Instead, we provide the library with pre-shifted iteration spaces and kernels with shifted and contracted array indexing, along with a guarantee that no loop-carried dependencies exist between statements of different kernels.

CLooG requires a client code generator to fill the loops it generates with appropriate kernels. The client supplies a unique identifier for a kernel when creating a polytope, and is provided with sequences of the same identifiers during fused code generation. One way to capture programmer-written kernels from the target application, as demonstrated in the TaskGraph [4] library, is to use template metaprogramming to build a high-level representation of the kernel which can later be unparsed back to text. This approach provides a semantic advantage and opportunities to modify the kernel. However, it imposes a syntactic structure that is limited in flexibility and familiarity to the programmer. We chose a less intrusive approach, using a simple pre-processing script to copy kernels from C++ source files into strings within the skeleton classes. In the future we could use source-to-source translators, such as ROSE [19], to perform optimisations on the string-based kernels.

Kernel chaining and array contraction are applied in a pattern matching pre-generation pass. The *inN* and *outN* references from programmer-defined kernels are chained together with unique arrays called *_named_arrX*. These arrays are instantiated with the contracted sizes computed in Section 2.2. They are freed after the loops have finished. User-supplied input and output arrays are referenced directly and are not involved in contraction. Listing 1.3 shows a fragment of CLooG's output for the degraining algorithm. Loop shifting, unrolling (not shown here), fusion and array contraction have all taken place to orchestrate the fully optimised algorithm. In the most aggressively fused case, the complete listing extends to over fifteen thousand lines of code, ninety loops and numerous unrolled fragments.

```
for (y=29;y<=paddedHeight-16;y++) {
  ...
  for (x=6;x<=9;x++) {
    // Vertical DWT
    {__m128 vValT = _mm_load_ps(&_named_arr0[y-1][x][0]);
     __m128 vValM = _mm_load_ps(&_named_arr0[y][x][0]);
     __m128 vValB = _mm_load_ps(&_named_arr0[y+1][x][0]);
     _named_arr2[i&3] = (vValM-(vValT+vValB)*vPoint5)*vPoint5;
     _named_arr3[i&3] = vValM-_named_arr2[i&3];}

    ...
    // Vertical DWT
    {__m128 vValT = _named_arr5[((-2-2)*paddedWidth+i)&32767];
     __m128 vValM = _named_arr5[((-2)*paddedWidth+i)&32767];
     __m128 vValB = _named_arr5[((+2-2)*paddedWidth+i)&32767];
     _named_arr6[i&7] = (vValM-(vValT+vValB)*vPoint5)*vPoint5;
     _named_arr7[i&7] = vValM-_named_arr6[i&7];}
  }
}
```

Listing 1.3. A fragment of CLooG's output for degraining

3   Experimental Results

The degraining algorithm is implemented in C++ with our skeleton optimisation framework. Two implementations are considered throughout this chapter: one written with scalar operations and the other with SSE intrinsics. This computation is trivially parallelised by statically partitioning the image to utilise all cores of a multicore system. We allow the compiler to vectorise the scalar code as it sees fit, but in practice it is able to do very little. Our target compiler is Intel C/C++ 10.0.025 on the Linux 2.6 operating system, in 64-bit mode where processor support was available. A brief comparison with GCC 4.1.2 showed this to be the favourable choice for performance on all benchmarking systems. We use the flag set '-O3 -funroll-loops' and append an architecture-specific optimisation flag as recommended by the manual – using -xW for non-Intel processors.

Before looking at the experimental results it is worth noting a design decision which impacts performance throughout this chapter. All of our benchmarks operate upon three-component interleaved RGB single-precision floating-point data. In order to simplify the vector processing front-end, we chose to pad this data to RGBA with an unused alpha channel in the SSE intrinsic implementations. This raises memory pressure over the scalar implementations and introduces significant redundant computation. One alternative design that we considered involved separating colour channels into contiguous regions. Another used loop unrolling to process RGBR, GBRG and BRGB pixel fragments. Both of these approaches relieve memory pressure but complicate the front-end or back-end of our optimisation framework. We leave these considerations for future work.

3.1   Baseline Performance

Figure 4 introduces the baseline performance of our algorithm in scalar and SSE intrinsic forms. A spectrum of benchmarking platforms spreads the observed

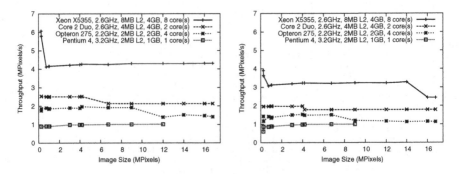

Fig. 4. Baseline throughput for scalar (**left**) and SSE intrinsic (**right**) implementations of degraining on interleaved RGB data for a range of practical image sizes. The SSE implementation pads RGB to RGBA before processing and unpads afterwards.

throughput to between 1 MPixel/s and 4 MPixels/s for useful image sizes. There is a clear reduction in performance on three out of four systems with the SSE implementation. In spite of the greater computational performance of SSE instruction units, memory performance dominates and suffers from the 33% larger RGBA pixels. On the Xeon, this almost perfectly correlates to a 33% drop in perfomance as the eight-core compute-heavy architecture is largely memory bound in this algorithm.

We build upon this data by recording the significant memory allocations and deallocations made by the algorithm during its lifetime. A single image size of 4000x3000x3 is used for comparison in later subsections; measurements scale proportionally to other image sizes. Peak memory consumption is a performance-limiting factor here – 970MiB for the scalar implementation and 1210MiB for SSE. This clearly demonstrates the padding that has occurred in order to simplify SSE application. Correlating this information with Figure 4 explains the absence of data for the Pentium 4 on images larger than 12 MPixels. The peak memory consumption exceeds the benchmarking system's capacity, resulting in page swapping and unstable performance. We omit data points where this has occurred due to the difficulty in obtaining representative samples.

3.2 Fusion within a Single Iteration

We now explore the benefits of loop fusion and array contraction within a single iteration of degraining. In fact, these transformations could also be applied across iterations of the algorithm to achieve maximal fusion. This comes at the expense of large loop shifts and an explosion in loop fragments in the output code, however. The impact of these factors is explored in Section 3.3, but we begin by constraining our transformations to a single iteration of the algorithm.

Figure 5 reports degraining performance with loop shifting and fusion applied to all components in the graph. First we show results of fusiona alone; shortly we show the impact of array contraction. Speed-ups are reported relative to the

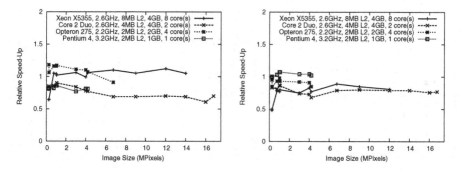

Fig. 5. Fused (but not contracted) speed-ups for scalar (**left**) and SSE intrinsic (**right**) implementations of degraining on interleaved RGB data, relative to the faster baseline implementations in Figure 4. The SSE implementation pads RGB to RGBA before processing and unpads afterwards.

faster baseline results from Figure 4 – the scalar implementations in this case. Fusion is a risky optimisation in a component environment because it displaces the deallocations of temporary data from in-between loops. The fused loop nest accumulates a large number of allocations beforehand, leading to a 230% increase in peak memory consumption. Relative speed-ups are unimpressive and in fact degraded throughput has occurred in several cases.

Loop fusion is not applied in vain, however. By consolidating kernels inside a single loop nest, the transformation enables an array contraction optimisation. There is only a need to hold intermediate data for the duration of its reuse distance. We can communicate this information to the compiler by explicitly reducing the size of connecting data sets and by wrapping accesses to their arrays inside the contracted size. Figure 6 shows the final optimised speed-ups of degraining with loop shifting, fusion and array contraction applied. Performance is very positive in the scalar implementation with speed-ups ranging from 1.6x to 4.8x. Peak memory consumption has been reduced by 30% over the original implementation. Interestingly, the SSE implementation now begins to show promise with speed-ups between 3.4x and 5.3x.

3.3   Fusion across Multiple Iterations

In the preceding section we chose to arbitrarily constrain fusion to within one iteration of the degraining algorithm. We now explore the effects of fusion across multiple iterations, right up to complete fusion of the component graph. Crucially, fusing between iterations will result in loop shifts rising from 60KB to nearly 1MB because the vertical DWT component has a row-striding window. In addition, the amount of generated code grows superlinearly with the number of fusions applied. These effects result in larger working sets, greater register pressure and poorer instruction cache performance. Nevertheless, two large intermediate data sets can be contracted per iteration, following loop fusion, to improve memory performance.

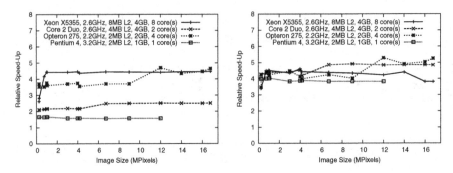

Fig. 6. Fused and contracted speed-ups for scalar (**left**) and SSE intrinsic (**right**) implementations of degraining on interleaved RGB data, relative to the fastest baseline implementations in Figure 4. The SSE implementation pads RGB to RGBA before processing and unpads afterwards.

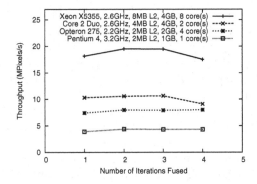

Fig. 7. Fusion and contraction within and across iterations of the SSE intrinsic implementation of degraining. At the fourth level of fusion, the entire algorithm is contained within a single aggressively fused loop nest.

Figure 7 presents results for fusion and contraction across one, two, three and four iterations of the algorithm. Only SSE intrinsic implementations are considered here, since they gave better average speed-ups in the preceding section. We find that performance isn't affected significantly in most cases. The Xeon system sees a small improvement with two fused iterations over one and experiences a similar drop from three to four fused iterations. We speculate that the heavily memory bound system benefits from inter-iterative contraction and suffers less from inflated working sets with its large L2 cache. The optimum average case fusion appears to be at two iterations.

3.4   Impact on Multicore Scalability

A final experimental analysis concerns the scalability of the pre- and post-optimised algorithm. The prevalence of multicore architectures places great

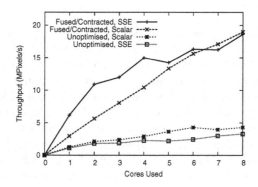

Fig. 8. Scalability of four implementations of degraining for a 4000x3000x3 image on a Dual Xeon X5355 2.6GHz (8 cores) with 8MB L2 cache and 4GB RAM in total

emphasis upon scalability for current and future performance gains. Our optimisations do not target this factor directly, but may indirectly shift scaling bottlenecks by reducing memory pressure.

Figure 8 graphs the throughput of four implementations of degraining on the Xeon system as they scale up to eight cores. These have been fully fused within iterations but not between. An ideal result here would be linear scalability, but contention for shared resources and redundant processing at the edges – a side effect of naive data parallelism, albeit small compared to the full data set – results in sublinear scalability in all cases. The post-optimised scalar implementation achieves closer to linear scalability than either pre-optimised case. However, the post-optimised SSE implementation experiences poor scalability after only two cores. It is worth noting that both implementations achieve roughly the same throughput with large numbers of cores – as both hit the memory wall – while SSE gives substantial improvements when fewer are in use.

Explaining these results is difficult because we have no direct method to determine which data points are CPU or memory bound. We believe that memory pressure is much lower in the optimised case, hence the large speed-ups, but that the algorithm remains memory bound. There is some indirect evidence to support this. Scalability is better when using scalar operations, particularly in the optimised case. Overall performance is of course lower but the algorithm scales more smoothly on a per-core basis. This is because SSE trades memory bandwidth for higher computational performance, so the vectorised cases exhibit high per-core performance but hit memory bottlenecks much sooner. Additional evidence comes from the speed-ups gained from vectorisation: 2.1x with one core in use and a little under 1.0x with eight cores. Padded data in the SSE implementation allows this figure to drop below one.

4   Related Work

Cross-component optimisation encompasses a spectrum of interprocedural techniques including data placement [6], loop transformation [1,18] and implementation selection [11]. The key challenge is to tunnel across the execution and code visibility barriers present in a component-based programming model without compromising the program structure. Two enabling technologies, delayed evaluation [5] and runtime code generation [5,4], have been demonstrated as effective and attractive infrastructure for cross-component optimisation [15]. Generative programming is a paradigm which encapsulates this functionality into metaprogrammed self-optimising libraries [22,10], termed active libraries. Kelly et al. proposed a metadata scheme [12] to carry information about component dependence to an optimising engine. This information is critical in ensuring correctness in code restructuring and efficiency in parallel data placement optimisations.

Algorithmic skeletons separate the problem-specific details of an algorithm, expressed in the full power of the underlying language, from structural features such as data dependence and iteration order. Skeletons have been researched extensively in parallel computing – as surveyed in [17] – as a programming model with explicit parallelism and communication semantics. Benoit et al. later refined the model to incorporate context-sensitive selection of operational parameters [7]. Adobe's Generic Image Library [8] is an implementation of the skeleton concept in the domain of image processing, enhancing fundamental data types with colour information and providing relevant algorithmic patterns.

Polytopes, in the context of software optimisation, are a mathematical formulation of loops, statements and dependence. In his seminal work on loop parallelisation [13] Lengauer illustrated the decomposition of a program into the polytope model and scheduling transformations to satisfy different processing goals. Code generation is a polyhedral scanning problem surveyed by Bastoul in [3] and incorporated into the CLooG library. Ongoing work by Pop et al. focuses on the integration of polytope transformations, through the CLooG library, into the GCC compiler [16]. Cohen et al. achieved similar integration with the Open64/ORC compiler [9], citing benefits in finding transformation sequences.

5   Conclusions and Further Work

In this paper we presented a visual effects library which takes an active role in the cross-component loop and data optimisations in a client application. We demonstrated the role of dependence metadata in replacing the complex program analyses previously required to apply these code transformations safely. Algorithmic skeletons underpin our metadata collection interface and proved flexible enough to annotate all of the components in the degraining algorithm. We implemented a code generation framework in the polytope model with the CLooG library, which proved robust enough to correctly generate over fifteen thousand lines of code and ninety loops in the most aggressively fused case.

Our evaluation showed that loop shifting and loop fusion alone were not sufficient to make gains in performance, and in many cases resulted in degraded throughput due to inflation of the memory profile. Array contraction substantially improved memory performance thereafter, giving 3.4x–5.3x speed-ups in the SSE vector implementation. Peak memory consumption was reduced by 30% as a side effect of this transformation. We explored the impact of our optimisations on multicore scalability and demonstrated closer to linear scalability in the post-optimised case. The SSE vector implementation initially scaled better but hit the memory wall after only four out of eight cores were in use.

The work described in this paper is part of an ongoing project to develop a domain-specific optimisation framework for industrial visual effects. Metadata underpins our approach to performance optimisation, retaining useful information that is lost or obscured within the program. We are presently exploring a range of increasingly complex visual effects in order to identify new metadata and to broaden the applicability of our collection system. In particular, we are investigating the limits of algorithmic skeletons as a means of describing the behaviour of industrial visual effects algorithms. We are also interested in identifying domain-specific metadata which may enable targeted optimisations in the visual effects field or for subsets of the algorithms within.

References

1. Ashby, T.J., Kennedy, A.D., O'Boyle, M.F.P.: Cross component optimisation in a high level category-based language. In: Danelutto, M., Vanneschi, M., Laforenza, D. (eds.) Euro-Par 2004. LNCS, vol. 3149, pp. 654–661. Springer, Heidelberg (2004)
2. Bacon, D.F., Graham, S.L., Sharp, O.J.: Compiler transformations for high-performance computing. ACM Comput. Surv. 26(4), 345–420 (1994)
3. Bastoul, C.: Code generation in the polyhedral model is easier than you think. In: PACT 13 IEEE International Conference on Parallel Architecture and Compilation Techniques, Juan-les-Pins, pp. 7–16 (September 2004)
4. Beckmann, O., Houghton, A., Mellor, M., Kelly, P.: Runtime code generation in C++ as a foundation for domain-specific optimisation. In: Lengauer, C., Batory, D., Consel, C., Odersky, M. (eds.) Domain-Specific Program Generation. LNCS, vol. 3016, pp. 291–306. Springer, Heidelberg (2004)
5. Beckmann, O., Kelly, P., Liniker, P.: Delayed evaluation, self-optimising software components as a programming model. In: Monien, B., Feldmann, R.L. (eds.) Euro-Par 2002. LNCS, vol. 2400, pp. 323–342. Springer, Heidelberg (2002)
6. Beckmann, O., Kelly, P.H.J.: Efficient interprocedural data placement optimisation in a parallel library. In: O'Hallaron, D.R. (ed.) LCR 1998. LNCS, vol. 1511, pp. 123–138. Springer, Heidelberg (1998)
7. Benoit, A., Cole, M., Hillston, J., Gilmore, S.: Flexible skeletal programming with eSkel. In: Cunha, J.C., Medeiros, P.D. (eds.) Euro-Par 2005. LNCS, vol. 3648, pp. 761–770. Springer, Heidelberg (2005)
8. Bourdev, L., Jin, H.: Generic Image Library design guide (December 2006), http://opensource.adobe.com/gil/gil_design_guide.pdf
9. Cohen, A., Girbal, S., Parello, D., Sigler, M., Temam, O., Vasilache, N.: Facilitating the search for compositions of program transformations. In: ACM Int. Conf. on Supercomputing (ICS 2005), Boston, Massachusetts (June 2005)

10. Czarnecki, K., Eisenecker, U.W., Glück, R., Vandevoorde, D., Veldhuizen, T.L.: Generative programming and active libraries. In: Jazayeri, M., Musser, D.R., Loos, R.G.K. (eds.) Dagstuhl Seminar 1998. LNCS, vol. 1766, pp. 25–39. Springer, Heidelberg (2000)

11. Furmento, N., Mayer, A., McGough, S., Newhouse, S., Field, T., Darlington, J.: Optimisation of component-based applications within a grid environment. In: Supercomputing 2001: Proceedings of the 2001 ACM/IEEE conference on Supercomputing (CDROM). ACM Press, New York (2001)

12. Kelly, P., Beckmann, O., Field, A.J., Baden, S.: THEMIS: Component dependence metadata in adaptive parallel computations. Parallel Processing Letters 11(4) (2001)

13. Lengauer, C.: Loop parallelization in the polytope model. In: Best, E. (ed.) CONCUR 1993. LNCS, vol. 715, pp. 398–416. Springer, Heidelberg (1993)

14. Nicolescu, C., Jonker, P.: EASY PIPE: An "easy to use" parallel image processing environment based on algorithmic skeletons. In: IPDPS 1901: Proceedings of the 15th International Parallel & Distributed Processing Symposium, p. 114. IEEE Computer Society Press, Los Alamitos (2001)

15. Osmond, K., Beckmann, O., Field, A.J., Kelly, P.H.J.: A domain-specific interpreter for parallelizing a large mixed-language visualisation application. In: Rauchwerger, L. (ed.) LCPC 2003. LNCS, vol. 2958, pp. 347–361. Springer, Heidelberg (2004)

16. Pop, S., Silber, G.-A., Cohen, A., Bastoul, C., Girbal, S., Vasilache, N.: GRAPHITE: Polyhedral analyses and optimizations for GCC. In: GNU Compilers Collection Developers Summit, Ottawa, Canada (2006)

17. Rabhi, F.A., Gorlatch, S. (eds.): Patterns and skeletons for parallel and distributed computing. Springer, London (2003)

18. Russell, F.P., Mellor, M.R., Kelly, P.H.J., Beckmann, O.: An active linear algebra library using delayed evaluation and runtime code generation. In: Library-Centric Software Design LCSD 2006 (2006)

19. Schordan, M., Quinlan, D.: A source-to-source architecture for user-defined optimizations. In: Böszörményi, L., Schojer, P. (eds.) JMLC 2003. LNCS, vol. 2789, pp. 214–223. Springer, Heidelberg (2003)

20. Song, Y., Xu, R., Wang, C., Li, Z.: Data locality enhancement by memory reduction. In: ICS 2001: Proceedings of the 15th International Conference on Supercomputing, pp. 50–64. ACM Press, New York (2001)

21. De Stefano, A., Collis, B., White, P.: Synthesising and reducing film grain. Journal of Visual Communication and Image Representation 17(1), 163–182

22. Veldhuizen, T.L., Gannon, D.: Active libraries: Rethinking the roles of compilers and libraries. In: Proceedings of the SIAM Workshop on Object Oriented Methods for Inter-operable Scientific and Engineering Computing (OO 1998). SIAM, Philadelphia (1998)

Supporting Huge Address Spaces in a Virtual Machine for Java on a Cluster

Ronald Veldema and Michael Philippsen

University of Erlangen-Nuremberg, Computer Science Department 2,
Martensstr. 3, 91058 Erlangen, Germany
{veldema,philippsen}@cs.fau.de

Abstract. To solve problems that require far more memory than a single machine can supply, data can be swapped to disk in some manner, it can be compressed, and/or the memory of multiple parallel machines can be used to provide enough memory and storage space. Instead of implementing either functionality anew and specific for each application, or instead of relying on the operating system's swapping algorithms (which are inflexible, not algorithm-aware, and often limited in their fixed storage capacity), our solution is a Large Virtual Machine (LVM) that transparently provides a large address space to applications and that is more flexible and efficient than operating system approaches.

LVM is a virtual machine for Java that is designed to support large address spaces for billions of objects. It swaps objects out to disk, compresses objects where needed, and uses multiple parallel machines in a Distributed Shared Memory (DSM) setting. The latter is the main focus of this paper. Allocation and collection performance is similar to well-known JVMs if no swapping is needed. With swapping and clustering, we are able to create a list containing 1.2×10^8 elements far faster than other JVMs. LVM's swapping is up to 10 times faster than OS-level swapping. A swap-aware GC algorithm helps by a factor of 3.

1 Introduction

There are problems that require extremely large numbers of objects (hundreds of gigabytes to terabyte(s)) and that are as such not bound by processor speed, but rather by the amount of available memory. Examples are simulations with large numbers of 'units', e.g., either molecular or fluid particles [16]; combinatorial search problems, e.g., finding the most frequent sub-graph in a set of other graphs, which requires to store all the graphs already processed; model checkers, which run a program on top of a (simulated) non-deterministic Turing machine (NDTM) and for each non-deterministic choice, the NDTM creates a copy of the simulated machine to explore both choices to check that no illegal program states can occur. Memory requirements for all of the above range from multiples of hundreds of gigabytes to a terabyte and above.

Since it is too costly or impossible to plug in enough memory into a single machine, programmers squeeze their code and rely on the operating system's swapping. Both of which is suboptimal. Reimplementing data structures and algorithms to reduce memory consumption takes time that is better spent implementing functionality and ensuring program correctness. Also, the operating system's virtual address space implementation

V. Adve, M.J. Garzarán, and P. Petersen (Eds.): LCPC 2007, LNCS 5234, pp. 187–201, 2008.

not only does not know what data is truly most recently used, but also the amount of virtual memory available (including swap space) is fixed and limited. Extending the amount of swap space is a tedious task for the system administrator and permanently reduces the amount of disk space available to the user. Finally, few operating systems compress swap space or exploit the aggregate memory and swap space available in a cluster.

Our LVM (Large address space Virtual Machine) swaps objects to disk in compressed format and provides a simple distributed shared address space to use all of a cluster's memory and disk space. While this functionality could also be implemented by the programmer, a virtual machine solution provides a separation of concerns. The programmer can concentrate on the correctness and efficiency of the application code instead of optimizing the low-level address space consumption. Also, address space optimizations for one particular program are often useless for the next program whereas a large address space virtual machine can be reused. As we need to modify basic VM data structures, LVM is written from scratch.

In sections 2.1 and 2.2, we describe the virtual address space. LVM's object management is described in Sections 2.3 and 2.5. In Section 2.4 we describe our optimized class library. Section 3 and 4 present performance numbers and cover related work.

2   LVM Implementation

Our compiler frontend [18] generates a register-based intermediate representation which is similar to LLVM [12]. This is fed into LVM that employs both an interpreter and a Just-In-Time compiler (JIT) to execute the code. The code is first interpreted, and if found important enough, it is compiled to native code. To ensure portability, our JIT is very simple: we compile a LVM-function first to C-code and from there to a shared library that is dynamically linked while the program is running.

We chose to use our own register-based intermediate for LVM instead of standard Java bytecodes to easily experiment with language extensions, annotations, compiler optimizations, etc. without being encumbered by Java's bytecode verification, conversion from a stack machine to a register machine, etc.

In LVM we focus on memory-conserving compiler optimization. For example, LVM performs escape analysis [7,13,19] and allocates objects that do not escape the allocating function/thread on the stack instead of the garbage collected heap to reduce pressure on the garbage collector.

2.1   Implementing the Address Space

The main problem with implementing a huge, distributed address space is addressing objects flexibly and efficiently. Implementing an object reference as a direct memory pointer is inflexible because it does not allow objects to easily move in memory and because it provides little information for analysis. On the other hand, a reference should be small, since there usually are many references that need to be kept in memory and are manipulated often. For performance, they should not be larger than the operand width of machine instructions. For these reasons, we employ 64 bit references to encode an

Machine 16 bits	Segment 24 bits	Obj–ID 16 bits	Flags 8 bits

Fig. 1. Reference layout

object's location in memory in a cluster. Every access to an object thus first needs to decode the object reference to retrieve a local object pointer. While this translation costs at run time, it allows us to access an address space that spans multiple machines. This indirection scheme is fully Java compatible as references are transparent in Java.

Every cluster node's local address space is divided into segments (of a megabyte). Objects are allocated inside such segments. If an (array-) object larger than a single segment is required, a segment is allocated that is large enough to hold it. Otherwise, arrays are treated as ordinary objects. Note that segment size is a trade-off between false sharing (swapping in a segment may also swap in unused data) and disk bandwidth.

An object reference is structured as shown in Fig. 1. The machine field encodes the number of the cluster node on which the object is allocated, the segment field indicates which segment on that machine it resides, and the object-id fields gives the offset (in multiples of 32 bytes) at which the object is found in the segment.

Because references are no direct memory addresses they need to be decoded. Fig. 2 shows a snippet of Java code and its corresponding LVM code where this is required. The latter is simplified, as we have switched off escape analysis, type inference, method inlining, and the removal of superfluous reference decoding.

In *main()*, first a new *Data* instance is created. This results in the invocation of *new_object* (which returns a *reference*). The *reference* is passed to the constructor in argument register %R2_64. The constructor uses *refToObjectPtr* to decode the reference to a physical object pointer. Afterwards it performs the assignment. The invocation of

```
class Data {
    int value;
    Data() {
        value = 12345;
    }
    void foo() {}

    public static
    void main(String args[]) {
        Data d = new Data();
        d.foo();
    }
}
```

```
Data_Data__:
%R0_64 = call refToObjectPtr(%R2_64)
('i', (%R0_64 + 12L) ) = 12345

Data_main___3Ljava_lang_String_2:
%R2_64 = vtable_Data
%R0_64 = call new_object(%R2_64)
%R2_64 = %R0_64
%R0_64 = call Data_Data__(%R2_64)
local('l', _14E,-8 ) = %R0_64
%R2_64 = %R0_64
%R0_64 = call refToObjectPtr (%R2_64)
%R0_64 = *('l', (%R0_64 + 0) )
%R0_64 = *('l', (%R0_64 + 104) )
%R2_64 = local('l', _14E, - 8)
%R0_64 = indirect_call %R0_64(%R2_64)
```

Fig. 2. Java example and resulting LVM code

```
javaObject *                                    Segment*
refToObjectPtr(object_reference_t ref) {        locate_segment(int index) {
    if (gc_requested) gc_barrier_enter();           Segment *s = &seg_arr[index];
    if (ref == 0) throw_null_pointer_exception();   if (s->is_swapped_out()) {
    test_dsm(ref);                                      s->swap_in();
    Segment*s = locate_segment(ref.seg_number)          in_core_segments++;
    s->update_timestamp();                              if (in_core_segments > THRESHOLD)
    javaObject *q = s->data + (32 *                         swap_out_oldest_segment();
        ref.get_seg_index());                       }
    return q;                                       return s;
}                                               }


Segment   seg_arr[MAX_SEGMENTS_PER_MACHINE];
```

Fig. 3. Decoding a reference to an object

foo() in main() requires the *vtable* that is located in the first 8 bytes of the object. So again, the reference is decoded to a physical pointer by *refToObjectPtr*. The *vtable* is accessed, the method pointer is extracted, and foo() is invoked, passing the *reference* to *this* in %R2_64. With compiler optimization enabled, the superfluous calls to *refToObjectPtr* within a basic block are eliminated.

More interesting is how address encoding and decoding works in the presence of LVM's garbage collection in a distributed cluster environment, in the presence of multiple threads, and when swapping is integrated.

Fig. 3 shows the pseudo code for *refToObjectPtr*. Because of its ubiquity, *refToObjectPtr* is also used as the GC barrier. Whenever the garbage collector needs to wait for all threads to stop, all threads are gathered in gc_barrier_enter();

If it is not a null-pointer that has to be decoded, the current thread will either stay at the current cluster node if *test_dsm* determines that the reference addresses a local object. Otherwise, if it detects a remote access, the DSM system is called to migrate the currently executing thread to the cluster node that holds the addressed object.

Finally, the segment in which the object resides is retrieved. If necessary, the segment is swapped in from disk and decompressed. The offset within the segment is used to compute the object's address.

Whenever the limit of the number of in-memory segments has been reached, the oldest segment in memory is compressed[1] and swapped out. This ensures that the operating system's swapping mechanism is never triggered, as LVM will never use more memory than core memory. LVM speeds up swapping by delaying all swap-out operations until the next swap-in operation. Which segment is least recently used is determined by a logical clock that is set by *update_timestamp()* upon each access. *Update_timestamp()* increments a global variable and sets the segment's timestamp to it. This only takes a few machine instructions. To further increase performance, LVM can be directed to swap-out a number of its oldest segments instead of just one segment when a memory shortage is encountered. The result is that most disk-IO can be performed in parallel.

---

[1] For compression we use the LZO library since it combines high compression speed with reasonable compression ratios [1].

Note that after the operating system's page level swapping loads a page, the OS does not track individual page hits. In contrast, LVM knows exactly which segments have been used last.

To ensure safe multi-threaded access to the segments, segment access needs to be protected by a lock. However, most segments cannot be candidates for swapping because they are too new. For such segments, LVM bypasses the lock for performance reasons and updates the timestamp with an atomic increment.

2.2 DSM Support

Where most DSM systems fetch remote data whenever a non-local access occurs, LVM relies solely on thread migration. Upon detecting a non-local data access, the thread (in its entirety) migrates to the machine that hosts the data to be accessed.

We employ this strategy for two reasons. First, all DSM protocols that fetch data for their operation (lazy, entry, scope consistency protocols, etc.), all require caching of objects and/or maintenance of copies for later diffing to find local changes. Also, they need some extra memory to store administrative data per page/object (for example, which machine has a copy, and in which access mode). These memory overheads impact memory usage and are unacceptable for our target applications.

Secondly, we can assume that any non-trivial parallel application will touch large amounts of shared data. If the size of the data is in the range of terabytes, the bandwidth requirements for achieving good speedup will be extremely high. This again means that traditional DSM protocols will mostly be a no-go for our target applications.

Hence, conceptually a call of *test_dsm* returns at a different node if migration is necessary. Of course, the performance of thread migration itself is crucial in this approach. We found that the key is a slightly verbose, machine independent stack-frame and call stack format. First, we use a separate call stack that is independent of the C call stack. Second, both the JIT and the interpreter maintain the same (machine independent) stack frame formats. Whenever the intermediate code writes to a 'virtual register', instead of writing to a physical register, it writes to a thread-local variable. While this slows down sequential code, it allows very fast thread migration as stack frames do not need to be analyzed to locate live registers/variables; stack-frames can be copied between cluster nodes verbatim. The complete call stack is kept in a migration-friendly format for efficiency (at the cost in baseline-performance). A stack frame itself consists of a return address, a parameter block, and a local variable block. The return address is a tuple {function *prev_function, int prev_insn_in_func, int prev_frame_offset}.

Thread migration traverses the stack using the prev_frame_offset links. For each activation, a translation table entry of the form {prev_function->name, offset_in_stack} is added and sent with the stack to the receiver. The receiver uses the translation table to plug in new function addresses (as the receiver might have allocated functions at different addresses). Migration therefore takes a stack traversal at both sender and receiver with an additional hash look up per stack frame at the receiver to find function addresses for given function names.

To support efficient stack allocation of objects (escape analysis) under thread migration, we maintain a separate per-thread stack using a mark-release algorithm. Management of the non-escaped object stack is then as follows. At function entry, we record the top-of-the-stack pointer. Each non-escaped object allocation bumps the top-of-the-stack pointer to allocate memory. At function exit, the top-of-the-stack is restored, thereby freeing all objects pushed while the function was running. Of course, the compiler only generates code for the above if a function actually allocates an object on the stack.

We maintain a separate data structure for non-escaped objects for two reasons. First, it is difficult to allocate objects directly on a thread's call stack, because after a thread has moved, the call stack will likely be at a different address and also the stack-allocated objects. Any references to the object would need to be corrected to point to the new address. Second, the garbage collector needs to be able to determine if a value found on the stack is a reference or not, even if it is to a stack-allocated object. For this purpose, each run of the GC quickly builds a per-thread bitmap. An enabled bit here says that the address in the thread-local stack starts an object. Building the bitmap is easy as all non-escaped objects are allocated in one single stack data structure, allocated one after the other.

At thread migration, the stack-allocated objects are transferred along with the call stack of the thread. However, at the remote machine, each stack-allocated object will have an invalid method table pointer (which would be at a different address in each LVM instance). For each stack-allocated object, the sender of the stack therefore sends along a type descriptor of the object. The receiving machine uses the type descriptor to patch in the new machine-local method table references.

For speeding thread migration, we maintain both a thread pool of operating system threads and a pool of LVM-thread objects. When an LVM-thread migrates away, the LVM-thread object is put into an object pool and the operating system thread that executes the thread's instructions performs a longjmp back to its start routine where it waits for its reactivation. When an LVM-thread migrates to a machine, we thus only need to pick a preallocated LVM-thread object (which includes its call stack and thread-local heap), initialize it with the migrated LVM-thread's data, and activate a thread from the thread pool of operating system threads. Maintaining an object pool saves us the operating system interaction to allocate enough memory.

In addition to accessing remote objects, there are two other language features that require DSM support. First, to maintain Java's global variables, every write to a global variable is broadcast to all machines. A read of a global variable is therefore a purely local operation. Second, a distributed locking scheme is needed to support Java's 'synchronized' functionality. Each wait, lock, and unlock causes a message to be sent to the owner of the object on which the operation was called. The caller then waits for an acknowledge message. This acknowledgement is sent after the lock-owning machine has successfully executed the lock, unlock, or wait.

2.3   Object Allocation Strategies

LVM implements Java's automatic memory management. It tries to allocate objects in the following order: (1) try first to allocate the object in an in-core memory segment. If that fails due to lack of memory capacity, (2) try to allocate the object on a remote node of the cluster. If the cluster's core memories are full as well, (3) continue locally and try to allocate by swapping out some old segment. Only if the swap space is full as well, (4) a garbage collection is triggered to free local core memory. In short, LVM tries the cheapest allocation method first and proceeds to the most expensive one. Note that phases (2) and (3) can be reordered for a different allocation scenario.

If a program needs arrays larger than a single machine's memory, our HugeArray class should be used that internally fragments an array.

Because lack of object locality causes excessive thread migration, we allow the programmer to suggest object co-location. We do so by extending the semantics of *new* to express that the new object is best located near to or far away from another object. Since in general, establishing optimal co-allocation is very hard to perform by static compiler analysis, we chose to offer this optional annotation scheme to specify locality.

The syntax for our (optional) directive is:

- **new** /*$ *close_to(ref)* $*/ Type
- **new** /*$ *far_from(ref)* $*/ Type

where 'ref' is a reference to a previously allocated object. The directive is enclosed in Java style comments so that the code still compiles correctly when a standard Java compiler is used. We implement *close_to* by first trying to allocate the object on the same segment (potentially swapping it in). If that fails, LVM tries to at least allocate it on the same cluster node. With *far_from*, we explicitly try not to allocate the object on the same segment. However, we make no special effort to allocate it on a different cluster node. This allows the allocating machine to fill up first, plus it may reduce thread migration.

Close_to can also be used for maintaining load-balancing by the programmer forcing object allocation close-to its thread-objects (which are allocated round-robin by LVM).

2.4   Reducing Thread Migrations

There are a number of simple Java constructs that can potentially cause excessive thread migrations. See, for example, the code in Fig. 4. If the arrays 'a' and 'b' are allocated on two different cluster nodes, each array element comparison will cause two thread migrations (once to the machine holding 'a' and once for going back to access 'b').

For this reason, we provide a small class library containing elemental operations on arrays. To be exact, we provide methods for fast addition, subtraction, multiplication, and division of two arrays. In addition, Java's class library already offers *java.util. Arrays.equals()* and *java.lang.System.arraycopy()* to compare and copy two arrays. LVM's optimized methods test if both arrays are local, and if so, they do a local operation. If one of the two arrays is remote and the other one is local, the local array is sent to the remote cluster node which then executes the operation locally. This reduces

```
boolean equal_arrays(int[] a, int[] b) {
    for (int i=0; i<a.length; i++)
        if (a[i] != b[i]) return false;
    return true;
}
```

Fig. 4. Comparing two arrays

the communication load to a total of two messages instead of 2·N messages for an N element array. To reduce the load on the heap, LVM does not allocate the remote copy on the garbage-collected heap, but instead it is allocated on the system heap. This reduces the pressure on LVM's garbage collector. Note, that because we allocate objects on the system's heap we bypass LVM's swapping mechanism as well. For this reason we reserve a bit of the system's memory for this purpose in advance.

The same problem occurs when copying a graph of objects or when comparing two object graphs for equality if the objects are spread across the cluster. LVM solves both problems by means of a multi-machine object serialization. Object serialization is the process of converting a graph of connected objects into a byte array. Deserialization is the inverse operation. Multi-machine object serialization is specifically built to deal with object graphs that are potentially distributed across multiple cluster nodes. It serializes as many objects on a single machine as possible. It keeps already serialized objects in a hash table to guard against cyclic referencing of objects. Whenever a cycle is detected, a reference to the already serialized object is put into the byte array instead of the object's data. Whenever no more references to local objects can be serialized, the multi-machine serialization process continues on the first machine that holds a remote reference. To detect cycles that span machine boundaries, the hash table is sent along. Note that this scheme relies on LVM's property that references are cluster-wide valid.

Only when used for cloning of an object graph, the deserialization creates the object graph on the LVM heap. Otherwise, when serialization is used for testing equality of object graphs, the object graph is deserialized to the system heap using the system's malloc instead of LVM's garbage-collected heap.

2.5   Distributed Garbage Collection

Java prescribes the use of a garbage collector to automatically remove objects that are no longer reachable. Unfortunately, most of the (local or distributed) garbage collection schemes proposed in the past have high memory overheads. Since LVM must conserve memory whenever it can, the number of choices for designing LVM's GC are limited.

We preferred a distributed mark-and-sweep collector over a copying collector (generational or otherwise) since the latter waste half of the memory which is intolerable given our project's goal of an efficient huge object space (in our benchmarks, intra-segment free-list fragmentation is no problem). Moreover, unlike some distributed garbage collector schemes, we do not separate into local and a global garbage collection phases, again due to memory concerns: to support machine-local GC's, a machine must keep track of incoming references, which can grow to a large set. Also, the gains compared to only using a global GC are low [17]. Hence, LVM starts a garbage collection phase whenever a cluster node hits its local heap usage boundary. It then requests a GC thread to be started on every cluster node.

Instead of marking the objects themselves, mark-and-sweep collectors can also use *mark-bitmaps* to store the marks. In addition, we use an *allocated-bitmap* to mark a location as allocated when a *new* is executed. Only the bit for the start address is set. The garbage collector can efficiently check that an object reference is valid by testing a single bit in the *allocated-bitmap*. During the sweep phase, an object is quickly determined to be garbage if the corresponding bit in the *mark-bitmap* is unset. Because we allocate objects in 32 byte increments, we require a 4 Kbyte bit array to cover a 1MByte segment.

Naive collectors are costly if they cross high latency network boundaries too often (going to another cluster node, swapping a segment in/out). LVM uses a number of optimizations to keep these costs down. First, to reduce the amount of GC-induced swapping, as many in-core references as possible are marked before any objects are marked that are known to be swapped out. For this reason, we maintain two to-do lists: one list *Core* for in-core objects to be marked, and one set *Swap* for swapped-out objects to be marked. Second, we sort the references in the *Swap* set based on the reference's segment before starting the mark phase for the referred-to objects. This ensures that objects on the same segment are marked together, hence swapping is further reduced. To reduce the cost of sorting the *Swap* set, we implement the *Swap* set as a hash table of buckets. Only the individual buckets then need to be sorted. We will hereafter call a GC using swap sets *'lazy swap GC'* in the measurements.

Third, when a remote reference is seen, it is buffered till either the local machine has no more local marking to do, or the buffer is full (max. 1024 references per buffer). To ensure a level of flow-control, only one outstanding mark-buffer is allowed per target machine.

After the mark phase has finished, every machine independently sweeps its local memory. Segments that were left untouched during marking are freed in one go. Segments that are only partially filled have their free lists rebuilt.[2]

3 Performance

To demonstrate LVM's effectiveness we first need to show that it is competitive with a standard JVM for small memory demands and that it outperforms the OS swapping algorithms for larger memory footprints.

We measure on two different machines (as our cluster's policy does not allow long running jobs). For the micro-benchmarks, we use two 2 GHz Athlon machines equipped with 2 gigabyte RAM each. For the application benchmarks, we use a cluster of Intel machines with 3 GHz Woodcrest CPUs. Each machine is equipped with a SATA disk with at least 80 GByte free space. All machines are equipped with both 10 GBit Infiniband and 1 GBit Ethernet. In all cases, LVM is configured to use at most 1.7 gigabyte RAM per machine for storing Java objects and arrays. This leaves 300 megabyte for the operating system, networking software (communication buffers), the LVM garbage collector, the JIT-ed code, and the interpreter's data.

3.1 Micro Benchmarks

To measure the performance of object allocation and object access, we allocate (see Fig. 5) and traverse (see Fig. 6) linked lists of increasing lengths. To be exact, we start the program, create and traverse a list in a loop (10 iterations), and exit the program.

---

[2] Instead of using physical pointers that become invalid when a segment is swapped in at a different memory address, LVM implements the free list as offsets from the start of the segment to the next free space within the segment.

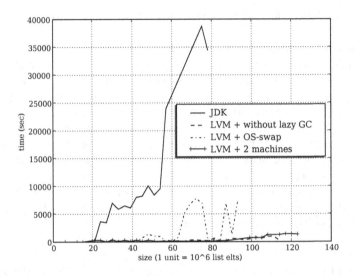

Fig. 5. LinkedList Creation

After a list summation, each list becomes garbage. The VM is restarted for each new list length.

We perform the same test both with SUN's JDK 1.6 and LVM. Starting at 2 Gbyte SUN's VM relies on the operating system's swapping mechanism whereas LVM already starts to swap at 1.7 GByte. LVM outperforms SUN's JVM in both list creation and list traversal as soon as swapping is needed. We stop measuring JDK's performance at lists with 7.8×10^7 elements due to the excessive time needed.

To show that LVM-directed swapping is much more efficient than OS-level swapping we disabled LVM's swapping module (see LVM+OS-swap numbers) and instead relied on the OS's virtual memory implementation. Note that in OS-LVM, the code still contains calls to *refToObjectPtr*. It is interesting to see that with OS-level swapping the system becomes very unresponsive as soon as the OS starts to compete for memory against the JVM or the LVM-OS version. This competition also impacts messaging speed as I/O buffers compete for memory as well. When LVM's internal swapping is enabled, OS performance does not suffer because enough memory is always reserved for it.

The irregularities in the results are caused by the GC. For example, if many GC passes occur when the lists are almost completely constructed, a lot of memory must be scanned, the reverse when lists are still small. The irregularities are thus a harmonic of both the heuristics LVM uses to decide when to collect garbage and the list sizes.

The builtin-swap version of LVM is slightly slower in object allocation due to the extra code needed (2 if statements) on the fast path to test for the need to swap. It is clear that data compression is not a bottleneck (LZO compresses at 100 MB/s and decompress at 310 MB/s on the 2Ghz Athlons). A 1 MByte LVM segment is, in the list benchmark, on average compressed to a 360 KByte file on disk (approx 36%) which reduces disk-I/O time and frees disk space. Using two machines, we first fill one machine's core memory, then the other's. The speedup is not caused by parallelism, as

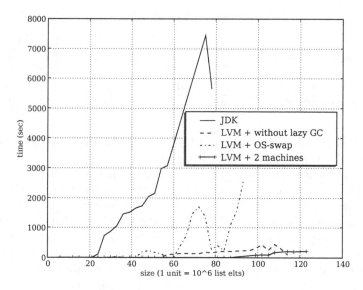

Fig. 6. LinkedList Traversal

there is still only one active thread in the cluster which migrates to the machine with free memory. The List/Node/Data constructors as well as all get/set methods are all inlined. Hence, method call overhead is thus not an issue in this benchmark.

LVM's performance greatly depends on the overhead of thread migration. Here, our implementation is extremely fast. A one-way thread migration takes just 54.9 μs over gigabit Ethernet. With Infiniband, the latency of thread migration drops to 19.9 μs. These times include thread exit, start, message transfer, and stack patching.

3.2   Application Benchmarks

JCheck is a **model checker** for a simplified Java dialect called Tapir. The model-checker tests all possible interleavings of thread-executions to find program bugs. Each state consists of a simulated heap and simulated threads. A Tapir program is translated into a simple bytecode format. At each point in the Tapir program where a context switch may occur, the Tapir compiler inserts a context switch bytecode instruction. Bytecode fragments delimited by context switch instructions are then emitted as separate Java functions.

To reduce the search space, each thread maintains a hash table of the states it has already seen. Before proceeding with a new state, a thread checks in the hash table if that state has already been visited. JCheck gives each thread its own private hash table to reduce synchronization costs. Once a new state is found, a thread publishes the new state by adding a reference to it to all the other thread's hash tables. As each thread maintains its own hash table, memory usage increases with cluster size.

For our LVM test, we wrote a simple Tapir program in which two processes alternatingly send an RPC to each other (which includes message delays and

Table 1. JCheck results

	1 machine	2 machines	4 machines	8 machines
Time, no-lazy-GC (seconds)	8830.2	3728.2	429.8	1553.6
Time lazy-gc (seconds)	3803.7	1077.9	412.7	1483.1
Avg. Heap (MByte total in cluster)	10196	9152	10857	24152
Avg. #thread migr. per machine (× thousand)	—	69.7	111.2	212.3

object-allocations). Note that this is almost the smallest problem to limit execution time (using SUN JDK, JCheck requires more than a day).

The memory requirements (see Table 1) are extreme due to the number of states that need to be explored and the corresponding hash tables for them. To reduce the number of thread migrations, JCheck heavily uses the optimized arraycopy, treeCopy, and treeEquals methods (see Section 2.4). Thread migration mostly happens whenever a thread attempts to publish a new state in hash tables belonging to other threads.

Lazy swap GC is a big gain for JCheck; GC is three times faster with it which shows most clearly on the 1 machine measurements (where run time is only 2.3 times faster as GC is only a portion of the run time). When using more than one machine, preformance is greatly influenced by the speed in which the thread's hash tables are kept up-to-date to allow pruning of the search space. With eight machines (threads), this becomes hard. The increased heap usage with eight machines is caused by missing search-space pruning opportunities (and thereby lowering speedup). Swap compression allows a 1 MB segment to be compressed to a 65 KB file on average.

The **Griso sub-graph locator** finds occurrences of a graph P in another graph K. Since nodes and edges may be rotated, a complicated graph isomorphism test is needed. The algorithm first creates a set of permutations of P with the outgoing edges of each node permuted to create a set. This set is reduced by only allowing canonical forms of the graphs into the set (while also converting K to its canonical form). The set is then partitioned into N parts, so that each of N worker threads can locate embeddings of a permutation of P in K.

Memory consumption (see Table 2) is large since all canonical forms of the permutations of P need to be stored (again excluding a standard JVM). Fortunately, with increasing numbers of machines, the memory requirements per machine drop such that with the graph sizes that we have chosen, with 8 machines the graphs almost fit in the cluster's memory (1864 MByte per node, with an LVM limit of 1700 MByte causes 164 MByte worth of graphs on average that need to be swapped). This results in the superlinear speedup seen when going from 4 to 8 machines. Unfortunately, Griso can take very little advantage of the class-libraries provided. This causes the high thread-migrations counts.

Table 2. Griso results

	1 machine	2 machines	4 machines	8 machines
Time (seconds)	274752	176400	29871	6962
Avg. Heap (MByte total in cluster)	15531	14838	15472	14912
Avg. #thread migrations per machine	—	34644978	25242531	12315766

Besides using a lot of objects, Griso also creates a lot of garbage. On 8 machines, 839 seconds is spent on garbage collection using lazy-swap-GC in 50 GC passes. Each GC pass takes about 16 seconds. Without lazy-swap-GC, this increases to 950 seconds total for GC, or 116 seconds longer. Each GC pass freed about a gigabyte of memory in mostly small arrays used to hold references to graph nodes (for cycle testing in graphs).

4 Related Work

LVM implements a host of techniques to increase available memory and performance. For each of these we will give a few entry points to the related work.

Operating systems. Swapping and compression of swap space is a technique usually associated with operating system implementations and out-of-core applications. In [8] Linux was adapted to compress MMU pages before swapping them out to disk. A small cache is used to store pages being compressed. In [5,15] Linux is adapted to divide memory into two parts. One holds compressed pages, the other uncompressed. Instead of swapping out an uncompressed page, the system first attempts to compress the page and to place it into the compressed memory area. That avoids many disk-IO operations. Our system is implemented on top of an OS. Hence, LVM is not restricted to the MMU's 4K page sizes, it is portable, and allows for multiple techniques to reduce memory pressure (escape analysis, lazy GC swapping, etc.).

Operating systems can also increase a process's available memory by remote swapping or remote paging. One approach is described in [10]. Here, a special I/O device 'nswap' is registered in the kernel. Related to this is [9], where the lowest-level page-manager in an operating system is made cluster-aware. Both approaches perform remote paging to allow idle nodes to cache pages of heavily loaded nodes to decrease reliance on slow disks for swapping. In contrast, LVM starts to remote-allocate objects once local memory is full and performs thread migration to access them afterwards.

Distributed garbage collection. A modified Linux notifies the Jikes RVM in [11] that a page is about to be swapped out. Whenever this happens, the GC creates a list of outgoing references from that page. Objects on that page are then part of the root-set for the GC's marking phase. All references to objects on swapped-out pages are ignored in subsequent collections. In contrast to LVM, RVM is restricted to a single machine and to the size of the OS level virtual address space. Closest to our distributed garbage collector is the system of [17]. However, it targets ABCL/f instead of Java, uses a traditional data fetching DSM system (with the associated memory overheads discussed above), and assumes that all data fits into core memory.

Locality directives. Related to our locality based directives is ccmalloc [6], an alternative to malloc that allows to allocate something close to some other ccmalloced block of memory. However, the authors' goal is cache optimization instead of swap optimization. Moreover, they target C instead of Java.

Out-of-core & DSM. There have been a number of Java-based DSM systems. An overview of DSM systems can be found in [14]. We will, however, concentrate on out-of-core in combination with DSM.

The interaction between, out-of-core applications, compilers, and execution on a DSM system is investigated in [2]. The authors perform source code analysis to add an inspector-executor style parallelization method. An inspector finds probable data usages and hands these over to the executor for the execution of the program. We perform no source code analysis to detect parallelism but rely on Java threads explicitly created by the programmer. Moreover, our different DSM style that relies on thread migration instead of data fetching is advantageous for memory-greedy applications. The compiler analysis for out-of-core applications in [3] inserts prefetch instructions to fetch array data from disk. The techniques described here are orthogonal to LVM: instead of inserting prefetch instructions, the LVM front-end compiler could try to call *refToObjectPtr* as early as possible.

LOTS [4] is closest to LVM. It is also a DSM that can swap out objects to disk. However, the mechanisms and techniques are quite different. LVM compresses data on disk while LOTS does not. Furthermore, LOTS can only use a third of the available memory/disk space for storing objects. LVM uses a virtual machine approach, while LOTS is provided as a C++ library. LOTS is an object-based DSM that migrates data and that therefore pays the memory penalty for storing proxy objects, diffs, and twins of pages. These overheads sum up significantly so that LOTS cannot support large address spaces, especially when large numbers of small objects are used. LVM uses thread migration and has no per-object DSM overheads. Finally, LVM manages standard Java code and migrates threads through a cluster automatically. LOTS requires manually inserted acquire and release statements to control data consistency and to use the C++ library constructs provided.

References

1. http://www.oberhumer.com/opensource/lzo/
2. Brezany, P., Choudhary, A.N., Dang, M.: Parallelization of irregular out-of-core applications for distributed-memory systems. In: Proc. of HPCN Europe 1997, Amsterdam, pp. 811–820 (April 1997)
3. Brown, A.D., Mowry, T.C., Krieger, O.: Compiler-based I/O prefetching for out-of-core applications. ACM Trans. Comput. Syst. 19(2), 111–170 (2001)
4. Cheun, B.W.L., Wang, C.L., Lau, F.C.M.: LOTS: A Software DSM Supporting Large Object Space. In: Proc. Cluster 2004, San Diego, CA, pp. 225–234 (September 2004)
5. Chihaia, I., Gross, T.: An analytical model for software-only main memory compression. In: WMPI 2004: Proc. of the 3rd workshop on Memory performance issues, Munich, Germany, pp. 107–113 (June 2004)
6. Chilimbi, T.M., Hill, M.D., Larus, J.R.: Cache-conscious structure layout. In: Proc. of the ACM SIGPLAN 1999 Conf. on Programming Language Design and Implementation, Atlanta, GA, pp. 1–12 (May 1999)
7. Choi, J.D., Gupta, M., Serrano, M., Sreedhar, V.C., Midkiff, S.: Escape Analysis For Java. In: Proc. of the 1999 ACM SIGPLAN Conf. on Object-Oriented Programming, Systems, Languages, and Applications (OOPSLA), Denver, CO, pp. 1–19 (November 1999)
8. Cortes, T., Becerra, Y., Cervera, R.: Swap compression: resurrecting old ideas. Software, Practice and Experience 30(5), 567–587 (2000)
9. Feeley, M.J., Morgan, W.E., Pighin, E.P., Karlin, A.R., Levy, H.M., Thekkath, C.A.: Implementing global memory management in a workstation cluster. SIGOPS Oper. Syst. Rev. 29(5), 201–212 (1995)
10. Finney, S., Ganchev, K., Klock, M., Newhall, T., Spiegel, M.: The NSWAP module for network swap. Journal of Computing Sciences in Colleges 18(5), 274–275 (2003)

11. Hertz, M., Feng, Y., Berger, E.D.: Garbage collection without paging. In: Proc. of the 2005 ACM SIGPLAN Conf. on Programming Language Design and Implementation (PLDI 2005), Chicago, IL, pp. 143–153 (2005)
12. Lattner, C., Adve, V.: LLVM: A Compilation Framework for Lifelong Program Analysis & Transformation. In: Proc. of the 2004 Intl. Symp. on Code Generation and Optimization (CGO 2004), Palo Alto, CA, pp. 75–85 (March 2004)
13. Lee, K., Fang, X., Midkiff, S.P.: Practical escape analyses: how good are they? In: Proc. of the 3rd Int'l Conf. on Virtual Execution Environments (VEE 2007), San Diego, CA, pp. 180–190 (2007)
14. Protic, J., Tomasevic, M., Milutinovic, V.: A survey of distributed shared memory systems. In: Proc. 28th Hawaii Intl. Conf. on System Sciences (HICSS 1995), pp. 74–84 (January 1995)
15. Rizzo, L.: A very fast algorithm for RAM compression. SIGOPS Oper. Syst. Rev. 31(2), 36–45 (1997)
16. Ryne, R., Habib, S., Qiang, J., Ko, K., Li, Z., McCandless, B., Mi, W., Ng, C., Saparov, M., Srinivas, V., Sun, Y., Zhan, X., Decyk, V., Golub, G.: The US DOE Grand Challenge in computational accelerator physics. In: Proc. Linear Accelerator Conference (LINAC 1998), Chicago, p. 603 (August 1998)
17. Taura, K., Yonezawa, A.: An Effective Garbage Collection Strategy for Parallel Programming Languages on Large Scale Distributed-Memory Machines. In: 6th Symp. on Principles and Practice of Parallel Programming (PPoPP), Las Vegas, NV, pp. 18–21 (June 1997)
18. Veldema, R., Hofman, R.F.H., Bhoedjang, R.A.F., Jacobs, C.J.H., Bal, H.E.: Source-level global optimizations for fine-grain distributed shared memory systems. In: 8th Symp. on Principles and Practices of Parallel Programming (PPoPP), Snowbird, Utah, pp. 83–92 (June 2001)
19. Whaley, J., Rinard, M.: Compositional Pointer And Escape Analysis For Java Programs. In: Proc. of the 1999 ACM SIGPLAN Conf. on Object-Oriented Programming, Systems, Languages, and Applications (OOPSLA), Denver, CO, pp. 187–206 (November 1999)

Modeling Relations between Inputs and Dynamic Behavior for General Programs

Xipeng Shen and Feng Mao

Computer Science Department
The College of William and Mary, Williamsburg, VA, USA
{xshen,fmao}@cs.wm.edu

Abstract. Program dynamic optimization, for being adaptive to runtime behavior changes, has become increasingly important for both performance and energy savings. However, most runtime optimizations often suffer from the lack of a global picture of a program's execution, and cannot afford sophisticated program analysis. On the other hand, offline profiling techniques overcome both obstacles but are oblivious to the effects of program inputs.

An approach in the between is to offline find the connections between program inputs and runtime behavior, and then apply the knowledge to runtime optimizations. Although it potentially gets the best of both worlds, it faces a fundamental challenge: How to discover and model the relations between inputs and runtime behavior for general programs.

This work tackles the problem from three aspects. It proposes an extensible input characterization language to resolve the complexity of program inputs. A translator to the langauage helps automatically convert a raw input into an attribute vector, which is then refined by a feature selector to remove redundancies and noises. Finally, statistical learning builds input-behavior models. Experiments on IBM XL compilers show accurate prediction of detailed execution profiles, helping profile-directed compilation outperform both static and offline profiling-based compilations, demonstrating the potential of the technique for continuous program optimizations.

1 Introduction

Program optimizations have evolved from static compilation to dynamic transformation, reflected by the increasingly growing interest in Just-In-Time compilers, continuous optimization techniques, and runtime compiling systems [3, 4, 7, 13, 14, 21]. During a program's execution, dynamic systems transform its code and data to better match the runtime behavior.

Most dynamic systems make optimization decisions upon the information collected through runtime sampling. The low tolerance of overhead makes it difficult if not impossible to capitalize on sophisticated program analysis or to discover important but costly behavior patterns (e.g. data access patterns). Moreover, most dynamic systems are reactive: they make decisions upon the just observed execution. An underlying assumption is that the program will behave the same as how it behaved. This assumption is fragile for program phases and runtime environment changes (e.g. garbage collections and interferences from other programs), and may mislead the optimizations.

V. Adve, M.J. Garzarán, and P. Petersen (Eds.): LCPC 2007, LNCS 5234, pp. 202–216, 2008.

On the other hand, profiling-directed compilation optimizes a program based on some profiling runs. Being an offline technique, the compilation can afford more analysis overhead. However, it is oblivious to the changes in program inputs, often resulting in inferior optimization decisions since the real runs of a program may differ substantially from the profiling runs due to the difference of their inputs [1].

A tradeoff in the between is to offline build an input-behavior model that can connect a program's inputs with its runtime behavior, and at the beginning of a real run, to predict the runtime behavior by plugging the new input into the input-behavior model, and then to optimize the program accordingly. The technique combines the strengths of the both worlds: By moving behavior data collection and analysis offline, it is more affordable to sophisticated behavior analysis than pure runtime techniques; by modeling input-behavior relations, it handles input-sensitive behavior better than profiling-directed compilations.

In order to apply input-behavior models to general programs, we have to address two issues: How to deal with the complexity of program inputs, and how to build the connections between inputs and runtime behaviors. Although there has been some work in utilizing program inputs for specific optimization decisions, e.g. the selection of algorithms for sequential sorting by Li et al. [16] and for parallel sorting and matrix multiplication algorithms by Thomas et al. [20], we are not aware of any systematic explorations in solving these two issues for *general* programs.

In this work, we develop three techniques to build input-behavior models. The first is an extensible input characterization language (XICL) for the formal expression of program inputs. The inputs to general programs can be as simple as an integer or as complex as an entire program with many options (e.g. inputs to a compiler). Furthermore, sometimes what matters to runtime behavior is the hidden attributes instead of literal value of an input. For instance, it is the size or content rather than the name of a file that determines the behavior of a file-compression. XICL is a mini-language for programmers to formally describe the format of program inputs and express a superset of the critical input attributes. After a programmer builds an input specification for a program using XICL, an interpretor can automatically translate any input of the program into an input vector with necessary attribute values. XICL makes input characterization tractable for general programs.

The second technique is input feature selection. From the input vector generated by XICL translator, this step finds the elements in the vector that are critical to the runtime behavior of interest. One input argument can have many attributes; some may be remotely relevant to the behavior, and some may strongly correlate with others. Feature selection can save the collection of redundant information, improving the generality of the constructed input-behavior model.

The third step is the construction of input-behavior models through statistical learning techniques. We explore various regression techniques and employ cross-validation to alleviate the overfitting problem. This step also marks unpredictable behaviors so that the runtime system can avoid poor predictions to those behaviors.

We apply the technique to 3 SPEC CINT2000 programs and a data mining program. The input-behavior models predict their detailed profiles with 90-99% accuracy. On an IBM Power4 machine, the predicted profiles help the IBM XLC compiler outperform both static and pure offline profiling-based compilations. It demonstrates the potential of the technique for continuous program optimizations.

In the rest of this paper, we present XICL in Section 3, feature selection in Section 4, model construction in Section 5, and evaluation in Section 6. In Section 7, we discuss the issues on training inputs and the ways to hide training process. Section 8 describes related work, followed by a short summary.

2   Program Behavior Model

Program dynamic behaviors fall into two categories depending on whether they are hardware-related or not. The goal of this work is to develop a technique for systematic detection and prediction of the effects of *inputs* on program behavior. Therefore, we concentrate on hardware-unrelated behaviors to avoid the distractions from other factors. But the techniques can be extended to hardware-related behaviors as well.

Program code and inputs are the only factors determining hardware-unrelated behaviors. A general formula is $B = g(P, I)$, where B is a hardware-unrelated behavior, P is a program, I is the program's input, and g represents the mapping function. In the study of input effects for a given program, P is constant and I is the only changing factor; thus we fold P into the mapping function and rewrite the formula as $B = f(I)$, where f is the mapping function from input I to behavior B.

Constructing an input-behavior model is to determine function f. With such a model, plugging any input into f will generate the predicted behavior of the program's execution on that input even without starting the real execution. One option to build the model is through symbolic analysis on program code, but it faces the difficulty of pointer analysis, alias analysis, and uncertainty of runtime behavior.

Our approach is to formalize the task as a statistical learning problem, and use regression analysis to solve it. By feeding a program with different inputs, $I_1, I_2, \ldots, I_N$, we observe the corresponding behavior of the program's executions, represented by $B_1, B_2, \ldots, B_N$. The input-behavior pairs, $< I_i, B_i > (i = 1, 2, \ldots, N)$, compose a training set. We use linear regression and regression trees to derive the approximation of f from the training set (Section 5.)

The complexity of program inputs is a major obstacle to the regression analysis. Developing a scalable technique to convert raw inputs to a clean form with critical input attributes contained is vital for input-behavior modeling.

3   Input Formal Expression

This section explains how XICL resolves input complexity. As illustrated by Figure 1, a typical program command-line in Unix/Linux consists of four components: command, options, option arguments, and operands. The last three form the content of a raw program input. In this work, we assume program inputs are given at the starting of the program's execution. Interactive programs can be addressed by incremental model building, a topic left for our future study.

Raw program inputs are not suitable for input-behavior analysis for four reasons. First, in many cases it is the attributes (e.g. the size of an input file) instead of the literal

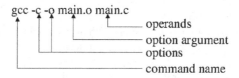

Fig. 1. Command-line components

values (e.g. the name of an input file) of a command-line component that determine a program's behavior. But it is not always possible to automatically determine what a raw input represents (e.g. a text file, a socket, or a graph) and what attributes should be included. Furthermore, some attributes are domain-specific and require programmers' knowledge. A typical example is the initial ordering of the input data for sorting [16, 20].

Second, input-behavior analysis requires the separation of qualitative attributes from quantitative ones. Unlike quantitative attributes (e.g. file size), qualitative attributes such as file types are categorical. Regression analysis treats them differently. Directly from raw inputs, it sometimes is difficult to separate them apart. For instance, the optimization level of a compiler is a qualitative attribute, even though it is an integer number.

The third reason is the relations among input components. Two arguments in an input can refer to the same option and one may overshadow the other. Raw inputs do not contain such information. Furthermore, finding the corresponding components between two raw inputs can be difficult if not knowing the format of the command line.

The last reason is that raw inputs don't contain the default values of input options. Although many programs allow a number of options, a command-line often has only several of them explicitly indicated, leaving other options carrying their default values. Without uncovering those values, most of the training data for the regression analysis would be incomplete, resulting in poor accuracy.

All of these suggest the necessity for a scheme which can deal with the complexity and convert raw inputs to a cleaner form with important input attributes contained; XICL is our solution.

3.1 Extensible Input Characterization Language (XICL)

XICL is a mini-language for programmers to formally describe the format and the potentially important attributes of a program's inputs. In order to enable the automatic translation of raw inputs to a well-structured format, the programmer of an application need write an input specification using XICL. The specification describes all the options and operands accepted by the program, in a format that a XICL translator can use to determine the role of each component in an arbitrary legal command-line and consequently convert the command-line to an input vector containing necessary attributes.

XICL Constructs. For the purpose of clarity, we will use the example contained in Figure 2 to show the use of XICL. The program is to find the shortest routes in a given graph. It allows three options: "-e", "–echo", and "-n". The first two options are equivalent to each other, determining whether intermediate results will be printed or not. The

SYNOPSIS: route [options] FILE

DESCRIPTION: A program to find the shortest path in a graph. FILE has node number at th
beginning followed by the graph structure.

OPTIONS:

    -e, --echo: print intermediate results. It is off by default.

    -n NUM: find NUM shortest paths. Default is 1.

(a) Usage of program *route*

option{ name = -e:--echo; has_arg = N; type = BIN; attr = VAL; default = 0; }
option{ name = -n; has_arg = Y; type = NUM; attr = VAL; default = 1; }
operand{ position = 1:1; type = FILE; attr = FSTN1:mEDGS; }

(b) Input specification in XICL. VAL and FSTN1 are predefined attributes, representing the va
an option and the first number in a file, while mEDGS is defined by a programmer as shown ir

```
ATTS * mEDGS (char * f) {
    n = readNumOfEdges(f);
    storeTo(n, patts->pAtt[0].value);
    patts->pAtt[0].isQuan = true;
    return patts;
}
```

Example command-line:
   route -n 3 graph1
where, graph1 contains 100 nodes
and 1000 edges.

Input vector produced by XICL translator:
   (0, 3, 100, 1000)

(c) An attribute-deriving procedure

(d) An example input and the produced vector

Fig. 2. An example illustrating the use of XICL

last option determines the number of shortest paths to find. Figure 2 (b) and (c) contain
the input specification and an attribute-deriving procedure written by a programmer.

The primary constructs of XICL include two structures, respectively for the description of options and operands in a command-line, as shown in Figure 3.

The first element of the option construct contains the possible names for the option.
An option can have multiple names equivalent to each other, which is common in the
Linux programs that conform POSIX conventions and have GNU long options. For
example, the first entry in Figure 2 (b) shows that "-e" and "–echo" are equivalent
option names. Options with equivalent names correspond to the same set of elements
in the input vector to be produced. The other elements of an option construct indicate
whether the option allows arguments, the predefined type of the option, the potentially
important attributes of the option, and the default value of the option.

The "position" element in an operand structure indicates that the specification of the
operand can be applied to all the operands in range [START, END] of the operand list in
the command-line. For instance, the third entry in Figure 2 (b) has "position" of "1:1",
showing that the entry is applicable to the first operand, 'FILE', in a command line. If
the "position" value is "1:3", the first three operands in a command-line will use that
entry's specification. Note, unlike equivalent option names, different operands, even if
having the same operand construct, correspond to different sets of elements in the input
vector to be produced.

```
option{
  name = NAME1:NAME2:...;  // names of the option
  has_arg = N/Y;      // has an argument or not
  type = TYPE;        // type of the option
  attr = ATT1:ATT2:...; // potentially important attributes
  default = DEFAULT; // default value
}


operand{
  position = START:END; // legal positions of the operand
  type = TYPE;        // type of the operand
  attr = ATT1:ATT2:...; // potentially important attributes
}
```

Fig. 3. Primary constructs in XICL

Two of the structure elements, "type" and "attr", deserve more explanations. For easier use, we predefine five types for commonly used options and operands. Each contains a group of predefined attributes that can be used for the value of "attr". The five types are BIN for binary values, NUM for numerical values, STR for strings, FILE for files, and OTH for others. Totally they have 25 predefined attributes [17].

The value of "attr" includes a group of attributes that the programmer regards as important ones to an option. Besides the predefined attributes, XICL allows programmers to write their own procedures to produce attributes for an option, providing the flexibility for addressing special and difficult attributes. The name of the procedure can be used in "attr" as part of the attributes of an option or operand. For example, the attribute "mEDGS" used in the third entry in Figure 2 (b) is such an attribute, supported by a function written by the programmer, "ATTS * mEDGS(char *f)" in Figure 2 (c) in order to determine the number of edges in the input graph file. During the translation of raw inputs, the translator will invoke the procedures to compute those attributes. In order to do that, the returned value of the procedures should be in structure ATTS defined as shown in Figure 4.

The ATTS structure allows a procedure to return a group of attributes, the value of each stored in a buffer. A boolean flag, "isQuan", indicates whether the value is quantitative or qualitative. Quantitative values are stored as floating-point type in the buffer.

XICL Translator and Input Vector. The XICL translator converts an arbitrary command-line into a vector containing the attributes of input components. Its input includes a command-line, the input specification of a program, the XICL library, and the library supporting programmer-defined attributes. It parses the command-line in light of the input specification and generates an input vector, whose format is illustrated in Figure 2 (d). Each element in the input vector is an attribute value. The vector length equals the total number of all options plus the attributes of the operands that appear in the command-line. Operands' attribute values always reside at the end of the input vector.

```
// structure of a single attribute
typedef struct ATT_{
    bool isQuan; // a quantitative or qualitative value
    char * value; // the attribute value
}ATT;

// structure of a set of attributes
typedef struct ATTS_{
    ATT* pAtt; // pointer of an ATT array
    int n;        // the number of attributes
}ATTS;
```

Fig. 4. Structures for programmer-defined attributes, used in attribute-deriving procedures in XICL description of program inputs

In the realm of software testing, there are some explorations on extracting program interfaces [8, 9, 12]. The key difference from XICL is that their main goal is to maximize the coverage of the program and they don't incorporate input attributes that determine program performance.

4   Feature Selection

The input vectors generated from the XICL translator tend to contain some redundancies. Since programmers are often not exactly sure what attributes are important, they tend to include anything potentially relevant. Moreover, relevant attributes may have strong correlation with each other (e.g. the number of words and the number of bytes in a file). These redundancies not only cause the overhead of collecting useless attributes, but more importantly, result in large regression coefficients in input-behavior models and hurt prediction accuracy.

Feature selection is to select the important attributes from preliminary input vectors. From the perspective of statistical learning, feature selection increases the relative coverage of the training data.

Suppose N is the dimensionality of input vectors, l_i and u_i are the lower and upper bounds of the possible input space in ith dimension, and along that dimension $\overrightarrow{l_i}$ and $\overrightarrow{u_i}$ are the lower and upper bound of the area that is covered by the training data. (For simplify, here we assume a continuous range in each dimension.) The upper bound of the covered area is thus a hypercubic with each side spanning from $\overrightarrow{l_i}$ to $\overrightarrow{u_i}$ ($i = 1, 2, \ldots, N$). It is embedded in the N-dimensional possible space defined by l_i and u_i. For an input vector whose corresponding point in the space falls out of the hypercubic, it is often difficult to predict the program's behavior on that input.

As the dimensionality N increases, the required number of training data increases exponentially in order to make the hypercubic cover a certain portion of the possible space. That is well known as the curse of dimensionality in statistical learning [10]. Feature selection reduces the dimensionality of input vectors, and hence increases the relative portion of the covered area.

We explore two methods for feature selection: principle component analysis (PCA), and selection upon T-test. PCA finds the directions in which the input data have the largest variances [10]. It converts the original input space to an orthogonal space (PCA space) and ranks the axes of the new space in terms of the data variances in their directions. The directions are called *principle components*. As PCA space is an orthogonal space, principle components have no correlations with each other. One can discard less-important components to reduce the effect of noises. Using data that are projected to PCA space has been shown beneficial for various regression and classification tasks. On the other hand, because every principle component is the combination of all input attributes, PCA does not eliminate the need for collecting any input attribute.

The second technique used in our exploration is based on T-test [10]. The T-statistic tests the hypothesis that the regression coefficient of an attribute is zero when the other attributes are in the model. T-test produces a P-value, *observed significance level*, for each attribute. Non-significant P-value of an attribute indicates that it does not have predictive capability in the presence of other attributes. We iteratively remove the non-significant attributes. In every iteration, no more than one attribute can be removed because an attribute that does not have predictive capability in the presence of the other attributes may have predictive capability when some of those are removed from the model.

The T-test method works in the original input space. Therefore, unlike the PCA method, it can *remove* non-important attributes and thus save the collections of redundant features. However, since the original input space is usually not orthogonal, it suffers from the correlations between input attributes. We explored both methods and selected T-test for its comparable effectiveness and the advantage in feature reduction.

Through feature selection, the input vectors are converted to *refined vectors* containing only the input information critical to the behavior of interest. Along with the behavior data collected during offline profiling, they compose the training data to the input-behavior model builder.

5   Model Building

Model building is the final step to determine the mapping function from program inputs to runtime behavior. We use linear regression and regression trees to uncover the linear and nonlinear relations between them.

Suppose f is the function mapping input $\overrightarrow{I}$ to a runtime behavior B for a given program. Given training data set $< \overrightarrow{I_i}, B_i > (i = 1, 2, \ldots, N)$, the goal of typical regression analysis is to find the approximation of function f, represented by $\hat{f}$, such that the sum of error square, $\sum_{i=1}^{N}(B_i - \hat{f}(\overrightarrow{I_i}))^2$, is minimized.

Linear regression assumes that function $f(\overrightarrow{X})$ is linear to the inputs. The problem is to determine the order and the coefficients of the function so that they minimize the sum of error square.

Nonlinear relations cannot be approximated well by linear regression. A branch in the code of *gzip*, for example, is not taken at all if the input size is larger than 90M; for smaller inputs, the number of times it is taken increases linearly to the input size. The cycles in Figure 5 show the observed behavior, that is, the number of times that branch

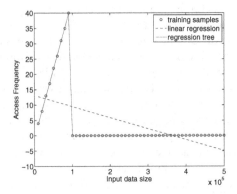

Fig. 5. Regress trees uncover nonlinear relationship between inputs and behavior

is taken for different size of inputs. We use regression tree to deal with the nonlinear relations.

Regression tree splits input space by applying information theory on the training data. By default, a regression tree uses the mean value in a leaf node as the prediction for any input that falls into that node. We build a linear model in each leaf node using linear regression to improve the accuracy. Figure 5 shows the fitting result from both linear regression and regression tree methods for the *gzip* example.

6   Evaluation

On an IBM Power4 machine, we collect detailed execution profiles through the profile-directed feedback (PDF) functionality in IBM XL compilers. The profile contains the number of times the basic blocks in a program are accessed during an execution, which are the behaviors to be predicted in the experiments. The reason for choosing block frequency is that its effect on program optimization (e.g. function inlining, block layout, loop transformation) is so important that IBM XL compilers mainly rely on it for profile-directed optimization.

6.1   Methodology

Our experiments use an IBM eServer pSeries 690 Turbo machine equipped with 1.7GHz Power4 processors. It runs AIX 5.1 with XL compiler version 6. Table 1 shows the benchmarks we used for our experiments. All programs are from SPEC CPU integer benchmarks except *kmlocal*, which is a K-means clustering program from University of Maryland [11]. Including *kmlocal* is for performance comparison with commercial compilers since those compilations often have already been tuned toward SPEC CPU benchmarks.

The third column of Table 1 shows the numbers of lines of source code in each benchmark. The next three columns show the number of inputs we used, the number of behaviors (block frequencies), and the difference of behaviors induced by those inputs. The 23 to 114 times difference indicates the high sensitivity of those programs on

Table 1. Benchmarks

benchmarks	description	lines	#inputs	#behaviors	behavior changes	#raw features	#selected features
gzip	spec2000	8614	50	1775	27X	18	2
mcf	spec2000	2412	250	289	114X	4	2
parser	spec2000	11391	40	4416	39X	7	1
kmlocal	data clustering	6617	50	3333	23X	12	1

their inputs. The last two columns contain the number of raw features provided by a programmer and the features selected by our technique. The selected features include the size and the type of the input file for *gzip*, the first two numbers in the input file for *mcf* (which correspond to the numbers of timetabled and dead-head trips), the number of lines in the input file for *parser*, and the number of points for *kmlocal*.

6.2 Accuracy of Behavior Prediction

IBM XL compilers have the functionality for profiling-directed feedback (PDF) compilation. The compilation includes three steps. It first instruments the program and let users run the executable on one or more training inputs to generate some profiles. A profile contains the number of times each basic block has been accessed in an execution. Multiple blocks can point to a single number in the profile if the compiler determines that they always have the same number of accesses. The compiler then recompiles the program using the profile(s). This is a typical offline profiling optimization technique.

In our experiments, we treat each frequency number in a profile as a program behavior. The goal is to predict the profile of an execution on a new input without even starting the execution.

Figure 6 shows the prediction accuracy. We use leave-one-out method to evaluate the prediction accuracy. Every time the method takes one data item out of the data set and uses the other data for model training. Then it measures the prediction error for the picked data. The process operates on every data and the average of the errors is taken as the estimation of the prediction error of the constructed model [10]. The formula for accuracy calculation is shown below, with f and $\hat{f}$ for the real and predicted behavior values. Using *max* in the divider is to normalize the accuracy to 0 to 1.

$$accuracy = 1 - \frac{|\hat{f} - f|}{max(f, \hat{f})}$$

Benchmarks *gzip* and *kmlocal* have less than 1% error for all behaviors, *parser* has 4% median error, and *mcf* has about 10% median error. The relatively larger error of mcf is due to its two quantitative features, requiring more training data than others.

We obtain the results using a combination of linear regression and regression trees. The model builder automatically chooses the better model for each behavior using 8-fold cross validation [10]. The idea is to take one eighth training data as validation data to measure the models trained by the remaining data.

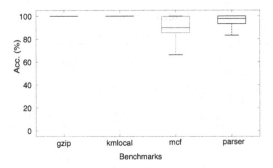

Fig. 6. Boxplot of the prediction accuracy for XL profiles. A box contains the median 50% results and the inside horizontal line shows the median value, with two outside horizontal lines for the maximum and minimum values.

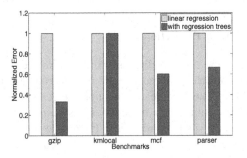

Fig. 7. Error reduction by regression trees

Regression trees improve prediction accuracy significantly. Figure 7 shows the prediction errors from pure linear regression methods and the above combined method. For legibility, we normalize the errors by those of pure linear regressions. Except *kmlocal*, all the other benchmarks show 33% to 68% error reduction. Program *kmlocal* does not need regression trees since it has only linear relations.

6.3   Effects on Optimizations

As a demonstration to the effects of the prediction errors on program optimization, we feed the predicted profiles to XL compiler and compare its PDF compilation results with those from static compilation and offline profile-directed compilation, which uses the average profile of training runs. Figure 8 shows the comparison on *kmlocal*. We use the result from the default level-2 optimization as the baseline. The level-2 PDF compilation using the predicted profiles produces an executable that is 10% faster. It is remarkable that the compilation, although using just "-O2" optimization level, beats the highest level compilation "-O5" by 5% and the offline compilation by 3.8%. (We didn't use PDF on level 5 because on that level the XL compiler failed in producing profiles for some programs for unclear reasons.) For the three SPEC benchmarks, we didn't see

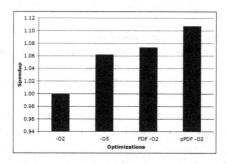

Fig. 8. Speedup of *kmlocal* with different optimizations: "-O2" for the level-2 optimization, "-O5" for the highest level optimization, "PDF-O2" for the "-O2" compilation directed by average profiles, "pPDF-O2" for the "-O2" compilation directed by predicted profiles

significant benefits from both PDF compilations. A possible reason reason is that the commercial compiler has been highly tuned to those benchmarks.

It is worth to note a desirable feature of the prediction model. During offline training, the model builder can mark the behaviors that are not predictable and avoid predicting them during runtime, which enables the avoidance of negative effects of poor predictions on optimizations.

We want to emphasize that the purpose of the experiment is to demonstrate the potential benefits input-behavior models can bring to program optimization. The experiment requires one binary version per input, which is obviously impractical. Although one may classify inputs and generate one version per class, a more proper use of the technique is in continuous (or runtime) program optimization, where, code optimizations occur during a program's execution and the input-behavior models can therefor provide useful guidance.

7 Training Inputs

This section discusses the effect of training inputs, the way to obtain training inputs, and how to hide the training process.

Training data determines the coverage of a model. The input space of a program can have many dimensions. However, typical uses of the program often form just a small subspace. For example, despite that *gzip 1.3.5* has 16 options, users often use few if any of them when compressing a file. This property along with feature selection techniques makes input-behavior modeling tractable. Focusing on typical uses of a program, the technique can avoid poor prediction by simply not predicting for inputs falling outside the covered area.

The distribution of training input in the covered area is important for model building. We conduct a comparison experiment on *gzip* by using two training sets with the size of 20 files distributed from 0 to 500MB respectively in a uniform and exponential distribution. All predictions using linear inputs have accuracy greater than 97.5%, while one thirds of the predictions using exponential inputs have errors larger than 10%. When collecting training data, it is therefore important to make training inputs well distributed in the covered area.

In our experiments, we use a semi-automatic way to generate training inputs. For each program, we create an input-generator based on the understanding of the program. For instance, for *gzip*, we pack a number of different types of files into a tar file and then use an input generator to randomly pick some parts of the file to compose training files of different sizes.

Collecting training inputs can be tedious. Much research is investigating automatic input generation in software engineering area [8, 9, 12]. Although most of the generators are designed for correctness testing, they are potentially usable for optimization purposes. Another possible solution is to implicitly collect inputs from users' real uses of an application. That is particularly useful for continuous optimizations where a program has the opportunity to be continuously optimized after its release. Training takes time. One way to hide the training process from users is to let computer systems start the training process when the machine is idle.

8   Related Work

Prior research in program optimizations falls into four categories in light of the treatment to program inputs. Static compilation either limits itself to the properties holding for any input, or uses ad-hoc estimations for dynamic behavior. For example, a loop is considered ten times more frequently accessed than others [5]. Offline profiling-based methods assume that the profiling runs are the representatives of the real runs and simply make optimization decisions upon those several runs [2]. Neither of them captures dynamic behavior for programs that are input-sensitive. Run-time methods make decisions by monitoring program behavior and trying different optimizations [3, 4, 7, 13, 14, 21]. Although they observe the actual behavior on an input directly, those methods suffer from run-time overhead and hence cannot afford sophisticated analyses. The last class of methods build models by applying machine learning techniques to offline training runs and conduct run-time prediction by plugging in the input characteristics of a real run [16, 20]. Compared to runtime techniques, they move most analysis to offline without sacrificing much confidence in the actual program behavior. However, the previous explorations are limited to several scientific computing kernels, including matrix multiplication and sorting. This work is an exploration to general programs. Ding et al. [6, 23] studied locality prediction across inputs but without dealing with input complexity and feature selection. Shen et al. [19] studied across-input phase sequence prediction based on locality phase analysis [18], but didn't resolve the complexity of inputs either. Berube and Amaral explore the use of Machine Learning techniques in benchmark design for profile-directed optimization [1], but didn't explore the input-behavior models in program optimizations.

For input characterization, some relevant work exists in the realm of software testing, the explorations in test data generation [8, 9, 12, 22]. Most of those techniques focus on the interface to program modules such as procedures or classes, rather than the input to the whole program. Behavior interface specification languages, like Java Modeling Language (JML), enable the specification of the constraints or contract between a class and its clients [15]. These constraints can be regarded as a kind of input attributes, but they are for correctness and don't capture the factors affecting program performance.

To our knowledge, this work is the first systematic study in tackling the complexity of raw inputs and providing a framework to consider general input attributes for performance optimizations.

9 Conclusion

This work develops a set of technique to uncover the relations between inputs and dynamic behavior for general programs. It proposes XICL to handle the complexity of program inputs and incorporate the critical input attributes into a formal format. It uses PCA and T-test to remove the redundancies and correlations inside the original input attribute set. It builds the statistical model through linear regression and regression tree methods. The experiments demonstrate the high prediction accuracy of detailed execution profiles for programs with complex control flows. The technique bridges program inputs and dynamic behavior, opening the opportunities for using input-behavior models in continuous program optimizations.

References

1. Berube, P., Amaral, J.N.: Benchmark design for robust profile-directed optimization. In: Standard Performance Evaluation Corporation (SPEC) Workshop (2007)
2. Chang, P.P., Mahlke, S.A., Chen, W.Y., Hwu, W.: Profile-guided automatic inline expansion for c programs. Software Practice and Experience 22(5) (1992)
3. Chen, W., Bhansali, S., Chilimbi, T.M., Gao, X., Chuang, W.: Profile-guided proactive garbage collection for locality optimization. In: Proceedings of ACM SIGPLAN Conference on Programming Languages Design and Implementation (2006)
4. Childers, B., Davidson, J., Soffa, M.L.: Continuous compilation: A new approach to aggressive and adaptive code transformation. In: Proceedings of 2003 International Parallel and Distribute Processing Symposium (IPDPS) (2003)
5. Dean, J., Chambers, C.: Towards better inlining decisions using inlining trials. In: Proceedings of ACM Conference on Lisp and Functional Programming (1994)
6. Ding, C., Zhong, Y.: Predicting whole-program locality with reuse distance analysis. In: Proceedings of ACM SIGPLAN Conference on Programming Language Design and Implementation, San Diego, CA (June 2003)
7. Diniz, P., Rinard, M.: Dynamic feedback: an effective technique for adaptive computing. In: Proceedings of ACM SIGPLAN Conference on Programming Language Design and Implementation, Las Vegas (May 1997)
8. Edvardsson, J.: A survey on automatic test data generation. In: Proceedings of the 2nd Conference on Computer Science and Engineering, pp. 21–28 (October 1999)
9. Godefroid, P., Klarlund, N., Sen, K.: Dart: Directed automated random testing. In: Proceedings of the Conference on Programming Language Design and Implementation (2005)
10. Hastie, T., Tibshirani, R., Friedman, J.: The elements of statistical learning. Springer, Heidelberg (2001)
11. Kanungo, T., Mount, D.M., Netanyahu, N., Piatko, C., Silverman, R., Wu, A.Y.: A local search approximation algorithm for k-means clustering. In: Proceedings of the 18th ACM Symposium on Computational Geometry (2002),
http://www.cs.umd.edu/users/mount/Projects/KMeans/

12. King, J.C.: Symbolic execution and program testing. Communications of the ACM 19(7) (1976)
13. Kistler, T.P., Franz, M.: Continuous program optimization: a case study. ACM Transactions on Programming Languages and Systems 25(4), 500–548 (2003)
14. Lau, J., Arnold, M., Hind, M., Calder, B.: Online performance auditing: Using hot optimizations without getting burned. In: Proceedings of the SIGPLAN Conference on Programming Language Design and Implementation (2006)
15. Leavens, G., Baker, A., Ruby, C.: Preliminary design of JML: A behavioral interface specification language for java. ACM SIGSOFT Software Engineering Notes 31(3), 1–38 (2006)
16. Li, X., Garzaran, M.J., Padua, D.: A dynamically tuned sorting library. In: Proceedings of the International Symposium on Code Generation and Optimization (2004)
17. Shen, X., Mao, F.: Modeling relations between inputs and dynamic behavior for general programs. Technical Report WM-CS-2007-07, Computer Science Dept., College of William and Mary (July 2007)
18. Shen, X., Zhong, Y., Ding, C.: Locality phase prediction. In: Proceedings of the Eleventh International Conference on Architect ural Support for Programming Languages and Operating Systems (ASPLOS XI), Boston, MA (2004)
19. Shen, X., Zhong, Y., Ding, C.: Phase-based miss rate prediction. In: Proceedings of the International Workshop on Languages and Compilers for Parallel Computing, West Lafayette, IN (September 2004)
20. Thomas, N., Tanase, G., Tkachyshyn, O., Perdue, J.: A framework for adaptive algorithm selection in stapl. In: Proceedings of ACM SIGPLAN Symposium on Principles and Practice of Parallel Programming (2005)
21. Voss, M., Eigenmann, R.: High-level adaptive program optimization with ADAPT. In: Proceedings of ACM Symposium on Principles and Practice of Parallel Programming, Snowbird, Utah (June 2001)
22. Whaley, J., Martin, M.C., Lam, M.S.: Automatic extraction of object-oriented component interfaces. In: Proceedings of International Symposium on Software Testing and Analysis (2002)
23. Zhong, Y., Dropsho, S.G., Shen, X., Studer, A., Ding, C.: Miss rate prediction across program inputs and cache configurations. IEEE Transactions on Computers 56(3) (2007)

Evaluation of RDMA Opportunities in an Object-Oriented DSM

Ronald Veldema and Michael Philippsen

University of Erlangen-Nuremberg, Computer Science Department 2,
Martensstr. 3, 91058 Erlangen, Germany
{veldema,philippsen}@cs.fau.de

Abstract. Remote Direct Memory Access (RDMA) is a technology to update a remote machine's memory without intervention at the receiver side. We evaluate where RDMA can be usefully applied and where it is a loss in Object-Oriented DSM systems. RDMA is difficult to use in modern OO-DSMs due to their support for large address spaces, advanced protocols, and heterogeneity. First, a communication pattern that is based on objects reduces the applicability of bulk RDMA. Second, large address spaces (meaning far larger than that of a single machine) and large numbers of machines require an address space translation scheme to map an object at different addresses on different machines. Finally, RDMA usage is hard since without polling (which would require source code modifications), incoming RDMA messages are hard to notice on time.

Our results show that even with RDMA, update protocols are slower than invalidation protocols. But RDMA can be successfully applied to fetching of objects in an invalidation protocol and improves performance by 20.6%.

1 Introduction

A Software Distributed Shared Memory (S-DSM) system allows for easy distributed programming by making a cluster seem like a single, big computer. The current proliference of Java programmers increases the importance of Java DSMs.

Recent cluster interconnects can directly and efficiently read/write another machine's memory by means of explicitly programmed Remote Direct Memory Access (RDMA). Note that an RDMA operation is performed without cooperation from the receiving machine, except for the initial setup of RDMA-able memory spaces. With Infiniband, RDMA can be up to 6-10 times faster than send/receive based primitives. For example, using 3Ghz CPUs, a 1 byte RDMA costs about 2 μs whereas a normal message send (including protocol processing to deliver the packet to the application layer) takes 17 μs. It therefore seems promising to employ RDMA in DSM systems to implement memory consistency protocols. However, due to a number of restrictions and the lack of message receipt notification, protocols can become more complex, so that performance is reduced.

Java DSMs must implement the Java memory model using some memory consistency protocol. There are two basic memory consistency protocols: invalidation protocols and update protocols. In an invalidation protocol, a machine asks a 'data-owning' machine (called the home-node), to send over the requested data (*fetch*), and caches it

V. Adve, M.J. Garzarán, and P. Petersen (Eds.): LCPC 2007, LNCS 5234, pp. 217–231, 2008.

locally until it is invalidated (and sent back, i.e., *flushed*). In an update protocol, a machine *broadcasts* its changes to all (accessing) machines so that a 'write' to some data causes communication while a read of some data will not cause communication. To reduce communication load, changes can be aggregated for delayed bulk broadcasts till a later synchronization action. Update protocols can be implemented solely by means of RDMA, i.e., without any explicit messaging.

Below, this paper investigates the RDMA opportunities in an invalidation protocol and in two update protocol alternatives.

Our prototype implementation uses Jackal [9,10], a Java based S-DSM system, because of its support for plugable DSM protocols and its simple mark-and-sweep Garbage Collector (GC) that makes RDMA-based DSMs easier to implement (as objects do not move during a program's runtime). Jackal compiles a Java program directly to an optimized native executable. We currently have code generators for x86, AMD64, PowerPC, and IA64. Any multi-threaded Java program can as such run *without change* on a cluster of workstations. Where some DSM systems transfer MMU pages over the network (fixed 1 to 4 Kbyte chunks of memory), Jackal's granularity is a region: a single Java object or a 64 KByte chunk of an array. This automatic array chunking reduces the possibility of false sharing.

Finally, Jackal is very flexible. It supports a very large virtual address space where each machine adds its memory to the global pool without limits on the number of participating machines. This large address space is one of the main obstacles for RDMA use. To build this large address space, it is necessary to translate object references between machines. This address translation scheme works as follows. At object allocation, each object is assigned a cluster-wide unique Global Object Reference (GOR). When sending an object reference to another machine, that objects's GOR is sent instead, combined with a type-descriptor structure of the object pointed to. When the target machine receives the GOR, it consults a hash table to see where the object's local copy is allocated. If no local copy has been allocated yet at that machine, the type-descriptor is used to locate the local machine's meta-class instance for that object. That meta-class contains enough information (type, size in memory, etc.) to allocate the local copy and store the new pointer in the table. Afterwards the local copy's address is used.

This scheme therefore has the following characteristics: copies of objects at different machines have different addresses, each reference sent over the network needs to be translated, and finally, copies are allocated lazily so that we cannot be sure that for each object a local copy always exists before sending references to other machines. These features make an RDMA based implementation harder.

2   Related Work

Both invalidation and update protocols exist in many variations and can operate under different memory models. For an (older) overview of DSM systems see [8].

To our knowledge, only few attempts have been made to use RDMA in a DSM protocol. In each of [7,2,5] a page oriented Home-based Lazy Release Consistency protocol (HLRC) is optimized with RDMA. In [7] multiple page diffs (the changes made by the local processor) are sent to their home via RDMA. In [2] diffs are applied by RDMA to the home-node copy. Our system, however, is not page based but object based. Also, we examine the opportunities offered by RDMA for both invalidation and update protocols. In [5] it is investigated how to allow multiple threads per process but by using VIA style network interconnects. Our system can use multiple threads per process as well, but uses different protocols to achieve this.

Other related works compare invalidation and update protocols (without RDMA usage) and program transformations to best utilize them. While the authors of [3] show some performance gains for update protocols, we avoid their extensive manual source-code transformations.

Munin [1] allows the programmer to choose from a time-out update protocol and a number of lazy release protocols. Whereas Jackal allows the protocol to be specified per object, in Munin this can be done per (global) variable. Munin's global address space is restricted. Both [3] and [1] do not use RDMA based protocol implementations and hence might benefit from the RDMA versions presented here.

3   DSM Protocol Template

Java's memory model prescribes that at the entry and at the exit of a synchronized block, any changes to memory caches made by a thread must be 'published' so that other threads can pick up those changes. Besides this, synchronized blocks guarantee mutual exclusion of threads. We implement the mutual exclusion part by sending a message to the owner of the object of the synchronized block and then waiting for an acknowledgement message. The owner will only send this acknowledgement if access to the synchronized block is granted. While an object has a lock associated with it, it is not eligible for home-migration (under invalidation protocols) to avoid having to migrate locking state across machines when migrating an object. Object.wait(), timed-wait(), notify(), and notifyAll() are implemented similarly.

Let us discuss the DSM protocol template first that works for both update and invalidation protocols. For concrete invalidation and update protocols different implementations of the three operations: *start_read(Region r), start_write(Region r)*, and *process_cached_regions()* need to be selected. In our implementation, these functions test some flag bits in a region and then pass control to the appropriate protocol handler for that region so that protocols (invalidation or update) can be specified per region.

Our compiler inserts conditional calls to *start_read* and *start_write* into the code. We call these 'access checks'. For example, the write access to the *'p'* field at line 4 of the source code on the left hand side of Fig. 1 causes the access check in lines 11–12 to be generated. A region is already locally available if the corresponding bit in the thread's *write_bitmap* is set. Optimization passes in the compiler remove as many superfluous access checks as possible, see [10]. If the region is not yet locally available, the *start_write* and *start_read* functions cause the DSM protocol to fetch a copy of the object. After mapping the copy locally, a reference to the mapped region is added to the thread's *cached list*. On this list update and invalidation managed regions co-exist. Whereas an invalidation protocol fetches a fresh copy of a region after every single thread synchronization statement (as the use of 'synchronized' causes data invalidations), the update protocol fetches it only once whereafter it remains mapped.

```
// Source:                          7 // Instrumented with pseudocode:
1 class A {                         8 void foo(int q) {
2    int p;                         9    process_cached_regions();
3    synchronized void foo(int q) { 10   lock(this);
4        this.p = q;                11   if (! current_thread.write_bitmap[this])
5    }                              12       start_write(this);
6 }                                 13   this.p = q;
                                    14   process_cached_regions();
                                    15   unlock(this);
                                    16 }
```

Fig. 1. DSM protocol template with object access and synchronization

At each *lock/unlock*, the *cached list* is traversed and each region is flushed (invalidation protocol) or broadcast (update protocol). In case of an invalidation protocol, a diff of a modified region is sent to the object's home-node. If the region was not modified, only a notification is sent that there is now one user less. These messages are used to implement lazy flushing, home-migration, home-only states, etc. Jackal's invalidation protocol is a multiple-writer protocol with home-migration similar to [4]. It uses lazy-flushing for cluster-wide read-only regions. In case of an update protocol, a diff is used to update all other existing copies.

As said before, Jackal uses an address translation scheme. Whenever a reference to an object is to be sent over the network, a GOR and some type-information is sent instead which the receiver maps to the local copy causing copies of objects to have different local addresses on different machines. In our prototype, the programmer can select an update protocol *per object/array* via a simple Java API. This sets the object's 'update protocol flag' and performs an all-to-all communication to exchange the local object addresses. This communication is required for RDMA protocols, as each machine needs to know the remote addresses of all the cached copies of an object. Each of *start_read/write* and *process_cached_regions()* test the object's 'update protocol flag' to determine the correct protocol handler. This all-to-all communication to exchange the addresses of local copies is needed only once at program start and is therefore not an issue for program performance. The following two sections study which parts of the general DSM protocol can/cannot benefit from RDMA.

4   Object Requests by Means of RDMA

Whenever an object is not locally available, the access check invokes either *start_read* or *start_write*, depending on the type of accesses that follow. The object is then requested. At receipt of the object by the requestor it is locally mapped by setting the thread's accessibility bits and by adding it to the cached-list of the requesting thread. This section shows that some parts of the object request protocol can be done by RDMA. Others must rely on regular send-receive pairs.

The fetch request itself *cannot be sent via RDMA* because of the following reasons. First, with RDMA, the home-node would have to periodically poll memory to determine message arrival. As the home-node will have other Java threads running, the program would need to be instrumented with polling statements. Due to Jackal's goal of running unchanged multi-threaded Java programs (not necessarily in SPMD style), we cannot require the Java programmers to insert polling statements in their codes. We therefore would have to resort to automatic insertion of polling statements. This causes performance problems as the frequency of polling is either too high or too low, both of which would adversely effect performance. Second, an RDMA-ed fetch request would need to correctly update any protocol state maintained at the home-mode. This would involve allocating and freeing data structures from memory, updating the accessibility state vectors, potentially sending invalidation messages, etc. These operations are too complex to manage by using only simple RDMA transfers.

We therefore need to apply a normal send-receive protocol for sending fetch-request messages. Message receipt at the home-node causes a special communication thread (an 'upcall thread') to wake up from a blocking-receive. It handles the message and sends the object back to the requestor. In contrast, object receipt by the requestor *can be handled by RDMA* as the receiver can actively wait for the message to arrive, since the message will (definitely) take only a short amount of time to arrive.

Fig. 2 shows the pseudocode for issuing fetch requests. First, the requestor figures out how large the combined received object and its protocol data will be. If this fits in a pre-allocated and pre-registered RDMA-able memory region (jackal_rdma_alloc), the fetch request is sent with the address of the local RDMA buffer. Otherwise the object will be sent by the home-node's communication thread as a normal message. An interesting insight is that the home-node cannot directly place the object's data into

```
void fetch_request(javaObject x) {
    // determine the size of the receive area to allocate:
    int reply_msg_size = 1 + x.size() + dsm_protocol_overhead_reply(x);
    int home = x.home_node();
    // allocate a RDMA receive area from the device's buffer pool
    jackal_rdma_t *rmda_descr = jackal_rdma_alloc(home, reply_msg_size);
    if (rdma_descr) { // a suitable RDMA receive area was found,
        byte *end_msg_byte = rdma_descr->memory[reply_msg_size];
        *end_msg_byte = 0;
        send_fetch_request_with_rdma_reply(home, rdma_descr);
        // wait for the RNIC to copy the data in place
        while (*end_msg_byte == 0) {}
        process_object_reply_message(rdma_descr->local_memory);
        jackal_rdma_free(rdma_descr);
    } else {
        ack_t ack; // create a condition variable
        send_fetch_request_with_normal_reply_msg(home, &ack);
        // wait for then signal from by process_object_reply_message()
        thread_condition_wait(&ack);
    }
}
```

Fig. 2. An efficient way to use RDMA for fast object fetching

the requestor's memory because in general the requestor needs to execute additional protocol code upon message receipt. For example, in a situation where there are other threads that are concurrently executing at the requestor and that already had write access to the requested object, tests need to prevent their changes from being overwritten. A naive RDMA-write initiated by the home-node cannot detect such concurrent writes as it would require it to examine the requestor's states, the (current) requestor's copy and its twin.

We therefore RDMA the complete reply message in the format of the normally sent protocol message. In other words, process_object_reply_message is always invoked for a fetch-reply message, regardless of whether the message is received normally or via RDMA. The overhead of active polling for the (RDMA-ed) message receipt is acceptable even if concurrent threads at the requestor may be slowed down that way. Note that the active memory polling for message receipt in the RDMA cannot be circumvented, nor can the CPU be freed in the meantime. We can't free the CPU using thread-yield or sleep statements as either causes slow operating system calls or takes longer than a message latency. It can be argued that polling memory in a tight loop could saturate the memory bus. Fortunately however, the reads from memory in the polling loop run out of the processor's cache which is updated by a processor's internal consistency protocols on modern CPUs.

To summerize, for fetching objects, we must send the request as a normal mesage while the reply message can be sent by RDMA. The reply message, cannot write to the object in place in order to allow multi-threaded execution. Note that our RDMA-rpc implementation is similar to what certain MPI implementations do internally for managing acks. See for example [6].

We will now examine the opportunities of RDMA use (regardless of a performance gain/loss) when we need to update copies of objects on other machines.

5   Processing the List(s) of Cached Objects

Each thread maintains four lists of cached objects, one for machine local read-only regions where some other machine(s) are modifying it (local read-only), one for cluster-wide read-only regions (lazy flushing), one for objects that are used by only one machine (home-only), and one for locally modified objects. At each entry and exit of a synchronized block, all regions on these lists must be examined and processed (except those on the lazy flush list). Depending on a region's flag, the region is managed by the invalidation protocol handler or by an update protocol handler. This section discusses where RDMA can be used in those protocol handlers.

5.1   Invalidation Protocol Handlers

For each region on the list of locally modified regions we create a diff. These diffs are then streamed to the home-node in 4 KByte packets. By streaming the diffs (instead of buffering them to send them all at once) the home-node can already process incoming diffs while the invalidator still continues to create them. Likewise, for each region on the thread's read-only list, one-user-less messages are streamed to the home-node.

The region is removed from either list as soon as the messages have been sent. The home-only/lazy-flush lists are left alone. Upon receiving a diff or a one-user-less message, a state-machine quickly performs any necessary state changes to implement home migration, invalidation, or read-only replication.

Due the same reasons that prevented RDMA from being applicable to object requests (polling requirements, too complex for RDMA management, etc.), diff messages and one-user-less messages in the invalidation protocol cannot be transferred by means of RDMA either. Hence, invalidation protocols cannot exploit RDMA capabilities when propagating changes.

5.2 RDMA-Based Update Protocol Handlers

We have developed two alternative update protocols that solely use RDMA. The first one updates remote objects/arrays in place. Diffs between modified regions and their twins are created and applied (by RDMA) to the remote copies at all other machines. This is a true zero-copy protocol performing RDMA from one Java heap to another. The second update protocol stores the above diffs in a large intermediate array first, one per target machine. These arrays are then broadcast via RDMA to all other machines for local processing at their earliest convenience.

For simplicity of our prototype implementation, our current update/RDMA protocols do not allow objects containing reference fields. For such objects the invalidation protocol handler must be used. To illustrate the problem, consider the example in Fig. 3. Here we have two machines, 0 and 1. Machine 0 initially holds objects A and B, where A is marked for update-protocol management. The addresses of the copies of A are therefore known at all machines. However the addresses of the copies of B at the other machines are unknown.

Now a thread at machine 0 writes a reference to B in the R field of A. This eventually causes a broadcast of A to machine 1. However, to ensure correctness, the R field of A at machine 1 should be translated to the local copy of B (and potentially allocating the copy of B if it did not already exist). A simple RDMA of A however would not do this,

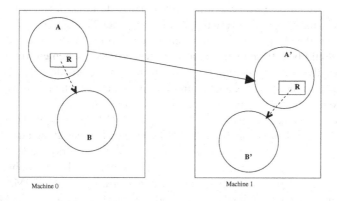

Fig. 3. Reference transfers

and write a copy of A with an illegal R field. Any circumvention of this problem would no longer make the protocol zero-copy.

To allow references in update-protocol managed objects the best solution would be to create a copy of the object in RDMA-able memory, replace references to their remotely valid equivalents, and RDMA the copy one-after-the-other to each machine. This is problematic as we need to know the remote addresses of *any* referred to objects, not only for update-protocol managed objects. This would cause memory shortage problems for maintaining the translation tables and additionally, large processing overheads as each machine would need to translate each reference for each machine to broadcast to.

Because of the difficulties outlined above, we support update protocols only for objects containing no reference fields at all (and default to an invalidation protocol for these).

Alternative 1, updating objects in place. To allow broadcasts of local modifications to objects to their copies on remote nodes by means of in-place RDMA, the entire Java object heap must be mapped and registered with the RDMA-device. Fortunately, this is not a problem with modern Infiniband hardware. Modifications to a region are found by comparison against its twin, which is a copy of the region from since it was last processed. Conceptually, for each region in the list of modified regions we invoke the update method shown in Fig. 4.

```
void update(Region r) {
    diff_t d = changes to r in respect to twin(r); apply 'd' to twin(r);
    for all machines p:
        int64_t remote_address = r->region_hash[p], remote_twin = r->twin_hash[p];
        RDMA 'd' to 'p' at remote_address and remote_twin;
}
```

Fig. 4. Update protocol handler, alternative 1: update in place

Note that we must update both the remote object and its remote twin because of the following scenario. Assume two machines that write to an object with two fields, X and Y. One machine exclusively modifies X the other Y. Machine 0 writes to X. It then broadcasts the change to machine 1 and updates its own twin. If the other twin on machine 1 would be left untouched, the next synchronized statement (by machine 1) would cause a diff to be created for field X, causing X to be broadcast back to machine 0 overwriting any changes to X at machine 1 made in between the two broadcasts. Our solution is to update both the remote region and the remote twin.

This protocol is a zero-copy protocol, since we RDMA the changed fields from one object directly over the corresponding fields in the object copies at the other machines.

To increase performance, we deal with ranges of fields or array elements that have changed at a time instead of processing single fields at a time. This intra-object coalescing of fields and array-element indexes allows to perform *some* bulk-RDMA. The same coalescing of changed fields inside single objects is used in Alternative 2 of the update protocol below as well.

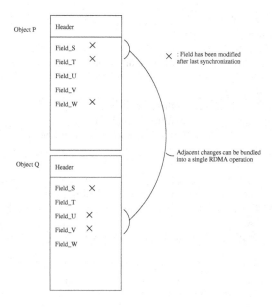

Fig. 5. Bulk communication example

To illustrate what exactly can and what cannot be shipped by bulk-RDMA, consider Fig. 5. Here, two objects, P and Q, have been allocated consecutively in memory. Each object is prefixed with an object header that contains information for the garbage collector, DSM, and the object's meta-information (pointer to the method table for the object, etc.). After the object-header reside the object's fields. The fields marked with an 'X' have been changed since the last lock/unlock (read: Java's synchronized).

During diff-creation, we first process object P, and create one RDMA-range for the combined fields S and T, and another RDMA-range for its field W. For object Q, we create RDMA-ranges for its field S and another for the combination of its fields U and V. To apply the diffs, we therefore have to perform four single RDMA-puts. We cannot merge the RDMA-ranges of P's W and Q's S due to the intervening object header (as the header is not read-only and furthermore, machine-local).

To summarize, this update protocol can be implemented with RDMA only. The upside of this update-protocol version is thus that there is virtually no overhead per object: (ranges of) changes in objects are copied from one machine directly to the copy on another machine. The downside is that there is no inter-object bulk-communication; only some intra-object bulk-communication is possible.

Alternative 2, RDMA-broadcast of diff-arrays. A potential problem with alternative 1 of the RDMA-update protocol is that there is little potential for bulk communication (it only supports some intra-object bulk communication). The second update protocol rectifies this by supporting inter-object bulk communication. It builds arrays of diffs and broadcasts these arrays in one go by means of RDMA, to all machines. Each machine then needs to periodically poll local memory to see if a new set of diffs has arrived and then process them. If polling is performed often enough, and if the received

```
void process_arrived_diff_arrays() {
    for each machine m and m != myself:
        patch m.diff_array in locally;
        RDMA m.diff_array.seq_num to 'm' at m.diff_array.remote_ack_seq_num
}
void find_locally_created_changes() {
    for all update_region r on thread->cached_modified_list:
        for each machine m: append diff(r) to m.diff_array,
                            m.diff_array.seq_number = m.current_bcast_seq_num;
}
void broadcast_new_diff_array() {
    for each machine m:
        while m.current_bcast_seq_num != m.diff_array.acked_seq_num:
            ; // wait RDMA-ed ack
        m.current_bcast_seq_num++;
        RDMA m.diff_array to 'm' at 'm.remote_diff_array';
}
```

Fig. 6. Update protocol handler, alternative 2: the three steps to process diff-arrays

diff-arrays are easy to process, overheads are low. In our implementation, diff-array elements consist of a target address, a length in bytes, and the changed bytes. The methods needed to process the list of modified regions are given in Fig. 6.

For the example of Fig. 5, we would create one diff-array containing the diff-ranges {P.S-P.T}, {P.W}, {Q.S}, and {Q.U-Q.V}. These diff-ranges are then copied into RDMA-able memory and copied by one single RDMA to all other machines.

The diff-array protocol therefore globally performs the following three steps. We first check for diff-arrays that have arrived from other machines. Any incoming diffs are applied to the local regions and their twins. Secondly, we create local diff-arrays, one for each target machine (for regions that are not already handled by the invalidation protocol). Finally, the diff-arrays are broadcast by RDMA. Note that a shipment of a diff-array must have been acknowledged before shipping the next diff-array.

To understand the need for an ack-protocol, think of two machines 0 and 1, and two objects, A and B. Machine 0 first updates A and broadcasts its modifications by placing them into the diff-array in machine 1. Let us assume that directly afterwards, machine 0 were to update B and broadcast the changes to B with a new diff-array. If machine 1 had not yet acked the processing of the first diff(-array), the second broadcast would overwrite the first diff(-array). The first diff and the update to A would be lost. We therefore need an acknowledgment scheme.

We have implemented the acknowledgments with single-word RDMA-writes for efficiency. As soon as a machine has processed a diff-array it performs a single-word RDMA to the diff-array originator. The acknowledgement protocol itself has thus a very low overhead.

To summarize, this second update protocol can also be implemented with RDMA only. The upside of this update-protocol version is that we allow both intra- and inter-object bulk-communication to occur by sending arrays of diffs at a time. The downside of this protocol is that the receiver needs to periodically test if a diff has to be processed.

If the receiver does not react quickly enough, the sender will need to wait a long time for diff-processing acknowledgements.

6   Performance

Two aspects are important for DSM performance, the latency of fetching objects and the available bandwidth for flushing or broadcasting modifications. This section analyzes performance with some micro-benchmarks and two applications. We use *Water* and *LU* from the SPLASH benchmark suite [11]. Both are irregular and challenging and thus stress the DSM protocols. Regular applications or applications with little communication are not well suited for showing protocol performance as differences are rarely visible. Also, Water and LU form the extremes of a spectrum: whereas Water uses many small objects, LU uses only one single array with larger contiguous modifications.

Our measurements were performed on a cluster of dual Xeon 3.20 GHz "Nocona" machines (800 MHz bus, 666 MHz front-side bus) with 2 GByte RAM each. The cluster uses an Infiniband interconnect (10 GBit/s). We use our own low-latency communication package that maps directly to the Infiniband driver's libraries. Our communication package maps RDMA-puts directly on top of the Infiniband verbs layer to get the best possible performance out of Infiniband. Note that normal message sends also use the Infiniband verbs layer directly so that both normal message sends and RDMA sends are fully optimized.

Micro-benchmarks. We first evaluate Jackal's performance for some simple primitive operations so that we can eliminate these as the sources of overhead in later benchmarks. The relevant data is given in the upper part of Table 1 (to simplify presentation, we only present numbers for 1, 2, and 8 machines (read: '1, 2 and many')).

To perform a synchronized block in a loop using one or two machines costs about the same (568181 vs. 566051 locks per second). This is due to the low contention ratio for the lock. The communication costs are very low given that only very small messages are needed and most of the time these messages are handled entirely by the communication thread (the thread that handles all incoming normal messages; RDMA messages of course bypass this thread). On eight machines, the machine that holds the lock object becomes overloaded with request and release messages. Hence, performance drops. Lock contention does not yet seem to be a problem however.

Table 1. Micro-benchmark results

	1 machine	2 machines	8 machines
# Locks/second	568181	566051	1768
# Barriers/second	—	15015	9174
Object-request latency (no RDMA)	—	49.9 μs	49.9 μs
Object-request latency (RDMA)	—	24.6 μs	24.6 μs
RDMA-invalidation-flush-bandwidth	1.0 GByte/s	64.0 MByte/s	13.3 MByte/s
RDMA-in-place-update bandwidth	1.2 GByte/s	91.0 MByte/s	9.6 MByte/s
RDMA-diff-array-update bandwidth	1.2 GByte/s	84.0 MByte/s	7.7 MByte/s

For the barrier micro-benchmark we use a Java object that consists of two fields, a barrier-entry limit and a barrier-entry counter. The main work is performed in a synchronized method that increments the counter. If the counter reaches its limit, the methods calls *Object.notifyAll()*, otherwise *Object.wait()*. Each entry/exit of the synchronized method and the execution of the *wait* method causes an invalidation of the cached objects and sends the barrier object to its home.

The *lock, unlock, Object.notify()*, and *Object.wait()* are implemented as normal messages sent to the home-node of the barrier object where they attempt to locally lock the object. If the lock succeeds or the wait finishes, acknowledgement messages are sent back to the remote machine to allow it to continue. In total, including flush messages and synchronization messages, we achieve a barrier time of 109 μs per barrier on 8 machines ($\frac{1}{9174}$). While the absolute number may seem high, given the much lower latencies for, say, an MPI barrier on Infiniband, Java's semantics add significant overhead to a barrier. For example, to handle multi-threading, Java requires an implementation to flush working memory, to send synchronization related messages, to handle Object.wait() and Object.notify(), and finally to wake up threads from thread-pools to handle protocol messages. With all this overhead, 109 μs is quite good.

Object request speed is measured by traversing a linked list. Each access to the 'next' field in a linked node causes that node to be fetched. For a list containing N elements, we thus get 2 N messages (one request message, one reply message with the node's data). We then take the average time required for a single list node fetch. Enabling RDMA for object requests almost halves the latency for fetching a node (even though only one side of the round trip can be optimized via RDMA). The numbers include the time needed for state updates, address translations, and for allocating a local copy for every list node. Regardless of whether 2 or 8 machines are used, the times are the same due to the low protocol processing overheads.

User level bandwidth is measured as follows. All machines (1 thread per machine) concurrently execute a loop and change each N-th element of a 32KByte array. The modifications are propagated via a single, empty synchronized block. This inner loop is performed 20.000 times to give us an indication of the application-level bandwidth available (32K * 20.000 / # seconds used). The same benchmark is used for the invalidation protocol and the two update protocols. When only 1 or 2 machines are used, both update protocols outperform the invalidation protocol. With larger numbers of machines, the invalidation protocol wins due to the high overheads in both update protocols. Note that for all bandwidth measurements, RDMA is also used for region requests (repeatedly for the invalidation protocol, once for the update protocols).

Water performs an (N-square) N-body simulation of water molecules coded as in Fig. 7. We simulate only 1728 molecules to stress protocols. The innermost array elements (the NUM_ATOMS dimension of MolData), contain the actual molecule data. The other data here is read-only and is cluster-wide read-only replicated by the protocols. Note that NUM_ATOMS equals '3' here (for two hydrogen atoms and one oxygen atom). This stresses protocols as modified data is encapsulated in many of these small arrays.

```
class MolData {
    double [][]data = new double [NUM_DIMENSIONS] [NUM_ATOMS];
    ...
}

class MoleculeEnsemble {
    MolData[][] f = new MolData [MAX_ORDERS] [ getNumMolecules() ];
    ...
}
```

Fig. 7. Water's main datastructures

An invalidation protocol with switched on RDMA-request, improves performance by 20.6% on 8 machines (13.1 seconds with RDMA-request versus 16.5 seconds with regular messaging, see Table 2).

Regardless of the number of machines used, both update protocols are slower as we pay two penalties. First, although changes are broadcast to every machine (eliminating the need to explicitly fetch them), the changes are not used by *every* processor. The exact set of consumers is hard to detect by the DSM protocol without changing Water's source code. In contrast, the invalidation protocol pulls the changes to only those machines that require them.

The second penalty is due to Java's lack of true multi-dimensional arrays (Java provides only arrays of references to sub-arrays). Since the data of all the innermost 1D arrays are not contiguous in memory, the first RDMA update protocol (updates in place) needs a large number of RDMA transfers. On the other hand, the diff-array RDMA update protocol version has a lot of administrative overhead for each diff-array. Even the higher efficiency of the RDMA hardware (compared to normal send/receive) cannot overcome this. The slight advantage of diff-array RDMA-update protocol on only two machines is quickly lost with increasing numbers of machines.

LU factorizes a dense matrix, encoded as a single flattened array of doubles. Due to the blocking technique used, every machine accesses only a few linear segments of array elements. Hence the number of region fetches needed is less than in Water. Use of RDMA improves the performance of the invalidation protocol only slightly by 3.6% (19.6 versus 18.9 seconds).

Table 2. Application results in walltime (seconds)

	1 machine	2 machines	8 machines
Water, no RDMA	56.4	41.2	16.5
Water, RDMA-request invalidation	56.4	40.2	13.1
Water, RDMA-in-place-update	56.9	41.1	26.8
Water, RDMA-diff-array-update	56.9	36.6	20.0
LU, no RDMA	47.3	30.1	19.6
LU, RDMA-request invalidation	47.3	32.9	18.9
LU, RDMA-in-place-update	47.0	37.5	26.1
LU, RDMA-diff-array-update	47.0	41.1	23.2

The update protocols are always a loss for LU. Unlike Water, LU's threads write larger consecutive chunks in a single linearized matrix. Because of array chunking, fewer updates and hence fewer RDMA broadcasts are needed. A few hundreds of 2 KByte array segments are broadcast instead of tens of thousands of 24 byte broadcasts as in Water. LU also suffers from the effect that broadcast data is often not (immediately) used by the receiving CPUs. Hence the invalidation protocol (with RDMA fetch) is faster.

Finally, there are many array sections on the list of modified regions that are actually *unmodified* since the last list processing. This happens because in update protocols, modified regions are never removed from the modified-regions list, causing many empty diffs. However, since we still need to test every single array element for potential modifications at each synchronization, the processing requirements of the update protocols increase. In Water, this effect does not occur since each processor writes the same water molecules each time. Of course, the invalidation protocol does not suffer from this effect as its regions are removed from the modified-regions list at invalidation time (but each access afterward triggers an access check to add it again to one of the flush-lists).

7   Conclusions

In our system, invalidation and update protocol managed regions can coexist. We found that RDMA can be successfully applied to invalidation protocols and have designed two update protocols that solely use RDMA. We have seen performance inprovements of up to 20.6% using RDMA for object-fetching. Without source code changes (for example, those suggested by [3]), even when modern RDMA hardware is used throughout, update protocols are still slower than invalidation protocols. This is because of three main reasons. First, when adding address translation to allow large address spaces, the cost of protocol processing grows large in update-protocols as they need, per-machine processing.

Second, message aggregation is hard to do with current Infiniband RDMA implementations as they currently lack remote scatter. Ideally, we would like to present the RDMA hardware with two lists of I/O vectors. One I/O vector for where to copy the data from at the local machine, and another I/O vector for where to copy the data to at the target machine. The current Infiniband VERBS allows only very limited use of I/O vectors.

Finally, another RDMA-feature currently missing is signalled-IO. Signalled RDMA would cause an interrupt at the receiver once data has been copied. This would not only allow to free the CPU when waiting for message replies but it would also allow us to immediately reply to unexpected incoming messages (instead of periodically tested for them).

References

1. Carter, J.B., Bennett, J.K., Zwaenepoel, W.: Techniques for reducing consistency-related communication in distributed shared-memory systems. ACM Trans. Comput. Syst. 13(3), 205–243 (1995)

2. Eichner, H., Trinitis, C., Klug, T.: Implementation of a DSM-System on Top of InfiniBand. In: Proc. 14th Euromicro Intl. Conf. on Parallel, Distributed, and Network-Based Processing (PDP 2006), Washington, DC, pp. 178–183 (February 2006)

3. Falsafi, B., Lebeck, A.R., Reinhardt, S.K., Schoinas, I., Hill, M.D., Larus, J.R., Rogers, A., Wood, D.A.: Application-specific protocols for user-level shared memory. In: Supercomputing, Washington, DC, pp. 380–389 (November 1994)

4. Fang, W., Wang, C.L., Zhu, W., Lau, F.C.M.: A novel adaptive home migration protocol in home-based DSM. In: Proc. of the 2004 IEEE Intl. Conf. on Cluster Computing, San Diego, CA, pp. 215–224 (September 2004)

5. Iosevich, V., Schuster, A.: Multithreaded Home-Based Lazy Release Consistency over VIA. In: Proc. 19th IEEE Intl. Parallel and Distributed Processing Symp (IPDPS 2004), Santa Fe, New Mexico, pp. 59–70 (April 2004)

6. Liu, J., Jiang, W., Wyckoff, P., Panda, D., Ashton, D., Buntinas, D., Gropp, W., Toonen, B.: Design and Implementation of MPICH2 over InfiniBand with RDMA Support. In: Int'l Parallel and Distributed Processing Symposium (IPDPS 2004), Santa Fe, NM (April 2004)

7. Noronha, R., Panda, D.K.: Reducing Diff Overhead in Software DSM Systems using RDMA Operations in InfiniBand. In: Workshop on Remote Direct Memory Access (RDMA): RAIT 2004 (Cluster 2004), San Diego, CA (September 2004)

8. Protic, J., Tomasevic, M., Milutinovic, V.: A survey of distributed shared memory systems. In: Proc. 28th Hawaii Intl. Conf. on System Sciences (HICSS 1995), pp. 74–84 (January 1995)

9. Veldema, R., Hofman, R.F.H., Bhoedjang, R.A.F., Bal, H.E.: Runtime-Optimizations for a Java DSM. In: Proc. ACM 2001 Java Grande Conf., San Francisco, CA, pp. 89–98 (June 2001)

10. Veldema, R., Hofman, R.F.H., Bhoedjang, R.A.F., Jacobs, C.J.H., Bal, H.E.: Source-level global optimizations for fine-grain distributed shared memory systems. In: 8th Symp. on Principles and Practices of Parallel Programming (PPoPP), Snowbird, Utah, pp. 83–92 (June 2001)

11. Woo, S.C., Ohara, M., Torrie, E., Singh, J.P., Gupta, A.: The SPLASH-2 Programs: Characterization and Methodological Considerations. In: Proc. 22nd Intl. Symp. on Computer Architecture, Santa Margherita Ligure, Italy, pp. 24–36 (June 1995)

Automatic Communication Performance Debugging in PGAS Languages

Jimmy Su[1] and Katherine Yelick[1,2]

[1] Computer Science Division, University of California at Berkeley
[2] Lawrence Berkeley National Laboratory
{jimmysu,yelick}@cs.berkeley.edu

Abstract. Recent studies have shown that programming in a Partition Global Address Space (PGAS) language can be more productive than programming in a message passing model. One reason for this is the ability to access remote memory implicitly through shared memory reads and writes. But this benefit does not come without a cost. It is very difficult to spot communication by looking at the program text, since remote reads and writes look exactly the same as local reads and writes. This makes manual communication performance debugging an arduous task. In this paper, we describe a tool called `ti-trend-prof` that can do automatic performance debugging using only program traces from small processor configurations and small input sizes in Titanium [13], a PGAS language. `ti-trend-prof` presents trends to the programmer to help spot possible communication performance bugs even for processor configurations and input sizes that have not been run. We used `ti-trend-prof` on two of the largest Titanium applications and found bugs that would have taken days in under an hour.

Keywords: PGAS languages, automatic performance debugging.

1 Introduction

Titanium is a Partitioned Global Address Space language. It combines the programming convenience of shared memory with the locality and performance control of message passing. In Titanium, a thread running on one processor can directly read or write the memory associated with another. This feature significantly increases programmer productivity, since the programmer does not need to write explicit communication calls as in the message passing model. Unfortunately, this is also a significant source of performance bugs. Many unintended small remote reads and writes go undetected during manual code audits, because they look exactly the same as local reads and writes in the program text. Furthermore, these performance bugs often do not manifest themselves until the program is run with large processor configurations and/or large input sizes. This means the bugs are caught much later in the development cycle, making them more expensive to fix.

In this paper, we describe an automatic communication performance debugging tool for Titanium that can catch this type of bugs using only program runs with small processor configurations and small input sizes. Trends on the number of communication

V. Adve, M.J. Garzarán, and P. Petersen (Eds.): LCPC 2007, LNCS 5234, pp. 232–245, 2008.
© Springer-Verlag Berlin Heidelberg 2008

calls are presented to the programmer for each location in the source code that incurred communication during the program runs. Each trend is modeled by a linear function or a power law function in terms of the number of processors or the input problem size. The models can be used to predict communication performance bottlenecks for processor configurations and problem sizes that have not yet been run. We used the debugging tool on two of the largest Titanium applications and report the bugs that were found using the tool.

2 Motivating Example

To illustrate the difficulty of manual performance debugging in a PGAS language like Titanium, we will use a simple sum reduction example in this section. Processor 0 owns a double array. We would like to compute the sum of every element in the array. To spread the workload among the processors, each processor gets a piece of the array and computes the sum for that part. At the end, the partial sums are added together using a reduction.

Two versions of the code are shown in Figure 1 and Figure 2. The code in Figure 1 has a performance bug in it. The two versions are identical except for two lines of code. The loop that computes the actual sum is identical. In the buggy version, each processor only has a pointer to the array on processor 0. `array.restrict(myPart)` returns a pointer to a subsection of `array` that contains elements from `startIndex` to `endIndex`. Each dereference in the foreach loop results in communication to processor 0 to retrieve the value at that array index. Processor 0 becomes the communication bottleneck as all other processors are retrieving values from it.

```
1   double [1d] array;
2   if (Ti.thisProc() == 0){
3       array = new double[0:999];
4   }
5   array = broadcast array from 0;
6   int workload = 1000 / Ti.numProcs();
7   if (Ti.thisProc() < 1000 % Ti.numProcs()){
8       workload++;
9   }
10  int startIndex = Ti.thisProc() * workload;
11  int endIndex = startIndex + workload - 1;
12  RectDomain<1> myPart = [startIndex:endIndex];
13  double [1d] localArray = array.restrict(myPart);
14  double mySum = 0;
15  double sum;
16
17  foreach (p in localArray.domain()) {
18      mySum += localArray[p];
19  }
20   sum = Reduce.add(mySum, 0);
```

Fig. 1. Sum reduction example with performance bug in it (Version 1)

```
12   RectDomain<1> myPart = [startIndex:endIndex];
13   double [1d] localArray = new double[myPart];
14   localArray.copy(array.restrict(myPart));
15   double mySum = 0;
16   double sum;
17
18   foreach (p in localArray.domain()) {
19     mySum += localArray[p];
20   }
21
22   sum = Reduce.add(mySum, 0);
```

Fig. 2. Sum reduction example without the performance bug (Version 2)

Figure 2 shows the version without the performance bug in it. Each processor first allocates space for the localArray, then it retrieves the part of array that it needs into localArray using one array copy call. The array copy results in one bulk get communication. The subsequent dereferences inside the loop are all local.

Although this is a very simple example, this kind of communication pattern is quite common, especially in the initialization phase of a parallel program, where processor 0 typically processes the input before distributing the workload to the rest of the processors. It is difficult to catch this type of bugs manually in Titanium, since the two versions of the program look very similar. For small processor configurations, the performance degradation may not be noticeable given that the initialization is run only once.

We would like a tool that can alert the programmer to possible performance bugs automatically earlier in the development cycle, when we are only testing the program with small processor configurations and small input sizes. For this example, the number of communication calls at the array dereference in the buggy version can be expressed as $(1-1/p)*size$, where p is the number of processors and size is the size of the array. If we fix the array size at 1000 elements, then we can see that the number of communication calls at the array dereference varies with the number of processors as in Figure 3. The graph shows the actual observed communication calls at the array dereference for 2, 4, and 8 processors along with the predicted curves for both versions of the code.

In the rest of this paper, we will describe a tool called ti-trend-prof that can present communication trends automatically given only program traces for small processor configurations and/or small input sizes.

3 Background

Before getting into the details of ti-trend-prof, we will give the necessary background information in this section. This includes brief introductions on Titanium, GASNet trace, and trend-prof.

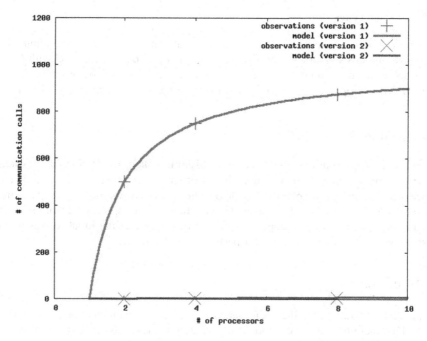

Fig. 3. The number of communication calls at the array dereference is expressed in terms of the number of processors for a fixed array size of 1000 elements for both versions of the program. The X axis is the number of processors, and the Y axis is the number of communication calls. Version 1 is clearly not scalable. For larger array sizes, the gap between version 1 and version 2 would widen.

3.1 Titanium

Titanium is a dialect of Java, but does not use the Java Virtual Machine model. Instead, the end target is assembly code. For portability, Titanium is first translated into C and then compiled into an executable. In addition to generating C code to run on each processor, the compiler generates calls to a runtime layer based on GASNet [2], a lightweight communication layer that exploits hardware support for direct remote reads and writes when possible. Titanium runs on a wide range of platforms including uniprocessors, shared memory machines, distributed-memory clusters of uniprocessors or SMPs (CLUMPS), and a number of specific supercomputer architectures (Cray X1, Cray T3E, SGI Altix, IBM SP, Origin 2000, and NEC SX6).

Titanium is a single program, multiple data (SPMD) language, so all threads execute the same code image. A thread running on one processor can directly read or write the memory associated with another. This feature significantly increases programmer productivity, since the programmer does not need to write explicit communication calls as in the message passing model.

3.2 GASNet Trace

Titanium's GASNet backends include features that can be used to trace communication using the GASNet trace tool. When a Titanium program is compiled with GASNet trace enabled, a communication log is kept for each run of the program. In this communication log, each communication event along with the source code line number is recorded.

3.3 Trend-Prof

`trend-prof` [7] is a tool developed by Goldsmith, Aiken, and Wilkerson for measuring empirical computational complexity of programs. It constructs models of empirical computational complexity that predict how many times each basic block in a program runs as a linear or a power law function of user-specified features of the program's workloads. An example feature can be the size of the input. It was previously used on sequential programs for performance debugging.

4 Bug Types

In parallel programming, there are many causes for communication performance bugs. This includes excessive amount of communication calls, excessive volume of communication, and load imbalance. Our work so far in `ti-trend-prof` has been focused on finding the first type of bugs automatically. Our framework can be extended to address the other two types of bugs. In Titanium, there are two main causes for excessive amount of communication calls:

1. Remote pointer dereference
2. Distribution of global meta-data

The first case can come up in two situations. One is when a processor has a shallow copy of an object that contains remote references in its fields. Even though the object is in local memory, accessing its field that contains remote reference would result in a round trip of small messages to a remote processor. If the field is accessed frequently during program execution, it can significantly degrade performance. The second situation comes up during workload distribution among processors. In parallel program, it is often the case that one processor does I/O during initialization, and then the workload is distributed among all processors. The motivating example in Section 2 fits this description.

The second case comes from distribution of global meta-data. In parallel programs, it is often desirable to have global meta-data available to each processor so that it can find remote objects by following pointers. Each processor owns a list of objects. A naïve way of programming the distribution of meta-data is by broadcasting each pointer individually. This performance bug would not be noticeable when the number of objects is small. Only a large problem size would expose this problem, which is likely to be much later in the development cycle.

In the experimental section, we will show that these types of performance bugs exist in two of the largest Titanium applications written by experienced programmers, and `ti-trend-prof` allowed us to find the bugs automatically within an hour instead of days through manual debugging.

5 `ti-trend-prof`

In this work, a new tool called `ti-trend-prof` is developed to combine the use of GASNet trace and `trend-prof` to do communication performance debugging for parallel programs. `ti-trend-prof` takes GASNet trace outputs for small processor configurations and/or small input sizes, and feeds them to a modified version of `trend-prof` that can parse GASNet trace outputs. The output is a table of trends per Titanium source code location that incurred communication for the input traces.

The number of processors and the input problem size can be used as features. The linear function $a + bx$ and the standard power law function with offset $a + bx^c$ are used to model the trend at each source code location. The function which minimizes error is picked to be the model. For example, if we fixed the problem size and varied the number of processors, then the trend would tell us how does the number of communication calls change at this location as we vary the number of processors. Similarly, if we fixed the number of processors and varied the problem size, then the trend would tell us how does the number of communication calls change as we vary the problem size. These trends can be used to predict communication performance bottlenecks for processor configurations and input sizes that we have not run yet. This is particularly useful in the beginning of the development cycle, where we do most of the testing on small processor configurations and small inputs. In the table, the trends are first ranked by the exponent, then by the coefficient. Larger values are placed earlier in the table. The goal is to display trends that are least scalable first to the programmer.

In practice, many of the communication patterns can be modeled by the linear function or the power law function. But there are algorithms that do not fall into this category, such as a tree based algorithms or algorithms that change behavior based on the number of processors used. We don't intend to use the linear or power law trends as the exact prediction in communication calls, but rather as an indicator for possible performance bugs. For example, if the number of communication calls at a location is exponential in terms of the number of processors, then `ti-trend-prof` would output a power law function with a large exponent. Although this does not match the actual exponential behavior, it would surely be presented early in the output to alert the programmer.

6 Experimental Results

In this section, we show the experimental results on running `ti-trend-prof` on two large Titanium applications: heart simulation [6] and AMR [12]. To obtain the GASNet trace files, the programs were run on a cluster, where each node has a dual core Opteron. We used both cores during the runs. This means that intra-node communication is through shared memory, which does not contribute to communication calls in the GASNet trace counts.

6.1 Heart Simulation

The heart simulation code is one of the largest Titanium applications written today. It has over 10000 lines of code developed over 6 years. As the application matures, the focus has been on scaling the code to larger processor configurations and larger problem sizes. The initialization code has remained largely unchanged over the years. Correctness in the initialization code is crucial. But we have not done much performance tuning on the initialization code, since it is run only once in the beginning of execution.

Recently, we had scaled the heart simulation up to 512 processors on a 512^3 problem. On our initial runs, the simulation never got passed the initialization phase after more than 4 hours on the 512 processors. The culprit is in the following lines of code.

```
// missing immutable keyword
class FiberDescriptor{
    public long filepos;
    public double minx, maxx, miny, maxy, minz, maxz;
    . . .
}

/* globalFibersArray and the elements in it live on
processor 0 */
FiberDescriptor [1d] globalFibersArray;
FiberDescriptor [1d] local localFibersArray;
. . .
localFibersArray.copy(globalFibersArray);
foreach (p in localFibersArray.domain()){
    FiberDescriptor fd = localFibersArray[p];
    /* Determine if fd belongs to this processor by ex-
amining the fields of fd */
    . . .
}
```

Fig. 4. Fiber distribution code containing a performance bug due to lack of immutable keyword

The programmer meant to add the "immutable" keyword to the declaration for the FiberDescriptor class. But the keyword was missing. Immutable classes extend the notion of Java primitive type to classes. For this example, if the FiberDescriptor were immutable, then the array copy prior to the foreach loop would copy every element in the globalFibersArray to the localFibersArray including the fields of each element. Without the "immutable" keyword, each processor only contains an array of pointers in localFibersArray to FiberDescriptor objects that live on processor 0. When each processor other than processor 0 accesses the fields of a FiberDescriptor object, a request and reply message would occur between the processor accessing the field and processor 0. This performance bug is hard to find manually because the source of the bug and the place where the problem is observed are far from each other.

When the processor configuration is small and the number of `FiberDescriptor` objects is small, the effects of this performance bug are hardly observable. Only when we start scaling the application over 100 processors on the 512^3 problem did we notice the problem. The size of the `globalFibersArray` grows proportionately to the problem size of the input. As we increase the number of processors for the same size problem, the number of field accesses to `FiberDescriptor` objects increases linearly. Each processor reads through the entire array to see which fiber belongs to it. Every field access to a `FiberDescriptor` object results in messages to processor 0. At large processor configurations and large problem sizes, the flood of small messages to and from processor 0 becomes the performance bottleneck.

`ti-trend-prof` can catch this bug earlier in the development cycle using only program runs from small processor configurations and small input sizes. It presents the trends in the communication performance both in terms of the number of processors and the input size. Trends are presented for each location in the source code that incurred communication as reflected in the GASNet traces. For a large application such as the heart code, there are many places in the program where communication occurs. In order to present the most interesting results to the user first, trends are sorted first by the exponent followed by the coefficients. Large values get placed earlier in the table. This allows users to see the least scalable locations predicted by the trends first.

Table 1. Trends output from `ti-trend-prof` for the heart simulation given the GASNet traces for the 128^3 size problem on 4, 8, 16 and 32 processors

Location	Operation	Feature	Max
FFTfast.ti 8727	Get	$41p^2 - 416$	198400
FFTfast.ti 8035	Put	$41p^2 - 416$	198400
MyMailBox.ti 384	Put	$9p^2 - 789$	404120
MetisDistributor.ti 1537	Get	$304690p - 1389867$	18330567
FluidSlab.ti 3685	Put	$200p$	12800
FluidSlab.ti 3725	Put	$200p$	12800

Table 1 shows the trends presented by `ti-trend-prof` given GASNet traces for the heart code on 4, 8, 16, and 32 processors for the 128^3 problem. The trend for the performance bug is in red. The trend shows that the number of get calls on line 1537 in the MetisDistributor file is a linear function with a large coefficient. This clearly alarms the programmer since the number of communication calls should be zero at this location if the "immutable" keyword were not missing. Figure 5 shows the power law model for the buggy line along with observed data.

`ti-trend-prof` can find this same bug in another way. Figure 6 shows the trend when given GASNet traces for the 32^3, 64^3, and 128^3 size problems on 8 processors. The trend for the performance bug location in terms of the input size also clearly indicates that there is a performance bug here. The number of get calls grows super linearly with the problem size. If the "immutable" keyword were there, there should not be any communication calls for this location.

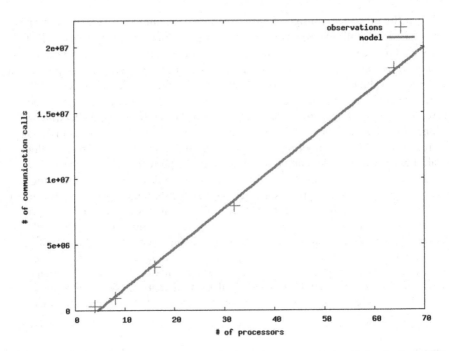

Fig. 5. Graph of the power law function generated by `ti-trend-prof` for the buggy line along with actual observations of communication counts. The X axis is the number of processors, and the Y axis is the count of communication calls.

We also note that not all trends presented by `trend-prof` are performance bugs. For example, the first trend presented in Table 1 represents the communication pattern during the global transpose in the FFT. The global transpose uses an all to all communication pattern, which makes the number of communication calls grow as the square of the number of processors. The trend presented by `trend-prof` confirms this.

6.2 Adaptive Mesh Refinement

Adaptive Mesh Refinement (AMR) is another large Titanium application. AMR is used for numerical modeling of various physical problems which exhibit multiscale behavior. At each level of refinement, rectangular grids are divided into boxes distributed among processors. Using `ti-trend-prof`, we were able to find two performance bugs in AMR, where one was known prior from manual debugging and the other was not found previously.

6.2.1 Excessive Use of Broadcasts
The first bug appears in the meta-data set up of the boxes at each refinement level. Boxes are distributed among all the processors. But each processor needs to have the

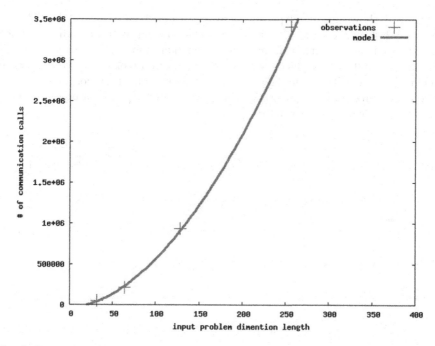

Fig. 6. Graph of the power law function generated by `ti-trend-prof` for the buggy line along with actual observations of communication counts. The X axis is the dimension length of the input problem, (dimension length)^3 gives us the input problem size. The Y axis is the communication count.

meta-data to find neighboring boxes that may live on another processor. Figure 7 shows the code for setting up the meta-data. Instead of using array copies to copy the array of pointers from each processor, it uses one broadcast per box to set up the global box array TA. For a fixed size problem, the number of broadcasts due to the code in Figure 7 is the same regardless of the number of processors. But each processor must wait for the broadcast value to arrive if the broadcast originates from a remote processor. As more processors are added for the fixed size problem, more of the values come from remote processors. Subsequently, each processor performs more waits at the barrier as the number of processors increases, and the total number of wait calls sum over all processors increases linearly as shown in Figure 8. If array copies were used, the number of communication calls should only increase by $2p-1$ when we add one more processor.

```
/* Meta-data set up*/
for (k=0;k<m_numOfProcs;k++)
    for (j=0;j<(int single)m_layout.numBoxesAt(k);j++)
        TA[k][j]=broadcast TA[k][j] from k;
```

Fig. 7. Fiber distribution code containing a performance bug due to lack of immutable keyword

Figure 8 shows the trend presented by `ti-trend-prof` given the GASNet traces for 2, 4, 6, and 8 processors for the 128^3 problem. It clearly indicates to the programmer that the increase in number of communication calls is larger than expected. Prior to the development of `ti-trend-prof`, it took three programmers to find this bug manually in four days. Similar to the bug in the heart code, the bug was caught late in the development cycle. This performance bug did not become noticeable until we ran the code beyond 100 processors.

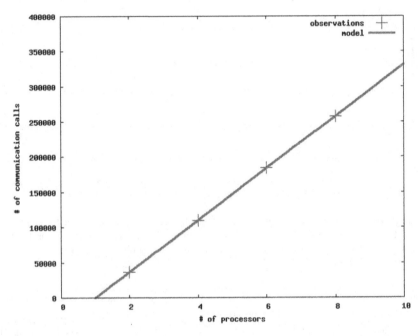

Fig. 8. Graph of the power law function generated by `ti-trend-prof` for the excessive broadcast along with actual observations of communication counts. Each processor must wait at the broadcast if the broadcast originates from a remote processor. As the number of processor increases for a fixed size problem, more of the broadcast values come from remote processors.

6.2.2 Shallow Copy of Meta-data

After the set up of meta-data, each processor only has a pointer to boxes that live remotely. Whenever it needs to perform operations on the underlying array for the box, it needs to call an accessor method for the box, which incurs communication if the box is remote. The number of calls that require communication increases with the number of processors, because more neighboring boxes become remote as processors are added. `ti-trend-prof` reports that the number of communication calls resulting from the accessor method grows almost as the square of the number of processors. If we had a deeper copy of the meta-pointer, which includes the caching of the pointer to the underlying array, we would avoid a majority of the communication calls at the accessor method. The meta-data for the boxes are reused over many iterations. This bug was not found previous through manual performance debugging.

7 Related Work

There has been vast amount of work in the area of performance debugging in both sequential programs and parallel programs. For sequential programs, gprof [8] is a widely used tool for estimating how much time is spent in each function. Gprof samples the program counter during a single run of the program. Then it uses these samples to propagate back to the call graph during post processing. The key difference is that we use multiple runs of the program to come up with trends that can predict performance problems for processor configurations and/or problem sizes that have not been run. Gprof only gives performance information for a single run of the program.

Kluge et al. [9] focus specifically on how the time a MPI program spends communicating scales with the number of processors. They fit these observations to a degree two polynomial, finding a, b, and c to fit $y = a+bx+cx^2$. Any part of the program with a large value for c is said to parallelize badly. Our work differs in that we can use both the number of processors and the input size as features to predict performance. We have used our tool on large real applications. The experiment in [9] only shows data from a Sweep3D benchmark on a single node SMP. Their technique is likely to have much worst errors when used on a cluster of SMPs. They are modeling MPI time, which would be affected by how many processors are used within a node to run MPI. All processors within a node share resource in communication with other nodes. Furthermore, our target programs are written in a PGAS language instead of MPI, which are much harder to find communication locations manually by looking at the program text.

Vetter and Worley [11] develop a technique called performance assertions that allows users to assert performance expectations explicitly in their source code. As the application executes, each performance assertion in the application collects data implicitly to verify the assertion. In contrast, ti-trend-prof does not require additional work from the user to add annotations. Furthermore, it may not be obvious to the programmer as to which code segment should have performance assertions. ti-trend-prof found performance bugs in code segments where the user didn't think was performance critical. But those performance bugs severely degrade performance only on large processor configurations and large problem sizes, and ti-trend-prof helps the user to identify them by presenting the trends.

Coarfa et al. [4] develop the technique for identifying scalability bottlenecks in SPMD programs by identifying parts of the program that deviates from ideal scaling. In strong scaling, linear speedup is expected. And in weak scaling, constant execution time is expected. Call path profiles are collected for two or more executions on different numbers of processors. Parts of the program that do not meet the scaling expectations are identified for the user.

Brewer [3] constructs models to predict performance of a library function implementation as a function of problem parameters. The parameters are supplied by the user. For example, the radix width can be a parameter for an implementation of the radix sort algorithm. Based on those parameters, the tool picks the implementation that the model predicts to be the best. Our tool does not require the user to have the knowledge to supply such parameters.

There are also vast amount of work based on the LogP [5] technique. In particular, Rugina and Schauser [10] simulate the computation and communication of parallel programs to predict their worst-case running time given the LogGP [1] parameters for the targeted machine. Their focus is on how to tune a parallel program by changing communication patterns given a fixed size input.

8 Conclusion

In this paper, we described a tool called `ti-trend-prof` that can help Titanium programmers to do communication performance debugging automatically. Given only program traces from small processor configurations and/or small input sizes, `ti-trend-prof` provides trends for each source code location that incurred communication. Trends are modeled as a standard power law function with offset. Programmers are alerted to trends with large exponents and coefficients, which correspond to possible communication performance bug in the program. The technique is completely automatic without any manual input from the user.

We used `ti-trend-prof` on two large Titanium applications, and we found three real performance bugs in the code. Two of them were known previously from time consuming manual debugging. The third was unknown prior to the use of the tool. These results show the feasibility of using an automatic tool to find communication performance bugs in PGAS languages, given only the program traces from small processor configurations and small input sizes.

Acknowledgements

The authors would like to thank Simon Goldsmith and Daniel S. Wilkerson for introducing us to `trend-prof`. Their enthusiasm and persistence greatly encouraged us to adapt `trend-prof` for our needs. Simon Goldsmith also helped us in implementing the parsing of GASNet trace outputs. Thanks go to the members of the Titanium research group, who provided valuable suggestions and feedbacks about this work. We would also like to thank the anonymous reviewers for their helpful comments on the original submission.

This work was supported in part by the Department of Energy under DE-FC02-06ER25753, by the California State MICRO Program, by the National Science Foundation under ACI-9619020 and EIA-9802069, by the Defense Advanced Research Projects Agency under F30602-95-C-0136, by Microsoft, and by Sun Microsystems.

References

1. Alexandrov, A., Ionescu, M.F., Schauser, K.E., Scheiman, C.: LogGP: Incorporating long messages into the LogP model. Journal of Parallel and Distributed Computing 44(1), 71–79 (1997)

2. Bonachea, D.: GASNet specifications (2003)
3. Brewer, E.A.: High-level optimization via automated statistical modeling. In: PPOPP 1995: Proceedings of the 5th ACM SIGPLAN Symposium on Principles and Practice of Parallel Programming, pp. 80–91. ACM Press, New York (1995)
4. Coarfa, C., Mellor-Crummey, J., Froyd, N., Dotsenko, Y.: Scalability Analysis of SPMD Codes Using Expectations. In: PPOPP (2007)
5. Culler, D.E., Karp, R.M., Patterson, D.A., Sahay, A., Schauser, K.E., Santos, E., Subramonian, R., von Eicken, T.: LogP: Towards a realistic model of parallel computation. In: Proceedings 4th ACM SIGPLAN Symposium on Principles and Practice of Parallel Programming, pp. 1–12 (1993)
6. Givelberg, E., Yelick, K.: Distributed Immersed Boundary Simulation in Titanium (2004)
7. Goldsmith, S., Aiken, A., Wilkerson, D.: Measuring Empirical Computational Complexity. Foundations of Software Engineering (2007)
8. Graham, S.L., Kessler, P.B., Mckusick, M.K.: Gprof: A call graph execution profiler. In: SIGPLAN 1982: Proceedings of the 1982 SIGPLAN Symposium on Compiler Construction, pp. 120–126. ACM Press, New York (1982)
9. Kluge, M., Knüpfer, A., Nagel, W.E.: Knowledge based automatic scalability analysis and extrapolation for MPI programs. In: Cunha, J.C., Medeiros, P.D. (eds.) Euro-Par 2005. LNCS, vol. 3648. Springer, Heidelberg (2005)
10. Rugina, R., Schauser, K.: Predicting the running times of parallel programs by simulation. In: Proceedings of the 12th International Parallel Processing Symposium and 9th Symposium on Parallel and Distributed Processing (1998)
11. Vetter, J., Worley, P.: Asserting performance expectations. In: SC (2002)
12. Wen, T., Colella, P.: Adaptive Mesh Refinement in Titanium. In: IPDPS (2005)
13. Yelick, K., Semenzato, L., Pike, G., Miyamoto, C., Liblit, B., Krishnamurthy, A., Hilfinger, P., Graham, S., Gay, D., Colella, P., Aiken, A.: Titanium: A high-performance Java dialect. In: Workshop on Java for High-Performance Network Computing (1998).

Exploiting SIMD Parallelism
with the CGiS Compiler Framework

Nicolas Fritz*, Philipp Lucas*, and Reinhard Wilhelm

Universität des Saarlandes, 66041 Saarbrücken, Germany
{cage,phlucas,wilhelm}@cs.uni-sb.de

Abstract. Today's desktop PCs feature a variety of parallel processing units. Developing applications that exploit this parallelism is a demanding task, and a programmer has to obtain detailed knowledge about the hardware for efficient implementation. CGiS is a data-parallel programming language providing a unified abstraction for two parallel processing units: graphics processing units (GPUs) and the vector processing units of CPUs. The CGiS compiler framework fully virtualizes the differences in capability and accessibility by mapping an abstract data-parallel programming model on those targets. The applicability of CGiS for GPUs has been shown in previous work; this work presents the extension of the framework for SIMD instruction sets of CPUs. We show how to overcome the obstacles in mapping the abstract programming model of CGiS to the SIMD hardware. Our experimental results underline the viability of this approach: Real-world applications can be implemented easily with CGiS and result in efficient code.

1 Introduction

Recent hardware development is leading from traditional core frequency increase towards parallelism [3]. Even standard PCs feature parallelism on several levels of granularity. Multiprocessor systems support a MPMD model, which distributes tasks to different cores. GPUs (graphics processing units) [15] and SIMD units of CPUs follow the SPMD paradigm. Exploiting this parallelism, however, is not sufficiently supported by common programming languages, which are still tightly coupled to the sequential computing model. Algorithms using SIMD instructions are commonly written in assembly language or low level programming language extensions (intrinsics) [22].

The CGiS system strives to open up the parallel programming capabilities of commodity hardware to ordinary programmers. It raises the abstraction level high enough, so that the developer is kept away from all hardware intricacies. A CGiS program consists of parallel forall-loops iterating over streams of data and sequential kernels called from those loops. The CGiS compiler framework supports both CPUs and GPUs as targets, exploiting their characteristics automatically. For GPUs this has been presented in [9]. The paper in hand focuses on

---

* In part supported by DFG grant WI576/10.

V. Adve, M.J. Garzarán, and P. Petersen (Eds.): LCPC 2007, LNCS 5234, pp. 246–260, 2008.

the SIMD back-end of the CGiS compiler generating code for Freescale's AltiVec and Intel's SSE, and presents a number of transformations and optimizations.

Modern GPUs offer hundreds of floating point units, which can work in a SIMD fashion on vectorial values or on any kind of scalar data [14]. Thus, GPUs can even execute scalar operations in parallel, offering heterogenous parallelism. In contrast to that, the SIMD units of PowerPCs and various generations of Intel Pentiums have only up to three 4-way SIMD processing units. This means that GPUs offer both SIMD parallelism in a single element and across a multitude of elements, whereas only the element-wise parallelism is exploitable by SIMD CPUs.

CGiS offers two levels of explicit parallelism, large scale SPMD parallelism by the iteration over streams and small scale SIMD parallelism by vectorial data types. A CGiS back-end needs to map these parallelisms to the ones offered by the target architecture. For GPUs this is a one-to-one mapping; for SIMD CPU architectures, the back-end has to chose which parallelism opportunity to map to the hardware features.

A method to map SPMD parallelism to the SIMD hardware is *kernel flattening*. This operation breaks down compound data into scalars to enable sensible packing of new vectors for parallel execution. To ensure the preservation of the program semantics, static program analyzes are used to guarantee the premises. This also requires automatic reordering of the input data which can be done locally to the routine or globally for all routines.

In many algorithms memory accesses dominate the computations. This makes the overall performance dependent on the memory connection. Hardware developers incorporate caches to speed up the access, but computations on large data sets make evictions inevitable. To make best use of the caches, a mechanism for loop sectioning is integrated in our SIMD back-end. The iteration of the data streams is adapted to the cache size and the stream layout.

The remainder of this paper is organized as follows. Section 2 gives a short overview of the current SIMD instruction sets and Section 3 provides a more in-depth look on CGiS, comparing it to related work. The SIMD back-end and its optimizations are set forth in Section 4, and examples and experimental results are presented in Section 5. Future work is discussed in Section 6, and Section 7 concludes the paper.

2 Hardware

The first SIMD instruction set in commercially successful desktop processors, the *Multimedia Extensions (MMX)* [11], was introduced by Intel in 1997. MMX extended the core instruction architecture with eight 64-bit registers and provided only integer instructions. It was followed by the Streaming SIMD Extensions (SSE) [7] in 1999. The first version of SSE provided eight 128-bit registers and a set of floating-point instructions. The SSE instruction set was successively extended by introducing integer support and horizontal operations (SSE2 and SSE3). SSE4 promises a broader connection to the SIMD processing unit as well as more horizontal instructions to speed up common algorithms.

The PowerPC architecture was augmented with the Velocity Engine or *AltiVec* [5,6] in 1999. It provides thirty-two 128-bit registers to hold vectors and supports integers of various widths as well as floating-point data. In contrast to SSE, AltiVec supports very powerful data reordering or permutation instructions, allowing arbitrary interchange of input vectors.

3   The CGIS Framework

CGIS [9,10] is a data-parallel language for GPUs and CPUs. The CGIS language and the runtime system abstract the target in a uniform way. In particular, it is invisible to the programmer on which target the generated code is executed. CGIS is not intended to replace a programming language for a complete application. Instead, a data-parallel algorithm can be expressed in CGIS and then called as a simple subprogram of an application.

3.1   CGIS

Figure 1 shows the usage pattern of CGIS. A source code file is fed to the compiler, which outputs code for the desired target (here: SIMD CPU code) and code for interfacing with the main application. The programmer interacts only with this interface code in a uniform way.

For an example of a CGIS program, see the code in Figure 2. It presents the rc5 cipher encryption [19] with a static number of 31 rounds. CGIS files are divided into three sections. An **INTERFACE** section defines the global data of the program; in this case, a one-dimensional stream of unspecified size of integer tuples (the stream to be encrypted) and a field of 32 integer key pairs. A **CODE** section defines the *kernels* operating in parallel on elements of *streams*. Here, the procedure rc5 operates on stream element **AB**. It is an **inout** parameter, meaning it is read and written in the same iteration. The second parameter S is a reference to a stream, denoted by **<_>**. The called procedure **load** looks up the i-th element of S and stores it in S01. The suffixes .x and .y on vectorial values denote component-selection: A vectorial value with a size of at most four can be treated as a structure with components x, y, z, w. The **CONTROL** section initiates a computation

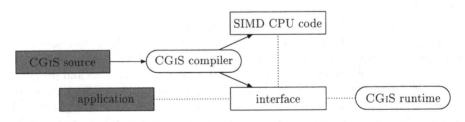

Fig. 1. Using CGIS. Arrows denote in- and output, dotted lines denote linkage. The filled rectangular nodes are user supplied code. The oval nodes are part of CGIS, and the other code components are generated by the CGIS compiler.

```
PROGRAM rc5_encryption;

INTERFACE
extern in uint2 S<32>;
extern inout uint2 ABs<SIZE>; // The stream to be encrypted.

CODE
procedure encrypt(inout uint2 AB, in uint2 S<_>)
{
  uint2 S01; uint i = 0;
  load(S,i,S01); // Get key-pair at 0.
  uint A = AB.x+S01.x, B = AB.y+S01.y;
  while(i<31) {
    i = i + 1;
    load(S,i,S01);  // Get key-pair at i.
    A = ((A^B)<<<B) + S01.x; // <<< is a left-
    B = ((B^A)<<<A) + S01.y; //     rotation.
  }
  AB.x = A; AB.y = B;
}

CONTROL
forall(AB in ABs) encrypt(AB,S);
```

Fig. 2. CGiS encryption of a stream with 31 rounds of rc5. A stream element consists of a pair of unsigned integers.

on streams. In this case, the kernel rc5 is invoked for the elements of the stream ABs. The computations on the elements get scheduled in parallel (SPMD).

CGiS features a relatively standard, imperative programming language to describe the kernels in the CODE section. It is based on C, but lacks pointers: Arrays are always accessed with indices, and function outputs are implemented with pass-by-value-result parameters. These restrictions are a consequence of CGiS' ancestry as a GPU programming language. Also stemming from this are the native vectorial types and operations, special instructions for reordering components and guarded executions. Element types are single-precision floating point or signed or unsigned integer.

Streams can be accessed through read-write iterators, with relative and absolute read accesses, and absolute write accesses. The kernels are scheduled by a simple language featuring sequential specification of parallel executions in the CONTROL section. The runtime system is responsible for synchronization and sequencing of memory accesses to ensure a well-defined semantics. The INTERFACE section declares the interface to other CGiS programs and to the application: The application passes pointers to the input data and receives the output data through C functions generated for the interface code. The target remains hidden in this approach: The main application uses the generated code as a black-box, consuming streams of input data and producing streams of output data.

CGIS was originally deceived as a language for general-purpose computations on GPUs [10,15]. As such, much of its syntax and semantics are owed to the hardware peculiarities of GPUs. SIMD CPUs can also make use of floating point vectors, but they lack the abundance of execution units. Therefore, a translation based on the same kind of parallelism available on GPUs is bound to produce lackluster results. From the two levels of parallelism mentioned above, SIMD parallelism on vectors and SPMD parallelism on stream elements, CPUs lack the GPU's large parallelism of the second kind. Section 4 shows that, with appropriate transformation on the source code inside the compiler, data-parallel algorithms expressed in CGIS can nevertheless also efficiently be executed on SIMD CPUs.

3.2   Related Work

Exploiting SIMD parallelism from standard C code is a complicated task. Common C compilers like gcc or icc are facing a multitude of problems both in analyzing the input code and in mapping it efficiently to the restricted SIMD hardware; many algorithms are still implemented by hand in assembly code or intrinsics, or using prefabricated libraries [17,22]. CGIS features a stream programming model, avoiding some of these problems and offering new opportunities to overcome others. The expressibility is restricted with respect to the full possibilities of C code, but it allows easier exploitation of parallelism.

The CGIS SIMD back-end shares a set of common problems with other SIMD code generation approaches. One of the major problems is data alignment, because SIMD hardware usually is limited to accessing 16-byte aligned addresses [16]. Because CGIS operates solely on non-overlapping arrays (streams) with indexed accesses, alignment analysis becomes easier and permutation operations can be kept local. Also control flow prevents parallelization, and for SIMD traditional control flow conversions have to be employed [1,23].

Other problems are avoided by language design or have to be tackled differently. As explicit data parallelism is mandatory for CGIS programs, extensive data-dependency analyses are obsolete. Specialized operations such as saturated operators or bit rotation operation are common to multimedia applications. These operations have to be reconstructed from C code by idiom recognition [17,18], whereas they are present in CGIS. To utilize SIMD potential on scalar code, superword level parallelism is able to recognize isomorphic operations on sequential, scalar code [8,21]. CGIS offers small (up to four components) vectorial types and componentwise operations, enabling the programmer to express isomorphic operations in their natural form. Exploiting SIMD parallelism from scalar code [13] is handled by cross-kernel-parallelism due to a transformation called kernel flattening. Conversion between element types of different length is a severe problem in C based approaches [22]; in CGIS, all data types are 32-Bit long.

4   The SIMD Back-End

This section deals with the transformations and optimizations which are necessary for the SIMD back-end of the CGIS compiler.

The challenges in generating efficient SIMD code differ from the ones in generating GPU code. Increased performance compared to scalar execution can only be achieved by exploiting vector parallelism. Each vector register of the supported SIMD hardware is 128 bit wide and can contain 4 floating-point or 4 (signed or unsigned) integer values. Mapping the stream computation to this hardware is hindered by the following issues:

- *Misalignment and data layout.* CGiS allows streams of arbitrary data elements allocated by standard allocation functions in the application. Because data can only be accessed with 16-byte aligned loads[1], in general, data must be reordered at some point. Consider the example in Figure 2 which describes a CGiS function encrypting a stream of pairs of unsigned integers with the rc5 encryption algorithm. With two integers per element, every odd element is not aligned for SIMD hardware.[2]

  The stream elements are compounds and the operations work on single components. There is no efficient SIMD exploit when processing one or two stream elements at a time as computations on the components are not uniform. Neither the data layout nor the alignment of the tuples match the requirements for SIMD vectorization.
- *Gathering operations.* Accesses to the main memory of a CPU are inherently slow. Thus, on-chip caches are employed to speed up the access to re-used data. Apart from arbitrary stream *lookups*, the CGiS language allows stream element loads or *gathers* relative to the element currently processed (neighborhood operations). Depending on the organization of the stream data and the shape of the accessed neighborhood, the CGiS compiler can adapt the stream iterations to increase cache performance.
- *Control flow.* Vectorizing code with control flow structures requires code transformation to ensure each of the stream elements processed in parallel enters the correct control flow branch. As in traditional vectorization, this is done by if- and loop-conversion and inlining.

4.1 Kernel Flattening

The main challenge in generating efficient SIMD code is data arrangement and meeting the alignment requirements of data accesses. A solution to this alignment and data layout problem is *kernel flattening*.

Kernel flattening is a code transformation on the intermediate language. It processes a single kernel and splits all stream elements and variables into scalar variables. This also includes operations on those variables: Every operation is copied and executed on each former component of the variable. Figure 3 shows the flattening operations applied to a simple CGiS procedure, transforming YUV color values into RGB values. The parameters YUV and RGB and the constant

---

[1] The unaligned loads supported by SSE2 severely impact execution time.

[2] We assume that at least the first element of every stream processed is 16-byte aligned. Another example of a stride-one stream where not every stream element is aligned is the YUV-stream depicted in Figure 3.

```
procedure yuv2rgb(in float3 YUV, out float3 RGB)
{
  RGB = YUV.x + [ 0, 0.344, 1.77 ] * YUV.y + [ 1.403, 0.714, 0] * YUV.z;
}

procedure yuv2rgb_f (in   float YUV_x, in   float YUV_y, in   float YUV_z,
                     out float RGB_x, out float RGB_y, out float RGB_z)
{
  float cy = 0.344, cz = 1.77, dx = 1.403, dy = 0.714;
  RGB_x = YUV_x +               dx * YUV_z;
  RGB_y = YUV_x + cy * YUV_y + dy * YUV_z;
  RGB_z = YUV_x + cz * YUV_y;
}
```

Fig. 3. The procedure yuv2rgb transforms YUV color values into RGB. As in common GPU languages, scalar operands are replicated to match the number of components of the target or operation. yuv2rgb_f is the result of the flattening transformation applied to yuv2rgb. Each component becomes a single scalar variable or parameter and all vector operations are replaced by scalar ones.

vectors are split into 3 scalar variables each. The assignment to RGB and the computations are split as well.

The procedure resulting from kernel flattening can be executed in parallel. After compound variables have been broken down to scalar ones, these can be subjected to SIMD vectorization. Four consecutive elements for each scalar variable stream can now be loaded into one vector register, and immediate constants are replicated into a vector. Because the original data elements of the stream are possibly ordered in tuples (e. g., the YUV-stream in Figure 3), data has to be reordered during execution or beforehand. The SIMD back-end supports local and global data reordering depending on the re-usability of the reordered data. Whereas global reordering is basically a reordering in memory, local reordering inserts code that reorders these elements in registers at the beginning of the function and at the end. For the previous example the possible stream access patterns are shown in Figure 4. Sequential execution accesses one YUV-triple per iteration. Global reordering splits the YUV-stream into three streams. Thus, in each iteration, four elements of each former component can be loaded into a vector register and processed. Local reordering takes the stream as it is and inserts permutation operations at the start and the end of the flattened procedure.

Per default, the CGiS back-end uses local reordering, but the programmer can force global reordering by annotations. Global data reordering requires input stream data to be loaded before and output stream data to be stored after execution. Thus, the higher reordering costs with respect to local reordering are amortized only if the reordered stream is processed several times with gathers and lookups.

Lookup and gather operations are split as well. In case of global reordering, the gathers and lookups are straightforward, because only alignment has to be taken

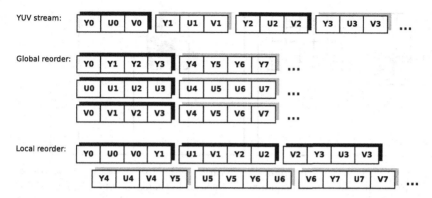

Fig. 4. Streams can be reordered globally or locally. Global reordering copies the data in memory before and/or after execution, depending on the data flow of the stream. Local reordering uses SIMD permutations. The layout of the data in memory remains unchanged. Different shades denote consecutively accessed data per iteration.

care of. As for local reordering, on gather operations the loaded and reorganized data can be kept minimal as the offset from the current element is statically known. On the other hand, data-dependent lookups result in four different scalar loads and the reconstruction of a vector. With too many of these lookups the benefit of vectorizing the function might get negated.

For the rc5 encryption, this means that the inout parameter AB is split into an inout parameter AB_x and an inout parameter AB_y. All operations are made scalar enabling SLP execution. Data reordering instructions are inserted allowing stride-one access to AB_x and AB_y. From the perspective of data layout and alignment, four elements can be processed in parallel. The lookup function load only depends on the scalar i. With data-flow analysis it can be determined that i is constant across all elements processed in parallel. CGiS allows the user to annotate uniform variables to guide the compiler. Each of the parallely processed elements wants to load the same value. So the desired vector can be reconstructed from one SIMD load and one or two permutations.

4.2 Loop Sectioning

Many data parallel algorithms, especially in image processing, require the gathering of nearby data elements. One example for such an image processing algorithm is the *Gaussian blur* described in Section 5.2. CGiS supports gathering operations that let the programmer access stream elements relative to the current position in the stream. When iterating over a two-dimensional stream column-by-column or row-by-row, it is possible that data elements already loaded and present in the data cache are evicted and have to be loaded again. To make best use of the cached data, the CGiS compiler can adapt the iterations over the stream dividing the field into smaller stripes that better match the cache size and organization of the processor. This optimization was inspired by [2].

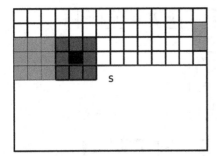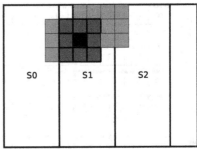

Fig. 5. The CGiS compiler can adapt the iteration order to increase cache hit rates in gather operations. Blue (light) squares are cached elements, the black square is the currently processed element and the red (dark) ones are the neighborhood accessed in this iteration. The left picture shows row-by-row iteration. In the right picture stripe-by-stripe is processed, showing the benefit of additional overlapping of cached data.

With the smaller width of the stripes, there is more overlapping in-between row iteration.

This is possible only on architectures which allow a direct control of the iteration order. As for example GPUs do not allow this detailed iteration control, the GPU back-end of the CGiS compiler cannot make use of this optimization.

As an example, consider Figure 5. A two-dimensional field S is processed, and for each element its 8 immediate neighbors are gathered. The blue (light) squares are data elements that have been loaded in former iterations and are thus present in the data cache. The currently iterated element is colored black, and the gathered elements are red (dark). In the left part, the iteration sequence is simply row-by-row. The right part shows the same field subdivided into smaller stripes S_i. Each S_i is also processed row-wise. But with the reduced row width, the cache hit rate is increased, because there is still data present in the cache from the last processed row.

The size of the stripes is determined by the cache size and the memory requirements as follows. To determine the dimension in which the stripes run, we investigate the access pattern of the gather operations. The dimension which gives rise to the most data accesses defines the run direction. We assume that the two-dimensional stream is stored row-wise in memory. The stripes then run column-wise. Iteration is row-wise inside the stripes. For each stream, o determines the maximum of iteration lines or rows crossed by the access pattern, e.g., in Figure 5 o is 3. o is the sum of maximum absolute offsets in stripe direction plus one for the current line. For a given parallel kernel-execution k, the CGiS compiler decides the width of the stripes S_k from the cache size C, the cache line size l and the size of the stream elements read and written. (Different architectures with different cache sizes are selected at compile-time.) δ is a constant number that represents the local data that is needed in each iteration such as intermediates and other stack data. Assume that k accesses stream elements with an element size of a_i and the gathers for a_i cross o_i lines. These parameters are statically known and result in a simple heuristic for computing the stripe width:

$$S_k = \lfloor (C - \delta)/(\textstyle\sum o_i \cdot a_i) \rfloor_l.$$

$\lfloor \rfloor_l$ rounds down to the nearest multiple of l. S_k does not need to be constant across a whole program but is adapted to each specific kernel execution.

Should the size of the field not match a multiple of the stripe width, the remaining elements are processed by normal iteration.

4.3   Control Flow Conversion

The three main control flow constructs of CGiS are procedure calls, conditionals and loops. Breaks are represented as modifying the loop control variable, so that each loop has exactly one exit. All transformations of the control flow conversion are executed on the intermediate representation of the CGiS program.

By default, calls are fully inlined in the SIMD back-end, although it is possible to force separate functions. We found that generating true calls increases the runtime of the application. Most parameters are present in vector registers, and passing those as arguments induces additional stores and loads.

If-conversion is the traditional way to convert control-dependencies into data-dependencies. A *mask* is generated for the condition. The execution of each statement in the conditional body is guarded by that mask [23]. In CGiS, the masks are the results of vector compare operations. These component-wise operations yield a vector that contains all 0s at an element if the comparison failed for that element, all 1s otherwise. Because current SIMD hardware does not feature guarded assignments, the Allen-Kennedy algorithm of [23] has to be adapted in the following way.

Let I be a basic block containing an if-statement with condition C_I and its associated mask M_I. For simplicity, we consider only a simple conditional body, with one block T_I in the **true**-branch and one block F_I in the **false**-branch. The control flow join is denoted J_I. Let L_I be the set of variables live at J_I, W_T the set of variables written in T_I and W_F is the set of variables written in F_I. The algorithm which inserts the additional operations required for the if-conversion is given in pseudo-code in Figure 6.

During the if-conversion phase, for each I the sets S_T and S_F are determined. For each control flow branch, copies of the variables written and live after the branch are inserted at the beginning of the respective branch. After the end of a branch, select instructions (like ϕ-functions from SSA [12]) are inserted which select the new value for the written variable depending on the generated mask.

The conversion of loops is pretty straight forward. For the loop condition, a mask is generated as well, and the loop is iterated as long as the mask is not completely 0 (signifying that *all* elements or the SIMD-tuple have finished iteration). If the mask is completely 0, then the loop can be exited.

Conversion of nested control flow statements is also supported. When the mask of a condition is generated for a nested statement, it is always combined with the mask of the control flow statement via binary **and**.

```
Use live variables analysis to determine L_I
Use reaching definitions analysis to determine W_T and W_F
Build intersections S_T = W_T ∩ L_I and S_F = W_F ∩ L_I
Foreach v_T ∈ S_T
    insert v_T' = v_T at the beginning of T_I
    insert select(v_T, v_T', M_I) at the end of T_I
Foreach v_F ∈ S_F
    insert v_F' = v_F at the beginning of F_I
    insert select(v_F', v_F, M_I) at the end of F_I
```

Fig. 6. Pseudo code for additional insertion of copies and select operations used in if-conversion

5   Examples and Evaluation

Three data parallel algorithms from different application domains will demonstrate the fitness of the SIMD back-end to the CGIS framework. Though all naturally parallel, each of those algorithms requires different optimization to run efficiently. Thus, they serve as representatives for larger categories of similar applications.

The two target platforms were a Freescale PowerPC G5, 1.8 GHz, running under Mac OSX, and an Intel Core 2 Duo 1.83 GHz running under Linux. The generated intrinsics code was compiled with gcc 4.0.1. Figure 7 shows the aggregation of the experiments for both hardware platforms. Speedup factors for SIMD only differ in the rc5 example as the SSE hardware does not support rotates or register-dependent shifts.

5.1   rc5 Encryption

rc5 [19] is a block cipher encryption that works on a stream of integer tuples. Each tuple gets modified by rotating and binary xor over a certain number of rounds. A parallel implementation of rc5 encryption requires the data to be reordered. Global data reordering via memory copy is not a valid option as it increases overall computation time drastically and does not amortize by the gain in computation speed. The alternative is local data reordering and is a automatically done by kernel flattening. For the tests, the message length to be encrypted is between 64k and 320k integers.

Figure 8.a holds the results of the generated SSE code. Because the Streaming SIMD Extensions do not support vector register dependent shifts or rotates, these operations must be done by the ALU, forcing data to go through memory twice. This has a severe impact on the computation time. The average increase of SIMD with respect to scalar code is about 20%. The results of the AltiVec implementation are shown in Figure 8.b. For all input sets the speedup is about 400%. As gcc did not recognize the shift patterns as rotates, it did not use the scalar rotate of the PowerPC, decreasing the scalar performance.

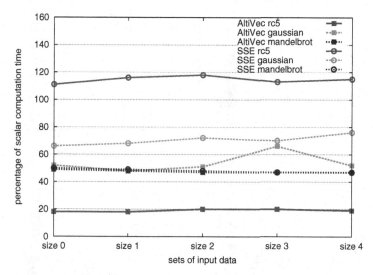

Fig. 7. Execution times of AltiVec and SSE hardware relative to scalar execution of PowerPC and Core 2 Duo. While Mandelbrot and Gaussian blur perform equally well on both architectures, rc5 is significantly slower on the Core 2 Duo due to the missing hardware rotation.

5.2 Gaussian Blur

Gaussian blur is an image processing algorithm to produce a blurring effect. For each pixel, its color and the colors of its neighbors are weighted and combined into a new color. Here the memory accesses strongly dominate computations. Our image data is stored in RGBA format, of which only the RGB values are considered. To increase performance in the gathering operations, cache sensitive iteration tries to make best use of the data already present in the cache. For the tests, an input image has been scaled, doubling the image size per test case.

The SSE results in Figure 8.c do not show large improvement over the scalar implementation. The increased memory accesses together with the weak memory connection of the SSE unit thwart any performance gain by the parallel execution. The execution times on AltiVec hardware in Figure 8.d show an improvement of roughly 50% and scale well with the size of the inputs.

5.3 Mandelbrot Set

Computing the Mandelbrot set is a well-known, computationally heavy algorithm. For a point $z \in \mathbb{C}$ in the complex plane, the sequence $z_0 = z$, $z_n = z_{n-1}^2 + z$ is computed until $|z_n^2| \geqslant 2$ for some n or a maximal iteration count n' is reached. Afterwards, the final iteration count n is mapped onto a color.

Parallelization of this algorithm is only possible with control flow conversion. For this example, both SSE and AltiVec implementation show speedups of factor 2 (Figure 8.e–f) across all inputs. While the SSE instruction set offers the

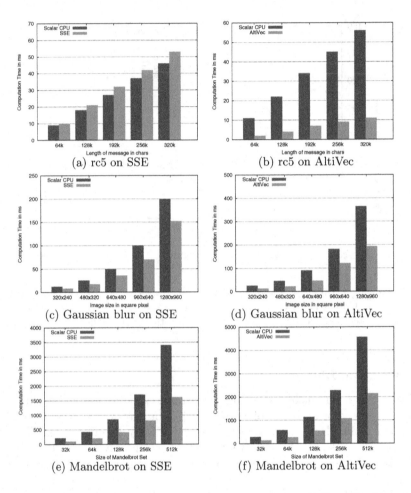

Fig. 8. Performance evaluation of three test sets on SIMD CPUs. The left column shows the computation times on SSE, the right one the computation times on AltiVec.

possibility to read the results of a compare directly to scalar hardware, for AltiVec writing of control register bits must be enabled and conditional jumps depending on those control bits are introduced.

6   Future Work

The SIMD back-end of the CGiS compiler is still under development. The main focus up to this point was to generate efficient code, i.e., faster than scalar code, for suitable applications. The next goal is the refinement of the existing optimizations. More program analyzes and better heuristics should replace the current heuristics.

Although intrinsics are a comfortable way of generating SIMD code, they have limitations. The conditional jumps using the control register of the PowerPC have to be inserted via inline assembly resulting in inefficient code. Furthermore, with pure assembly code emittance the compiler has more control over register allocation, which is imperative on the SSE architecture. This also enables the optimization of register caching for gather operations [20]. Compiling directly to assembly would offer also easy access to other processor features. For example, conditionals in loops can be optimized by introducing flags to avoid the generation of the masks for the if-statement, should there be no else-branch associated with the if. Also, we plan to extend the compiler to the Cell processor, which offers parallelism on several kinds [4]. We believe that the CGiS model can efficiently be mapped to the parallelisms allowed by the Cell processor.

7 Conclusion

This paper presents the SIMD back-end of the CGiS compiler framework in its current state. Generating efficient SIMD code for data parallel algorithms is a demanding task as many restrictions like data layout, control dependencies and other characteristics of the hardware avoid vectorization.

We introduce the program transformation of kernel flattening combined with local data reordering to solve the problem of data layouts that are not suitable for stream processing otherwise. On memory dominated algorithms, we try to increase performance by making best use of data caches by adapting the iteration sequence. Control flow is straightened by full if- and loop-conversion offering the possibility to parallelize functions with control dependencies. The experimental results show the viability of this approach. Though the number of examples is not exhaustive, the applications each stand for a whole category of similar applications in the field of encryption, image processing and mathematical calculations.

References

1. Allen, R., Kennedy, K.: Optimizing Compilers for Modern Architectures. Morgan Kaufmann, San Francisco (2002)
2. Coleman, S., McKinley, K.S.: Tile size selection using cache organization and data layout. In: Proceedings of PLDI, pp. 279–290 (1995)
3. Culler, D.E., Singh, J.P., Gupta, A.: Parallel Computer Architecture: A Hardware/Software Approach. Morgan Kaufmann, San Francisco (1999)
4. Eichenberger, A.E., O'Brien, K., O'Brien, K., Wu, P., Chen, T., Oden, P.H., Prener, D.A., Shepherd, J.C., So, B., Sura, Z., Wang, A., Zhang, T., Zhao, P., Gschwind, M.: Optimizing compiler for a cell processor. In: Proceedings of PACT (2005)
5. Freescale. AltiVec Technology Programming Interface Manual. ALTIVECPIM/D 06/1999 Rev. 0 (June 1999)
6. Freescale. AltiVec Technology Programming Environments Manual. ALTIVECPEM/D 04/2006 Rev. 3 (April 2006)
7. Intel. Intel 64 and IA-32 Architectures Optimization Reference Manual (May 2007)

8. Larsen, S., Amarasinghe, S.: Exploiting superword level parallelism with multimedia instruction sets. Technical Report LCS-TM-601, MIT Laboratory for Computer Science (November 1999)
9. Lucas, P., Fritz, N., Wilhelm, R.: The CGiS compiler—a tool demonstration. In: Mycroft, A., Zeller, A. (eds.) CC 2006. LNCS, vol. 3923, pp. 105–108. Springer, Heidelberg (2006)
10. Lucas, P., Fritz, N., Wilhelm, R.: The development of the data-parallel GPU programming language CGiS. In: Alexandrov, V.N., van Albada, G.D., Sloot, P.M.A., Dongarra, J. (eds.) ICCS 2006. LNCS, vol. 3994, pp. 200–203. Springer, Heidelberg (2006)
11. Mittal, M., Peleg, A., Weiser, U.: MMX technology architecture overview. Intel Technology Journal Q3(12) (1997)
12. Muchnick, S.S.: Advanced Compiler Design and Implementation. Morgan Kaufmann, San Francisco (1997)
13. Nuzman, D., Rosen, I., Zaks, A.: Auto-vectorization of interleaved data of simd. In: Proceedings of PLDI (2006)
14. NVIDIA. CUDA Programming Guide Version 0.8 (February 2007)
15. Owens, J.D., Luebke, D., Govindaraju, N., Harris, M., Krüger, J., Lefohn, A.E., Purcell, T.J.: A survey of general-purpose computation on graphics hardware. Computer Graphics Forum 26(1), 80–113 (2007)
16. Pryanishnikov, I., Krall, A., Horspool, R.N.: Compiler optimizations for processors with SIMD instructions. Software—Practice & Experience 37(1), 93–113 (2007)
17. Ren, G., Wu, P., Padua, D.: An empirical study on the vectorization of multimedia applications for multimedia extensions. In: IPDPS (2005)
18. Ren, G., Wu, P., Padua, D.A.: A preliminary study on the vectorization of multimedia applications for multimedia extensions. In: Rauchwerger, L. (ed.) LCPC 2003. LNCS, vol. 2958, pp. 420–435. Springer, Heidelberg (2003)
19. Rivest, R.L.: The RC5 encryption algorithm. In: Practical Cryptography for Data Internetworks. IEEE Computer Society Press, Los Alamitos (1996)
20. Shin, J., Chame, J., Hall, M.W.: Compiler-controlled caching in superword register files for multimedia extension architectures. In: Proceedings of PACT, pp. 45–55 (2002)
21. Tenllado, C., Piñuel, L., Prieto, M., Catthoor, F.: Pack transposition: Enhancing superword level parallelism exploitation. In: Proceedings of Parallel Computing (ParCo), pp. 573–580 (2005)
22. Wu, P., Eichenberer, A.E., Wang, A., Zhao, P.: An integrated simdization framework using virtual vectors. In: Proceedings of the 19th Annual International Conference on Supercomputing (ICS), pp. 169–178 (2005)
23. Zima, H.P., Chapman, B.: Supercompilers for Parallel and Vector Computers. ACM Press, New York (1990)

Critical Block Scheduling: A Thread-Level Parallelizing Mechanism for a Heterogeneous Chip Multiprocessor Architecture

Slo-Li Chu

Department of Information and Computer Engineering,
Chung Yuan Christian University, Chung-Li, Taiwan, R.O.C.
slchu@cycu.edu.tw

Abstract. Processor-in-Memory (PIM) architectures are developed for high-performance computing by integrating processing units with memory blocks into a single chip to reduce the performance gap between the processor and the memory. The PIM architecture combines heterogeneous processors in a single system. These processors are characterized by their computation and memory-access capabilities. Therefore, a novel mechanism must be developed to identify their capabilities and dispatch the appropriate tasks to these heterogeneous processing elements. Accordingly, this paper presents a novel parallelizing mechanism, called Critical Block Scheduling to fully utilize all of the heterogeneous processors in the PIM architecture. Integrated with our thread-level parallelizing system, Octans, this mechanism decomposes the original program into blocks, produces corresponding dependence graph, creates a feasible execution schedule, and generates corresponding threads for the host and memory processors. The proposed Critical Block Scheduling not only can parallelize programs for PIM architectures but also can apply on other Multi-Processor System-on-Chip (MPSoC) and Chip Multiprocessor (CMP) architectures which consist of multiple heterogeneous processors. The experimental results of real benchmarks are also discussed.

Keywords: Chip Multiprocessor (CMP), Processor-in-Memory, Critical Block Scheduling, Octans.

1 Introduction

In current high-performance computer architectures, the processors run many times faster than the computer's main memory. This performance gap is often referred to as the Memory Wall. This gap can be reduced using the System-on-a-Chip or Chip Multiprocessor [18] strategies, which integrates the various processors and memory on a single chip. The rapid growth in silicon fabrication density has made this strategy possible. Accordingly, many researchers have addressed integrating computing logic/ processing units and high density DRAM on a single die [9][11][12][14][15] [17] [18]. Such architectures are also called Processor-in-Memory (PIM), or Intelligent RAM (IRAM).

V. Adve, M.J. Garzarán, and P. Petersen (Eds.): LCPC 2007, LNCS 5234, pp. 261–275, 2008.

Integrating DRAM and computing elements on a single chip generates PIM architecture with several desirable characteristics. First, the processors are heterogeneous for their purpose. Second, instead of traditional off-chip communication, the on-chip communication between processor-to-processor and processor-to-memory are very wide and fast. Third, eliminating off-chip drivers reduces the power consumption and latency [17].

This class of architectures constitutes a hierarchical hybrid multiprocessor environment by the host (main) processor and the memory processors. The host processor is more powerful but has a deep cache hierarchy and higher latency when accessing memory. In contrast, memory processors are normally less powerful but have a lower latency in memory access. The main problems addressed here concern the method for dispatching suitable tasks to these different processors according to their characteristics to reduce execution times, and the method for partitioning the original program to execute simultaneously on these heterogeneous processor combinations.

Since the mechanisms of partitioning and scheduling for heterogeneous multicomputers are classical NP-Hard problems, many researches propose their mechanisms for distributed-memory parallel computers. Opportunistic Load Balancing algorithm assigns each task, in arbitrary order, to the next available machine, regardless of the task's expected execution time on that machine [2]. Min-min algorithm minimizes the completion time for each task is computed for all machines. The newly mapped task is removed, and the process repeated until all tasks are mapped [2]. These methods are focus on how to reduce the communication cost of the parallel program. However, in PIM architecture, the communication cost is not the most significant factor of overall performance. Hence we veer to thread-level parallelizing mechanisms. Cintr et al. [6] present a architectural support thread-level parallelization framework, which can obtain more potential parallelism by their speculative thread-level parallelizing mechanism with hardware support, especially for the modified CC-NUMA architecture. Arora et al. [3], Zhou et al. [21], and Agrawal et al. [1] propose their mechanisms to dynamically schedule the threads in the thread queue to reduce memory access cost and improve cache locality. These mechanisms improve the capabilities of thread scheduler of the targeted operating system, but can not apply on parallelizing compiler for static scheduling. Llosa, et al. [13] propose a software pipelining mechanism, called Swing Modulo Scheduling (SMS), to partition iteration spaces of loops according to their dependence graph. This algorithm provides iteration-based mechanism that can improve the potential parallelism of the loops and reduce the usage of registers. It is also adopted in GNU Compiler Collection (GCC) Version 4.0. However SMS focuses on scheduling iterations of given loops but not restructure whole program. It isn't suitable for parallelizing program and generating corresponding threads for different heterogeneous processors. Therefore we have to consider other mid-grained approach instead of traditional fine-grained mechanism based on iteration analysis.

From the aspect of compilation for PIM architectures, previous approaches [8] [10] concentrate on instruction-level parallelization and loop vectorization to increase speedup, rather than on the figure out the capability difference between the host and memory processors. However, such approaches do not exploit the real advantages of PIM architectures. Accordingly we design a thread-level parallelization system,

Octans, which integrates statement splitting, weight evaluation and a scheduling mechanism. The original PSS scheduling [5] mechanism focuses on a simplified configuration of PIM architecture that only consists one-P.Host and one-P.Mem processors. Since PSS scheduling can not deal with multiple P.Mem processors and fully utilizes all heterogeneous computing resources, we design a new mechanism, Critical Block Scheduling, to generate a superior execution schedule to fully utilize all heterogeneous processors in the PIM architecture. A weight evaluation mechanism is established to collect characteristics of varied and estimate a precise execution time then generate a normalized value, called weight. The Octans system can automatically analyze the sequential program, partition program into several blocks, determine the weights of each block, produce a good executing schedule, and finally generate parallel threads for execution on the host and memory processors accordingly.

The rest of this paper is organized as follows: Section 2 introduces the PIM architecture. Section 3 describes our Octans system and the Critical Block Scheduling algorithms. Section 4 presents experimental results. Conclusions are finally drawn in Section 5.

2 The Processor-in-Memory Architecture

Fig. 1 depicts the organization of the PIM architecture evaluated in this study. It contains an off-the-shelf processor, P.Host, and four PIM chips. The PIM chip integrates one memory processor, P.Mem, with 64 Mbytes of DRAM. The techniques presented in this paper are suitable for the configuration of one P.Host and multiple P.Mems, and can be extended to support multiple P.Hosts.

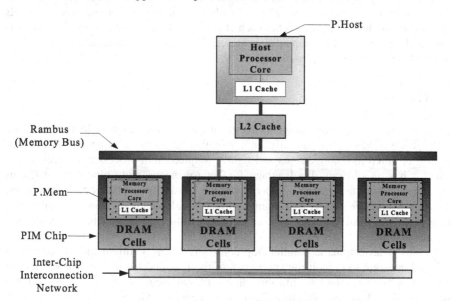

Fig. 1. Organization of the PIM architecture

Table 1. Parameters of the PIM architecture

P.Host	P.Mem	Bus & Memory
Working Freq: 800 MHz	Working Freq: 400 MHz	Bus Freq: 100 MHz
Dynamic issue Width: 6	Static issue Width: 2	P.Host Mem RT: 262. 5 ns
Integer unit num: 6	Integer unit num: 2	P.Mem Mem RT: 50. 5 ns
Floating unit num: 4	Floating unit num: 2	Bus Width: 16 B
FLC_Type: WT	FLC_Type: WT	Mem_Data_Transfer: 16
FLC_Size: 32 KB	FLC_Size: 16 KB	Mem_Row_Width: 4K
FLC_Line: 64 B	FLC_Line: 32 B	
SLC_Type: WB	SLC: N/A	
SLC_Size: 256 KB		
SLC_Line: 64 B		
Replace policy: LRU		
Branch penalty: 4	Branch penalty: 2	
P.Host_Mem_Delay: 88	P.Mem_Mem_Delay: 17	

* FLC stands for the first level cache, SLC for the second level cache, BR for branch, RT for round-trip latency from the processor to the memory, and RB for row buffer.

Table 1 lists the main architectural parameters of the PIM architecture. P.Host is a six-issue superscalar processor that allows out-of-order execution and runs at 800MHz, while P.Mem is a two-issue superscalar processor with in-order capability and runs at 400MHz. There is a two-level cache in P.Host and a one-level cache in P.Mem. P.Mem has lower memory access latency than P.Host since the former is integrated with DRAM. Thus, computation-bound codes are more suitable for running on the P.Host, while memory-bound codes are preferably running on the P.Mem to increase efficiency.

The PIM chip is designed to replace regular DRAMs in current computer systems, and conform to a memory standard that involves additional power and ground signals to support on-chip processing. One such standard is Rambus [7], so the PIM chip is designed with a Rambus-compatible interface. The private interconnection network of the PIM chips is also provided.

3   The Octans System

Most current parallelizing compilers focus on the transformation of loops to execute all or some iterations concurrently, in a so-called iteration-based approach. This approach is suited to homogeneous and tightly coupled multi-processor systems. However, it has an obvious disadvantage for heterogeneous multi-processor platforms because iterations have similar behavior but the capabilities of heterogeneous processors are diverse. Therefore, a different approach is adopted here, using the statements in a loop as a basic analysis unit, called statement-based approach, to develop the Octans system.

Octans is an automatic parallelizing compiler, which partitions and schedules an original program to exploit the specialties of the host and the memory processor. At first, the source program is split into blocks of statements according to dependence relations [5]. Then, the Weighted Partition Dependence Graph (WPG) is generated, and the weight of each block is evaluated. Finally, the blocks are dispatched to either the host or the memory processors, according to which processor is more suitable for

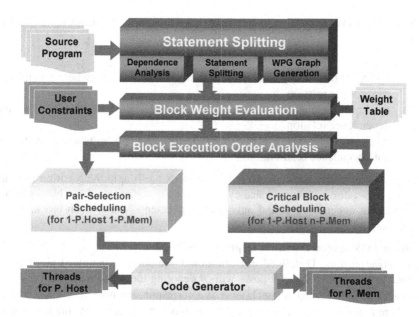

Fig. 2. The sequence of compiling stages in Octans

executing the block. The major difference between Octans and other parallelizing systems is that it uses a statement rather than an iteration as the basic unit of analysis. This approach can fully exploit the characteristics of statements in a program and dispatch the most suitable tasks to the host and the memory processors. Fig. 2 illustrates the organization of the Octans system.

3.1 Statement Splitting and WPG Construction

Statement Splitting splits the dependence graph by Node Partitioning as introduced in [5]. WPG Construction constructs the Weighted Partition Dependence Graph (WPG), to be used in the subsequent stages of Weight Evaluation, Wavefront Generation and Schedule Determination.

The definitions relevant to Statement Splitting are introduced as below.

Definition 1 (Loop Notation)
A loop is denoted by $L = (i_1, i_2, \ldots i_n)(s_1, s_2, \ldots s_k)$, where i_j, $1 \leq j \leq n$, is a loop index, and s_k, $1 \leq k \leq d$, is a body statement which may be an assignment statement or another loop.   ∎

Definition 2 (Node Partition Π)
For a given loop L on the dependence graph G, we define a node partition Π for the statements set $\{s_1, s_2, \ldots s_d\}$ in such a way that s_k and s_l, $1 \leq k \leq d$, $1 \leq l \leq d$, $k \neq l$, are in the same block (cell) π_i of the partition Π if and only if $s_k \Delta s_l$ and $s_l \Delta s_k$ where Δ is an indirect data dependence relation.

On the partition $\Pi=\{\pi_1,\pi_2,\ldots,\pi_n\}$, we define partial ordering relations α, $\alpha^\wedge$, and α° as follows.

For $i \neq j$:
1) $\pi_i \alpha \pi_j$ iff there exist $s_k \in \pi_i$ and $s_l \in \pi_j$ such that $s_k \delta s_l$, where δ is the true dependence relation .
2) $\pi_i \alpha^\wedge \pi_j$ iff there exist $s_k \in \pi_i$ and $s_l \in \pi_j$ such that $s_k \delta^\wedge s_l$, where $\delta^\wedge$ is the anti dependence relation.
3) $\pi_i \alpha^\circ \pi_j$ iff there exist $s_k \in \pi_i$ and $s_l \in \pi_j$ such that $s_k \delta^\circ s_l$, where δ° is the output dependence relation.   ∎

Based on the definition, the statements form a block (cell) π_i in the partition Π if and only if there is a directed dependence cycle among the statements. Two blocks have a true/anti/output dependence if and only if two statements, one in each block, exist a true/anti/output dependence.

Definition 3 (Weighted Partition Dependence Graph)

Given a node partition Π defined in Definition 2, we define a weighted partition dependence graph $WPG(B,E)$ as follows with B denoting the set of nodes and E denoting the set of edges. For each $\pi_i \in \Pi$, there is a corresponding node b_i (I_i, S_i, W_i, O_i) $\in B$, where I_i denotes the set of loop indices in block π_i; S_i represents the set of statements in block π_i; W_i is the weight of block π_i in the form of W_i (PH,PM) with PH and PM being the weights (i.e., the expected execution time) for the P.Host and P.Mem, respectively; and O_i is the execution order for block π_i. There is an edge $e_{ij} \in E$ from b_i to b_j if b_i and b_j have dependence relations α, $\alpha^\wedge$, and α° defined in Definition 1. These dependence relations are respectively denoted by $\xrightarrow{}$, $\xrightarrow{anti}$, and $\xrightarrow{o}$.   ∎

Based on these three definitions, we propose a *Statement Splitting* algorithm (Algorithm 1) to partition the loops:

Algorithm 1. (Statement Splitting Algorithm)
Given a loop $L = (i_1, i_2, \ldots i_n)$ ($s_1, s_2, \ldots s_d$)
Step 1: Construct dependence Graph G by analyzing subscript expressions and index pattern by using Polaris [4].
Step 2: Establish a node partition Π on G as defined in Definition 2. If there are large blocks caused by control dependence relations, convert control dependence into data dependence first [5], and then partition the dependence graph.
Step 3: On the partition Π, establish a weighted partition dependence graph WPG(B,E) defined in Definition 3.

3.2 Weight Evaluation

Two approaches to evaluating weight can be taken. One is to predict the execution time of programs by profiling the dominant parts. The other considers the operations in a statement and estimates the program execution time by looking up an operation weight table [20]. The former method called code profiling may be more accurate, but the predicted result cannot be reused; the latter called code analysis can determine statements for suitable processors but the estimated program execution time is not sufficiently accurate. Hence, the Self-Patch Weight Evaluation scheme was designed

Algorithm 2. (Critical Block Scheduling Algorithm)

[Input]

    $WPG=(P,E)$: original weighted partition dependence graph after weight is determined.

[Output]

    An critical block execution schedule CPS, where CPS = {CPS_1, CPS_2, …,CPS_i}. CPS_i ={CP_i, IWF_i} where CP_i = {Processor(b_a)} where processor is PH or PM . IWF_i ={$PH(b_a)$, $PM_1(b_b)$, $PM_2(b_c)$,…} means that in Inner Wavefront i, $PH(b_a)$ means that block b_a will be assigned to P.Host, $PM_1(b_b)$ means that blocks b_b will be assigned to P.Mem$_1$, $PM_2(b_c)$ means that blocks b_c will be assigned to P.Mem$_2$.

[Intermediate]

    W: a working set of nodes ready to be visited.

    EO_temp: a working set for execution order scheduling.

    iwf_temp: a working set for Inner Wavefront scheduling.

    max_EO: the maximum number of execution order.

    min_pred_O(b_i): the minimum execution order for all b_i's predecessor blocks.

    max_pred_O(b_i):the maximum execution order for all b_i's predecessor blocks.

    min_succ_RO(b_i):the minimum execution order for all b_i's successor blocks.

    max_succ_RO(b_i):the maximum execution order for all b_i's successor blocks.

    PHW(b_i): the weight of b_i for P.Host.

    PMW(b_i): the weight of b_i for P.Mem,

    $Rank_u(b_i)$: the trace up value of b_i used for finding CP

    $Rank_d(b_i)$: the trace down value of b_i used for finding CP

[Method]

    Step 1: For each block of the WPG, initializes the execution order, obtains the weights of P.Host and P.Mem by using the weight evaluation mechanism.

    Step 2: Travel down all blocks of the WPG to determine its $rank_d$ which is the maximal $rank_d$ of the parent blocks, add itself P.Mem weight and increase its execution order according to the maximal execution order of its parent blocks.

    Step 3: Travel up all block to determine the $rank_u$ by current block's P.Mem weight plus the max of children block's $rank_u$.

    Step 4: Travel all block find out the critical block that $rank_u$ + $rank_d$ equal to the $rank_d$ of the starting block, and then append the block into CP_temp and its order into CP_O.

    Step 5: In CP_temp, when a critical block's PHW is less than PMW, assign it to PH, otherwise assign it to PM$_1$. Append the block into CP_k, where k is CP_O of the block.

    Step 6: Split all block to subset by CP_O, the subset doesn't include the critical block, and then perform each subset by follow step.

        6.1 Split subset to new subset iwf_temp by order number.

        6.2 Check the PH_Used and PM1_Used between CP_O for each iwf_temp.

        6.3 Sort iwf_temp in decreasing order by the PMW.

        6.4 If the PH_Used of iwf_temp is false then find the minimal PHW block to set PH tag.

        6.5 Other block of iwf_temp set PM_k and append to IWF_i.

    Step 7: Append CP_i and IWF_i to CPS_i set, and then append all CPS_i to CPS set to generate the execution schedule.

    Step 8: Perform each IWF_i by follow steps to modify the execution schedule to fit the limitation of PM number.

        8.1 Sort IWF in decreasing order by the block's weight.

        8.2 If the PH_Used of IWF is false then find the minimal load of PH + PHW and set it to PH and add the PMW of block to PH load.

        8.3 Find the PM with minimal load then reassign the block to it.

        8.4 Repeat Step 8.3 until all blocks of IWF is done.

to combine the benefits of both approaches. It integrates these two approaches together by analyzing code and searching weight table first to estimate the weight of a block. If the block contains unknown operations, the patch (profiling) mechanism is then activated to evaluate the weights of unknown operations. The obtained operation weights are added into the weight table for next look-up. For a detailed description of this scheme, please refer to [5].

3.3   The Critical Block Scheduling Mechanism

Here we propose the Critical Block Scheduling mechanism to achieve an optimal schedule for utilizing all of the memory processors in PIM architecture. At first, the redundancy and synchronization between processors are critical factors that affect the performance of task scheduling for multiprocessor platforms. A critical block mechanism is used to minimize the frequency of synchronization. Then the WPG is then partitioned into several Sections according to the critical blocks and the dependence relations between these nodes. In a Section, the blocks are partitioned into several Inner Wavefronts in the following stages. Finally, the execution schedule for all P.Host and P.Mems is obtained. If the number of occupied memory processors exceeds the maximum number of processors in the PIM configuration, then the execution schedule will be modified accordingly. Algorithm 2 presents the main steps of this scheduling mechanism.

The algorithm includes eight major steps. In Step 1, the algorithm initiate the necessary variables and determine the P.Host and P.Mem weights of each blocks determined by the weight evaluation mechanism.

This algorithm figures out the critical nodes to partition WPG into *Sections*, so the critical blocks must be determined. Then the attributes, $rand_u$ and $rank_d$, of block b_i in WPG are defined by the following equations.

$$rank_u(b_i) = PMW(b_i) + \max_{b_j \in succ(b_i)}(rank_u(b_j))$$

$$rank_d(b_i) = \max_{b_j \in pred(b_i)}\{rank_d(b_j) + PMW(b_j)\}$$

Here, $succ(b_i)$ and $pred(b_i)$ represent all of the successors and predecessors of b_i, respectively.

The *critical block* is defined as the following equation.

A block b_i is *critical block*, if and only if $rand_u(b_i) + rank_d(b_i) = rand_u(b_s)$, where b_s is the start block of the WPG, and b_i is called the *critical block*.

According to the above definitions, the *critical block* can be determined by Step 2 to Step 4. Step 2 determines the $rand_d$ and the execution order of each block. In Fig.3 the $rand_u$ of b1 is zero and PWM(b1) is 2, that we can determine the $rand_d$ of b2...b6 are 2. The execution order O is the max execution order O increase. By this way we can determine the $rand_d$ and the execution order of each block. Step 3 determines the$rand_u$ of each block. The $rand_u$ determine by the max $rand_d$ of child block add the PWM of current block. Then, the algorithm determines which blocks are *critical blocks* in Step 4. In Fig.3 we can find the $rank_d$ +$rand_u$ of {b2,b15,b21,b29} equal to the $rand_u$ of b1, those block are the critical block. In order to split block set, we need to save the information of critical block for step 6.

Fig. 3 illustrates the WPG of the synthetic program, which is processing in stages stated above. In this WPG, the colored blocks are critical blocks.

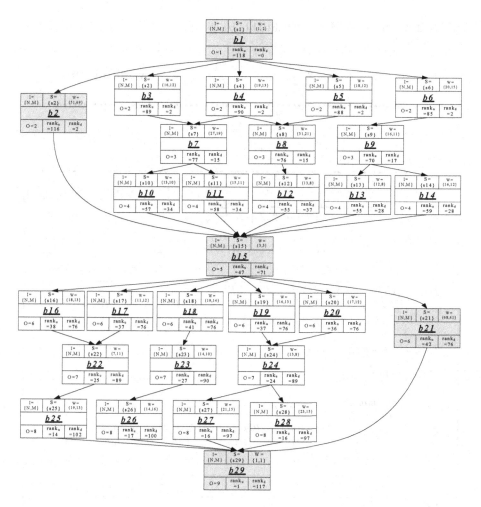

Fig. 3. WPG of a synthetic example

When the critical blocks are determined in Step 5, it partition all blocks in the WPG into several Sections. Fig. 4 illustrates the result of the given WPG, which is partitioned into five Sections, Section1:{b1}, Section 2: {b2, b3, b4, b5, b6, b7, b8, b9, b10, b11, b12, b13, b14}, Section 3:{b15}, Section 4: {b16, b17, b18, b19, b20, b21, b22, b23, b24, b25, b26, b27, b28} and Section 5:{b29}. The execution order of Sections is governed by their dependence relations. After the critical blocks are identified, the remaining blocks are partitioned into several Inner Wavefronts according to the order of execution and the dependence relations. In Fig. 4, Section 2 of the WPG is used to explain how blocks are scheduled in a Section. Since b2 is the critical block in Section 2, Step 5 is firstly used to schedule b2 to reduce the waiting and synchronization frequencies. The remaining blocks are partitioned in to three wavefronts according to the Oi of each block, by calling Step 6. Finally, iw1={b3, b4, b5, b6}, iw2={b7, b8, b9}, iw3={b10, b11, b12, b13} are determined.

Section 2={b2,b3,b4,b5,b6,b7,b8,b9,,b10,b11,b12,b13}
Critical block ={b2}

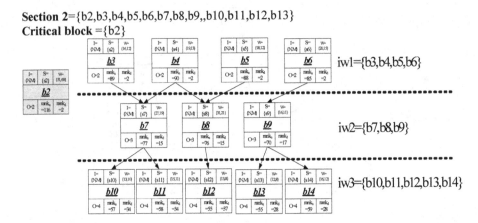

Fig. 4. Scheduled WPG of *Section* 2

$CPS = \{CPS1 , CPS2 , CPS3 , CPS4 , CPS5\}$
$= \{\{CP1 , IWF1\}, \{CP2 , IWF2\}, \{CP3 , IWF3\}, \{CP4 , IWF4\}, \{CP5 , IWF5\}\}$

CPS_1 : /*Section 1*/
$CP_1=\{PH(b1)\},$
$IWF_1=\{\phi\}$

CPS_2 : /*Section 2*/
$CP_2=\{PH(b2)\},$
$IWF_2=\{iwf1, iwf2, iwf3\} =\{\{PM_1(b3), PM_2(b4), PM_3(b5), PM_4(b6)\}, \{PM_1(b7),$
$PM_2(b8), PM_3(b9)\}, \{PM_1(b10), PM_2(b11), PM_3(b12), PM_4(b13),$
$PM_5(b14)\}\}$

CPS_3 : /*Section 3*/
$CP_3=\{PH(b15)\},$
$IWF_3=\{\phi\}$

CPS_4 : /*Section 4*/
$CP_4=\{PM_1(b21)\},$
$IWF_2=\{iwf1, iwf2, iwf3\} =\{\{PH(b16), PM_1(b17), PM_2(b18), PM_3(b19),$
$PM_4(b20)\}, \{PH(b22), PM_1(b23), PM_2(b24)\}, \{PH(b25), PM_1(b26),$
$PM_2(b27), PM_3(b28)\}\}$

CPS_5 : /*Section 5*/
$CP_5=\{b29\}, IWF_5=\{\phi\}$

Fig. 5. Output of the Critical Block scheduling algorithm

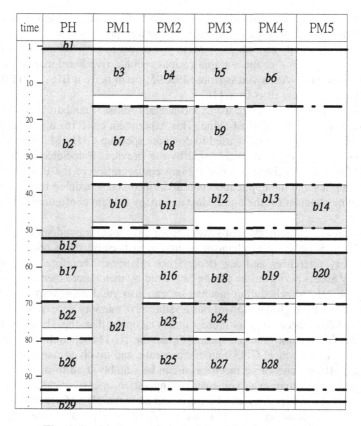

Fig. 6. Graphical execution schedule of the given example

In Step 7, the execution schedule is generated as shown in Fig. 6. Fig. 5 shows the graph-mode of the execution schedule. The shaded blocks represent the execution latency. The blank blocks indicate that the processor is waiting for other processors to synchronize. The bold and dotted lines determine the point of synchronization of Section and Inner Wavefront respectively.

Sometimes, the execution schedule may occupy more processors than are present in the architectural configuration. Therefore, Step 8 modifies the execution schedule as necessary. The sub-step of Step 8 is finding the minimal load processor and place the comport block. If PH is idle, find the maximal PHW block to fill it. Then using a loop to find minimal load processor to fill it and plus the PMW of block to its load. Redo this loop until all block fit in processor.

4 Experimental Results

The code generated by our Octans system is targeted on our PIM simulator that is derived from the FlexRAM simulator developed by the IA-COMA Lab. at UIUC [11] based on MINT simulator [14]. Table 1 lists the major architectural parameters. In this experiment, the configuration of one P.Host with many P.Mem processors is modeled to reflect the benefits of the multiple memory processors.

This experiment utilizes multiple P.Mem processors in the PIM architecture to improve performance. The evaluated applications include five benchmarks: cg is from the serial version of NAS; swim is from SPEC95; strsm is from BLAS3; TISI is from Perfect Benchmark, and fft is from [16].

Table 2 and Fig. 7 summarize the experimental results. "Standard" denotes that the application is executed in P.Host alone. This experiment concerns a general situation of a uniprocessor system, and is used to compare speedup. "1H-1M" implies that the application is transformed and scheduled by our previous Pair-Selection Scheduling (PSS) [5] for the one-P.Host and one-P.Mem configuration of the PIM architecture. "1H-nM" implies that the application is transformed and scheduled by Critical Block Scheduling mechanism for the one P.Host and many P.Mem configuration of the PIM architecture.

Table 2 and Fig. 7 indicate that swim and cg have quite a good speedup when the Critical Block Scheduling mechanism is employed because these programs contain many memory references and few dependence relations. Therefore, the parallelism and memory access performance can be improved by using more memory processors. Applying the 1H-1M scheduling mechanism can also yield improvements. strsm exhibits an extremely high parallelism but a rather few memory access, so the Critical Block Scheduling mechanism is more suitably adopted than the 1H-1M scheduling mechanism. TISI cannot generate speedup when the 1H-1M scheduling mechanism is applied, since it is a typical CPU bounded program, and involves many dependencies. The Critical Block Scheduling mechanism can be suitably used to increase speedup. Finally, in fft, the program is somewhat computation-intensive and sequential, and therefore only a little speedup can be improved after the 1H-1M schedulin g mechanism is applied. However, an additional overhead is generated when the Critical Block Scheduling mechanism is applied. Accordingly, 1H-1M and Critical Block Scheduling mechanisms are suitable for different situations. Choosing the 1H-1M or Critical Block Scheduling mechanism more heuristically in the scheduling stage of the Octans system will improve performance.

Table 2. Execution cycles of five benchmarks

Bench mark	Standard	1H-1M	1H-nM	Speedup		
				1H-1M	1H-nM	n (Occupied P.Mem)
swim	228289321	116669760	52168027	1.96	4.38	6
cg	91111840	51230772	32124287	1.78	2.84	4
TISI	133644087	173503404	91098174	0.77	1.47	2
fft	117998621	101841407	110399171	1.16	1.07	2
strsm	201133647	139990872	53711479	1.44	3.74	5

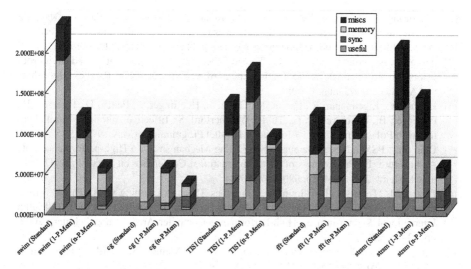

Fig. 7. Execution times of five benchmarks obtained by Standard, 1H-1M and 1H-nM

5   Conclusions

This study proposes a new scheduling mechanism, called Critical Block Scheduling, with Octans system for a new class of high-performance SoC architectures, Processor-in-Memory, which consists of a host processor and many memory processors. The Octans system partitions source code into blocks by statement splitting; estimates the weight (execution time) of each block, and then schedules each block to the most suitable processor for execution. Five real benchmarks, swim, TISI, strsm, cg, and fft were experimentally considered to evaluate the effects of the Critical Block Scheduling. In the experiment, the performance was improved by a factor of up to 4.38 while using up to six P.Mems and one P.Host. The authors believe that the techniques proposed here can be extended to run on DIVA, EXECUBE, FlexRAM, and other high-performance MPSoC/CMP architectures by slightly modifying the code generator of the Octans system.

Acknowledgement

This work is supported in part by the National Science Council of Republic of China, Taiwan under Grant NSC 96-2221-E-033 -019-.

References

[1] Agrawal, K., He, Y., Hsu, W.-J., Leiserson, C.: Shared Memory Parallelism: Adaptive Scheduling with Parallelism Feedback. In: Proceedings of the Eleventh ACM SIGPLAN Symposium on Principles and Practice of Parallel Programming (2006)

[2] Armstrong, R., Hensgen, D., Kidd, T.: The Relative Performance of Various, Mapping Algorithms is Independent of Sizable Variances in Run-Time Predictions. In: Proceedings of 7th IEEE Heterogeneous Computing Workshop, March 1998, pp. 79–87 (1998)

[3] Arora, N., Blumofe, R., Plaxton, C.: Thread Scheduling for Multiprogrammed Multiprocessors. In: Proceedings of the Tenth Annual ACM Symposium on Parallel Algorithms and Architectures (January 1998)

[4] Blume, W., Eigenmann, R., Faigin, K., Grout, J., Hoeflinger, J., Padua, D., Petersen, P., Pottenger, B., Rauchwerger, L., Tu, P., Weatherford, S.: Effective Automatic Parallelization with Polaris. International Journal of Parallel Programming (May 1995)

[5] Chu, S.L.: PSS: a Novel Statement Scheduling Mechanism for a High-performance SoC Architecture. In: Proceedings of Tenth International Conference on Parallel and Distributed Systems, July 2004, pp. 690–697 (2004)

[6] Cintra, M., Torrellas, J.: Eliminating Squashes Through Learning Cross-Thread Violations in Speculative Parallelization for Multiprocessors. In: Proceedings of 2002 Eighth International Symposium on High-Performance Computer Architecture, February 2002, pp. 43–54 (2002)

[7] Crisp, R.: Direct Rambus Technology: the New Main Memory Standard. In: Proceedings of IEEE Micro, November 1997, pp. 18–28 (1997)

[8] Hall, M., Anderson, J., Amarasinghe, S., Murphy, B., Liao, S., Bugnion, E., Lam, M.: Maximizing Multiprocessor Performance with the SUIF Compiler. IEEE Computer (December 1996)

[9] Hall, M., Kogge, P., Koller, J., Diniz, P., Chame, J., Draper, J., LaCoss, J., Granacki, J., Brockman, J., Srivastava, A., Athas, W., Freeh, V., Shin, J., Park, J.: Mapping Irregular Applications to DIVA, a PIM-Based Data-Intensive Architecture. In: Proceedings of 1999 Conference on Supercomputing (January 1999)

[10] Judd, D., Yelick, K.: Exploiting On-Chip Memory Bandwidth in the VIRAM Compiler. In: Proceedings of 2nd Workshop on Intelligent Memory Systems, Cambridge, MA, November 12 (2000)

[11] Kang, Y., Huang, W., Yoo, S., Keen, D., Ge, Z., Lam, V., Pattnaik, P., Torrellas, J.: FlexRAM: Toward an Advanced Intelligent Memory System. In: Proceedings of International Conference on Computer Design (ICCD), Austin, Texas (October 1999)

[12] Landis, D., Roth, L., Hulina, P., Coraor, L., Deno, S.: Evaluation of Computing in Memory Architectures for Digital Image Processing Applications. In: Proceedings of International Conference on Computer Design, pp. 146–151 (1999)

[13] Llosa, J., Gonzalez, A., Ayguade, E., Valero, M.: Swing Module Scheduling: a Lifetime-Sensitive Approach. In: Proceedings of the 1996 Conference on Parallel Architectures and Compilation Techniques, October 1996, pp. 80–86 (1996)

[14] Oskin, M., Chong, F.T., Sherwood, T.: Active Page: A Computation Model for Intelligent Memory. Computer Architecture. In: Proceedings of the 25th Annual International Symposium on Computer Architecture, pp. 192–203 (1998)

[15] Patterson, D., Anderson, T., Cardwell, N., Fromm, R., Keeton, K., Kozyrakis, C., Tomas, R., Yelick, K.: A Case for Intelligent DRAM. IEEE Micro, 33–44 (March/April 1997)

[16] Press, W.H., Teukolsky, S.A., Vetterling, W.T., Flannery, B.P.: Numerical Recipes in Fortran 77. Cambridge University Press, Cambridge (1992)

[17] Snip, A.K., Elliott, D.G., Margala, M., Durdle, N.G.: Using Computational RAM for Volume Rendering. In: Proceedings of 13th Annual IEEE International Conference on ASIC/SOC, pp. 253–257 (2000)

[18] Swanson, S., Michelson, K., Schwerin, A., Oskin, M.: WaveScalar. MICRO-36 (December 2003)

[19] Veenstra, J., Fowler, R.: MINT: A Front End for Efficient Simulation of Shared-Memory Multiprocessors. In: Proceedings of MAS-COTS 1994, January 1994, pp. 201–207 (1994)

[20] Wang, K.Y.: Precise Compile-Time Performance Prediction for Superscalar-Based Computers. In: Proceedings of ACM SIGPLAN 1994 Conference on Programming Language Design and Implementation, pp. 73–84 (1994)

[21] Zhou, Y., Wang, L., Clark, D., Li, K.: Thread Scheduling for Out-of-Core Applications with Memory Server on Multicomputers. In: Proceedings of the Sixth Workshop on I/O in Parallel and Distributed Systems (May 1999)

Capsules: Expressing Composable Computations in a Parallel Programming Model

Hasnain A. Mandviwala[1], Umakishore Ramachandran[1], and Kathleen Knobe[2]

[1] College of Computing, Georgia Institute of Technology
{mandvi,rama}@cc.gatech.edu
[2] Intel Corporation Inc.
kath.knobe@intel.com

Abstract. A well-known problem in designing high-level parallel programming models and languages is the "granularity problem", where the execution of parallel task instances that are too fine-grain incur large overheads in the parallel runtime and decrease the speed-up achieved by parallel execution. On the other hand, tasks that are too coarse-grain create load-imbalance and do not adequately utilize the parallel machine. In this work we attempt to address this issue with a concept of expressing "composable computations" in a parallel programming model called "Capsules". Such composability allows adjustment of execution granularity at run-time.

In Capsules, we provide a unifying framework that allows composition and adjustment of granularity for both data and computation over iteration space and computation space. We show that this concept not only allows the user to express the decision on granularity of execution, but also the decision on the granularity of garbage collection, and other features that may be supported by the programming model.

We argue that this adaptability of execution granularity leads to efficient parallel execution by matching the available application concurrency to the available hardware concurrency, thereby reducing parallelization overhead. By matching, we refer to creating coarse-grain Computation Capsules, that encompass multiple instances of fine-grain computation instances. In effect, creating coarse-grain computations reduces overhead by simply reducing the number of parallel computations. This leads to: (1) Reduced synchronization cost such as for blocked searches in shared data-structures; (2) Reduced distribution and scheduling cost for parallel computation instances; and (3) Reduced book-keeping cost maintain data-structures such as for unfulfilled data requests.

Capsules builds on our prior work, TStreams, a data-flow oriented parallel programming framework. Our results on an SMP machine using the Cascade Face Detector, and the Stereo Vision Depth applications show that adjusting execution granularity through profiling helps determine optimal coarse-grain serial execution granularity, reduces parallelization overhead and yields maximum application performance.

1   Introduction

Parallel programming is difficult [18]. Even more daunting is the task of writing a parallel program that executes efficiently on varying amounts of available concurrency

V. Adve, M.J. Garzarán, and P. Petersen (Eds.): LCPC 2007, LNCS 5234, pp. 276–291, 2008.
© Springer-Verlag Berlin Heidelberg 2008

without source code modification. Different platforms provide a different level of hardware parallelism, for example, the Cell B.E. processor has 1 Power Processing Element (PPE) and 8 Synergistic Processing Elements (SPEs), whereas the Intel Core2 Duo processor has upto four general purpose cores. In all these examples, the available hardware parallelism varies depending on the platform. Even on a given platform, depending on the workload mix, the parallelism available for a given application may change over time. Clearly, an application programmer would like to exploit all available hardware parallelism without having to re-compile code (on the same platform). The traditional solution was to extract all potential application parallelism and map it evenly among the available processors. However, if the granularity of parallel tasks is too fine, and the available hardware concurrency does not match the application concurrency, the application would incur excessive run-time overhead in executing the fine-grain computations on the limited available hardware. Ideally, one would like to shield the application programmer from the vagaries of resource availability while maximizing performance. Therefore, there is a need to dynamically adapt the application granularity (without change in source code) to match the available hardware parallelism and thus reduce the *parallelization overhead*.

Current parallel programming models lack the semantic ability to express a granularity adaptation mechanism for parallel tasks, where the granularity of execution could be changed for greater execution efficiency. Previous high-level parallel programming models such as Jade [9, 16, 17], Cilk [2], OpenMP [3, 6, 8] and even surveys [1] on parallel programming trends have acknowledged the problem of high run-time overhead when executing fine-grain computations. However, the granularity problem is not addressed at the programming model level and the programmer is left to encode parallel tasks to have sufficient granularity to avoid high parallelization overheads.

In this paper, we introduce the Capsules parallel programming model, which exposes the notion of composable computations and in-turn allows the dynamic adjustment of execution granularity for concurrent tasks. The application is written with the granularity that makes sense from the point of view of the application. Capsules provides software abstractions that allow dynamic composition of fine-grained computations into coarser grain modules when there are insufficient hardware resources. Such a dynamic composition results in a two-fold advantage: (1) The run-time needs to manage fewer parallel tasks thus reducing the book-keeping, scheduling, and distribution overheads. (2) The synchronization costs for shared data access is reduced by amortizing these overhead costs within the more useful work done for the composed coarse-grain computations.

We show that the Capsules model is a unifying framework that allows the application programmer to not only make decisions on adjusting the granularity of execution, but also allows him/her to adjust the granularity of other features. Features such as garbage collection (GC) of items can be made to occur at different granularities depending on how aggressive the programmer would like it to be. Similarly, features such as checkpointing and debugging can also occur at different granularities.

To evaluate the Capsules programming model and its run-time, we have parallelized two applications, namely: (1) The Cascade Face Detector (FD) [19] and (2) the Stereo Vision Depth (SV) [20] algorithm. Our results show that increasing the execution granularity helps reduce run-time overhead, and simultaneously yield an increase in performance.

2   Reducing Run-Time Overhead

In most parallel programming models, overhead is caused during *synchronization points*, which represents access to shared data either through explicit *put/get* [7, 11, 13, 14, 15] calls or implicitly through data access mechanisms such as *closures* and *continuations* [2] or *access declarations* [16]. There may also be book-keeping costs incurred to track the data requirement of computations/tasks running concurrently. Scheduling and distribution of tasks also contribute to this overhead. Therefore, the total overhead cost in such parallel systems is directly proportional to the number of concurrent tasks that execute and the number of synchronization points reached by those concurrent tasks during the entire application execution.

Therefore, in the absence of sufficient hardware concurrency, it is important to reduce this cost of parallelization. This can be achieved partially by reducing the total number of parallel tasks the run-time system needs to manage during the execution of a parallel program. Reducing the total number of tasks means increasing the amount of computation each parallel task needs to achieve. We refer to this as increasing the granularity of parallel tasks. Decreasing the number of parallel tasks can also decrease the number of synchronization points required to access shared data, which is also composed to a coarser granularity. Synchronization points are reduced by moving the shared data accesses to the boundary of coarser-grain composed computations.

Our approach towards reducing the number of concurrent tasks is to create coarser-grain tasks from finer-grain tasks dynamically during the parallel execution. The finer-grain computations inside the coarse-grain computation then execute serially. We introduce the notion of composable computations to the programming model level that enables instances of fine-grain computations to be merged together to form coarse-grain computations and at the same time reduce overall parallelization overhead.

3   Composing Computations Dynamically

In our work, we build upon the TStreams [7] parallel programming model to incorporate the notion of Composable Computations to enable adjustable granularity. We call our new parallel programming model *Capsules*. A user of Capsules can express maximum potential application parallelism by defining an application task-graph using finest-grain computational pieces and finest-grain data abstractions. Then, fine-grain computations can be dynamically composed together by the user to form more efficient coarse-grain computations. The mechanisms for composability are divided into two sub-mechanism that work orthogonal to each other. They are: (1) *Composition by Iteration Space*, and (2) *Composition by Computation Space*. Each mechanism is dynamic, and allows run-time determination of granularity that can affect application performance.

3.1   Software Abstractions: Step, Item, and Tag Capsules

In this section we describe software abstractions that allow expressing composable computation within a parallel programming model. These abstractions are (1) *StepCapsules*, (2) *ItemCapsules* and (3) *TagCapsules*. These abstractions are similar to the primary objects in TStreams [7], and differ only in the extra information they encapsulate to allow

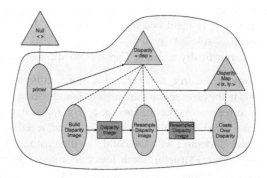

Fig. 1. Stereo Vision Depth application graph in Capsules

composability. Each Capsule object either contains only *one* object instance, or a *collection* of object instances representing a coarser-granularity. The granularity of these Capsules is user-defined, and can be dynamically adjusted at run-time.

To make a distinction between static and dynamic information about capsule objects, each object abstraction is separated into *Spaces* [7] and *Instances*. The notion of Capsule Spaces is analogous to the notion of *Classes* in Object Oriented Programming (OOP), which refers to the static specification of the object. Capsule Instances, therefore, are dynamic incarnations that conform to the specification of a Capsule Space (or object class). These distinctions provide Capsules with clean object oriented semantics, making it an easy development model for parallel programming.

Figure 1 illustrates an application constructed using Capsules. The task-graph denotes Capsule Spaces and relationship edges that remain static during program execution. The triangular shapes represent TagCapsule Spaces that denote iteration spaces for computation and data. The relationship between the iteration spaces and the computation and/or data is denoted by the dotted line. The oval shapes here represent computations or StepCapsule Spaces. Finally, the rectangular shapes represent data or ItemCapsule Spaces. These store data objects communicated between computations during program execution.

Listed below are the three basic objects found in TStreams that we use and extend from in Capsules:

Tag Instances are unique identifiers for a given Step or an Item instance (similar to Tuples in Linda [5]). Tags are multi-dimensional, where each dimension represents an iteration dimension specifying a range of possible values. These dimensions can be of any arbitrary type but only integer Tag dimensions are supported in the current implementation. A Collection of Tag Instances are called TagCapsule Instances.

Step Instances are function calls to the finest-grain user-defined indivisible computations. Each step instance is uniquely identified by a parametrizing Tag instance. Step instances produce Item instances or Tag instances via the producer relation. They also produce ItemCapsule instances and TagCapsule instances. Step instances also consume Item instances and ItemCapsule instances via the consumer relationship. A collection of finer-grain Step Instances is called a StepCapsule Instance.

Item Instances are fine-grain data produced by other computation Step instances. Each item instance is uniquely identified by a Tag instance. A collection of Item Instances is called an ItemCapsule Instance.

Now we list objects specifically added to Capsules to allow for composability:

TagCapsules Instances are *tree* structures that store multiple Tag instances in a compressed form. This is the abstraction that enables composition over iteration space. The depth i of the tree represents the dimension i of a Tag instance. Each tree node consist of a Tag dimension value. Enumeration of Tags is achieved by the cross-product of a Tag dimension value at depth i with the child Tag dimension values at depth $i + 1$. Since trees have a hierarchical structure with fewer root nodes than child nodes, this structure also specifies the hierarchical compression of the Tags dimension values at different dimensions. Tag dimension values that are higher in the tree are compressed more (have fewer nodes representing them) than Tag dimension values lower in the tree.

StepCapsule Instances are coarse-grain computations that are composed from other coarse-grain Step, Item and Tag Capsules enabling composition over computation space. StepCapsules play a dual role in the composable computation paradigm. They not only represent coarse-grain computations, but also represent the GC boundary for an automatic constrained GC mechanism (described in detail in sec. 4.3). StepCapsule instances are also hierarchical tree data-structures, where each non-leaf node represents a coarse-grain computation and a leaf-nodes represents fine-grain Step instances.

ItemCapsule Instance is also a collection of Items forming a coarse-grain data Capsule. It is also a tree structure similar to the TagCapsule instance tree. Each node at depth i of the ItemCapsule instance tree represents the Tag dimension value of the parametrizing TagCapsule instance tree at the same depth i. At the leaf-nodes of the tree, the actual items are stored. The items stored in a leaf-node are parametrized by the Tags represented by the parent hierarchy of the leaf-node.

Finally, we enumerate the Capsule primitives that specify the static relationships in the application task-graph. These Spaces, encapsulate the common denominator properties of Capsule object instances that belong to the same space.

TagCapsule Spaces, contain the static dimension information, namely, the number of dimensions in the iteration space and the name of each dimension. TagCapsule Spaces also store information about the objects they *parametrize*. Parametrization is a relationship between TagCapsule Spaces and other ItemCapsule Spaces or StepCapsule Spaces that specify which objects the TagCapsule instances uniquely identify.

StepCapsule Spaces contain static information about its parent StepCapsule Space, its parametrizing TagCapsule Space and child that are contained within it. They also contain producer/consumer relationship information between itself and other ItemCapsule and TagCapsule Spaces.

ItemCapsule Spaces also contain static information about its parametrizing TagCapsule Space and its parent StepCapsule Space.

3.2   Reducing Synchronization Points

In Capsules, synchronization points or data-access points to shared data structures can be reduced by creating coarser-grain data objects and coarser-grain computations. The synchronization points accessing coarse-grain data are moved to the *border* of the coarse-grain computations. Each coarse-grain computation requires a *serialization schedule* that defines the execution order of its constituent fine-grain computation. For StepCapsules created by composing over iteration space, the serialization schedule is determined by inspecting the StepCapsule instance's parametrizing TagCapsule instance. For StepCapsules created by composing over computation space, the serialization schedule requires analysis of data-dependencies between the component computations.

Moving synchronization or data-access points to the border of the serialization schedule refers to the transformation required to the data-access pattern and the granularity of input ItemCapsules, such that the total number of synchronization points in the application execution are reduced. When a StepCapsule instance is composed over iteration space, moving synchronization points to the boundary of the coarse-grain StepCapsule depends on the relationship of the dimensions between the producer/consumer StepCapsule Space and its ItemCapsule Space. However, for a StepCapsule instance composed over computation space, moving synchronization points requires analysis of the producer/consumer edge information between the composed coarse-grain StepCapsule Space and its ItemCapsule Spaces.

4   Composing by Computation Space

Composition over Computation Space is based on the notion of combining distinct computations or distinct pieces of code to create coarse-grain computations. Furthermore, these composed computations allow further composability by combining with other computation pieces like an erector set. This is a concept derived from functional and procedural languages where a coarse-grain function can be composed from fine-grain functions.

4.1   Serialization Order When Composing over Computation Space

To execute coarse-grain StepCapsules created by composition over computation space, a serial execution schedule is required to define the execution order of the fine-grain computations contained within it. We call this the serialization order for the coarse-grain StepCapsule. In Capsules, programmers are only required to provide data-dependencies between computation with the help of producer and consumer edges. Therefore, in order to construct a non-blocking serial execution schedule, a-priori resolution of data-dependencies via edge analysis is required. We have not yet implemented the automatic generation of a serialization schedule and leave it for future work.

4.2   Moving Synchronization Points to Coarse-Grain Computation Boundary

When composing over computation space, data access information for the composed coarse-grain StepCapsule Space needs to be distilled from the application graph. Explicit *get()* calls to retrieve data from external ItemCapsule Spaces are only required at the beginning of the coarse-grain StepCapsule. Likewise, *put()* calls to produce data and instantiate further StepCapsule instances are only needed at the end of the composed coarse-grain computation. This transformation has also not been implemented and is part of our future work.

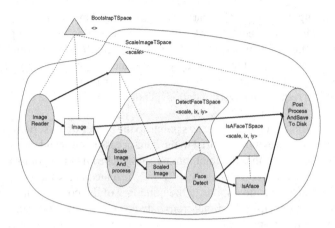

Fig. 2. Cascade Face Detector application, with a hierarchy of StepCapsule Spaces composed over computation space. The *ScaleImageAndProcess* and *FaceDetect* StepCapsule Spaces, along with the *ScaleImage* ItemCapsule Space and the *DetectFaceTSpace* TagCapsule Space are composed into one *coarse-grain* StepCapsule Space. This StepCapsule Space and the remainder objects form the outermost StepCapsule Space.

4.3   StepCapsule Space: A Software Abstraction Enabling Composition over Computation Space

A StepCapsule Space is constructed by combining together Step/Item/Tag Capsule Spaces. We refer to these finer-grain Spaces composed to form a coarse-grain StepCapsule Space as *Inner Spaces*. A composed StepCapsule Space also contains information about the producer/consumer relationships between the inner spaces.

A Hierarchy of Composable Computations. As fine-grain StepCapsule Spaces are composed into coarse-grain StepCapsule Spaces, a hierarchical StepCapsule tree is formed. Each *finest-grain* Step, Item and Tag Capsule Space in the application task-graph occurs *exactly once* as a *leaf node* of this tree. Each intermediate node of the tree represents the coarse-grain *composed* StepCapsule Spaces. For a given application, a StepCapsule Space hierarchy tree can be constructed in multiple ways using an API. Figures 1 and 2 illustrate two applications in their composed hierarchical form.

Selecting a Computation Space Hierarchy. Constructing the right computation space hierarchy is dependent on how the application needs to be partitioned along its data and computation boundaries to extract parallelism. Selecting the best hierarchy is dependent on complex variables such as available resources (memory and hardware concurrency), hardware platform characteristics such as shared memory or distributed memory, and exploitable application parallelism. Furthermore, in future hardware platforms, which will likely have hierarchical memory structures, the ability to hierarchically express computations for locality would be significant for performance. For our current system, we leave the determination of composable computation hierarchy to the application developer.

It is important to distinguish that the computation space hierarchy is statically defined by the user using the composition API. This hierarchy *cannot* change once the application begins execution. However, the decision to use the composed StepCapsule Space for coarse-grain serial execution is made dynamically at run time for each StepCapsule instance. Different StepCapsule instances can therefore be made to execute either serially in their coarse-grain form or simply allow the inner fine-grain StepCapsules instances to execute in parallel.

StepCapsule as a Boundary for GC and Scope. The coarse-grain StepCapsule instance also acts as a data-structure to maintain a GC boundary for all the ItemCapsules contained within it. Once all inner StepCapsule instances are done executing, the coarse-grain parent StepCapsule instance is marked *executed*, allowing all inner ItemCapsule instances to be GC'ed.

From a scoping perspective, inner ItemCapsule instances are visible only to inner StepCapsule instances contained within the same coarse-grain StepCapsule instance. However, inner StepCapsule spaces have visibility to Item/Tag Capsule spaces defined anywhere in their parent StepCapsule Space hierarchy.

4.4   Rules for Constructing a StepCapsule

The rules for composition over computation space are summarized as restrictions that guarantee the composed coarse-grain StepCapsule Space to be (1) atomic in execution, (2) to be uniquely tagged, (3) to terminate and (4) to not contain any non-reachable computations. These rules rules keep the execution model simple and avoid dead-locks during parallel execution.

5   Composition over Iteration Space

In this section we describe the notion of composing over iteration space within the context of parallel programming models.

Iteration space simply refers to all possible values that Tag instances can have. For example, a TagCapsule Space $< int\ x, int\ y >$ can span the entire space of two dimensional positive integer values. Therefore, the notion of composition over iteration space is defined by a collection of Tag instances put together over one or more dimensions of a TagCapsule Space. Since Tag instances actually parametrize computations (Steps) and data (Items), composition over iteration space is said to be a generalized form of the concept of composing together multiple instances of the same computation or composing together multiple instances of the same data-type.

5.1   Serialization Order When Composing over Iteration Space

Similar to coarse-grain computations created by composition over computation space, coarse-grain computations created by composition over iteration space also require a serialization schedule for execution. The serial execution schedule of a StepCapsule is based on the structure of its parametrizing TagCapsule instance tree. The schedule

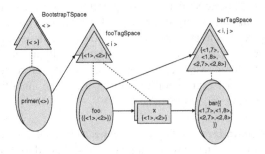

Fig. 3. An example of Composition by Iteration Space

simply traverses the sparse TagCapsule tree *in-order*, and appends the Tag dimension value found at depth i as the value for Tag dimension i. At every leaf node at depth N, the fine-grain StepCapsule instance is executed with the specified Tag Instance.

Clearly, the serial execution order is dependent on the order of Tags in the TagCapsule instance tree. As Tag dimension values at any level of a TagCapsule tree are created by a user-defined fine-grain StepCapsule function, the serialization order is therefore created by these producers by virtue of their serial creation order.

5.2   Moving Synchronization Points to Coarse-Grain Computation Boundary

Reducing the number of synchronization points means reducing the number of accesses to ItemCapsule Spaces. This requires the ItemCapsule instances to be coarse-grain so as to satisfy the data-requirements of the coarse-grain StepCapsule instance.

Retrieving any ItemCapsule instance in the Capsules programming model requires the run-time to define its parametrizing TagCapsule instance. This TagCapsule instance is derived from the parametrizing TagCapsule instance of the executing StepCapsule instance. Specifically, the matching dimensions between the parametrizing TagCapsule spaces of both the ItemCapsule space and the StepCapsule space determine what sub-tree in the StepCapsule instance's TagCapsule instance will be used to retrieve the ItemCapsule instance. The rules for valid producer and consumer relationships between StepCapsules and ItemCapsules are summarized in the next section. The ability to express coarse-grain ItemCapsules and performing data-access on them reduces the total number of synchronization points during program execution.

The following code example is used to explain the transformation that reduces synchronization points by moving them to the coarse-grain computation boundary:

```
foo() parametrized by TagCapsule Space <i, j>: foo<i, j>
foo<i, j> requires a[i] and b[j] as input
foo<i, j> produces c[i][j] as output

    Ai = getItem(A, <i>);
    Bj = getItem(B, <j>);
    Cij = foo(Ai, Bj);
    putItem(Cij, <i, j>);
```

Here, if *foo()* is executed in its finest granularity, there are $(I * J)$ instances of *foo()*, each performing *one* synchronized *get()* on each Item Spaces *A* and *B* and *one* synchronized *put()* on Item Space *C* to satisfy its input/output data requirements. Therefore, overall $2(I * J)$ *get()* calls and $(I * J)$ *put()* calls are performed. However, if *foo()* is composed along a dimension of its parametrizing iteration space i, there should then only be J coarse-grain instances of *foo()*. Each coarse-grain instance of foo$< j >$ performs only one synchronized *get()* on *A[0:I]* and one on *B[j]*. Overall, there are only $(2 * J)$ synchronized *get()* calls. Similarly, each coarse-grain instance of foo$< j >$ performs one *put()* of *C[0:I,j]*. Below is a code representation of the transformation:

```
Aall = getItem(A, <0:I >);
Bj   = getItem(B, <j >);
for(int i = 0; i <= I; i++) {
  Cj[i] = foo(Aall[i], Bj);
}
putItem(Cj[0:I], <0:I, j >);
```

This transformation reduces the number of synchronization points required for foo$<$ $i,j >$ by creating coarse-grain serial executions of foo$< j >$.

5.3 TagCapsule Space: A Software Abstraction Enabling Composition over Iteration Space

Similar to Tag Spaces in TStreams, TagCapsule Spaces in Capsules *parametrize* Item/-Tag Capsules Spaces. Although more general, TagCapsules enable a behavior similar to that of tiling [4].

Since a TagCapsule instance represents a collection of Tag instances, when a Tag-Capsule instance parametrizes a StepCapsule instance, each inner Tag instance inherently parametrizes a Step instance to form a collection of parametrized Step instances. However, from the stand point of the Capsules parallel programming model, all step instances parametrized by the TagCapsule are denoted as *one* coarse-grain StepCapsule instance that executes *atomically* and *serially* over the finer-grain Step instances.

TagCapsule instances denote the same granularity for ItemCapsule instances as they do for the StepCapsule instances they parametrize. This implies that for a given Tag-Capsule instance only *one* coarse-grain ItemCapsule instance would exist, where the inner fine-grain item instances would have a one to one mapping with the inner fine-grain Tag instances in the TagCapsule. For example, in fig. 3, the *fooAndItemTagSpace* parametrizes both the *foo()* StepCapsule space and the ItemCapsule Space. Therefore, the granularity of the TagCapsule instances in *fooAndItemTagSpace* denotes the granularity of ItemCapsule instances in ItemCapsule Space.

5.4 Rules for Composition over Iteration Space

In this section, we discuss rules that define composition over iteration space. In general, these rules provide restrictions on certain application graphs that make composability either expensive or impossible. We eliminate this class of application graphs to maintain a balance between a simple and efficient parallel run-time and a parallel programming model that is general enough to sufficiently address the composability requirements for the class of high performance vision applications targeted in this work.

To elaborate further, these rules describe restrictions on the *dimensions* of object spaces with producer/consumer relationships between them. In order words, these rules define what producer/consumer relationships/edges are allowed between StepCapsule Spaces and other Tag/Item Capsule Spaces.

For simplification, let us call the dimensions of the parametrizing TagCapsule Space of an Item/Step Capsule Space as the dimensions of that Item/Step Capsule Space.

The rules of composition limit StepCapsule Spaces to emit into Item/Tag Capsule Spaces that have the same number or more dimensions as itself (i.e. *dimensional expansion*), with matching dimensions listed in the same order. This disallows any case of *dimensional reduction*, where the produced objects have fewer dimensions that the producer. Such cases, which could lead to Tag value collisions, are invalid in the Dynamic Single Assignment (DSA) [12] property of the underlying programming mode [7].

Consumer StepCapsule Spaces, on the other hand, can have fewer or greater dimensions that their input ItemCapsule Spaces. If a consumer StepCapsule has fewer dimensions, the extra dimensions on the ItemCapsule Space can be defined with the help of *dimension definition functions* specified for the input edge. These functions can also inspect other ItemCapsule Spaces (also known as dependent edges) to define the missing dimensions. However, these dependent ItemCapsule Spaces should have dimensions fully specified by the consumer StepCapsule's dimensions. Although an implementation specific restriction that can be removed with additional support in the API, cycles are also currently disallowed in the application task-graph.

5.5 ItemCapsule Spaces: Composed over Iteration Space

When creating coarse-grain computations by composing over iteration space (sec. 5), it is crucial to also have the ability to change the granularity of data objects. We call these composable data objects, ItemCapsules. The granularity of an ItemCapsule instance depends on the granularity of the TagCapsule instance that parametrizes it. As described earlier in sec. 3.1, ItemCapsules are tree data-structures that mimic the structure of their parametrizing TagCapsule instance. This is essential to allow efficient querying of the ItemCapsule tree for relevant Items that are required to fulfill the data request of executing StepCapsule instances.

6 SMP Run-Time Implementation

The current C++ Capsules SMP run-time supports only composition over iteration space.

The run-time implementation is based on a simple execution model of work queues. Each processor or processing core is considered as a separate Processing Element (PE) with each PE assigned a unique work queue and a work thread. The work threads continuously pop StepCapsule instances from the head of the work queue for execution, whereas new StepCapsule instances are inserted at the tail of the queue.

Each StepCapsule instance is either a fine-grain StepCapsule instance or is a composed StepCapsule instance of multiple Step/Item/Tag Capsule instances. In the case it is an indivisible StepCapsule instance, the execution invokes the serialization schedule of the StepCapsule and executes all the fine-grain Step instances represented by the parametrizing TagCapsule instance. Composed StepCapsule instances can be operated on in one of two ways. They can also be executed serially, requiring a serialization schedule that would define the execution order of the inner StepCapsule instances, or they can be used as a GC container. The inner StepCapsule instances in this case are executed in parallel in work queues, whereas the composed StepCapsule GC container keeps track of executed inner StepCapsules with the help of a counter. Once all inner StepCapsule instances are done executing in parallel, the GC container and all inner Item/Tag Capsule instances are GC'ed.

Every application execution is encapsulated in a default StepCapsule GC instance that contains all application StepCapsule instances. Application termination is achieved once this outermost StepCapsule GC container is GC'ed.

7 Performance Evaluation and Results

In this section we describe our evaluation methodology, test cases and results.

7.1 Evaluation Methodology

The metrics used to evaluate the application performance and the underlying Capsule mechanisms are as follows:

The **Normalized Execution Time** is the ratio of the parallel execution time with respect to the serial execution time of the original unmodified application.

The **Percentage Overhead** represents the fraction of the CPU time spent in the Capsules run-time with respect to the total work done on all PEs. The run-time overhead consists of all non-application related operations performed by the system. The overhead percentage represents the efficiency with which the Capsules programming model is able to execute the application in parallel.

The OProfile [10] statistical sampling tool was used to measure the run-time overhead. Samples gathered in application functions were separated from samples captured in the run-time to compute the application percentage overhead. Samples were captured at every 90K clock cycle intervals with a call-graph depth size of 10.

The hardware platform used was an 8-Way SMP machine with 2 x 1.6GHz Intel Quad Core, Core 2 Duo Clovertown processors, with 2 GB RAM. A 32bit Fedora Core 6 Linux OS with kernel 2.6.20-1.2962 was used.

7.2 Applications

We parallelized two applications using Capsules: (1) The Cascade Face Detector (FD) [19] (fig. 2) and (2) a Stereo Vision depth (SV) algorithm [20] (fig. 1).

The face detector applies a cascade of pre-computed simple facial features on a window of fixed size in the image to detect whether a face exists in that window or not. This detection process is performed over the entire input image by shifting the window over the X and Y axes of the image to detect faces on different locations in the image.

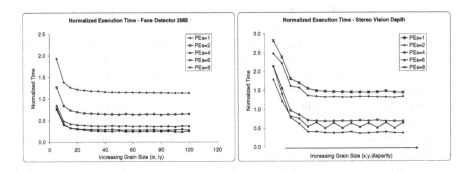

Fig. 4. Performance, Normalized Execution Time:*(left to right)*: Cascade Face Detector, Stereo Vision Depth; x-axis: Increasing Granularity; y-axis: Normalized time

In order to detect faces of different sizes, the image is scaled down and the detection process is repeated over again. This scaling and re-detection is repeated until the image scales down to the size of the feature detection window. A post processing phase, takes all detected faces and prunes duplicates that are close to each other.

The Stereo correlation algorithm is used to detect how far objects are placed in a given scene. It outputs a depth map from two stereo input images. The first stage in the algorithm consists of building multiple disparity-maps for the two input images. The second stage re-samples the disparity-maps to find the highest disparity values. The final stage composes the re-sampled disparity-maps to create the final depth-map.

7.3   Results

Figure 4 illustrates the *normalized execution time* of the two applications on different number of available PEs. The x-axis for the FD graph represents the granularity selected for the detection windows in both the x and y axis location in the image $< ix, iy >$. The total number of detection windows grouped together is therefore the square of the granularity selected. The x-axis for the SV graph represents a three-dimensional

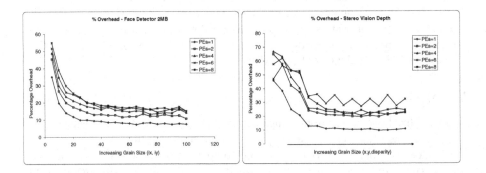

Fig. 5. Performance, Percentage Overhead: *(left to right)*: Cascade Face Detector, Stereo Vision Depth; x-axis: Increasing Granularity; y-axis: Percentage Overhead

granularity parameter $< ix, iy, disparity >$. The first-two parameters are again the x and y pixel locations grouped together for the first phase of processing. The third dimension disparity represents the disparity-maps grouped together for processing of the second phase of the algorithm.

Figure 5 illustrates the *percentage overhead* of all run-time mechanisms with respect to the total work done by all the PEs for a given execution.

Figure 4 clearly shows that increasing the granularity on different dimensions increases the performance of the application's parallel execution regardless of the number of PEs. Both applications speed-up by several factors with the help of granularity adjustment. Furthermore, percentage overhead in fig. 5 shows that increasing the granularity actually increases the efficiency of the parallel execution with less overhead incurred by the run-time. This is due to several factors. There is a total reduction in Step-Capsule instances created during the application execution, which in-turn reduces the total overhead due to synchronization, distribution and scheduling, and book-keeping cost. The percentage overhead confirms the hypothesis that composability in Capsules, even though more memory intensive due to its dynamic data-structures than other systems such as Cilk, can be used to dynamically create efficient coarse-grain computations to reduce the total overhead of parallelization. The fewer coarser-grain computations reduce the overhead to useful work ratio of resources and thereby improve the application's efficiency in using the underlying hardware concurrency for speed-up.

Figure 4 shows that application speed-up becomes constant beyond a certain point and does not change with further increasing granularity. A similar trend is seen in fig. 5 where the percentage overhead does not go down any further beyond increasing the granularity after a certain point. This is due to the fact that the dynamic data-structures required to enable coarse-grain computations begin to out-weigh the marginal gain achieved by reducing the cost of parallelization.

8   Conclusion

We introduce *Capsules*, a parallel programming model that brings together two distinct forms of composability namely, *composability over computation space* and *composability over iteration space*. Composability at the programming model level enable a user to dynamically adjust the granularity of parallel tasks and reduce system overhead. We show in our experiments that overhead due to synchronization and run-time book-keeping costs can be minimized by adjusting the granularity of an application's concurrent tasks and moving the synchronization points to the boundary of those coarse-grain computations. Overall, composability at the programming model level enables the application developer to write a parallel application once, and tune its granularity parameters later to extract the optimal amount of potential application parallelism required to efficiently utilize the hardware concurrency.

Acknowledgments

The work has been funded in part by an NSF ITR grant CCR-01-21638, NSF NMI grant CCR-03-30639, NSF CPA grant CCR-05-41079, and the Georgia Tech Broadband

Institute. The equipment used in the experimental studies is funded in part by an NSF Research Infrastructure award EIA-99-72872, and Intel Corp. We thank the members of the Embedded Pervasive Lab at Georgia Tech (http://wiki.cc.gatech.edu/epl/) for their helpful feedback on our work.

References

1. Asanovic, K., Bodik, R., Catanzaro, B.C., Gebis, J.J., Husbands, P., Keutzer, K., Patterson, D.A., Plishker, W.L., Shalf, J., Williams, S.W., Yelick, K.A.: The Landscape of Parallel Computing Research: A View from Berkeley. Technical Report UCB/EECS-2006-183, EECS Department, University of California, Berkeley (December 2006)
2. Blumofe, R.D., Joerg, C.F., Kuszmaul, B.C., Leiserson, C.E., Randall, K.H., Zhou, Y.: Cilk: An Efficient Multithreaded Runtime System. In: PPOPP 1995: Proceedings of the Fifth ACM SIGPLAN Symposium on Principles and Practice of Parallel Programming, pp. 207–216. ACM Press, New York (1995)
3. Board, O.A.R.: OpenMP: Simple, Portable, Scalable SMP Programming (2006)
4. Carter, L., Ferrante, J., Hummel, S.F., Alpern, B., Gatlin, K.-S.: Hierarchical Tiling: A Methodology for High Performance. Technical Report CS-96-508, University of California at San Diego, San Diego, CA (1996)
5. Gelernter, D.: Generative communication in Linda. ACM Transactions on Programming Languages and Systems 7(1), 80–112 (1985)
6. Intel. C++ Compiler 9.1 for Linux
7. Knobe, K., Offner, K.: TStreams: How to Write a Parallel Program. Technical Report HPL-2004-193, Hewlet Packard Labs - Cambridge Research Laboratory, Cambridge, MA (2004)
8. Kusano, K., Satoh, S., Sato, M.: In: Valero, M., Joe, K., Kitsuregawa, M., Tanaka, H. (eds.) ISHPC 2000. LNCS, vol. 1940, p. 403. Springer, Heidelberg (2000)
9. Lam, M.S., Rinard, M.C.: Coarse-grain parallel programming in Jade. In: PPOPP 1991: Proceedings of the third ACM SIGPLAN symposium on Principles and practice of parallel programming, pp. 94–105. ACM Press, New York (1991)
10. Levon, J.: OProfile, a system-wide profiler for Linux systems
11. Nikhil, R.S., Ramachandran, U., Rehg, J.M., Halstead Jr., R.H., Joerg, C.F., Kontothanassis, L.: Stampede: A programming system for emerging scalable interactive multimedia applications. In: Carter, L., Ferrante, J., Sehr, D., Chatterjee, S., Prins, J.F., Li, Z., Yew, P.-C. (eds.) LCPC 1998. LNCS, vol. 1656. Springer, Heidelberg (1999)
12. Offner, C., Knobe, K.: Weak Dynamic Single Assignment Form. Technical Report HPL-2003-169R1, Hewlet Packard Labs - Cambridge Research Laboratory, Cambridge, MA (2003)
13. Ramachandran, U., Nikhil, R., Rehg, J.M., Angelov, Y., Adhikari, S., Mackenzie, K., Harel, N., Knobe, K.: Stampede: A Cluster Programming Middleware for Interactive Stream-oriented Applications. IEEE Transactions on Parallel and Distributed Systems (2003)
14. Ramachandran, U., Nikhil, R.S., Harel, N., Rehg, J.M., Knobe, K.: Space-Time Memory: A Parallel Programming Abstraction for Interactive Multimedia Applications. In: Proc. Principles and Practice of Parallel Programming (PPoPP 1999), Atlanta, GA (May 1999)
15. Rehg, J.M., Knobe, K., Ramachandran, U., Nikhil, R.S., Chauhan, A.: Integrated Task and Data Parallel Support for Dynamic Applications. Scientific Programming 7(3-4), 289–302 (1999); Invited paper selected from 1998 Workshop on Languages, Compilers, and Run-Time Systems
16. Rinard, M.C., Scales, D.J., Lam, M.S.: Heterogeneous Parallel Programming in Jade. In: Supercomputing 1992: Proceedings of the 1992 ACM/IEEE conference on Supercomputing, pp. 245–256. IEEE Computer Society Press, Los Alamitos (1992)

17. Rinard, M.C., Scales, D.J., Lam, M.S.: Jade: A High-Level, Machine-Independent Language for Parallel Programming. Computer 26(6), 28–38 (1993)
18. Sutter, H., Larus, J.: Software and the Concurrency Revolution. Queue 3(7), 54–62 (2005)
19. Viola, P., Jones, M.: Rapid Object Detection using a Boosted Cascade of Simple Features. CVPR 01, 511 (2001)
20. Yang, R., Pollefeys, M.: A Versatile Stereo Implementation on Commodity Graphics Hardware. Journal of Real-Time Imaging 11, 7–18 (2005)

Communicating Multiprocessor-Tasks

Jörg Dümmler[1], Thomas Rauber[2], and Gudula Rünger[3]

[1] Chemnitz University of Technology
djo@informatik.tu-chemnitz.de
[2] University Bayreuth
rauber@uni-bayreuth.de
[3] Chemnitz University of Technology
ruenger@informatik.tu-chemnitz.de

Abstract. The use of multiprocessor tasks (M-tasks) has been shown to be successful for mixed task and data parallel implementations of algorithms from scientific computing. The approach often leads to an increase of scalability compared to a pure data parallel implementation, but restricts the data exchange between M-tasks to the beginning or the end of their execution, expressing data or control dependencies between M-tasks.

In this article, we propose an extension of the M-task model to communicating M-tasks (CM-tasks) which allows communication between M-tasks during their execution. In particular, we present and discuss the CM-task programming model, programming support for designing CM-task programs, and experimental results. Internally, a CM-task comprises communication and computation phases. The communication between different CM-tasks can exploit optimized communication patterns for the data exchange between CM-tasks, e.g., by using orthogonal realizations of the communication. This can be used to further increase the scalability of many applications, including time-stepping methods which use a similar task structure for each time step. This is demonstrated for solution methods for ordinary differential equations.

1 Introduction

The implementation of modular programs on parallel platforms can be supported by multiprocessor task programming (M-task programming). Each M-task represents a part of a program which can be executed in parallel by an arbitrary number of processors. The entire program consists of a set of M-tasks; a coordination structure specifies how the M-tasks of one specific program cooperate with each other and which dependencies have to be considered for the execution. For the coordination of M-tasks different parallel programming models have been proposed [13, 14, 15, 21]. A coordination structure in form of SP-graphs (serial parallel graphs) has been used in the TwoL model [15]. Using M-tasks often leads to a better scalability compared to a pure data parallel implementation due to a decrease of the communication overhead. Executing M-tasks concurrently on smaller subsets of processors reduces the internal overhead for collective communication of the M-tasks, thus reducing the overall communication overhead.

V. Adve, M.J. Garzarán, and P. Petersen (Eds.): LCPC 2007, LNCS 5234, pp. 292–307, 2008.

An M-task can use data produced by another M-task, leading to dependencies between M-tasks that have to be considered for their execution. A dependency between two M-tasks may require communication to achieve a data re-distribution such that a data structure is reordered at the end of one M-task A to be available in a data distribution expected by another M-task B before the execution of B starts. This restricts the data exchange between M-tasks to the beginning or the end of their execution.

In this article, we extend the standard M-task model as used in the TwoL model to the model of communicating M-tasks (CM-tasks) which allows a more complex graph structure and an additional kind of communication between M-tasks. The extension includes modified M-tasks which have the ability to communicate with other M-tasks during their execution. This new feature can capture the behavior of applications from scientific computing or numerical analysis in which modules exchange information during their execution. Examples are modules with internal iterations exchanging data with other modules after each iteration step. The CM-task model can also benefit from specific communication patterns. For example, it is possible to organize the communication phases between CM-tasks in an orthogonal fashion, thus enabling a more efficient realization of array-based applications on many execution platforms.

The CM-task programming model requires new scheduling and load balancing algorithms to achieve an efficient execution. The scheduling has to ensure that CM-tasks which communicate with each other are executed concurrently to each other on disjoint sets of processors. The scheduling has to be based on a cost model which also takes the internal computations and the external communications between CM-tasks into consideration. To support the programming in the CM-task model we have designed a transformation framework including a specification mechanism for CM-task programs and transformation steps which create an executable parallel program.

In the following, we present the parallel programming model of CM-tasks in Section 2 and discuss the programming support in Section 3. As example applications, we consider parallel Adams methods [16] which are solvers for systems of ordinary differential equations (ODEs) with potential method parallelism and show experimental results in Section 4. Section 5 discusses related work and Section 6 concludes.

2   Programming Model of CM-Tasks

The CM-task programming model exhibits two levels of parallelism: an upper level that captures the coarse-grain task structure of the application and a lower level that expresses parallelism within the tasks of the upper level. A CM-task program consists of a collection of CM-tasks which form the tasks of the upper level. Each CM-task is implemented in a way that allows its execution on an arbitrary number of processors. A CM-task can be a parallel module performing parallel computations (basic CM-task) or can have an internal structure activating other CM-tasks (composed CM-task). The internal parallelism of basic CM-tasks is realized by an SPMD programming approach; message passing may be used for distributed memory platforms while an implementation based on Pthreads or OpenMP may be advantageous on clusters with large SMP nodes. But within one CM-task program, the same SPMD model for the basic CM-tasks is used. In this article, we assume that CM-tasks are based on message passing using

MPI and have an internal data distribution for each of their input and output variables. On the upper level, the CM-tasks of the same parallel program can cooperate with each other in two different ways:

1) **P-relation:** CM-tasks A and B have a precedence relation (P-relation) if CM-task B requires input data from CM-task A before it can start its execution. This relation is not symmetric and is denoted by $A\delta_P B$.

2) **C-relation:** CM-tasks A and B have a communication relation (C-relation) if A and B have to exchange data during their execution to be able to continue their execution correctly. This relation is symmetric and is denoted by $A\delta_C B$.

In contrast, previous programming models based on M-tasks allow only P-relations between the tasks. The P- and C-relations determine some constraints on the potential execution order of CM-tasks:

• If there is a P-relation between two CM-tasks A and B, they have to be executed one after another. If B expects its input data in another data distribution as it is produced by A, a re-distribution operation has to be used to make the data available in the distribution expected. This re-distribution has to capture the situation that the processor sets executing A and B are not identical and may even be disjoint.

• If two CM-tasks A and B have a C-relation, both tasks have to be executed concurrently to realize the specified data exchange during their execution. Therefore, A and B are executed on disjoint sets of processors and cannot be executed one after another.

• Due to the constraints on CM-tasks with C-relations to be executed at the same time and for CM-tasks with P-relation to be executed one after another, there cannot be both a P-relation and a C-relation between two CM-tasks.

• If there is no P-relation and no C-relation between two CM-tasks A and B, they can be executed concurrently to each other but also one after another.

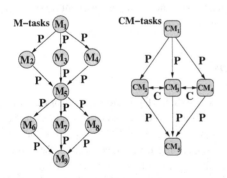

A CM-task program can be represented as a CM-task graph $G = (V, E)$ where the set of nodes $V = \{A_1, \ldots, A_n\}$ represent the CM-tasks. The edges are composed of two sets $E = E_c \cup E_p$ with $E_c \cap E_p = \emptyset$; E_p contains directed edges and represents the P-relations between CM-tasks; E_c contains bidirectional edges and represents the C-relations between CM-tasks.

Figure 1 illustrates an M-task graph (left) and a CM-task graph (right) for a typical task graph structure occurring in time stepping methods, e.g. for the solution of ODEs. The M-task graph captures two time steps where M-tasks M_2, M_3,

Fig. 1. M-task graph (left) with P-relations and CM-task graph (right) with P- and C-relations

and M_4 perform independent computations within one time step and the tasks M_6, M_7, and M_8 perform analogous computations for the next time step. In between, M_5 combines the results, e.g. for error control or information exchange. In the M-task model (with P-relations only), M_2 and M_6 cannot be combined because the result of M_2 is used by M_5. In the CM-task model, such combinations are possible, see Figure 1 (right). The CM-tasks CM_2, CM_3, and CM_4 are used to perform the independent computations within a series of time steps and to combine the results at the end of each time step. Data exchanges with other program parts are captured by C-relations.

The CM-task graph of a CM-task program illustrates constraints on the execution order. Different execution orders are possible, but will usually result in different execution times. The goal is to find a schedule and mapping for the CM-tasks of one program which fulfills the constraints given by the CM-task graph and leads to a minimum execution time on a given parallel execution platform.

3   Programming Support

To support the development of CM-task programs, a specification language, a cost model, and a transformation framework with support tools have been developed.

3.1   Specification Language

The specification language is used to describe the upper-level of CM-task programs by giving a list of CM-task declarations. The dependencies (P-relations) and interactions (C-relations) between CM-tasks are expressed by variables which carry the information to be communicated. For a P-relation between CM-tasks A and B, specific variables are produced by A as output data and are required by B as input data. For a C-relation between CM-tasks A and B, specific variables are exchanged between A and B or are sent from A to B (or from B to A) during the execution of A and B.

A CM-task specification of an application consists of data type declarations, data distribution type declarations, declarations of CM-tasks supplied by the user (basic CM-tasks), and definitions of CM-task graphs (composed CM-tasks). As data types we consider scalars and multi-dimensional array structures. For the data distribution, arbitrary block-cyclic and replicated distributions over multi-dimensional processor meshes are available. The specification contains only the interface definition of the CM-tasks. The implementation of the basic CM-tasks are provided separately by the programmer using the corresponding data distribution.

The declaration of a basic CM-task starts with the keyword **cmtask** followed by a unique name and two parameter lists: an input/output parameter list in round brackets for variables that are communicated over the P-relations at the beginning or the end of the CM-task and a communication parameter list in square brackets for variables that are exchanged during the execution of the CM-task. Each parameter has a name and a data type. The input/output parameters additionally have an access type (in, out, inout) and array variables have a data distribution type. An estimation of the execution time based on the cost model, see Subsection 3.2, can also be specified.

Composed CM-tasks are defined by using the keyword **cmgraph** followed by the name and the input/output parameter list similar to the parameters for basic CM-tasks. One composed CM-task is defined as the main entrance point of the CM-task program; this CM-task is denoted by using the keyword **cmmain** instead of **cmgraph**. The body

Listing 1. Specification program for the PAB method

```
const K=8, n=320000;
type vector = array[n] of double;

distrib vector:replic = [REPLIC(p)];
cmtask pab_stage (stage:int:in, xs,xe,h:double:inout,
  yps:vector:inout:replic)[xchg:vector] with runtime
  n/p*T_eval+(2*K+1)*n/p*T_op+T_mb(p, n/p);
cmmain pab (xs,xe,h:double:in, yps:vector[K]:inout:replic) {
  var vecxchg : vector;
  parfor (i = 0:K-1) {
    pab_stage (i, xs, xe, h, yps[i])[vecxchg]; } }
```

of composed CM-tasks may include the declaration of local variables using the keyword
var. Loops and conditional statements are available to define the internal task structure
of composed CM-tasks. Different types of loop structures are supported: sequential **for**
and **while**-loops can be used to define the sequential execution of CM-tasks. Parallel
parfor-loops can be used to activate a set of CM-tasks that are executed concurrently
on disjoint subsets of processors. The iteration space of the **for** and **parfor**-loops has to
be known at compile time (constant loop bounds) whereas the **while**-loop contains an
estimation of executed iterations. Conditionals are expressed by using the keyword **if**
and may contain an optional **else** branch.

The activation of a CM-task is specified by giving the name of the CM-task, an
input/output parameter list (for the P-relations), and a communication parameter list
(for the C-relations). The P-relations and C-relations of a CM-task graph are defined
implicitly by using variable names in the parameter lists. The transformation steps of
the framework annotate additional information to the composed CM-task definitions
including the explicit specification of the relations, scheduling and load balancing decisions, and information about necessary data re-distribution operations; see Subsection
3.3 for more details.

Example. As an example for scientific applications that can benefit from the CM-task
programming model we consider parallel Adams methods which are solution methods for ordinary differential equations (ODEs). These methods have been developed
for a parallel implementation in [20] and include the explicit parallel Adams-Bashforth
(PAB) methods as well as the implicit parallel Adams-Moulton (PAM) methods. Combining the PAB method with the PAM method in a predictor-corrector scheme results
in an implicit ODE solver (PABM) with fixed point iteration using the PAB method as
predictor. In [16], a detailed description of a parallel implementation is given.

Both, the PAB and PABM methods compute a fixed number K of stage vectors in
each time step which are then combined to compute the final solution vector of the
time step. In the M-task model, the stage vectors of one time step can be computed by
separate M-tasks which are executed concurrently by disjoint sets of processors. This
has the advantage that the internal communication of the M-tasks (which is dominated
by a gather operation, e.g. MPI_Allgatherv()) is restricted to a subset of the processors.

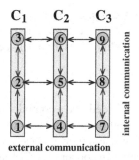

Fig. 2. Orthogonal communication between CM-tasks: Processor subsets C_i with $C_1 = \{1, 2, 3\}$, $C_2 = \{4, 5, 6\}$ and $C_3 = \{7, 8, 9\}$ are used for executing CM-task $CM_i, i = 1, 2, 3$. Orthogonal communication for communication between CM-tasks is performed within the subsets $\{1, 4, 7\}$, $\{2, 5, 8\}$, and $\{3, 6, 9\}$.

At the end of each time step, global communication is required to construct the solution vector of the time step. For x time steps, the total number of M-tasks is $x \cdot K$. Using the CM-task model, it is now possible to define CM-tasks such that one CM-task is responsible for the computation of the corresponding stage vectors in all x consecutive time steps, i.e. a total number of K CM-tasks is used, independently from the number of time steps. This enables the use of orthogonal communication between the CM-tasks at the end of each time step to construct the solution vector of the time step. For many array-based algorithms from scientific computing with potential CM-task parallelism, this can reduce the communication overhead tremendously.

The term orthogonal communication denotes a communication pattern for processors arranged in a two-dimensional mesh structure and divided in two different ways into subsets of processors with corresponding communicators. The first division into subsets of processors $C_1, \ldots, C_K$ is used to execute CM-tasks $CM_1, \ldots, CM_K$ in parallel, each one executing one CM-task. The internal communication of CM-task CM_i is executed within subset $C_i, i = 1, \ldots K$. The second division into subsets results by building new subsets across the subsets $C_1, \ldots, C_K$; these orthogonal sets of processors contain one processor of each of the subsets $C_1, \ldots, C_K$ and are used for the communication between concurrently running CM-tasks, see Figure 2 for an illustration. In the example, the second communicator is used for the data exchange after each time step using a multi-broadcast operation and includes all processors with the same rank within the first communicator.

Listing 1 shows the specification program for the PAB method with $K = 8$ stage vectors for an ODE of size $n = 320000$. For the replicated storage of the stage vectors a data type `vector` and a distribution type `replic` (for replicated distribution) are declared. The CM-task that computes the stage vectors is called `pab_stage` and requires the stage number `stage`, the starting time `xs`, the ending time `xe`, and the step size `h` as an input. The parameter `yps` inputs the initial stage vector and outputs the final result after all time steps have been computed. The communication parameter `xchg` is used to exchange information with the CM-tasks computing the other stage vectors after each time step. The cost information provided is discussed in Subsection 3.2. The composed

CM-task pab is the main part of the application. It consists of a parallel loop that creates K independent CM-tasks pab_stage. Because all loop iterations access the same local variable vecxchg, there is an implicit C-relation between each pair of iterations.

3.2   Cost Model

The specification language is embedded into a compiler framework which supports design decisions for the parallel execution on a specific execution platform, like the execution order of independent CM-tasks, assigning processors to CM-tasks, and determining required data re-distributions between cooperating CM-tasks. The design decisions are based on estimated costs for the execution of CM-tasks and the communication between them. Usually, different execution orders are possible for a given specification program, and each possible execution order may result in different estimated costs. The compiler framework selects the execution with the smallest estimated costs for the execution platform considered.

The cost model is based on symbolic runtime formulas which estimate the expected execution time of CM-tasks for a specific set of processors on the given machine and for a specific size of the input data. The cost model captures the expected execution times of the basic CM-tasks and the communication costs resulting from data re-distribution operations induced by the P-relations. The costs for a basic CM-task consist of computation costs for the arithmetic operations and communication costs for internal communication; also costs for data exchanges as specified by the C-relations are considered. The data re-distribution costs depend on the size of transmitted data in bytes and on the platform dependent startup time and byte-transfer time; the size of transmitted data can be computed within the framework based on the data types and data distribution types. Costs for composed CM-tasks can be built up from costs of basic CM-tasks and communication times for P-relations and C-relations according to the hierarchical CM-task structure: For a concurrent execution of CM-tasks CM_1 and CM_2, the maximum of their cost formulas is taken; for a consecutive execution, the sum of their cost formulas is used. The costs for the CM-task **cmmain** determine the costs for the entire program.

The symbolic runtime formulas are based on application dependent information and platform dependent information. The application dependent information includes the number of arithmetic operations and the number and types of communication operations. The platform dependent information includes the average execution time for an arithmetic operation and formulas describing the execution time for the communication operations depending on the number of transmitted data items and the number of participating processors. The cost information is included in the CM-task specification and can be provided manually by the programmer if simple cost formulas are used or can be extracted automatically by a compiler tool by inspecting the internal SPMD structure of the CM-task implementations.

In [11] it has been shown that symbolic runtime formulas can give realistic predictions of the runtime of the PAB and the PABM method. For the CM-task pab_stage of the PAB method the cost formula $T_{pabstage}(n,p) = (n/p * T\_eval + (2 * K + 1) * n/p * T\_op) + T\_mb(p, n/p)$ has been derived, see Listing 1. In this formula, K represents the number of stage vectors, n is the size of the ODE system, p is the number of processors, T_eval is the time to evaluate a single component of the ODE

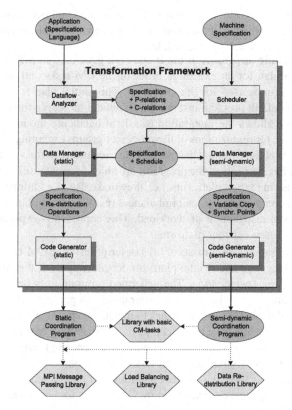

Fig. 3. Overview of the transformation framework

system, T_op is the time to execute an arithmetic operation and T_mb is the runtime of a multi-broadcast operation (MPI_Allgatherv()) depending on the number of processors and the size of the data. All values, except p, are known at compile-time. This results in the cost formula $K \cdot T_{pabstage}(n, p)$ for one time step of a data parallel version of the PAB method executing all stage vectors one after another by all processors.

3.3 Transformation Framework

A compiler framework is provided to transform CM-task programs specified in the specification language into executable parallel MPI programs. The framework integrates scheduling and load balancing methods, data distribution methods, as well as a generation process for the final MPI program. The framework supports two different approaches to generate parallel programs:

- The **static approach** of the framework generates an MPI program (in C) with a fixed schedule, i.e. the execution order of the CM-tasks and the size of the processor groups used for the execution is fixed at compile time and cannot be changed at runtime. The fixed schedule is created for a given problem instance (e.g. a fixed system size) and a specific target platform with a fixed number of processors. This approach is especially suited for dedicated homogeneous platforms and requires an accurate cost model for a good schedule.

- The **semi-dynamic approach** of the framework generates an MPI program (in C) with an initial plan for an execution order of the CM-tasks and an initial size of the processor groups used for the execution. This initial plan is based on a fixed schedule for a default problem instance and a default target platform. The MPI program generated allows the integration of a load balancing module that is able to arrange dynamic reorganizations of the processor groups executing CM-tasks based on observations of the dynamic behavior of the execution progress and possible load imbalances. Thus, semi-dynamic programs are able to adapt to different problem instances and varying target platforms, i.e., they make use of additional processors, if available, and compensate for load imbalances resulting from platform heterogeneity or an uneven distribution of workload. This approach is especially suited for non-dedicated heterogeneous platforms.

The input to the framework consists of (a) a description of the CM-task application in the specification language and (b) the platform dependent part of the cost information in a separate *machine specification*. The generated program uses implementations of basic CM-tasks that are provided by the programmer as parallel MPI functions. The interface of each of these MPI functions has to match the specification, i.e., the number and types of the parameters have to match; the data distribution types are used to select appropriate re-distribution operations. At runtime, the generated program provides two kinds of communicators to the basic CM-tasks: (a) a group communicator for group internal communication and (b) a cluster communicator that includes all processes that execute CM-tasks that are interconnected by C-relations for communication between running CM-tasks.

The programs generated by the semi-dynamic approach additionally use a load balancing library and a data re-distribution library. The load balancing library is initialized at program start with the CM-task graph of the application and is invoked during the execution of the application with measured runtimes of executed CM-tasks and may output an adapted schedule. The data re-distribution library provides runtime support for copying and re-distributing data structures.

The transformation framework includes a number of transformation steps where each step generates new information and adds it to the application description. Additionally, support tools are provided to visualize the progress of the framework and to give the programmer a possibility to interact with the framework, e.g., to influence or change decisions made by the framework. Figure 3 gives an overview of the transformation system. In the following, we describe the transformation steps in more detail.

The **Dataflow Analyzer** uses a data dependency analysis to detect the P-relations and C-relations that are defined implicitly in the initial specification program. For the P-relations, three different kinds of data dependencies are considered between the input/output parameter lists of the CM-tasks forming a CM-task graph: a WR data dependency occurs when a CM-task A writes a variable that is subsequently read by a CM-task B; a RW data dependency emerges when a CM-task A reads a variable that is subsequently written by a CM-task B; a WW data dependency arises when CM-tasks A and B subsequently write to the same variable. In each of these cases a P-relation between CM-tasks A and B is inserted; for WR data dependencies this P-relation is additionally annotated with the name of the variable, denoting that a data re-distribution between A and B might be necessary.

The C-relations of a CM-task graph are constructed using an analysis of the communication parameter lists of the CM-tasks. Two cases are considered: (a) two CM-tasks A and B access the same communication variable denoting a point-to-point communication between A and B during their execution and therefore a single C-relation is created; (b) more than two CM-tasks access the same communication variable resulting in collective communication between these CM-tasks and therefore C-relations between each pair of these CM-tasks are inserted.

The **Scheduler** determines a global hierarchical schedule consisting of a starting point in time and an executing processor group for each CM-task in a given specification of a CM-task application. Heuristics or hand-coded scheduling can be used for the scheduling decisions.

The **Static Data Manager** inserts descriptions of data re-distribution operations into the specification language. Such a description consists of the starting point in time, the source and target processor groups and a list of variables that should be re-distributed. For each variable, the name, the data type and the source and target distribution type is specified. The required data re-distribution operations are determined by an inspection of the P-relations within each composed CM-task.

The **Static Code Generator** produces a static coordination program that utilizes the MPI message passing library for the processor group management and for the realization of the data re-distribution operations. The coordination program consists of an initialization phase that creates all required communicators, a coordination function for each composed CM-task, and a finalization procedure that disposes all created communicators. A coordination function may contain declarations of local variables, constructs to guide the control flow (if-statement, for-loop) and code to execute CM-tasks and data re-distribution operations. The data re-distribution operations are performed in three steps: first, all sending processors pack their data into a sending buffer; second, the data is transmitted over the network; and third, the receiving processors unpack the data into the appropriate memory locations.

The **Semi-dynamic Data Manager** contributes to the transformation process in two ways. First, it marks the positions in the specification program where the load balancing should be performed. By default, the marked positions are points in time where all processors are available to allow a global restructuring and within loops to allow an adaption of the schedule based on previous loop iterations. Second, this transformation step decides which variable accesses are performed to the original variable and for which accesses a copy of the original variable should be supplied. The original variable may only be accessed by at most one CM-task at any given point in time. Write accesses use the original variable to ensure that it always contains the most recent values. This approach provides a flexible way to deal with a changing processor group layout without having to recompute all required re-distribution operations at runtime.

The **Semi-dynamic Code Generator** produces a coordination program that consists of a coordination function for each composed CM-task. Before starting a CM-task the required communicators are created and the data re-distribution library is invoked to ensure a correct data distribution of the input data. The runtimes of the executed CM-tasks are measured and provided to the load balancing library at the positions marked by the previous transformation step.

4 Experimental Evaluation

In the following, we illustrate the CM-task model for solution methods of ODEs. In particular, we consider the PAB and PABM methods that have been introduced as examples in Subsection 3.1. For the runtime tests we consider three different program versions using a static schedule:

- The pure data parallel version computes the stage vectors one after another using all available processors. Communication between the different stage vector computations is not required.
- The task parallel version uses K disjoint processor groups of equal size to compute the K stage vectors in parallel. Internally, each task is executed in an SPMD fashion resulting in mixed task and data parallelism for the entire program. Additional communication operations are required at the end of each time step to exchange the stage vectors. This communication is realized by an intra group broadcast followed by an inter group data exchange.
- The orthogonal version uses the same task layout as the task parallel variant. The exchange of stage vectors is performed using concurrent multi-broadcast operations between processes with the same group rank.

The runtime tests shown are made for ODE systems that result from a spatial discretization of the 2D Brusselator equation [7]. The resulting ODE systems are sparse: each component of the right-hand side function $\mathbf{f}$ of the ODE system has a fixed evaluation time that is independent of the size of the ODE system; thus, the evaluation time for the entire function $\mathbf{f}$ increases linearly with the size of the ODE system. The figures show the execution time of one time step, obtained by dividing the total execution time by the number of time steps performed. A typical integration may consist of tens of thousands of time steps, thus leading to a large overall execution time.

Figure 4 (left) shows the runtimes for a Xeon cluster consisting of 16 dual SMP nodes with an SCI interconnection network using ScaMPI. For two processors, no task parallel implementation is given because at least $K = 4$ processors are required for task parallelism. The runtimes for $p = 24$ are worse compared to the results for $p = 16$ because two processes need to be started on some nodes making the network interface on these nodes a bottleneck. For $p = 32$ the amount of data per node decreases leading to faster execution times. There is no speedup for the task parallel version because the communication overhead outweighs the additional computational power.

Figure 4 (right) shows the execution times of the PABM method on the CLiC cluster. This cluster is built from 528, 800 MHz, Pentium III processors connected by a fast-Ethernet network. For this cluster, the task parallel implementation is significantly faster than the data parallel implementation which is further improved by exploiting orthogonal communication structures. The impressive decrease in runtime when using concurrent multiprocessor tasks instead of data parallelism can be explained by the large communication overhead for collective communication operations on the CLiC due to

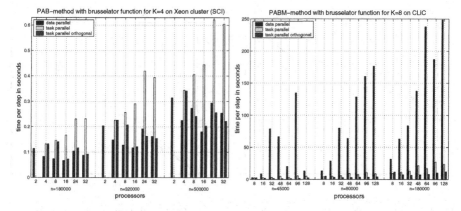

Fig. 4. Runtimes of one time step of the PAB method for Brusselator on SCI Xeon cluster with $K = 4$ (left) and runtime of the PABM method on CLiC with $K = 8$ (right)

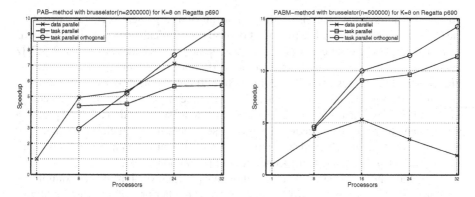

Fig. 5. Speedups of the PAB (left) and PABM (right) methods for Brusselator on IBM Regatta with $K = 8$

its interconnection network. From the figure, it can be seen that for a larger number of processors, the task parallel implementations with orthogonal communication (as it is supported by the CM-task model) usually leads to the fastest runtimes.

Figure 5 shows the speedups of the different program versions for the PAB and PABM methods for an IBM Regatta system; this system uses 32, 1.7 GHz, Power4 processors per SMP node and has 41 nodes. The results show that the orthogonal program version can outperform a data parallel execution scheme even on shared memory platforms. The PABM method requires a higher computational effort compared to the PAB method and therefore also higher speedups are possible. Group based communication also plays a more important role in the PABM method, leading to a decrease of the speedups for the data parallel version for more than 16 processors.

The speedups for the PAB method on the CHiC cluster are presented in Figure 6 (left) for the sparse Brusselator system and in Figure 6 (right) for the dense Schrödinger system. The Schrödinger system uses a right-hand side function **f** for which the evalua-

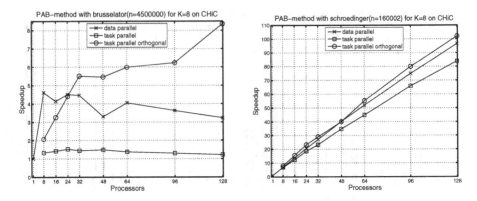

Fig. 6. Speedups of the PAB-method with $K = 8$ on the CHiC with Infiniband network using a sparse ODE system (left) and a dense ODE system (right)

tion of each component depends on all components of its argument vector and therefore the evaluation time of the entire function **f** depends quadratically on the size of the ODE system. The CHiC cluster consists of 538 dual Opteron 2218 nodes clocked at 2.6 GHz interconnected by a 10GBit/s Infiniband network. For the benchmark tests the MVA-PICH2 MPI library was used. The computation to communication ratio of the dense system is much higher compared to a sparse system leading to much higher speedups. The number of executed arithmetic operations per node is identical in all three program versions and therefore the speedups for the dense system lie much closer together. For the sparse system, the achieved speedups are limited because the amount of communication and computation are of the same order of magnitude.

Altogether, the results show that the orthogonal program version, as one example for communication between CM-tasks, outperforms both other program version in almost all cases. Especially for cluster systems with a slower interconnection network, such as the CLiC cluster (see Figure 4 (right)) optimizations such as orthogonal task parallel versions are required to achieve competitive performance results. But also for platforms with a fast interconnection network like the CHiC cluster, significant performance improvements can be obtained, especially for a larger number of processors.

5   Related Work

In the past decade, several research groups have proposed models for mixed task and data parallel executions with the goal to obtain parallel programs with faster execution time and better scalability properties, see [2, 18] for an overview of systems and approaches and see [3] for a detailed investigation of the benefits of combining task and data parallel executions. An exploitation of task and data parallelism in the context of a parallelizing compiler with an integrated scheduler can be found in the Paradigm project [9, 14]. The approach in this article is an extension of these approaches which captures additional communication patterns.

Other environments for mixed parallelism in scientific computing are language extensions, see [6] for an overview. In contrast to our approach, these environments leave the task placement, i.e. the scheduling, to the programmer and do not have an explicit specification language. The Fx compiler[19] extends the HPF data parallel language with statements that allow the partitioning of processor groups into disjoint subgroups whose size may be determined at runtime offering a semi-dynamic execution. [4] describes a concept to combine the task parallel Fortran M with the data parallel Fortan D or HPF to derive a mixed parallel execution. This concept allows communication between concurrently running parallel programming parts but lacks an automatic data re-distribution between data parallel tasks. Opus[5] uses Shared Data Abstractions (SDAs) for synchronization and communication between parallel program parts. The Tlib library [17] is a realization of the TwoL model as runtime system.

Scheduling algorithms for computing an appropriate mix of task and data parallel executions for M-task programs are presented in [21, 22]. For the decision, the scalability characteristics of the M-tasks and the communication costs between the M-tasks are taken into account. A comparison of different scheduling algorithms for M-task programs is given in [13]. These scheduling algorithms cannot be applied directly to CM-task programs, since they do not capture the C-relations between CM-tasks.

The use of skeletons to coordinate different program parts was considered within the Lithium environment [1]. Task and data parallel skeletons are available and can be nested within each other. Skeletons were also used in the $COLT_{HPF}$[12] compiler to create mixed parallel coordination programs providing a runtime system that controls communication and supports the dynamic loading of additional tasks. A lot of research has been invested in the development of the BSP (bulk synchronous parallelism) model and there exists a programming library (Oxford BSP library) that allows the formulation of BSP programs in an SPMD style [8]. NestStep extends the BSP model by supporting group-oriented parallelism by nesting of supersteps and a hierarchical processor group concept [10]. NestStep is defined as a set of extensions to existing programming languages like C or Java and is designed for a distributed address space.

6   Conclusions

In this paper, we have presented a parallel programming model with mixed task and data parallelism for coding modular applications. This model is based on M-tasks where each M-task is a parallel program part which can be executed on an arbitrary set of processors and can be hierarchically decomposed into further M-tasks. Programming models for M-tasks usually consider task graphs with control or data dependencies (precedence constraints). We have extended the M-task model by communication between concurrently running M-tasks. The model is able to capture communication between M-tasks, thus providing a flexible way to structure complex modular applications. In particular, the model is able to structure the communication between M-tasks such that orthogonal communication patterns can be exploited. Experimental results for solution methods for ODEs show a significant performance improvement compared to data parallel or pure task parallel execution schemes. Another area of examples which are expected to benefit from the CM-task model are modular simulation algorithms, e.g., from atmospheric simulation. For the implementation of efficient programs in the CM-task model, we have proposed a step-wise transformation process that is realized by a transformation framework. This framework supports the development of efficient CM-task programs by an automated transformation process and a toolset of interacting software tools to transform a specification into an executable program.

References

[1] Aldinucci, M., Danelutto, M., Teti, P.: An advanced environment supporting structured parallel programming in Java. Future Generation Computer Systems 19(5), 611–626 (2003)
[2] Bal, H., Haines, M.: Approaches for Integrating Task and Data Parallelism. IEEE Concurrency 6(3), 74–84 (1998)
[3] Chakrabarti, S., Demmel, J., Yelick, K.: Modeling the benefits of mixed data and task parallelism. In: Symposium on Parallel Algorithms and Architecture, pp. 74–83 (1995)
[4] Chandy, M., Foster, I., Kennedy, K., Koelbel, C., Tseng, C.-W.: Integrated support for task and data parallelism. The Int. Journal of Supercomputer Applications 8(2), 80–98 (1994)
[5] Chapman, B., Haines, M., Mehrota, P., Zima, H., Van Rosendale, J.: Opus: A coordination language for multidisciplinary applications. Sci. Program. 6(4), 345–362 (1997)
[6] Fink, S.J.: A Programming Model for Block-Structured Scientific Calculations on SMP Clusters. PhD thesis, University of California, San Diego (1998)
[7] Hairer, E., Nørsett, S.P., Wanner, G.: Solving Ordinary Differential Equations I: Nonstiff Problems. Springer, Berlin (1993)
[8] Hill, M., McColl, W., Skillicorn, D.: Questions and Answers about BSP. Scientific Programming 6(3), 249–274 (1997)
[9] Joisha, P., Banerjee, P.: PARADIGM (version 2.0): A New HPF Compilation System. In: Proc. 1999 International Parallel Processing Symposium (IPPS 1999) (1999)
[10] Keßler, C.W.: NestStep: Nested Parallelism and Virtual Shared Memory for the BSP model. The Journal of Supercomputing 17, 245–262 (2001)
[11] Kühnemann, M., Rauber, T., Rünger, G.: Optimizing MPI Collective Communication by Orthogonal Structures. Journal of Cluster Computing 9(3), 257–279 (2006)
[12] Orlando, S., Palmerini, P., Perego, R.: Coordinating HPF programs to mix task and data parallelism. In: SAC 2000: Proceedings of the 2000 ACM symposium on Applied computing, pp. 240–247. ACM Press, New York (2000)
[13] Radulescu, A., Nicolescu, C., van Gemund, A., Jonker, P.P.: CPR: Mixed task and data parallel scheduling for distributed systems. In: Proceedings of the 15th International Parallel and Distributed Symposium (2001)
[14] Ramaswamy, S.: Simultaneous Exploitation of Task and Data Parallelism in Regular Scientific Applications. PhD thesis, University of Illinois at Urbana-Champaign (1996)
[15] Rauber, T., Rünger, G.: A Transformation Approach to Derive Efficient Parallel Implementations. IEEE Transactions on Software Engineering 26(4), 315–339 (2000)
[16] Rauber, T., Rünger, G.: Execution Schemes for Parallel Adams Methods. In: Danelutto, M., Vanneschi, M., Laforenza, D. (eds.) Euro-Par 2004. LNCS, vol. 3149, pp. 708–717. Springer, Heidelberg (2004)
[17] Rauber, T., Rünger, G.: Tlib - A Library to Support Programming with Hierarchical Multi-Processor Tasks. J. of Parallel and Distributed Computing 65(3), 347–360 (2005)
[18] Skillicorn, D., Talia, D.: Models and languages for parallel computation. ACM Computing Surveys 30(2), 123–169 (1998)
[19] Subhlok, J., Yang, B.: A new model for integrated nested task and data parallel programming. In: Proceedings of the sixth ACM SIGPLAN symposium on Principles and practice of parallel programming, pp. 1–12. ACM Press, New York (1997)

[20] van der Houwen, P.J., Messina, E.: Parallel Adams Methods. J. of Comp. and App. Mathematics 101, 153–165 (1999)

[21] Vydyanathan, N., Krishnamoorthy, S., Sabin, G., Catalyurek, U., Kurc, T., Sadayappan, P., Saltz, J.: An integrated approach for processor allocation and scheduling of mixed-parallel applications. In: Proc. of the 2006 International Conference on Parallel Processing (ICPP 2006). IEEE, Los Alamitos (2006)

[22] Vydyanathan, N., Krishnamoorthy, S., Sabin, G., Catalyurek, U., Kurc, T., Sadayappan, P., Saltz, J.: Locality conscious processor allocation and scheduling for mixed parallel applications. In: Proc. of the 2006 IEEE Int. Conf. on Cluster Computing. IEEE, Los Alamitos (2006)

An Effective Automated Approach to Specialization of Code

Minhaj Ahmad Khan, H.-P. Charles, and D. Barthou

University of Versailles-Saint-Quentin-en-Yvelines, France

Abstract. Application performance is heavily dependent on the compiler optimizations. Modern compilers rely largely on the information made available to them at the time of compilation. In this regard, specializing the code according to input values is an effective way to communicate necessary information to the compiler.

However, the static specialization suffers from possible code explosion and dynamic specialization requires runtime compilation activities that may degrade the overall performance of the application.

This article proposes an automated approach for specializing code that is able to address both the problems of code size increase and the overhead of runtime activities. We first obtain optimized code through specialization performed at static compile time and then generate a template that can work for a large set of values through runtime specialization.

Our experiments show significant improvement for different **SPEC** benchmarks on Itanium-II(IA-64) and Pentium-IV processors using *icc* and *gcc* compilers.

1 Introduction

The classical static compilation chain is yet unable to reach the peak performance proposed by modern architectures like Itanium. The main reason comes from the fact that an increasing part of the performance is driven by dynamic information which is only available during execution of the application. To obtain better code quality, a modern compiler first takes into account input data sets, and then optimizes code according to this information.

Static specialization of integer parameters provides to the compiler the opportunity to optimize code accordingly, but it comes at the expense of large code size. A wide range of optimizations can take advantage of this kind of values: branch prediction, accurate prefetch distances (short loops do not have the same prefetch distance as loops with large iteration count), constant propagation, dead-code elimination, and complex optimizations including loop unrolling and software pipelining etc. can then be performed by the compiler.

The dynamic behavior of the applications and unavailability of information at static compile time impact the (static) compilation sequence and result in specialization of code to be performed at runtime. The code is specialized and optimized during execution of the program. It is mostly achieved by dynamic code generation systems [1,2,3,4,5] and offline partial evaluators [6,7]. These

V. Adve, M.J. Garzarán, and P. Petersen (Eds.): LCPC 2007, LNCS 5234, pp. 308–322, 2008.

```
void smvp (int nodes, params..) {
  for (i = 0; i < nodes; i++) {
    Anext = Aindex[i];
    Alast = Aindex[i + 1];
    sum0 = A[Anext][0][0]*v[i][0] + A[Anext][0][1]*v[i][1] +
    A[Anext][0][2]*v[i][2];
    sum1 = A[Anext][1][0]*v[i][0] + A[Anext][1][1]*v[i][1] +
    A[Anext][1][2]*v[i][2];
    sum2 = A[Anext][2][0]*v[i][0] + A[Anext][2][1]*v[i][1] +
    A[Anext][2][2]*v[i][2];
    Anext++;
    ...
  }//end for
}//end function
```

Fig. 1. 183.equake benchmark

systems perform runtime activities including analysis and/or computations for code generation and optimizations. All these activities incur a large overhead which may require hundreds of calls to be amortized.

For the hybrid specialization approach proposed in this paper, we do not require such time-consuming activities. The runtime specialization is performed for a limited number of instructions in a generic binary template. This template is generated during static compilation and is highly optimized since we expose some of the unknown values in the source code to the compiler. This step is similar to static specialization. The template is then adapted to new values during execution thereby avoiding code explosion as in other existing specializers. This step is similar to dynamic specialization with a very small runtime overhead. We have applied our method to different benchmarks from SPEC CPU2000 [8] suite.

The remainder of the paper is organized as follows. Section 2 describes the main principle on which hybrid specialization is based. Section 3 provides the required context that is essential to apply this technique and Section 4 elaborates the main steps included in the algorithm. The implementation details describing the input and output of each phase are provided in Section 5. Sections 6 and 7 present respectively the experimental results including the overhead incurred. A comparison with other technologies has been given in Section 8 before concluding in Section 9.

2   Principle of Hybrid Specialization

Consider the code in Figure 1 of the most time-consuming function *smvp* from 183.equake benchmark. Code specialization is oriented towards improving the performance by simplification of computations (through constant propagation, dead code elimination), or by triggering other complex optimizations such as software pipelining. It however may result in code explosion if performed at static compile time. Although the runtime optimizations may take advantage of known input, the cost of these optimizations makes them inappropriate to be performed at runtime.

If the parameter `nodes` is specialized with constants from 1 to 8192, we obtain different versions of code. We categorize them into different *classes* where each class differs from others in terms of optimizations but contains versions which are similar in optimizations. The versions in a class must differ only by some immediate constants. These differences occur due to different values of a specialized parameter.

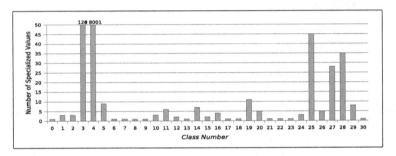

Fig. 2. *Classes* obtained for *183.equake* benchmark

Analyzing object code generated through Intel compiler *icc V9*, we find only 31 *classes* of code. Figure 2 shows the classes obtained after specialization together with the number of versions in each class. Any version in the class can serve as a *template* which can be instantiated at runtime for many values. Such behavior of compilers is similar for other benchmarks as well, even for different architectures.

The principle of the optimization we propose relies on the fact that while versioning functions for different parameter values, the compiler does not generate completely different codes. For some parameter value range, these codes have the same instructions and only differ by some constants. The value range to consider can be defined by several approaches: profiling, user-input, or static analysis. The idea is to build a binary template, which if instantiated with the parameter values, is equivalent to the versioned code. If the template can be computed at compile time, the instantiation can be performed at run-time with little overhead. We therefore have the best of versioning and dynamic specialization, i.e., we take advantage of complex static compiler optimizations and yet obtain the performance of versioned code without paying the cost of code expansion.

The hybrid specialization approach is depicted in Figure 3. The first step consists of versioning a function for appropriate parameters. From these versions, a template is extracted if this is possible. The template generation also includes the generation of a dynamic specializer together with specialized data for the template. The final hybrid code therefore comprises template versions, dynamic specializer and the original compiled code (as a fallback).

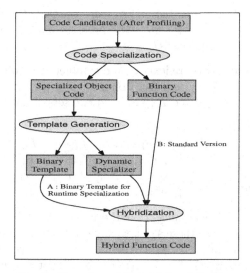

Fig. 3. Overview of Hybrid Specialization

3   Template Creation and Efficient Runtime Specialization

We define the notion of template as an abstraction of binary code with some slots (locations in the binary code) corresponding to parameters specialized. These slots can be filled with the constant values instantiating the template. Let $T_{X_1...X_n}$ denote a binary template with slots $X_1,...,X_n$. The instantiation of this template with the constant integer values $v_1,...,v_n$ is written $T_{X_1...X_n}[X_1/v_1,...,X_n/v_n]$, and corresponds to a binary code where all slots in the template have been filled with values. The complexity of instantiation of a template is $O(n)$ which is very low as compared to full code generation and optimizations performed at runtime.

3.1   Equivalence of Specialized Binaries

Now consider the code of a function F to be optimized, we assume without loss of generality that F takes only one integer parameter X. This function is compiled into a binary function $C(F)(X)$, where C denotes the optimization sequence and code generation performed by the compiler. By versioning F with a value v, the compiler generates a binary $B_v = C(F_v)$, performing better than $C(F)(v)$. We define an equivalence between specialized binaries:

Definition 1. *Given two specialized binaries B_v and $B_{v'}$, B_v is equivalent to $B_{v'}$ if there exists a template $T_{X_1...X_n}$ and functions $f_1 \ldots f_n$ such that*

$$T_{X_1...X_n}[X_1/f_1(v),...,X_n/f_n(v)] = B_v, \ T_{X_1...X_n}[X_1/f_1(v'),...,X_n/f_n(v')] = B_{v'}.$$

In other words, the two specialized binaries are equivalent if they are instantiations of the same template with the same function applied to their specialized value. Let R denote this equivalence.

This is indeed an equivalence: reflexivity and symmetry are obvious, and for the transitivity: Assume $B_v \mathcal{R} B_{v'}$ and $B_{v'} \mathcal{R} B_{v''}$, for $v \neq v''$, this means that there exist two templates $T_{X_1 \ldots X_n}$ and $T_{Y_1 \ldots Y_m}$, and two sets of functions $f_1 \ldots f_n$ and $g_1 \ldots g_m$ such that:

$$T_{X_1 \ldots X_n}[X_1/f_1(v), \ldots, X_n/f_n(v)] = B_v$$
$$T_{X_1 \ldots X_n}[X_1/f_1(v'), \ldots, X_n/f_n(v')] = B_{v'}$$
$$T_{Y_1 \ldots Y_m}[Y_1/g_1(v'), \ldots, X_m/g_m(v')] = B_{v'}$$
$$T_{Y_1 \ldots Y_m}[Y_1/g_1(v''), \ldots, X_m/g_m(v'')] = B_{v''}$$

Assume, without loss of generality, that the first p slots $Y_1, \ldots, Y_p$ correspond to the slots $X_1, \ldots, X_p$. For these slots, we deduce from the preceding equations that $f_i(v') = g_i(v')$, for all $i \in [1..p]$. We define $m - p + 1$ new functions on v' and v'' by $f_{i-p-1+n}(v') = g_i(v')$, $f_{i-p-1+n}(v'') = g_i(v'')$ for $i \in [p + 1..m]$. Finally, we define these functions for v as the value in the binary B_v taken in the slot Y_i, $i \in [p + 1..m]$. To conclude, we have defined a new template $T_{X_1 \ldots X_n Y_{m-p-1} \ldots Y_m}$ such that the instantiation of this template with the functions f_i in v, v' and v'' gives the binaries $B_v, B_{v'}$ and $B_{v''}$. These three binaries are equivalent, and R is an equivalence relation.

Computing the minimum number of templates necessary to account for all specialized binaries B_v when $v \in [lb, ub]$ boils down to computing the equivalence classes $\{B_v, v \in [lb, ub]\}/\mathcal{R}$ incrementally. Given below is the relation between specialized binaries and templates:

Interval of values	Specialized binaries	Binary templates
$[lb, ub]$ $\longrightarrow$	$\{B_v, v \in [lb, ub]\}$ $\rightleftharpoons$	$\{B_v, v \in [lb, ub]\}/\mathcal{R}$

As shown in the motivating example, there are many more specialized binaries than binary templates. Given the range of values to specialize for, compilation of the specialized binaries from the original code is achieved by a static compiler. Computation of the templates is likewise at static compile time. Instantiation of the templates then corresponds to the efficient dynamic specialization, performed at run-time.

3.2   Minimizing Overhead of Template Specialization

The overhead of template specialization is reduced through the generation of template at static compile time together with generation of specialized data requiring no calculation at runtime.

To compute the specialized data for instantiation of templates, we proceed after having found the *classes*. For each *class* computed from specialized binaries, let $v_t = v_1$ be first value for the *class* whose version will act as a template.

For values $v_2, v_3, \ldots, v_n$, occurring in the same equivalence *class* (producing n versions in the class),

- Initialize a linear data list with immediate values which exist in version specialized with v_t and do not exist in version specialized with v_2.
- Insert into the data list the values that differ (at corresponding locations) in the version specialized with v_t and those in versions specialized with $v_2, v_3, \ldots, v_n$.
- Generate the formula corresponding to the starting index of the element for the *class* in the data list.

By using this specialized data, it is easier to instantiate the template without calculating the runtime values.

4   Optimization Algorithm

We describe in this section the main steps that are required to perform hybrid specialization, incorporating both static and dynamic specializations. After obtaining intervals of values of the parameters, the following steps are performed.

1. Code specialization and analysis of object code;
   Different specialized versions of the function may be generated where its integer parameters are replaced by constant values. The specialized object code is analyzed to obtain a template that can be used for a large range of values. This search is performed within profiled values to meet the conditions described in Section 3. The equivalent specialized code versions differ in immediate constants being used as operands in object code. The instructions which differ in these versions will be termed as *candidate* instructions.
2. Generating statically specialized data list;
   The runtime specialization overhead is minimum if necessary data required for specialization of binary code has already been computed at static compile time. This specialized data (to be inserted into binary instructions) can be obtained for values in the interval corresponding to each *candidate* instruction as given in Section 3.2. The specialized data approach not only transfers the complexity of runtime computations to static compile time but also reduces the overhead of possible code size increase.
3. Generation of runtime specializer and template;
   For the *classes* containing more than one value, a runtime specializer is generated. The runtime specializer contains the code to search for the proper template and subsequently modify binary instructions of that template. Information regarding locations of each *candidate* instruction can be easily gathered from object code. The template in hybrid specialization therefore comprises all the *candidate* instructions to be modified during execution. The modification of instructions can then be accomplished by self-modifying code.
   This approach ensures that the cost of runtime code generation/modification is far less than that in existing specializers and code generators. The optimizations on the template have already been performed at static compile time due to specialization of code.

5   Implementation Framework and Experimentation

The hybrid specialization approach (depicted in Figure 3) has been automated for function parameters of integral data types in *HySpec*[5] framework. It takes input configuration file containing the functions, parameters, the intervals and compilation parameters. The intervals can be specified based on application-knowledge, otherwise code is first instrumented at *routine* level with *HySpec* to obtain the value profile [9] for integral parameters of the functions.

In addition to instrumentation for value profiling, *HySpec* performs different steps to generate hybridly specialized code which are given below.

5.1   Code Specialization and Object Code Analysis

Within interval values, code is specialized by exposing the values of function parameters. The code is parsed[1] to generate another specialized version. This is followed by an analysis of object code to search for *classes* of code, so that within a *class* the versions differ only in immediate constants. For example, for

Table 1. Object code generated over Itanium-II and Pentium-IV

Value	IA-64	P-IV
nodes=19	cmp.ge.unc p6,p0=**19**,r54	cmpl **$19**, %eax
nodes=17	cmp.ge.unc p6,p0=**17**,r54	cmpl **$17**, %eax

`183.equake`, the object code generated by `icc` compiler, when specialized with the value *nodes*=17 and the one generated for *nodes*=19 differs only in some constants as shown in Table 1. These instructions correspond to the value of specialized parameter.

5.2   Generation of Specialized Data and Runtime Specializer

Automatic generation of specialized data and the runtime specializer renders hybrid specialization to be a declarative approach. For an interval, all the values corresponding to each instruction differing in equivalent versions are used to generate a linear array of specialized data. This array represents the actual values with which the binary code is specialized during execution. The offset of data from where the values start for an instance of a template, are also computed at static compile time.

The template can be specialized by modifying instructions at runtime. This is accomplished by the runtime specializer which is able to efficiently insert values at specified locations. These locations are also calculated during analysis of object code. As shown in Figure 4 (on the right), each invocation of *Instruction Specializer* puts statically specialized data into template slots. This is followed by activities for cache coherence (required for IA-64).

---

[1] Only the C language is supported.

The *Instruction Specializer* is implemented as a set of macros which may have different functionality for different processors due to different instruction set architecture. For Itanium-II, the offset contains the bundle number and instruction number within that bundle, whereas for Pentium-IV, it contains exact offset of the instruction to be modified.

5.3 Final Wrapper Code

Figure 4 (on the left) shows the pseudo-code for the wrapper. It first searches for the template for which the new (runtime) value is valid. The branches in the wrapper are used to redirect control to the proper version. For each template, the current implementation supports dynamic specialization with a software cache of single version. We intend to implement the software cache with multiple clones to mitigate the problem of parameters with repeated patterns.

```
static long old_Param[]={...};      Offset = Location of candidate inst.
void WrapperFunction (Parameters)   Data = Pointer to specialized data
    Let TN = FoundTemplate          BA = Function's Base Address
    if TN>0 then                    void BinaryTemplateSpecializer{
        if Param <> old_Param[TN]       InstSpec(BA+offset_0, Data[0])
            Branch to Specializer[TN]    InstSpec(BA+offset_1, Data[1])
            Update old_Param            InstSpec(BA+offset_2, Data[2])
        end if                          InstSpec(BA+offset_3, Data[3])
        Branch to Template[TN]          .........
    else                                .........
        Branch to Standard code         .........
End Function                         }
```

Fig. 4. Wrapper code (left) and invocation of Instruction Specializer(right)

6 Experimental Results

The specialization approach has been applied to hot functions in SPEC CPU2000 benchmarks with reference inputs. The experiments have been performed over platforms with the configurations given in Table 2. This section describes the results of these benchmarks together with optimizations performed by compilers due to specialization.

Figure 5 shows the speedup percentage obtained w.r.t standard (original) code. For these benchmarks, the speedup largely depends upon the use of parameters in the code. The hot code of these benchmarks does not always include

Table 2. Configuration of the Architectures Used

Processor	Speed	Compilers & optimization level
Intel Itanium-II (IA64)	1.5 GHz	gcc v 4.3, icc v 9.1 with -O3
Intel Pentium-4 (R)	3.20 GHz	gcc v 4.3 , icc v 8.0 with -O3

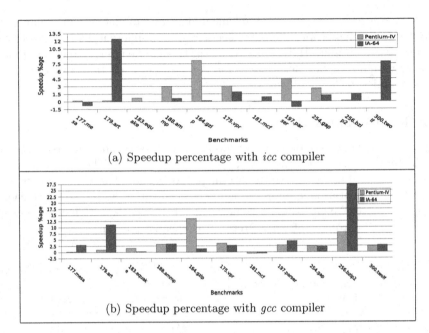

(a) Speedup percentage with *icc* compiler

(b) Speedup percentage with *gcc* compiler

Fig. 5. Performance Results of SPEC CPU2000 Benchmarks

integer parameters, and in some cases, the candidate parameters were unable to impact overall execution to a large factor.

For benchmark *mesa*, the compilers were able to perform inlining and partial evaluation. However, these optimizations did not put any significant impact on execution time. In *art* benchmark, the main optimizations were data prefetching and unrolling which resulted in good performance on IA-64 architecture. However, the compilers did not make any big difference w.r.t standard code on Pentium-IV architecture.

For *equake*, the large values of specializing parameters resulted in code almost similar to that of un-specialized version with small difference in code scheduling. Similarly, the *gzip* benchmark benefits from loop optimizations and code inlining on Pentium-IV, however on Itanium-II, the compilers generated code with similar unroll factor for both the standard and specialized versions.

In the *ammp*, *vpr*, *mcf*, *parser* and *gap* benchmarks, a large part of hot functions does not make use of integer parameters and the large frequency of variance in runtime values reduces the performance gain after hybrid specialization.

In case of the *bzip2* benchmark, the *gcc* compiler performed partial evaluation and the loop-based optimizations which did not exist in un-specialized code. With the *icc* compiler, the loop-based optimizations were similar in both the specialized and un-specialized code with small difference due to partial evaluation.

The *twolf* benchmark benefits mainly from data cache prefetching, reduced number of loads and better code scheduling on IA-64 with *icc* compiler, whereas

Table 3. Summarized analysis for SPEC benchmarks

Benchmark	Number of static versions reqd.	Percentage of re-instantiations				Number of Templates				Percentage of code size increase (w.r.t. un-specialized benchmark)			
		IA-64		P-IV		IA-64		P-IV		IA-64		P-IV	
		icc	gcc	icc	gcc	icc	gcc	icc	gcc	icc	gcc	icc	gcc
177.mesa	9	8%	8%	36%	8 %	9	9	2	9	10%	1%	1%	1%
179.art	5	1%	1%	1%	1%	4	5	5	4	9%	8%	9%	1 %
183.equake	1	0%	0%	0%	0%	1	1	1	1	8%	7%	1%	7%
188.ammp	1	0%	0%	0%	0%	1	1	1	1	1%	2%	1%	3%
164.gzip	15	43%	86%	43%	86%	2	1	2	1	1%	2%	1%	3%
175.vpr	8444	1%	1%	1%	1%	3	3	11	4	1%	1%	1%	1%
181.mcf	10	1%	1%	1%	1%	3	1	3	1	19 %	38 %	19%	1%
197.parser	40	21%	42%	21%	42%	2	1	2	1	4%	1%	4%	1%
254.gap	53	8%	16%	8%	63%	8	4	8	1	34%	10%	1%	5%
256.bzip2	5	21%	42%	21%	21%	2	1	2	2	2%	1%	1%	5 %
300.twolf	2	49%	49%	49%	49%	1	1	1	1	1%	1%	1%	1%

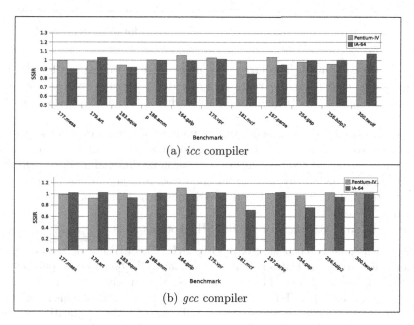

(a) *icc* compiler

(b) *gcc* compiler

Fig. 6. Speedup to Size Increase Ratio(SSIR) for SPEC Benchmarks. SSIR=1 means that the speedup obtained is equal to the code size expansion.

for the remaining platform configurations, the compilers were limited to performing inlining and partial evaluation.

Table 3 shows (in column 1) the number of versions that were required for static specialization together with percentage of re-instantiations of the same

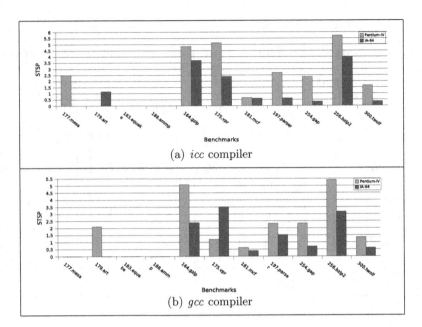

Fig. 7. Slot to Template Size Percentage (STSP) for SPEC Benchmarks

template (in column 2). The large percentage of re-instantiations for the *gzip*, *parser* and *twolf* benchmarks represents repeated pattern of values. This factor can only be minimized through software cache of templates which is part of future work.

Columns 3 and 4 show respectively the number of templates and the percentage of code size increase w.r.t. un-specialized code. The compilers show variant behaviour in terms of code size after code specialization mainly due to different optimizations. This is why, sometimes code with a large number of specialized versions/templates may result in less size than with a small number of specialized versions.

The speedup to size increase ratio (SSIR) computed as $\frac{Speedup}{\left(\frac{Size\ of\ code\ after\ specialization}{Size\ of\ unspecialized\ code}\right)}$ for SPEC benchmarks has been given in Figure 6. The SSIR metric is a measure of efficiency for our specialization approach (similar to the one used for parallelism). The SSIR is not large over both the processors even with benchmarks having large speedup, e.g., *art*. This is due to the fact that for benchmarks with the large speedup, standard (un-specialized) code size of entire application is small, and addition of hybrid code with specialized versions, template and specializer code thereby reduces the SSIR factor.

The Figure 7 shows the largest slot to template size percentage (STSP) for each benchmark. It is calculated as: $\left(\frac{No.\ of\ slots\ reqd.\ for\ dynamic\ specialization}{Total\ no.\ of\ instructions\ in\ template}\right) * 100$. For benchmarks *mesa*, *equake*, *ammp*, where the number of static versions required is equal to the number of templates, it becomes zero. However, it is less than 6%

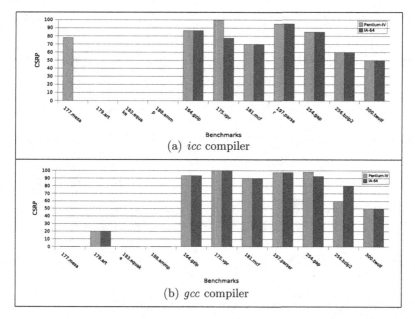

(a) *icc* compiler

(b) *gcc* compiler

Fig. 8. Code Size Reduction Percentage(CSRP) for SPEC Benchmarks w.r.t equivalent static specialization. 50% would mean that the number of templates is half the number of static versions required to cover the same specialized values.

for all benchmarks which shows that our specialization method incurs the smallest possible overhead at runtime.

The effectiveness of hybrid specialization also lies in code size reduction w.r.t static specialized code for the same input intervals. In this regard, the metric *Code Size Reduction Percentage* calculated as, $\left(1 - \frac{Number\ of\ Templates\ found}{Number\ of\ Static\ Versions\ Required}\right) * 100$, has been given in Figure 8. For the benchmarks *mesa*, *art*, *equake* and *ammp*, the *CSRP* is very small since the number of templates is very close to the number of versions required for static specialization. For other benchmarks, this factor becomes large since a single template is used to serve a very large number of values.

7 Specialization Overhead

A summarized view of overhead with respect to application execution time is shown in Figure 9. The reduced overhead results in good performance for SPEC benchmarks. It is due to the fact that the templates and the values to be inserted at runtime are entirely generated at static compile time. The modification of a single instruction takes an average[2] of 9 cycles on Itanium-II and 2 cycles on Pentium-IV. This overhead of generation of instructions is far less than that in existing dynamic compilation/specialization systems e.g. Tempo [6] or Tick C [1],

---

[2] The binary instruction formats require extraction of different numbers of bit-sets.

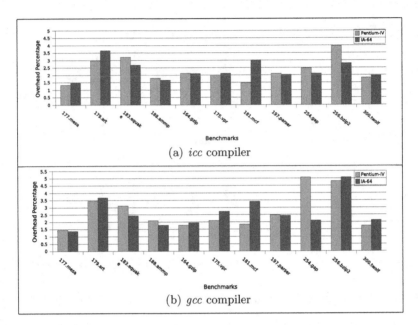

Fig. 9. Overhead of Specialization w.r.t Execution Time

where it takes 100 cycles with the VCODE interface (with no optimizations) and 300 to 800 cycles using the ICODE interface (with optimizations) to generate a single instruction.

Moreover, the time taken to generate templates at static compilation depends upon the size of intervals. For benchmark with the largest interval size, i.e. *vpr*, it takes 5 hours for *gcc* on IA-64, otherwise it takes 3 hours for all other configurations.

8   Related Work

The C-Mix [10] partial evaluator works only at static compile time. It analyzes the code and makes use of specialized constructs to perform partial evaluation. Although it does not require runtime activities, it is limited to optimizing code for which the values already exist. The scope therefore becomes limited since a large part of application execution is based on values only available during execution.

The Tempo [6] specializer can perform specialization at both static compile time and runtime. At static compile time, Tempo performs partial evaluation that is only applicable when the values are static (i.e. already known). In contrast, hybrid specialization makes the unknown values available and uses a template that is already specialized at static compile time. Therefore, the template is more optimized in our case than the one generated through the Tempo specializer. Similarly, another template-based approach of specialization has been given in [4,5]. They suggest the use of affine functions to perform runtime code specialization. The scope of templates therefore becomes very limited since the number of constraints for generating templates is very large. Moreover, the runtime computations required for specialization of templates reduce the impact of optimizations.

The Tick C('C)[1] compiler makes use of the *lcc* retargetable intermediate representation to generate dynamic code. It provides ICODE and VCODE interfaces to select the trade-off between performance and runtime optimization overhead. A large speedup is obtained after optimizations during execution of code. However, its code generation activity incurs overhead that requires more than 100 calls to amortize. In case of the hybrid specialization approach, we minimize the runtime overhead through generation of optimized templates and specialized data at static compile time. Similarly, most of the dynamic code generation and optimization systems like Tick C [1], DCG [11] or others suggested in [2,12,7] are different in that these can not be used to produce *generic* templates thus requiring large number of dynamic template versions for each different specializing value. The runtime activities other than optimizations, such as code buffer allocation and copy, incur a large amount of overhead thereby making them suitable for code to be called multiple times.

In runtime optimization systems, Dynamo [13] and ADORE [14] perform optimizations and achieve good speedup, but these systems do not provide the solution to control code size increase caused by dynamic versions.

9   Conclusion and Future Work

This article presents a hybrid specialization approach which makes use of static specialization to generate templates that can be specialized at runtime to adapt them to different runtime values. For many complex SPEC benchmarks, we are able to achieve good speedup with minimum increase in code size. Most of the heavyweight activities are performed at static compile time including the optimizations performed by compilers. The code is specialized statically and object code is analyzed to search for templates followed by generation of a runtime specializer. The specializer can perform runtime activities at the minimum possible cost.

A generalization mechanism makes the template valid for a large number of values. This new concept of template serves two purposes: to control the code size with minimum runtime activities and benefit from optimizations through specialization performed at static compile time.

The current implementation framework of hybrid specialization is being embedded into XLanguage [15] compiler with additional support of software cache containing more clones of same templates.

References

1. Poletto, M., Hsieh, W.C., Engler, D.R., Kaashoek, F.M.: 'C and tcc: A language and compiler for dynamic code generation. ACM Transactions on Programming Languages and Systems 21, 324–369 (1999)

2. Grant, B., Mock, M., Philipose, M., Chambers, C., Eggers, S.J.: DyC: An expressive annotation-directed dynamic compiler for C. Technical report, Department of Computer Science and Engineering, University of Washington (1999)

3. Leone, M., Lee, P.: Optimizing ml with run-time code generation. Technical report, School of Computer Science, Carnegie Mellon University (1995)

4. Khan, M.A., Charles, H.P.: Applying code specialization to FFT libraries for integral parameters. In: 19th Intl. Workshop on Languages and Compilers for Parallel Computing, New Orleans, Louisiana, November 2-4 (2006)

5. Khan, M.A., Charles, H.P., Barthou, D.: Reducing code size explosion through low-overhead specialization. In: Proceeding of the 11th Annual Workshop on the Interaction between Compilers and Computer Architecture, Phoenix (2007)

6. Consel, C., Hornof, L., Marlet, R., Muller, G., Thibault, S., Volanschi, E.N.: Tempo: Specializing Systems Applications and Beyond. ACM Computing Surveys 30(3es) (1998)

7. Consel, C., Hornof, L., Noël, F., Noyé, J., Volanschi, N.: A uniform approach for compile-time and run-time specialization. In: Danvy, O., Thiemann, P., Glück, R. (eds.) Partial Evaluation, Dagstuhl Seminar 1996. LNCS, vol. 1110, pp. 54–72. Springer, Heidelberg (1996)

8. SPEC: SPEC Benhmarks: SPEC (2000), http://www.spec.org/cpu2000/

9. Calder, B., Feller, P., Eustace, A.: Value profiling. In: International Symposium on Microarchitecture, pp. 259–269 (1997)

10. Makholm, H.: Specializing C— An introduction to the principles behind C-Mix. Technical report, Computer Science Department, University of Copenhagen (1999)

11. Engler, D.R., Proebsting, T.A.: DCG: An efficient, retargetable dynamic code generation system. In: Proceedings of Sixth International Conf. on Architectural Support for Programming Languages and Operating Systems, California (1994)

12. Leone, M., Lee, P.: Dynamic Specialization in the Fabius System. ACM Computing Surveys 30(3es) (1998)

13. Bala, V., Duesterwald, E., Banerjia, S.: Dynamo: a transparent dynamic optimization system. ACM SIGPLAN Notices 35(5), 1–12 (2000)

14. Lu, J., Chen, H., Yew, P.C., Hsu, W.C.: Design and Implementation of a Lightweight Dynamic Optimization System. Journal of Instruction-Level Parallelism 6 (2004)

15. Donadio, S., Brodman, J., Roeder, T., Yotov, K., Barthou, D., Cohen, A., Garzaran, M., Padua, D., Pingali, K.: A language for the comParallel Architectures and Compilation Techniques representation of multiple program versions. In: Ayguadé, E., Baumgartner, G., Ramanujam, J., Sadayappan, P. (eds.) LCPC 2005. LNCS, vol. 4339. Springer, Heidelberg (2006)

Flow-Sensitive Loop-Variant Variable Classification in Linear Time

Yixin Shou[1], Robert van Engelen[1,*], and Johnnie Birch[2]

[1] Florida State University, Tallahassee FL 32306
{shou,engelen}@cs.fsu.edu
[2] University of Texas at San Antonio, San Antonio TX 78249
birch@cs.utsa.edu

Abstract. This paper presents an efficient algorithm for classifying generalized induction variables and more complicated flow-sensitive loop-variant variables that have arbitrary conditional update patterns along multiple paths in a loop nest. Variables are recognized and translated into closed-form functions, such as linear, polynomial, geometric, wrap-around, periodic, and mixer functions. The remaining flow-sensitive variables (those that have no closed forms) are bounded by tight bounding functions on their value sequences by bounds derived from our extensions of the Chains of Recurrences (CR#) algebra. The classification algorithm has a linear worst-case execution time in the size of the SSA region of a loop nest. Classification coverage and performance results for the SPEC2000 benchmarks are given and compared to other methods.

1 Introduction and Related Work

Induction variables (IVs) [1,9,11,12,13,23] are an important class of loop-variant variables whose value progressions form linear, polynomial, or geometric sequences. IV recognition plays a critical role in optimizing compilers as a prerequisite to loop analysis and transformation. For example, a loop-level optimizing compiler applies array dependence testing [23] in loop optimization, which requires an accurate analysis of memory access patterns of IV-indexed arrays and arrays accessed with pointer arithmetic [8,21]. Other example applications are array bounds check elimination [10], loop-level cache reuse analysis [3], software prefetching [2], loop blocking, variable privatization, IV elimination [1,9,11,22], and auto-parallelization and vectorization [23].

The relative occurrence frequency in modern codes of flow-sensitive loop-variant variables that exhibit more complicated update patterns compared to IVs is significant. The authors found that 9.32% of the total number of variables that occur in loops in CINT2000 are conditionally updated and 2.82% of the total number of variables in loops in CFP2000 are conditionally updated. By contrast to IVs, these variables have no known closed-form function equivalent. As a consequence, current IV recognition methods fail to classify them.

---

* Supported in part by NSF grant CCF-0702435.

V. Adve, M.J. Garzarán, and P. Petersen (Eds.): LCPC 2007, LNCS 5234, pp. 323–337, 2008.
© Springer-Verlag Berlin Heidelberg 2008

The result is a pessimistic compiler analysis outcome and lower performance expectations.

Closer inspection of these benchmarks reveals that value progressions of *all* of these flow-sensitive variables can be bounded with tight bounding functions over the iteration space. Typically a pair of linear lower- and upper-bound functions on variables that have conditional increments suffices. Bounding the value progressions of these variables has the advantage of increased analysis coverage. Bounding also significantly alleviates loop analysis accuracy problems in the presence of unknowns. Most compilers will simply give up on loop analysis and optimization when a single variable with a recurrence in a loop has an unknown value progression. With the availability of tight functional (iteration-specific) bounds on variables, analysis and optimization can continue. For example, in [6,20] it was shown that dependence analysis can be easily extended to handle such functional bounds. We believe this approach can also strengthen methods for array bounds check elimination, loop-level cache reuse analysis, software prefetching, and loop restructuring optimizations that require dependence analysis.

Automatic classification of flow-sensitive variables poses two challenges: 1) to find accurate bounds on the value progressions of variables that are conditionally updated, conditionally reinitialized, and, more generally, exhibit multiple coupled assignments in the branches of a loop body. And 2) to find a polynomial time algorithm with sufficient accuracy to classify and bound these variables.

A search method that uses full path enumeration to collect coupled variable update operations in a loop body may require an exponential number of steps to complete in the worst case. Furthermore, the use of bounds should be restricted to the necessary cases only. This means that the "traditional" form of IVs in loops should still be classified as linear, polynomial, and geometric. Thus, speed of a classification algorithm can only be traded in for accuracy of classifying flow-sensitive variables that have (multiple) conditional updates in loops.

While the recognition of "traditional" forms of IVs is extensively described in the literature, there is a limited body of work on methods to analyze more complicated flow-sensitive loop-variant variables that have arbitrary conditional update patterns along multiple paths in a loop nest. We compared this related work to our approach. To compare the capabilities of all of these approaches, Figure 1 shows four example loop structures[1] with a classification of their fundamentally different characteristics.

The method by Gerlek, Stoltz and Wolfe [9] classifies IVs by detecting *Strongly Connected Components* (SCCs) in a FUD/SSA graph using a variant of Tarjan's algorithm [16]. Each SCC represents an IV or a loop-variant variable. A collection of interconnected SCCs represent a set of interdependent IVs. The IV classification proceeds by matching the update statement patterns for linear, geometric, periodic, and polynomial IVs and by constructing the closed-form characteristic function of each IV using a sequence-specific recurrence solver. Induction variable substitution (IVS) is then applied to replace induction expressions with equivalent closed-form functions. The method suggests a *sequence strengthening*

---

[1] All examples in this text will be given in *Single Static Assignment* (SSA) form.

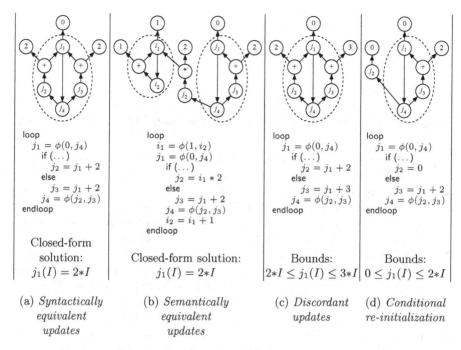

loop
$j_1 = \phi(0, j_4)$
  if $(\dots)$
    $j_2 = j_1 + 2$
  else
    $j_3 = j_1 + 2$
    $j_4 = \phi(j_2, j_3)$
endloop

Closed-form
solution:
$j_1(I) = 2*I$

(a) *Syntactically equivalent updates*

loop
$i_1 = \phi(1, i_2)$
$j_1 = \phi(0, j_4)$
  if $(\dots)$
    $j_2 = i_1 * 2$
  else
    $j_3 = j_1 + 2$
    $j_4 = \phi(j_2, j_3)$
$i_2 = i_1 + 1$
endloop

Closed-form solution:
$j_1(I) = 2*I$

(b) *Semantically equivalent updates*

loop
$j_1 = \phi(0, j_4)$
  if $(\dots)$
    $j_2 = j_1 + 2$
  else
    $j_3 = j_1 + 3$
    $j_4 = \phi(j_2, j_3)$
endloop

Bounds:
$2*I \leq j_1(I) \leq 3*I$

(c) *Discordant updates*

loop
$j_1 = \phi(0, j_4)$
  if $(\dots)$
    $j_2 = 0$
  else
    $j_3 = j_1 + 2$
    $j_4 = \phi(j_2, j_3)$
endloop

Bounds:
$0 \leq j_1(I) \leq 2*I$

(d) *Conditional re-initialization*

Fig. 1. Loops with Flow-Sensitive Loop-Variant Variable Updates

method to handle restricted forms of conditionally-updated variables. However, the variables in Figure 1(a) and (c) would be loosely classified as a *monotonic variables*, without identifying its linear sequence or bounds.

Loops with *syntactic and semantically equivalent updates* Figure 1(a,b) require aggressive symbolic analysis and expression manipulation to prove equivalence of updates in branches. Haghighat and Polychronopoulos [11] present a *symbolic differencing* technique to capture induction variable sequences by applying abstract interpretation. Symbolic differencing with abstract interpretation is expensive. They do not handle the classes of loops shown in Figure 1(c,d).

Wu et al. [24] introduce a loop-variant variable analysis technique that constructs a lattice of *monotonic evolutions* of variables, which includes variables with *discordant updates* Figure 1(c). However, her approach only determines the *direction* in which a variable changes and other information such as strides are lost. Closed-form functions of IV progressions are not computed.

Recent work by several authors [5,15,17,18] incorporates the *Chains of Recurrences* (CR) algebra [25] for IV recognition and manipulation. The use of CR forms eliminates the need for a-priori classification, pattern matching, and recurrence solvers. All of these approaches use a variation of an algorithm originally proposed by Van Engelen [18] to construct CR forms for IVs. The primary advantage of these methods is the manipulation of CR-based recurrence forms rather than closed-form functions, which gives greater coverage by including the recognition and manipulation of IVs that have no closed forms.

$$i_1 = \{0, 1, 2, 3, 4, \ldots\}$$
$$j_1 = \{99, 0, 1, 2, 3, \ldots\}$$

Fig. 2. SCC of the SSA Form of an Example Loop with a Wrap-around Variable

An extensive loop-variant variable recognition approach based on CR forms is presented in [20]. The approach captures value progressions of all types of conditionally-updated loop-variant variables Figure 1(a-d). The method uses *full path enumeration* on *Abstract Syntax Tree* (AST) forms. The algorithm has an exponential worst-case execution time as a consequence of full path enumeration.

The class of *re-initialized variables* Figure 1(d) and *wrap-around variables* shown in Figure 2 are special cases of "out-of-sequence" variables, which take a known sequence but have exceptional (re)start values. Even though the relative percentage of these types of variables in benchmarks is low (0.55% in CINT2000 and to 0.62% in CFP2000), their classification is important to enable loop re-structuring [11]. A wrap-around variable is flow-sensitive: it is assigned a value outside the loop for the first iteration and then takes the value sequence of another IV for the remainder of the iterations. These variables may cascade: any IV that depends on the value of a wrap-around variable is a wrap-around variable of one order higher [9] (two iterations with out-of-sequence values).

This paper presents a linear-time flow-sensitive loop-variant variable analysis algorithm based on the method by Gerlek et al. [9] and the CR# (CR-sharp) algebra [19]. This approach enables the analysis of coupled loop-variant variables in multiple SCCs Figure 1(a-b) (both formed by conditional and unconditional flow) and is essential to construct lower- and upper-bounding functions for flow-sensitive variables Figure 1(c-d).

The contributions of this paper can be summarized as follows:

- A systematic classification approach based on new CR# algebra extensions to analyze a large class of loop-variant variables "in one sweep" without the need for a-priori classification and recurrence solvers.
- A new algorithm for classification of flow-sensitive variables that are updated in multiple branches of the loop body, with a running time that scales linearly with the size of the SSA region of a loop nest.
- An implementation in GCC 4.1 of the classifier.

The remainder of this paper is organized as follows. Section 2 gives CR# algebra preliminaries. Section 3 presents the linear time, flow-sensitive IV classification algorithm based on the CR# algebra. In Section 4 results are presented using an implementation in GCC 4.1. Performance results on SPEC2000 show increased classification coverage with a very low running time overhead. Section 5 summarizes the conclusions.

2   Preliminaries

The CR notation and algebra was introduced by Zima [25] and later extended by Bachmann [4] and Van Engelen [18]. A *basic recurrence* Φ_i is of the form:

$$\Phi_i = \{\varphi_0, \odot_1, f_1\}_i$$

which represents a sequence of values starting with an initial value φ_0 updated in the next iteration by operator $\odot_1$ (either $+$ or $*$) and stride value f_1. When f_1 is a non-constant function in CR form this gives a *chain of recurrences*:

$$\Phi_i = \{\varphi_0, \odot_1, \{\varphi_1, \odot_2, \{\varphi_2, \cdots, \odot_k, \{\varphi_k\}_i\}_i\}_i\}_i$$

which is usually written in flattened form

$$\Phi_i = \{\varphi_0, \odot_1, \varphi_1, \odot_2, \cdots, \odot_k, \varphi_k\}_i$$

The value sequences of three example CR forms is illustrated below:

iteration $i =$	0	1	2	3	4	5	...
$\{2, +, 1\}_i$ value sequence $=$	2	3	4	5	6	7	...
$\{1, *, 2\}_i$ value sequence $=$	1	2	4	8	16	32	...
$\{1, *, 2, +, 1\}_i$ value sequence $=$	1	2	6	24	120	720	...

Multi-variate CRs (MCR) are CRs with coefficients that are CRs in a higher dimension [4]. Multi-dimensional loops are used to evaluate MCRs over grids.

The power of CR forms is exploited with the CR algebra: its simplification rules produce CRs for multivariate functions and functions in CR form can be easily combined. Below is a selection of CR algebra rules[2]:

$$c * \{\varphi_0, +, f_1\}_i \Rightarrow \{c*\varphi_0, +, c*f_1\}_i$$
$$\{\varphi_0, +, f_1\}_i \pm c \Rightarrow \{\varphi_0 \pm c, +, f_1\}_i$$
$$\{\varphi_0, +, f_1\}_i \pm \{\psi_0, +, g_1\}_i \Rightarrow \{\varphi_0 \pm \psi_0, +, f_1 \pm g_1\}_i$$
$$\{\varphi_0, +, f_1\}_i * \{\psi_0, +, g_1\}_i \Rightarrow \{\varphi_0*\psi_0, +, \{\varphi_0, +, f_1\}_i*g_1 + \{\psi_0, +, g_1\}_i*f_1 + f_1*g_1\}_i$$

CR rules are applicable to IV manipulation. For example, suppose i is a loop counter with CR $\{0, +, 1\}_i$ and j is a linear IV with CR $\{j_0, +, 2\}_i$ which has a symbolic unknown initial value j_0. Then expression $i^2 + j$ is simplified to

$$\{0, +, 1\}_i * \{0, +, 1\}_i + \{j_0, +, 2\}_i \Rightarrow \{0, +, 1, +, 2\} + \{j_0, +, 2\}_i \Rightarrow \{j_0, +, 3, +, 2\}_i$$

The closed form function f of this CR is $f(I) = j_0 + I * (I + 2)$, which is derived by the application of the CR inverse rules defined in [17]. A lattice of CR forms for simplification and methods for IV analysis is introduced in [19].

The CR# (CR-sharp) algebra is an extension of the CR algebra with new operators, algebra rules, and CR form alignment operations to derive CR bounding functions. The #-operator of the CR# algebra has the following semantics.

Definition 1. *The* delay operator # *is a right-selection operation defined by*

$$(x \# y) = y \qquad \text{for any } x \text{ and } y.$$

---

[2] See [17] for the complete list of CR algebra simplification rules.

CRs with #-operators will be referred to as *delayed CRs*. The #-operator allows several initial values to take effect before the rest of the sequence kicks in:

iteration $i =$	0	1	2	3	4	5	...
$\{9, \#, 1, +, 2\}_i$ value sequence =	9	1	3	5	7	9	...
$\{1, *, 1, \#, 2\}_i$ value sequence =	1	1	2	4	8	16	...

Delayed CRs are an essential instrument to analyze "out-of-sequence" variables.

To analyze conditionally updated variables in a loop, new rules for CR# alignment and CR# bounds construction are introduced. Two or more CR forms of different lengths or with different operations can be aligned for comparison.

Definition 2. *Two CR forms Φ_i and Ψ_i over the same index variable i are aligned if they have the same length k and the operators $\odot_j$, $j = 1, \ldots, k$, form a pairwise match.*

For example, $\{1, +, 1, *, 1\}$ is aligned with $\{0, +, 2, *, 2\}_i$, but $\{1, +, 2\}_i$ is not aligned with $\{1, *, 2\}_i$ and $\{1, +, 2\}_i$ is not aligned with $\{1, +, 2, +, 1\}_i$.

A set of Lemmas that provide concept and proof of a simple algorithm for alignment of CR forms can be found in a technical report [14]. After alignment, the minimum and the maximum bounding CRs of two arbitrary CR forms is inductively defined, see also [14].

Consider two example CR forms, $\Phi_i = \{1, \#, 1, +, 2\}_i$ represents a wrap-around variable and $\Psi_i = \{1, *, 2\}_i$ is geometric. First, Φ_i and Ψ_i are aligned:

$$\Phi_i = \{1, \#, 1, +, 2\}_i = \{1, \#, 1, +, 2, *, 1\}_i$$
$$\Psi_i = \{1, *, 2\}_i = \{1, \#, 2, *, 2\}_i = \{1, \#, 2, +, 2, *, 2\}_i$$

Then both sequences are bounded by the min and max sequences:

$$\min(\{1, \#, 1, +, 2, *, 1\}_i, \{1, \#, 2, +, 2, *, 2\}_i) = \{1, \#, 1, +, 2, *, 1\}_i$$
$$\max(\{1, \#, 1, +, 2, *, 1\}_i, \{1, \#, 2, +, 2, *, 2\}_i) = \{1, \#, 2, +, 2, *, 2\}_i$$

3   Flow-Sensitive Loop-Variant Variable Classification

This section presents an algorithm to classify flow-sensitive loop-variant variables in linear time based on CR forms. The algorithm has three parts: COLLECT-RECURRENCES, CR-CONSTRUCTION and CR-ALIGNMENT-AND-BOUNDS. These routines are described first, followed by an analysis of complexity and accuracy.

3.1   Algorithms

1. Collect Recurrence Relations. The first phase of the algorithm is performed by COLLECT-RECURRENCES shown in Figure 3. The routine computes the set of recurrence relations for a variable v defined in an assignment S and this is repeated for each variable of a loop header ϕ-node. The algorithm visits each node in each SCCs to compute sets of recurrence relations of loop-variant

Algorithm COLLECT-RECURRENCES(v, S)
- **input:**   program in SSA form, SSA variable v, and assignment S of the form $var = expr$
- **output:** recurrence sequence pair or recurrence sequence list
if $expr$ is of the form x **then** $rec :=$ CHECK(v,x), store (var, rec) and Return rec
else if $expr$ is of the form of $x \odot y$ **then**
    $rec :=$ CHECK$(v,x) \odot$ CHECK(v,y), store (var, rec) and Return rec
else if $expr$ is a loop header node $\phi(x,y)$ (x is defined outside the current loop and
    y is defined inside the current loop) **then**
    $I :=$ CHECK(var,x) and $Seq :=$ CHECK(var,y)
    Construct Pair $p := \langle var, (I, Seq)\rangle$
    Return p
else if $expr$ is a conditional node $\phi(b_1, \cdots, b_n)$ **then**
    Check each branch of conditional ϕ node:
    $B_1 := Check(v, b_1), \cdots, B_n := Check(v, b_n)$
    Construct sequence list $Seq := (B_1, \cdots, B_n)$, Compute bound on the Seq
    if the length of the Seq list $> N_{\text{thresh}}$ **then** Return $\perp$
    Store (var, Seq) and Return Seq
else Return $\perp$
endif

Algorithm CHECK(v, x)
- **input:**   loop header ϕ-node variable v and operand x
- **output:** recurrence sequence expression list
if x is loop invariant or constant **then** Return x
else if x is an SSA variable **then**
  if x is v **then** Return x
  else if x has a CR form or recurrence Φ stored **then**
    if Φ's index variable loop level is deeper than current loop level **then**
      Apply the $CR\#^{-1}$ rules to convert Φ to closed form $f(I)$
      Replace I's in $f(I)$ with trip counts of index variables of the loop
      Return f
    else Return Φ
    endif
  else if the loop depth where x located is lower than the loop depth where v located **then**
    Return x
  else
    Return COLLECT-RECURRENCES$(v,$ the statement S that defines $x)$
  endif
endif

Fig. 3. Collecting the Recurrence Relations from the SCCs of an SSA Loop Region

variables. The sets are cached at the nodes for retrieval when revisited via a cycle, which ensures that nodes and edges are visited only once.

The process is illustrated with an example code in SSA form and corresponding SCC shown in Figures 4(a) and (b). The loop exhibits conditional updates of variable j. Starting from the loop header ϕ-node j_1, the algorithm follows the SSA edges recursively to collect the recurrence relations for each SSA variable in the SCC. The ϕ function for j_1 merges the initial value 0 outside the loop and the update j_7 inside the loop. Since conditional ϕ-node j_7 merges two arguments j_5 and j_6, to collect the recurrence sequence for j_7, the recurrence sequences for j_5 and j_6 must be collected first, which means j_7 depends on j_5 and j_6. Thus, j_5 was checked first for j_7 and j_4 was reached by following the SSA edges from j_5. The search continues until the starting loop header ϕ-node j_1 is reached. The symbol j_1 was returned and the recursive calling stops. Therefore, the recurrence sequence for j_2 can be obtained based on j_1, which is $j_1 + 1$. Similarly, based on this dependence chain, the recurrences propagated for each SSA variable are shown in Figure 4(c).

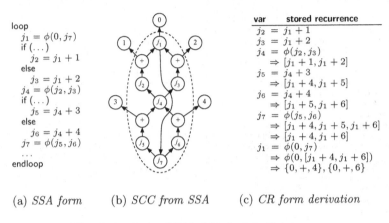

(a) *SSA form*   (b) *SCC from SSA*   (c) *CR form derivation*

Fig. 4. Analysis of SSA ϕ-Node Join Points

Note that due to control flow variable j_4 has two recurrences. Consequently, all variables that depend on j_4 have at least two recurrences. However, as the recurrences are propagated they degenerate into lower and upper sequences to limit the algorithmic complexity. Finally, the recurrence pair for loop header ϕ-node j_1 is constructed with initial value 0 and bounding recurrence sequences $j_1 + 4$ and $j_1 + 6$.

To compute the recurrences for variables in a multi-dimensional loop, the algorithm starts with the analysis of the inner loop. More details with examples of multiple-dimensional loops can be found in a technical report [14].

2. Constructing CR Forms for Recurrences Relations.

Algorithm CR-CONSTRUCTION(p) shown in Figure 5 converts recurrence relations of a variable into CR form (the last step of the example shown in Figure 4(c)), where p denotes a recurrences sequence pair with initial value v_0 of variable v and recurrence sequence S. If variable v does not appear in recurrence sequence S, then v is a conditionally reinitialized variable or wrap around variable of any order.

To illustrate this process, consider a classic form of a wrap-around variable shown in Figure 2. The CR forms are derived as follows, where j_1 is a first-order wrap-around variable:

$$i_1 : \quad \langle i_1, (0, i_1 + 1) \rangle \Rightarrow \{0, +, 1\}$$

$$j_1 : \quad \langle j_1, (99, i_1) \rangle \Rightarrow \{99, \#, 0, +, 1\}$$

$$j_1 + 1 = \{99, \#, 0, +, 1\} + 1 = \{100, \#, 1, +, 1\}$$

Now CR-CONSTRUCTION takes the pair $\langle i_1, (0, i_1 + 1) \rangle$ for variable i_1 as the input. The CR form for i_1 is computed with rule **(1)** of the algorithm. Similarly, the CR form for j_1 is computed based on rule **(5)** of the algorithm. The application of the CR# algebra enables efficient manipulation and simplification of expressions with wrap-around variables, such as the analysis of array subscript $j_1 + 1$ in Figure 2.

Algorithm CR-ALIGNMENT-AND-BOUNDS(pl)
- **input:**   recurrences sequence list pair $pl = \langle v, (I, Seq) \rangle$
- **output:** CR Bounds solution
if length of the Seq list $n > N_{\text{thresh}}$ **then** Return $\perp$
$cr := $ CR-CONSTRUCTION($\langle v, (I, \text{first recurrence in } Seq \text{ list}) \rangle$)
for each remaining recurrence e in Seq
    Construct pair $p := \langle v, (I, e) \rangle$
    $cr_1 := $ CR-CONSTRUCTION(p)
    Align cr with cr_1
    if CR alignment succeeds **then** Compute the bounds of cr and cr_1 to cr
    else Return $\perp$
    endif
enddo
Store (v, cr) and Return cr

Algorithm CR-CONSTRUCTION(p)
- **input:**   recurrences sequence pair $p = \langle v, (v_0, S) \rangle$, where v_0 is initial value
            of variable v and S is the recurrence sequence for v
- **output:** CR Solution
(1) **if** S is of the form $v + \Psi$ (Ψ can be CR or constant) **then**
    $\Phi := \{v_0, +, \Psi\}_{loop}$, where $loop$ is the innermost loop v located
(2) **else if** S is of the form $v * \Psi$ (Ψ can be CR or constant) **then**
    $\Phi := \{v_0, *, \Psi\}_{loop}$
(3) **else if** S is of the form $c * v + \Psi$, where c is constant or a singleton CR form and
    Ψ is a constant or a polynomial CR form **then**
    $\Phi := \{\varphi_0, +, \varphi_1, +, \cdots, +, \varphi_{k+1}, *, \varphi_{k+2}\}_{loop}$, where
    $\varphi_0 = v_0; \quad \varphi_j = (c-1) * \varphi_{j-1} + \psi_{j-1}; \quad \varphi_{k+2} = c$
(4) **else if** S is variable v **then**
    $\Phi := \{v_0\}_{loop}$
(5) **else**
    $\Phi := \{v_0, \#, S\}_{loop}$
    endif

Fig. 5. Constructing CR Forms for Recurrence Relations

3. CR Alignment and Bounds.

To handle conditionally updated variables in a loop nest, we introduce an algorithm for CR alignment and bounds computation. The key idea is that two or more CR forms of different lengths or with different operations can be aligned to enable pair-wise coefficient comparisons to efficiently construct bounding functions on the combined sequences. The CR-based bounds are important to determine the iteration-specific bounds on sequences as illustrated in Figures 1(c) and (d).

Algorithm CR-ALIGNMENT-AND-BOUNDS shown in Figure 5 aligns multiple CRs and computes bounding functions, which are two CR forms that represent lower- and upper-bound sequences.

Consider an example variable j_1 which has three different recurrences due to control flow. The input recurrence list pair for the algorithm CR-ALIGNMENT-AND-BOUNDS is:

$$pl = \langle j_1, (1, \ j_1 + 3 \ \rightarrow \ 2 * j_1 + 1 \ \rightarrow \ 2 * j_1 \ ) \rangle$$

Algorithm CR-CONSTRUCTION computes CR forms for each recurrence in this list. We have three different CR forms:

$$cr_1 = \{1, +, 3\} = \{1, +, 3, *, 1\}$$
$$cr_2 = \{1, +, 2, *, 2\} = \{1, +, 2, *, 2\}$$
$$cr_3 = \{1, *, 2\} = \{1, +, 1, *, 2\}$$

where cr_1, cr_2, and cr_3 are computed with rules **(1)**, **(3)** and **(2)** in CR-CONSTRUCTION, respectively. CR form cr_1 is aligned using Lemma 3 of [14] and cr_3 is aligned using Lemma 1 of [14]. The minimal and maximum bound of these CR forms is obtained with Definition 3 in [14] as follows:

$$\min(\{1,+,3,*,1\},\{1,+,2,*,2\},\{1,+,1,*,2\})=\{1,+,1,*,1\} \overset{CR\#^{-1}}{\Rightarrow} I+1$$
$$\max(\{1,+,3,*,1\},\{1,+,2,*,2\},\{1,+,1,*,2\})=\{1,+,3,*,2\} \overset{CR\#^{-1}}{\Rightarrow} 3*2^I-2$$

Therefore, we have the bounds $I+1 \leq j_1 \leq 3*2^I-2$ for iteration $I=0,\ldots,n$.

3.2   Complexity

In the worst case there are 2^n cycles in the SCC for n number of ϕ-node join points, see Figure 6. Methods based on full path enumeration require 2^n traversals from j_1 to j_n. However, the presented algorithm is linear in the size of the SSA region of a loop nest as explained as follows.

The algorithms COLLECTRECURRENCES and CHECK perform a recursive depth-first traversal of the SSA graph to visit each node to collect recurrences. When the COLLECT-RECURRENCES algorithm visits a node in the SSA graph, the recurrence collected for this SSA variable is stored in a cache for later retrieval. Whenever this node is visited again via another data flow path, the cached recurrence forms are used. Thus, it is guaranteed that the algorithm visits each node and each edge in the SSA graph only once, which has the same complexity as Tarjan's algorithm [16].

For example, in Figure 4(c) each SSA node in the SCC cycle has recurrences stored and updated during the traversal of the SCC. Assume that the algorithm visits the leftmost successor of ϕ-nodes first. To get the recurrence for variable j_7, the edges from j_5 was followed first to collect the recurrence for node j_4 in depth-first manner. The recurrence stored for j_4 guarantee all the successor node of j_4 in the graph and the node j_4 itself will not be revisited via edge from j_6.

Note that each time a new set of recurrence pairs at a conditional ϕ-node is merged this potentially increases the recurrence set by a factor of two. However, the set is reduced immediately by eliminating duplicate recurrence relations and eliminating relations that are already bounded by other relations, see e.g. Figure 4. The size of the set of recurrence relations cannot exceed N_{thresh}, which is a predetermined constant threshold. A low threshold speeds up the algorithm but limits the accuracy. Since the average size of the recurrence list of the benchmark

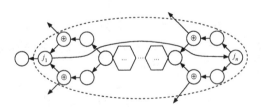

Fig. 6. An SCC with 2^n Cycles Constructed from a Loop with n ϕ-Nodes

```
i = 0                Path 1:                  Variable| Min CR    | Max CR
j = n                  i = {0, +, 1}          i       | {0}       | {0, +, 1}
do                     j = n                  j       | {n, +, −1}| {n}
  if (...)             s = j - i = {n, +, −1} s = j-i | {n, +, −2}| {n}
    i = i + 1        Path 2:
  else                 j = {n, +, −1}
    j = j − 1          i = 0
    s = j − i          s = j - i = {n, +, −1}
    ...              Solution for iteration I:
while (s > 0)          0 ≤ i ≤ I
                       n−I ≤ j ≤ n
                       s = {n, +, −1}
```

(a) *Loop*   (b) *Full path search results*   (c) *Linear-time results*

Fig. 7. Comparison of Full Path Search and Linear Time Algorithms

in CINT2000 ranges from 2.04 to 2.32, we found that $N_{thresh} = 10$ is sufficiently large to handle the SPEC2000 benchmarks accurately.

Because the cost for analyzing an SSA node operation is constant and the cost of recurrence updates at nodes is bounded by N_{thresh}, the worst-case complexity is $\mathcal{O}(|SSA|)$, where $|SSA|$ denotes the size of the SSA region.

3.3 Accuracy

The algorithm recognizes IVs with closed forms accurately when IVs are not conditionally updated, thereby producing classifications that cover linear, polynomial, geometric, periodic, and mixer functions, similar to other nonlinear IV recognition algorithms [9,11,22]. For conditionally updated loop-variant variables that have no closed forms the algorithm produces bounds.

By comparison, in certain exceptional cases, the full path analysis algorithm [20] is more accurate in producing bounds than the linear time algorithm presented in this paper. This phenomenon occurs when variables are coupled or combined in induction expressions. In that case their original relationship may be lost, which results in looser bounds than full path analysis. However, the greatest disadvantage of the full path analysis method is its exponential execution time.

To illustrate the effect of coupling on the accuracy of the algorithms, an example comparison is shown in Figure 7 for a Quicksort partition loop. The full path search results are shown in Figure 7(b) and the linear-time results is in Figure 7(c). Full path analysis computes CR solution for variable i, j, and s in the example loop separately for two paths of the program. The CR result $\{n, +, −1\}$ for variable $s = j − i$ is equal in two paths because on of the updates $i = i + 1$ and $j = j − 1$ is always taken. Instead of the single CR form for s, the CR solutions of the faster algorithm for variable s are bounded by $\{n, +, −2\}$ and $\{n\}$, which is less accurate than full path search.

4   Implementation and Experimental Results

The following classes of loop-variant variables are recognized and classified by the algorithm.

```
while (k++ < AttrCount) {
    CppObjectAddr = (addrtype )((char *)CppObjectAddr + Base01Offset);
    DbObjectAddr = (addrtype )((char *)DbObjectAddr + BaseDbOffset);
    ...
    Base01Offset += Attr01Size;
    BaseDbOffset += AttrDbSize;
}
```

(a) *Polynomial IV from* 255.vortex

```
for (n=1; n<=...; n*=10 ) {
    ...
}
```

(b) *Geometric IV from* 254.gap

```
j = 1;
for (i=0; i < j; ) {
    i = j;
    j = 2 * j + 1;
    largest_block = i;
}
```

(c) *Mixed IV from* 197.parser

```
while (...) {
    iside = iside + 1;
    if (iside > 3) {
        pindex++;
        iside = 0;
    }
    ...
}
```

(d) *Re-initialized IV*
from 175.vpr

```
a = 1; b = 0;
while ( o != 0 ) {
    t = b;
    b = a - (k/o) * b;
    a = t;
    ...
}
```

(e) *Cyclic IV*
from 254.gap

```
offset = 0;
for (ipin=0;...;ipin++) {
    ...
    if (ldots) {
        times_listed[bnum] = 0;
        unique_pin_list[inet][offset] = bnum;
        offset++;
    }
}
```

(f) *Conditionally updated*
IV from 175.vpr

Fig. 8. Example Loops from the SPEC2000 Benchmarks

Linear induction variables are represented by nested CR forms $\{a, +, s\}_i$, where a is the integer-valued initial value and s is the integer-valued stride in the direction of i. The coefficient a can be a nested CR form in another loop dimension. Linear IVs are the most common IV category.

Polynomial induction variables are represented by nested CR forms of length k, where k is the order of the polynomial. All $\odot$ operations in the CR form are additions, i.e. $\odot = +$. For example, the variable CppObjectAddr and DbObjectAddr in Figure 8(a) are pointer IV with polynomial CR form $\{DbObjectAddr, +, 0, +, AttrDbSize\}$ and $\{CppObjectAddr, +, 0, +, Attr01Size\}$.

Geometric induction variables are represented by the CR form $\{a, *, r\}_i$, where a and r are loop invariant. For example, the variable n in Figure 8(b) are Geometric induction variable with CR form $\{1, *, 10\}$.

Mix induction variables with CR forms that contain both $\odot = +$ and $*$. For example, the variable i and j in Figure 8(c) have CR form $\{0, +, 1, *, 2\}$ and $\{1, +, 2, *, 2\}$ respectively.

Out-of-sequence (OSV) variables are *re-initialized variables* and *wrap-around variables*. They are represented by (a set of) CR forms $\{a, \#, s\}_i$, where a is the initial out-of-sequence value and s is a nested CR form. In Figure 8(d), variable iside in the loop of 175.vpr benchmark is bounded by the CR-form range $[\{-1, \#, +, 0\}, \{-1, \#, +, 1\}]$ (iside is a re-initialized variable).

Cyclic induction variables who have cyclic dependence between the recurrence relations of variables. For example, in Figure 8(e) variables a and b from

Table 1. Loop-variant Variable Classification in SPEC2000

Benchmark	Linear	Polyn'l	Geom.	OSV	Cyclic	Cond'l	Mix	Unknown
CINT2000								
164.gzip	59.45%	0.00%	0.00%	0.79%	0.00%	7.48%	0.00%	32.29%
175.vpr	59.47%	0.00%	0.21%	0.21%	0.00%	9.05%	0.00%	31.07%
181.mcf	38.18%	0.00%	0.00%	0.00%	0.00%	10.91%	0.00%	50.91%
186.crafty	47.91%	0.00%	0.00%	0.00%	0.00%	12.71%	0.00%	39.37%
197.parser	35.19%	0.00%	0.00%	0.51%	0.00%	5.22%	0.51%	58.58%
254.gap	62.73%	0.00%	2.52%	1.00%	0.33%	5.85%	0.38%	27.51%
255.vortex	66.06%	3.03%	0.61%	2.42%	0.00%	15.15%	0.00%	12.73%
256.bzip2	54.67%	0.00%	0.93%	0.00%	0.00%	12.15%	1.40%	30.84%
300.twolf	40.21%	0.00%	0.00%	0.00%	0.00%	5.35%	0.00%	54.45%
Average	51.54%	0.34%	0.47%	0.55%	0.04%	9.32%	0.25%	37.53%
CFP2000								
168.wupwise	80.20%	0.00%	0.00%	0.00%	0.00%	0.00%	0.00%	19.80%
171.swim	96.30%	0.00%	0.00%	0.00%	0.00%	0.00%	0.00%	3.70%
172.mgrid	84.06%	0.00%	0.00%	0.00%	0.00%	0.00%	0.00%	15.94%
173.applu	94.77%	0.00%	0.00%	0.00%	0.00%	1.31%	0.00%	3.92%
177.mesa	79.57%	0.00%	0.30%	0.00%	0.00%	12.73%	0.00%	7.40%
179.art	73.12%	0.00%	0.00%	0.00%	0.00%	4.30%	0.00%	22.58%
183.equake	81.25%	0.00%	0.00%	2.08%	1.04%	3.12%	0.00%	13.54%
187.facerec	86.92%	0.00%	0.42%	0.00%	0.00%	2.53%	0.00%	10.13%
188.ammp	59.89%	0.00%	0.00%	2.54%	0.00%	3.95%	0.00%	33.62%
189.lucas	87.68%	0.00%	1.48%	0.00%	0.00%	1.97%	0.99%	7.88%
200.sixtrack	83.87%	0.00%	2.15%	2.15%	0.00%	1.08%	1.08%	9.68%
Average	82.51%	0.00%	0.40%	0.62%	0.09%	2.82%	0.19%	13.47%

cyclic IVs. In some cases cyclic IVs can be represented by geometric sequences [9,11], but most cyclic forms represent special functions (e.g. the Fibonacci sequence is such an example). Some cyclic forms can be degenerated into monotonic sequences, by replacing a variable's update with an unknown [19].

Conditional induction variables are represented by the CR $\{[a, b], \odot, s\}$, where s is a nested bounded CR form and $\odot$ can be $+$, $*$, or $\#$. Variable offset in Figure 8(f) is bounded by the CR sequence range $[0, \{0, +, 1\}]$.

Unknown variables have unknown initial values or unknown update values. These unknown are typically function returns, updates with (unbounded) symbolic variables, or bit-operator recurrences. Some of these are identified as monotonic. For example, an IV with initial value 0 and a "random" positive stride function has a CR $\{0, +, \top\}$, where the stride is represented by the lattice value $\top$.

Table 1 shows the experimental results of all induction variables categorized in SPEC2000[3] with our algorithm. The first column in the table names the benchmark. The columns labeled "Linear", "Polynomial", "Geometric", "OSV", "Cyclic", "Conditional", "Mix" and "Unknown" show the percentage of each loop-variant variable category as a percentage of the total number of loop-variant variables in each benchmark.

From the results of Table 1 the percentage of conditional induction variables ranges from 5.22% to 15.15% in CINT2000, with 9.32% on average. None of these

---

[3] Three CINT2000 and three CFP2000 benchmarks results are not listed because of GCC 4.1-specific compilation errors that are not related to our implementation.

are detected by GCC as well as other compilers, such as Open64 and Polaris [7] (Polaris uses advanced nonlinear IV recognition algorithms [13]). Our algorithm also identifies all polynomial, geometric, mix, cyclic and wrap-around induction variables. None of these are currently detected by GCC implementations.

To evaluate the execution time performance of our CR implementation in GCC, we measured the compilation time of CR construction for the SPEC2000 benchmarks. CR construction accounts for 1.75% percent of the compilation time of GCC in average. The additional time is less than one second for most benchmarks. This shows that the performance of our algorithm is quite good.

5   Conclusion

This paper presented a linear-time loop-variant variable analysis algorithm that effectively analyzes flow-sensitive variables that are conditionally updated. We believe that the strength of our algorithm lies in its ability to analyze nonlinear and non-closed index expressions in the loop nests with higher accuracy than pure monotonic analysis. This benefits many compiler optimizations, such as loop restructuring and loop parallelizing transformations that require accurate data dependence analysis.

The experimental results of our algorithm applied to the SPEC2000 benchmarks shows that a high percentage of flow-sensitive variables are detected and accurately analyzed requiring only a small fraction of the total compilation time (1.75%). The result is a more comprehensive classifications of variables, including additional linear, polynomial, geometric, and wrap-around variables when these are conditionally updated.

References

1. Aho, A., Sethi, R., Ullman, J.: Compilers: Principles, Techniques and Tools. Addison-Wesley Publishing Company, Reading (1985)
2. Allen, R., Kennedy, K.: Optimizing Compilers for Modern Architectures. Morgan Kaufmann, San Francisco (2002)
3. Andrade, D., Arenaz, M., Fraguela, B., no, J.T., Doallo, R.: Automated and accurate cache behavior analysis for codes with irregular access patterns. In: Concurrency and Computation: Practice and Experience (to appear, 2007)
4. Bachmann, O.: Chains of Recurrences. PhD thesis, Kent State University, College of Arts and Sciences (1996)
5. Berlin, D., Edelsohn, D., Pop, S.: High-level loop optimizations for GCC. In: Proceedings of the 2004 GCC Developers' Summit, pp. 37–54 (2004)
6. Birch, J., van Engelen, R., Gallivan, K., Shou, Y.: An empirical evaluation of chains of recurrences for array dependence testing. In: PACT 2006: Proceedings of the 15th international conference on Parallel architectures and compilation techniques, pp. 295–304. ACM Press, New York (2006)
7. Blume, W., Doallo, R., Eigenmann, R., Grout, J., Hoeflinger, J., Lawrence, T., Lee, J., Padua, D., Paek, Y., Pottenger, B., Rauchwerger, L., Tu, P.: Advanced program restructuring for high-performance computers with Polaris. IEEE Computer 29(12), 78–82 (1996)

8. Franke, B., O'Boyle, M.: Array recovery and high-level transformations for dsp applications. ACM Transactions on Embedded Computing Systems (TECS) 2(2), 132–162 (2003)
9. Gerlek, M., Stolz, E., Wolfe, M.: Beyond induction variables: Detecting and classifying sequences using a demand-driven SSA form. ACM Transactions on Programming Languages and Systems (TOPLAS) 17(1), 85–122 (1995)
10. Gupta, R.: A fresh look at optimizing array bound checking. SIGPLAN Not. 25(6), 272–282 (1990)
11. Haghighat, M.R., Polychronopoulos, C.D.: Symbolic analysis for parallelizing compilers. ACM Transactions on Programming Languages and Systems 18(4), 477–518 (1996)
12. Muchnick, S.: Advanced Compiler Design and Implementation. Morgan Kaufmann, San Fransisco (1997)
13. Pottenger, W., Eigenmann, R.: Parallelization in the presence of generalized induction and reduction variables. Technical report, 1396, Univ. of Illinois at Urbana Champaign, Center for Supercomputing Research & Development (1995)
14. Shou, Y., van Engelen, R., Birch, J.: Flow-sensitive loop-variant variable classification in linear time. Technical report, TR-071005, Computer Science Dept., Florida State University (2007)
15. Shou, Y., van Engelen, R., Birch, J., Gallivan, K.: Toward efficient flow-sensitive induction variable analysis and dependence testing for loop optimization. In: Proceedings of the ACM SouthEast Conference, pp. 1–6 (2006)
16. Tarjan, R.: Depth first search and linear graph algorithms. SIAM Journal of Computing 1(2), 146–160 (1972)
17. van Engelen, R.: Symbolic evaluation of chains of recurrences for loop optimization. Technical report, TR-000102, Computer Science Dept., Florida State University (2000)
18. van Engelen, R.: Efficient symbolic analysis for optimizing compilers. In: Wilhelm, R. (ed.) CC 2001. LNCS, vol. 2027, pp. 118–132. Springer, Heidelberg (2001)
19. van Engelen, R.: The CR# algebra and its application in loop analysis and optimization. Technical report, TR-041223, Computer Science Dept., Florida State University (2004)
20. van Engelen, R., Birch, J., Shou, Y., Walsh, B., Gallivan, K.: A unified framework for nonlinear dependence testing and symbolic analysis. In: Proceedings of the ACM International Conference on Supercomputing (ICS), pp. 106–115 (2004)
21. van Engelen, R., Gallivan, K.: An efficient algorithm for pointer-to-array access conversion for compiling and optimizing DSP applications. In: Proceedings of the International Workshop on Innovative Architectures for Future Generation High-Performance Processors and Systems (IWIA) 2001, Maui, Hawaii, pp. 80–89 (2001)
22. Wolfe, M.: Beyond induction variables. In: ACM SIGPLAN 1992 Conf. on Programming Language Design and Implementation, San Fransisco, CA, pp. 162–174 (1992)
23. Wolfe, M.: High Performance Compilers for Parallel Computers. Addison-Wesley, Redwood City (1996)
24. Wu, P., Cohen, A., Hoeflinger, J., Padua, D.: Monotonic evolution: An alternative to induction variable substitution for dependence analysis. In: Proceedings of the ACM International Conference on Supercomputing (ICS), pp. 78–91 (2001)
25. Zima, E.: Recurrent relations and speed-up of computations using computer algebra systems. In: Fitch, J. (ed.) DISCO 1992. LNCS, vol. 721, pp. 152–161. Springer, Heidelberg (1993)

Using ZBDDs in Points-to Analysis

Ondřej Lhoták[1], Stephen Curial[2], and José Nelson Amaral[2]

[1] D.R. Cheriton School of Computer Science, University of Waterloo
[2] Department of Computing Science, University of Alberta

Abstract. Binary Decision Diagrams (BDDs) have recently become widely accepted as a space-efficient method of representing relations in points-to analyses. When BDDs are used to represent relations, each element of a domain is assigned a bit pattern to represent it, but not every bit pattern represents an element. The circuit design, model checking, and verification communities have achieved significant reductions in BDD sizes using Zero-Suppressed BDDs (ZBDDs) to avoid the overhead of these *don't-care* bit patterns. We adapt BDD-based program analyses to use ZBDDs instead of BDDs. Our experimental evaluation studies the space requirements of ZBDDs for both context-insensitive and context-sensitive program analyses and shows that ZBDDs can greatly reduce the space requirements for expensive context-sensitive points-to analysis. Using ZBDDs to reduce the size of the relations allows a compiler or other software analysis tools to analyze larger programs with greater precision. We also provide a metric that can be used to estimate whether ZBDDs will be more compact than BDDs for a given analysis.

1   Introduction

This paper describes improvements to Binary-Decision-Diagram-based implementations of pointer analysis used in ahead-of-time compilation and program analysis frameworks. The main benefit of BDDs [3] in program analysis is a reduction in the memory requirements of otherwise infeasible analyses: BDDs yield scalable highly context-sensitive may-point-to and call-graph-construction analyses [2,12,27,30,29]. The improvements presented in this paper further reduce the storage requirements, thus enabling more precise variations of the analysis to be computed for larger programs.

When various context-sensitive pointer analyses, such as that of Whaley and Lam [27] and object-sensitive analysis [16,17,18], were applied to object-oriented programs such as javac, soot, and the DaCapo benchmarks, the more precise variations (especially 3-object-sensitive, 1H-call-site sensitive, and Whaley/Lam) failed to complete due to memory limitations [13]. Although the running time of the most expensive analyses in [13] was several hours, none of the infeasible analyses failed to complete due to lack of time; they all failed due to excessive space requirements. A more compact BDD representation lowers the memory requirements of these analyses and allows them to scale to larger programs.

A BDD is a data structure representing a function that maps a vector of bits (the *BDD variables*) to a boolean value. When BDDs are used for program

V. Adve, M.J. Garzarán, and P. Petersen (Eds.): LCPC 2007, LNCS 5234, pp. 338–352, 2008.

analysis, each element of the analysis is represented using some bit pattern. In general, however, not every bit pattern corresponds to an element, and these *don't-care* bit patterns unnecessarily increase BDD size.

A variation of BDDs, known as Zero-Suppressed BDDs (ZBDDs), are a promising alternative to eliminate the overhead of don't-care bit patterns [19,23]. ZBDDs have been very effective at reducing BDD size in applications such as circuit design, model checking, and verification. Like these applications, program analyses use BDDs to represent and manipulate sets of elements chosen from a domain. Therefore, it is reasonable to expect these techniques to also reduce BDD size in program analysis. However, up to now there has been no description or evaluation of the use of ZBDDs in program analysis.

The main contributions of this paper are:

- A ZBDD representation of relations, and an algorithm, based on ZBDD multiplication, to compute the *relational product* on this representation. The combination of this representation and this algorithm makes it possible to use ZBDDs in relation-based program analysis.
- A ZBDD variation of the BDD-based points-to analysis of Berndl *et al.* [2].
- An empirical study of the space requirements of the ZBDD encodings of the relations in Berndl *et al.*'s analysis, Whaley and Lam's joeq/bddbddb [27], and Lhoták and Hendren's Paddle framework [10,13].
- A relation-density metric that predicts whether a relation will be represented more compactly by a BDD or by a ZBDD.

The number of ZBDD variables used to represent a relation is the sum of the sizes of the domains of the relation. In analyses expressed using relational operations, the domains are sets of syntactic entities (such as statements, variables, etc.) of the program being analyzed, so this sum is linear in the size of the input. However, the context-sensitive call-graph specialization algorithm used in joeq/bddbddb [27] uses a special BDD operation with no relational equivalent to construct a single domain whose size is exponential in the size of the input. It is unlikely that an analogous operation can be practical for ZBDDs because it would have to construct a ZBDD over an exponential number of variables. Thus, we do not propose a ZBDD analogue of the joeq/bddbddb algorithm. However, other algorithms that use only relational operations and represent contexts as relations of syntactic entities can be implemented with our ZBDD representation. This includes the context-sensitive analyses in Paddle.

The rest of the paper is organized as follows. Section 2 gives background on pointer analysis, BDDs, and ZBDDs. Section 3 describes how ZBDDs can be used for program analysis. Section 4 compares the sizes of BDDs and ZBDDs used in pointer analysis. Section 5 reviews related work, and Section 6 concludes.

2   Background

A pointer analysis computes a static abstraction of the run-time relationships between pointers and their targets [6,8]. For each static abstraction of a pointer

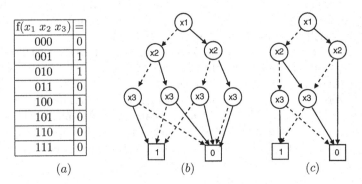

f($x_1\ x_2\ x_3$)	=
000	0
001	1
010	1
011	0
100	1
101	0
110	0
111	0

(a)   (b)   (c)

Fig. 1. The function f($x_1\ x_2\ x_3$) (a), and the OBDD (b) and ROBDD (c) representing it. Solid edges represent 1-edges and dotted edges represent 0-edges.

variable, a points-to analysis computes a points-to set of the abstract target locations to which the variable points at run time. This work focuses on *may-*point-to information and on *subset-based* analysis. The result of a may-point-to analysis over-approximates the run-time relationships. In a *subset-based* analysis, also called Andersen-style analysis, points-to sets are computed by solving a collection of subset constraints [1]. Subset constraints are often solved by propagation. For example, the constraint $A \subseteq B$ can be satisfied by propagating the contents of A into B. Such propagation is done repeatedly for all the constraints in the system until a fixed-point solution satisfying all the constraints is reached.

A key difficulty is that the points-to sets can become very large, especially when precise abstractions of the run-time behavior are used. Recent research focus on efficient data structures and propagation algorithms. A BDD [3] is one such data structure [2,29].

2.1 BDDs

A BDD represents a function that maps vectors of bits (the *BDD variables*) to boolean values. This function can be viewed as the set of bit vectors that the function maps to true. A BDD is a directed acyclic graph where a terminal node represents `true` and another terminal node represents `false`. Each non-terminal node, which specifies a BDD variable, has two outgoing edges to other nodes, a `one` edge and a `zero` edge. The value of the function for a given valuation of the BDD variables is determined by a traversal starting at the root node. At each node, the traversal follows either the one edge or the zero edge, depending on the value of the BDD variable associated with that node. The function has the value of the terminal node reached by the traversal.

An Ordered BDD (OBDD) is a BDD with a fixed variable ordering. Every path through an OBDD evaluates the variables in the given order. An OBDD can be reduced to remove redundant nodes, by following two reduction rules:

1. When two BDD nodes p and q are identical, edges leading to q are changed to lead to p, and q is eliminated from the BDD.
2. A BDD node p whose one-edge and zero-edge both lead to the same node q is eliminated from the BDD and the edges leading to p are redirected to q.

For any given function, the resulting Reduced Ordered BDD (ROBDD) is unique. Figure 1 shows an example function, an OBDD, and the ROBDD representing it. In practice, BDDs are always maintained in reduced ordered form. The remainder of this paper uses the abbreviation BDD to mean ROBDD.

In the BDD representation of a set, each element of each domain is encoded as a binary string. This encoding ideally uses the minimum number of bits required to assign each element to a unique binary string. A relation is formed by two or more attributes. Each attribute belongs to a domain and thus has a binary string representation. A relation can be represented as a set of binary strings by concatenating the binary encoding of each attribute. For example, assume a domain D with elements $\{a, b, c\}$ encoded as $\{00, 01, 10\}$, respectively, and a relation R that has 2 attributes $R_1 \in D$ and $R_2 \in D$. If R contains the tuples $\langle a, a \rangle$, $\langle a, b \rangle$ and $\langle c, b \rangle$, then R can be represented by the set $S = \{0000, 0001, 1001\}$. The BDD encoding of S evaluates to true for the strings in S and false for the strings not in S.

2.2   Solving Subset Constraints Using BDDs

Berndl et al. [2] and Zhu [29] show how to solve points-to subset constraints using BDDs. They encode both the points-to sets and subset constraints as relations represented with BDDs. Propagation is performed using the relational-product BDD operation. For example, consider a program with pointers p and q and abstract objects X and Y, with initial points-to sets $pt(p) = \{X\}$ and $pt(q) = \{Y\}$, and a subset constraint $pt(p) \subseteq pt(q)$. The relationships between pointers and abstract objects in this program are represented as a points-to relation $\{\langle X, p \rangle, \langle Y, q \rangle\}$ and a constraint relation $\{\langle p, q \rangle\}$. The result of propagating the original points-to sets along the constraint (which adds X to $pt(q)$) is computed by finding the relational product of the two relations (which evaluates to the relation $\{\langle X, q \rangle\}$).

2.3   ZBDDs

Zero-suppressed binary decision diagrams (ZBDDs) are like BDDs (see Section 2.1), but the second reduction rule is changed to:

2. A BDD node p whose one-edge leads to the zero terminal node and whose zero-edge leads to a node q is removed from the BDD and the edges leading to p are redirected to q.

Because of the difference in the reduction rules, the interpretation of a ZBDD is slightly different than a BDD. To determine the value of the function for a given valuation of the ZBDD variables, the ZBDD is traversed like a BDD,

following either the one or zero edge of each node
depending on the value of the variable tested by
the corresponding node. However, the final value
is true only if the traversal ends at the true terminal node *and every variable whose value is 1 has
been tested during the traversal.* Otherwise, the final value is false. For example, the function that
was presented in Figure 1(a) is represented by the
ZBDD in Figure 2. For instance, according to the
ZBDD interpretation, the bit pattern 011 maps to
false because the true terminal is reached without testing variable x3. Because of the difference

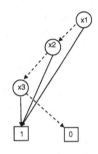

Fig. 2. ZBDD representation
of the function from Figure 1

in reduction rules, ZBDDs can represent some functions more compactly than
BDDs, and vice versa.

3   Encoding Relations in ZBDDs

In a one-of-N encoding, the number of bits used is equal to the size of the domain.
Each element is associated with one bit in the vector. Each element is represented
by a bit vector with 1 for the corresponding element and 0 elsewhere. ZBDDs
are particularly suited to manipulate sets encoded using a one-of-N encoding.
According to Meinel and Theobald [15, p. 224], ZBDDs compactly encode sets
of bit vectors that are sparse in the sense that: (i) the set contains only a small
number of bit vectors relative to the number of all possible combinations of n
bits; and (ii) each bit vector in the set contains few one bits.

The first condition holds in many practical problems involving sets. The
second condition is a consequence of the one-of-N encoding. ZBDDs are more
efficient than BDDs in many set-based applications, such as combinatorial problems [20], problems in graph theory [4], and traversal of Petri nets [28]. Since
points-to analysis also requires manipulation of (points-to) sets, ZBDDs should
also work well for points-to analysis.

Although one-of-N encodings implemented using ZBDDs have been used successfully in problems involving sets, relatively little attention has been paid to
encoding relations. A relation is a subset of a cross product of its attributes.
The size of this universal set is the product of the sizes of the attribute domains,
which can be very large. Encoding a relation in a ZBDD as a subset of this
universal set is not practical because the number of bits required is equal to the
size of the universal set. Yoneda *et al.* come close to manipulating relations in
ZBDDs [28]. Although they do not represent relations explicitly, they define new
ZBDD operations that have the effect of applying a transition relation to a set
of Petri-net states encoded in a ZBDD.

We propose a new technique to represent a relation in a ZBDD: allocate
one bit for each element of every attribute domain. Thus, the number of bits
required is the sum, rather than the product, of the sizes of the attribute domains.
A tuple containing one element from each attribute is represented as a set of

those elements. For example, suppose a domain D with elements $\{a, b, c\}$, and a relation R with two attributes R_1 and R_2 with domain D. Encode this relation as a ZBDD on six bits, namely $a_1, b_1, c_1, a_2, b_2, c_2$, where the bits with subscript 1 represent elements in attribute 1, and the bits with subscript 2 represent elements in attribute 2. Then the tuples $\langle a, a \rangle$, $\langle a, b \rangle$ and $\langle c, b \rangle$ are represented by the sets $\{a_1, a_2\}$, $\{a_1, b_2\}$, and $\{c_1, b_2\}$, and encoded with the binary strings 100100, 100010, and 001010, respectively.

This representation encodes each tuple as a bit vector. Therefore the standard ZBDD set operations defined on sets of bit vectors (union, intersection, difference) implement the corresponding operations on the relations. The replace operation can be implemented on ZBDDs in the same way as on BDDs.

The relational product operation is central to relation-based points-to analysis. To our knowledge, there is no practical algorithm to compute the relational product in ZBDDs. In BDDs a relational product is a conjunction followed by an existential quantification — implementations combine them into a single, more efficient, operation. In ZBDDs, the analogue of the conjunction is a multiplication followed by removal of tuples containing more than one element of the attribute being compared.

For instance, the example from Section 2.2. has points-to relation $\{\langle p, X \rangle,$ $\langle q, Y \rangle\}$ and subset constraints relation $\{\langle p, q \rangle\}$. These relations can be represented using ZBDDs with bits X, Y, p, q, p', q', where the primed bits represent elements in the second attribute of the relation. The points-to relation is represented by a ZBDD for the set of subsets $\{Xp, Yq\}$, and the subset constraints relation is represented by $\{pq'\}$. The product of these ZBDDs is $\{Xpq', Yqpq'\}$. The second tuple is removed because it contains two elements (p and q) from the attribute being compared. Finally, the equivalent of an existential quantification removes the p from Xpq', yielding the correct final result $\{Xq'\}$.

Although an algorithm for ZBDD multiplication is given by Minato [21, p. 75], there are two other operations for which algorithms have not been designed: (1) removal of tuples with multiple elements from the same attribute; and (2) existential quantification. We present a modification of the ZBDD multiplication algorithm (see Figure 3) that performs all three operations in a single pass through the ZBDD. ZRELPROD takes an additional parameter pd, the set of ZBDD variables representing the relation attributes being compared. Let x be the variable tested by the top node of the operand ZBDDs. When x is not in pd, line 14 performs the standard multiplication.[1] However, when x is in pd, line 12 returns the union of two relational products: the product of the 0-cofactors with respect to x and the product of the 1-cofactors with respect to x. This result contains exactly those tuples in which the value of x is equal in both operands. Tuples in which the value of x is zero appear in the 0-cofactors, and those in which x is one appear in the 1-cofactors. ZRELPROD combines into a single step the ZBDD multiplication, the removal of tuples with multiple elements

---

[1] Compared to Minato's ZBDD multiplication algorithm, line 14 lacks the terms $p1 * q1$ and $p0 * q1$. This is a relational-product behaviour-preserving optimization: when x is not in pd but it is tested by p, it cannot also be tested by q, so $q0 = q$ and $q1 = 0$.

ZBDD ZRELPROD(ZBDD p, ZBDD q, SET⟨VARIABLE⟩ pd)

```
 1   if p.top < q.top
 2      then return ZRELPROD(q, p, pd)
 3   if q = 0
 4      then return 0
 5   if q = 1
 6      then return SUBSET0(p, pd)
 7   x ← p.top
 8   (p0, p1) ← factors of p by x
 9   if x ∈ pd
10      then
11              (q0, q1) ← factors of q by x
12              return ZRELPROD(p1, q1, pd) + ZRELPROD(p0, q0, pd)
13      else
14              return x · ZRELPROD(p1, q, pd) + ZRELPROD(p0, q, pd)
```

Fig. 3. The Relational Product Algorithm for ZBDDs

from the same attribute, and the computation of the existential quantification. The following theorem shows its correctness.

Theorem 1. *Let $V = \{v_1 \ldots v_n\}$ be a set of ZBDD variables, ordered such that if a ZBDD node testing v_i is a child of a ZBDD node testing v_j, then $i < j$ (i.e. v_1 is closest to the terminal nodes). Partition V into three disjoint subsets V_1, V_2, V_3 representing the domains unique to the left-hand-side relation, the domains common to both relations, and the domains unique to the right-hand-side relation. Let $P \subseteq \mathcal{P}(V_1 \cup V_2)$ and $Q \subseteq \mathcal{P}(V_2 \cup V_3)$ be arbitrary sets of subsets of $V_1 \cup V_2$ and $V_2 \cup V_3$ represented as ZBDDs. Define*

$$P \times Q = \{s_1 \cup s_3 : \exists s_2 \subseteq V_2.s_1 \cup s_2 \in P \wedge s_2 \cup s_3 \in Q \wedge (s_1 \cup s_3) \cap V_2 = \emptyset\}$$

Then $\text{ZRELPROD}(P, Q, V_2) = P \times Q$. *That is,* ZRELPROD *correctly computes the relational product of the relations represented by P and Q.*

Proof. Define $k(P) = \max\{i : v_i \in S \wedge S \in P\}$, with $k(P) = 0$ when P is the empty set or contains only the empty set. Then the top (root) node of the ZBDD representing P tests variable $v_{k(P)}$, since a node that tests $v_{k(P)}$ must appear in the ZBDD in order for $v_{k(P)}$ to appear in a set in P, and the maximality of $k(P)$ ensures that this node is at the top of the ZBDD. Define operations $s0(P, v_i) = \{S : S \in P \wedge v_i \notin S\}$ and $s1(P, v_i) = \{S \setminus \{v_i\} : S \in P \wedge v_i \in S\}$, which partition P into those sets that do not contain v_i and those that do, and remove v_i from each set in the latter partition. The cofactor ZBDD operation computes $s0$ and $s1$.

The proof is by induction on $K = \max\{k(P), k(Q)\}$. In the base case, $k(P) = k(Q) = 0$, so Q is either the empty set or contains only the empty set. When $Q = \emptyset$, $P \times Q = \emptyset$, and line 4 correctly returns the ZBDD representing the empty set. When Q is the set containing the empty set, $P \times Q$ is the set of sets from

P not containing any elements of V_2. The SUBSET0 ZBDD operation computes this set in Line 6.

In the inductive case, if $k(P) < k(Q)$, the algorithm switches P and Q; since $\times$ is symmetric, we need only consider the case when $k(P) \geq k(Q)$, so $K = k(P)$. When $k(Q) = 0$, the same argument as for the base case applies. Thus, consider the case when $k(Q) > 0$, so line 7 of the algorithm is reached. There are two cases to consider: either $v_{k(P)} \in V_1$ or $v_{k(P)} \in V_2$.

Case 1: $v_{k(P)} \in V_1$: Partition $P \times Q$ into $R1 = \{s \in P \times Q : v_{k(P)} \in s\}$ and $R0 = \{s \in P \times Q : v_{k(P)} \notin s\}$. Define $v_{k(P)} \cdot X = \{S \cup \{v_{k(P)}\} : S \in X\}$. From the definition of $\times$, $s0(P, v_{k(P)}) \times Q = R0$, and $v_{k(P)} \cdot (s1(P, v_{k(P)}) \times Q) = R1$. Since $v_{k(P)} \notin V_2$, the condition in line 9 fails and line 14 is executed. By the definition of the cofactor operation, neither $p0$ nor $p1$ contains any sets containing $v_{k(P)}$, so $k(p0) < k(P) = K$ and $k(p1) < k(P) = K$. Since no set in Q contains an element of V_1, $k(Q) < k(P) = K$. Thus, the inductive hypothesis can be applied to the relational products in line 14 to show that they compute $s1(P, v_{k(P)}) \times Q$ and $s0(P, v_{k(P)}) \times Q$, respectively. Adding $v_{k(P)}$ (i.e. x) to each set in the former and taking their union, as done in line 14, gives $R1 \cup R0 = P \times Q$ as required.

Case 2: $v_{k(P)} \in V_2$: In the definition of $\times$, for each element of $P \times Q$, there must exist some s_2. Partition $P \times Q$ into $R1$ containing those elements for which $v_{k(P)} \in s_2$, and $R0$ containing those elements for which $v_{k(P)} \notin s_2$. From the definition of $\times$, $s1(P, v_{k(P)}) \times s1(Q, v_{k(P)}) = R1$ and $s0(P, v_{k(P)}) \times s0(Q, v_{k(P)}) = R0$. Since $v_{k(P)} \in V_2$, the condition in line 9 succeeds and lines 11 and 12 are executed. Again, by the definition of the cofactor operation, $k(p0), k(p1), k(q0)$, and $k(q1)$ are all strictly less than $k(P) = K$, so the inductive hypothesis can be applied to show that the relational products in line 12 correctly compute $s1(P, v_{k(P)}) \times s1(Q, v_{k(P)})$ and $s0(P, v_{k(P)}) \times s0(Q, v_{k(P)})$. Line 12 returns their union, which is $R1 \cup R0 = P \times Q$ as required.   □

One other issue with ZBDDs is that the set-complement operation cannot be performed efficiently because the complement of a sparse set is no longer sparse. The BDD-based points-to analyses of Berndl et al. [2] and of Whaley and Lam [27] do not use set complement. The Paddle framework [10] uses set complement for convenience (in cases where it is more natural to write $R_1 \cap \overline{R_2}$ instead of $R_1 \setminus R_2$) but not in essential ways. Paddle could be restructured to avoid using set complement.

4   Experimental Evaluation

The program analysis community started using BDDs to represent relations without investigating whether a variant representation could be more compact. The experiments presented in this section test whether ZBDDs are a better choice of data structure for program analyses.

The results indicate that ZBDDs are consistently more space efficient than BDDs for relations in context-sensitive points-to analyses, but yield little improvement for the dense relations found in context-insensitive points-to analyses.

4.1   Experimental Setup

This experimental study evaluates ZBDDs in the context of three program-analysis frameworks.

- The first framework is the context-insensitive points-to analysis developed by Berndl *et al.* [2]. In this implementation, Soot [26] and its Spark points-to analysis framework [9,11] are used to generate a system of subset constraints to be solved. The constraints are then read in and solved by a solver written in C using the BuDDy BDD library [14].
- The second framework is the joeq/bddbddb system of Whaley and Lam [27]. In this implementation, the joeq compiler pre-processes the code to be analyzed, generates a system of subset constraints to be solved, and outputs the initial relations as BDDs. The algorithm to solve the constraints is specified as a Datalog program. The bddbddb tool reads the Datalog program and the initial relations, and solves the system of constraints. We evaluated ZBDDs within the context-insensitive points-to analysis implemented in joeq/bddbddb. As explained in the introduction, we did not apply ZBDDs to the context-sensitive analysis in joeq/bddbddb because it uses a "new primitive" BDD operation to construct domains of exponential size [27].
- The third framework is Lhoták and Hendren's Paddle framework [10,13]. Unlike the other two systems, Paddle integrates the BDD-based analysis into the compiler (Soot). Paddle is implemented in the Jedd language [12], an extension of Java for expressing program analyses in terms of relations, which the Jedd runtime represents and manipulates using BDDs. All modifications are confined to Jedd. Of the variations of context sensitivity supported by Paddle, we evaluated the 1-object-sensitive analysis, which was identified in earlier work as being precise at a modest cost, relative to other context sensitivity variations [13].

This study uses a representative subset of the benchmarks from Lhoták and Hendren's study [13] of context-sensitive points-to analysis. Three (`antlr`, `bloat`, `chart`) are from the Dacapo suite, version beta050224 [5], four (`jack`, `javac`, `jess`, `raytrace`) are object-oriented programs from the SPEC JVM 98 suite [25], and three (`polyglot`, `sablecc`, `soot`) are other object-oriented Java programs. These benchmarks have been used in many previous points-to analysis studies. All of the benchmarks are analyzed with the standard class library from the Sun JDK 1.3.1.

Operations on BDDs and ZBDDs have the same asymptotic complexity. Packages such as BuDDy contain tuned implementations of BDD operations. We did not perform a comparison of running time because we do not have access to a carefully-tuned ZBDD implementation. Unlike running time, the number of nodes is not affected by the fine tunning of the decision diagram implementation.

4.2   ZBDDs

This study compares ZBDDs to BDDs in two ways. First, we wrote a variation of the BDD-based points-to analysis implementation of Berndl *et al.* [2]

that represents the same relations in ZBDDs instead of BDDs. This variation uses ZBDD operations, including the relational-product operation presented in Section 3, instead of BDD operations to manipulate relations. Second, we instrumented Paddle [10,13] and joeq/bddbddb [27] to dump the relations computed during the analysis. Then we developed a tool to read these relations into both a BDD and a ZBDD. This infrastructure allows for the comparison of the number of nodes in each BDD with the number of nodes in the corresponding ZBDD representing the same relation.

A fair comparison must use an appropriate ordering of the variables in the BDD and ZBDD because the size of these representations can vary significantly depending on the choice of ordering. Berndl *et al.* found that requiring that all the bits representing a given attribute be grouped together consecutively in the ordering is a suitable restriction for BDD-based program analyses [2]. Thus, for each relation, we searched exhaustively for the BDD ordering that obeys this restriction and produces the smallest BDD: for a relation with n attributes, we evaluated the $n!$ possible orderings of the attributes. The ordering found by this exhaustive search on a representative benchmark (antlr) was applied to the corresponding relations in the analysis of all the benchmarks.

Since the BDD and ZBDD representations of a relation are defined in terms of different sets of bits, an appropriate ZBDD variable ordering that corresponds to a given BDD variable ordering must be selected. To be consistent with BDD orderings and to limit the search space of possible orderings, the restriction that the bits representing a given attribute be grouped together consecutively is also maintained for ZBDD orderings. Given this restriction, the only choice remaining is the relative ordering of different attributes. It turns out that for most of the relations examined, the best BDD variable ordering is also the best ZBDD ordering. For all but one relation, using the best BDD ordering for the ZBDD results in a ZBDD no more than 5% larger than the ZBDD with the best ZBDD ordering.

The resolvedSpecials relation in Paddle is an interesting outlier. Using the best BDD ordering results in a ZBDD 76% larger than the ZBDD with the best ZBDD ordering. However, when the best ZBDD ordering is applied to BDDs it yields only 7% more nodes than the best BDD ordering. We will continue to study such outliers for more insights on BDD and ZBDD orderings. However, for the most part, good BDD orderings tend to also be good ZBDD orderings. The experiments reported in the remainder of this paper use the best BDD ordering for both BDDs and ZBDDs. Therefore, the results are slightly biased in favour of BDDs.

The graphs in Figure 4 show the relative size of the BDD and ZBDD for each relation of each benchmark. Points below the diagonal line represent relations for which the ZBDD is smaller than the BDD. Points above the line represent relations for which the BDD is smaller. Larger decision diagrams, which affect analysis cost more significantly, appear to the right and top of each graph. Note that the three graphs in Figure 4 have different scales.

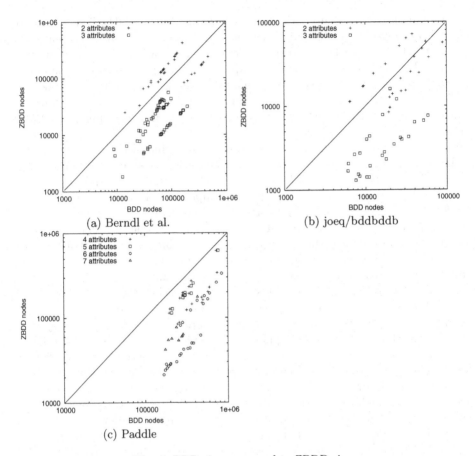

Fig. 4. BDD size compared to ZBDD size

In the Berndl *et al.* analysis, although most relations are represented more efficiently by ZBDDs than BDDs, the reverse is true for a significant number of relations, some of them large. Closer examination reveals that in every benchmark, the relations represented more efficiently by BDDs than ZBDDs are always the `pointsTo` and `typeFilter` relation, both of which are manipulated frequently by the analysis. Thus, the data indicates that there is no clear advantage in using ZBDDs over BDDs, or vice versa, for the Berndl *et al.* analysis.

Results for the joeq/bddbddb analysis are similar to those of the Berndl *et al.* analysis. The relations for which BDDs are smaller than ZBDDs are mainly `vPfilter` (the joeq/bddbddb equivalent of `typeFilter`), and in several benchmarks `vP` (equivalent of `pointsTo`).

In both the Berndl *et al.* and joeq/bddbddb analyses, the relative size of BDDs and ZBDDs favours ZBDDs more strongly in relations with three attributes than those with two attributes. Therefore, for context-sensitive analyses, which use additional attributes to represent contexts, we expected ZBDDs to be significantly smaller than BDDs. Indeed, Figure 4(c) shows that in the

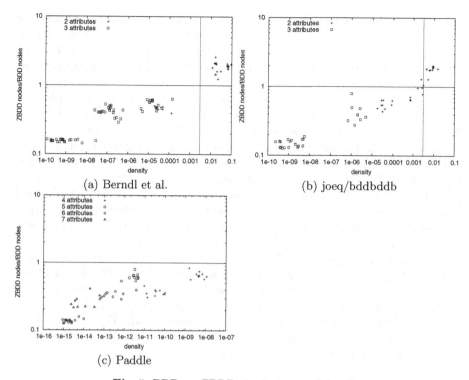

Fig. 5. BDD vs. ZBDD size in terms of density

Paddle context-sensitive analysis every relation in every benchmark is smaller when represented by a ZBDD than by a BDD. The differences ranged up to a factor of eight! However, the link with the number of attributes is less clear in the Paddle results: (1) the BDD and ZBDD sizes for 6-attribute relations are very close to those for 4-attribute relations; and (2) the ZBDD vs. BDD advantage is smaller for 7-attribute relations than for a large set of 6-attribute relations.

These results indicate that for context-insensitive points-to analyses, ZBDDs are generally smaller than BDDs, but the advantage is too small and inconsistent to allow a general recommendation that ZBDDs be used instead of BDDs. However, for analyses using relations with more attributes, and for context-sensitive points-to analysis in particular, we expect ZBDDs to be significantly and consistently smaller than BDDs representing the same relations.

When should we use ZBDDs? Given the mixed results for points-to analyses in the question of the size of ZBDDs vs. BDDs for the same relations, a metric that indicates whether ZBDDs or BDDs are expected to be more compact would be useful for the program analysis community. Such a metric could be used when a designer is considering the use of a BDD representation for a relation-based analysis that has not yet been implemented using BDDs.

The metric that we propose is *density* and it is equal to the number of tuples in the relation divided by the size of the full domain of possible tuples. This metric is inspired by Meinel and Theobald's recommendation that ZBDDs be used for boolean functions whose on-set (those input vectors that the function maps to one) is small, and whose bit vectors in the on-set contain few one-bits [15]. The density metric covers both parts of this qualitative recommendation, since the number of tuples in a relation is equal to the total number of one-bits in all the bit vectors in the on-set of a one-of-N encoding of the relation, multiplied by the number of attributes. The density metric measures the density of a relation. Thus it applies to relations independently of the ZBDD representation.

Figure 5 plots the ratio of ZBDD vs. BDD size as a function of the density metric. Points below the horizontal line represent relations whose ZBDD is smaller than the BDD. In all three graphs, as density increases, the advantage of ZBDDs over BDDs decreases. At a density of around 3×10^{-3}, BDDs and ZBDDs are approximately equal in size. This threshold is indicated in the graphs by a vertical dotted line. Of all the relations that we observed, two had a density lower than this threshold but were represented more compactly by a BDD than a ZBDD; they appear slightly to the left of and above the crossing lines in Figure 5(b). The context-sensitive relations extracted from Paddle, which are represented more compactly by ZBDDs than BDDs, have low densities. Because the size of BDDs and ZBDDs strongly depends on the contents of the relation being represented, density can only serve as a rough guide. However, we hope it will be a useful metric for analysis designers considering ZBDDs or BDDs for other program analyses.

5   Related Work

ZBDDs were introduced by Minato, and found to scale better than BDDs when representing large combinatorial circuits [19]. Minato showed that ZBDDs are likely a better choice than BDDs if there are many input variables, variables default to 0, or very few elements in a set are asserted.

Okuno applied ZBDDs to the N-Queens problem. He reports that for this problem, the ZBDD representation is about a factor of N smaller than the corresponding BDD version [24, summarized in [21]].

Yoneda et al. applied ZBDDs to Petri-net state-space exploration, and compared their performance to BDDs [28]. They found the ZBDD representation to be one half to one third the size of the BDD representation. They also report that the ZBDD implementation was several times faster for some benchmarks.

Coudert used ZBDDs to efficiently solve graph optimization and routing problems [4].

Since then, ZBDDs have been used to efficiently solve several combinatorial problems as well as fault simulation, logic synthesis, processing of petri nets and manipulation of polynomial formulas [22,23].

BDDs were first applied to points-to analysis by Zhu and Berndl et al. [29,2]. These context-insensitive analyses were then generalized to context-sensitive analysis by Zhu and Calman and by Whaley and Lam [30,27]. Hardekopf and Lin compared several non-BDD and BDD implementations of a context-insensitive points-to analysis [7], including a hybrid implementation in which only the points-to sets are represented by BDDs, and the rest of the analysis uses traditional data structures. This implementation used less than one-fifth of the memory of a non-BDD implementation. ZBDDs could be substituted for BDDs in this implementation, possibly yielding further reductions in memory usage.

6 Conclusion

Although BDDs have been successfully used for points-to analysis, alternative BDD representations were not evaluated by this community. This paper develops the techniques that allow the use of ZBDDs for such analyses. The new relational-product operator described here allows for the immediate use of ZBDDs in points-to analysis. The experimental results indicate that non-trivial reduction of BDD sizes can be realized when ZBDDs are used for context-sensitive points-to analysis.

References

1. Andersen, L.O.: Program Analysis and Specialization for the C Programming Language. PhD thesis, DIKU, Univ. of Copenhagen (DIKU report 94/19) (May 1994)
2. Berndl, M., Lhoták, O., Qian, F., Hendren, L., Umanee, N.: Points-to analysis using BDDs. In: Proceedings of PLDI 2003, pp. 103–114 (2003)
3. Bryant, R.E.: Symbolic boolean manipulation with ordered binary-decision diagrams. ACM Comput. Surv. 24(3), 293–318 (1992)
4. Coudert, O.: Solving graph optimization problems with ZBDDs. In: EDTC 1997: Proceedings of the 1997 European Conference on Design and Test, p. 224 (1997)
5. DaCapo Project. The DaCapo benchmark suite,
   http://www-ali.cs.umass.edu/DaCapo/gcbm.html
6. Emami, M., Ghiya, R., Hendren, L.J.: Context-sensitive interprocedural points-to analysis in the presence of function pointers. In: Proceedings of PLDI 1994, pp. 242–256 (1994)
7. Hardekopf, B., Lin, C.: The ant and the grasshopper: Fast and accurate pointer analysis for millions of lines of code. In: Proceedings of PLDI (2007)
8. Hind, M.: Pointer analysis: haven't we solved this problem yet? In: Proceedings of PASTE 2001, pp. 54–61. ACM Press, New York (2001)
9. Lhoták, O.: Spark: A flexible points-to analysis framework for Java. Master's thesis, McGill University (December 2002)
10. Lhoták, O.: Program Analysis using Binary Decision Diagrams. PhD thesis, McGill University (January 2006)
11. Lhoták, O., Hendren, L.: Scaling Java points-to analysis using Spark. In: Hedin, G. (ed.) CC 2003. LNCS, vol. 2622, pp. 153–169. Springer, Heidelberg (2003)
12. Lhoták, O., Hendren, L.: Jedd: a BDD-based relational extension of Java. In: Proceedings of PLDI 2004, pp. 158–169. ACM Press, New York (2004)
13. Lhoták, O., Hendren, L.: Context-sensitive points-to analysis: is it worth it? In: Mycroft, A., Zeller, A. (eds.) CC 2006. LNCS, vol. 3923, pp. 47–64. Springer, Heidelberg (2006)
14. Lind-Nielsen, J.: BuDDy, A Binary Decision Diagram Package,
   http://www.itu.dk/research/buddy/

15. Meinel, C., Theobald, T.: Algorithms and Data Structures in VLSI Design. Springer, New York (1998)
16. Milanova, A.: Precise and Practical Flow Analysis of Object-Oriented Software. PhD thesis, Rutgers University (August 2003)
17. Milanova, A., Rountev, A., Ryder, B.G.: Parameterized object sensitivity for points-to and side-effect analyses for Java. In: Proceedings of ISSTA 2002, pp. 1–11. ACM Press, New York (2002)
18. Milanova, A., Rountev, A., Ryder, B.G.: Parameterized object sensitivity for points-to analysis for Java. ACM Trans. Softw. Eng. Methodol. 14(1), 1–41 (2005)
19. Minato, S.: Zero-suppressed BDDs for set manipulation in combinatorial problems. In: DAC 1993: 30th International Conf. on Design Automation, pp. 272–277 (1993)
20. Minato, S.: Calculation of unate cube set algebra using zero-suppressed BDDs. In: 31st ACM/IEEE Design Automation Conference (DAC 1994), pp. 420–424 (1994)
21. Minato, S.: Binary decision diagrams and applications for VLSI CAD. Kluwer Academic Publishers, Dordrecht (1996)
22. Minato, S.: Zero-suppressed BDDs and their applications. International Journal on Software Tools for Technology Transfer (STTT) 3(2), 156–170 (2001)
23. Mishchenko, A.: An introduction to zero-suppressed binary decision diagrams. Technical report, Portland State University (June 2001)
24. Okuno, H.G.: Reducing combinatorial explosions in solving search-type combinatorial problems with binary decision diagrams. Trans. of Information Processing Society of Japan (IPSJ) (in Japanese) 35(5), 739–753 (1994)
25. Standard Performance Evaluation Corporation. SPEC JVM98 benchmarks (1998), http://www.spec.org/osg/jvm98/
26. Vallée-Rai, R., Gagnon, E., Hendren, L.J., Lam, P., Pominville, P., Sundaresan, V.: Optimizing Java bytecode using the Soot framework: Is it feasible? In: Watt, D.A. (ed.) CC 2000. LNCS, vol. 1781, pp. 18–34. Springer, Heidelberg (2000)
27. Whaley, J., Lam, M.S.: Cloning-based context-sensitive pointer alias analysis using binary decision diagrams. In: Proceedings of PLDI 2004, pp. 131–144 (2004)
28. Yoneda, T., Hatori, H., Takahara, A., Minato, S.: BDDs vs. zero-suppressed BDDs: for CTL symbolic model checking of petri nets. In: Srivas, M., Camilleri, A. (eds.) FMCAD 1996. LNCS, vol. 1166, pp. 435–449. Springer, Heidelberg (1996)
29. Zhu, J.: Symbolic pointer analysis. In: Proceedings of the 2002 IEEE/ACM International Conference on Computer-Aided Design, pp. 150–157 (2002)
30. Zhu, J., Calman, S.: Symbolic pointer analysis revisited. In: Proceedings of PLDI 2004, pp. 145–157 (2004)

Author Index

The application of flow birefringence
to rheological studies of polymer melts

The application of flow birefringence to rheological studies of polymer melts

J. L. S. WALES

Delft University Press / 1976

ISBN 978-90-298-0102-7   ISBN 978-94-010-1556-1 (eBook)
DOI   10.1007/978-94-010-1556-1

Contents

Acknowledgements

The author wishes to thank Dr. A. Schors, Director of the Centraal Laboratorium TNO, for his permission of publishing the investigations described in this thesis.

Particularly warm thanks are due to Mrs R. Massa, formerly Miss R. de Zeeuw, for her help in the experimentation; to Mrs H.E. Koot for carefully typing the manuscript, and to Messrs G.H.J. van Velzen and J. Jansen for the preparation of the drawings.

The author is greatly indepted to Messrs R. Nauta, J. Schijf, A.L. Baas and J.E.A. van Schie who helped either in the design or in the building of the various apparatuses, none of which are commercially available.

My final words of thanks must be directed to my colleagues Dr. J.L. den Otter, U. Daum and J. Heijboer, and to Prof. Dr. F.R. Schwarzl for their discussions during various phases of the investigation, and also to Professors J. Meissner and W. Philippoff for some of their measurements. My particular thanks are due to Dr. J.L. den Otter for his dynamic mechanical measurements shown in various figures throughout the work, and to Prof. Dr. H. Janeschitz-Kriegl for his guidance and enthusiasm.

1. Introduction

1.1 Preamble

The science to which this work is appended is termed rheology and rheology means the study of flow and deformation of liquids and solids with emphasis on the underlying physical processes.

Characteristic for solids is that they respond to a force by deforming, and, on removal of the force, by returning to their original shape. This type of response is termed elastic. Characteristic for liquids is that they deform and continue to deform as long as the force is present. This type of response is termed viscous.

The two definitions just given for viscous and elastic response represent two extremes of response to an external force. Materials do not always fall readily into one or the other of the above-mentioned categories. An additional parameter is needed to describe material response more fully. The extra parameter is time. As a general rule the faster the deformation the closer the response is to being elastic, the slower the deformation the closer the response is to being viscous. Slow and fast are factors relative to some natural time, τ, of the material. This natural time may be thought connected with the rates of spontaneous diffusion of its molecular and atomic constituents. For everyday fluids as water, the natural time is very short, of the order of 10^{-10}s [1] and hence for most purposes is considered as being viscous. For a material such as glass, the natural time is very long, and consequently this material is bracketed as being elastic. Materials with natural times of the order of daily events (seconds, minutes, hours) are defined as being viscoelastic. The materials of this investigation fall into this class.

The forces on a material element can act internally (gravity, electrical and magnetic fields) or externally on the surfaces of the element. In the latter case the forces on the element are defined by the stress tensor p_{ij} (i=1,2,3,). With an arbitrary coordinate system with base vectors $\underline{e}_1$, $\underline{e}_2$, $\underline{e}_3$, the force $\underline{f}_i$ on a unit surface of normal $\underline{e}_i$ is obtained by the relation:

$$\underline{f}_i = \sum_{j=1}^{3} p_{ij}\underline{e}_j \qquad (1.1.1)$$

As a consequence of the balance of angular momentum, the stress tensor is symmetric, i.e. $p_{ij} = p_{ji}$. The last result holds only in the absence of internal spin and in the absence of certain magnetic and electrical fields.

Simple shear flow is an important class of flow and forms the major subject in this work. Using a right handed coordinate system to define the flow, the usual convention is retained with: 1 - the flow direction; 2 - the direction of the flow gradient, and 3 - the neutral direction. If a particle in simple shear flow is given coordinates (ξ_1,ξ_2,ξ_3) at some time time t_1 previous to the present time t then the present coordinate position (x_1,x_2,x_3) reads:

$$x_1 = \xi_1 + q(t - t_1)\xi_2 \qquad (1.1.2)$$
$$x_2 = \xi_2 \qquad (1.1.3)$$
$$x_3 = \xi_3 \qquad (1.1.4)$$

where q is the shear rate and the macroscopic deformation is $s = q(t - t_1)$.
Also present in simple shear flow is a shear stress p_{12}. This quantity represents a force in the flow direction but acting on a unit surface normal to
the 2-direction.

The relationships between the stresses, the deformations and time is the
essence of rheology: in the following section we begin with the linear theory.

1.2 Linear Viscoelasticity

The basic premise of the linear theory is found in the Boltzmann superposition principle[2]. The following form is convenient:

$$p_{12}(t) = \int_{-\infty}^{t} q(t_1)G(t - t_1)dt_1 \qquad (1.2.1)$$

where $p_{12}(t)$ is the shear stress at time t, $q(t_1)$ the shear rate at time t_1,
and $G(t - t_1)$ is a time-dependent modulus which decreases as the interval
$(t - t_1)$ increases. Physically, the principle relies on the linear additivity
of the stress increments from past deformations. Each deformation $q(t_1)dt_1$ at
some time t_1 in the past contributes to the stress at time t by an amount
$G(t - t_1)q(t_1)dt_1$. The sum over all past deformations defines the present
state of stress. Similar formulations can be made for deformations other than
simple shear.

The steady shear viscosity defined as the ratio of the equilibrium shear
stress to the constant shear rate q follows immediately:

$$\eta = \int_{0}^{\infty} G(\tau)d\tau \qquad (1.2.2)$$

The transformation $t - t_1 = \tau$ has been made for convenience. It is possible to
construct an expression similar to 1.2.1 but giving the deformation as a function of the past stress and a compliance $J(t - t_1)$. The time-dependent modulus G and the compliance J are interrelated by[3]:

$$\int_{0}^{t} G(t_1)J(t - t_1)dt_1 = t \qquad (1.2.3)$$

In this linear theory the material shows an interesting elastic property: the
material recovers a part of the impressed deformation when the force is removed. For simple shear flow the "shear recovery" is defined as the total recovery at infinite time after cessation of steady shearing:

$$s_{\infty} = J_e \eta q \qquad (1.2.4)$$

where J_e is called the steady shear compliance.

$$J_e = \frac{1}{\eta^2} \int_{0}^{\infty} \tau G(\tau)d\tau \qquad (1.2.5)$$

So far we have only considered steady shearing; time-dependent motions are
also important and a particularly important one is obtained by sinusoidal
stressing with deformations of small amplitude. In general, the stress is out
of phase with the strain. However, the stress can be decomposed into two com-

2

ponents, one in-phase and one 90° out of phase with the movement. Division of the amplitudes of these stress components by the strain amplitude defines a complex modulus as consisting of an in-phase component and an out-of-phase component. The in-phase component or storage modulus is termed G' and represents the stored energy, the out-of-phase component or loss modulus is termed G'' and represents the dissipated energy. The phase angle between the in- and out-of-phase components is given by $\tan \delta = G''/G'$, and the ratio of the peak stress to the peak strain is called the absolute value of the dynamic modulus $|G^*|$:

$$|G^*| = [G'^2 + G''^2]^{\frac{1}{2}} \qquad (1.2.6)$$

Equivalently, the results of dynamic experiments can also be expressed through the J's. It is also possible to define a real η' and an imaginary η'' component of viscosity from the moduli G'' and G':

$$\eta' = G''/\omega \qquad (1.2.7)$$

$$\eta'' = G'/\omega \qquad (1.2.8)$$

where ω is the applied circular frequency. The dynamic moduli are expressed in terms of a continuous distribution of relaxation times since in practice it is found that a single relaxation time is insufficient to describe the behaviour of most materials.

$$G' = \int_{-\infty}^{\infty} H(\tau) \, \frac{\omega^2 \tau^2}{1 + \omega^2 \tau^2} \, d(\ln \tau) \qquad (1.2.9)$$

$$G'' = \int_{-\infty}^{\infty} H(\tau) \, \frac{\omega \tau}{1 + \omega^2 \tau^2} \, d(\ln \tau) \qquad (1.2.10)$$

where $H(\tau)$ is habitually called the relaxation time spectrum; an unfortunate name since $H(\tau)$ has the dimension of a modulus and does not only convey the meaning of a statistical frequency. All the above relations can be developed from the Boltzmann principle[3]. The conditions to be met are those of linearity: a change of amplitude of the applied deformation may not effect the derived moduli. It appears that these requirements are always met with polymer solutions and pure melts, even at rather large strain amplitudes: many other liquid systems which are structured (e.g. clay suspensions, certain soaps[4]) and most solids - including some metals[5], do not show linearity except at extremely low deformations.

1.3. Normal Stresses in Simple Shear Flow

Associated with the shear stress in simple shear flow are stresses acting perpendicular to the normal surfaces formed by the coordinate axes. According to classical fluid mechanics these normal stresses, p_{ii}, are all equal to the local pressure and hence normal stress differences $p_{ii} - p_{jj}$ (no summation over the indices) are zero. For non-Newtonian fluids such as polymer melts and solutions at high shear rates, these normal stress differences do not

3

vanish. As a result, the cross of the principal axes of stress is inclined with respect to the stream lines. Its position can be described by a single angle for which the one smaller or equal to 45° is chosen*.

To explain deviations from 45°, as found by early workers, at the turn of the century postulations were made that elastic liquids of the type proposed by Maxwell, should possess unequal normal stresses (see Section 1.4). These early ideas seem to have been lost and at a later date it was left to K. Weissenberg[6] to devise the first apparatus for the measurement of the normal stress differences.

At the present time, extensive measurements of normal stresses have been carried out on polymer solutions. Polymer melts have not been so extensively investigated and other non-Newtonian fluids hardly at all.

The Boltzmann principle of the previous section does not predict unequal normal stresses in shear flow. Lodge[7] overcame this problem by using a description of strain that was applied earlier by Weissenberg in his non-linear theories of elasticity. Lodge adapted this description for a description of liquid behaviour.

In developing his theory, he used a particular model: the temporary network model for concentrated solutions and melts. However, the results are probably of more general validity. He proposed the following equation of state:

$$p_{ij}(t) = \int_{-\infty}^{t} N(t - t_1) \frac{dx_i}{d\xi'_m} \frac{dx_j}{d\xi'_m} dt_1 - P_0 \delta_{ij} \qquad (1.3.1)$$

where $N(\tau)$ is a "memory function" and the usual summation has been applied to repeated indices; P_0 is a hydrostatic pressure, and x_i and ξ'_i denote the coordinates of the positions occupied by particles at the time of observation t and at a previous time t'_1, the x_i being expressed as functions of the ξ'_i. The physical basis for the above model is the same as that of the Boltzmann principle: the linear addition of past deformations coupled with a time-dependent modulus gives the present state of stress. However, non-linear terms in the strain tensor must be taken into account for the calculation of the normal stresses.

For the case of steady shear flow given by equations (1.1.1) to (1.1.3) there has been obtained:

$$p_{12} = q \int_0^{\infty} N(\tau)\tau d\tau \qquad (1.3.2)$$

$$p_{11} - p_{22} = q^2 \int_0^{\infty} N(\tau)\tau^2 d\tau \qquad (1.3.3)$$

$$p_{22} - p_{33} = 0 \qquad (1.3.4)$$

These equations show that for steady shearing the shear stress is proportional to the gradient q; the normal stress difference $p_{11} - p_{22}$ is proportional to the square of the gradient and the normal stress difference $p_{22} - p_{33}$

---

*The reader is reminded that for Newtonian fluids the principal stresses lie at 45° to the flow direction.

should be zero. The state of affairs where the viscosity is independent of the gradient (the so-called Newtonian region) and the normal stress differences proportional to the square of the gradient leads to the term second order region. Classical (i.e. linear) viscoelasticity has also a constant viscosity independent of the gradient.

If $G(t)$ vanishes at infinite time, $N(\tau)$, $G(\tau)$ and $H(\tau)$ can be related[8]:

$$N(\tau) = -\frac{dG(\tau)}{d\tau} = \int_0^\infty \frac{H(s)}{s^2} e^{-\tau/s} \, ds \qquad (1.3.5.)$$

In subsequent chapters equations 1.3.2. and 1.3.3. are expressed in terms of $H(\tau)$ instead of $N(\tau)$.

A set of equations can be derived from this theory relating the orientation angle χ_m of the stress tensor in steady shear flow, the recovery s_∞ after steady flow, and the phase angle δ in oscillatory shear:

$$\cot 2 \chi_m = \frac{p_{11} - p_{22}}{2 \, p_{12}} = J_e \eta q = J_e p_{12} \qquad (1.3.6)$$

$$s_\infty = \cot \delta = \cot 2 \chi_m \qquad (1.3.7)$$

where δ is to be evaluated at a low frequency equal to the shear rate at which the corresponding steady shear flow experiment is carried out.

1.4 Flow Birefringence

Most molecules are optically anisotropic. When the molecules in an assembly are completely randomly distributed then the assembly behaves as an isotropic medium. If the assembly can be brought either partially or fully into a state of orientation by any means whatsoever, then double refraction (birefringence) will occur. Orientation in liquids may be achieved by the application of electrical fields (Kerr effect), magnetic fields (Cotton-Mouton effect), acoustic waves (Lucas effect) or by flow (Maxwell effect). The general problem of double refraction including flow birefringence, was considered by Peterlin and Stuart[9]. Other reviews, discussing particular and general aspects of flow birefringence, have also appeared from time to time[10-16]. The most recent account with particular emphasis on macromolecular fluids has been given by Janeschitz-Kriegl[8].

Definition of the terms extinction angle and birefringence

The liquid is viewed through crossed polarizing devices so that light travels perpendicularly to both the stream lines and the velocity gradient. The field appears dark when the liquid is at rest. Under the influence of the hydrodynamic forces the fluid becomes optically biaxial, i.e. it possesses three different principal axes with three different principal refractive indices. One of these axes coincides with the direction of the light beam and the other two lie in the plane of observation. The field now appears dark or light depending on whether the orientation of the crossed polarizers corresponds with the orientation of these two principal axes or not.

The extinction angle χ is defined as the smaller of the two angles between the shearing planes and the vibration planes of the polarizers, which give rise to the dark field. According to this definition, χ lies between 0° and 45°.

When linearly polarized light of wavelength λ (in vacuo) passes through a length d of doubly refracting medium it is resolved into two linearly polarized components one along each principal axis in the viewing plane. These components emerge with a phase difference δ (radians) which is given by $\delta = 2\pi d\Delta n/\lambda$. In this formula Δn ($= n_I - n_{II}$) is the difference between the principal refractive indices in the viewing plane, which we call the birefringence. The principal refractive index n_I is, in accordance with the previously given definition of the extinction angle, taken from that principal axis which points between the flow vector and the gradient vector. The sign of the birefringence is positive or negative as n_I is greater or less than n_{II}.

Historical background of the stress-optical effect

The discovery of artificial double refraction by stress was made by Brewster in 1816[17]. He found that a plate of glass under simple tension aquired the properties of a uniaxial crystal. Further experimentation on solids carried out by Neumann and later by Maxwell[18,19] culminated in the formulation of stress-optical laws before the discovery of double refraction induced by flow. Formulated in the terms of stress these laws are:

1) At any point in a stressed transparent solid the axes of polarization of light passing through the solid are parallel to the directions of the principal stresses in the plane of the wave front at that point.

2) The differences of the velocities of the two oppositely polarized rays at the point is proportional to the difference of their two principal stresses, and is independent of stresses perpendicular to the wave front.

In simple shear the refractive index tensor has components n_{ij} corresponding to the stress components p_{ij}. Explicitly, the non-zero components are n_{11}, n_{22}, n_{33} and n_{12}. The birefringence Δn in the 1-2 plane and the extinction angle χ are formally related to the stress components by:

$$\Delta n \sin 2\chi = 2 n_{12} = 2 Cp_{12} \tag{1.4.1}$$

$$\Delta n \cos 2\chi = n_{11} - n_{22} = C(p_{11} - p_{22}) \tag{1.4.2}$$

where C is called the stress-optical coefficient.
The first published, qualitative, observations on flow birefringence were made by Mach[20] in 1873 on viscous substances such as Canada Balsam and strong metaphosphoric acid. Maxwell[21] described in 1874 a concentric cylinder apparatus used by him in earlier experiments on Canada Balsam. The first real attempts to get quantitative measurements and a theory for streaming double refraction were made by Kundt[22]. According to his view, each elemental volume is subjected to tensile and compressive stresses along two directions which are mutually perpendicular and inclined at 45° to the lines of flow. These stresses are proportional to ηq where η is the viscosity and q the velocity gradient.

6

Kundt assumed, thus, stresses produce double refraction in a liquid just as they do in a solid. The optic axes were assumed coincident with those of stress. According to the ideas at that time, χ should be 45° and any departure from this value was an unexplainable anomaly. Several such cases were found. An attempt to explain such departures was first made by Schwedoff[23]. He rejected the possibility that the optic axes do not coincide with the axes of stress and concluded that the latter do not always lie at 45°. This amounts in modern terms to the view that additional forces vectored in the gradient and flow directions are induced by the flow and that these normal forces are not equal. Moreover, Schwedoff deduced a relation between χ and a quantity related to the (fugitive) elasticity of the fluid as defined by Maxwell[24]. Later, Nantonson[25] obtained the modern looking equation:

$$\cot 2\chi = q\tau \qquad\qquad (1.4.3)$$

As will be seen later, first in Fig. 2.6b, this equation gives a qualitatively correct description of the so-called extinction angle curve: starting at 45° to the flow direction, this angle decreases, in general, monotonically with increasing shear rate. (At the same time, birefringence Δn increases continuously from zero, and, sometimes, shows a tendency of saturation within the accessible range of shear rates, cf. e.g. Fig. 2.6a).

Thus, the initial ideas concerning double refraction in streaming flow were basically that the birefringence was caused by stresses just as in solids. Later, alternative proposals were made[14] that the movement and reorientation of the constitutive particles should be considered[14,26] and, further, that a distinction should be made between rigid and flexible particles. This is, essentially, the modern standpoint. Advancing swiftly to more recent times, Lodge was apparently the first to suggest that for sufficiently flexible, amorphous, polymers in solution a stress-optical relation, as defined at the beginning of this section, should hold. He substantiated his proposals by re-examining[27] some old results of Signer, amongst others. Re-appraisal of these earlier investigations showed that the quantity $\Delta n \sin 2\chi / p_{12}$ where p_{12} is the shear stress, was essentially independent of the gradient even though χ showed considerable deviations from 45°. As the measurement of normal stresses was not thought of at the time of the original measurements, it was not possible to make direct comparison of the extinction angle χ with the orientation of the stress axes. Lodge was able to show, using his network model, that the coefficient of the stress optical law should be the same as that for crosslinked elastomers of the same polymer. As is known, for this latter case, the coefficient is independent of the concentration of effective chains and of their lengths[28]. Philippoff and co-workers[29,30a], in following up these proposals, could show that in some cases the quantity $\Delta n \sin 2\chi / p_{12}$ was constant over many decades of the shear stress, as theory required, independent of gradient, concentration and molecular weight of the polymer. He was able to demonstrate for some solutions that the optical and mechanical "extinction" angles had the same value[30b].

Experimentally, the bounds of validity of the stress-optical relation have not yet been fully defined. Consequently, the usefulness of the relation in determining stress distributions in complicated flows of viscoelastic materials cannot be guaranteed as yet. We expect deviations to occur from the simple linear stress-optical relation when motions are unsteady or the stresses are too high. Moreover, there will be qualitative differences between diluted solutions and melts.

With diluted solutions, high shear stresses (i.e. greater than 10^4 N/m^2) are not usually attainable. We do not expect deviations to occur on this account. It appears with these fluids that the stress-optical relation holds to a good approximation in oscillatory experiments. In one case of a high molecular weight material, deviations between the stress and optical phase angles first occur at frequencies about two decades higher than the reciprocal natural time of the system[31]. Therefore we believe the relation to be of general applicability as long as the solutions are amorphous and the molecular weights are sufficiently high.

Few results have been established for melts; the stress-optical relation for steady flow is, in part, the subject of this study. It is known that, in oscillatory testing near the glass temperature T_g, the stress and the birefringence can be out-of-phase with one another as well as with the imposed deformation[32] In the true melt region (at least 40 °C above T_g), however, no results appear to have been published. We may, however, expect that for sufficiently fast changes the stress-optical relation will not hold in principle. How fast these changes should be with respect to the materials times in order to obtain serious deviations from this law, remains open. One may expect that deviations occur at frequencies at which the glass transition is reached. However, there is one example of a non-steady flow for which the stress-optical relation has been investigated. The case in mind is melt spinning, where very high transient stresses can be generated. For some systems the birefringence remains linear in the stress over the complete measurement range (up to 10^7 N/m^2), for others the birefringence reaches saturation[33]. Deviations from linearity do not occur below stresses of the order of 10^6 N/m^2. This has a parallel in the behaviour of rubbers where a linear stress-optical relation also holds for stresses up to this order[28]. In the case of rubbers it is known that the deviations are a function of the degree of crosslinking[34]. The higher the degree of crosslinking the lower the stress level at which deviations from linearity become significant. In some cases[28] of low degree of crosslinking the linearity is retained up to 7×10^6 N/m^2. In rubbers the origin of the non-linearity at the higher stresses is thought to be the length of the chains between the crosslinks being too short for the applicability of the ideal Gaussian chain model[34] (see Section 4.1).

The present author does not believe that these points will be of serious matter for shearing flow in normal solutions and melts since (deviatoric) stress levels do not ever greatly exceed 10^6 N/m^2 even during the injection moulding cycle. Moreover, the polymers in normal use have higher molecular weights (longer chain lengths) than the materials used ordinarily in spinning.

1.5 Scope of the Investigation

The major concern of this investigation is the experimental use of flow birefringence to measure and characterize molten polymers of the type that are of industrial interest; only a few model fluids will be used. Owing to the relative simplicity of the methods of flow birefringence it has been found possible to develop instruments which can completely define the anisotropy of the refractive index tensor in steady shear flow. Specifically, direct determinations of the quantities n_{12}, $n_{11}-n_{22}$, $n_{11}-n_{33}$ and $n_{33}-n_{22}$ will be reported. Next, experimental evidence will be presented, as far as possible, for the validity of the stress-optical law as defined in Section 1.4. The obtained optical quantities will then be used for the evaluation of a few molecular theories which predict relations between molecular weights and J_e. Next, the data found from steady shearing will be used to examine theoretical relations between the stress tensor in steady shear flow and quantities which can be obtained from (small deformation) measurements of the dynamic moduli. The interest being here the perhaps distant possibility that dynamic measurements could predict even non-linear steady flow behaviour. Finally, a study has been made of a case where the developed methods for the measurement of the birefringence in steady flow could be used in practise. The example chosen is injection moulding where in some cases the degree of molecular orientation is predictable in the ejected parts; the importance being that some mechanical properties are extremely sensitive to the orientation frozen in during the injection cycle.

References

1) J. Frenkel, *"Kinetic Theory of Liquids"*, Clarendon Press, Oxford 1946, Ch. 4.

2) L. Boltzmann, *Pogg. Ann. Phys.* 7, 624 (1876).

3) J.D. Ferry, *"Viscoelastic Properties of Polymers"*, J. Wiley and Sons, New York 1961.

4) P. Pacor, L.H. Larder, J.M.P. Papenhuijzen, *Rheol. Acta 9*, 455 (1970).

5) J. Fleeman and G.J. Dienes in *"Rheology: Theory and Application"*, Vol. 1, F. Eirich Ed., Academic Press, New York 1856, Ch. 7.

6) K. Weissenberg, *Proc. 1st Int. Congr. on Rheology*, North-Holland Publ., Amsterdam 1949.

7) A.S. Lodge, *Trans. Farad. Soc.* 52, 120 (1956).

8) H. Janeschitz-Kriegl, *Adv. Polymer Sci.* 6, 170 (1969).

9) A. Peterlin, H.A. Stuart in *"Die Physik der Hochpolymeren"*, Vol. 2, Springer Verlag, Berlin 1953, Ch. 12.

10) A. Peterlin in *"Rheology, Theory and Applications"*, Acad. Press, New York 1956.

11) G. Boehm in *"Handbuch der biologischen Arbeitsmethoden"*, Vol. 2, Part 3, Urban u. Schwarzenburg, Berlin and Vienna 1939, p. 2929.

12) J.T. Edsall, *Adv. Colloid Sci. 1*, 169 (1942).

13) J.T. Edsall, *Fortschr. Chem. Forsch. 1*, 119 (1949).

14) H.G. Jerrard, *Chem. Rev. 59*, 345 (1959).

15) R. Cerf, *Adv. Polymer Sci. 1*, 382 (1959).

16) V.N. Tsvetkov in *"Newer Methods of Polymer Characterization"*, Interscience, New York 1964, p. 563.

17) D. Brewster, *Trans. Roy. Soc. (London)*, p. 156 (1816).

18) H.T. Jessop and F.C. Harris, *"Photoelasticity Principles and Methods"*, Cleaver-Hume Press, London 1949.

19) E.G. Coker and L.N.G. Filon, Revised by H.T. Jessop, *"A Treatise on Photo-Elasticity"*, Cambridge University Press, Cambridge 1957.

20) M.E. Mach, *"Optisch-Akustische Versuche"*, Calve, Prague 1873.

21) J.C. Maxwell, *Proc. Roy. Soc. (London) A 22*, 46 (1873); *Sci. Papers, Vol. 2*, Cambridge University Press, London 1890.

22) A. Kundt, *Pogg. Ann. 153*, 10 (1874); *Wied. Ann. 13*, 110 (1881).

23) T. Schwedoff, *J. Phys. 1 (3)*, 49 (1892).

24) J.C. Maxwell, *Phil. Trans.*, 157 (1867); *Phil. Mag. 35*, 129 (1868); *Sci. Papers, Vol. 2*, p. 26, Cambridge University Press (1890).

25) M.L. Nantonson, *Bull. Int. Acad. Sci. Cracovie 1*, 1 (1904).

26) H. Zocher, H. Freundlich, F. Stapelfeld, *Z. physik. Chemie 114*, 161, 190 (1925).

27) A.S. Lodge, *Nature 4487*, 838 (1955).

28) L.R.G. Treloar, *"The Physics of Rubber Elasticity"*, Clarendon Press, Oxford 1958, Ch. 10.

29) J.G. Brodnyan, F.A. Gaskins, W. Philippoff, *Trans. Soc. Rheol. 1*, 109 (1957).

30) a: W. Philippoff, *Trans. Soc. Rheol. 4*, 159 (1960).
    b: Ibid, p. 169.

31) A.B. Thurston, Discussion of Paper at *"6th Int. Congr. of Rheology"*, Lyon, September 1972. See also: W. Philippoff, *"Proc. 5th Int. Congr. on Rheology"*, Vol. 4, p. 3 (1968).

32) B.E. Read, *Polymer 5*, 1 (1964).

33) A. Ziabicki, K. Kedzierska, *J. Appl. Polymer Sci. 6*, 111, 361 (1962).

34) D.W. Saunders in *"The Rheology of Elastomers"*, Eds P. Mason and N. Wookey, Pergamon Press, London 1958, p. 30.

2. Apparatus

APPARATUS

2.1 The Cone-and-Plate Apparatus

The first apparatus to be built was made to measure the flow birefringence in the 1-2 plane. The quantities measured are the birefringence Δn, and the orientation angle of the ellipse to the stream lines. The choice fell on a cone--and-plate device in view of the experience that this geometry has been proven to be more useful in viscometry of elastico-viscous fluids like polymer melts than the co-axial cylinder type. Amongst other advantages, filling is easier.

Figure 2.1 gives a schematic representation. The conical surface is formed by the inner end-surface of disk C, which is stationary. The plane surface is on disk D, which forms the rotor. Axle A on which disk D is mounted, fits into a combined thrust and axial bearing, B_1, and is driven by gear box G. The gear box is itself driven via a set of interchangeable reduction gears, by an elec-tronically controlled variable speed motor (Contraves, Zürich). With a cone angle ε of 1°8' and a disk diameter of 50 mm, the range of shear rates is from 10^{-4} to 10^2 s^{-1}.

The units B_1, D and C fit into a cylindrical block B_2 which is surrounded by the heating elements H. The temperature is controlled by a thermocouple in-serted into the back of block B_2.

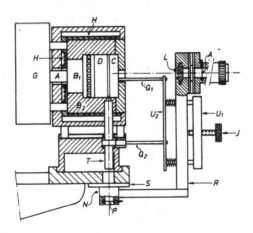

Fig. 2.1 Schematic diagram of cone-and-plate apparatus and auxiliary equipment:
(C) cone; (D) disk (i.e. plate); (B_1) bearing; (A) axle; (G) gear box;
(P, A) polarizer and analyzer (polarizing sheets); (T) tube-shaped
window holder; (S) drum scale. The remaining symbols are explained in
the text.

The light beam enters from below through polarizer P and passes tube T which serves as a holder for the lower window. The window is indicated by a half sphere on top of tube T. Here the light beam enters the gap between plate D and cone C in a radial direction. The upper window is not shown in Fig. 2.1. Inside parts C and D there is, besides the window, also a prismatic mirror which reflects the light beam so that it leaves the unit in a horizontal direction.

Details of this arrangement are shown in Fig. 2.2. From this figure it is seen that a relatively large chamber which is symmetric with respect to the axis of revolution, is inside parts C and D. In this chamber part E is fitted. It is rigidly connected with the stationary conical part C. Both parts are pressed with the aid of cover Z against disk K. Disk K, which rests on bearing B_1, ensures the correct distance between the parts D and C, so that the geometrical apex of the cone is exactly on the geometrical plane of the front surface of D.

Inside part E there is cylinder V, which can be rotated about the incident light beam. It contains the upper window W_2 and the reflection prism M. Q_1 is a handle, the function of which will be described later. F is a bore into which the filling device fits. (A rod of material is melted in a reservoir and pushed into the unit with the aid of a piston.)

The glass used for both the windows and the prismatic mirror (optical glass BK 7, Schott and Gen. (Borfe)) has a low coefficient of cubical expansion ($\alpha = 2.3 \times 10^{-5}$ °C^{-1}) and a low homogeneous residual birefringence. Its index of refraction is $n_d = 1.5163$ and its dispersity between the C and F lines is 0.0081. The body of the unit as well as parts C, D, E, and V are made of nitrided steel.

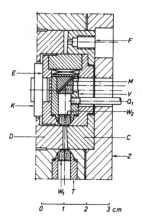

Fig. 2.2 *Detailed scale drawing of heart of cone-and-plate system: (C) cone; (D) plate; (W_1, W_2) windows, (M) reflection prism. The action of the other parts is described in the text.*

The windows, W_1 and W_2, are hemispherical. Parallel flat surfaces are ground vertically to the equatorial plane into the glass body of each window. These surfaces fit between the jaws on top of the holders (parts T and V). In this way, the windows must rotate together with the holders. Near the jaws the window rests with its equatorially cut surface on the flat area of the holder top. To prevent the spherical surface from acting as a lens, a very small plane surface is ground on top of the window. The surface of this is also polished.

It is seen from Fig. 2.2 that the light beam passes only through one side of the ring-shaped gap. In fact, if it were not led out near the centre, the birefringence on one side would be compensated by the birefringence on the other side of the centre.

Returning to Fig. 2.1, the light beam is followed on its horizontal path. It passes lens L and analyzer A before it reaches the ocular which is only schematically drawn. Part R remains to be described. It consists of a horizontal bar which is soldered to nave N, and a vertical beam which carries on its upper end the telescopic tube for the ocular. It is seen from the drawing how lens L and analyzer A are mounted on part R. Between L and A there are two slide channels: one in a vertical, the other in a horizontal direction. These slide channels serve for the insertion of a compensator in the correct attitude. The part designated U consists of two parts, U_1 and U_2, which are connected by two shafts fitting into horizontal bores in part R. The spiral springs on these shafts are counteracted by screw J. In this way part U can be moved in both directions by turning screw J. U_2 contains two holes in which handles Q_1 and Q_2 are fit. These handles are connected with parts T and V.

Now the working of the apparatus can be described. For the determination of the extinction positions, polarizer P is set parallel with the plane of incidence of mirror M. In this way, the mirror is extinguished when analyzer A is put into the crossed position. This adjustment is carried out with the rotor at rest. With turning rotor the melt in the gap is birefringent. To seek the extinctions, part R is turned around the axis of the incident light beam. Due to the action of handle Q_1, mirror M is turned together with part R so that the relative positions of the polarizer and mirror are maintained. The positions of dark field are read from drum scale S. The function of Q_2 is to let window W_1 rotate with window W_2. It appears that in this way occasional strains in the windows are released. The angular positions of the flow lines on the arbitrary scale S on the stand is not known better than to within 4° owing to small variations in the clamping position in day-to-day use. To find the true extinction angle the motor is normally reversed and a second extinction is found. The two extinction positions are symmetric with respect to the flow lines and the true extinction can then readily be found.

For the determination of the birefringence, polarizer and analyzer are rotated 45° in their fittings, and the compensator is inserted in the suitable slide channel to give subtraction with the combined birefringence of polymer melt and reflection prism. The latter value can be calculated from the Fresnel equations for total reflection. The formula reads[2]:

$$\tan (\phi/2) = \frac{\cos u \ (n^2 \ \sin^2 u - 1)^{\frac{1}{2}}}{n \ \sin^2 u} \qquad (2.1.1)$$

where ϕ is the phase difference due to the mirror, u is the incident angle of light to the plane of mirror, and n is the refractive index of glass relative to air. The theoretical value of the path difference caused by the prism is

60 mµ in green (548 mµ) light. Experimentally the path difference due to the
mirror is measured with the rotor still. The values found are in the range
56 mµ to 64 mµ. This difference between the experimental and theoretical is
probably ascribable to slight setting faults in the prism. If the angle of
incidence u were increased from 45° to 46°, then the theoretical value would
increase to about 64 mµ.

2.1.1 Limitations of Cone-and-Plate Apparatus

Boundary Conditions

One great difference with conventional cone-and-plate devices is contained
in the boundary conditions. Normally, the boundaries are formed by the metal
surfaces $\theta = \pi/2$ and $\theta = \pi/2 - \epsilon$ (spherical polar coordinates), and there is
a free boundary with the atmosphere. In the present case, in addition to the
metal boundaries at $\theta = \pi/2$ and $\theta = \pi/2 - \epsilon$, there are cylindrical metal boundaries at $r = r_1$ and $r = r_2$. This means deviations from the assumed flow pattern at or near these boundaries. For small values of ϵ it is known that the
flow field in a symmetrically adjusted cone-and-plate is given by the equation[3,4]:

$$V_\phi = \omega \; \frac{r \cos \theta}{\sin \epsilon} \qquad\qquad (2.1.2)$$

where ω is the angular velocity of the cone about its axis. We now assume
that the actual cylindrical boundaries at r_1 and r_2 may be replaced by
spherical ones in the case of small ϵ. The requirements now has to be made
that $V_\phi = 0$ at $r = r_1$ and at $r = r_2$ in order to satisfy the condition of no
slip at the metal boundaries. The exact solution for this problem could be
sought by trying to solve the vector Laplace equation in spherical polar coordinates which governs the slow motion of viscous liquids. In attempting this,
the author was unsuccessful. To obtain some estimate for the expected deviations of the flow field from the flow pattern undisturbed by the side walls
at r_1 and r_2 the flow was likened to the flow in a rectangular duct, one large
side wall of which is moving parallel with the channel with a constant speed
V_0. This may be justified by the intuitive consideration that errors induced by
the metal surfaces at $r = r_1$ and $r = r_2$ will only seriously effect the flow at
radial distances from r_i of the order of the gap between the cone and the
plate at r_i. The gap is ϵr_i where ϵ is the angle between the cone and the
plate. The gap is small compared with the local radius and so we do not expect
the curvature of the system to influence the flow field calculations seriously.

The sides of the duct are given by the cartesian coordinate surfaces $z = 0$,
$z = b$, and $y = 0$, $y = a$; the flow field is of the assumed form $V = [V(z,y),0,0]$
with $V(z,a) = V_0$ and $V(z,o) = V(o,y) = V(b,y) = 0$. The error estimate is only
made for Newtonian liquids.

Since the conduit is closed, there can be no pressure gradient in the flow
direction, x. The equation of motion for slow flows then has the simple form:

$$\frac{\partial p_{xy}}{\partial y} + \frac{\partial p_{xz}}{\partial z} = 0 \qquad\qquad (2.1.4)$$

14

With the given assumption that no transverse flow occurs ($V_y = 0$) we have for Newtonian liquids with viscosity η:

$$p_{xy} = \eta \partial V_x / \partial y \qquad (2.1.5)$$

$$p_{xz} = \eta \partial V_x / \partial z \qquad (2.1.6)$$

The equations of motion found by substitution of (2.1.5) and (2.1.6) in (2.1.4) is the Laplace equation:

$$0 = \frac{\partial^2 V_x}{\partial z^2} + \frac{\partial^2 V_x}{\partial y^2} \qquad (2.1.7)$$

The solution for V_x with the given boundary conditions is known as a series of eigen functions which conveniently form a Fourier series. A detailed discussion on this is given by Morse and Feshback[5].

The solution for the velocity distribution reads:

$$V_x = \frac{4V_o}{\pi} \sum_{n \text{ odd}}^{\infty} \frac{1}{n} \sin \frac{n\pi z}{b} \frac{\sinh \dfrac{n\pi y}{b}}{\sinh \dfrac{n\pi a}{b}} \qquad (2.1.8)$$

This result is also quoted by McKelvey[6]. This expression is now used to estimate the possible errors.

A) The velocity gradient dV_x/dy

Light passes through the system in the z direction. The velocity gradient dV_x/dy is chiefly responsible for the birefringence. Seen in the microscope are the metal surfaces $y = 0$ and $y = a$ of the rotor and stator. We are mainly interested in the central region $y = \frac{1}{2} a$, as this corresponds to the centre of the optical image and is therefore the most convenient for observation. For this central region, an average value of the velocity gradient dV_x/dy over the z coordinate is first calculated, in order to find the effect of the boundary surfaces at $z = 0$ and $z = b$. We find:

$$< \frac{\partial V}{\partial y} > = \frac{8}{\pi^2} \frac{V_o}{a} \sum_{n \text{ odd}}^{\infty} \frac{x \cosh xn/2}{n \sinh nx} \, , \qquad x = \frac{\pi a}{b} \qquad (2.1.9)$$

For the cone-and-plate in question $b = 10$ mm and (a) varies from 0.3 to 0.5 mm. For calculation the latter value was used as it leads to more pessimistic estimates of the errors and thus may give an upper bound to them (the largest value of the depth to breadth ratio is involved). The above series is known to converge slowly. Machinal computation is the only practical method of evaluation. To this end use was made of a Bull-General Electric computer type GE-265. After fifty terms the calculated average gradient was constant at 97.79 % of the nominal value, V_o/a. Calculation was stopped after 100 terms. The error in this average velocity gradient is thus less than 2.3 %.

15

To give an impression of the variation of the velocity gradient in the 1-2 plane from the nominal gradient, Fig. 2.3 was prepared. The average gradient in the field of view was calculated as a function of the distance between the still boundary surface (y = 0) and the moving boundary surface (y = a). As can be expected very near the moving boundary surface the average gradient shows important deviations from the nominal value, here taken as 1 s^{-1}. From the figure it can be seen also that the position of closest agreement with the nominal gradient lies at about two thirds of the distance between the still and the moving boundaries. Taking ± 2 % as acceptable for the deviation of the average shear gradient from the nominal gradient, Fig. 2.3 indicates that measurements should be carried out between 0.53 and 0.76 of the distance between the still and the moving boundaries.

B) *The parasitic velocity gradient dV_x/dz*

This gradient differs considerably from zero only near the small side walls in which the windows are placed. Its maximum value is situated on the windows, i.e. at z = 0 and at z = b. Figure 2.4 has been prepared to show the variation of this parasitic gradient on one of the windows as one progresses from the still boundary surface, at y = 0, to the moving boundary surface at y = a. Near the still metal boundary the parasitic gradient is zero; in the middle it takes a value equal to the nominal value of the principal gradient dV_x/dy. It is infinite at the moving boundary. In connection with the observations made at the end of paragraph A) it is useful to see how fast the parasitic gradient dV_x/dz dies on moving from the window surface. Machine calculations based on equation (2.1.8) indicated that at 0.5 mm from the window the parasitic gradient in the centre of the field of vision had dropped to 8.6 % of its value at the window and at 1 mm to 0.01 % of the latter value. Figure 2.5 shows the course of the parasitic gradient as one progresses from one window to the other in the direction of the light beam. The influence of this gradient is such that, in the centre of field of view it induces on the window surface an optical effect equal to the birefringence $(n_{11} - n_{33})$ of the principal gradient[*]. This helps us to estimate the effect of the parasitic gradient on the measured quantities.

If the birefringence is small, contributions to it can simply be added in a vector diagram. Under these circumstances one obtains the following results: for X close to 45° the disturbances at the windows will decrease the limiting birefringence by about 2% and increase the departure of X from 45° by about the same amount. For X is this completely unimportant and the error is acceptable for Δn. When the extinction angle is close to the stream direction (X ∿ 0) the birefringence is hardly changed and again X will be about 2 % too small. This result holds for the central plane (y = a/2) and was obtained from the data shown in Fig. 2.5 and from the course of the shear rate in the 1-2 plane. The errors due to the disturbances caused by the boundaries at r = r$_1$

---

[*]This birefringence is the Δn value measured in the 1-3 plane and is related to $p_{11} - p_{33}$. It is only measureable if the large side walls of the channel are transparent. Cf. Chapter 2.2.

and $r = r_2$ are thus acceptable within the approximation chosen. The actual apparatus has certain features which make the given calculations only rather rough. The windows are not fully flush with the metal boundaries at $r = r_1$ and $r = r_2$. They are sunk by about 0.2 mm. Moreover, the corners of the rectangular cross-section are not infinitely sharp. These complications cannot be properly taken into account.

Apart from the effects just mentioned, the disturbances at the windows cause depolarization at high gradients and as a result further measurement becomes impossible. It usually appears that depolarization occurs at a shear stress of about 10^4 N/m^2 or a little higher. The determining factor is not so much the relative magnitude of the parasitic birefringence, but its absolute magnitude. Light through a stack of randomly orientated plates can be extinguished between polarizing devices only, when the path differences of each plate are very small. When these path differences are not small, extinction is not possible, except when the plates are equally directed. Thus the limiting conditions under which the cone-and-plate device will give measurements are determined by magnitude of the gradients and by the nature of the material under study.

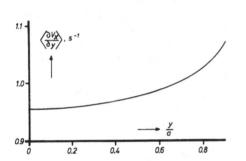

Fig. 2.3 The average value of the principal shear gradient evaluated between the windows, given as a function of the distance y/a between the still and moving boundaries.

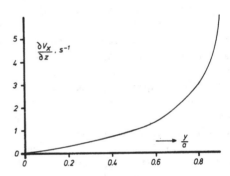

Fig. 2.4 The parasitic gradient at the window, given as function of the distance between the still and moving boundaries. The principal gradient is nominally, 1 s^{-1}.

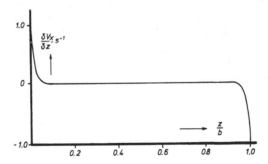

Fig. 2.5 The parasitic gradient in the central place as a function of the distance between the windows. The nominal gradient is 1 s^{-1}.

17

It should always be possible to measure at high shear stresses with optically weak materials if their extinction angles remain close to 45°. On the other hand, an optically strong material should be equally measureable at high gradients if it readily orientates in the flow field, i.e. approaches the orientation of the birefringence caused by the parasitic gradient.

2.1.2. Thermal Stability

All experimental work at elevated temperatures is bounded by the thermal stability of the substance concerned. We can class materials in two groups. The first group spontaneously change or degrade with or without an incubation period. PVC is an example. For this group of materials the cone-and-plate apparatus is at a disadvantage since filling and cleaning are time consuming.

The second group contains materials which are susceptible to attack from the environment. This is generally the oxygen in the atmosphere. Polyolefins are examples here. Against this attack the present cone-and-plate apparatus has great advantages over other cone-and-plate apparatuses: the material is totally enclosed by the metal surfaces. As an added precaution, material obtained from granulate or flocculated suspensions can be pre-moulded under vacuum in order to minimize a possible source of oxygen during the preparatory stage. In order to test the thermal stability of a member of this group and to determine the allowable measurement period, a 24 hours' test was carried out for a sample of high density polyethylene at the unusually high temperature of 240 °C[*]. If exposed to the atmosphere at this temperature, the given polymer would turn brown within a few minutes and char completely within two hours. At regular intervals during the 24 hours' period, the birefringence and the extinction angle were measured; Figs 2.6a and b show the obtained results, which also may serve as an example of the type of measurements, which can be obtained with the described apparatus. For the birefringence, only very small changes were found: a slight increase with time in the region of low gradients. Figure 2.6b shows the results obtained for the extinction angle. Here the changes are clearer: within the first hour nothing happens; after three hours the extinction angle has decreased and continues to decrease during the whole 24 hours' period. The greatest changes occur at the lowest shear gradients.

Normally, measurements are carried out at much lower temperatures. A temperature of 200 °C is quite normal for rheological experiments on this type of material. It was concluded that it would normally be safe to measure at 200 °C on the same sample for three or four hours. Nevertheless, when it was necessary to measure on a polymer for this length of time,"degradation" was checked by a repeat of the measurements made at the beginning of the interval.

---

[*]No extra stabilizer was added to that possibly present in the granules.

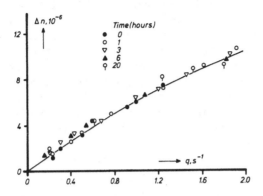

Fig. 2.6a Example of birefringence measurements obtained with the cone-and--plate apparatus during a 24 hours' test.
The material is a high density polyethylene (Marlex 6050) and the temperature is 240 °C. The example shows the good stability of the material when examined by this apparatus.

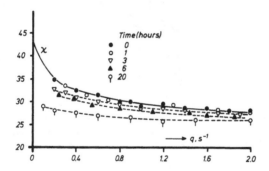

Fig. 2.6b The extinction angle X accompanying Fig. 2.6a. The extinction angle is seen to be more sensititve to degradation effects than the birefringence.

2.2 The Slit Apparatus : Measurements in the 1-3 Plane

The use of slit and capillary devices for the measurement of birefringence effects extends back prior to polymer research[7]. Previous investigations were in the main concerned with non-polymeric liquids such as V_2O_5 sols[8] and experiments were carried out at or near room temperature. Work of this type was carried out in the years before the second world war in order to obtain qualitative information with streaming birefringence in the 1-3 plane. It was considered a great disadvantage that with slits and capillaries the optical effect is an average quantity over the flow field. For this reason, quantitative interpretation was considered impossible[7,8]. Unaware of this historical background, the present author could show that the averaging is very specific and with a few restrictions, quantitative values of the difference $n_{11} - n_{33}$ at the large slit wall can be obtained[9]. With a slit one can also make observations in the 1-2 plane. However, for reasons which will be discussed later, it does not appear possible to make good measurements in this plane.

The present instrument, built for transparent, but also merely translucent materials, such as rubber-modified polystyrene, is of a rugged construction. It was developed from slit viscometers used in flow visualisation studies[10]. In this study slits of differing dimensions were used. They were all built according to the same principle of construction. A schematic drawing of one such slit is given in Fig. 2.7.

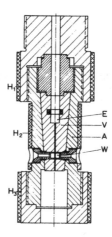

Fig. 2.7 Schematic drawing of essential components of apparatus: H_1, H_2, and H_3 – heating bands; V – conical inner section containing slit; A – outer body; W – windows and holder for 1-3 plane measurements; E – entrance to slit.

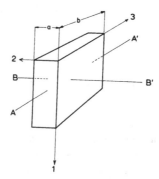

Fig. 2.8 Geometry of flow through the slit: 1, 2 and 3 indicate coordinate system: 1 is flow direction; 2 is the direction of changing shear gradient. AA' for 1-2 plane measurements; BB' for 1-3 plane measurements.

The essential component of the apparatus is a conical member V which fits into a correspondingly machined outer body A. Part V has been split and a slit channel has been machined into it. The width of the channel is here 10 mm and the depth 1 mm. Fitted into the system are a set of glass windows of which two are clearly indicated (W in Fig. 2.7). These windows are situated 35 mm from the entrance of the slit and viewing through them corresponds to viewing along direction BB' in Fig. 2.8. The other four windows correspond with direction AA' in Fig. 2.8. Two of the latter windows are near the entrance, E, of the slit and the other two are situated at the same level as W. The windows fit sufficiently well to avoid perturbation of the flow (they may protrude into the channel by at most 0.02 mm). The temperature of the whole is determined by three independently controlled heating bands H_1, H_2 and H_3. The apparatus can either be mounted on a screw extruder for high shear rates (up to 10^3 s^{-1}) or onto a ram extruder for low shear rates (0.5 to 15 s^{-1}).

If the slit is of a sufficiently large cross-section ratio (width/depth $\geq$ 10) the flow gradient will change sharply only in the 2-direction, and it will be constant over the major portion of the 3-direction of the slit. With plane polarized light in direction AA' any measured birefringence will correspond to the 1-2 plane (Fig. 2.8) and vary with the position of the microscope with respect to the 2-direction. Near the walls of the slit the birefringence will be maximum and in the centre it will be zero. That means that one is not able to obtain measurements near the centre, where one would expect the highest accuracy from the point of view of undisturbed light propagation. Birefringence measurements taken in the direction BB', correspond to the 1-3 plane and the optical effect gives $n_{11} - n_{33}$. However, in the direction BB' the path difference is the sum over an inhomogeneous stress field since the shear stress is zero in the centre plane of the slit and maximum at the walls (see Section 2.5). The optical result then corresponds to an average value over the whole stress field. Actually measured by the compensator is the path difference P. If one takes a shear layer,dy, at a distance from the centre plane of the slit, then its contribution to the total path difference will be:

$$dP = (n_{11} - n_{33})\,dy \qquad\qquad (2.2.1)$$

The total path difference will be:

$$P = 2 \int_0^{a/2} (n_{11} - n_{33})\,dy \qquad\qquad (2.2.2)$$

where, a, is the depth of the slit in the direction BB'.

This is an equation of the type which will also be met in the section on slit viscometry. It is based on the assumption of symmetry with respect to the central plane. To obtain the solution, the assumption is made that the shear stress, τ, varies linearly in the direction BB'. This is always true when the pressure distribution along the slit is linear and a very good approximation when the pressure distribution is non-linear (corrections of the order $a^3\,d^3P/dx^3$ need to be added). Equation (2.2.2) then becomes on using the proportionality of the shear stress to y:

$$P = \frac{a}{\tau_w} \int_0^{\tau_w} (n_{11} - n_{33}) d\tau \qquad (2.2.3)$$

where τ_w is the shear stress at the wall. The average birefringence is simply P/a. If this is termed, ϕ, then the solution of the above equation, as obtained by a rearrangement and differentiation with respect to τ_w, is:

$$(n_{11} - n_{33})_w = \phi(1 + \frac{d \ln \phi}{d \ln \tau_w}) \qquad (2.2.4)$$

where the subscript, w, indicates that the quantities concerned are to be taken at the wall of the die. Quantity ϕ is measured as a function of τ_w and the relation (2.2.4) allows one to calculate $(n_{11} - n_{33})_w$ as a function of τ_w.[*] The restrictions on the validity of this relation are not so severe as in the case of the corresponding Rabinowitsch equation for the velocity gradient (see Section 2.5). In steady flow, at a given stress level, the birefringence is either independent of the temperature or only a weak function of it. Also it is probable that pressure can only exert a very weak effect although there have been no experiments to confirm this. However, the above result, i.e. (2.2.4) is only of general validity at sufficiently large distances downstream so that the entrance stresses due to longitudinal gradients have died away.

More than one slit was used in this investigation. The essential dimensions of all the slits which were used, are given in the Table 2.1.

Table 2.1

slit	length (l) (mm)	depth (a) (mm)	breadth (b) (mm)	l/a
A	50	1	10	35;15
B	50	1	30	35;15
C	50	2.5	30	15;6
C1	58	1	20	60
C2	58	0.6	2	96
D	50	1	10	35

The slit C was large enough for slits C1 and C2 to be inserted into its channel. All slits, except slit D, had flat entrances. Slit D has a gradual opening at its entrance as it was built to avoid dead corners with PVC extrusion. The object in using so many slits was to check the influence of the slit aspect ratio on the optical performance and secondly to examine the influence of the channel length on the orientation.

[*]Later in the text the symbol $<n_{11} - n_{33}>$ is sometimes used instead of ϕ.

Measurements in the 1-2 plane

The slit device can also be used for measuring the birefringence
$\Delta n(= n_I - n_{II})$ in the 1-2 plane, where the principal values n_I and n_{II} should
not be confused with the components n_{11} and n_{22} which are related to the corresponding normal stresses p_{11} and p_{22}. (Cf. Eqs (1.3.3), 1.3.6) and (1.4.2)).
Measurement takes place in the direction AA' (Fig. 2.8). In view of the linear
stress field which should be seen in the ocular, one expects zero optical effect
in the centre of the field and an increasing optical effect on both sides of a
central dark line. In white light this means coloured bands on either side of
a symmetrically placed black line. In addition, one expects an extra black band
parallel to the central band (line) but positioned according to extinction
angle, χ: at an arbitrary orientation of the crossed polarizers somewhere on
one side of the central line, the main directions of the refractive index
ellipsoid will coincide with the directions of the polarizers. On rotation of
the polarizers, a dark line should shift over the whole field. However, it
turns out to be very difficult to make effective measurements in this plane.
The first difficulty, which arises from alignment, is here more important than
in other devices, owing to the non-homogeneous structure of the flow field. A
good alignment is obtained by illuminating the slit with convergent light and
adjusting the slit until the outcoming reflections from the two walls are symmetrically placed. The finer adjustment by which the image in the microscope
is made perfectly symmetrical, then follows. It now turns out that with polymer melts and white light, there is no central black fringe except when the
analyzer-polarizer combination is orientated in the stream direction or when
the outputs are relatively low. The cause of this effect, which was not originally foreseen, is a parasitic shear flow (q_{13}) against the viewing windows.
More serious is the absence of a clear fringe which should represent the extinction angle. The best that can be seen with polyethylene and polystyrene
melts is a shadow covering one half of the image. The reasons for this failure
are still not fully clear. There appear to be two main causes, both of which
can give rise to the mixing of phase differences. As a consequence of these
effects the extinction angle becomes indistinct.

A) *Wall effects* : Owing to the absence of slip, the orientation of the material is determined by a parasitic shear stress on the window as well as by the
main shear stress on the larger wall. As a result, the light beam passes
through regions of different orientation. This leads to errors of the kind mentioned at the end of 2.1.1. A further complication, possibly associated principally with the wall effect in as far as the birefringence is highest there,
is the splitting of the light beam into ordinary and extraordinary beams. This
manifestation has been seen with polyethylene melts where at very high shear
stresses the emerging (and diverging) light beam contains differently polarized
elements even when the ingoing light was unpolarized.

B) *Friction heating* : Friction heating always takes place. In equilibrium at
some distance from the entrance to the conduit, the melt will be at a higher
temperature in the centre than at the walls. The melt then acts as a lens diverging any passing light. The existence and importance of this effect could be

23

demonstrated by observations on a highly viscous PMMA. This material is optically isotropic at temperatures of about 150 °C. Extrusion of this material at this temperature was associated with a large lens effect; the temperature distribution could be measured with the help of the requisite Schlieren optics. It appears that even quite small temperature gradients are sufficient to cause serious mixing of light rays passing zones of varying birefringences.

Measurements in the 1-2 plane may nevertheless become necessary in order to estimate the stress optical coefficient required for further interpretation of the 1-3 plane measurements with a slit. For example, some materials, such as rigid PVC are unsuitable for measurement with the cone-and-plate apparatus at elevated temperatures (circa 200 °C). The stress optical coefficient then has to be estimated from the 1-2 plane results of the slit via the relation:

$$\Delta n \sin 2X = 2Cp_{12} \qquad\qquad (2.2.5)$$

One uses monochromatic light. The analizer and polarizer are crossed and set parallel and perpendicular to the flow direction. The distribution of fringes is measured in a microscope. Each fringe corresponds to a path difference $m\lambda$ ($m = 0, 1, 2, \ldots$), where λ is the wave length of the light concerned. The measurements at one output then lead to the relation between the shear stress and Δn. Measurements can also be made at a second output as a check. It appears that the procedure always is accompanied by a large amount of scatter. The polystyrenes and the polyethylenes are not measurable at very high shear stresses owing to the lens effect arising from A or B. The value found for Δn from each fringe is set out against the shear stress calculated for the location of the fringe, on the assumption that the shear stress increased linearly from the central plane to the wall. The shear stress at the wall is found by slit-viscometry (see Ch. 2.5). The initial slope of Δn vs shear stress (linear paper) is evaluated to obtain the stress optical coefficient C ($\sin 2X = 1$ in the limit of zero shear stress). A few examples of this method will be shown in Chapter 5.

In one recent publication, other authors obtained, with a slit apparatus very similar to the one described, successful optical measurements, including the extinction angle, in the 1-2 plane[11]. We point out here, however, that they only showed results for the low stress region, i.e. less than 10^4 N/m². The present attempts were more aimed at the high stress region, i.e. 10^5 N/m² and higher, as the low stress region was covered by the cone-and-plate apparatus.

2.3 The Capillary Apparatus : Measurements in the 2-3 Plane

Freundlich[12] shew the existence of non-zero $n_{22} - n_{33}$ for V_2O_5 sols by viewing along the axis of a short capillary. Later, Philippoff made the first serious attempts to quantify and classify different materials by this method[13]. With the help of a capillary and, at a later date, with the help of a slit, by viewing along the axis between crossed nicols, he tried to measure the optical effect ascribable to $n_{33} - n_{22}$. With the polymeric materials he examined, which were in the freely flexible state, he was unable to detect an effect and therefore concluded that for these systems $n_{22} - n_{33}$ must be zero. The solutions that he examined were highly elastic; melts of high viscosity were not examined. He could show, as is expected theoretically, that suspensions of rigid particles (also certain polymer solutions with suitable solvent) gave a very strong effect corresponding to a non-zero $n_{22} - n_{33}$. For the examination of molten polymers, this author built a sturdy device based on the apparatus of Philippoff. Figure 2.9 is a diagrammatic representation of the main features

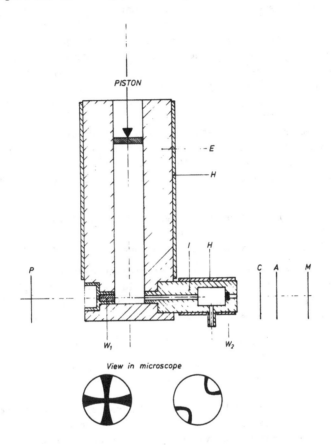

Fig. 2.9 *Diagrammatic representation of the main features of the apparatus.*
E (cylinder); H (heating bands); W_1 and W_2 (windows); I (capillary);
C (compensator); P (polarizer); A (analyzer); M (microscope).

of the apparatus. The body of the apparatus is formed by a hollow cylinder of nitrided steel E, inner diameter 15 mm, outer diameter 75 mm. At the lower end the cylinder E has been drilled to make room for a window W_1 and for the capillary I. The capillary projects out of the cylinder. The inner diameter of the capillaries was usually 2.67 mm and the inner surface was honed. Three capillaries of length 40 mm, 20 mm and 7 mm were used. Heating elements H completely surround all parts. Temperature can be controlled to within 1 °C at four places in the system (one in the capillary and three in block E). The light path is schematically given in this figure; light passes through a polarizing sheet P, then through a first window W_1, axially along the capillary, through a second window W_2. Finally it passes through a compensator C and analyzing polaroid, and into the observer's microscope M.

The reservoir R is first filled either with granulate or with melt. The necessary time is allowed for thermal equilibrium and the piston which is controlled by a variable speed motor,is set in motion. In the viewer's microscope (Fig. 2.9 under) a typical Maltese cross is seen on flow, with the microscope focussed in the capillary. During compensation (the compensator is set at 45° to the crossed polarized sheets) the cross splits into two fringes which move towards the edge formed by the wall of the capillary. Compensation is achieved when the apex of each fringe is judged to be at the wall of the die. In general the view in the microscope is fairly symmetric, considering the amount of gel particles and dust always present in commercial melts, and the fact that the downward exit from the chamber before W_2 had to be placed asymmetrically. Measurements could not ordinarily be carried out at gradients which would lead to birefringences much greater than 10^{-5}, as extinction with the compensator became progressively difficult. This, we must assume, is the result of depolarization caused by:

1) the bending over of the flow lines near the entrance and the exit;
2) a mixing effect due to frictional heating;
3) a mixing effect caused by beam splitting due to the birefringence.

The last effect is perceptible in any birefringent medium of sufficient working thickness, when the light beam does not coincide with a principle optic axis.

The shear stress was not obtained directly with the apparatus. Instead, the measured path differences were correlated to the reduced output D_c.

$$D_c = \frac{4}{\pi} \frac{Q}{R^3} \qquad (2.3.1)$$

where Q is the volume output per unit of time and R is the radius of the capillary.

Each material investigated had to be calibrated so that a correction (the so-called Rabinowitsch correction) could be applied to obtain the gradient at the walls of the die from the D_c values[14]. In order to examine the influence of the entrance and the exit disturbances, the optical effects were measured with a set of capillaries of varying length and set out against the length of the capillary.

2.4 Measurement of the Path Difference

There are many methods, a full description of all of them is beyond the scope of the present work. In the simplest case the phase difference between two plane polarized rays of monochromatic light vibrating in perpendicular planes amounts to an integral multiple of 2π, say, $2\pi m$. The emergent light is then extinguished by the analyzer. The birefringence is then given by:

$$\Delta n = m \frac{\lambda}{d} \qquad (2.4.1)$$

where λ is the wavelength of the light concerned, and d the thickness of the working section. In liquids, m can be found for monochromatic light by steadily increasing the shear stress and counting the extinctions as they pass by: the first gives m = 1, the second m = 2, etc.

Under normal circumstances, one requires measurements of path differences which are fractions of the wavelength being used. In the present work, this was achieved chiefly by the use of the Ehringhaus compensator[15], well-known to the users of polarizing microscopes. The principal of this compensator lies in the use of a rotating combination of two crystals of quartz or calcite. The combination is placed in the path of the light ray immediately after the double refracting material to be measured. The crystals have been cut and combined, so that no phase difference is present when the combination is in an exactly perpendicular position with respect to the light beam. On rotation about a principal axis perpendicular to the light path, a birefringence effect is produced. By placing the axis of rotation of the instrument successively in two mutually perpendicular positions, the subtraction position can be found and, in this way, the sign of the birefringence effect can be determined. In use the apparatus is simple: it is set so that the axis of rotation of the crystal coincides with one of the extinction directions of the material to be measured. The crystal is rotated, producing a phase shift, which either adds to or subtracts from the phase shift produced by the material. With monochromatic light extinction is then obtained when the sum of the path differences is an integral multiple of 2π. In normal use the subtraction position is used and the method is one of compensation. The relation between the crystal rotation, read from a scaled drum, and the phase shift, is supplied in a manual of the manufacturer (Carl Zeiss, Oberkochen, Württ.). The tables were spot checked and found to be very accurate. Compensation carried out in this way always gives the phase difference apart from some multiple of 2π. The multiple is not directly obtainable in monochromatic light, but is usually evident if one, for instance, works with steadily increasing stresses. It can also be determined by using white light as extinction only occurs in this case, when the phase shift produced by the crystals is equal but opposite in sign to that of the material.

2.5 The Slit Viscometer

Viscosities can be determined with dies of rectangular cross-section. When the ratio of the longer side to the shorter side, i.e. the aspect ratio, is sufficiently great, the system approximates to two parallel plates. The advantage of slit viscometry over the more common capillary viscometry using capillaries of circular cross-section, is that the measurement of the pressure gradient in the flow direction is easily made at the wall of the die. An essential requirement for such measurements is that the pressure device does not influence the flow. For this reason measurements of the pressures are made with electronic pressure gauges[16], for which the transducer displacement is very small, relative to the dimensions of the slit channel.

For Newtonian fluids the influence of the edge effects in infinitely long ducts is known exactly for all aspect ratios of the slit - at least in the slow flow region. Experimental investigations have verified the solutions for slits of aspect ratios less than ten[17]. In a previous investigation[18] with polyethylene melts, it was found that there were no measurable, systematic, differences between dies of aspect ratios 10 : 1, 20 : 1, and 30 : 1.

The assumption is now made that, for experimental purposes, an aspect ratio of 10 : 1 or greater is sufficient to achieve a reasonable approximation to fluid behaviour between two infinite parallel planes.

The physically measured quantity is the distribution of the normal pressure, P_{22}, along the wall of the slit channel. When the distribution is linear, the shear stress at the wall of the die is given by the slope of the pressure distribution.

$$P_{21,w} = \tau_w = -\frac{b}{2}\frac{dP_{22}}{dx} \qquad (2.5.1)$$

where b is the depth of the slit and x is the distance of a pressure gauge from the slit entrance. Often a linear pressure distribution along the die is not obtained. In this case equation (2.5.1) gives the local shear stress at the wall of the die to within a very good approximation. The full expression contains higher derivatives as well, but these lead to corrections of the order of 0.01 % only. The normal pressure, P_{22}, consists of a hydrostatic component and a deviatoric component. The deviatoric component for the usual conditions of flow rate, temperature, etc., is estimated to be of the order of a few bars at most and, probably nearly constant along the slit. Its precise value is determined by the stress conditions at the die exit. Under the conditions of this work, P_{22}, can be equated to the hydrostatic pressure.

To obtain the viscosity, having obtained the shear stress at the wall, one needs the velocity gradient at the wall. This is obtained from a version of the Rabinowitsch correction already known for capillary flow[14]. The volumetric output, Q, per unit of time is to the usual approximation given by:

$$Q = 2 b \int_0^{a/2} V(y)dy \qquad (2.5.2)$$

where b is the breadth of the slit and V(y) the velocity at a distance y from the plane of flow symmetry (conditions of laminar flow). The first assumption needed for the present purpose is, that slip does not occur at the die wall. Partial integration then leads to:

$$Q = 2 b \int_0^{a/2} y \frac{dV}{dy} dy \qquad (2.5.3)$$

The absence of slip condition has been experimentally confirmed for unfilled polymers under normal processing conditions by direct observation on several systems[10,19]. The variable under the integral may be transformed by using the already mentioned linear relation between the shear stress and the distance y of a shear plane from the central plane. In this way one finds:

$$\frac{6 Q}{ba^2} = D_s = \frac{3}{\tau_w^2} \int_0^{\tau_w} \tau q d\tau \qquad (2.5.4)$$

28

where q (= dV/dy) is the shear gradient and τ is the shear stress at y. Quantity D_s is called the reduced output. By introducing the factor 6 on both sides of the equation, D_s has become the shear rate at the wall, if the investigated fluid is Newtonian. The solution to (2.5.4) is found by rearrangement and by differentiation with respect to τ_w. There is obtained:

$$q_w = D_s \left[\frac{2}{3} + \frac{1}{3} \frac{d \ln D_s}{d \ln \tau_w} \right] \qquad (2.5.5)$$

There are two restrictions to the above relation. The flow should be isothermal and the viscosity should not depend on the hydrostatic pressure. The isothermal condition means that not only should the melt entering the duct be at the correct temperature, but also shear heating should be absent. The pressure condition can be relaxed by evaluating the shear stress at a constant pressure level, i.e. at places along the slit which depend on the reduced output D_s. Usually, the shear stress is evaluated at the exit of the slit, corresponding to zero hydrostatic pressure. When the above conditions are fulfilled the relation between the shear gradient at the wall and the reduced output becomes:

$$q_w = D_s \left(\frac{2 + n}{3} \right) \qquad (2.5.6)$$

where n = d log D_s/d log τ_w is simply the slope on a log-log plot of the experimental relation between D_s and τ_w. This relation in combination with the shear stress at the wall allows one to determine the viscosity as function of the shear gradient. The corresponding relation for circular capillaries reads[14]:

$$q_w = D_c \left(\frac{3 + n}{4} \right) \qquad (2.5.7)$$

where D_c is given by (2.3.1) and n = d log D_c/d log τ_w for this case.

A slight peculiarity of the slit (or capillary) viscometer method becomes apparent: one obtains properties of the material at an interface. One cannot be completely sure that this is not somehow different from the properties of the bulk material.

Since, however, the boundary surfaces are not smooth on a molecular scale, the foregone results for finding the stress and the gradient at the wall must allude to an average boundary formed in part by the container walls and in part by the bulk material. If, in fact, the interface was important, then changes in the container, in material, in surface smoothness, should produce noticeable effects. Whilst such effects have been reported from time to time[20] there does not seem to be any reason that for normal, unfilled, polymer melts of this investigation a wall effect might be present (cf. Ref. 10).

References

1) J.L.S. Wales, H. Janeschitz-Kriegl, *J. Polymer Sci.* A2 *5*, 781 (1967).

2) A.C.S. van Heel, *"Inleiding in de Optica"*, M. Nijhoff, s-Gravenhage 1958, p. 133.

3) A.N. Fredrickson, *"Principles and Applications of Rheology"*, p. 209, Prentice Hall, Englewood Cliff 1964.

4) J.G. Oldroyd, *Proc. Roy. Soc. (London)* A *245*, 278 (1958).

5) P.M. Morse and H. Feshback, *"Methods of Theoretical Physics"*, p. 706, New York 1953.

6) J.M. McKelvey, *"Polymer Processing"*, J. Wiley, New York, London 1962, p. 99.

7) G. Boehm, *"Handbuch der biologische Arbeitsmethoden"*, *Vol. 2, Part 3/2*, Ed. E. Abderhalden, Urban and Schwarzenberg, Berlin, Vienna 1939, p. 3939.

8) H. Freundlich, F. Stapelfeld, H. Zocher, *Z. phys. Chem. 114*, 161 (1924-1925).

9) J.L.S. Wales, *Rheol. Acta 8*, 38 (1969).

10) J.L. den Otter, J.L.S. Wales, J. Schijf, *Rheol. Acta 6*, 205 (1967).

11) C.D. Han, L.H. Drexler, *J. Appl. Polymer Sci. 17*, 2329 (1973).

12) H. Diesselhorst and N. Freundlich, *Physik. Z. 16*, 419 (1915).

13) W. Philippoff, *Trans. Soc. Rheol. 5*, 149 (1961).

14) B. Rabinowitsch, *Z. phys. Chemie 145*, 1 (1929).

15) A. Ehringhaus, *Z. Kristallog. 76*, 315 (1931).

16) J. Schijf, *Plastica 20*, 156 (1967).

17) D.B. Holmes, *K.N.C.V. Symposium "Hanteren van Viskeuze Vloeistoffen"*, *Deel* 319 May (1967).

18) J.L.S. Wales, J.L. den Otter, H. Janeschitz-Kriegl, *Rheol. Acta 4*, 146 (1965).

19) G.J. Reusswig, F.G. Ling, *Appl. Sci. Res. 21*, 260 (1969).

20) R. Berger, *Plast. u. Kautschuk 19/2*, 113 (1972).

3. Materials

Most measurements described in this work were performed on melts of poly-styrene (PS), low density polyethylene (LDPE), high density polyethylene (HDPE), polydimethylsiloxane (PDMS), polypropylene (PP), and polyvinylchloride (PVC). The following table gives the specific materials used, the experiments carried out, and the temperature of measurement.

Table 3.I

polymer	name	temperature(s)	measurements
PS	Styron 666	140-200	1,2,3,5,6
	Styron 678	140-190	1,3,4,5,6
	Styron 475	140-190	3
	BASF 3	150-220	1,3,4,6
	S111	190	1,3,5,6
	PC 3a	200	1,3,5
	PC 4a	168	1
	PC 5a	200	1
	PC 6a	214	1,3,5
	PC 7a	158	1,3,5
	PC 14a	242	1
LDPE	Alkathene 2	190	3
	LDND	150	1,5
	LDBD	150	1,5
	IUPAC A	150,190	1,3,4,5
HDPE	HDND	150	1,5
	HDBD	150	1,5
	Marlex 6050	190	1,3,4,5,6
PDMS	Siloprene RS	22	1,4,5,6
	E 302	22,105,190	1
PP	PPND	210	1,5
	PPBD	210	1,5
PVC	Solvic 229	180-210	2

The measurements performed were:

1 = Δn and χ in the 1-2 plane with the cone-and-plate apparatus

2 = Δn in the 1-2 plane with the slit apparatus

3 = $(n_{11} - n_{33})$ of the 1-3 plane with the slit apparatus

4 = $(n_{22} - n_{33})$ of the 2-3 plane with the capillary apparatus

5 = viscosity with either capillary, slit or cone-and-plate apparatus

6 = dynamic shear moduli $G'(\omega)$ and $G''(\omega)$

Styron 666, 678 and 475 are general purpose and injection moulding grades
of polystyrene produced by the Dow Chemical Corporation, Midland, Michigan,
U.S.A. The same company kindly supplied the narrow molecular weight distribution polystyrene S111. PC 3a to 14a are polystyrenes of narrow molecular
weight distribution supplied by the Pressure Chemical Company of Pittsburgh,
Pennsylvania, U.S.A. BASF 3 was obtained from the BASF, Ludwigshafen, Germany.

The polyethylenes were obtained from I.C.I., Welwyn Garden City, England
(Alkathene 2); Monsanto Chemicals Limited, Newport, Monmouth, England (LDND
and LDBD)*; BASF (IUPAC A); and Dow Chemicals (HDBD and HDND). The last mentioned polymers have been the subject of IUPAC Working Party investigations[3)7)].

The polypropylenes were from the Shell Plastics Laboratory, Delft, Holland
(PPND and PPBD).

The polydimethylsiloxanes were commercial polymers supplied by Bayer, Lever-
kusen (Siloprene RS) and by Midland Silicones (E 302).

The polyvinylchloride, Solvic 229, was supplied by Solvay & Cie, Brussels,
Belgium.

Molecular Weights

One of the aims of this investigation is to study the relation between the
molecular weight and its distribution on the rheological properties. A full and
complete knowledge of the molecular weight distribution is not possible. The
nearest approximation that exists is a Gel Permeation Chromatogram (GPC). However, the details of the high molecular weight tail, so important for the rheological properties, is often obscured and the interpretation of GPC curves is
still a matter for investigation. In practice only two molecular weight averages are regularly determined: M_n the number average molecular weight, and M_w
the weight average molecular weight. Even these quantities are difficult to obtain with confidence to within 10 % and literature values for commercial polymers can show disparities as great as 50 %. [In the table 3.2. examples of
such great disparities are to be found.] The higher averages M_z and M_{z+1} can be
determined either from sedimentation equilibrium experiments (ultracentrifuge)
or from an analysis of the GPC curves. The accuracy of these latter methods for
the higher averages is less than that for the number and weight average molecular weights. The data available on the measured polymers is given in the following table, together with the source.

*LD = low density; HD = high density; ND = narrow, BD = broad distribution of
  molecular weights.

Table 3.2

material	molecular weights in 100,000				source
	M_n	M_w	M_z	M_{z+1}	
1a	1.54	1.6	-	-	1
	2.54	1.63	1.76	(2.26)	2
3a	3.92	3.93	-	-	1
	4.02	3.93	4.21	-	2
4a	0.98	0.96	-	-	1
	-	0.94	0.98	-	2
5a	4.04	5.07	-	-	1
	4.35	5.20	5.93	(6.77)	2
6a	7.35	8.62	-	-	1
	-	7.90	8.30	-	2
7a	0.49	0.51	0.54	-	2
14a	16.1	17.0	-	-	1
	-	14.2	15.8	-	2
S111	2.14	2.24	-	-	3
Styron 666	1.08	2.71	6.0	12.0	4
	0.92	2.3	-	-	5
	1.66	3.66	-	-	6
Styron 678	0.90	2.40	5.3	11.0	4
BASF 3	0.82	4.1	12.5	18.0	2
HDND	0.11	0.44	-	-	3
HDBD	0.11	1.6	12	-	3
LDND	0.2	1.0	3.0	-	3
LDBD	0.15	2.5	24	-	3
IUPAC A	1.17	5.4	-	-	7
Marlex 6050	0.1	0.84	-	-	8
	0.12	1.53	9	-	9
Solvic 229	0.67	1.4	2.5	3.7	4

Literature

1) Data Pressure Chemical Company.

2) H. Scholte, Dutch State Mines, Private Communication.

3) See J.L.S. Wales, *Pure and Applied Chemistry 20*, 331 (1969).

4) J.L.S. Wales, *TNO Internal Report*.

5) I.J. Chen, D.C. Bogue, *Trans. Soc. Rheol. 16:I*, 59 (1972).

6) H.J. Karam, K. Hyon, J.C. Bellinger, *Trans. Soc. Rheol. 13:2*, 209 (1969).

7) J. Meissner, IUPAC Working Party "The Relation between Structure and Properties of Commercial Polymers", Report to be published.

8) R. Precher, R. Panaris, H. Benoit, *Die Makrom. Chemie 156*, 39 (1972).

9) R. Koningsveld, A.J. Staverman, *J. Polymer Sci. A2*, 325 (1968).

34

4. Theories

4.1 Molecular Theories

Molecular theories of the hydrodynamic behaviour of polymeric systems began to appear some thirty years ago with the work of Kuhn[1]. At that time particular interest was paid to dilute solutions. The first requirements of any molecular theory are expressions for the refractive index and the stress tensors. For relations with these quantities only some special features are identical. and melts, the same or similar expressions may be used for the contribution of each molecular chain to the total macroscopic effect. Sometimes a whole molecule is considered as a "chain", sometimes only a segment of a molecule, e.g. between two "entanglements". The final macroscopic effect is to be obtained by the simple sum over all the chains present.

The Stress Tensor

The contribution, Δp_{ij}, of a single chain to the macroscopic stress, p_{ij}, is given by:

$$\Delta p_{ij} = - \langle x_i F_j \rangle \tag{4.1.1}$$

where x_i is the x_i $(i = 1,2,3)$ coordinate of one chain end with respect to an origin of coordinates at the other end and is, therefore, essentially the probability that the chain crosses a unit area on the j,k plane; F_j is the x_j component of the statistical force exerted between the chain ends and $\langle \ \rangle$ signifies that the whole needs to be averaged by the distribution function of the chain ends. The above expression has been derived in a simple way by Hermans[2] and more rigorously by Kramers[3]. Similar expressions have also been given by Kirkwood and Riseman[4] (using the Oseen expression for the perturbation of the solvent velocity field); Fixman[5], and others[6-9] who studied the application of the time correlation method to polymer chain dynamics.

To (4.1.1) there should be added a term due to the momentum transfer between the particles. This correction is important for low molecular weight liquids, but along with other corrections is considered negligible for polymeric solutions and melts in the normal range of shear rates. The macroscopic stress p_{ij} is obtained by summing over all the molecular chains, m, present and reads:

$$p_{ij} = - \sum_m \frac{N_a c_m}{M_m} \langle x_i F_j \rangle_m \tag{4.1.2}$$

where N_a is Avogadro's number and c_m the concentration of the chains of molecular weight M_m. The simple addition of the supposed average contribution of each molecule to form the total macroscopic stress is one of the basic hypothesis of these molecular theories. The traditional model thus assumes all interactions can be smoothed out in order to form the average medium in which each molecule is free to react to the forces acting upon it.

The Refractive Index Tensor

Refraction is described by a refractive index n related to the polarization, β_m, per molecule formed by the chain elements in vacuum and the reaction field from the surrounding elements.

$$\frac{n^2 - 1}{n^2 + 2} = \frac{4}{3} \pi \sum_m \beta_m \frac{N_a c_m}{M_m} \qquad (4.1.3)$$

where again N_a is Avogadro's number, c_m the concentration, and M_m the molecular weight of the species m. The above is the Lorentz-Lorenz relation which is only strictly valid if the molecular dipoles are in structures of cubic or tetrahedral symmetry[10]. For the anisotropic state the above relation is assumed valid when corresponding components of the refractive index and polarizability tensors replace n and β_m[11]. This leads to:

$$[\frac{n^2 - 1}{n^2 + 2} - \frac{6n^2}{(n^2 + 2)^2}] \delta_{ij} + \frac{6n}{(n^2 + 2)^2} n_{ij} = \frac{4}{3} \pi \sum_m \beta_{ij}^m \frac{N_a c_m}{M_m} \qquad (4.1.4)$$

where n is now the average refractive index given by $3n = n_{11} + n_{22} + n_{33}$.

The quantities which are obtainable from birefringence experiments are $n_{11} - n_{22}$, $n_{11} - n_{33}$, $n_{22} - n_{33}$ and n_{12}. We are not interested in the isotropic term factoring δ_{ij}.

For the measurable quantities there is obtained:

$$n_{ii} - n_{jj} = \frac{2\pi}{9} \frac{(n^2 + 2)^2}{n} \sum_m \frac{N_a c_m}{M_m} (\beta_{ii} - \beta_{jj})_m \qquad (4.1.5)$$

There is now needed an expression for $\beta_{ii} - \beta_{jj}$, the anisotropy of the molecule. We follow the path originally taken by Kuhn and Grün[12], and smooth out the real optical structure of the chain by using average random link quantities. The assumption is made that the polarizabilities of the random links are additive and independent of the various chain conformations. Both assumptions are disputable; the reaction field round a dipole is a function of the neighbours of the dipole and their orientation.

The process of averaging out the bond polarizabilities into polarizabilities of random links takes the first point, at least partially, into account. In doing this we lose, however, the possibility of interpreting the results quantitatively in terms of the molecular structure of the chains. The second point implies that the Lorentz-Lorenz field will not be correct when the material is seriously orientated. This point will be discussed later.

To each of the N random links, which constitute the chain, is assigned a polarizibility α_1 in the axial direction and a polarizability α_2 perpendicular to this direction. Kuhn and Grün showed that as long as one can neglect saturation effects (which is the case for deformations small compared with the chain contour length), the mean optical anisotropy of a chain, $\Delta\gamma$, after averaging over all possible conformations at fixed end-to-end distance r, is given by:

$$\Delta\gamma = \frac{3}{5}(\alpha_1 - \alpha_2)\frac{r^2}{r_0^2} \tag{4.1.6}$$

where $(\alpha_1 - \alpha_2)$ is the optical anisotropy of the random link; r_0^2 the mean square of the end-to-end distance of the chain in undeformed state. The components of the chain polarizability, β_{ij}, in the laboratory frame of reference are given by:

$$\beta_{ij} = \langle\gamma_2\rangle\,\delta_{ij} + \langle(\gamma_1 - \gamma_2)\cos\theta_i\cos\theta_j\rangle \tag{4.1.7}$$

where θ_i is the angle between the chain end-to-end vector and the i coordinate axis; $(\gamma_1 - \gamma_2) = \Delta\gamma$. Also $\langle\gamma_2\rangle$ is a function of the chain stretching and is given by:

$$\langle\gamma_2\rangle = N\left(\frac{\alpha_1 + 2\alpha_2}{3}\right) - \frac{1}{5}(\alpha_1 - \alpha_2)\frac{\langle r^2\rangle}{r_0^2} \tag{4.1.8}$$

where N is the number of random links. If one end of the chain is held at the origin of coordinates and the other at (x_1, x_2, x_3), $\cos\theta_i$ reads:

$$\cos\theta_i = \frac{x_i}{r} \tag{4.1.9}$$

By substituting (4.1.6) with (4.1.9) in (4.1.7) there is obtained for β_{ij}:

$$\beta_{ij} = \langle\gamma_2\rangle\delta_{ij} + \frac{3}{5}(\alpha_1 - \alpha_2)\frac{\langle x_i x_j\rangle}{r_0^2} \tag{4.1.10}$$

and for the birefringence:

$$n_{ii} - n_{jj} = \frac{6\pi}{45}\frac{(n^2 + 2)^2}{n}(\alpha_1 - \alpha_2)\,\Sigma\,\frac{N_a c_m}{M_m}\frac{\langle x_i^2 - x_j^2\rangle_m}{r_0^2} \tag{4.1.11}$$

The extinction angle, X, for shear flow in the 1-2 plane follows:

$$\cot 2X = \frac{n_{11} - n_{22}}{2\,n_{12}} = \frac{\langle x_1^2 - x_2^2\rangle}{2\langle x_1 x_2\rangle} \tag{4.1.12}$$

The Stress-Optical Relation

Let us remark that if the linear expression from rubber elasticity for the force between the chain ends is applied, we automatically obtain the stress-optical relations 1.4.1. and 1.4.2.

The force between the chain ends is[11]:

$$\underline{F} = -2\mu\, kT\,\underline{r} \tag{4.1.13}$$

37

where μ is a function of the mean square end-to-end distance in equilibrium.

$$\mu = 3/2r_o^2 \qquad (4.1.14)$$

When this expression is combined with (4.1.2) it is immediately found that the orientations of the stress tensor and the optic tensor coincide and that the deviatoric components are related by linear relations[13].

$$n_{11} - n_{22} = C(p_{11} - p_{22}) \qquad (4.1.15)$$

$$n_{11} - n_{33} = C(p_{11} - p_{33}) \qquad (4.1.16)$$

$$n_{12} = C\ p_{12} \qquad (4.1.17)$$

where C is a deformation independent parameter, i.e. the stress optical coefficient given by:

$$C = \frac{2\ \pi}{45\ kT}\ \frac{(n^2 + 2)^2}{n}\ (\alpha_1 - \alpha_2) \qquad (4.1.18)$$

4.2 The Distribution Function (Basic Theory)

The averages $<F_i x_j>$ and $<x_i x_j>$ needed for the stress and refractive index tensors, have to be supplied by a distribution function. In the course of this chapter it will be seen that it is often only necessary to obtain the differential equation governing the distribution function and not have to solve it explicitly. The basic procedure is to obtain a Smoluchowski equation for chains. In one of the original treatments, Kirkwood[14] formulated the equation in terms of a real chain space. Kirkwood hoped to relate the hydrodynamic behaviour of the real chain to the hydrodynamic resistances of its individual atomic groups. This is now thought to have been too optimistic and consequently one replaces the atomic structure by a model structure. The real chain is hereby replaced by a row of N point resistances – "beads" – connected by springs, subject to ordinary hydrodynamic friction. The points are sufficiently far apart that their actions are uncorrelated; a complete description of all their movements therefore requires a 3N-dimensional space.

One begins by writing down the equation for the conservation of mass. In terms of the distribution function ψ which represents the probability function for the density of the segments; this has the form:

$$\frac{\partial \psi}{\partial t} + \text{Div}(\psi \phi) = 0 \qquad (4.2.1)$$

where ϕ is the flux of segments in 3N-dimensional configurational space.

We now need expressions for this flux. In doing this, we shall follow the path usually taken by polymer scientists. There are two sources of flux: $\underline{\phi_1}$ and ϕ_2. The first, $\underline{\phi_1}$, is simply the macroscopic flow, $\underline{V}$.

38

$$\underline{\phi}_1 = \underline{V} \qquad\qquad (4.2.2)$$

The second, $\underline{\phi}_2$, is formed by the forces on the chain. Magnetic, electrical and acceleration forces involving the masses of the beads are neglected. The further assumption is made that a force $\underline{F}$ will give a flux $\underline{\underline{D}}.\underline{F}/kT$ where the components of the (symmetric) tensor $\underline{\underline{D}}$ are diffusion constants of individual beads, to be defined later. The two forces acting are:

a) *Brownian motion:* According to Zimm[16], the theories of Brownian motion[17,18] show that a bead acts as if it were subject to a force $-kT\ \mathrm{grad}\ (\ln\ \psi)$. This relation is not explicitly given by quoted references. From their results it can be shown nevertheless, that this should be a suitable relation provided the deviations from equilibrium are small.

b) *Restoring force:* To prevent the beads diffusing apart, a restoring force $\underline{F}$ must be present. In the absence of the macroscopic flow, $\underline{V}$, this force will be in equilibrium with the Brownian motion force, a). At present $\underline{F}$ is not stipulated, it may be a non-linear function of the state variables.

Equation (4.2.1) becomes on substituting the sources of flux, the diffusion equation in 3N-dimensional vector space.

$$\frac{\partial\psi}{\partial t} + \mathrm{Div}\ [\underline{V}\psi + \underline{F}.\underline{\underline{D}}\ \frac{\psi}{kT} - \underline{\underline{D}}.\mathrm{grad}\ \psi] = 0 \qquad (4.2.3)$$

Equation (4.2.3) is a version of the Smoluchowski equation of diffusion. Somewhat confusingly, it is also referred to often as the Fokker-Planck equation. When the linear relation (4.1.13) is used for $\underline{F}$ we have the diffusion equation in basic form, as seen in the theories of Kuhn[1], Hermans[2], Rouse[15] and Zimm[16]. For this case, we may put the equation in a form which emphasizes the linearity of the theory.

$$\frac{\partial\psi}{\partial t} + \mathrm{Div}\ [\underline{V}\psi - \underline{\underline{D}}.(\mathrm{grad}\ \psi - \mathrm{grad}\ \psi_0)] = 0 \qquad (4.2.4)$$

where ψ_0 is the distribution function in the undisturbed state. Indeed we could have obtained the result directly by appealing to the Onsager relations from irreversible thermodynamics.

$$\mathrm{Flux} = L_{pq}\ F_q(\alpha_1\ ....\ \alpha_n) \qquad\qquad (4.2.5)$$

where α_p (p = 1 .... n) is the deviation of the pth state variable from the value at thermal equilibrium, F_q is the thermodynamic force defined as the derivative of entropy ($kT\ \log\ \psi$) with respect to α_q, and L_{pq} are (symmetric) transport coefficients. The forces F_q are considered to be linear in the deviations α_p. When now the α_p are considered to be the state variables instead of the deviations of the state variables from equilibrium the flux due to the forces has just the form of the ϕ_2 term as given in (4.2.4).

In this work we are chiefly interested in steady flow for which $\frac{\partial \psi}{\partial t} = 0$ and (4.2.4) takes the explicit form when the suffixes are added for the N beads[19] in cartesian coordinates.

$$\sum_{p,q}^{N} \nabla_{Rp}\{\delta_{pq}\nabla_q\psi + D_{pq}F_q \frac{\psi}{kT} - D_{pq}\nabla_{Rq}\psi\} = 0 \qquad (4.2.6)$$

The symbol R indicates that further suffixes have to be added for the three space directions. The physical interpretation of D_{pq} is that it represents the diffusion constant of bead p as modified by bead q. In dilute solutions the need for this refinement can readily be seen as the flow at bead q will disturb the flow around bead p; in the extreme case the solvent becomes entrapped in the coil.

For melts and concentrated solutions on the other hand, it is considered that the bead q has no influence on the bead p. The reason for this belief lies in the observation that the interpenetration of neighbouring coils ensures that the surroundings of a segment move on average with the macroscopic flow field since the surroundings are coils whose centres of gravity drift with the average flow field[20]. In the context of the last remark, it is possible that low molecular weight components in a polydisperse mixture might be entrained in the way described for very dilute solut⌐. An additional and more pragmatic reason for ignoring hydrodynamic interaction in melts is contained in the difficulty of handling; there does not se⌐ to be any non-Newtonian equivalent to the Oseen tensor[4] which has been so useful in describing the interaction for dilute solutions.

Since in this work we are not directly concerned with dilute solutions, we will ignore the possibility that the diffusion constant is a function of the bead position along the chain and treat it as a constant tensor.

$$D_{pq} = D\delta_{pq} \qquad (4.2.7)$$

The above indices refer to the bead number; D may still be an anisotropic function in space, however. Equation (4.2.6) then simplifies to the following equation when the summation over the space coordinates are explicitly included:

$$\sum_{i,j=1}^{3} \sum_{p=1}^{N} \frac{\partial}{\partial x_i^p} [D_{ij} \frac{\partial \psi}{\partial x_j^p} - D_{ij}F_j^p \frac{\psi}{kT} - V_i^p\psi] = 0 \qquad (4.2.8)$$

where i,j refer to the ordinary ($1 \equiv x$, $2 \equiv y$, $3 \equiv z$) space coordinates; x_i^p is the i-component (x, y, or z) of the p bead based on the space coordinates; D_{ij} are the components of the diffusion tensor; V_i^p is the i-component of the macroscopic flow at bead p, i.e. the macroscopic fluid velocity at that place. The diffusion coefficients D_{ij} are for polymers invariably chosen from the translational diffusion coefficients of the hydrodynamic centres of resistance (beads). The terms involving the rotation diffusion coefficients of the beads are neglected. In principle, each segment both rotates and translates. However, with increasing distance from the hydrodynamic centre of the total molecule, the translational resistance dominates.

4.3 The Elastic Dumbbell Model

This model originated from the pens of Kuhn[1] and Hermans[2]. In recent times it has waned in relative importance against the Rouse[15], Bueche[21], Zimm[16] models and their modifications[22]. Nevertheless, the model has been found useful since features of more involved models can be explored in a tentative way.

The model represents the polymer chain by two spheres connected by an elastic spring. All the hydrodynamic forces on the chain segments are lumped together and assumed to act only on the end spheres. The elastic spring is a representation of the statistical forces acting to balance the hydrodynamic forces. In the original models hydrodynamic interaction between the spheres was neglected. For reasons previously given, this aspect is also neglected here.

The origin of the space coordinates is set on one of the spheres. The coordinate of the other sphere with respect to this origin of coordinates, is simply:

$$\underline{r} = (x_1, x_2, x_3) \tag{4.3.1}$$

The diffusion tensor is assumed to be spherically symmetric; $D_{ij} = D\delta_{ij}$. Further, the assumption is made that the force between the beads is given by the linear expression from rubber elasticity, i.e. relation (4.1.13). This expression for the force was obtained by considering the average force between the chain ends when they are held $\underline{r}$ apart. The same linear approximation is obtained for the average distance between the chain ends when they are subject to a given force. When the deformation becomes significant with respect to the chain contour length and higher order terms have to be included, this correlation does not hold[23]. Thus, the extension of (4.1.13) to include non-linear terms, gives rise to conceptual difficulties.

With steady shear flow given by a gradient q in the x_2 direction, we have:

$$\underline{V} = (qx_2, 0, 0) \tag{4.3.2.}$$

Equation (4.2.3) becomes:

$$\text{Div } [\underline{V}\psi - 2\mu D \underline{r}\psi - D \text{ grad } \psi] = 0 \tag{4.3.3}$$

Following J.J. Hermans[2] we now multiply the above in turn by x_1x_2, x_1^2, x_2^2, x_3^2 and integrate over all space. In doing this, the reasonable assumption is made that ψ decreases exponentially at large distances from the origin. It is then possible to derive the following averages needed for the stress and refractive index components: $\langle x_1x_2 \rangle$, $\langle x_1^2 \rangle$, $\langle x_2^2 \rangle$, $\langle x_3^2 \rangle$. The results are:

$$\langle x_1^2 \rangle = \langle x_2^2 \rangle + 2q^2\tau^2\langle x_2^2 \rangle \tag{4.3.4}$$

$$\langle x_2^2 \rangle = \langle x_3^2 \rangle = 1/2\mu = r_0^2/3 \tag{4.3.5}$$

$$\langle x_1 x_2 \rangle = q\tau\langle x_2^2 \rangle \tag{4.3.6}$$

where $\tau = (4\ \mu D)^{-1}$ is called the relaxation time of the system.
The gradient dependency of the extinction angle for a monodisperse system is given by (4.1.12):

$$\cot 2X = q\tau \tag{4.3.7}$$

i.e. a relation of the type proposed by Nantonson (see Introduction).
It is seen that: the mean square projections of the dumbbells length onto the x_2 and x_3 axes are unaltered by the flow; the shear component $\langle x_1 x_2 \rangle$ is linearly proportional to the gradient q, and that the normal component $\langle x_1^2 \rangle$ is changed proportional to the square of the gradient. This model therefore predicts:

1) The stress-optical law: since the expression for the force in the chain has been taken from the linear approximation.

2) Newtonian viscosity: since $\langle x_1 x_2 \rangle$ is proportional to q. The full expression for the shear stress in steady shear flow reads when the sum over all molecules is included (4.1.2):

$$P_{12} = q \sum_m \frac{RT\ c_m}{M_m} \tau_m \tag{4.3.10}$$

where $\tau_m = 1/4\ \mu D = fM_m^2$. Here it has been assumed that the diffusion constant D is inversely proportional to the molecular weight and f is a material constant which is a function of the polymer type and its surroundings. Factor f is related to the friction constant of a single segment. The expression (4.3.10) can be rewritten:

$$P_{12} = qcRTfM_w \tag{4.3.11}$$

3) A normal stress difference $P_{11} - P_{22}$ proportional to the square of the gradient. In a similar way to the last paragraph we find:

$$P_{11} - P_{22} = 2q^2 \sum_m \frac{RTc_m}{M_m} \tau_m^2 \tag{4.3.12}$$

and

$$P_{11} - P_{22} = 2q^2 cRTf^2 M_{z+1} M_z M_w \tag{4.3.13}$$

4) A normal stress difference $P_{22} - P_{33}$ equal to zero.

$$P_{22} - P_{33} = 0 \tag{4.3.14}$$

42

The Dumbbell Extended

We would like to see under which conditions the simple dumbbell model would give a behaviour qualitatively more in keeping with the experimental reality. Specifically, we are interested in obtaining unequal normal stresses p_{22} and p_{33} in the second order region. We do not consider rigid dumbbells, as these have been extensively considered[24,25], and because the stress-optical relation is not valid for these systems. Instead, we investigate two modifications in a simple way:

A) The expression for the force is left undefined, and the diffusion constant is again isotropic. In this way, the possible effects of non-linear springs can be examined.

B) The rubber elasticity expression for the force is retained, but it is assumed that the diffusion tensor of a typical segment between the chain ends has cylindrical symmetry. The diffusion constant of the end bead is in turn assumed to have a symmetry, determined by the average spatial orientation of all segments between the beads. It then turns out that the average diffusion tensors of the end beads have the same symmetry as the stress tensor in the liquid, e.g. $D_{13} = D_{23} = 0$ (cf. equations (4.1.10) or (4.3.27)). There are two reasons why we expect this to be a better and more realistic model. The first is the need for a self-consistency condition in the melt, but possibly not in very dilute solutions. The molecular theories predict various anisotropic properties of the liquid in flow (stress, birefringence, etc.). In the melt we have to assume that by summing over all chains, we simultaneously arrive at the average properties of the medium surrounding the chains. If the chains become distorted, it is only logical that the medium becomes anisotropic and hence the diffusion should not, in general, be isotropic except possibly for small deformations. Some authors[26,27] believe that this is the cause of the Mooney C_2 term in rubber elasticity and point out that C_2 decreases with increasing swelling by solvent. The second ground for relaxing spherical symmetry with the diffusion tensor is the simple observation that a chain is a flexible linear string and it is more logical to use the symmetry of the hydrodynamic resistance of a cylinder or ellipsoid to define the components of the diffusion tensor of a typical segment.

Case A

The diffusion equation (4.2.8) for simple steady shear flow reads:

$$-qx_2 \frac{\partial \psi}{\partial x_1} - \frac{D}{kT}\left[\frac{\partial}{\partial x_1}(F_1\psi) + \frac{\partial}{\partial x_2}(F_2\psi) + \frac{\partial}{\partial x_3}(F_3\psi)\right] + D\left[\frac{\partial^2 \psi}{\partial x_1^2} + \frac{\partial^2 \psi}{\partial x_2^2} + \frac{\partial^2 \psi}{\partial x_3^2}\right] = 0 \quad (4.3.15)$$

This is multiplied in turn by x_1x_2, x_2^2, and x_3^2, and integrated through space with the same assumption as in the last section. This gives:

$$q\langle x_2^2\rangle + \frac{D}{kT}\langle x_1F_2 + x_2F_1\rangle = 0 \qquad (4.3.16)$$

$$\frac{D}{kT}\langle x_2F_2\rangle + D = 0 \qquad (4.3.17)$$

$$\frac{D}{kT}\langle x_3F_3\rangle + D = 0 \qquad (4.3.18)$$

From the last two equations it is seen that for steady shearing flow $\langle x_2F_2\rangle = \langle x_3F_3\rangle =$ constant. On comparison with (4.1.1), we may conclude that in this model the second normal stress difference, $p_{22} - p_{33}$, will always be zero, even when the spring force is an arbitrary non-linear function. When this is true, then the model fails by not giving the required behaviour. A further objection to modifications on these lines is that the stress-optic relation will break down.

Case B

We start again with the equation for a dumbbell, but write it out for the general case when $\underline{F}$ is not specified and D_{ij} has the symmetry of stress (the assumption is not necessary, but can be proven). In full for steady shear flow:

$$\frac{\partial}{\partial x_1}\left(D_{11}\frac{\partial\psi}{\partial x_1} + D_{12}\frac{\partial\psi}{\partial x_2}\right) + \frac{\partial}{\partial x_2}\left(D_{12}\frac{\partial\psi}{\partial x_1} + D_{22}\frac{\partial\psi}{\partial x_2}\right) + \frac{\partial}{\partial x_3}D_{33}\frac{\partial\psi}{\partial x_3} - qx_2\frac{\partial\psi}{\partial x_1} -$$

$$-kT\left[\frac{\partial}{\partial x_1}(D_{11}F_1 + D_{12}F_2)\psi + \frac{\partial}{\partial x_2}(D_{12}F_1 + D_{22}F_2)\psi + \frac{\partial}{\partial x_3}D_{33}F_3\psi\right] = 0 \qquad (4.3.19)$$

We now substitute the rubber elasticity expression for the force in the chain (4.1.13) and assume that the diffusion tensor has been pre-averaged for the gradient q. As in the preceding cases, we multiply the above by x_1x_2, x_1^2, x_2^2 and x_3^2 in turn and integrate over all space. This yields the following set of equations:

$$q\langle x_2^2\rangle - 2\mu(D_{11} + D_{22})\langle x_1x_2\rangle - 2\mu D_{12}\langle x_1^2 + x_2^2\rangle + 2D_{12} = 0 \qquad (4.3.20)$$

$$q\langle x_1x_2\rangle - 2\mu D_{11}\langle x_1^2\rangle - 2\mu D_{12}\langle x_1x_2\rangle + D_{11} = 0 \qquad (4.3.21)$$

$$-2\mu D_{12}\langle x_1x_2\rangle - 2\mu D_{22}\langle x_2^2\rangle + D_{22} = 0 \qquad (4.3.22)$$

$$-2\mu D_{33}\langle x_3^2\rangle + D_{33} = 0 \qquad (4.3.23)$$

From the last of these it follows that, as with the simple dumbbell, $\langle x_3^2\rangle$ remains unchanged by the flow. Yet, the above system of equations gives unequal normal stresses p_{22}, p_{33} and refractive indexes n_{22}, n_{33}. The stress-optic law is included by virtue of the assumption concerning the chain force. Let us now

estimate the ratio of the refractive index difference $n_{22} - n_{33}$ to $n_{11} - n_{33}$.
To begin, (4.3.23) is combined with (4.3.22) and (4.3.21) in turn.
This yields:

$$- 2\mu D_{12} \langle x_1 x_2 \rangle + 2\mu D_{22} \langle x_3^2 - x_2^2 \rangle = 0 \qquad (4.3.24)$$

$$q \langle x_1 x_2 \rangle - 2\mu D_{12} \langle x_1 x_2 \rangle + 2\mu D_{11} \langle x_3^2 - x_1^2 \rangle = 0 \qquad (4.3.25)$$

whence the ratio of the two differences is:

$$\frac{n_{22} - n_{33}}{n_{11} - n_{33}} = \frac{\langle x_2^2 - x_3^2 \rangle}{\langle x_1^2 - x_3^2 \rangle} = - \frac{D_{11}}{D_{22}} \frac{2\mu D_{12}}{2\mu D_{12} - q} \qquad (4.3.26)$$

According to the assumption of cylindrical symmetry, D is given by:

$$D_{ij} = D_2 \delta_{ij} + (D_1 - D_2) \langle \frac{x_i x_j}{r^2} \rangle \qquad (4.3.27)$$

where D_1 and D_2 are proportional to the principal diffusivities of a typical
random link. D_1 is proportional to the diffusivity of a link along its axis,
and D_2 is proportional to the diffusivity perpendicular to its axis. The above
equation is a general relation for the components of a tensor of cylindrical
symmetry onto a cartesian coordinate system. When the coil is undistorted
$\langle x_i x_j / r^2 \rangle = \frac{1}{3} \delta_{ij}$ and the diffusion of the end bead is spherically symmetric
with $D_{ij} = [(D_1 + 2 D_2)/3] \delta_{ij}$. In this case, the diffusion of the end bead is
determined by the average value of the segment diffusivities. On flow the coil
becomes distorted and the spherical symmetry is lost. In order to calculate
this case, the average product of the direction cosines $\langle x_i x_j / r^2 \rangle$ is approximated to $\langle x_i x_j \rangle / \langle r_0^2 \rangle$. This is a fair approximation as long as the coil dis-
tortion remains small. The limiting value for D_{12} as q approaches zero is then
given by:

$$D_{12} = (D_1 - D_2) \frac{\langle x_1 x_2 \rangle}{\langle r_0^2 \rangle} \qquad (4.3.28)$$

In the same limit $\langle x_1 x_2 \rangle$ is given by (see Eq. (4.3.6)):

$$\langle x_1 x_2 \rangle = \frac{q \langle x_2^2 \rangle}{4\mu \langle D \rangle} \qquad (4.3.29)$$

where $\langle D \rangle = (D_1 + 2 D_2)/3$. The ratio of the refractive index differences can
then be evaluated easily and the result is:

$$\frac{n_{22} - n_{33}}{n_{11} - n_{33}} = - \frac{D_1 - D_2}{D_1 + 5 D_2} \qquad (4.3.30)$$

45

There is now needed an expression for the ratio of the diffusivities D_1 to D_2. This ratio is determined by the ratio of the hydrodynamic resistances of a random link when it is translated either parallel or perpendicular to its axis. Account has to be made of the fact that the diffusivity of a link is inversely proportional to its hydrodynamic resistance. In the present case the ratio D_1/D_2 was found by modeling a link to an infinitely long but thin cylinder. This gives the same result, as would be obtained by modeling the link to an ellipsoid of infinite axial ratio. In this limiting case D_1 is equal to $2D_2$. More general results for ellipsoids and cylinders of various shapes are to be found in the literature[28,29].

The ratio of the refractive index differences is then:

$$\frac{n_{22} - n_{33}}{n_{11} - n_{33}} = -\frac{1}{7} \tag{4.3.31}$$

If the link were modeled to a cylinder with length to diameter ratio of 10:1, which is more reasonable considering that Kuhn's random link often contains about ten monomer units, the ratio of the refractive indexes should be about −0.1.

From (4.3.31) we see that, if the normal stress difference ($p_{11} - p_{33}$) or the refractive index differences ($n_{11} - n_{33}$) are positive, it then follows that the differences $n_{22} - n_{33}$ and $p_{22} - p_{33}$ are negative. Later it will appear that (4.3.31) gives the correct sign and magnitude found in experimental measurements both of normal stress differences and of refractive index differences.

According to the above, the ratio of the differences should be independent of concentration, molecular weight, and molecular weight distribution of the polymer. It should only depend on the "stiffness" of the component random links.

It is interesting to compare these results with the behaviour of rigid particles of cylindrical symmetry, the subject of extensive study[24,25,30]. For this case, the stress optical law does not hold when the extinction angle deviates from 45°. Giesekus[24] has examined the normal stress differences in the second order region and found for the two extremes of needles (ellipses of infinite axial ratio) and platelets (infinitely small axial ratio), ($p_{33} - p_{22}$)/($p_{11} - p_{22}$) lay between 1/6 and 0.4 with a minimum of 0.08 at an axial ratio of 6:1. The corresponding ratios for the refractive index differences have never been given. From calculations using the theory of Peterlin and Stuart[31], it can be shown that the ratio should vary monotonically between 2.5 (plates) and 0.4 (needles). Thus, for rigid particles, the theoretical ratio of the normal component differences is markedly different for stress tensor components and refractive index tensor components. In fact, the ratio from the optical components would be the most suitable in determining shapes of particles, should one be required to do this by rheological means.

The extended dumbbell model also predicts a weak non-Newtonian viscosity and normal stresses which show a more complicated dependency on q than the strictly quadratic one in the original dumbbell model. However, we do not believe that such a linear theory can be used to explain non-Newtonian behaviour (see Section 6.2). We only suggest the model, as it gives possible mechanism for the inequality of the p_{22} and p_{33} in and near the second order region. The origin of non-Newtonian viscosity and other non-linear effects should be sought elsewhere.

When consideration is made of the viscoelastic parameters G' and G", it appears that dumbbell models can only supply a limited number of relaxation mechanisms whilst polymer solutions and melts require a wide spectrum of relaxation times for a satisfactory phenomenological description of experimental results.

We now pass on to the most well-known of polymer models which possesses the latter possibility.

4.4 The Rouse Model

In this model the macromolecule is represented by a set of N identical beads joined by N-1 identical segments[15]. The number of real atomic units between each bead is supposed so great that Gaussian chain statistics may be assumed to hold between the beads. As in the dumbbell model, all hydrodynamic effects are assumed to act on the beads via an isotropic diffusion tensor. The model, while often associated with the name of Rouse, seems to have been developed to the same degree, but independently by others[32,21]. Originally the theory was developed to describe the behaviour of dilute solutions. When applied to melts it will be referred to as the modified theory of Rouse. The application to melts is essentially based on the interpretation of entanglements due to Ferry and others[33,34,35] in which entanglements are supposed to contribute an excess friction to segments of polymer molecules. Thus, each molecule behaves at low deformation rates as if it were immersed, independently of the other molecules, in a medium of increased viscosity.

The mean force acting between beads p and p+1 is given by the linear relation:

$$F_{p,p+1} = - 2\mu \ kT(r_p - r_{p+1}) \tag{4.4.1}$$

where 2μ now equals $3/b^2$; b^2 is the mean square distance between consecutive beads. The force acting on the p bead originating from the segments p-1 to p, and p to p+1, is then represented by the vector equation:

$$\underline{F} = - 2 \ kT \ \underline{\underline{A}} \cdot \underline{r} \tag{4.4.2}$$

where $\underline{\underline{A}}$ is the interaction tensor of order N with components

$$A_{11} = A_{NN} = 1$$

$$A_{ii} = 2 \ ; \ i \neq N \ , \ 1$$

$$A_{ij} = -1; \ |i-j| = 1 \tag{4.4.3}$$

$$= 0 \ ; \ |i-j| > 1$$

47

The matrix A is basic and familiar to the theories of linear systems. Thus A is associated with the vibrations of uniformly weighted strings[36] and vibrations in crystal lattices[37]. It has been humorously suggested that A stands for Archimedes[38]. Owing to the interaction term, the diffusion equation is not readily soluble. Solution is achieved by use of a coordinate transformation which diagonalises A. The transposed forces are then used in the diffusion equation.

When the procedure is followed, the distribution function ψ can be written in the form of a product of distribution functions ψ_p for each normal mode.

$$\psi = \Pi \psi_p \tag{4.4.4}$$

Each ψ_p is governed by a diffusion equation of the dumbbell type:

$$\text{Div}[-\underline{V}\psi_p + 2\mu\lambda_p D\underline{r}_p\psi_p + D \text{ grad } \psi_p] = 0 \tag{4.4.5}$$

where λ_p is a diagonal element of the transformed matrix A and for large N:

$$\lambda_p = \frac{p^2}{N^2} \pi^2 \quad ; p = 1, 2, 3 \ldots \tag{4.4.6}$$

By comparison with the results of the previous Section 4.3, it is evident that the model is characterised by a distribution of relaxation times:

$$\tau_p = (4 \mu D \lambda_p)^{-1} \tag{4.4.7}$$

With the omission of a hydrostatic pressure component, the components of the stress tensor are:

$$P_{12} = q \sum_m \frac{RTc_m}{M_m} \sum_{p=1}^{N} \tau_{pm} \tag{4.4.8}$$

$$P_{11} = 2q^2 \sum_m \frac{RTc_m}{M_m} \sum_{p=1}^{N} \tau_{pm}^2 \tag{4.4.9}$$

$$P_{22} = P_{33} = 0 \tag{4.4.10}$$

In view of the stress-optical relation which immediately follows from the model, the refractive index components are not given.

To obtain the components of the dynamic viscosity at frequencies ω, the quantity $\partial\psi/\partial t$ in (4.2.3) is not set equal to zero. The determination of the stress components follows a similar course to the steady shear case. When this is done, the dynamic moduli are found to be:

48

$$G''(\omega) = \sum_m \frac{RTc_m}{M_m} \sum_p \frac{\omega\,\tau_{pm}}{1 + \omega^2\tau_{pm}^2} \tag{4.4.11}$$

$$G'(\omega) = \sum_m \frac{RTc_m}{M_m} \sum_p \frac{\omega^2\tau_{pm}^2}{1 + \omega^2\tau_{pm}^2} \tag{4.4.12}$$

In the limiting case of zero frequency, a simple relation results between the measurable quantities of steady and oscillatory shearing.

$$p_{12} = G''(\omega)\,, \qquad q = \omega \text{ as } \omega \to 0 \tag{4.4.13}$$

$$p_{11} - p_{22} = 2G'(\omega)\,, \qquad q = \omega \text{ as } \omega \to 0 \tag{4.4.14}$$

The above result is well-known and is quite general for simple (i.e. un-structured) liquids, as it can be obtained from more general considerations[39]. The relaxation times are found by combining (4.4.6) and (4.4.7):

$$\tau_p = N^2/4\mu D\pi^2 p^2 \tag{4.4.15}$$

In the model the diffusion constant D, the segment length b, and the number N of segments, are all adjustable parameters as they cannot be independently chosen. We expect the number of segments to be proportional to the molecular weight. The relaxation times are therefore written for each species m.

$$\tau_{pm} = fM_m^2\, p^{-2} \tag{4.4.16}$$

where f is a parameter determined by D and the chosen relation between M, N and b. As

$$\sum_{p=1}^{\infty} p^{-2} = \frac{\pi^2}{6}$$

the shear stress becomes:

$$p_{12} = qcRTfM_w\pi^2/6 \tag{4.4.17}$$

This result differs from the dumbbell result only by a numerical factor. The shear stress and hence viscosity, should be proportional to the concentration and the weight average molecular weight. From experiments it is known, that the viscosity is not such a simple function of the molecular weight. At low degrees of polymerization (less than 600), the viscosity is indeed roughly proportional to M, but at higher degrees of polymerization it is proportional to a higher power of the molecular weight, usually the 3.4 power. To overcome this difficulty it must be assumed that f is also a function of the molecular weight. Experimentally, it is found that η is determined mainly by M_w[40,41,42], although with some very broad distributions higher averages of the molecular weight distribution may play a role[43]. The correct dependency of η on the molecular weight is obtained by assuming f is proportional to $M_w^{2.4}$ in the higher molecular weight region.

For the normal stress difference one finds:

$$P_{11} - P_{22} = 2q^2 cRTf^2 M_{z+1} M_z M_w \pi^4 / 90 \qquad (4.4.18)$$

The steady shearing compliance J_e is obtained by combining (1.3.6), (4.4.18) and (4.4.17):

$$J_e = \frac{P_{11} - P_{22}}{2\,P_{12}^2} = \frac{2}{5}\,\frac{M_{z+1} M_z}{M_w cRT} \qquad (4.4.19)$$

For melts, the concentration is replaced by the density ρ. When the melt has a narrow distribution of molecular weights, the compliance should read:

$$J_e = \frac{2}{5}\,\frac{M}{\rho RT} \qquad (4.4.20)$$

J_e should not depend on the f factor. Again the only difference from the dumbbell model turns out to lie in a numerical constant. (For the dumbbell, 2/5 is replaced by unity.)

The measurement of the steady state compliance J_e is now a favoured way for checking molecular theories for slow flow and small, cyclic, deformation behaviour. The viscosity is no longer used since its application needs the interpretation of f in (4.4.17). Some earlier authors did this successfully[44] by reducing the problem of f to that of an atomic friction factor which, however, remained empirical. The use of J_e instead of the viscosity avoids any interpretation of f since f is eliminated.

There is no longer great optimism for applying the molecular theories in their present form to the flow of melts. Following the initial investigations of Ferry[34] and coworkers, there was considerable hope that the modified Rouse theory was applicable to melts. Indeed, it was found with some melts that J_e followed the molecular weight behaviour given by the modified theory - polyvinyl acetate[45,46] and polymethyl methacrylate[47]. Certain moderately concentrated solutions also seemed to obey the predicted behaviour[48,49,50]. These early hopes were dashed when polystyrene came to be examined.

As the nature of the described theory is semi-empiric, a short discussion of recent mechanical experiments seems justified. The Japanese investigators have been particularly active. Dynamic testing has been the popular mode of investigation. In one study, Onogi and coworkers found that for narrow distribution polystyrenes[51] η_0 was proportional to $M^{3.7}$ and J_e to M^0 for samples with molecular weights higher than a critical molecular weight M_c^*. J_e was proportional to M for molecular weights lower than M_c^*. In this region, agreement with the Rouse theory was achieved but the proportionality constant was incorrect by a factor five.

In a further investigation, this time on blends[52], the same group found that η_0 was determined by M_w, but that J_e was proportional to w_2^2 where w_2 is the weight fraction of the highest molecular weight component. They also concluded that the low molecular weight component in binary blends does not contribute to J_e in the high concentration region, even when their molecular weight exceeds M_c. This means that the basic rule, given by (4.1.2) might be invalid.

Results of many J_e investigations on polystyrene melts are given in Fig. 4.1. Other materials have been investigated in individual papers[53,54,55], but

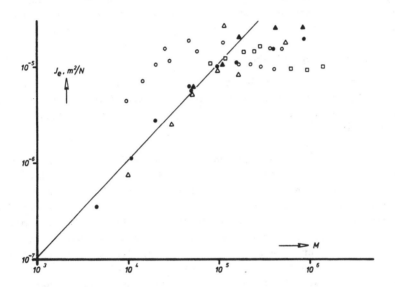

Fig. 4.1 The steady shearing compliance as function of molecular weight for polystyrenes of narrow molecular weight distribution.
Drawn line ... Rouse theory.
o ... Ref.[51]; □... Ref.[56]; ● ... Ref.[57]; △ ... Ref.[58];
▲ ... Ref.[59].

it is only with polystyrene that extensive work has been carried out allowing cross-checking of different methods. In Fig. 4.1 data are shown from stress relaxation in tensile tests[56]; from dynamic moduli with a concentric cylinder viscometer[51], and with a cone-and-plate[57,58]; and, from the steady shear behaviour of the shear stress and the normal stress difference[59]. Values of J_e from the latter work were increased by a factor two in order to correspond with the definition of J_e used in this work. The above list is by no means exhaustive. When all results are placed together in the above manner, the general result is a little muddy, but a census of opinion is present. J_e is independent of the molecular weight above a certain critical molecular weight. Below this critical weight, J_e is roughly proportional to M in the manner demanded by the theory.

Graessly has recently[60] proposed a modification of the theory to overcome the difficulty. His main point seems to be that in applying the Rouse Theory to melts (entangling systems), account should be made for the differing friction which entanglements have, dependent on their position. Thus, the diffusion coefficient is not completely smoothed and he chooses $D_{ij} = D(p)\delta_{ij}$ where p is the bead number. He obtained an expression for J_e in the form $J_e = 0.7M_c/\rho RT$ for all high molecular weight polymers. This leads to a value of J_e for polystyrene which is too small by a factor of about two only. He also obtained a dependency on the polydispersity weaker than the original theory: J_e proportional to M_z/M_w instead of $M_{z+1}M_zM_w^2$. According to his own remarks, the Rouse theory gives a better description of the influence of polydispersity than the modified theory does[60].

4.5 Molecular-Phenomenological Theories

In this section, mention is made of a few theories developed particularly to describe non-Newtonian aspects of polymer melt flow. Characteristic of the theories is a mixture of intuitive reasoning and molecular concepts; "pure" statistical premises are not present.

Graessly Model: Graessly[61] used the concept of entanglements for an intuitive development of non-Newtonian flow. In this he did not use the rotation of the molecules, as had been done by Bueche[62], but rather, the changing distances between molecules. Since the kinetics of junction formation and breakdown are unknown, Graessly took a mechanistic view. In the shear field, when the molecules are close, entanglements can form. After molecules pass one another, disentanglement must occur. For an entanglement to be reformed, molecules must lie within reach of one another and remain within reach for a sufficient length of time. With increasing shear rate, this "contact time" decreases and entanglements with long diffusion times are not re-formed. The entanglement density decreases and consequently, the viscosity decreases. To specify the model, Graessly used diffusion times, obtained from the Rouse model applied to the melt. In order to satisfy the needs of self-consistency, the diffusion times are a function of the shear rate, q, and are determined by the viscosity of the melt at that shear rate.

As a result of these considerations, the limiting behaviour at high shear rates should be given by the relation: $\eta(q) \propto q^{-3/4}$.

In an ensuing development[63], Graessly also considered the possibility that the friction factor would decrease during flow. For this latter model, the following limit relation was obtained for the high shear rate region: $\eta(q) \propto q^{-9/11}$. Alternatively, the limit relations for the viscosity can be re-phrased as limit relations for the "power law" flow curve. The exponent in the relation $q \propto p_{12}^n$ should, according to the latter version, be less than 5.5. For some systems, e.g. PVC gels, rubbers, and very high molecular weight polystyrene, exponents higher than 5.5 are often found.

In both of the models, the second normal stress difference $(p_{22} - p_{33})$ should be zero. In the first model, $p_{11} - p_{22}$ should remain proportional to the square of the shear stress. In the section on results, it will be seen that this is a feature of polystyrene melts (but not of many other systems). The latter model of Graessly makes no pronouncement on $p_{11} - p_{22}$ behaviour.

Schroff[64] claims that for the latter model, the results of Graessly may be put in the convenient form:

$$\eta(q) = \int_{-\infty}^{\infty} H(\tau)K(\tau q) \, d\tau \qquad (4.5.1)$$

where $K(\tau q)$ is a kernel, determined by the changing number of entanglements and the changing diffusion constant.

Maximum Energy Model: Recently, Booij[65] proposed an energy threshold model to account for non-linear behaviour in polymer fluids. The basic postulate is: "A mode of relaxation characterized by a time τ cannot store an amount of free energy greater than kTb^2 where b is a constant. The mode disappears when this limit value is exceeded during the deformation process". The parameter b was assumed independent of τ. The physical picture in the model is that modes with long relaxation times are more deformed than modes with short relaxation times. As an example, one imagines that an entanglement between two molecules which happens to be far from the chain ends of both molecules, will take longer to diffuse out than an entanglement near their periferies. Owing to the longer diffusion time of deeply located entanglements, chains connecting these entanglements become more highly deformed. Eventually, the chain forces exceed the entanglement's strength. Consequently, the entanglement is destroyed.

The model thus resembles the Graessly model. However, the maximum energy model has advantages, in that it is more general, and detailed dynamics of chain motion do not need to be considered. Moreover, it may be applied to non-polymer systems.

The practical problem is to relate b to measurable quantities. This was tackled by considering a generalisation of the Rouse-Bueche approach and by using solutions of the diffusion equation to calculate the increase of the free energy of a mode. For the special case of steady shear flow, there was found:

$$\Delta F(\tau) = q^2\tau^2 kT < kTb^2 \qquad (4.5.2)$$

where $\Delta F(\tau)$ is the increase of the free energy over the undisturbed state of the considered mode. The influence of volume changes has been neglected in the above. The consequence of the model in the case of steady shear flow is, that an upper limit is set to the intervals over which the integrals for the flow quantities are taken. The formulae for the shear stress and the first normal stress differences are[65] (cf. Eqs (1.3.2) and (1.3.3)):

$$p_{12} = q \int_0^{\tau_m} H(\tau) \, d\tau \qquad (4.5.3)$$

$$p_{11} - p_{22} = 2q^2 \int_0^{\tau_m} H(\tau)\tau \, d\tau \qquad (4.5.4)$$

where τ_m is the maximum permitted relaxation time:

$$\tau_m = b/q \qquad\qquad (4.5.5)$$

Ajroldi, Garbuglio and Pezzin[66] suggested earlier that the integral expression in (4.5.3) would be a suitable quantity for the differential viscosity dp_{12}/dq.

The above model can give a fair description of non-linear behaviour including stress overshoot[*]. However, as appears from the few studies made[65], simple termination of the relaxation spectrum at a particular value τ_m is not consistent with both the gradient dependency of the shear stresses and the normal stresses. For example, a more gradual truncation is possible, yielding the same viscosity function and a better agreement with the gradient dependency of the normal stresses.

In addition to the above described model, other rupture models exist. The Leonov thixotropic model[67] and the Simmons-Tanner model[68] are examples. It appears that the results of these theories can also be put in the form of (4.5.3) amd (4.5.4).

The application of any kind of truncation procedure is equivalent to the introduction of a shape function $K(q\tau)$ in the integrand. Integration is retained over the whole time scale and $K(q\tau)$ ensures that the contributions of the longer times become progressively smaller.

$$P_{12} = q \int_0^\infty H(\tau)K(q\tau)\ d\tau \qquad\qquad (4.5.6)$$

$$P_{11} - P_{22} = 2q^2 \int_0^\infty H(\tau)K(q\tau)\tau\ d\tau \qquad\qquad (4.5.7)$$

The idea of introducing a kernel into the expressions from the linear theory in order to describe non-linear behaviour is not new. Various proposals for suitable forms for $K(q\tau)$ have been given, including suggestions using the Ree-Ehring theory for rate processes[66,69-71] and the Graessly theory described previously[63,64].

In our final remarks we wish to point out that the theories described in this section, are essentially linear theories since the postulates on which they are based, are linear postulates. In the Graessly theory, for instance, the coil deformation and orientation are ignored. This is perhaps justified by the experimental fact that polymer melts retain a linear behaviour up to very

---

*Stress overshoot is a phenomenon associated with experiments where a constant flow gradient is suddenly applied. At low rates of applied shearing, the stresses rise monotonically to equilibrium. At high shear rates, the stresses rise and overshoot the equilibrium value before decreasing to equilibrium (if obtainable). The phenomenon is particularly associated with low density polyethylene.

high deformations in dynamic testing. Nevertheless, the non-Newtonian flow is obtained by a trick which may or may not have a sound basis in a suitably modified form of the diffusion equation. By these remarks we only mean that these theories are based on ad hoc assumptions which need to be experimentally evaluated for a true assessment of their merits. It is always possible that the approach will give a good description of experimental findings and can be of assistence in the classification of materials.

References

1) W. Kuhn and H. Kuhn, *Helv. Chim. Acta 26*, 1394 (1943).

2) J.J. Hermans, *Physica 10*, 777 (1943).

3) H.A. Kramers, *Physica 11*, 1 (1944).

4) J.G. Kirkwood and Riseman, *J. Chem.Phys. 16*, 565 (1948).

5) M. Fixman, *J. Chem. Phys. 42*, 3831 (1965).

6) W.H. Stockmayer, W. Gobush, Y. Chikahisa, D.K. Carpenter, *Disc. Farad. Soc. 49*, 182(1970).

7) R. Zwanzig, *Ann. Rev. Phys. Chem. 16*, 67 (1965).

8) R.M. Mazo, *Statistical Mechanical Theories of Transport Processes*, Pergamon Press, Oxford 1967.

9) Y-H. Pao, *J. Macromol. Sci. B1*, 289 (1967).

10) D.G. LeGrand, *Macromolecules 3*, 764 (1970).

11) L.R.G. Treloar in *"The Physics of Rubber Elasticity"*, Oxford, Clarendon Press, 1958, Ch. 9.

12) W. Kuhn and F. Grün, *Kolloid-Z. 101*, 248 (1942).

13) H. Janeschitz-Kriegl, *Makromol. Chem. 40*, 140 (1960).

14) J.G. Kirkwood, *J. Polymer Sci. 12*, 1 (1954).

15) P.E. Rouse, *J. Chem. Phys. 21*, 1272 (1953).

16) B.H. Zimm, *J. Chem. Phys. 24*, 269 (1956).

17) M.C. Wang and G.E. Uhlenbeek, *Rev. Mod. Phys. 17*, 323 (1945).

18) S. Chandrasasekhar, *Rev. Mod. Phys. 15*, 1 (1943).

19) R. Zwanzig, *Adv. Chem. Phys. 15*, 325 (1969).

20) F. Bueche, *J. Chem. Phys. 210*, 1959 (1952).

21) F. Bueche, *J. Chem. Phys. 22*, 603 (1954).

22) C. Reinhold, A. Peterlin, *J. Chem. Phys. 44*, 4333 (1966).

23) M.V. Volkenstein, *"Configurational Statistics of Polymeric Chains"*. Interscience, (1963), Ch. 8.

24) H. Giesekus, *Rheol. Acta 2*, 50 (1962).

25) R.B. Bird, H.R. Warner, D.C. Evans, *Adv. Polymer Sci. 8*, 1 (1971).

26) E.A. DiMazzio, *J. Chem. Phys. 36*, 1563 (1962).

27) J.L. Jackson, M.C. Shen and D.A.McQuarrie, *J. Chem. Phys. 44*, 2388 (1966),

28) J.M. Burgers in *"Second Report on Viscosity and Plasticity"*, North-Holland Publ., Amsterdam 1955, Ch. 3.

29) C.H. Sadron in *"Flow Properties of Disperse Systems"*, J.J. Hermans, Ed., North-Holland Publ.,Amsterdam 1953, Ch. 4.

30) J.T. Yang, *J. Am. Chem. Soc. 80*, 1783 (1958).

31) A. Peterlin, H.A. Stuart, *Z. Physik. 112* (1939).

32) V.A. Kargin, G.L. Sloimskii, *Dokl. Akad. Nauk. SSSR 62*, 239 (1948).

33) J.D. Ferry, R.F. Landel and M.L. Williams, *J. Appl. Phys. 26*, 359 (1955).

34) J.D. Ferry, *"Viscoelastic Properties of Polymers"*, New York, London, John Wiley (1961).

35) A.J. Chompff and H.A. Duizer, *J. Chem. Phys. 45*, 1505 (1966).

36) F.B. Hildebrand, *"Methods of Applied Mathematics"*, Ch. 3, Prentice Hall, Englewood Cliff 1952.

37) R.A. Smith, *"Wave Mechanics in Crystalline Solids"*, Chapman and Hall, London 1961.

38) R.A. Orwell, W.H. Stockmayer, *Adv. Chem. Phys. 15*, 305 (1969).

39) B.D. Coleman and H. Markovitz, *J. Appl. Phys. 35*, 1 (1964).

40) P.J. Flory, *J. Am. Chem. Soc. 62*, 1057 (1940).

41) T.G. Fox, P.J. Flory, *J. Am. Chem. Soc. 70*, 2384 (1948); *J. Appl. Phys. 21*, 582 (1950); *J. Polymer Sci. 14*, 315 (1954).

42) T.G. Fox, S. Gratch, S. Loshaek, *"Rheology"*, F.R. Eirich Ed., Academic Press Inc., New York, Vol. 1, Ch. 12 (1956).

43) F. Bueche, *J. Polymer Sci. 43*, 527 (1960).

44) V.R. Allen, T.G. Fox, *J. Chem. Phys. 41*, 337 (1964); *J. Chem. Phys. 41*, 344 (1964).

45) K. Ninomiya, J.D. Ferry, *J. Phys. Chem. 67*, 2292 (1963).

46) Y. Oyanagi, J.D. Ferry, *J. Colloid Sci. 21*, 547 (1966).

47) T. Masuda, K. Kitagawa, S. Onogi, *Polymer J. 1*, 418 (1970).

48) L.A. Holmes, J.D. Ferry, *J. Polymer Sci C23*, 291 (1968).

49) S. Kusamizo, L.A. Holmes, A.A. Moore, J.D. Ferry, *Trans. Soc. Rheol. 12*, 559 (1968).

50) E. Ashare, *Ibid 12*, 535 (1968).

51) S. Onogi, T. Masuda, K. Kitagawa, *Macromol. 3*, 109 (1970).

52) T. Masudo, K. Kitagawa, T. Inoue, S. Onogi, *Macromol. 3*, 116 (1970).

53) H. Odani, S. Kitamura, N. Nemoto, M. Kurata, *Rep. Prog. Poly. Phys. Jap. 10*, 321 (1967).

54) T. Fujimoto, N. Ozaki, M. Nagasawa, *J. Polymer Sci. A2, 6*, 129 (1968).

55) N. Nemoto, M. Moriwaki, H. Odani, M, Kurata, *Macromol. 4*, 215 (1971).

56) G. Akovali, *J. Polymer Sci. A2, 5*, 875 (1967).

57) W. Prest, R.S. Porter, J.M. O'Reilly, *J. Appl. Polymer Sci. 14*, 2697 (1970).

58) N.J. Mills, A. Nevin, J. McAinsh, *J. Macromol. Sci., Phys. B4*, 863 (1970).

59) H.J.M.A. Mieras, C.F.H. van Rijn, *Nature 218*, 865 (1968).

60) W.W. Graessly, *J. Chem. Phys. 54*, 5143 (1971).

61) W.W. Graessly, *J. Chem. Phys. 43*, 2696 (1965).

62) F. Bueche, S.W. Harding, *J. Polymer Sci. 12*, 177 (1958).

63) W.W. Graessly, *J. Chem. Phys. 47*, 1942 (1967).

64) R.N. Schroff, *J. Appl. Phys. 41*, 3652 (1970).

65) H.C. Booij, Thesis, Leiden 1971.

66) G. Ajroldi, C. Garbuglio, G. Pezzin, *J. Polymer Sci A2, 5*, 289 (1967).

67) A.I. Leonov, *J. Appl. Mech. Techn. Phys 4*, 78 (1964).

68) R.I. Tanner, J.M. Simmons, *Chem. Eng. Sci. 22*, 1803 (1967).

69) J.A. Faucher, *J. Appl. Phys. 32*, 2336 (1961).

70) H. Eyring, T. Ree, *J. Appl. Phys. 26*, 793 (1955).

71) A.J. de Vries, J. Tochon, *J. Appl. Polymer Sci. 7*, 315 (1963).

5. Results

5.1 The Stress-Optical Law

We recall the stress-optical law as developed by Maxwell and Neumann, where for simple shear (Section 1.4) the results can be expressed by the relations:

$$\Delta n \sin 2\chi = 2\, n_{12} \qquad = 2\, Cp_{12} \qquad (5.1.1)$$

$$\Delta n \cos 2\chi = n_{11} - n_{22} = C(p_{11} - p_{22}) \qquad (5.1.2)$$

$$n_{22} - n_{33} = C(p_{22} - p_{33}) \qquad (5.1.3)$$

Lodge[1] emphasized in his original proposal for the stress-optical law (as applied to polymeric, amorphous liquids) that the relation rests on two hypotheses. One is that the off-diagonal components of the optical and the mechanical tensors are directly proportional to one another. The other is that the mechanical and optical tensors are coaxial. The first has been checked in this work for many materials in steady shear flow. This was achieved by examining the constancy of the ratio $\Delta n \sin 2\chi/2p_{12}$. As the theory required, this ratio was found to be independent of shear rate, molecular weight, and molecular weight distribution and agreed with results on elastomers and dilute solutions of the same polymer. The molecular weights were sufficiently high (> 20,000) for the avoidance of short chain effects. The second hypothesis has also been checked for a few cases where mechanical measurments were kindly made available to this author by other authors.

All measurements were made with cone-and-plate apparatuses. Most of them took place in a shear rate region not far from the Newtonian region of viscosities (exceptions are the high density polyethylenes of broad molecular weight distribution).

At present, there do not exist any means of measuring the normal stresses $p_{11} - p_{33}$, etc., in the region of shear stresses higher than about 10^4 N/m^2. It is, therefore, not possible to check the stress-optical relation at shear stresses higher than this. However, indirect evidence derived from measurements of frozen stresses and birefringences in injection moulding will be given,

5.1.1 The Constancy of $\Delta n \sin 2\chi/2p_{12}$ in Steady Shearing

Polystyrenes

The following materials of narrow molecular weight distribution have been measured: Pressure Chemical 3a, 6a, and 7a, and Dow S111. The following polymers of relatively broad molecular weight distribution were also investigated: Dow Styron 666, Styron 678, and BASF 3. It was not possible to measure every material at one given temperature, owing to the extreme range of viscosities involved. Where possible, a standard temperature of 190 °C was used. The low molecular weight polymers were measured at a lower temperature than this, and the high molecular weight polymers were measured at a higher temperature.

The optical equivalent to stress overshooting (see Section 4.5: Maximum Energy Model) did not appear to be present with any of these materials. The upper limit to the experimental shear rate range was imposed by depolarization which was probably due to parasitic gradients at the windows. The shear stress vs shear rate relations were obtained with a slit apparatus (Section 2.3). It was usually possible to measure the viscosity with the slit down to about 0.1 s^{-1}. For this purpose, a specially made electronic pressure gauge with a range 0-15 bar, was used. In some cases, the Newtonian viscosity was obtained by extrapolation and in others, it was measured. The results on the polystyrenes of narrow molecular weight distribution are given in Fig. 5.1. The range of the molecular weights was 50,000 (7a) to 860,000 (6a). Shown in each figure is the course of the viscosity and the absolute value of the ratio

$$C = \Delta n \, \sin 2\chi / 2 p_{12}$$

as a function of the shear rate. In fact, Δn is negative for polystyrene, when χ is defined as in Section 1.4. It is seen that, in every case, the ratio is a constant, independent of molecular weight (and temperature). However, it is also to be noticed that at the highest shear rates, which could be used in the cone-and-plate apparatus for birefringence, the steady shearing viscosity does not deviate significantly from the viscosity at zero shear rate. With these polystyrenes of narrow molecular weight distribution it was not possible to measure the birefringence and the extinction angle far into the region of non-Newtonian flow. Possibly as a consequence, the term $\sin 2\chi$ did not make a significant contribution to the constancy of the ratio $\Delta n \, \sin 2\chi / 2 p_{12}$, as the extinction angle deviated by less than 15° from 45°. Thus, these particular results do not form a strong evidence for the general applicability of the stress-optical relation. On the other hand, results with the commercial polystyrenes Styron 666, Styron 678, and BASF 3, which are shown in Fig. 5.2, do. These materials have a fairly wide distribution of molecular weights with M_w/M_n ranging from 2 to 5 (Table 3.2). We again find that the quantity $\Delta n \, \sin 2\chi / 2 p_{12}$ is independent of the gradient and has, for Styron 678, values near to those found for the polystyrenes of narrow molecular weight distribution. These commercial polymers are distinguished by the possibility of demonstrating the constancy of the ratio $\Delta n \, \sin 2\chi / p_{12}$ well into the region of non-Newtonian flow. The term $\sin 2\chi$ also makes a significant contribution to the constancy of the mentioned ratio, as the extinction angle deviates by up to 25° from 45°. The stress-optical coefficient, C, of Styron 666 and BASF 3, was significantly lower than that of the other polystyrenes (4.1 nm^2/N compared with about 5 nm^2/N). It is possible that the lower value is due to the presence of various processing aids which associate with the chains to alter their effective anisotropy. The values for C found here, are in agreement with the sparce measurements of C from tensile experiments with polystyrene elastomers[2,3], and with many results obtained with solutions of polystyrenes in matching solvents (solvents of the same refractive index)[4-5].

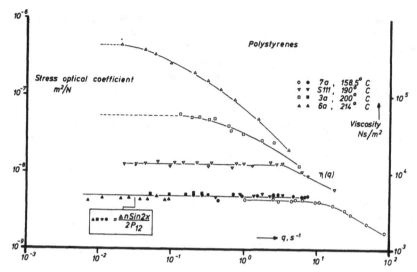

Fig. 5.1 The steady flow viscosity (open symbols) and the absolute value of
the stress-optical coefficient (filled symbols) for polystyrenes of
narrow molecular weight distribution as a function of the gradient
q.

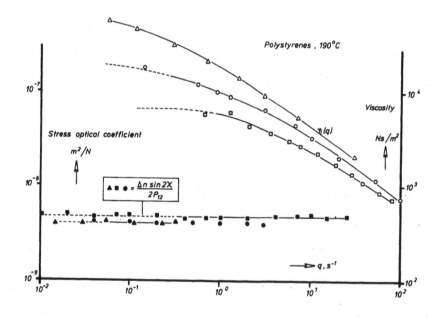

Fig. 5.2 The steady shearing viscosity (open symbols) and the absolute value
of the stress optical coefficient (filled symbols) for commercial
polystyrenes, as a function of gradient q.
□, ■... Styron 678; o,● ... Styron 666; Δ,▲ ... BASF 3.

Polyethylenes

The following polymers have been measured: HDND and HDBD (high density with respectively narrow and broad molecular weight distributions), LDND and LDBD (low density polymers) and material A (also low density). The birefringence measurements in the cone-and-plate apparatus were discontinued when either depolarization precluded measurement or stationary results were not obtained within a reasonable time (15 minutes at each speed). The latter problem often occurs with low density polyethylenes when the shear rate is too high and stress overshoot occurs. For the above materials, the dependency of the viscosity on the shear rate was obtained with cone-and-plate apparatus of the Kepes type. The only exception was material A, where a Weissenberg apparatus was used. The data are also to be found in the literature[6,7]. The temperature of measurement was mainly 150 °C. As with the polystyrenes, the quantity $C = \Delta n \sin 2X / 2p_{12}$ has been plotted against the shear rate along with the viscosity function. In Figs 5.3 and 5.4, the constancy of C can be seen despite a great variation in molecular weight, molecular weight distribution and non-linear behaviour. For HDBD, measurements were only possible in the non-Newtonian region of viscosity.

The low density polyethylenes of Fig. 5.4, have different molecular weight distributions, but similar flow behaviour (see Table 3.2). The flow behaviour of linear polymers, such as the high density polyethylenes, is much more sensitive to variations in the molecular weight and its distribution. This fact is generally ascribed to the chain branching in low density polyethylene. In the figure, the coefficient C appears to have a value somewhat smaller than the value for the high density polyethylenes (see also Table 5.1). The lower value could also be a result of branching in low density polyethylenes. If true, we expect the decrease with respect to the high density polymers to be proportional to the number of branches since the segment polarizability at a branch root will be more optically isotropic than at other places along the chain. This appears to be true, as the present author has found a linear relation between the stress-optical coefficient and the branching index of a series of low density polymers.

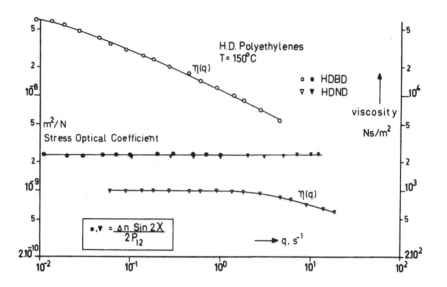

Fig. 5.3 *The viscosity (open symbols) and stress-optical coefficient (filled symbols) for two high density polyethylenes of widely differing molecular weight distributions.*

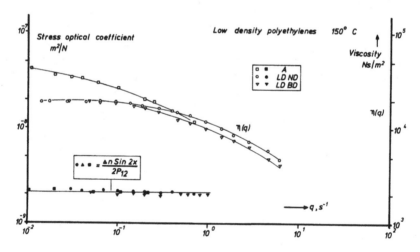

Fig. 5.4 *The viscosity (open symbols) and stress-optical coefficient (filled symbols) for low density polyethylenes of widely differing molecular weight distributions.*

The other materials measured were two polypropylenes and a polydimethyl-siloxane. The polypropylenes were of similar weight average molecular weight, but of different molecular weight distribution. As a result, their zero shearing viscosity was similar, but their non-linear behaviour and normal stresses were distinctly different[8]. The results are shown in Fig. 5.5. The scatter in the viscosity measurements is a consequence probably of oxygen attack for which polypropylene is extremely susceptible at high temperatures (see also Section 2.1.2). Nevertheless, it is clear as with the other polymers, that the stress-optical coefficient is constant independent of molecular weight and non-linear behaviour.

The results obtained for the silicone oil Siloprene RS, are shown in the following Fig. 5.6. The viscosities at low shear rates were kindly supplied by W. Philippoff. The result is the same as with the previous polymers: the stress optical coefficient is independent of the applied steady shearing gradient. This material has a distorted extrudate when it is pressed through capillaries at shear rates greater than about 30 s^{-1}. At this critical speed, the flow curve also shows a sharp bend. This is a general phenomenon which can be loosely called melt fracture. Most polymers show this pehnomenon at shear rates higher than are experimentally available with cone-and-plate apparatuses. This material is exceptional in that such shear rates were measurable. No kind of flow instability was observed in these experiments, however.

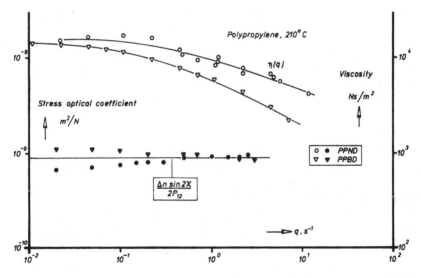

Fig. 5.5 The viscosity (open symbols) and the stress-optical coefficient (filled symbols) as a function of the shear rate for two poly-propylenes of nearly the same weight average molecular weight, but different distributions.

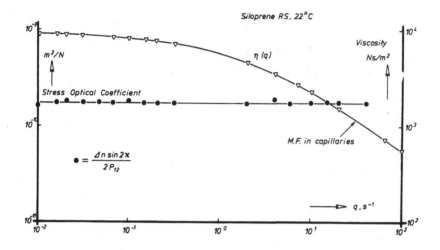

*Fig. 5.6 The viscosity (open symbols) and the stress-optical coefficient
(filled symbols) for a silicone oil. The results at low rates
were supplied by W. Philippoff.*

5.1.2 The Coaxiality of the Stress and Optical Tensors

Owing to the general unavailability of direct measurements of the normal
stress differences, the coaxiality of the tensors could be checked for two
polymers only: the two polypropylenes, and the low density polyethylene A.
The normal stress differences were determined with cone-and-plate apparatuses
of the Weissenberg type[7,8], together with the viscosity. Displayed in Figs
5.7 and 5.8 are the extinction angle X_0 obtained in the course of the streaming birefringence experiments, and the mechanical orientation X_m defined in
terms of the shear stress p_{12} and the first normal stress difference $p_{11} - p_{22}$.

$$\tan 2X_m = \frac{2\ p_{12}}{p_{11} - p_{22}} \qquad (5.1.4)$$

The correspondence between the mechanical and the optical orientations is
good and clearly justifies the application of the stress-optical relation - at
least for the systems and conditions investigated.

It has to be admitted in the case of the low density polyethylene that, at
higher shear rates than the ones shown, there appeared to be differences in
that, at long times, the optical extinction angle was a few degrees higher
than the mechanical. This appeared to be associated with the appearance of
stress-overshoot with both the mechanical and the optical quantities. Under
these conditions, of course, conditions of steady flow were unobtainable. It
was very difficult to decide whether the results represented a physical re-

ality or could still be due to an experimental artifact (see also Section 6).
Qualitatively, the behaviour of the extinction angles under these conditions,
is interesting as,with high shear rates,the extinction angle tends to increase
after some time instead of decrease, which is the normal behaviour.

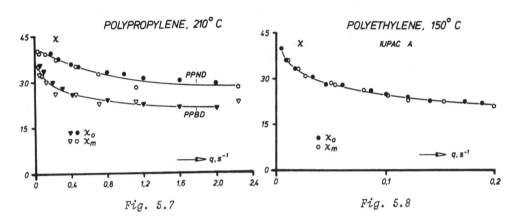

Fig. 5.7   Fig. 5.8

*The optical extinction angle, X_0, and the mechanical orientation angle of the
principal stresses, X_m, for polypropylenes (left) of narrow and broad molecular weight distribution,and for a low density polyethylene (right).*

5.1.3 Indirect Evidence of the Validity of the Stress-Optical Law at High
Shear Stresses

Indirect evidence was obtained for polystyrene during the course of injection moulding experiments with Styron 678[9]. Other results concerning injection moulding are discussed in a later section (5.5.2). When parallel sided
strips are moulded by injection at one end, the flow is mainly shear. After
the plate is ejected from the machine, processing stresses remain frozen in
the material. These stresses are composed of packing stresses, which effect
the density and of deviatoric stresses, which largely account for the warping
of the product on ageing or heat treatment. The deviatoric stresses (shear
and normal) are accompanied by frozen birefringence.

The magnitude of the shear stress frozen into the plate, can be estimated
from the time course of the pressure distribution along the cavity during injection. On sectioning the plates parallel to their longest edge, and perpendicular to their largest surface, one can examine the birefringence in the
1-2 plane of the frozen flow. In this way, edge effects are avoided which
would otherwise make examination of the flowing melt in the 1-2 plane difficult. The sections are placed under a polarizing microscope, with or without
a surrounding medium, and the extinction angles and birefringences are measured. In white light the extinction angle is derived from the position of a
sharp black line parallel to the edges. This line moves on rotation of the
crossed polaroids. (The reader will note that the extinction angle could not

65

be sharply determined with the flowing melt - Section 2.2: Measurements in the 1-2 plane.) The results were then used to check the constancy of the ratio $\Delta n \sin 2\chi / 2p_{12}$ as a function of the shear stress.

In the outlined experiments, the dimensions of the mould cavity were $2 \times 65 \times 300$ mm^3; the mould temperature was 50 °C; and the melt temperature varied from 210 °C to 250 °C.

Typical results are shown in Fig. 5.9. The upper part shows the required pressure distribution[9] and the central part the birefringence. Behind the flow front, the material freezes first at the walls. As a result, the direct proximity of the walls shows an optical structure, more or less independent of the filling conditions, e.g. injection pressure. In the central planes of the cavity the effects of longitudinal gradients are noticeable. In this central region, the optical pattern is the most strongly influenced by any relaxation phenomena after the mould filling cycle.

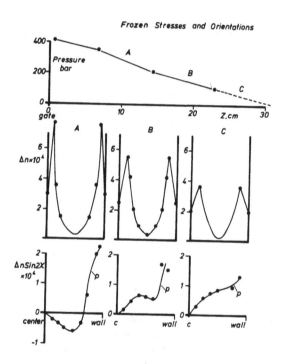

Fig. 5.9 *Typical results from injection moulding experiments on Styron 678.*
   Moulding conditions: melt temperature 230 °C; mould temperature 50 °C; injection pressure 510 bar.
   Upper : *the longitudinal pressure distribution before the gate freezes.*
   Centre : *birefringence distribution in the 1-2 plane for regions A,B and C of the upper figure.*
   Lower : *distribution of the optical shear component across the section for regions A, B and C of the upper figure.*

On account of these considerations it is believed that, during the mould filling process, the flow near the birefringence peak (Fig. 5.9 centre) makes the closest approximation to steady shearing flow.

The region of the peak in the birefringence pattern was therefore used to evaluate the course of the stress-optical coefficient at high shear stresses.

The distribution of the shear component $\Delta n \sin 2\chi$ is shown in the lower portion of Fig. 5.9. In the region of the peak, the extinction angle is small - between 4° and 10° in the investigated cases - and $\sin 2\chi$ is subject to considerable error. $\Delta n \sin 2\chi$ might be expected to vary linearly over the plate cross-section. This does not appear to occur. The strongest deviations from linearity are near the gate and are probably the result of back flow after the mould was filled. On occasions the back flow near the gate can be seen in the frozen birefringence pattern by the presence of secondary peaks or in the stress, by a change in sign of the pressure distribution. A full account of all these and other details cannot be given as yet. They are, of course, important for the process but not for the point to be made here.

From a series of plates made by injection at various pressures, the ratios $\Delta n \sin 2\chi / 2p_{12}$ were determined and plotted, in Fig. 5.10, against the shear stress. The latter was estimated from the frozen longitudinal pressure gradient, using the depth of the cavity and the position of the peak (cf. formula 2.5.1). The results for true steady shearing flow are also shown for comparison. Scatter with the injection moulding experiments is large, but it is clear that the ratio of the shear components is an essentially constant quantity over the whole range of shear stresses.

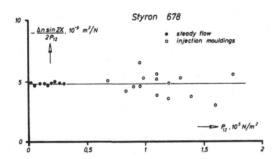

Fig. 5.10 *The stress optical coefficient as a function of shear stress for steady shearing experiments and from the stresses and birefringence frozen in injection mouldings.*

The upper shear stress limit to the measurements on injection moulded plates was about six times that with the cone-and-plate experiments. This factor would seem to be relatively small but it should be born in mind that, owing to the extreme non-linear behaviour of the viscosity function, shear rates under isothermal conditions - at 190 °C - would have to range up to 10^4 s^{-1} in a laboratory apparatus to cover the same shear stress region. This cannot be achieved at present with any apparatus.

5.1.4 Temperature Dependence of the Stress-Optical Coefficient

The stress-optical coefficient C for amorphous melts is, according to the theory, a function of the structure of the monomeric units. Inspection of the expression given by the simple theory (Equation 4.1.18) shows that the coefficient may change with temperature by three mechanisms:

1) The ubiquitous kT factor - C should decrease with increasing temperature, but by a small amount since the temperature T is in degrees Kelvin, and often only a moderate temperature range is available.

2) Density changes - these alter the refractive index and the Lorentz-Lorenz factor. The influence of density changes is very small, however, and can be neglected for most work. For example taking polydimethylsiloxane, the effect is no more than 3 % in going from 20° to 190 °C.

3) Conformation changes altering the anisotropy of the random link - for the real polymer chain, the frequency and ordering of the rotational isomers determines the effective segment anisotropy[10,11]. Temperature changes can be expected to alter this balance[38]. As a consequence, the stress-optical coefficient can be temperature dependent. The exact theory can be given in a formal way only[12]. For applications, simplifications have to be made, and doubts remain as to the correctness of the basic premisses, e.g. additivity of bond polarizabilities. Nevertheless, the stress-optical method has had some use for the substantiation of proposed models for the real-chain sequencing of the rotational isomers.

As a result of changes to the isomer distribution, C may either decrease or increase with increasing temperature - ignoring the first effects 1) and 2). Three of the materials chosen for this work show the three different types of behaviour possible. The stress-optical coefficient of polystyrene is independent of temperature, that of polyethylene decreases slightly with increasing temperature, but that of polydimethylsiloxane increases with increasing temperature. The same behaviour of the stress-optical coefficient is also found by static stretching of elastomers of the same polymers[2,13-17].

The most striking effect is with the silicones. Figure 5.11 shows the evaluated stress-optical coefficients for the polydimethylsiloxane E302 at 22, 105 and 190 °C. For comparison, other results for elastomers from the same polymer type, but crosslinked by various methods, are also shown. A fair agreement is found between values and temperature dependencies of the stress-optical coefficient as determined by the various methods. The stress-optical coefficient of polydimethylsiloxane is small and sensitive to chemical impurities[18]. This latter fact may explain the dependency on the method of crosslinking and the result that C from flow birefringence is greater for Siloprene RS than for E302 (see Table 5.1).

A smaller relative change in C with temperature was found for polyethylene. For the high density type, the stress-optical coefficient decreased from 2.4×10^{-9} m^2/N at 150 °C to 1.8×10^{-9} m^2/N at 190 °C. This decrease appears to be in agreement with results obtained for elastomers of this material[15].

The physical origin of the marked increase in C with increasing temperature for the silicone oil is thought to be a decrease in population of bonds in the trans conformation. The coil expands since the corresponding increase in the number of bonds in the "gauche" position causes an increase in the chain end-to-end distance.

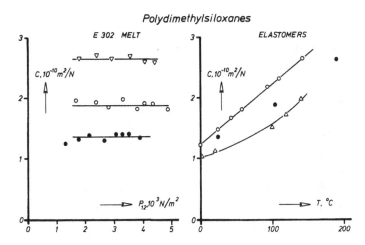

Fig. 5.11 Left: The stress optical coefficient for a silicone oil as a function of shear stress at o ... 20 °C, o ... 105 °C; ∇ ... 190 °C. Right: The stress-optical coefficient of silicone elastomers as a function of temperature. Δ ... crosslinked with 8 % "hydride" (Ref. [17]); o ... crosslinked by 1 % dichlorobenzoyl peroxide, giving same results as by irradiation (Refs[17] and[16]); ● ... this work.

The same mechanism is also thought to cause the stress-optical coefficient and the chain end-to-end distance of polyethylene to decrease with increase of temperature. This remarkable difference in behaviour between the two polymers is to be explained apparently[17] by the difference of the two bond angles OSiO and SiOSi, whereby the trans form of the chain is coiled-up for the silicone. The trans form of the polyethylene chain is the fully stretched chain.

Table 5.1

Stress-Optical Coefficients

material	M_W		temp.	C
	(10^5)		(°C)	$(10^{-9}\ m^2/N)$
HDBD			150	2.4
HDBD			190	1.8
HDND			150	2.35
A			150	2.1
LDND	1		150	2.1
LDBD	4.2		150	2.0
PPND	5	(1)	210	0.9
PPBD	4	(1)	210	0.9
Siloprene	3.8	(2)	22	0.175
E302	7.7	(2)	25	0.135
E302	7.7	(2)	105	0.19
E302	7.7	(2)	190	0.265
Styron 666	3.7		190	4.1
Styron 678			190	4.8
BASF 3	4.1		178	4.5
BASF 3	4.1		188	4.6
BASF 3	4.1		200	4.4
BASF 3	4.1		214.5	4.2
S111	2.2		190	5
3a	3.9		200	5.2
6a	8.6		214	4.4
7a	0.51		158.5	5

(1) M_v in Decaline at 135 °C
(2) M_v in Toluene at 25 °C

5.2 Intrinsic Quantities at Zero Shearing

In view of the great interest in the molecular theories, part of this work was carried out with a series of polystyrenes of narrow molecular weight distribution. The range of molecular weights was 5×10^4 to 1.8×10^6. For practical reasons, the temperature was varied between 150 °C and 240 °C, depending on the molecular weight under examination. Measurement of each polymer at one temperature would require an apparatus capable of covering a viscosity range of nearly five decades. To convert to the isothermal standard of 190 °C, the results were adjusted with the aid of experimentally determined temperature shift factors (Section 5.3.3) from some members of the series (S111, 6a and 3a).

The zero shearing limits (intrinsic values) of the following quantities were determined:

$$A = \frac{n_{12}}{q} = \frac{\Delta n \sin 2X}{2q} \tag{5.2.1}$$

$$B = \frac{n_{11} - n_{22}}{q^2} = \frac{\Delta n \cos 2X}{q^2} \tag{5.2.2}$$

Twice the zero shearing limit of the first quantity is sometimes called the intrinsic Maxwell constant. Apart from the numerical factor, this is the optical equivalent to the zero shearing viscosity. The second quantity B is the optical equivalent of the coefficient of the first normal stress difference. Figure 5.12 shows the experimental ratios A and B as a function of the shear rate at the temperature of measurement for each member of the series. Two members of low molecular weight (51,000 and 97,000) were measurable in the region of second order flow only and, as a consequence, the ratios remained unchanged within the shear rate range. For the other, higher, molecular weights both A and B decreased with increasing gradient, but extrapolation to the second order region was still possible. The zero shear limits of A and B were then shifted to correspond to 190 °C and the results were plotted in Fig. 5.13 to show the molecular weight dependency.

From the results shown in Fig. 5.13, the following relations were empirically found to describe the relationships between the intrinsic quantities and the molecular weight:

$$\lim_{q \to o} \frac{n_{12}}{q} = 2 \times 10^{-22} M^{3.3}, \quad T = 190 °C \tag{5.2.3}$$

$$\lim_{q \to o} \frac{n_{11} - n_{22}}{q^2} = 2.2 \times 10^{-40} M^{6.6}, \quad T = 190 °C \tag{5.2.4}$$

The first relation corresponds well with the relation for the molecular weight dependency of the Newtonian viscosity. Fox and Flory[19] gave an exponent of 3.4 for the viscosity relation and other authors have given other values close to this.

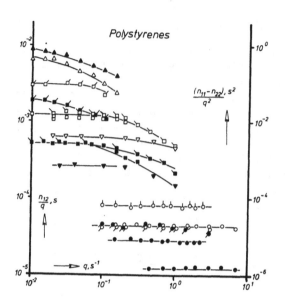

Fig. 5.12 *The optical equivalents of the viscosity and the coefficient of the first normal stress difference. Open symbols ... n_{12}/q, closed symbols ... $(n_{11} - n_{22})/q^2$. ●○ ... 7a, ▲▽ ... 4a, ◗◖ ... S111, ▼▽ ... 1a, ■□ ... 3a, ◗□ ... 5a, ◗□ ... 6a, ▲△ ... 14a. For the temperatures of measurement, see Table 3.1.*

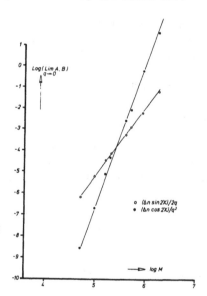

Fig. 5.13 *Intrinsic quantities at zero shear rate for polystyrenes of narrow molecular weight distribution. All results converted to 190 °C.*
○... Lim q→0, n_{12}/q, ● ... Lim q→0, $(n_{11} - n_{22})/q^2$.

Using these results and a stress-optical coefficient of 5×10^{-9} m^2/N (see Table 5.1), the following relation for J_e was determined with the aid of Eq. (1.3.6):

$$J_e = 1.4 \times 10^{-5} \text{ m}^2/\text{N} \qquad (5.2.5)$$

for all molecular weights.

However, the normal stress function is very sensitive to molecular weight and the applied shear gradient. It is also possible that, at the higher molecular weights, the results were not ideally extrapolated to zero shear rate. For the determination of J_e a better extrapolation method is to use the ratio of half the normal stress difference to the square of the shear stress. This ratio becomes equal to J_e in the limit of zero shear stress, yet it is far less shear rate dependent than the viscosity and normal stress coefficients individually. Figure 5.14 shows the shear rate dependency of the ratio of the corresponding optical quantities $\frac{1}{2}(n_{11} - n_{22})/n_{12}^2$, which we shall define as J_{eo}.

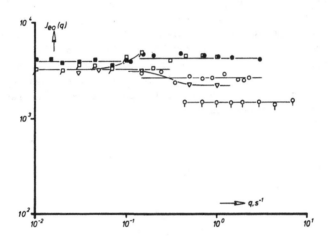

Fig. 5.14 *The optical corollary $J_{eo} = \frac{1}{2}(n_{11} - n_{22})/n_{12}^2$ to the steady shearing compliance, plotted as a function of the shear rate q. The results show that J_{eo} is insensitive to the shear rate for these polymers of narrow molecular weight distribution, even when the viscosity is non-Newtonian.*

φ *7a .. at 158 °C; o 4a .. at 168 °C; ∇ 1a .. at 165 °C; $\bullet$ ... S111 at 196 °C; $\square$ 5a .. at 200 °C; $\blacksquare$ 6a .. at 214 °C; $\square$ 14a .. at 242 °C.*

We find within the scatter of the measurements, independency of the shear rate, even in the region where a pronounced non-Newtonian viscosity is found (compare Fig. 5.1).

According to the results shown in Fig. 5.14, a weak dependency of J_{eo} on the molecular weight is found, which was lost by the previous analysis of the data in Fig. 5.13. J_{eo} appears to increase with molecular weight to reach a plateau

73

at a molecular weight of about 200,000. By a simple multiplication by the stress-optical coefficient, J_e is calculated for the plateau region to be about 1.8×10^{-5} m^2/N, which is in good agreement with the work of others (see Fig. 4.1).

5.3 Results with the Slit Apparatus

5.3.1 The Influence of the Aspect Ratio

As a check on the important supposition that the edge effects were not of great influence, the birefringence, $n_{11} - n_{33}$, of a low density polyethylene was measured with slits A, B and C (see Table 2.1). Slit B with an aspect ratio of 30 : 1, was used for measurements at a distance of L/a = 15 and L/a = 35 from the entrance. Slit C with an aspect ratio of 12.5 : 1, was used for measurements at L/a = 15, whilst slit A with an aspect ratio of 10 : 1, was used for measurements at L/a = 35 from the entrance. Slits A and C have nearly the same aspect ratio (order of 10 : 1). It was found that the slits of aspect ratio 10 : 1 gave exactly the same results as the slit of aspect ratio 30 : 1. These results for a polyethylene are shown in Fig. 5.15. The same independency on the aspect ratio was also found for the polystyrene Styron 678. Since a very large range of non-Newtonian viscosity behaviour was covered by these two materials, it is believed that these results confirm from the experimental standpoint the sufficiency of slits of aspect ratio 10 : 1. The two curves in Fig. 5.15, indicate that, whilst the aspect ratio has no influence on the results, the distance of the measuring point from the entrance has. This is the subject of the next section.

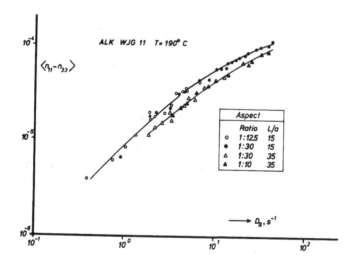

Fig. 5.15 The influence of the aspect ratio on measurements of the 1-3 plane birefringence with slits. The two different curves were obtained by measurement at two different reduced distances from the entrance.

5.3.2 The Influence of Pre-history

As a measure of the pre-history in ducts, we may take the distance of the observers window from the entrance to the channel. However, other factors play a role as well. Such factors are for instance the method of filling or the shape of the entrance. The first point to be noted is that different materials show widely different types of behaviour in this respect. The polystyrenes examined did not show a pronounced influence of pre-history: the same birefringence was obtained when measurements were made at $L/a = 35$ or $L/a = 96$ from the entrance. For this material, the entrance effects die out at quite a short distance from the entrance. On the other hand, low density polyethylenes formed an exceptional class of materials as they often did not reach a state of equilibrium flow - even with the longest slits available. The material of Fig. 5.15 was such an example. For the determination of $n_{11} - n_{33}$ with a view to obtaining equilibrium quantities, it is therefore essential to check by measuring at two or more positions in the slit. For an examination of the changes occurring in the duct in the direct neighbourhood of the entrance, the present slit dies are unsuited. In order to get an impression of the birefringence changes near the entrance, measurements have been made with short glass capillaries mounted in a holder in the reservoir of a piston driven viscometer. The outer surface of the capillary was thus surrounded by polymer. This lessened the influence of the hydrostatic pressure on the capillary glass and at the same time almost completely nullified the lens effect of the outer surface of the capillary. The complete capillary was viewed via windows mounted in the wall of the reservoir and the birefringence determined in the usual way. With flat entrances to the capillaries, the findings had the general shape of the findings for slits. With polystyrenes equilibrium was reached, however, at very short distances from the entrance and for those measured (Styron 666 and BASF 3) this was less than 10 diameters.

With glass capillaries the field is non-uniform, but compensation can be achieved readily along the axis. In the equilibrium region this is related via a relation similar to (2.2.4) to the birefringence at the wall. For quantitative measurements glass capillaries are less suited than slits in that the results are less reproducible. The strains in the glass form one factor. The other is that glass is a bad conductor of heat, and temperature variations can more readily occur. Examples showing the monotonic decrease of the birefringence as the fluid flows along a slit and along a glass capillary, are shown in Fig. 5.16. The left hand part shows that, with the LDPE Alkathene 2, equilibrium is not reached in any slit of length less than 100 depths. The right hand part shows, on the other hand, that for the polystyrene, Styron 666, equilibrium is consistently reached within 5 capillary diameters.

In the above, the orientation decreased to an equilibrium value. This decrease is modified when the material is pressed into the duct by a screw extruder instead of by a piston as in the above examples. It is also modified when the material passes a restriction at the entrance to the capillary. When a screw extruder was used with low density polyethylene, the birefringence still decreased along the slit, but started at a lower value, later to coincide with that found in experiments with a piston driven viscometer. After passing a restriction it is even possible for the birefringence to increase in

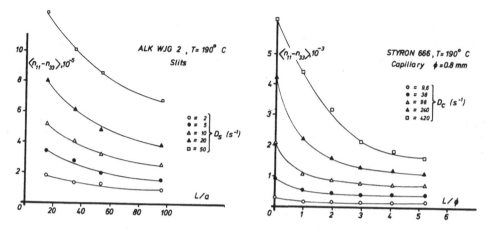

Fig. 5.16. Left: Plotted against the reduced distance from the entrance, L/a,
is the birefringence in the 1-3 plane for LDPE in slits. For practical purposes, equilibrium flow in ducts does not exist with this
material.

Right: For comparison, the birefringence in the 1-3 plane for a
polystyrene in a capillary. The extremely short reduced distance
needed to reach equilibrium is typical of this material.

the direction of flow. In this case the equilibrium length of the capillary
seems to be greater than without the restriction. Such an entrance has been
used to study the orientation induced by injection moulding where at the entrance to the mould, a "gate" is present[9].

The explanation of these results can only be given in a qualitative way.
It would appear that, in both cases, the polymer has been badly mauled
before entering the capillary proper. As a result, its viscosity just inside
the entrance is lower than it would otherwise have been. Qualitative support
for this view is to be found in the widely experienced observation that after
steady shearing at a high shear rate, e.g. with a cone-and-plate apparatus,
the viscosity at a lower shear rate is initially lower than the equilibrium
viscosity for that shear rate.

5.3.3 The Equilibrium Quantity $n_{11} - n_{33}$

Temperature Superposition: Figure 5.17 shows results of measurements on Sty-
ron 666 of the average birefringence $\phi = \langle n_{11} - n_{33} \rangle$ at various temperatures
between 130 °C and 220 °C in the reduced output range $D_s = 0.3$ to 10 s^{-1}. By
shifting along the shear rate or D_s axis with a factor a_T, the measured curves
are superimposable. The procedure of shifting along a rate axis to obtain superposition is termed time-temperature superposition, and was briefly alluded to
in previous chapters. By the procedure it is possible to derive, by measuring
at a different temperature, the probable behaviour of a given property in a
rate region outside of the experimental window. The procedure has a strong em-

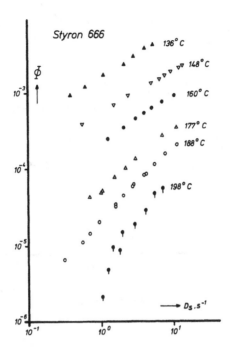

Fig. 5.17. The birefringence, φ, for the polystyrene Styron 666 measured with the slit apparatus for reduced outputs, D_s. The measurements were made at a distance of 35 slit depths from the entrance.

pirical basis for the linear viscoelastic region. However, for non-linear properties, although generally believed valid, there is not a great accumulation of experimental evidence to support its use. The physical root on which time--temperature superposition depends, is that all relaxation times of the flow processes in the material change with temperature by the same factor. For the linear region, the quantitative relation between the shift factor and the temperature is often of the WLF kind (Ref.[34]) of Chapter 4). The master curves obtained by superposition for Styron 666 and for S111 with BASF 3, are shown in Figs 5.18 and 5.19, respectively. In these figures, an additional vertical shifting by ρT factors has also been carried out[*].

For Styron 666, a few measurements were obtained with the same slit fed by a screw extruder. In this way, it was possible to make direct measurements at outputs up to 300 s^{-1} at 190 °C, and compare these with the results deduced at 300 s^{-1} from the temperature shift method. The agreement is good. The shift

[*]Within experimental error the extra vertical shifting is an unnecessary refinement to obtain superposition. The procedure was carried out merely to comply with the normal methods in dynamic mechanical studies.

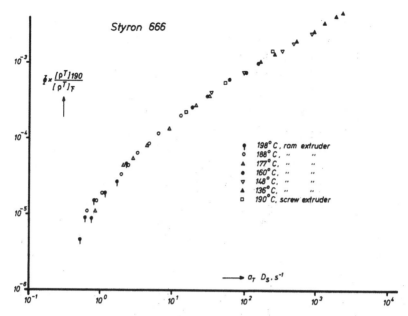

Fig. 5.18 Master plot showing reduction of measured birefringence (φ) at various temperatures to 190 °C for Styron 666.

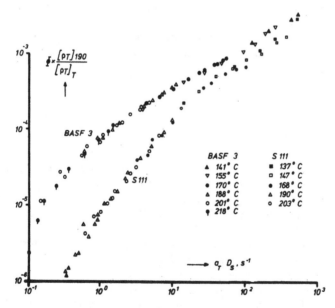

Fig. 5.19 Master plot showing reduction of measured birefringence (φ) at various temperatures to 190 °C for BASF 3 and S111.

factors are collected in Fig. 5.20 for Styron 666 and Fig. 5.21 for BASF 3 and S111. In both cases, 190 °C is the base temperature. The shifts found from measurements of G' and G" as a function of ω and T are also shown. It is clear

78

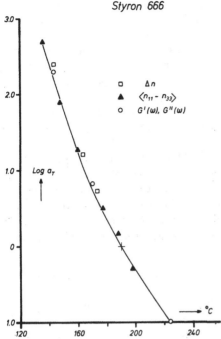

Fig. 5.20 Temperature shift factors obtained for polystyrene from measurements of the streaming birefringence in a cone-and-plate, in a slit die and from dynamic mechanical measurements.

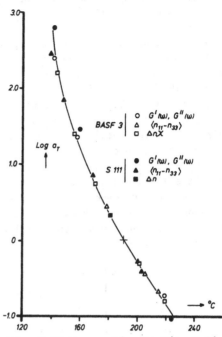

Fig. 5.21 See caption to Fig. 5.20.

that all the different techniques give the same results. Thus, for polystyrene we conclude that the same time-temperature superposition is valid for the linear and the non-linear regions of rheological behaviour, as well as for optical and mechanical quantities.

The procedure will have to be refined in the case of the optical measurements when the stress-optical coefficient is a function of temperature. In this event, additional vertical shifting will be needed to obtain coincidence of the mechanical and optical rate-shift factors. This was observed with the silicone oils where the shifts to obtain superposition long the rate axis, were different for the extinction angle and the birefringence. The extinction angle gave the same results as found with mechanical measurements.

One may conjecture that comparison of the optical and the mechanical shifts along the rate axes might help one to determine the temperature dependency of the stress-optical coefficient of materials such as polyethylene over a much wider range of temperatures than is possible by the usual method of stretching the crosslinked material in an inert atmosphere. The usual procedure is not suitable for many polymers owing to stability problems and the difficulty of crosslinking some polymers. In particular, temperatures of the order of 300 °C should become accessible by the proposed method. Such measurements could be helpful in studies of the rotational isomer balance in polymeric systems.

Molecular Weight Dependency - Polystyrenes: This was generally determined with slit A at a distance L/a =.35 from the entrance. Both polymers of narrow molecular weight distribution (7a, S111, 5a and 6a) and commercial polymers were measured. The polymer with the highest molecular weight, 14a, was also measured, but the results could not be used as the flow was not uniform in the 3-direction. Pressures were measured simultaneously with the ram speed and the birefringence. The results have been set out in Fig. 5.22 with the birefringence as a function of the shear stress at the wall of the slit. The quantity $\langle n_{11} - n_{33} \rangle$ is seen to vary approximately as the square of the shear stress (drawn lines), except at the highest shear stresses where in one case (S111) there is a clear tendency for the birefringence to increase at a faster rate. The reason for this is unknown, but it is noted that indications of similar behaviour have been found with normal stresses $p_{11} - p_{22}$ and polystyrene solutions at lower shear stresses than the present[20].

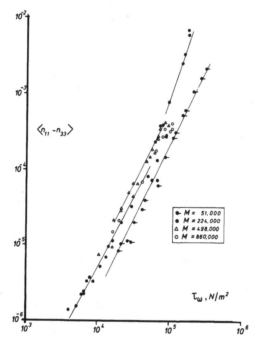

Fig. 5.22 *The measured birefringence in the 1-3 plane as a function of shear stress τ_w with the slit apparatus: polystyrenes of narrow molecular weight distribution. At high molecular weights the birefringence is nearly independent of the molecular weight.*

The ratio $\langle n_{11} - n_{33} \rangle / p_{12}^2$ seems to increase with molecular weight up to a critical molecular weight above which it remains constant. These results closely follow results with J_{eo}, as seen in Fig. 5.14. In analogy with the relation of J_{eo} to the normal stress differences we define an optical quantity G_{eo} which is equal to the ratio $\frac{1}{2}(n_{11} - n_{33})/n_{12}^2$. In the limit of zero shearing, this should be equal to J_{eo}, according to the basic molecular theories (Rouse, etc.) since for these $n_{22} = n_{33}$. In the extended model, described in Section 4.3, G_{eo} should be up to 15 % smaller than J_{eo}. Indeed, it was always found that G_{eo} was smaller than J_{eo}, the average difference being about 15 % of J_{eo}. The precision of the method is, however, not sufficient for a more quantitative comparison with the theory outlined in that section. The value of $n_{22} - n_{33}$ depends on the difference between two quantities, the absolute precision of each is not better than 10 %.

The basic molecular models appear to be unsatisfactory in not giving the correct dependence of J_{eo} and G_{eo} upon the molecular weight. However, they additionally suggest that J_{eo} and G_{eo} shoud be sensitive to the broadness of the molecular weight distribution. The broader the molecular weight distribution, the larger the value of each quantity. In Fig. 5.23 the measured values of $\langle n_{11} - n_{33} \rangle$ are given for BASF 3, Styron 678 and S111. The commercial polymers, which have much wider molecular weight distributions than S111, show distinctly greater effects than S111. BASF 3, at equal shear stress, produces six times the birefringence which S111 gives. This is less than that would be expected on the basis of the polydispersity factor of the Rouse theory (about 9). However, it is greater than indicated in one model of Graessly (end Section 4.4) where optical strengths of these two materials should be proportional to M_z/M_w and accordingly (see Table 3.2), BASF 3 should have been only about three times stronger than S111. Similarly, the optical strength of Styron 678 seems to lie between the two models.

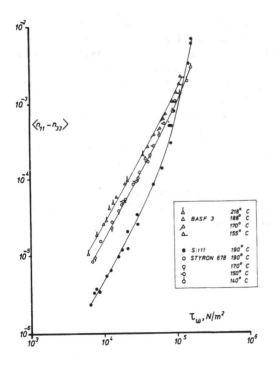

Fig. 5.23 The measured birefringence in the 1-3 plane as a function of shear stress τ_ω with the slit apparatus: S111 and two commercial polystyrenes. At low shear stresses, the differing polydispersities determine the birefringence level.

5.3.4 Measurements in the 1-2 Plane

The experimental procedure was outlined in Section 2.2. The method should be used only when other methods of obtaining the stress-optical coefficient fail. This may occur when the material is either too viscous or too unstable (thermally). The coefficient is evaluated from the initial slope of the birefringence - shear stress relation. The birefringence, Δn, is given as:

$$\Delta n = (4\, n_{12}^2 + (n_{11} - n_{22})^2)^{\frac{1}{2}} \qquad (5.3.1)$$

Assuming that the stress-optical relation holds and relation (4.1.17) is valid there follows:

$$\Delta n = 2\, Cp_{12}(1 + (\frac{n_{11} - n_{22}}{2\, n_{12}})^2)^{\frac{1}{2}} \qquad (5.3.2)$$

At low shear rates $\frac{1}{2}(n_{11} - n_{22}) = J_{eo}n_{12}^2$. Substitution of this relation and expansion leads to:

$$\Delta n = 2\, Cp_{12} + C^3 J_{eo}^2 p_{12}^3 + \ldots \ldots \qquad (5.3.3)$$

The experimental results are to be fitted by a least squares procedure to a cubic polynomial of the form $Ap_{12} + Bp_{12}^3$. (In general, Δn is an odd function of p_{12}.) The numerical values of A and B yield the stress-optical coefficient, C, and J_{eo}.

Figure 5.24 shows the results of measurements on Styron 666 at 190 °C. The drawn curve follows the computed cubic. The dashed line has slope A and therefore represents the shear component of the total birefringence. The difference between the dashed and the full line represents the contribution from the second term in (5.3.3). The value found for C was 3.8×10^{-9} m^2/N compared with 4.1×10^{-9} m^2/N from the more accurate cone-and-plate measurements. J_{eo} was found to be 0.7×10^4 compared with 1×10^4 from the cone-and-plate measurements. It is seen that both quantities are of the correct order, the error in C being about 10 % The results were also evaluated with an added term proportional to p_{12}^5. The stress-optical coefficient then decreased to 3.5×10^{-9} m^2/N, and J_{eo} increased to 1×10^4.

Figure 5.25 shows the results of similar measurements on Solvic 229, a rigid PVC, at 210 °C. The initial slope gave a C value of 4.2×10^{-10} m^2/N from the cubic, and 3.8×10^{-10} m^2/N from the pentic polynomial, respectively.

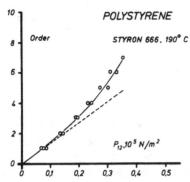

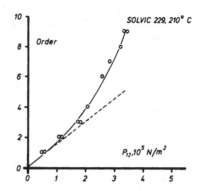

Fig. 5.24 Path difference, by counting
isochromes in 1-2 plane, as a function
of shear stress for a slit of section
10 mm × 1 mm. The material is polystyrene.
The dashed line determined by regression gives the initial slope and the
stress-optical coefficient.

Fig. 5.25 See caption to 5.24.
The material is rigid PVC.

The table below gives values of the stress-optical coefficient found by the
slit method (cubic polynomial) in the temperature range 180 °C to 210 °C.

Table 5.2

Stress-Optical Coefficients of Rigid PVC

Temp. (°C)	C (m^2/N)
180	4.3×10^{-10}
192	5.5
205	5.3
210	4.2

Considering that determination of C by this method for the polystyrene led
to too small a value, it is expected that the real stress-optical coefficient
of rigid PVC is little higher than the values given in the table.

It is seen that the stress-optical coefficient is appoximately independent
of the temperature in the range considered. This is of interest since rigid
PVC is believed to undergo in this temperature region, a change in its flow

mechanism from particulate or supramolecular to molecular*. The values found
for C in the above, are somewhat higher than values in the literature[21]
(3 to 4 × 10^{-10} m^2/N). However, the latter were obtained from creep measurements extrapolated to the region of steady flow at temperatures of the order
of T_g ($\sim$ 70 °C).

5.4 Results with the Capillary Apparatus (n_{22} - n_{33})

5.4.1 The Influence of Entrance and Exit Effects

Figures 5.26 and 5.27 show the basic experimental results obtained with
capillary instruments on the silicone, Siloprene RS, and on the low density
polyethylene, IUPAC A, respectively. In both cases the measured optical effect,
proportional to n_{33} - n_{22}, was positive. This was seen from the position of the
compensator and of the extinction fringe.

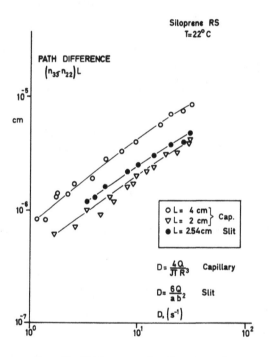

Fig. 5.26 The measured path difference in the 2-3 plane at the wall for a silicone oil as a function of the shear gradient for various capillaries
and a slit with lengths, L, indicated.

*In our case, the particles must have been smaller than the wavelength of light
since optical measurements were possible. It is not possible to satisfactorily
measure PVC melts at lower temperatures on account of the strong depolarization that occurs (particle flow?).

84

The silicone oil is an optically weak material (see Table 5.1) and could not be measured with the shortest capillary. Instead, an additional measurement was made with a slit, lent by W. Philippoff. An attachment was fitted to the apparatus of Fig. 2.9. With this arrangement, the field of view was different to that in Fig. 2.9 bottom. On onset of flow with the polaroids crossed at 45 °C to the axes of flow symmetry, the central region of the split remained

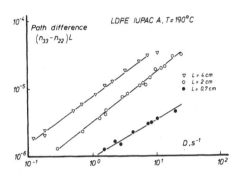

Fig. 5.27 The measured path difference in the 2-3 plane for a low density polyethylene as function of shear rate for different capillary lengths.

dark, and the region near the wall lighted up. On compensation, a dark fringe moved from the central region to the wall. Compensation was taken when the fringe was judged to be at the wall. The obtained path differences at the wall were then correlated with the reduced output, D, for the slit. The gradient at the wall was obtained from D with the help of Rabinowitsch correction factors from previous calibrations of the material. For the silicone under discussion, the corrections are very nearly the same (within 10 %) for both slits and capillaries. It is therefore justifiable to compare results as a function of reduced outputs for slits and capillaries in the same figure as is done in Figs 5.27 and 5.28. The latter shows the dependency on the capillary length.

Clearly, the optical path difference increases essentially linearly with the capillary length. This indicates that the measured effect is either a real material effect indicative of non-zero $n_{22} - n_{33}$ and/or a window effect. If the whole effect were determined by the entrance flow, then one could not expect the path difference to depend on the capillary length. In the case of silicone oil, the lines, extrapolated to zero capillary length, go within experimental uncertainty through the origin of the coordinate system. For this material one concludes that, within experimental error, the optical effect is entirely due to the flow in the capillaries, and entrance or exit flows make no important contribution. In the case of low density polyethylene(IUPAC A)(Fig.5.29)on the other hand, the linear plot extrapolated through the experimental results, indicates the existence of an entrance correction which is, however, negative. In this case, the optical effect is partially caused by entrance-exit flows. However, the entrance flow apparently compensates for the orientation formed in the capillary. Again the greatest part of the measured effect must be ascribed to

85

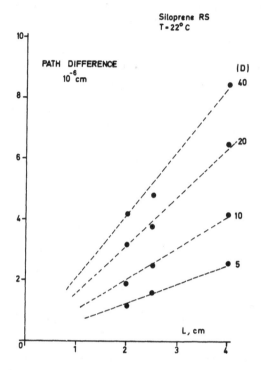

Fig. 5.28 Data from Fig. 5.26, replotted to show that the measured effect in the 2-3 plane is proportional to the capillary length and that entrance/exit effects are negligible. The reduced outputs, D, are in-indicated.

flow in the capillary.

Similar measurements have also been made for the polystyrene Styron 678 and BASF 3 (not shown). Again, for these materials, the optical effect varies essentially linearly with the capillary length, and entrance-exit effects were insignificantly small compared with the capillary effect. For these polystyrenes the sign of the effect was reversed, i.e. $n_{22} - n_{33}$ was found to be positive. This is in keeping with the principal anisotropies of polystyrene for which $n_{11} - n_{22}$ is negative. So, for the polystyrenes the ratio $(n_{22} - n_{33})/(n_{11} - n_{22})$ is also a negative quantity, just as with the silicone oil and the low density polyethylene.

A remarkable result of the present findings is that the optical effect is a linear function of the capillary length. This might not have been expected after the results for the corresponding quantity $n_{11} - n_{33}$ (Section 5.3.2). The explanation is, presumably, the fact that $n_{11} - n_{33}$ may contain effects of longitudinal gradients which are optically ineffective in the 2-3 plane.

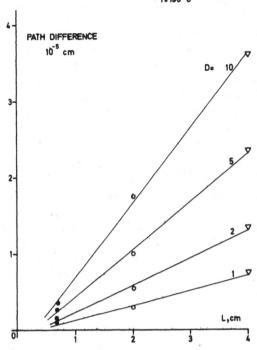

Fig. 5.29 Data from Fig. 5.27, replotted to show that the measured effect in
the 2-3 plane is proportional to the capillary length. A small en-
trance/exit effect is present in this case.

5.4.2 The Influence of the Window Strain

One expects the window strain to be a function of the hydrostatic pressure
on the windows and hence, on account of this alone, one might expect the optical effect to increase linearly with the capillary length. Fortunately, window strain can be discounted as being of serious importance for the results on
account of the following:

1) By compensation with the slit measurements (silicone only), a dark fringe
   moved parallel to the centre line of flow symmetry towards the wall. The
   symmetry of the windows is cylindrical. If window strain were serious one
   would expect with the slit the image in the microscope to be the same as in
   Fig. 2.9 under. This was not observed.

2) The window strain was measured by blocking the exit and measuring without
   flow the birefringence of the windows as a function of the superimposed
   pressure. The effect due to the window strain was small, giving about
   3×10^{-6} cm path difference at a pressure of 200 bar on both windows (see

Fig. 2.9), and gave a negative apparent birefringence. During flow, pressure is only exerted on one window. The other, opposite the exit of the capillary, is not subject to such high pressures. The highest pressures obtained with the experiments on the silicone were of the order of 70 bar. One may therefore estimate a correction of 5×10^{-7} cm, at most, to a measured effect of about 90×10^{-7} cm path difference. Owing to window strain in this case, the real optical effect should be about 5 % higher than the measured effect. This has not been taken into account in the further evaluation of the results owing to the fact that for the one material where it might be important; the error remains acceptable. For the other melts, the problem is completely absent as they are 10 to 30 times more optically sensitive than the silicone oil and possible corrections for window strain lie well within the experimental error.

5.4.3 Comparison of $n_{22} - n_{33}$ with $n_{11} - n_{22}$ and $n_{11} - n_{33}$

In Fig. 5.30, for Siloprene RS at room temperature, the obtained values of $(n_{33} - n_{22})$ are set out against the shear gradients at the wall of the die. The same figure includes results of $n_{11} - n_{22}$ and Δn measurements with the cone-and-plate apparatus and a concentric cylinder apparatus. It is seen that $n_{33} - n_{22}$ is about 10 % of $n_{11} - n_{22}$. Strangely, $n_{33} - n_{22}$ seems to lie more parallel to Δn than to $n_{11} - n_{22}$. However, the effect is partly illusionary, and with increasing q the ratio of $n_{33} - n_{22}$ to $n_{11} - n_{22}$ does not decrease greatly.

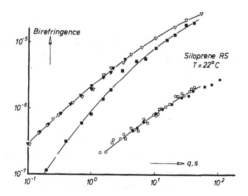

Fig. 5.30 Various birefringences plotted as a function of the shear rate, q, for a silicone oil. ▼ ... Δn (concentric cylinder); ▽ ... ∇n (cone-and-plate); ■ ... $n_{11} - n_{22}$ (cone-and-plate); o●□ ... $n_{33} - n_{22}$ (capillaries).

In Fig. 5.31 the obtained values of $n_{33} - n_{22}$ for LDPE, IUPAC A at 190 °C, are plotted against the calculated gradients at the wall of the die. Also included in this figure are measurements of $n_{11} - n_{22}$ and Δn obtained with the cone-and-plate apparatus, and $n_{11} - n_{33}$ obtained with the slit apparatus. The cone-and-plate measurements were carried out at 150 °C and transposed to 190 °C by temperature shifting. (The particular low density polyethylene was not thermally very stable.) The unfilled squares represent extrapolated equilibrium values of $(n_{11} - n_{22})$ with the cone-and-plate and are seen to agree very well with the $(n_{11} - n_{33})$ measurements with the slits.

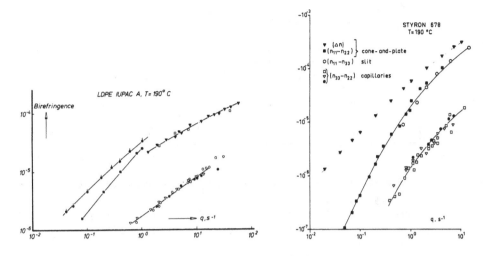

Fig. 5.31   Fig. 5.32

Comprehensive plots showing the gradient dependency of the various deviatoric combinations as determined by various apparatuses. Fig. 5.31 ... polyethylene low density; ● ... Δn (cone-and-plate); ■□... $n_{11} - n_{22}$ (cone-and-plate); ▼ ... $n_{11} - n_{33}$ (slits); ●○▽ ... $n_{33} - n_{22}$ (capillaries) Fig. 5.32 ... polystyrene.

In Fig. 5.31 there is an apparent discontinuity at about 1 s^{-1}, which marks the onset of overshoot phenomenon with the cone-and-plate measurements. True equilibrium was not attainable within experimental time available just in the shear rate region where overshoot, and possible structural breakdown, first occur. At high shear rates in the overshoot region, equilibrium is obtained after a few minutes. As the shear rate is decreased, the equilibrium time strongly increases (becomes hours), and it is no longer possible to make a satisfactory extrapolation to steady flow conditions: measurements are again "constant" after about five minutes. This difficulty often occurs with low density polyethylenes. Apart from this blemish $n_{33} - n_{22}$ is seen to be about 10 % of $n_{11} - n_{22}$ and $n_{11} - n_{33}$.

Figure 5.32 gives the results for Styron 678 at 190 °C. Again $n_{11} - n_{22}$, Δn, $n_{11} - n_{33}$ and $n_{33} - n_{22}$ are plotted against the gradient. Only the overlap region is shown; results for higher gradients with the slit and lower gradients with the cone-and-plate have been left out.

All the results concerning the $n_{22} - n_{33}$ effect have been collected and re-plotted in the following figure (Fig. 5.33) to show the ratio $(n_{33} - n_{22})/(n_{11} - n_{22})$ as a function of the shear gradient.

A few results, obtained by Philippoff (23 % PIB in oil) using the same method are also shown. The value of the ratio 0.05 to 0.14 is of the order found with the most reliable normal stress measurements[23]. A few results with the narrow molecular weight polystyrene, S111, were determined by using the

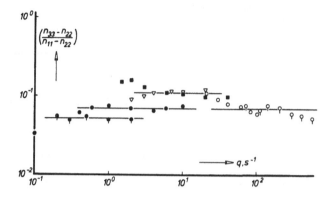

Fig. 5.33 Plot of ratio $(n_{33} - n_{22})/(n_{11} - n_{22})$ for various melts. Data on a polyisobutylene melt (Oppanol B5) and a solution from Ref.[22] are also shown. • ... Styron 678; ❡ ... BASF 3; ■ ... Silopren RS; ▽... IUPAC A; o ... Oppanol B5; ♀ ... 23 % PIB in oil.

indirect method of Section 5.3.3. These are also in agreement (ratio was about 0.08) with the results in Fig. 5.33.

Remarkable is the constancy of the ratio for the polystyrenes and also for the low density polyethylene; both materials were in their non-Newtonian regions of flow.

The silicone oil and the polyisobutylenes tend to show a monotonic decrease in the ratio, as the shear rate is increased. However, the decrease is not considerable. Theoretically, we might expect the ratio not to be altered by an initial departure from second order flow (this can be proven for rigid particles of ellipsoidal shape). Ultimately, we expect the ratio to decrease to zero since in the case of extreme chain stretching the cross-section along the axial coordinate should become circularly isotropic. An attempt has been made to check this by examining sections of injection moulded polystyrene (see also Sections 5.1.3 and 5.5.2). Astonishingly, $n_{33} - n_{22}$ at the peaks (e.g. Fig. 5.9) was still about 10 % of $n_{11} - n_{33}$ ($\simeq \Delta n$), even under these extreme conditions. This particular experiment may not have been very meaningful because of the complicated stress pattern in injection moulding. Nevertheless, it remains an interesting point. There is no easy way of doing the same for the silicone oil.

5.5 Applications

5.5.1 The Relations between Steady Shearing Flow and Oscillatory Shearing

Cox and Merz[24] discovered a relation between the viscosity in steady shearing flow and the absolute value of the dynamic viscosity. The relation is expressed:

$$\eta(q) = |\eta^*(\omega)| \qquad ; \qquad \omega = q \qquad (5.5.1)$$

Probably, this result is only valid for polymer melts and for these systems it has been well established[25)26)]. A theoretical foundation for (5.5.1), either from molecular or from phenomenological theories of non-linear behaviour, has not yet been found.

As regards theories that compare high shear rate behaviour in steady flow with dynamic behaviour of polymeric systems, two types exist. The first group of theories assumes that the material is essentially unchanged during flow so that a suitable equation of state will describe both linear viscoelastic behaviour and flow at high shear rates. This was done by a number of authors: Bueche[27)]; Roscoe[28)]; Pao[29)]; Zapas[30)]. The second group of theories uses the assumption that the material changes during the steady flow because a structure (e.g. entanglements) is broken down: Yamamoto[31)]; Graessly[32)]; Schroff[33)]; Booij[34)].

Roscoe obtained:

$$\eta(q) = \eta'(\omega) \quad ; \quad \omega = mq \qquad (5.5.2)$$

$$(p_{11} - p_{22})/(2q^2) = G'(\omega)/\omega^2 \quad ; \quad \omega = mq \qquad (5.5.3)$$

$$\frac{1}{r+1} \left(\frac{p_{11} - p_{33}}{q^2} \right) = G'(\omega)/\omega^2 \quad ; \quad \omega = mq \qquad (5.5.4)$$

where m and r are material constants. In view of the experimentally found result that $p_{11} - p_{33}$ is close to $p_{11} - p_{22}$ for all the materials of this investigation r may be set equal to unity.

One can summarize the above system of equations by saying that the theory predicts a constant shift m along the logarithmic rate axis for superposition of steady flow and linear dynamic-mechanical quantities. The shift factors for the normal stress coefficients and the viscosity should be the same. A constant shift along the rate axis is not consistent with equation 5.5.1 nor with experiment. To a fair approximation, however, the experimental results are often consistent with the following empirical relationship[26)].

$$\eta(q) = |\eta^*(\omega)| = \eta'(\frac{\omega}{m}) \qquad m = m(\omega) > 1 \qquad (5.5.5)$$

$$\frac{1}{2}\left(\frac{p_{11} - p_{22}}{q^2} \right) \simeq \frac{1}{2}\left(\frac{p_{11} - p_{33}}{q^2} \right) = G'(\frac{\omega}{m})(\frac{m}{\omega})^2 \qquad (5.5.6)$$

Typical of the second group of theories is the theory of Schroff. This may be cast in the form:

$$\eta(q) = \int_{-\infty}^{\infty} H(\tau)K(\tau q)\tau d \ln \tau \qquad (5.5.7)$$

This is an integral equation for the steady shearing viscosity. The kernel $K(\theta)$ with $\theta = \tau q$ is in this theory given by the functions h and g of Graessly: $K(\theta) = h(\theta)g(\theta)^{3/2}$. The theory of Booij can also be cast in the form of equation (5.5.7). In this case the kernel is equal to unity for q less than b and to zero for q greater than b (see Section 4.5).

Some of the theories of the first group can also be cast in this general form. In, for example, that of Roscoe and in a simplified version of the Kaye-Bernstein-Kearsley-Zapas theory[35] where the kernel has the form:

$$K(\theta) = (1 + 2\theta^2/9)^{-1} \quad , \quad \theta = \tau q$$

By curve fitting it is always possible to find a kernel which will fit given experimental results either for the viscosity or for the normal stress function. The question arises: is it possible to use the same kernel for the normal stresses and the viscosity, and can the same kernel be used for different polymeric systems. For the normal stresses the relation should read:

$$\tfrac{1}{2}(\frac{p_{11} - p_{22}}{q^2}) = \int_{-\infty}^{\infty} H(\tau)K(\tau q)\tau^2 d \ln \tau \tag{5.5.8}$$

For polymer solutions the problem has already been examined by Tanner[36]. He concluded from examination of available literature that this was not possible in general. The kernel from the viscosity curves causes appreciable error in predicting normal stresses. However, smaller errors in predicting viscosities were found if the kernel was obtained from the normal stress data. His method of tackling the problem was to use the experimental data and treat (5.5.7) and (5.5.8) as Fredholm equations and find F by iterative means. This is somewhat unsatisfactory as $H(\tau)$ needs to be found by a separate inversion of linear viscoelastic data and the experimental region is often restricted. It will be recalled that, in principle, inversion is only possible if one knows the behaviour over the entire frequency range zero to infinity. These problems may be overcome by finding a linear combination of $\eta'(\omega)$ and $\eta''(\omega)$, which agrees with the viscosity in steady shear over the experimental range (up to five decades in rate). For the polystyrenes S111, BASF 3, Styron 678 and Styron 666, the same relation was found to hold for the viscosity:

$$n(q) = \eta'(\omega) + \frac{1}{3} \eta''(\frac{\omega}{2.5}) \quad , \quad \omega = q \tag{5.5.9}$$

This experimental relation is just as good as the relation of Cox and Merz. The experimental support for this contention is plotted in Figs 5.34 to 5.36. The advantage of (5.5.9) over the Cox and Merz relation is that it is linear. After considering the integral forms for $\eta'(\omega)$ and $\eta''(\omega)$ - see equations (1.2.7) through (1.2.10) - the kernel follows immediately:

$$K(\theta) = \frac{1}{1 + \theta^2} + \frac{1}{3} \frac{(\theta/2.5)}{1 + (\theta/2.5)^2} \quad , \quad \theta = q\tau \tag{5.5.10}$$

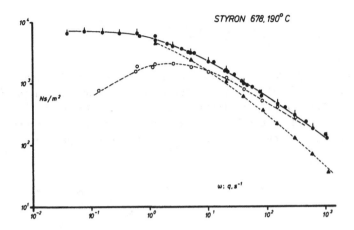

Fig. 5.34 *Comparison of steady flow viscosity with dynamic viscosities:*
$\circ$ ... $\eta(q)$; $\circ$ ... *relation (5.5.9)*; Δ ... $\eta'(\omega)$; $\circ$ ... $\eta''(\omega)$.

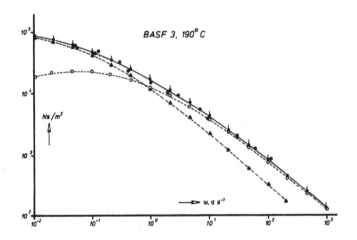

Fig. 5.35 *Comparison of steady flow viscosity with dynamic viscosities:*
$\circ$ ... $\eta(q)$; $\circ$ ... *relation (5.5.9)*; Δ ... $\eta'(\omega)$; $\circ$ ... $\eta''(\omega)$.

The normal stress coefficients as obtained from birefringence measurements, were difficult to fit. Just as with the viscosities, there are many ways of obtaining superposition. The best one found is indicated by the following equation:

$$\frac{(p_{11} - p_{22})}{2q^2} = \frac{G'(\omega)}{\omega^2} + \lambda\{\eta_0 - \eta'(\omega/2.5)\}/\{\omega/2.5\} , \quad \omega = q \qquad (5.5.11)$$

The above relation gives a kernel of the same form as the kernel for the steady flow viscosity, but the factor 1/3 in (5.5.9) is replaced by a parameter λ. The kernel becomes

$$K(\theta) = \frac{1}{1 + \theta^2} + \lambda \frac{(\theta/2.5)}{1 + (\theta/2.5)^2} \quad , \quad \theta = q\tau \qquad (5.5.12)$$

The values of λ were 1/4 for S111, 1/30 for BASF 3 and 1/20 for Styron 678. Resulting fits of the normal stress coefficients to the dynamic-mechanical quantities via (5.5.12) are shown in Figs 5.37 to 5.39. The normal stress coefficients were obtained in the lower shear rate range with the cone-and-plate apparatus and in the high shear rate range with the slit apparatus.

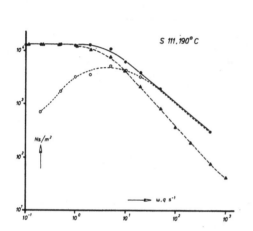

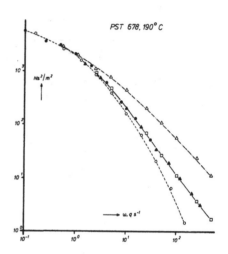

Fig. 5.36 Comparison of steady flow viscosity with dynamic viscosities:
● ... η(q); ▲ ... η(ω); o ... η"(ω);
the drawn line is relation 5.5.9.

Fig. 5.37. Comparison of steady flow elastic properties with dynamic data:
▲ ... ½(p₁₁ – p₂₂)/q²; o ... G'(ω)/ω²;
□ ... *relation (5.5.11)*; Δ ... *from relation (5.5.10).*

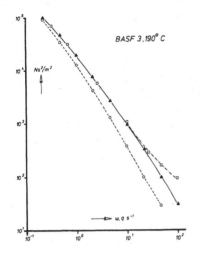
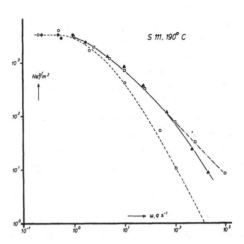

Fig. 5.38 *Comparison of steady flow elastic properties with dynamic data:* ▲ ... $\frac{1}{2}(p_{11} - p_{33})/q^2$ *(slit);* ○ ... $G'(\omega)/\omega^2$; □... *relation (5.5.11).*

Fig. 5.39 *Comparison of steady flow elastic properties with dynamic data:* ▲ ... $\frac{1}{2}(p_{11} - p_{22})/q^2$; ○ ... $G'(\omega)/\omega^2$; □ ... *relation (5.5.11).*

In the latter case, experimental data were all increased by 10 % to eliminate the slight difference between $n_{11} - n_{33}$ and $n_{11} - n_{22}$. In one figure, normal stress coefficients have also been predicted from the kernel for the viscosity function, i.e. by using 1/3 instead of 1/20 for Styron 678. The prediction was poor and can be seen in Fig. 5.37. The reverse procedure was also tried, i.e. trying to fit viscosity data with the kernel from the normal stresses. This was just as unsuccessful. Similar results were also found for the other commercial polystyrenes. We can conclude that it is not generally possible to interchange the normal stress and the viscosity kernels.

However, for S111 which has a narrow distribution of molecular weights, the kernels for the viscosity and the normal stresses are very nearly equal.

Schroff[33] used a kernel from the theory of Graessly to calculate the steady shear viscosity from the spectrum of relaxation times $H(\tau)^*$. The materials he examined, were high-density polyethylene melts, and the kernel he used, showed a much sharper cut-off than the kernels found here. Computer calculations with his kernel and the spectrum $H(\tau)$ evaluated from dynamic moduli measurements, failed to reproduce the steady flow curves shown here for S111. At the highest shear rates the calculated viscosity was too low by a factor four and the normal stress coefficient by a factor of twenty. Other theoretically based kernels

It is not sure that the proposal of Schroff is consistent with the ideas propounded by Graessly.

have been investigated as well. One was $\sin^{-1}(q\tau)/q\tau$ which has been proposed on the basis of the Ree-Ehring theory for non-Newtonian flow[37]. This was also inadequate: at the highest shear rates, the viscosity was a factor three too high and the normal stress coefficient a factor twenty too high.

Other systems have also been investigated, but the results were not so conclusive. Measurements on the low density polyethylenes LDND and LDBD (see Table 3.1) showed in a IUPAC Working Party investigation that the zero shearing viscosity did not agree with the real part of the dynamic viscosity at low frequencies[6]. This discrepancy has also been found on occasions by other workers with low density polyethylenes.On account of this difficulty and the problem that equilibrium measurements of $n_{11} - n_{33}$ are for practical purposes non-existent for these materials (see Section 5.3.2), at very high shear rates, further investigation of the kernel approach seemed of limited value.

5.5.2 The Orientation in Injection Moulding

The control of product anisotropy can be of importance to the producer, since some important properties of the finished product are sensitive to the degree of orientation present. Thus, it is known that impact strength and environmental stress resistence are considerably affected by the degree of molecular orientation determined by birefringence. In conjunction with J. van Leeuwen and R. van der Vijgh, the present author has shown [9] that, in the case of moulded strips (see Section 5.1.3), the peak orientation in the strip is related to the orientation in steady, isothermal, flow.

The basis of this investigation is the result mentioned in 5.1.4, that the birefringence induced in polystyrene by steady flow, is governed by the shear stress, regardless of temperature. This prompted the suggestion that, for molecular orientation occurring during the non-isothermal cavity filling process, the shear stress might be an appropriate and exclusive variable provided relaxation of the orientation which is temperature dependent, does not get the chance to disturb the situation appreciably.

The slit apparatus is appropriate to characterize steady, isothermal flow orientation. In fact, only with this apparatus is it possible to measure at the high shear stresses which occur during injection moulding.

The materials were a straight polystyrene (Styrene 678), a rubber modified polystyrene (Styrene 475) and an acrylonitrile-butadiene-styrene copolymer (ABS). The latter compounds were only translucent in thicknesses of less than one millimeter. This was sufficient, however, for measurements in the 1-3 plane. Owing to the depolarizing effects of the rubber particles, birefringence measurements could not be carried out in the other two planes. With the slit apparatus both these compounds showed the same qualitative behaviour as the straight polystyrene, i.e. the birefringence was essentially a function of the shear stress only.

Figures 5.40 and 5.41 show results of the tests in steady, isothermal flow with these compounds. These results are interesting in that the stress-optical relation is not expected to hold for these two phase materials. The reason for the simple behaviour may lie in the probable fact that only the polystyrene phase is considerably deformed during melt flow and that the stress-optical coefficient of the polystyrene phase is predominant.

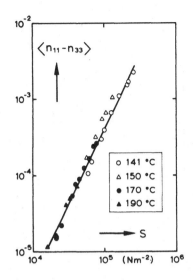

Fig. 5.40 Styron 475.

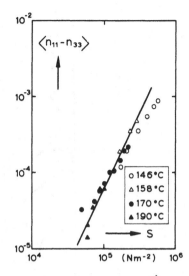

Fig. 5.41 ABS (ref.[9]).

Flow birefringence in 1-3 plane for steady isothermal flow. A simple relation between the orientation and the shear stress is retained at all temperatures, even for these two-phase materials.

The orientation formed during the filling process and frozen in the injection mouldings, show a complicated pattern. Simplest is to view the whole plates in a perpendicular direction between crossed polaroids, and to count isochromes in order to obtain the longitudinal distribution of birefringence in the 1-3 plane. Figure 5.42 shows an example of this for Styron 678 at various moulding conditions. Typically, one finds a peak or plateau near the gate, whilst at the frozen flow front there is no optical effect.

For the interpretation of the results, only the peak value of the birefringence in the 1-3 plane was used. This was directly compared to the equilibrium birefringence in steady, isothermal flow. The parameter of comparison being the shear stress. The shear stress in the mould was defined by the average slope of the pressure distribution in the mould just before the hydraulic pressure was shut-off. Two types of moulding conditions can occur:

a) Short - the mould is just filled or incompletely filled. The melt-entry pressure is then a direct measure for the shear stress.

b) Flash - the mould is overfilled and the melt-entry pressure gives an overestimation for the shear stress in the mould.

Both of the above conditions were examined with two moulds. The first, of the butterfly type, had relatively short and loss-free runners (runners are the channels through which the melt flows before reaching the cavity). The cavity of this mould had dimensions $1 \times 65 \times 65$ mm^3. With this mould it was

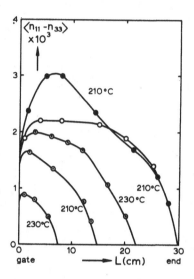

Fig. 5.42 Typical examples of the birefringence in the 1-3 plane in injection moulded plates of straight polystyrene Styron 678. Open symbols ... short condition; filled symbols ... just flash condition.

only possible to measure the melt entry pressure and not the pressure distribution in the mould. The rubber modified polystyrene and the ABS were measured with this mould in a study of the influence of moulding conditions on orientation and product properties [9]. The cavity of the second mould had dimensions $2 \times 65 \times 300$ mm^3. With this mould the pressure distribution could be measured for a wide range of conditions using the straight polystyrene. Figures 5.43 through 5.45 show plots of the peak values of $n_{11} - n_{33}$ in the 1-3 plane as a function of the shear stress at the wall at the end of the cavity filling process for rubber modified polystyrene and straight polystyrene, respectively. Comparison with the isothermal data, as represented by the drawn lines, shows good agreement for all short data although the scatter is considerable. The flash data for the rubber modified polystyrene and the ABS deviate in a direction to be expected from an overestimation of the shear stress in the mould.

In spite of the difficulties for a detailed interpretation of all observations, the fact remains that the birefringence in injection moulded objects can be explained and predicted semiquantitatively from the flow birefringence in steady shear flow. Other mould geometries, where radial fow plays an important role, may give different details. There is no doubt, however, that they will show similar general features.

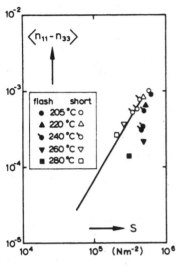

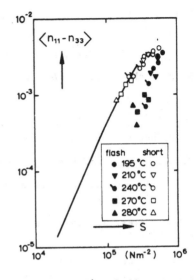

Fig. 5.43   Fig. 5.44

*The maximum birefringence in the 1-3 plane of mouldings as a function of the
shear stress at the cavity wall for the short and the flash conditions. The
drawn line represents isothermal, equilibrium, flow conditions. With the
mould used, the shear stress is overestimated under flash conditions.*

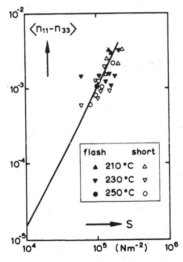

*Fig. 5.45 Straight polystyrene Styron 678. See captions to Figs 5.43 and 5.44.
With this mould the shear stress should be estimated equally well
for both flash and the short conditions.*

References

1) A.S. Lodge, *Nature*, 4487, 838 (1955).

2) N.I. Shishkin, M.F. Milagin, A.D. Gabaraeva, *Soviet Physics-Solid State* 5, 2535 (1964).

3) A.N. Gent, T.H. Kuan, *J. Polymer Sci.* 9 A2, 927 (1971).

4) H. Janeschitz-Kriegl, *Die Makromol. Chemie 33:1*, 55 (1959).

5) W. Philippoff, *Proc. 5th International Congress on Rheology*, held at Kyoto, Japan, 1968, Tokyo, 1970, *Vol. 4*, p. 3.

6) J. Wales, *Pure and Applied Chemistry 20*, 331 (1969).

7) J. Meissner, *IUPAC Working Party Report*, to be published.

8) J.W.C. Adamse, H. Janeschitz-Kriegl, J.L. den Otter, J.L.S. Wales, *J. Polymer Sci. A26*, 871 (1968).

9) J.L.S. Wales, J. van Leeuwen, R. v.d. Vijgh, *Polymer Eng. Sci. 12*, 358 (1972).

10) M.V. Volkenstein, *"Configurational Statistics of Polymeric Chains"*, *Interscience*, New York, London 1963.

11) D.W. Saunders in *"The Rheology of Elastomers"*, Ed. Mason and Wookey, Pergamon, 1958.

12) K. Nagai, *J. Chem. Phys. 40*, 2818 (1964).

13) R.J. Volungis, R.S. Stein, *J. Chem. Phys. 23*, 1179 (1955).

14) D.W. Saunders, *Trans. Faraday Soc. 52*, 1414 (1956).

15) D.W. Saunders, D.R. Lightfoot, D.A. Parsons, *J. Polymer Sci. A2, 6*, 1181 (1968).

16) V.N. Tsvetkov, A.Ye. Grishchenko, *Vysokovolekul. Soedin. 5*, 817 (1965).

17) N.J. Mills, D.W. Saunders, *J. Macromol. Sci.-Phys. B2*, 369 (1968).

18) E.V. Friswan, A.K. Dadivanyan, *J. Polymer Sci., Part C, No. 16*, 1001 (1967).

19) T.G. Fox, P.J. Flory, *J. Am. Chem. Soc. 70* (1968) 2384; *J. Appl. Phys. 21* (1950) 582; *J. Polymer Sci. 14* (1954) 315.

20) W. Philippoff, R.A. Stratton, *Proc. 5th International Congress on Rheology 4*, 13 (1968).

21) R.D. Andrews, Y. Kazama, *J. Appl. Phys. 38*, 4118 (1967).

22) J.L.S. Wales, W. Philippoff, *Rheol. Acta 12*, 25 (1973).

23) R. Tanner, *6ᵉ Congrès de Rhéologie*, Lyon 1972.

24) W.P. Cox, E.H. Merz, *J. Polymer Sci. 28*, 619 (1958).

25) S. Onogi, T. Fujii, H. Kato, S. Ogihara, *J. Chem. Phys. 68*, 1598 (1964).

26) J.L.S. Wales, J.L. den Otter, *Rheol. Acta 9*, 115 (1970).

27) F. Bueche, *J. Chem. Phys. 22*, 1570 (1954).

28) R. Roscoe, *Brit. J. Appl. Phys. 15*, 1095 (1964).

29) Y.H. Pao, *J. Appl. Phys. 28*, 591 (1957).

30) L.J. Zapas, *J. Res. Nat. Bur. Standards 70A*, 525 (1966).

31) M. Yamamoto, *J. Phys. Soc. Japan 11*, 413 (1956); *12*, 1148 (1957), *13*, 1200 (1958).

32) W.W. Graessly, *J. Chem. Phys. 47*, 1942 (1967).

33) R.N. Schroff, *J. Appl. Phys. 41*, 3652 (1970).

34) H. Booij, *Thesis*, Leiden 1971.

35) See S. Middleman *"The Flow of High Polymers"*, Interscience, 1968. Kaye's name is now associated with that of Bernstein, Kearsley and Zapas, as he had previously published an almost identical theory.

36) R.I. Tanner, G. Williams, *Trans. Soc. Rheol. 14:1*, 19 (1970).

37) A.J. de Vries, J. Tochon, *J. Appl. Polymer Sci. 7*, 315 (1963).

38) J.W.M. Noordermeer, R. Darynani, H. Janeschitz-Kriegl, *Polymer 16*, 359 (1975).

6. Discusion

6.1 The Stress-Optical Relation

   In the preceding sections we have shown that the stress-optical law holds
for amorphous melts during steady shear flow. The simple stress-optical law is
remarkable in that it bridges the macroscopic stress with the microscopic inner
processes, i.e. the rotations and deformations of the atomic bondings. Remarkable too, because relations between the stresses and strains or strain rates
are non-simple, and not usually of general applicability. In fact, in the world
of mechanics, the molecular theory of the stress-optical relation in polymers
gives the only theoretical relation between measurable quantities which actually works over a wide range of conditions and variables. To exemplify this
remark we recall that the stress-strain relations for rubbers are not understood since the ad hoc C_2 term of Mooney-Rivlin has to be added in order to
achieve curve fitting. The value of C_2 is not even constant but changes for a
given material when the type of deformation is changed: C_2 is smaller in simple
shear than in uniaxial extension[1]. The situation is even more complicated for
solutions and melts since it can still be safely said that non-Newtonian flow
is not fully understood. Yet, for both solutions and melts, when one takes the
simplest theory, eliminates the strain rate from the stress-strain rate and
strain rate-birefringence relations, one obtains the same simple relation between the stresses and the birefringence which is obtained for rubbers by eliminating the strain from the stress-strain and strain-birefringence relations.
The proportionality factor is typical for a given polymer type independent of
whether the polymer has been crosslinked, diluted or left undiluted, has low
or high molecular weight, has a broad or a narrow molecular weight distribution
or is being sheared or uniaxially stretched at low or high deformations.

   The reason for the success of the stress-optical relation and the relative
lack of success of relations between strain rates or strains and the stresses
or birefringence is not sure. It must be admitted that a chance compensation
may have taken place between factors not taken into account by the simpler molecular theory. The factors we have in mind are the internal field on the one
hand and the crowding problem for chain statistics on the other. The first involves the Lorenz-Lorentz field which must be too crude when the system becomes deformed.

   Orientation of the chains, effects the internal field in two ways: through
the intra-molecular orientation and through the inter-molecular orientation.
The intra-molecular effect is always present, but the inter-molecular effect,
depending on the changing distance between the chains, should be reduced by
the addition of solvent, because at high dilutions the chains are so far apart
that small relative changes in inter-chain distances have no appreciable effect.

   Legrand[2] has made a start on this particular problem by treating the case
of simple extension. More general results are not available. According to Legrand, a careful account of the influence of deformation on the internal field
should also account for the C_2 term in rubber elasticity since the van der Waals

binding forces are also determined local dipole interactions. It is supposed that the intermolecular cause will be the dominant factor for the determination of C_2.

The second factor referred to in the above has been taken into account by Jacksen and co-authors[3]. These authors point out that the Gaussian or random walk model for chain statistics is based on assumptions that the medium in which the chain acts, is isotropic in action. This is clearly an unreasonable assumption for an undiluted system, because when the individual chains are deformed, the medium becomes anisotropic. Chain steps should not be equally probable in all directions. To be properly self-consistent, the model should take this bias into account. The afore-mentioned authors did this for simple extension and obtained the right kind of behaviour for elastomers.

Since both of these theoretical possibilities have the same qualitative effect, it is just possible that their combination will still lead to the same, simple, stress-optical relations, as discussed earlier. If this speculation is true, we should then only speak of a quasi-linearity in the relations between the stresses and the birefringences.

For another class of amorphous materials - filled systems - we do not expect the stress-optical relation to hold, except for very special cases. Depolarization due to particle scattering, makes any experimental investigation with filled systems very difficult. Nevertheless, there exist a few filled systems which show but a small degree of depolarization. One such material, a clear acrylonitrile-butadiene-styrene copolymer, was presented very kindly by J. Young of Borg-Warner Chemicals. Scattering in this material has been reduced by matching the refractive index of the components. The 1-2 plane birefringence, the extinction angle χ are shown in Fig. 6.1 for this material.

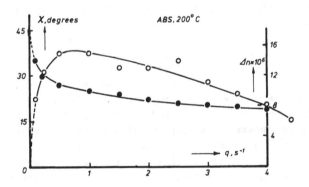

Fig. 6.1 The gradient dependency of the extinction angle χ and the birefringence Δn in the 1-2 plane for a clear ABS. The stress-optical relation fails for this material. ● ... χ; o ... Δn. The birefringence was negative for this material.

103

The stress-optical relation fails because, whereas the extinction angle monotonically decreases and the shear stress monotonically increases, the birefringence goes through a maximum. A similar behaviour also occurs with dilute non-
matching solutions of polystyrene[4]. The birefringence is then the sum of a
positive form effect, and a negative "eigen" effect of the polystyrene. Both
effects have differing shear rate dependencies and the sum behaviour is similar
to that in the figure.

For non-steady flows, the bounds of validity of the stress-optical relation
are still to be delineated. For matching solvents there is already in existence
a theory[5,6], which seems to be successful in describing deviations from the
stress-optical law at higher frequencies[7]. A phase difference between the
stress and the birefringence is caused by the presence of internal friction (a
force in the chain caused by the rate of relative movement between its parts,
it should also be active in the absence of any surrounding medium). The same
internal friction causes the viscosity η' to level-off at high frequencies to
a constant value instead of steadily decreasing as in the Rouse or Zimm theory.
The ratio $\eta'(\infty)/\eta'(o)$ is directly proportional to the internal friction and is
a direct measure of the latter's relative importance. The introduction of internal friction might therefore be a good trick to obtain a molecular description of actual melt behaviour. It appears, however, that $\eta'(\infty)/\eta'(o)$ is so extremely small (< 0.01) for melts that internal friction can be neglected. Thus,
if one uses the device of internal friction, one does not expect in the first
instance any serious deviations from the stress-optical law.

Continuing with the question of non-steady flows, it may become necessary to
distinguish between time-dependent motions at temperatures close to T_g and
time-dependent motions at temperatures far removed from T_g. Below T_g, the birefringence is determined principally by bond deformations, whereas above T_g
it is determined mainly by long-range rearrangement of the chains. Traversing
T_g by decreasing the temperature, the long-range processes become frozen. According to the empirical time-temperature superposition, one can approach T_g
at temperatures above T_g by increasing the time rate of a motion. Therefore,
at temperatures not too far removed from T_g, we do not expect the stress-optical relation to hold for non-steady motions of the material. Polymers which
probably suffer this restriction are polymethyl methacrylates, polyvinyl-
chlorides and polystyrenes, since these are not normally examined at temperatures far removed from their glass temperature. Other polymers might not suffer this disadvantage, although, as indicated, a full investigation has not
been performed. Under the aegis of a IUPAC Working Party, a few experiments
have been made to examine the stress-optical rule on IUPAC A, a low density
polyethylene (see Section 3)[8]. The experiments were steady shearing after
sudden starting of the rotor of a cone-and-plate. The optical quantities were
compared with the time dependencies of the shear and the normal stresses under
the same circumstances. The optical behaviour was qualitatively the same as
the mechanical, but quantitative differences were present. The shear components
showed good agreement as the ratio $\Delta n \sin 2\chi / 2p_{12}$ remained constant, equal to
the value for steady shearing. The ratio $\Delta n \cos 2\chi / (p_{11} - p_{22})$ was too high at
low shear rates and too low at high shear rates. The maximum difference was
about 20 %. Definite conclusions cannot be drawn as yet from these experiments,

as there are difficulties in the measurement of the time dependency of the normal stresses with the Weissenberg apparatus. A particularly important feature is that the time dependency is a function of the angle between the cone and the plate. At short times, the overshoot increases with increasing angle until an angle of about 8° is reached where the signal becomes consistent[8]. The origin of this unwished-for effect is the small displacement needed to measure the normal force. The birefringence apparatus differs in that stresses are not measured, friction is not important, and any displacement between the cone and the plate should be prevented by the thrust bearings.

The definitive experiments on this subject will have to be carried out with better apparatuses whereby, in the case of flow birefringence, the laborious compensation of the optical effect from the prism will have to be avoided. In the case of the normal stresses, the displacement problem will have to be solved as wide angle cones could lead to incorrect results on account of secondary flows or intractable boundary conditions.

6.2 The Diffusion Equation

It is worth-while spending a little time considering the diffusion equation 4.2.8. In the general form quoted, F, is supposed capable of being a non-linear function of the distance between the end points of the chain. Indeed, some authors have used non-linear forms of the chain force, e.g. a Langevin function[9,10]. Their idea was to obtain non-linear macroscopic behaviour from the diffusion equation. The basic philosophy lies close to that in the quasi-static model for streaming flow. The forces in the chain are supposedly related to the average deformation of the chain as if the material were an elastomer and equilibrium conditions could exist. The justification for the procedure is that in the absence of flow, V is equal to zero and ψ in 4.2.8 becomes, as it must, equal to ψ_0. There are several comments to be made at this point. The first is, that such approaches rely heavily on theoretical results for non-linear behaviour of elastomers, whilst ignoring the fact that there is as yet no conclusive evidence that such theories hold even for the systems they are intended. Secondly, there are other possible extensions to account for non-linear behaviour. For example, one could consider the term inside the inner brackets of equation 4.2.4, as the first term of a Taylor series, and simply add further terms, such as $(S - S_0)\mathfrak{A}(S - S_0)$ with $S=kT$ gradlog ψ.

We suspect that the aforesaid approach might be incorrect, because the derivation of the Brownian motion force in the original equations was made for small deviations from equilibrium. For a proper account of non-linear effects, the writer fears that one will have to return to a basic statistical hypothesis, such as the "Master" equation of Markoff, relating the probability in momentum and configuration space to the transition probabilities[*]. The derivation of a diffusion equation from the "Master" equation depends on a series of linearizations in the momentum space[11]. As an example, the basic form of the Fokker-Planck equation obtained during the derivation of the Smoluchowski equation from first principles, is of the form:

[*]Fears, because the theory will become even more indigestible and it would seem inevitable that uncontrolable parameters will be introduced.

$$\frac{\partial \phi}{\partial t} = - a_1 \frac{\partial \phi}{\partial x} + a_2 \frac{\partial^2 \phi}{\partial x^2} \qquad (6.1)$$

It contains two constants a_1 and a_2 which represent the first and second moments of the deviations (fluctuations) in the momenta. The second constant a_2 represents the diffusion constant. Higher order terms have been neglected. Owing to this latter approximation, one suspects that the diffusion equation in present use is not really suitable for the prediction of non-linear phenomena. A parallel state of affairs already exists in the theory of (Nyquist) noise in electrical circuits. These systems, apparently, are also governed by a Fokker-Planck equation. In this electrical analogy it can be proven that it is impossible to obtain the macroscopic behaviour from the (microscopic) diffusion equation by allowing in an ad hoc way, the coefficients a_1 and a_2 to be non-linear functions of the state variables[12]. It is necessary to add third and higher moments of the fluctuations giving third and higher order derivatives in the diffusion equation. Whether this stringent conclusion is of serious consequence for the case in hand, is unknown since the Smoluchowski equation contains a further series of approximations[11].

Having made these remarks, it is interesting to note that in amorphous rubbers, the diffusion of small molecules is unaffected by the degree of stretching of the matrix as long as the latter does not crystallize[13]. This might be interpreted to mean that the Brownian motion of the segments in the chain is unaltered by the stretching process. If this is a correct interpretation of the findings, then it is very possible that, notwithstanding the remarks of this section, the diffusion equation as represented by 4.2.3 is still a very useful starting point and can lead to meaningful results.

6.3 The Deviatoric Components

The existence of the deviatoric combination $n_{22} - n_{33}$ has been demonstrated. The ratio of this difference to the first difference $n_{11} - n_{22}$ is of the order of magnitude expected from determinations of the first and second normal stress differences. The ease and accuracy of the optical determinations far exceeds that from stress measurements. In principal, it is possible to determine the value of $n_{22} - n_{33}$ independent of $n_{11} - n_{22}$ or $n_{11} - n_{33}$ whilst the accuracy of the second normal stress difference depends on the accuracy of the determinations of $p_{11} - p_{22}$ and $p_{11} - p_{33}$.

The value of the experimentally determined ratio $(n_{33} - n_{22})/(n_{11} - n_{22})$ was remarkably constant and always seemed to lie in the range 0.05 to 0.14. The ratio was clearly independent of the molecular weight and the molecular weight distribution of the polymer type. The above-mentioned range of experimental values for the optical ratio is, however, distinctly lower than the value derived in the model theory of Chapter four. The value obtained (= 1/8) in that chapter was in fact a limiting upper bound which could never be reached in practice. The reason for this is that the ratio of the principal diffusivities for rod- or ellipsoid-like particles reaches a value of two only in the case of extremely great length to diameter ratios. Significant deviations from the limiting case are still present for length to diameter ratios of one hundred. The reason for this is that the limiting condition is only reached as fast as log (L/d) approaches infinity. Perhaps it would have been more physically realistic to assume that the rod had a length to diameter ratio equal to that of the random link in the theory of chain dimensions. For many polymers, the random link contains about ten C-C bonds and so to an intuitive approximation, the length to diameter ratio of the diffusion units should also be about ten to one. When this assumption is made, the optical ratio lies within the range of the experimentally found values.

The last result lends some credulity to the theory of Chapter four. Further support comes from the concentration dependence of the ratio $n_{33} - n_{22}$ to $n_{11} - n_{22}$ for a given polymer. According to the model, the ratio should be independent of the concentration of the polymer. Whilst this work has not been concerned with solutions, a few incidental measurements have been made to check the point. It was found that ten and fifteen percent solutions of BASF 3 in Aroclor at room temperature gave the same value for the ratio as the melt. Also, a four percent solution of a National Bureau of Standards polystyrene gave values for the ratio of about 0.08 which is in agreement with the results for the other polystyrenes. For these reasons, we feel that the model theory given in Chapter four gives, at least the correct physical origins of the second normal stress difference in polymers, whilst retaining the stress-optical relationship.

As a corollary for very stiff molecules, e.g. solutions of cellulosic derivatives or polar molecules in ionic solvents, we expect the ratio of the second to the first difference to be somewhat higher than the present values and nearer the limiting theoretical value. This prediction needs experimental confirmation.

The idea to use the anisotropy of diffusivity of the segments to obtain $n_{22} - n_{33}$ arose from a paper of Copic[14] concerning the anisotropy of diffusivity due to the working of the hydrodynamic interaction between the spheres in a dumbbell model. As he was only interested in non-Newtonian viscosity, he did not include the normal stress components in his calculations. In the limit of infinite shearing, he found the same ratio of two for the principal diffusivities. There is thus some connection with his ideas and the results presented here. The difference lies in that the present approach accounts for near neighbour interactions in the bead model, whereas his calculations were concerned with long-range interactions.

The dependency of $(n_{11} - n_{33})$ on the shear stress was found to be quadratic for several monodisperse polystyrenes and very nearly quadratic for the commercial polystyrenes. One polystyrene with a narrow distribution of molecular weight (S111) distribution showed an increased sensitivity at the very highest shear stresses, whilst another, with a lower molecular weight (Pressure Chemical No. 7a), retained even at the highest shear stresses its approximate quadratic behaviour. In the high shear-stress region, S111 shows a nearly quartic relation between $(n_{11} - n_{33})$ and the shear stress. We cannot offer any explanation for the increased sensitivity of S111. It may be remarked, however, that a similar kind of behaviour has been found for solutions of polystyrene, but again only for materials of narrow molecular weight distribution[15]. Materials with a very broad molecular weight distribution, such as the polyethylenes of this investigation, show a decreased sensitivity to the shear stress when one leaves the quadratic region. The constant, nearly quadratic, dependency of some polystyrenes up to the very highest shear stresses, is therefore a compensation of two different causes. Tanaka[16] and others have shown for a model of non-linear behaviour how the various types of behaviour could be related to the shape of the relaxation spectrum.

6.4. The Molecular Models Applied to Melts

The results of the present investigation with melts are in line with the results of other workers who used different experimental techniques. As indicated earlier, the general opinion is at present that the Rouse theory is not sufficient to describe melt behaviour, the molecular weight dependency of the compliance J_e being the great stumbling block. However, it should not be forgotten that the prediction in the theory is born out remarkably in the region of low molecular weights: quantitative agreement is obtained (see Fig. 4.1). The same results were obtained in this investigation. Additional support for the spirit of the basic molecular model, are the results for the second normal stress difference which would also seem to follow the predictions of the diffusion theory given in Chapter four. Rejection of the Rouse model applied to melts, would probably imply rejection of theory and interpretation of the results for the ratio $(n_{33} - n_{22})$ to $(n_{11} - n_{22})$. We remark at this point that we do not expect any further extension of the dumbbell model to the multi-bead case would lead to differing results for the ratio $(n_{33} - n_{22})$ to $(n_{11} - n_{22})$. This writer feels that it is still possible that the basic premises of the Rouse model are good. It may be necessary, however, to make minor modifications to the theory or improve the experimentation. It is noticeable that the friction factor in the theory has to be adjusted in an ad hoc way to comply with the molecular weight dependency of the viscosity. The mixing rule (eq. 4.1.2) for polymers should also be examined carefully. The ratio $(n_{33} - n_{22})$ to $(n_{11} - n_{22})$ would appear to be independent of any mixing rule or assumption about the friction factor, and this may be the strongest support for the molecular approach.

A good description of non-linear behaviour and molecular weight dependency of J_e is still problematic. However, the modifications proposed by Graessly (see Section 4.5) could be on the right lines. Two of the polystyrenes in this thesis fall within the scope of his second, more elaborate, theory for non-Newtonian flow[17]. Styron 678 has M_w/M_n ratio of about two and S111 has M_w/M_n ratio of about one; for both eventualities tables are available of the viscosity and the reduced shear rate $q\tau$, where τ is the longest relaxation time of the Rouse theory[17]. For Styron 678 at 190 °C, τ is about 0.25 s and for S111 about 0.5 s. The latter value is in good agreement with the longest relaxation time from stress-relaxation experiments on S111 at the same temperature[18]. When these data are used, the viscosity curve (Fig. 5.34) for Styron 678 was in almost perfect agreement with Graessly's predicted curve - ± 5 %. The fit for S111 was less good, but still acceptable. We use these results to show that present developments in the molecular theories, although in some aspects rather unsatisfactory, are very close to a correct description of experimentally found behaviour.

6.5 Steady Shearing - Oscillatory Shearing

The validity of the Cox-Merz relation was reconfirmed in all cases. The possibility of more general relations between quantities in steady shearing and oscillatory shearing have been examined. For this purpose, linear combinations $\eta'(\omega)$ and $\eta''(\omega)$ were used to reproduce the steady flow data. In this way, kernels could be generated to predict steady flow data from dynamic, linear viscoelastic, flow data. It was found that a single kernel could be used to describe the steady flow viscosity of several polystyrenes. However, the determined kernel may not have been unique as for each of the polystyrenes other combinations of η' and η'' gave an adequate description of the steady flow viscosity. The quoted combination was the only one which worked satisfactorily for all polystyrenes, the same relation did not work equally well for the polyethylenes.

For the application of the viscosity kernel to the normal stresses, the conclusion must be that this is generally not possible if accurate data are required.

The experimentally found kernels were not in good agreement with most of the theoretical proposals, which are to be found in the literature, as most of the latter show too sharp a decay.

Notwithstanding the problem of obtaining exact data, there is plenty of semi-quantitative agreement between the kernel method and the approach, whereby a sharp cut-off of the relaxation spectrum $N(\tau)$ is used. To illustrate this, let us evaluate to a first approximation the simple cut-off function, as defined by Booij [19] in the case of non-Newtonian viscosity.

We seek a solution for τ_m in the equality

$$\eta(q) = \int_0^{\tau_m} H(\tau)\, d\tau = \int_0^\infty H(\tau)K(q\tau)\, d\tau \tag{6.2}$$

For the present results we approximate the kernel $K(q\tau)$ to $[1 + c^2q^2\tau^2]^{-1}$.

This is equivalent to assuming that $\eta(q)$ and $\eta'(\omega)$ can be superimposed by horizontal shifts along the rate axis by a factor c^{-1}. As indicated earlier this is not a good description of the results, but it is far better than the assumption that $\eta(q)$ and $\eta'(\omega)$ superimpose directly and it gives the first approximation. The next step is to approximate $N(\tau)$ by the box function $\tau N(\tau) = H_0(\tau) = 1$, $0 < \tau < \tau_c$; $\tau N(\tau) = 0$, $\tau > \tau_c$. There is obtained for the physically realistic case $[\tau_m < \tau_c]$:

$$\tau_m = \frac{1}{qc} \tan^{-1}(qc\tau_c) \sim \frac{\pi}{2qc} \tag{6.3}$$

For this very simple model, the cut-off time of equation (6.2) is inversely proportional to q, a result born out by experience [19]. From the present data for Styron 666, the parameter c varies from 0.6 to 0.3 in the range $0 < p_{12} < 10^5$ N/m^2. One therefore deduces that non-Newtonian flow will be defined by a shearing of $q\tau = \frac{1}{2}\frac{\pi}{c} \sim 3$ units at the lower shear rates. This is close to the findings of Booij for other systems. These considerations may also be extrapolated to stress overshoot. To qualitatively describe this latter phenomenon, we consider that the deformation of a Maxwell element is of the order of $q\tau$, where τ is the relaxation time of the element. If q is greater than $1/\tau$ then the molecule will, from rest, follow the macroscopic deformation until the critical deformation is reached. The internal deformation (i.e. of the molecular elements) will not increase any further than the equivalent of this shearing and might even decrease. We expect that the peak in overshoot experiments will occur at a shear of the order of 3 units for polystyrenes. The measurement of the birefringence overshoot with polystyrenes was not successful in this investigation. However, a few stress overshoot results have been published for Styron 666; the measurements were at 200 °C and the shear rates were low[20]. The peaks occurred at shears between two and three units in quantitative agreement with the above expectations.

References

1) L.R.G. Treloar in *"The Physics of Rubber Elasticity"*, Clarendon Press, Oxford 1958, Chapter 8.

2) D.G. LeGrand, *Macromolecules 3*, 764 (1970); see also R.S. Stein, *J. Polymer Sci. A2, 7*, 1021 (1969).

3) J.L. Jacksen, M.C. Shen, D.A. McQuarrie, *J. Chem. Phys. 44*, 2326 (1966).

4) H. Janeschitz-Kriegl, *Adv. Polymer Sci. 6*, 170 (1969).

5) A. Peterlin, *Polymer Letters 5*, 113 (1967).

6) A. Peterlin, *Kolloid Z. 209*, 181 (1966).

7) G.B. Thurston, *J. Chem. Phys. 47*, 3582 (1967).

8) J. Meissner, To be published.

9) Ch. Reinhold, A. Peterlin, *J. Chem. Phys. 44*, 4333 (1966).

10) A. Peterlin, *Polymer 2*, 257 (1961).

11) H.J. Merk, Collegedictaat *"Stochiastische Problemen in de Lineaire Constitutietheorie"*, Delft 1971.

12) N.G. van Kampen, *Adv. Chem. Phys. 15*, 65 (1969).
For application of the Fokker-Planck equation to other physical problems, see also M. Lax, *Rev. Mod. Phys. 38*, 541 (1966).

13) See J. Crank, G.S. Park (Eds) *"Diffusion in Polymers"*, London, Academic Press (1968).

14) M. Copic, *J. Chim. Phys. 53*, 440 (1956).

15) W.W. Graessly, L. Segal, *Macromolecules 2*, 49 (1969).

16) T. Tanaka, N. Yawamoto, Y. Takano, *J. Macromol. Sci. Phys. B4*, 931 (1970).

17) W.W. Graessly, *J. Chem. Phys. 47*, 1942 (1967).

18) J.L.S. Wales, *Pure and Appl. Chem. 20* (1969) p. 331.

19) H. Booij, *Thesis*, Leiden 1971.

20) I-Jen Chen, D.C. Bogne, *Trans. Soc. Rheol. 16:1*, 59 (1972).